The Great Philosophers

BY THE SAME AUTHOR:

Worlds to Know: A Philosophy of Cosmic Perspectives (1962)
The Ways of Genius (1949)
Ethics (1947; Revised Edition, 1955)
The Moral Ideals of Our Civilization (1942)
Religious Crossroads (1942)
The Nature of Evil (1931)
The Problem of Immortality: Studies in Personality and Value (1924)

THE GREAT
PHILOSOPHERS

SECOND EDITION

RADOSLAV A. TSANOFF

Rice University

Harper & Row, Publisher
New York, Evanston, and [...]

Contents

IV. The Philosophers of the Nineteenth and Twentieth Centuries

Preface to the Revised Edition

In preparing this revised edition of *The Great Philosophers*, I have kept in mind those aspects of the work which have been tested favorably in its wide use in college classes during the past decade, as well as some suggestions for improvement of its plan and execution. In my close rereading of the text I have aimed at simple and clear exposition and at the right degree and direction of emphasis. The principal revision, and it has been extensive, has been motivated by the purpose, expressed in its title, to concentrate on the leading minds in the history of philosophy. The first edition of the book did realize this purpose to a certain degree, but not enough. In a general, undergraduate course in the history of philosophy, a one-volume text, to be accompanied by selected readings from the primary sources, must of necessity be limited to the major thinkers. The lesser minds can at best receive only passing mention which scarcely engages the student's interest or advances real understanding.

I have carried out this sort of revision with fair thoroughness, but also with some careful judgment. For there are several periods in the history of philosophy which are characterized precisely by a multiplicity of minds, without any one outstanding philosopher. For example, the exposition of the first chapter of ancient thought requires the tracing of the many initial explorations of the nature of things which were to be followed by the later great systems of Athenian philosophy. Likewise, in the radical turn from declining classical culture to medieval-Christian thought, not only the great variety, but also the confusion of controversial patristic doctrines must be noted. In this way also, we can understand and appreciate the transition from medieval to modern thought by surveying the fertile and sprouting new life in the Renaissance in all directions. No one mind—not even Leonardo or Giordano Bruno—can suffice here. A similar comment relates to the eighteenth-century Enlightenment. In brief, in my revision of this book I have concentrated on the great philosophers, but have been mindful of the importance of listening to the many voices which are necessary to give us the true expression of certain periods in the history of ideas.

With this I send forth this revised edition in the hope that it will continue to receive favorable reception, for which I am deeply grateful.

I wish to express my thanks to the staff of the Development Department at Rice University for the typing of my revised manuscript. I am indebted also to my colleague, Professor James Street Fulton, and to my daughter, Katherine Tsanoff Brown, for reading the manuscript carefully and for making many good suggestions for its improvement. My wife has given me steady and able help in all the planning and composition of the book, and in the proofreading.

I am grateful to the following publishers for permission to use quotations from works published as indicated below:
The Clarendon Press, Oxford: the Oxford edition of Aristotle's *Works;* Cyril Bailey's translation of Lucretius' *On the Nature of Things;* P. E. Matheson's translation of Epictetus' *Discourses and Manual;* A. C. Fraser's edition of Berkeley's *Works;* Selby-Bigge's edition of Hume's *Treatise of Human Nature* and Hume's *Enquiries;* F. H. Bradley's *Essays on Truth and Reality.* Longmans, Green & Co., London: T. H. Green and T. H. Grose's edition of Hume's *Essays;* T. K. Abbott's translation of Kant's *Critique of Practical Reason and Other Works on the Theory of Ethics.* The Macmillan Company, New York: F. Max Müller's translation of Kant's *Critique of Pure Reason;* A. N. Whitehead's *Process and Reality.* Kegan Paul, Trench, Trübner & Co., London, and Charles Scribner's Sons, New York: R. B. Haldane and J. Kemp's translation of Schopenhauer's *World as Will and Idea.* Charles Scribner's Sons, New York: R. D. Hicks' *Stoic and Epicurean.* Passages from the *Enneads* of Plotinus are quoted usually from Stephen MacKenna's translation, as selected and edited in *The Essence of Plotinus* by Grace H. Turnbull, published by Oxford University Press, New York. Shaftesbury's *Characteristics of Men, Manners, Opinions, Times, etc.* is quoted from J. M. Robertson's edition, published by Grant Richards, London.

RADOSLAV A. TSANOFF

Rice University

Introduction

This work is a history of philosophy in our western civilization. The word "philosophy" means love or pursuit of wisdom. Aristotle wrote on the first page of his *Metaphysics;* "All men by nature desire to know." Philosophy and science have been men's two ways of satisfying this natural desire of intelligence. Philosophy has shared with science the character of critical mental activity, but has differed from science in its scope and in its ultimate aim. The sciences are investigations of various fields or aspects of nature, each science seeking specific knowledge and systematic organization of the laws and principles of nature in its respective field. Philosophy is not so much the attainment of specific knowledge as the search for basic and ultimate understanding.

The state of human knowledge at any stage of intellectual development has influenced men's general outlook on nature, has influenced their philosophy. The first philosophers of Greece were also the pioneers in scientific investigation. The distinction between philosophical and scientific inquiry could not be made clearly in those first chapters in the history of critical thought, but the advance in the use of special inquiries in geometry or astronomy induced the progressive recognition of the main philosophical problems. Philosophers asked: What is real? What is the fundamental character and structure of nature? What is the relation of the world we know to our minds that know it? To these and similar questions many answers were offered, and this variety of theories, in turn, led philosophers to ask: How can the validity of our ideas be tested? What is true knowledge as distinguished from random opinion? While in all these inquiries philosophy was satisfying the normal desire for understanding, it also sought assurance of the abiding values of human life: What makes life worth living? What is really good?

Philosophical reflection has thus been marked by its persistent concentration on ultimate problems and issues. Beyond particular information and explanation, the philosophers have endeavored to attain an understanding of reality in a cosmic perspective; that is, the nature of the world and our own nature and role in it. Beyond the ascertainment of any specific knowledge, philosophy has tried to grasp the basic principles of knowledge itself: the meaning of truth. And in its inquiry and self-criticism the philosophic mind

I

has also aimed at wisdom in the right gradation and choice of values: the recognition and pursuit of the Highest Good.

These three—the Problem of Reality, the Problem of Knowledge, the Problem of Value—have engaged the best thought of philosophers down through the centuries, and they will continue to engage human reflection, for a final and definitive philosophy is no more available than is a final and definitive science. With every great advance in the various sciences, radically new ideas or reinterpretations of old principles in new perspectives enter the stream of critical thought. Philosophy is nourished by every great fertile idea which inquiring minds develop in any field. Note how the modern philosophical conceptions of nature and human nature have been influenced by the theory of evolution, not only in biology but in all humanistic inquiries.

While philosophy thrives on the advances in the special sciences, it cannot expect to attain their precise conclusions. Its very endeavor—to consider each principle in relation to the others, in a universal context, and as it magnifies the complexity of philosophical problems—limits the likelihood of definitely formulated and final solutions. This prospect in philosophy is due to the very character of its undertaking. Even so, as we climb a mountain range, the distant horizon of our view expands and changes with our ascent. Philosophy has been called the "eternal problem in eternal solution"; or, as we might rather put it: in continual solution—an unending problem.

This reasonable recognition of the course and destiny of ideas in science and philosophy does not warrant skepticism, but it does indicate the importance of critical judgment. In the special sciences, the experimental evidence and theoretical reasoning which lead to replacing one conclusion with another are both at hand, definitely formulated. The mind may move forward with assurance. Philosophy considers the larger and more remote implications of the reinterpreted or wholly new principle. The mind must proceed more cautiously here; yet its dominant interest in ultimate bearings accentuates its speculative tendency. This speculative *élan* affords various ideas a chance to have their way unhindered in the contemplative play of creative minds, and to reveal their merits and their defects. But if this philosophical drama is to be fruitful, it must be enacted in minds which are richly stored with great ideas and which are less likely to go astray in judging or interpreting some new doctrine.

The historical study of philosophy enables us to develop a critical appraisal of alternative ideas by seeing how they have fared in human reflection. Some ideas are like new roads that lead us to new lands, that open significant vistas on reality. But other ideas are dead-end trails that, like woodcutters' roads in the mountains, only mislead the traveler. Dante said that he wrote *The Divine Comedy* ". . . to procure [for himself] full experience." The study of the history of philosophy can give us a full measure of experience with the great ideas of the great minds.

The history of philosophy is enlightening in another way. It can reveal to us the inner spirit and motives of the various periods of civilization. Beneath the outward course of human events we can recognize the dominant principles and ideals of a period, the problems, convictions, or perplexities which engrossed men's thought, and the ideas or hopes that were emerging to change the future course of events. Our understanding of Athenian culture, for example, is deepened by knowing Plato's *Dialogues;* the decline and fall of Rome gain in significance as we view them in the perspective of St. Augustine's *City of God;* and through the philosophers of the Renaissance we can get a living sense of the emerging modern world.

The history of ideas reflects, as it also affects, the general course of history. Although we should not use too rigidly the conventional division of history into three general periods—ancient, medieval, and modern—these divisions will serve our purpose as well as the historian's. Each of the three stages of our culture is marked by its characteristic and deeply significant philosophical outlook: ancient—*classical,* medieval—*Christian,* and modern—*scientific.*

A few words may be added about the method of treatment adopted in this work as it is suggested by the title of the book. First, the emphasis on the great philosophers is intended to provide as fair an exposition of the principal systems of philosophical ideas as is possible within the compass of a single volume. Lesser thinkers are considered in so far as they help to clarify or to develop some relevant issue raised by the main philosophers. A great system of philosophical ideas is like a window of the mind opening on a cosmic prospect. In following the development of philosophy, we should first view these great and revealing vistas.

Secondly, while the title of this book, *The Great Philosophers,* does not imply an overemphasis on biography, the author hopes that the personality and the social-cultural background of each thinker will come alive in the chapter devoted to him to express the spirit and temper of his ideas, as well as to present a clear and reliable logical analysis of them.

General histories of philosophy usually reach to about the middle of the nineteenth century. Contemporary philosophy is an extensive subject, and a detailed treatment of it would exceed the limits of this work. But it is hoped that our final chapter will serve as an outline to indicate the main currents in recent philosophical thought.

SUGGESTED WORKS FOR FURTHER STUDY

The lists of books at the end of each chapter are intended as guides for the reader. Only English titles have been cited. For a comprehensive catalogue of philosophical literature the student should consult Benjamin Rand's *Bibliography* in J. M. Baldwin's *Dictionary of Philosophy and Psychology,* Vol. III, 1905. More recent titles may be found in F. Ueberweg's *History of Philosophy,* 11th or 12th German edition (*Grundriss der Geschichte der Philosophie*).

HISTORIES OF PHILOSOPHY.   Boas, George, *Dominant Themes of Modern Philosophy;* Collins, James, *A History of Modern European Philosophy;* Copleston, Frederick, *History of Philosophy;* Cushman, H. E., *A Beginner's History of Philosophy;* Durant, Will, *The Story of Philosophy;* Erdmann, J. E., *A History of Philosophy;* Fuller, B. A. G., *A History of Philosophy;* Janet, Paul, and Séailles, Gabriel, *A History of the Problems of Philosophy;* Lamprecht, S. P., *Our Philosophical Traditions;* Marvin, W. T., *The History of European Philosophy;* Mayer, Frederick, *A History of Ancient and Medieval Philosophy,* and *A History of Modern Philosophy;* Miller, Hugh, *An Historical Introduction to Modern Philosophy;* Radhakrishnan, S. *et al., History of Philosophy Eastern and Western;* Rogers, A. K., *A Student's History of Philosophy;* Russell, Bertrand, *A History of Western Philosophy;* Thilly, Frank, *A History of Philosophy;* Tomlin, E. W. F., *The Great Philosophers: The Western World;* Turner, William, *History of Philosophy;* Ueberweg, Friedrich, *A History of Philosophy;* Webb, Clement C. J., *A History of Philosophy;* Weber, Alfred, *History of Philosophy;* Windelband, Wilhelm, *A History of Philosophy.*

AESTHETICS.   Bosanquet, Bernard, *A History of Aesthetics;* Gilbert, Katherine, and Kuhn, Helmut, *A History of Esthetics.*

ETHICS.   Kropotkin, Peter A., *Ethics;* Rogers, A. K., *Morals in Review;* Rogers, R. A. P., *A Short History of Ethics;* Schweitzer, Albert, *Civilization and Ethics;* Sidgwick, Henry, *Outlines of the History of Ethics;* Tsanoff, Radoslav A., *The Moral Ideals of Our Civilization.*

LOGIC.   Adamson, Robert, *A Short History of Logic;* Enriques, Federigo, *The Historical Development of Logic.*

POLITICAL THEORY.   Catlin, George, *The Story of the Political Philosophers;* Dunning, W. A., *A History of Political Theories;* Gettell, R. G., *History of Political Thought;* Sabine, George H., *A History of Political Theory.*

PSYCHOLOGY.   Boring, E. G., *A History of Experimental Psychology;* Brett, George S., *A History of Psychology;* Dessoir, Max, *Outlines of the History of Psychology;* Klemm, Otto, *A History of Psychology;* Murphy, Gardner, *Historical Introduction to Modern Psychology.*

ANCIENT PHILOSOPHY.   Adamson, Robert, *The Development of Greek Philosophy;* Benn, A. W., *The Greek Philosophers;* Burnet, John, *Greek Philosophy;* Cornford, Francis M., *Before and After Socrates;* Fuller, B. A. G., *History of Greek Philosophy;* Gomperz, Theodor, *Greek Thinkers;* More, Paul E., *Hellenistic Philosophies;* Robin, Léon, *Greek Thought and the Origins of the Scientific Spirit;* Stace, W. T., *A Critical History of Greek Philosophy;* Warbeke, J. M., *The Searching Mind of Greece;* Zeller, Eduard, *Outlines of the History of Greek Philosophy.*

GENERAL WORKS ON GREEK THOUGHT, CULTURE, AND RELIGION.   Caird, Edward, *The Evolution of Theology in the Greek Philosophers;* Campbell, Lewis, *Religion in Greek Literature;* Dickinson, G. Lowes, *The Greek View of Life;* Livingstone, Sir Richard W., *Greek Ideals and Modern Life;* Murray, Gilbert, *Five Stages of Greek Religion;* Taylor, Henry Osborn, *Ancient Ideals.*

SELECTIONS FROM GREEK PHILOSOPHICAL AND RELIGIOUS WRITINGS.   Cornford, F. M., *From Religion to Philosophy;* Oakeley, Hilda D., *Greek Ethical Thought from Homer to the Stoics;* Smith, T. V., *Philosophers Speak for Themselves.*

I. THE PHILOSOPHERS OF CLASSICAL ANTIQUITY

1.   The First Explorers of Nature

The Beginnings of Philosophy in the Greek Colonies

The first chapters of science and philosophy were written by colonial Greeks in the sixth century before our Christian Era. A favorable combination of conditions in Greek life helped to stimulate these pioneers of western civilization. The Greek mainland has a very irregular and extensive coastline and a rough, mountainous interior. The narrow valleys and hilly stretches afforded poor roads; with little communication by land, the Greek tillers-of-the-soil developed many centers of local culture and government—the traditional city-states of Hellas. But everywhere the hillsides sloped to the sea. The Greek's travel was by water, and though he had slight contact with his own countrymen over the steep mountain ridges, he sailed overseas and knew strange peoples and strange ways of life and thought. In this environment both distinctive individuality and a broad, cosmopolitan outlook on life were stimulated.

The poor soil was a spur to industry and also to seafaring ventures in quest of more productive lands where the Greeks could trade and settle. All along the Aegean shores, on the Black Sea coast of Asia Minor, and throughout the eastern Mediterranean basin, this greater Greece was in direct contact with various other cultures. For this cultural interplay the Greek was preeminently fitted. He was versed in assimilating foreign ideas, and whatever he learned he transformed by his original interpretation. Neither his religion nor his social order was rigid. His worship of the Olympian deities was not marked by priestly conformity, creed, or orthodox theology. Homeric religion was an anthropomorphic polytheism that directed the imagination to poetry and mythology. Men were moved by the poetic inspiration of the old myths as Homer sang them, and by the beauty and power of the sculptor's art that gave the gods and goddesses tangible form.

The Greek tendency to popular government aroused discussion and argument; it cultivated critical intelligence in able minds. Where social policies were ever facing divided opinion, reflective men naturally sought the basic principles of social order. The seething contest of popular opinions engaged all minds. The market place was also a forum. Discussion came naturally to

7

the Greeks, who were continually vying with each other, body with body and mind with mind. The contention did not always aim at practical mastery; the play of ideas yielded intrinsic satisfaction. Said Socrates: "Is not the road to Athens made for conversation?" One can imagine such a question about our modern speedways, and the likely answer to it.

The Greek mind was thus free of some of the impediments to scientific-philosophical thinking that hampered other ancient cultures. Readily letting ideas and images have their way with him, yet always reserving his own judgment and never recognizing any authority as unquestionable, the Greek was prepared for investigation. But before this step could be taken, not only some myths, but mythology itself had to be discredited. Science and philosophy began in Greece when, no longer satisfied with telling tales, men asked questions that required analysis and explanation.

This radical shift in mental activity, from a mythology that personified every process in nature to objective exploration of the nature of things, did not take place on the Greek mainland, where the traditional anthropomorphism long prevailed. It was on the colonial outskirts of the Greek world, where widely traveled men heard the strange myths of other peoples and, of course, could not accept them all, that the belief in their own tales was undermined. The processes of nature and the course of human life yielded, in each country, a different mythological account. So Xenophanes wrote: "Ethiopians make their gods black and snub-nosed; Thracians give theirs blue eyes and red hair."[1] The more critical Greeks came to regard all mythology, including their own, with suspicion. But they went further; they did not merely reject the mythological answers, but they raised a different kind of question. They no longer tried to tell the right story, for example, as to whether it was Artemis or Aphrodite who caused trees to blossom in spring. They no longer asked: Who stirs the tempestuous sea and wrecks the helpless mariner? They wanted to understand the origin and nature of wind blasts and of lightning and thunder. Instead of wondering *who* made the world, men inquired, What is the world made *of?* This change in the mind's approach to nature was epoch-making. Mythology yielded to philosophy and to physical science.

The mythologists themselves had in part prepared the way for this great turn in thought. Hesiod, during the eighth century B.C., undertook to trace the order and succession of the gods in his *Theogony:* First came Chaos, then Gaia or Earth, then Eros or Love. But this speculation about the original divine powers, this theogony was in effect a cosmogony, an attempt of the mind to understand the primary agencies in the structure of nature. As we shall see, the early pioneers in science and philosophy did not break utterly with their mythological tradition, but their intention was definitely naturalistic.

[1] Charles M. Bakewell (ed.), *Source Book in Ancient Philosophy,* New York, Scribner, 1909, p. 8.

This early inquiry into the nature of things was marked by a characteristic detachment. Corresponding to the Greek's sheer delight in the visions of his imagination was the new pursuit of understanding. He learned his first geometry from the Egyptian rope-knotters who measured the lands of the rich, but he then tried to prove the Pythagorean theorem. He used the records of the Babylonian star-watchers to predict an eclipse, but he was mainly concerned with understanding the ways of the heavens, not with practicing divination. In the early speculations the practical motive sometimes persisted, but it was the exception. We may question the factual basis or the logic of this early speculation, but we cannot mistake its intellectual spirit of pure inquiry.

In thinking of Greek philosophy, we are apt to contemplate it in its classical Athenian setting where it reached its consummation. But Athens had no part in these beginnings. Nor should we expect to find among these early explorers of nature some one great philosopher. In poetry or religion, one preeminent genius has seemed to arrive sometimes unheralded, himself initiating the epoch which he has dominated. But in intellectual achievement it appears that many toilers have to open up the field before the master minds come to possess it. We shall be considering here at the outset several of the early explorers of nature, but the really great philosopher in this first chapter of western thought was the collective Greek mind which, in so many regions, was aroused to the problems of critical investigation.

Science and philosophy began in the Greek colonies, and first of all on the coast of Asia Minor. Let us imagine ourselves casting a glance eastward across the classical Aegean from Athens. The island of Samos projects from the Asiatic coast. A little to the northeast of it on the mainland is Ephesus, and fifteen miles beyond Ephesus, on the seashore, lies its rival and stubborn enemy, Colophon, claiming Homer as a native son. Not far to the south, near the mouth of the Meander river, is Miletus, most prosperous of Ionian cities and the founder of threescore settlements along the Euxine coast. In these four colonial districts, philosophy in western civilization had its origin. Its first cradle was Miletus.

The Milesians: Monistic Doctrines of the Primal Stuff of All Things

Several conditions in Greek life helped to induce scientific-philosophical inquiry, but these conditions alone cannot be said to provide adequate explanation. Even if we recognize the Greek eminence in theory or thorough insight, we should still have to explain why these qualities of mind emerged, in the sixth century B.C., with such creative power. The historian of that age is confronted with some baffling coincidences. Within the span of a short century or two a wave of spiritual upheaval seems to have swept over the entire world. From China to Hellas, major religions and philosophies of life had their inception in those days of fertile ideas: Confucianism, and perhaps Taoism, in China; Buddhism in India; Zoroastrianism in Persia; and in Israel, the ethical monotheism of Jeremiah and "Second Isaiah." In their criticism of the traditional cults, some of the Greek philosophers invite comparison with the Hebrew prophets, but the differences between them are more frequent and more important than the similarities. They bring out the characteristic bent of early Greek reflection, which sought primarily not righteousness, but understanding.

What the Greeks desired to know first of all was nature itself. That the nature of things was investigable and explicable seems to have been their initial conviction. There must be a cause for everything. This principle of necessity had deep roots in Greek thought. Beyond the gods and goddesses of the Homeric pantheon was the impersonal Moira, to the inflexible laws of which all wills, human and divine, were subject. Even in his mythology, the Greek recognized a certain necessary order or way of things. His reaction to it might be moral-religious and he would call it eternal justice or retribution, *Diké*, Nemesis. At a later age, Greek tragedy, as in Aeschylus, would be dominated by this conviction. But early inquirers in Miletus regarded this necessity as the natural course of things, and so they called it Nature, *physis*.

This view of the world as an investigable order of necessary caused events would seem to rule out both absolute creation and utter annihilation. The Milesians undertook to explain the varieties and order or structure of being— not the existence of matter itself, but the kinds and ways of matter. The outstanding fact in the world was the variety of forms and processes of things. This variety could not be ultimate; it required explanation. Right here we see two postulates of these first philosophers which are to raise problems for their successors. The Milesians assumed the existence of some primary substance or material stuff of which all things in nature were various forms or compounds; and they wished to know by what processes this primary stuff assumes all these various forms. They considered a farmer plowing and sowing his field in spring. Somehow, by the combined action of sunlight and rain and earth and grain, this sown field became a green wheat field and then a golden harvest, reaped and threshed, fed to men and beasts; it became animal and human bodies; and these in their due season died and turned to dust and ashes. What then was the primary substance of nature which in all these processes assumed all these different forms?

With inquiry of this sort, the Milesians were in effect undertaking to write the first page of chemistry, but for them it was a chemistry of a single element. In philosophical terminology we say that this first philosophy of nature was Monism. Starting with this principle, that the variety of things in the world points to some one primary substance, the Milesians asked: What is this basic stuff or element? How does it become differentiated in the course of existence?

THALES

The first of these explorers of the ultimate nature of things was Thales (640–546). He left no writings; our actual knowledge of him is scant and not very reliable. Antiquity agrees that he was a citizen of Miletus, but whether he was a native son or of mixed or foreign descent—perhaps Phoenician—seems uncertain. He is reported to have traveled far, learned geometry from the Egyptians, and to have measured the height of the pyramids by comparing the length of their shadows with that of a man. Using the calculations of Babylonian star-watchers, he predicted the total eclipse of the sun on May 28, 585 B.C. He was renowned as one of the Seven Wise Men, and the only one of these sages who investigated the nature of things. An inscription on his statue eulogized him as "wisest of mortals in all kinds of knowledge."[2]

Thales declared that the primary substance in all things is Water. It may seem strange that such a conclusion should have sealed the fame of a sage, and right here we should clarify our evaluation of these early theories. Important to science and philosophy has been the question which Thales raised regarding primary substance, rather than his answer to it. The answer itself is interesting in the history of ideas, for it reveals the persisting influence of traditional mythologies on these early intellectual radicals. How was Thales led to his doctrine that the world is made of water? Had he observed in his Egyptian travels that land and crops and people all depended on the inundations of the Nile? Or had he, as Aristotle said, noted that all life, germination and growth, require moisture? Aristotle also reminds us of the Greek myth that Ocean and Tethys were the parents of creation. This notion that all things have sprung out of the original watery chaos was widespread. Thales could have heard it from the Babylonian sages who recited their epic of the first beginnings, of the elemental being Apsu and of Tiamat, the all-encircling flood and streaming dragon of the deep, the primeval ocean, *tiamtu*, which Marduk split in two, separating the upper waters of heaven from those of the regions below the earth. We should note that Thales called the primeval elemental being neither Okeanos, oldest of the Titans, nor Tiamat, the dragon of the deep, but plain water. Was he always so naturalistic in his view of existence? His reported saying, "All things are full of gods,"[3] expresses the belief in hylozoism, that all things have a soul-like character—a view which the Milesians combined with their naturalism.

ANAXIMENES

The doctrine of Thales naturally suggested alternative versions. A later sixth-century Milesian, Anaximenes, said that air, or vapor, was the basic stuff of which all things are constituted. Like Thales, he viewed the world

[2] Diogenes Laertius, *The Lives and Opinions of Eminent Philosophers* (trans. C. D. Yonge), London, Bohn's Libraries, 1853, p. 10.
[3] Bakewell, *op. cit.*, p. 2.

as flat, like a table top. While Thales considered it a disk afloat on the en-
circling ocean, Anaximenes contemplated it as suspended in the cosmic vapor.
In the exploration of nature, this theory seems to be only a variant, not an
advance in thought. The greater significance of Anaximenes is that he considered the problem of transformation: how the world of various things as
we know it arose out of the primal stuff or matter. His answer to this question is free of mythology and expounds the mechanics of existence: Air or
vapor may be condensed or rarefied; condensation of air yields winds, clouds,
liquids and solids; by rarefaction, air becomes fire.

ANAXIMANDER

But early Greek naturalism had already reached deeper insight in the cosmology of Anaximander (611–547). Anaximander recognized the futility of
trying to discover the composition and structure of nature from any specific
kind of matter, be it water or air or fire or earth. He countered all such
obvious but inadequate solutions with a doctrine whose vagueness shows his
realization of the complexity of the problem. Every kind of matter that we
observe is of a particular, determinate nature, different from others, derived
in its own way from the primeval and basic reality. The ultimate stuff of
existence must be the matrix of all possible determinate things, but itself
must transcend all particular limitations. So Anaximander described it by a
name that expressed this elemental indeterminate character: the *apeiron*, the
boundless or the infinite. It is eternal, unbegotten, and indestructible.

This *apeiron* reminds us directly of Hesiod's Chaos, and in his cosmogony,
Anaximander combines mythological with naturalistic ways of thought.
Things, he says, originate or pass away as destiny orders; in overstepping
their bounds they must give satisfaction to one another. But he also explains
that the earth hangs free, supported by nothing, in the center of the universe,
because it is the most compact and solid. Abandoning the pancake cosmology
of Thales, Anaximander viewed the earth as cylindrical, "like a stone pillar."
We inhabit one of its flat ends. The sun, the moon, and the stars were
formed by rings or cartwheels that flew centrifugally from the central mass.
The earth is surrounded by circles of fiery vapor in which the stars are
visible through tube-like openings. The closing of these apertures produces
eclipses; the moon waxes or wanes owing to the widening or narrowing of
these holes or slits in the cosmic circles that surround us. The vapor drawn
up from the earth by the sun descends as rain. From the evaporated moisture
spring up living things of various sorts and shape according to their nourishment. Men sprang from some fishlike animal. Different species of animals
and plants thus come into being and pass away, and likewise all finite worlds,
but the infinite *apeiron* encompasses and transcends them all.

Here in the very first words of Greek philosophy are bold ventures of
thought: a definite, though not always steady, effort to explain the structure
of the world in nonmythological terms, a description of the mechanics of
nature, a due recognition of its complexity, a groping after the idea of

biological and cosmic evolution. To his speculation about the universe, Anaximander added more particular scientific competence. He is said to have constructed sundials that showed the solstices and the equinoxes. He is also reputed to be the first world map-maker.

We may be astonished or amused at this opening of the drama of science and philosophy; but we should remember that our primary sources for the study of the Milesian sages are very meager, only a few sentences. We have to rely on brief and vague comments by later writers, and we should beware of reading later meanings into their reported words. We must keep our sense of historical perspective, and it is well to take this warning to heart early in our study. Despite its occasional lapse into mythology, the Milesian cosmology was an exploration of nature seeking to derive its variety from some one primal and basic substance, and to describe the course of existence in terms of mechanical processes.

The Pythagorean "Number Philosophy" of Form, Relation, and Harmony

The echo of Pythagoreanism is vaster than the original sound. The persistent influence of this philosophy may be traced throughout classical antiquity, but its first statement has no reliable record. Some of the teachings that were ascribed to its founder are probably later in origin. This philosophy was the gathered tradition of a school or sect rather than the systematic work of one mind; its adherents were really votaries initiated into the saving truths of life. Pythagoreanism expounded ideas of great systematic importance, but its basic motivation was social-ethical and religious. Whereas the Milesians expressed the Greek naturalistic inquiry, the Pythagoreans exemplified the Greek pursuit of wisdom for the sake of achieving perfection.

PYTHAGORAS

The reputed founder of the school was Pythagoras, a sixth-century thinker born on the island of Samos. The many stories about his early life describe him as a far-ranging traveler who gathered his miscellaneous knowledge from Egypt, Phoenicia, and perhaps from Persia and even farther east. Banned from his native Samos by the tyrant Polycrates, he turned westward and settled at Crotona, a Dorian colony in southern Italy, where he established his school in 529 B.C. The school was really a secret fraternity of the strictest order, aristocratic in its social-political outlook, morally austere with rigid regulation of diet and daily conduct, ascetic in temper, and marked by mystical religious consecration. The disciples had to listen in silence to the words of the master and to follow implicitly his plan of personal reform and social reconstruction. The suspicious citizens of Crotona were stirred to violent hostility by some of their leaders, perhaps owing to Pythagoras' refusal to admit them to his inner circle. The fraternity house was attacked and burned about the year 500; Pythagoras and many of his votaries were slain. But refugee disciples scattered over the Greek world; about a century later Pythagoreanism was revived by Philolaus in Greek Thebes, and, in Plato's day, by Archytas at Tarentum in Italy. In the form of Neopythagoreanism it became one of the latest currents of declining Greek speculation.

The dominant moral-religious spirit of the Pythagorean school is apparent, but whether it stimulated among adherents an intellectual emphasis on Form, number relations, and harmony, or was itself a practical expression of their systematic philosophy, cannot be stated with assurance. To the historian of philosophy, the Pythagorean number formalism is of primary importance; despite its fanciful elaboration, this doctrine inspired fruitful work in mathematics and astronomy.

Instead of seeking to grasp the nature of things by discovering the primary and basic stuff of which all substances are composed, the Pythagoreans sought ultimate insight by analyzing the variety of existence into a system of principal forms. It is essential *form*, not primary *stuff*, that determines the nature of everything and every process in the world. For instance, take a most elusive reality like sound: Can you understand its varieties by describing them in terms of water or air? Pythagoras is said to have used, not the Greek seven-stringed lyre, but a simple instrument with one string, the monochord. He could readily show that a certain note was sounded by striking a certain length of string. Doubling the length of string gave him the octave of the original note, and he could reliably get other notes by observing the string-length ratio 3:2 or 4:3. The whole science of tones, in all their subtle and elaborate harmonies, could thus be grasped in a system of numerical relations.

Here, we may say, is the mathematical approach to reality. The Pythagoreans, fascinated by this idea, allowed no limit to its possible application. Number is all, physically and spiritually. Blending persistent analysis with stubborn occultism, they explored the properties and the mysteries of numbers. To illustrate, arrange the first four numbers in triangular order, thus:

$$
\begin{matrix}
& & \bullet & & \\
& \bullet & & \bullet & \\
\bullet & & \bullet & & \bullet \\
\end{matrix}
$$
$$\bullet \quad \bullet \quad \bullet \quad \bullet$$

In any position in which you may look at this triangle, the number of dots in the order 1, 2, 3, 4, adds up to the decad, the perfect number 10. This is "the holy tetractys" by which the Pythagoreans swore their oaths. The number explanation is applied generally. Thus, 1 is the point, 2 is the line, 3 is the plane, 4 is the solid. But numbers seem to be versatile in their occult essence. Thus, justice is designated as 4, presumably because it is the first square, expressing the idea of retribution—an eye for an eye and a tooth for a tooth. A Pythagorean would have said, "a two for a two," the square deal.

Marriage is 5—the union of the even (female) number 2 with the odd (male) 3.

We may see in the ramifications of this doctrine a Greek version of the number occultism which appears in so many religions with their triads, trinities, enneads, and the like. But Pythagorean analysis yielded here significant, scientific results. The bare mention of "the Pythagorean theorem" suggests other contributions to geometry which are said to have been extensive.

PHILOLAUS

Pythagorean astronomy deserves more explicit mention. As we noted, Anaximander rejected Thales' idea that the earth is like a disk floating on water, and regarded it as drum-shaped, a compact pillar suspended in the center of the universe. But Pythagoras declared that the earth is spherical, as are the other stars. Heaven itself is a harmony and a number; were it not for our incapable ears, we could hear the music of the spheres in their calculable revolutions. This doctrine of revolutions and orbits was developed with scientific intention by Philolaus, a Pythagorean of Thebes (born about 480 B.C.). Philolaus first conceived of the earth as revolving like the moon, the sun, and the other stars. That he believed in the rotation of the earth on its axis seems very unlikely; he maintained that the earth circulates on its orbit around a central point. This central point was not the sun, which, according to him, had its own orbit and revolution. Philolaus thought of the universe as a system of spheres: the sphere of the fixed stars, the five planets, the sun, the moon, and the earth. To these nine spheres he added a "counter-earth" to make the perfect number ten. These all revolved round a Central Fire, each in its orbit and period of revolution: the earth every twenty-four hours, the moon monthly, the sun annually. No one saw the counter-earth or the Central Fire, for the earth turned its uninhabited side toward them. Moving westward, the earth's revolution every day brings it from dawn to evening and, as it passes out of sight of the sun, to dark night.

ARISTARCHUS OF SAMOS

This astronomy of Philolaus could last so long as travelers and navigators did not cross the alleged limits of the inhabited half of the earth. But when sailors passed the Pillars of Hercules (Gibraltar) into the Atlantic, or when Alexander's legions advanced eastward to India, it was found that in neither west nor east was there any glare of the Central Fire, but always sunrise and sunset as in Greece. Then another Pythagorean, Aristarchus of Samos, about the middle of the third century B.C., reached the heliocentric idea—the earth revolves around the sun. But antiquity was then committed to a geocentric astronomy, with the earth at the center of the universe, and the Pythagorean's idea had to wait until the time of Copernicus in the Renaissance.

The dominant principle of form and harmony, which found expression in the doctrine of numbers and in the view of the world as a system of calculable relations, is directive also in the Pythagorean moral-religious philosophy of life. We may note here not so much a confusion as a tension of ideas. Nature is described as a harmony; but everywhere is the opposition of contraries, of which the Pythagoreans drew a whole table. Man's life is also a strife of contending powers. This dualism sounds a tragic note in the Pythagorean philosophy, which is expressed in their myth of Dionysus Zagreus. Dionysus, the son of Zeus and Persephone, was his father's favorite. The Titans, enemies of the great god, tried to destroy the youth, but he escaped them by the art of changing his shape. They finally captured and devoured him, all except his heart, which Athena rescued and gave to Zeus, who thereupon struck and consumed the Titans with his thunderbolts. From their ashes sprang the human race—partly divine Dionysian, but partly Titanic, coarse and evil. These two sides are ever contending in human nature. The Pythagorean philosophy and way of life aimed to achieve the victory of divine perfection in its followers. Philosophy is indeed a striving; the philosopher is not a sage or wise man, but one who loves and pursues wisdom, who seeks to recognize the world as a cosmos, a harmonious order of beauty, and to achieve the beauty of true harmony in his own life. Pythagoreanism taught the virtues of loyalty, fidelity, piety, and moderation, with harmony as the guiding principle. Man's span of life is a trial and probation, and death is not its end but only the transition to another rebirth according to the laws of retribution. This belief in metempsychosis or transmigration of souls was one of the firm tenets of Pythagoreanism, and it comes up again in the philosophy of Plato.

The Pythagorean teachings expressed the spiritual strivings of a critical age. They are marked by lofty aspiration and moral idealism, but they also lapse into occultism and fantastic vagaries. To systematic philosophy they contribute the important emphasis on formal analysis, mathematical methods, and the interpretation of nature as a system of calculable relations.

The Problem of Change and Permanence: Heraclitus vs. the Eleatic School

The Milesians sought the elemental stuff in nature which changes in all the various forms of things, but they did not recognize the basic problem of change itself. How can we say that the primordial air or water changes into iron or into brains? Anaximenes spoke of condensation and rarefaction; this only states hypothetically *how* air changes into a solid. There is the further question whether the primal substance does really change in becoming iron or wine or flame. If the primal air really changes in becoming fire, so that it is no longer air, then the basic substance ceases to exist, and how can that be accepted? But if it is the nature of air to be fire and all these other things, does it really change in becoming any one of them? And why should we call air as air more elemental than air in the form of bricks? We are led again to Anaximander's indeterminate *apeiron*, but the problem still faces us: Is there any real change in nature? How can we reconcile the changing variety of the world we see with the self-identical unity of basic stuff which the Milesians held as certain truth?

HERACLITUS

On this issue a new generation of Greek thinkers contended in stiff opposition. Heraclitus of Ephesus (*c*. 540–475) was a sage who derided the ignorance of the multitude but also the pride of the elite and their traditions and dignities. He renounced the royal priestly office to which he had been born and dedicated his life to meditation. King Darius invited him to his palace to explain his wisdom to the court, and promised him highest distinction and honor, but Heraclitus refused the Persian monarch; he was quite content with his lot, he replied, and lived to suit himself. He saw no reason for trying to make himself clear to people who could not understand anyhow. "Nature," said Heraclitus, "loves to hide."[4] Tradition called him the "dark" philosopher, which may have meant profound or only obscure, or even blind. He is represented as weeping, and the extant fragments of his writings express a dark, pessimistic view of the instability of human and cosmic affairs. He had seen the Ionian cities sacked by invading armies, and the proud prosperity of Miletus reduced to ashes and ruins by the Persians. Wherever he looked, the world manifested origin and decay, arising and passing away, but no basic permanence.

Thus, his was a philosophy of change. Change is the outstanding fact of nature; nature is an endless succession of changes. Heraclitus declared: All things are flowing; you cannot step twice into the same river. If, like the Milesians, you seek to know the basic stuff of nature, you may call it "fire," for fire is itself a process and a change of things from one form into another. Fire thickens into air or vapor, and vapor into water, into slime and solids. And the opposite process is always going on. Everything comes and goes, is and is not. A river, to be a river, must ever be and not be, forever filling and forever emptying. The death of plants and animals is our own food and life.

These two ideas, of universal flux and continuous strife in nature, dominate the thought of Heraclitus, but they do not lead him to conclude that nature is chaos. All things change, but they do not change in just any way. There is a law of change and there is a wisdom, a *logos*, or reason, in the behavior of nature which the wise man can perceive through understanding, provided he does not trust merely his senses, which are bad witnesses. By this law and order of change, nature is a cosmos. The gods may seem to play with human lives and destinies, but the law and reason of change rules the divine nature as well as our own.

[4] *Ibd.*, p. 35.

There is a conflict of principles in the thinking of Heraclitus which corresponds to the tensions he witnessed throughout nature. In the world he saw universal change but also everlasting law. "Nature loves to hide," yet our reason can understand its reasons and its laws. But if the world thus changes in a recognizable order and pattern, does it not manifest throughout all changes a certain permanence of character, and is not this, then, the basic nature of things? In still distant prospect is rationalistic metaphysics; nearer to view are more immediate explanations of change and permanence. But to evoke these explanations, a doctrine which denied the reality of change was required. This denial of change was the bold teaching of the Eleatics that reality is one, eternal and immovable.

XENOPHANES, THE FIRST ELEATIC

The Eleatic doctrine was, in the first place, a sharp criticism of the traditional anthropomorphic polytheism. The pioneer of the Eleatics, Xenophanes of Colophon, is believed to have been born in the third or fourth decade of the sixth century B.C. A refugee from home after the Persians had ravaged all the Ionian cities except Ephesus, he traveled far overseas and finally settled in Elea, a Greek city in southern Italy. In his castigation of popular superstitions and unworthy ideas of Deity, and in his advocacy of moral reforms, Xenophanes bears comparison with the Hebrew prophets. He denounced luxury, effeminacy, and drunkenness, but his scorn was poured out especially on corrupt and spurious beliefs about God. Not only the ignorant rabble, but also Homer and Hesiod portrayed the gods as thieves, liars, and adulterers. If cattle or horses had temples, they would worship therein deities bovine or equine.

Such worship was impious folly to Xenophanes. Deity, he felt, is beyond any evil or corruption, beyond multiplicity or change or limitation. Is this a spiritualized development of Anaximander's infinite *apeiron?* God is one and eternal, unlike mortals in body or in mind. He has no head or eyes or ears; He is all mind, all sight; He is supreme and abiding; there is no effort, no change or motion in Him.

The Deity of Xenophanes is not Jeremiah's universal-personal God of righteousness. The sage of Elea taught a philosophical pantheism; his God is the ultimate infinite Reality, beyond all limits and variation. In the Eleatic doctrine, early Greek meditation expressed its unqualified conviction of the basic unity of nature. Xenophanes gave this conviction a theological expression, but his pantheistic theology had explicitly philosophical implications. This more systematic analysis and exposition was achieved by his successor, the leading thinker of this school and the real head of the Eleatic philosophy, Parmenides.

PARMENIDES

Parmenides of Elea, born about 539 B.C., was of renowned family and broad culture. He saw a problem in the issue between the Heraclitean doctrine of universal flux and Xenophanes' conviction that Deity was one and unchanging. The dualism of human nature, divine-earthly, which the Pythagoreans taught, may have suggested to him the dualism in our views of the world—the contrast between appearance and reality. Truth and reality, according to Parmenides, were on the side of Xenophanes, and so Parmenides expounded this doctrine of the one ultimate Being as a systematic metaphysics.

In hexameter verse, Parmenides revealed the eternal essence of thorough pervasive truth and also exposed the unreliable opinions of mortals. The way of truth and reality is the way of reasoning, untroubled by the confusion and deception of the senses. The changes in and varieties of things which men observe are not real, for nothing really exists that is inconceivable to sound reasoning. How could we think of reality as that which is and also that which is not, as a primary substance which really becomes many other things that are the same as itself, being derived from it and yet not identical with it? How can we conceive of the ultimate Being as one and eternal, and also as a multiplicity of things that arise and pass away? No, Parmenides maintained, we can truly know and reason out only that which exists: a Being unitary, unmoved, and everlasting. Like a perfect sphere, it fills and is all space; it is all-pervasive and it alone abides. This absolute Being is one, continuous, indivisible, and self-identical throughout. We should err if we visualized it as a whole having parts, as being here rather than elsewhere, as occurring now rather than before or after. Its eternal reality transcends all such differences and limitations.

To speak of the origin or change, and transformation or motion, of Being, is to express ideas which cannot be reasoned out and are null and void. If Being ever began to exist, it could have come from either Being or non-Being. The first alternative reaffirms that Being is eternal; the second alternative is absurd, for out of nothing, nothing can arise. Likewise if Being is ever transformed, it must change into either Being or into non-Being. The first alternative denies the change that it would seek to prove, and the second alternative maintains absolute destruction, which is as absurd as the former second alternative of absolute origin. Again, if Being ever moves, it can do so only in space; but space is either Being or non-Being, and once more we should have to choose between a self-contradictory and an absurd alternative.

All the same, Parmenides takes notice of our sense perceptions, to which the world is manifested as various and changing, a world in which things combine and disintegrate, arise and pass away, adhere and move and follow each other in space and time. This way of viewing nature he calls the "way of opinion," and it is based on confused and deceptive appearances. Unlike Xenophanes, who brusquely denounced errors and superstitions, Parmenides leisurely exposed the opinions of men. Common daily impressions are cited in his verses, and traditional beliefs of the old mythology, but also some notions of the Ionian cosmologists. These vary as errors vary; they are more or less deceptive, but there is no real truth in any of them. Most men are content with random, hearsay opinions; they trust their senses and repeat the gossip of others without thorough reflection or analysis. They give full rein to their fancies, are charmed with untested illusions, and mistake them for profound wisdom.

So men have pictured the world as arising out of two opposite natures, one fine and subtle, celestial Fire, or Light, and the other dense or heavy Night. Dark necessity, Moira, drives the course of existence. The necessity is also an impulse that draws opposites to productive union. Men have called it "Eros," the first divine contriver that fructifies all nature by the union of male and female. Along with our random sense impressions and the fanciful or bold myths of tradition, Parmenides would include many cosmological doctrines of philosophical opinion: "How the earth and the sun and the moon, and the sky common to all things and the Galaxy, and uttermost Olympus and the hot strength of the stars came into being."[5]

Alongside of the Pythagorean doctrine of the Forms essential in the nature of things and the Pythagorean mathematical analysis, the metaphysics of Parmenides was the work of self-reliant reason, distrusting the alleged facts of daily sense experience, dismissing all changing particulars in its concentration on the one universal Being. But this august rationalism, with its denial of real multiplicity and change and motion, was unconvincing to common thought. Sense perception would not be ruled out of court. The later Eleatics undertook to elaborate the doctrine of Parmenides and to confirm the validity of his demonstrations by confuting sense experience.

ZENO THE ELEATIC

The controversial dialectician of the Eleatic school was the fellow townsman, and perhaps adopted son of Parmenides, Zeno (born about the beginning of the fifth century B.C.). He actually owes his fame in antiquity to the boldness with which he defended his denial of change and motion, and discredited the testimony of the senses and the idea that Being is divisible into parts.

If Being were a multiplicity, it would have to be either infinitely great or infinitely small, for its parts must be either divisible and discrete ad infinitum or indivisible, and so, as he judged, without any magnitude. The senses tell us of many things arising and passing away, but we should not trust them. If dropping a bushel of grain makes a noise, why can't a single grain be heard: or is a loud noise composed of a great many silences? Against the reality of motion, Zeno advanced several paradoxes which engaged ancient wits and which some modern mathematicians have revived. How can a courier cover a certain distance? He would have to pass through an infinite number of points. Let a moving body cover the first half of its journey, the half of that would remain, and so the half of the quarter, and the half of the remaining eighth, and so on indefinitely. Thus, in the famous paradox, if the

[5] M. T. McClure, *The Early Philosophers of Greece* (with translations by R. Lattimore), New York, Appleton-Century, 1935, p. 150.

tortoise had a start in its race with Achilles, the fleet hero would never overtake it, for while he was catching up with the distance he had to make up,
the tortoise would always have moved its little bit ahead. Take an arrow
supposedly in flight, at any moment it is at some point in space, and there
it is at rest. But how can you get a motion out of so many rests? Suppose
two chariots move with equal speed in opposite directions; they will pass
each other twice as fast as they will pass a stationary object of the same
length. In sum, motion—though apparent—is impossible; our reason cannot
entertain it without contradictions.

The conclusiveness of Zeno's arguments is very debatable, and the reader
may see directly the confusion in some of his paradoxes. But his dialectical
method was important in raising analytical problems in the conception of
space, time, motion, and matter. Say that an arrow in actual flight both is
and is not at different points in space—at different moments of time. Say that
Zeno, in considering the moving bodies passing each other in opposite directions, raises the problem of relativity but draws the wrong conclusion. Still
these paradoxes show analysis confusedly moving to deeper levels of reflection.

A basic difficulty in the Eleatic doctrine seemed to be its inability to include a plain recognition of change and motion in a strictly monistic conception of nature. But the opposite doctrine of universal flux could not be
accepted as final, and Heraclitus himself in effect modified it when he recognized a system of law and order of changes in the world. The Greek mind
required the recognition of both change and permanence. The new viewpoint
from which cosmology sought this reinterpretation of nature was pluralism.

Reconciliation of Change and Permanence: Pluralism and Atomism

The early Greeks were baffled by the problem of change because of their
monistic view of nature—their chemistry of one element. How can the one
basic substance alter in any way? The philosophy of change reported man's
common observation of things, but it could be confuted by able dialectic.
The philosophy of the one permanent Being could be reasoned out, but it
ran counter to man's plain daily experience. The pluralists met this tangle
of naturalism by rejecting the initial monism. The world is made of a number
of things. The general pattern of this new cosmology may be stated thus: in
the course of nature different elements form a changing variety of combinations, but each element retains its substantial identity throughout all changes.
With the Eleatics, these pluralists declare that there is universal permanence
(of the basic elements), but they agree also with Heraclitus that the world is
universal flux and change (of the combinations formed by the permanent
elements). On this common pluralistic basis, specific questions arise which
were answered differently: How many elements are there in nature? What

produces or breaks up their various combinations? Thus, there appeared contending theories of the complexity of structure in nature and of its process of operation.

EMPEDOCLES

The first doctrine of pluralism was advanced by Empedocles of Acragas in Sicily (*c.* 490–430). This pioneer in chemistry and biology was also a poet, a social-political reformer, a mystic, and a marvelous healer and wonderworker. Tradition or legend tells us that he delivered his people from oligarchic oppression and then refused to become their king; that he stopped a pestilence by cleaning up the marshes in the countryside; that he cut a passageway through a cliff to let in the invigorating north wind. With his healing art, he revived a woman who to all appearances had been dead for a month. Attired in purple with a golden girdle and a garland, he was adored as divine by his fellow countrymen. Legend has it, also, that after a feast he ascended to heaven in the fiery clouds of Mount Etna, and also that he leaped into the crater of the volcano. A more prosaic tradition related that he died an exile in the Peloponnesus.

Science and mythology vie in the philosophy of Empedocles, just as fact and legend are confused in the accounts of his life. He had followed the Pythagoreans as the votary of a cult; he believed in the transmigration of souls; in previous existences, he said, he had been a bird, a fish, a bush. But he also undertook an objective investigation of nature, ready to use both sense perception and reason in his search for the facts: "Come, learn with every bodily power the way in which each thing is clear."[6]

Empedocles agreed with the Eleatics that Being can neither arise from non-Being nor perish utterly. It is eternal and indestructible. But he did not admit the further inferences that Being is unitary, or that change and motion are inadmissible. The variety and complexity of nature manifest the operation of a number of basic substances. He recognized four elements or roots of existence: Fire, Air, Water, and Earth. Each of these four substances abides as self-identical, but they are ever brought together and torn asunder by two powers, or cosmic agencies, which Empedocles called "Love" and "Strife." If we said Attraction and Repulsion, we should be emphasizing the mechanical aspect of these agencies which Empedocles described not only as a scientist but also as a poet: "These [elements] never cease changing place continually, now being all united by Love into one, now each borne apart by the hatred engendered of Strife. . . ."[7]

The contemplation of this continual stir in nature led Empedocles to some bold ventures in cosmology. He imagined that all sorts of fortuitous combinations of the elements tangled the long evolution of living things, many of them monstrous: "Creatures arose with double faces and double breasts, off-

[6] *Ibid.*, p. 158.
[7] Milton C. Nahm (ed.), *Selections from Early Greek Philosophy*, New York, Crofts, 1934, p. 130.

spring of oxen with human faces. . . . Many heads grew up without necks, and arms were wandering about naked, bereft of shoulders, and eyes roamed about alone with no foreheads."[8] We shall meet this cosmological nightmare again in Lucretius, who, unlike Aristotle, admired the philosophical hexameters of the Sicilian sage. According to Empedocles, those misfit abortions perished, and suitable combinations in natural order multiplied themselves.

The entire course of nature, according to Empedocles, proceeds cyclically through four stages in the cosmic contest of Love and Strife. In the first stage, the four elements are joined by Love in perfect union. But then Strife breaks in and disrupts all order. So, in the third stage, there is complete isolation of substances in nature. Yet Love returns once more, to bring the elements together and achieve cosmic order. In this cyclic sweep of existence, worlds arise, dissolve, and are fashioned again and again. This doctrine of eternal recurrence, as we shall note later, is itself eclipsed and reappears in the history of cosmic speculation.

As an alternative version of pluralism, the doctrine of Empedocles was bound to give rise to critical objections. If a plurality of elements is recognized, why should their number be limited to four? The vast complexity of nature would seem to indicate an indefinite variety of basic substances. And furthermore, did Empedocles have four or six elements in his cosmology? What is the relation of Love and Strife to the four "roots" of Existence—Earth, Water, Air, and Fire? It seems confusing to regard Love and Strife as substances or elements of matter. Rather they are the powers or energies that determine the behavior of the elements in relation to each other. Thus, they determine the cosmic character of the elements, and are in a real sense the first principles of nature. Yet, the ways in which the elements are united or sundered by Love and Strife must somehow depend upon the nature of those four stuffs of being. These problems, and others implied in them, mark the development of Greek pluralism as it proceeds towards its culmination in the theory of Atomism.

ANAXAGORAS

Born about 500 B.C. in Clazomenae, Ionia, Anaxagoras early in life renounced wealth and political preferment to devote his life to reflection. In his thirties he settled in Athens and found there both high recognition and intense hostility. Pericles and the dramatist Euripides became his intimate friends, and young Socrates is said to have been his disciple for a time. His great learning and his personal dignity commanded wide respect, but adherents of the Homeric mythology suspected his radical views that the sun was not divine but only a glowing body of molten iron, and other similar dismissals of revered popular beliefs. Anaxagoras had been a resident of Athens for thirty years when, by the enemies of Pericles, he was charged with gross impiety. Anaxagoras was convicted and thrown into prison, from which he escaped to Lampsacus. This condemnation and the later, more momentous,

[8] *Ibid.*, p. 136.

condemnation of Socrates were two very exceptional departures from the general freedom of thought and speech in classical Greece.

Anaxagoras rejected the Eleatic view of the essential unity of all Being. His basic conviction was that things are infinitely various in number and in kind. This is qualitative pluralism. Empedocles' analysis seemed superficial and insufficient to Anaxagoras. Take wood, iron, hair, breath, blood: each of these is itself, irreducible to anything else. The number of different elements is vast beyond our power of reckoning. Anaxagoras called them the "seeds of existence." There is no limit to their accumulation, and they are infinitely divisible; yet they maintain their unique identity throughout. There is a less than the least, and there is a greater than the utmost, for nature cannot be limited. Nor can any of these particles in nature really be created or destroyed; they are eternal and in themselves abiding, but their relation to one another changes continually as they are commingled or separated. This is the world in actual operation.

The problem of explaining the orderly existence of things led Anaxagoras to his distinctive cosmic principle, and also to his confused conception of it. Left to themselves, the infinitely various seeds of existence would mix into an indiscriminate mass. This indeed was the supposed primordial state of being. It is as though we conceived of Anaximander's *apeiron* as an infinitely chaotic compound.

From this indistinct multifariousness a cosmos could arise only through the direction of an ordering agency. This cosmic operating activity Anaxagoras called *Nous*. The word means "Reason," but his use of it was not clear and consistent. He spoke of it as a directing, intelligent mind; he also treated it as a moving, rotating force that whirls and sorts masses of various seeds into appropriate compounds. In this way are formed worlds and systems of worlds, and in this way also come into being the great variety of things that we observe in nature.

Heraclitus had proclaimed a Law governing all changes, a Logos, or wisdom of things, in their universal flux. Anaxagoras saw in nature the evidence of an organizing rational power. This may be called his cosmic first principle, for it makes possible a cosmos or an order of nature. This recognition of the sovereignty of Mind was esteemed highly by Aristotle. Comparing Anaxagoras with the early philosophers who tried to explain the course and harmony of nature in merely mechanical terms, Aristotle praised him as a sober man among babblers. However, Aristotle criticized him for calling Mind the directive agency that constructs the universe, yet not really using mind to explain the detailed course of nature. This is also the criticism attributed to Socrates in Plato's *Phaedo*.

We might err if we regarded Anaxagoras as inconsistent in maintaining a distinction which perhaps he did not make at all. His *Nous* is the organizing agency in nature. Sometimes he felt obliged to view it explicitly as the designer and ruler of the cosmos, but again he described it as the finest and purest matter, the very opposite of the indiscriminate muddle of the seeds of existence when left to themselves. Anaxagoras did not discriminate be-tween rational system and merely mechanical succession or conglomeration. He followed the lead of his Ionian predecessors, like Anaximenes—who was perhaps his teacher—in explaining the course of nature mechanically by motion, contact and collision, condensation, and rarefaction. But while these early explorers of the constitution of things rejected the tales of the old anthropomorphic mythology, they retained some of its conviction that there was a kind of soul even in material things (hylozoism). When Anaxagoras dealt with processes that seemed to manifest intelligent direction, such as he felt in himself, he spoke of his *Nous* more definitely as Mind.

The above criticisms of Anaxagoras by Aristotle and Plato are the expres-sions of a later philosophy for which rational design and direction were dominant cosmic principles. But Anaxagoras was criticized also in the oppo-site way, for not explaining the course of things in strictly mechanical terms. This account of the explicit mechanics of nature was the doctrine of the Atomists.

DEMOCRITUS, THE ATOMIST

Democritus (born about 470 or 460 B.C.) is said to have been a native of Abdera in Thrace and a known contemporary of Socrates, whom he out-lived by thirty years. He boasted of his extensive travels, which perhaps took him to Egypt, Babylon, Persia, and India, and of his great erudition and versatile inquiry. But, of his scores of reputed treatises, only a few brief fragments have been preserved. The Epicureans must have known his works, for, as we shall note later, their philosophy was a development (Cicero calls it a repetition) of the Democritean atomism.

It is said that Democritus admired the Pythagoreans; with them he shared an emphasis on form and quantitative relations. But unlike them he did not recognize higher and lower, divine and titanic nature, or any qualitative differences in matter. In one sense he would agree with the Eleatics against his fellow pluralists: There are not different kinds of Being, neither four elements nor an infinity of them. Qualitatively existence is all one. The in-dubitable changes in nature must therefore be changes in shape or order or position. Change implies motion, and to Democritus motion implied an empty space in which things (filled space) can move. So the universe of Democritus is Being (matter) moving in non-Being (void or vacuum).

We may now consider the Democritean doctrine of atoms. Every thing we know can be divided; that is to say, it does not fill all the space that it seemingly occupies. Like a large gathering of men in one place, it can break up into smaller groups. And each group can similarly separate and be scat-tered. And each man likewise is a combination that can fall apart. Continue this process of division with each part of the body, with any object what-ever, be it the least that you can find, and always the various bits of matter that compose it in space can divide into still smaller ones. But there must be an end to this division of matter, for matter is not mere space, infinitely divisible, but matter *in* space. There must be indivisible bits of it, entirely filling the space which they occupy, and so Democritus called these ultimate particles "the indivisibles" or in Greek *atomoi*. The word comes from a root meaning "cut" or "section," preserved by us in words like appendec-*tomy*, or in en*tom*ology, the science of in*sect*s. Atoms are, if you please, "non-sects," without any parts or division. But we should not confuse them with mathematical points. These indivisibles are too small to be seen, but they have magnitude, and they have the quantitative distinctions of magnitudes; they differ in size, in shape, in position, in order, and in relation to other atoms. Qualitatively all alike, they are also alike in having motion inherent in their nature.

The world of Democritus is thus a world of atoms in motion in space. This is thoroughgoing materialism, and a strictly mechanistic cosmology. The last point is especially noteworthy. In order to explain the changing combination of their basic elements or particles, both Empedocles and Anaxagoras required cosmic agencies—Love and Strife, or *Nous*, Reason—a power or powers outside the elements or particles which combined, separated, or organized and directed them. To Democritus, all such cosmologies were defective. He required an account and explanation of the world that contained within itself the mechanism of its activity, without any Zeus or *Nous* to operate it. His world of atoms is a world that runs itself. In the doctrine of atomism the emancipation of the Greek mind from anthropomorphism and mythology seems to have been accomplished fully.

How does the Democritean world run itself? The motion of atoms in space brings them together, and their shape and position determine the nature and behavior of the resultant combinations or disintegrations of atomic masses. Imagine all the atoms falling in the boundless void, a sort of cosmic rain. The larger ones overtaking the smaller would collide with them; they would either join or bounce off each other in all conceivable directions. In this universal whirl or dance of atoms, clusters of various shapes or sizes would be formed, which in later collisions would either increase or break up. As the motion of the atoms would thus explain the whole sweep of existence, so the nature and behavior of each thing would be explained by the shape and size of the atoms composing it. Some atoms are rough, having crevices or hooks; they hang together. Other atoms are spherical or oval, and are very smooth; these are nimble and easily dissipated.

As are all other bodies in the heavens or on earth, so are we ourselves, whirling masses of atoms in space. Our so-called mind, or soul, is composed of the finest, smoothest, round or oval, and most delicately mobile atoms. With every breath we blow out some of them and breathe in others. They are distributed throughout our body, and the least motion around us stirs them. This is what we call their "sensitivity," and this is the mechanical process in every sensation—sight, hearing, etc. The senses perceive continually changing clusters of atoms, different for each perceiver or each moment of perception. They are unreliable witnesses and cannot yield universal knowledge, but only some conventional agreement; Democritus called it "bastard knowledge." It is by reason that we infer the truth about the nature of things—that they must all be changing compounds of minute and invisible unchanging atomic particles. Did Democritus mean to incorporate reason in his mechanical explanation of knowledge? He did not indicate clearly the distinction of the reliable, "legitimate" rational process, by which we recognize the ultimate particles of matter, from our shifting sensitivity to combinations of atoms. In any case, it would seem that we must proceed from mechanical processes to whatever can be meant by knowledge. Nothing exists or takes place but clusters of atoms, contacts and collisions of atoms. My idea of anything is literally my impression of it, the way it strikes me.

In this mechanics of human existence, could any recognition of moral activity be inferred? It is interesting to note that many of the preserved sayings of Democritus are ethical. He taught a way to happiness and tranquillity of mind by genial recognition of the nature of things, a life of moderate pleasures and equanimity, a philosophic resigned cheerfulness. Antiquity called him "the laughing philosopher."

The atomism of Democritus knits together many strands of the early Greek idea about the nature of things into a cosmological texture that is the culminating achievement of early Greek science; but it also raises some perplexing questions. The Greek undertook to explore and to understand the structure of nature. In describing and explaining the world by the strict mechanics of atoms in motion in space, Democritus was consistent enough to describe the so-called "process" of knowledge also atomistically. This involved him in the problem regarding the truth of our ideas. His way of dealing with this problem and its difficulties might, and did, give rise to skepticism. But in resisting skeptical doubts, other thinkers in the classical age of Athenian philosophy sought a sound basis for knowledge in rational insight. They turned from the Democritean whirl of atoms to a theory of nature in which reason could really abide, recognize and realize its true character.

SUGGESTED WORKS FOR FURTHER STUDY

SELECTIONS FROM EARLY GREEK PHILOSOPHERS. Bakewell, Charles M., *Source Book in Ancient Philosophy;* Fairbanks, Arthur, *The First Philosophers of Greece;* Kirk, G. S., and Raven, J. E., *The Pre-Socratic Philosophers;* McClure, M. T., *The Early Philosophers of Greece;* Nahm, Milton C., *Selections from Early Greek Philosophy.*

HISTORIES OF EARLY GREEK PHILOSOPHY. Burnet, John, *Early Greek Philosophy;* Cornford, F. M., *From Religion to Philosophy;* Guthrie, W. K. C., *History of Greek Philosophy,* Vol. I: *Earlier Pre-Socratics and the Pythagoreans;* Jaeger, Werner, *The Theology of the Early Greek Philosophers;* Scoon, R. M., *Greek Philosophy Before Plato.*

2. Socrates: Critical Philosophy of Life

Denial of Any Real Knowledge: the Sophists

The second chapter in the history of Greek thought reviews a period of transition marked by a radical shift in philosophical outlook and method. For a hundred and fifty years, men had inquired into the structure and order of nature. Their rich variety of cosmologies were more or less plausible, and they were expounded by able advocates. But they were inconsistent with each other and could not all be true. Was any one of them the really true account of nature? How could one ever know this? The Greek mind was thus confronted with the problem of knowledge and truth.

The title of this section indicates that the men called Sophists answered the question about knowledge with skeptical dismissal: Men's minds are not capable of attaining real truth. This was the eventual conclusion of the Sophists, and it produced a crisis in Greek science and philosophy; but it was not their initial teaching. A brief survey of their profession in Greek life is necessary, if we are to understand fairly how the Sophists acquired the disrepute with which Plato and Aristotle have familiarized us, and from which some modern scholars have tried to defend them.

The term "Sophists," or wise men, was at first generally applied to thinkers or inquiring minds before the designation "philosophers" gained currency. More particularly, a Sophist was an acknowledged expert, and versatile excellence swelled his fame. The early philosophers sought to probe the structure and the operation of nature, and some of them pursued inquiries in many special fields: geometry, astronomy, map making, agriculture, medicine, music, stagecraft, and sanitary engineering. But learned men of a new kind soon appeared in Greece, men who gained popularity by their practical exploitation of expert skill and who were ready to impart it to others. The technical manuals of these Sophists were eagerly bought by many who could not follow either general or special cosmological reflections. Such teachers

28

attracted disciples who were eager to learn from them and who paid them handsomely for their instruction. They traveled from one city to another and, eventually, to Athens, which had become the center of Greek life and culture.

In charging money for their teaching, the Sophists evoked from Socrates and others stern criticism, which has not impressed modern intellectual workers. We should remember that for the early explorers of nature knowledge and wisdom were treasures of the soul, sought for their own sake and freely shared. Socrates must have looked on those other mercenary sages as some of us regard professional athletes. But the traveling experts commanded popular applause, not only from their pupils who hoped to profit in their turn by what they could learn, but also from the throngs who were swept by admiration for their eloquent display of versatile mastery.

The Sophists, then, were distinguished by their mental attitude and aim. They were not pure seekers after understanding or, like the true philosophers, pursuers of wisdom. They were rather the purveyors of ideas for gain or fame or practical control. This emphasis on practice was motivated by various considerations of private advantage or social utility. The mastery which they imparted to their pupils was a marketable commodity. It not only enriched themselves and their pupils but it showed their eminence above ordinary men. An exceptionally able and cultivated person was self-reliant in any situation, not dependent upon others. Thus, the Sophist Hippias boasted that he could design and produce everything that he wore or used.

Above all other craft and wisdom was statecraft, the art of achieving social security and mastery. The importance of this political wisdom was impressed on Greek minds by the historical course of events, and nowhere more emphatically than in Athens and in the states that patterned themselves after her. The dominance of Athens was due not merely to her military and naval power nor to her industrial and commercial vitality, but mainly to her preeminence in statesmanship, to the large supply of astute leaders which her political organization elicited and developed. The social reforms in Athens that gained headway under the direction of Cleisthenes in the sixth century pointed toward middle-class government. Not the word of a king or a tyrant, but the vote of the people, decided what was law and how it was to be enforced. But in a social-political order maintained by suffrage, the supreme power was that of eloquent persuasion which could win popular support. In the execution of law in the courts one's conviction or acquittal depended on the effectiveness of a lawyer's pleading; similarly in the establishment of law, the astute, political use of ideas by the expert orator was decisive. To thousands of men, especially young men who aspired to leadership in the state, rhetoric became the chief art and science.

Thus, the naturalism of the earlier explorers of the cosmos was followed by the humanism of these ambitious public men. They were not stirred to speculation about the basic nature of things; their minds turned to the nature and course of men's beliefs and preferences, their loyalties, ambitions, and passions, and how they could be deeply moved and brought to decision and action. They pursued the art of social dominion. As in their mechanical crafts the Sophists were satisfied with various specific skills and had not inquired into the ultimate structure of nature, so in their political-social thinking they did not go beyond immediate expedience. When they taught Athenians, they were prepared to forget some of their teaching at Abdera or in Sicily. Right and wrong teaching varied with the place and time and the particular situation. The most statesmanlike orator was he who knew which line to follow most effectively with this or that assembly of men whom he was trying to sway. No ultimate principle concerned the Sophists but the belief or interest of the moment. If they had any basic conviction, it was a Heraclitean sense of the endless variety and flux of human affairs. But they did not, like Heraclitus, recognize any universal law in the flux of nature. Law to them was itself only changing custom; it was men's attachment to some adopted opinion; it was unstable, but supreme so long as it had popular support. The poet Pindar wrote: "Custom rules all men." But what were the foundations of custom? Men's varying opinions and feelings.

Step by step the Sophists were led away from the scientific-philosophical pursuit of understanding, from insight into the fundamental laws of nature and human nature, toward practical expediency, control, and management of the particular situation; away from the search after truth, to persuasion and effective direction of popular beliefs and opinions. Implied in all this astute trafficking in ideas was a finally skeptical state of mind, in both theory and practice. Rampant disputants like Callicles or Thrasymachus simply defied any appeals to sovereign right or sound reason as empty pretensions. But the more reflective Sophists undertook to reason out their denial of any valid reason, to prove that no conclusive proof, no knowledge was available.

GORGIAS AND PROTAGORAS

We have been tracing here a spreading tendency in Greek thought rather than the development of a philosophical system of ideas. Only a few sayings have been preserved even of the two most famous Sophists. Their skeptical conclusions enable us to understand the stern criticism to which both of them were subjected by Plato.

Gorgias was sent by his city, Leontini in Sicily, as an ambassador to Athens in the year 427 B.C. (the year of Plato's birth). He charmed the Athenians with his eloquence, and throughout Greece his golden tongue won him triumphant welcome. During his long life of over a century he was lauded as the master of oratory. It is strange that a man whose specialty was rhetoric and the art of persuasion reached in his philosophy the conclusion that ideas cannot really be communicated.

The skepticism of Gorgias has been recorded in the threefold inference he drew from the Eleatic doctrine of Being. Being does not exist; even if it did exist, we could not know it; and even if anyone knew it, he could not communicate his knowledge to others. Gorgias' arguments for the first proposition illustrate the grammatical, rhetorical, and logical artifices in which the Sophists excelled. When you say that non-Being is not, you admit that it *is* not; and when you say that Being is not non-Being, you admit that Being *is not* non-Being. So Being and non-Being are alike confusing, and since non-Being, of course, does not exist, no more does Being exist; Gorgias reached the same skeptical conclusion by showing that contradictory attributes can be plausibly ascribed to Being, without ground for conclusive preference either way. So Being is emptied of all reality.

In his second and third proposition, Gorgias was appealing directly to the perplexities of human experience. Neither by our sensations nor by any reasoning can we reach certain knowledge of the existence and nature of Being. By the very conception of this ultimate reality, we are bound to admit that it is beyond our reach. Yet, if peradventure you or I did possess such knowledge, how could we share it? Our communication of ideas is by means of words, and words have no settled meaning and are unreliable means of sharing ideas. From beginning to end, our minds proceed by opinion ever beset with uncertainties.

The preeminence of Protagoras of Abdera (*c.* 481–411) as a teacher matched Gorgias's fame for eloquence. Long trains of disciples followed him from one city to another. In the dialogue, *Protagoras*, Plato portrays vividly the enthusiasm of the Athenians for the celebrated Sophist: the mansion and the spacious court of Callias overflow with distinguished guests who hang on every word of the renowned sage. Yet, while Protagoras dominates the scene, two other Sophists, Hippias and Prodicus, are also there, each with his circle of admirers.

Protagoras rejected the distinction between sense perception and reason on which his fellow townsman, Democritus, relied for his conviction or "legitimate" knowledge about the atomic structure of things. What we call reason is itself reducible to a variety of sensations. This means that all our ideas of things are shifting, individual impressions. Each one of us can observe only the way a certain passing composition and condition of things affects him at the moment. How can any number of such reflections of a changing variety in a changing medium yield reliable knowledge, truth?

But, beyond these individual variations that invalidate any claim to universal truth, there is a basic defect in all our ideas. They are all limited by the processes and conditions of sense experience. We never possess nature itself; we have only our perceptions of things, our subjective reactions. The various qualities of things—colors, sounds, odors—depend upon our ways with them: seeing, hearing, smelling. So Protagoras reached his famous doctrine: "Man is the measure of all things, alike of their existence and their non-existence."[1] Protagoras, therefore, dismissed all proposed accounts of the real nature of things as vain pretensions. We have only men's versions of reality, versions that are shifting impressions, different for each man at each moment. Instead

[1] Diogenes Laertius, *The Lives and Opinions of Eminent Philosophers* (trans. C. D. Yonge), London, Bohn's Libraries, 1853, p. 397.

of formulating the laws of nature, a man should merely say, "It seems to me thus and so, here and now." No real knowledge is available.

This doctrine undermines science and philosophy, and it was bound to unsettle rational validity in all fields of reflection. We make lofty claims for virtue, right, and justice. But, according to the Sophists, our moral judgments are only the expressions of our peculiar likes and dislikes. Instead of declaring loftily, "This is good!" we should remark more properly that we happen to like it at the moment. As to justice and law, they are but the expressions of the prevailing will of those in power. Right is might. Nor does religious conviction fare any better. What to me is holy may move you to derision. Protagoras was acclaimed by the radical freethinkers in Athens, but he shocked the conservative believers by his essay, "On the Gods," which he read before a company at the home of the tragic poet Euripides: "As to the Gods, I know not whether they exist or not, or what they might be."[2]

The skeptical vein that marked many Greek minds during the latter half of the fifth century was not merely the effect of Sophistic teaching. The wide fame of the Sophists was itself due in part to their eloquent expression of the popular unsettling of all universal principles. The age of the Sophists, we should remember, was also the age of Greek tragedy. The old myths which were reenacted before the multitudes at the theater portrayed the character of the gods and goddesses in their dealings with men. The Greeks of the fifth century could not recognize divine perfection in these traditional deities. Zeus punished Prometheus for his generous gift of fire to men. The divine Furies tortured Orestes for obeying the behest of the god Apollo to avenge his father's murder by slaying the murderess, his mother, Clytemnestra. The people of Thebes were smitten with pestilence for the unwitting parricide and incest of their King Oedipus, who had been led to his dread destiny while forthrightly seeking to evade it. If even the Gods were thus confused in their ideas of good and evil, how were men to know the true and godly way of virtue? The perplexities to which Aeschylus, Sophocles, and Euripides were giving creative expression stirred the more reflective minds to productive criticism, but they also left large multitudes baffled.

Two profoundly significant results of Sophist teaching should be recognized. By turning the main direction of Greek thinking from doctrines about nature to the self-exploration of mind and the meaning and principles of knowledge and the other values of life, it opened the new classical period of Greek philosophy which was to reach its consummation in the rationalism of Plato and Aristotle. Furthermore, the Sophists' preoccupation with the art of persuasion, with rhetoric and the dialectical play of ideas, went beyond word-splitting artifices. It served to perfect a language that was to become a fine instrument for philosophical exposition. But the fuller realization of the new philosophy required deeper insight into both the purposes and the methods of productive thinking. Dialectic had to be raised from disputatious

2 *Ibid.*

skill to a fertile contention of ideas in the eliciting of truth. And the concentration on the mind's self-inquiry had to lead beyond the shifting confusions of sense to the laws and principles of reason. The pioneer in this reconstruction of Greek philosophy was Socrates.

The Life and Character of Socrates

The lifetime of Socrates (469–399) was a period of dramatic contrasts in Greek history. He was born at the close of the Persian Wars, and his youth and early manhood saw the rise of his native Athens to imperial and cultural dominance in Greece in the Golden Age of Pericles. In his later years, he witnessed the ruin of Greek cities in the Peloponnesian War and the subjugation of Athens by Sparta. His courage was as distinguished on the field of battle as in his resistance to the unjust designs and intrigues of politicians and tyrants at home. In his loyalty to the right, he faced death with equanimity. But his real struggles were in the inner life of the spirit; his great achievement was the discovery of man's soul and of his goal in life, the perfection of character through self-understanding.

Socrates' father was a sculptor and his mother was noted for her skill as a midwife. Perhaps Socrates himself tried his hand at sculpture, but he soon reached the conclusion that he was meant to be a molder and fashioner, not of stones, but of souls. He claimed that, in his own way, he was following his mother's profession. For men's minds were pregnant with knowledge; by right inquiry they could be led to give birth to true ideas. This was his art of *maieutic*, philosophical midwifery.

The Greeks had a conviction that beauty and goodness were kin, and they expressed it in their word for nobleness, *kalokagathia*, meaning beauty-goodness. To this Socrates was the outstanding exception, for his personal appearance belied his inner worth. This wisest and best and most righteous of men, as his disciples called him, was in outward form and looks the epitome of ugliness and coarse stupidity. With bulging eyes, swollen nostrils, and heavy lips; his short, stout body ill clad, unkempt, and ungainly, he looked like a satyr pacing barefoot through the streets of Athens. Yet Apollo himself could not have enchanted the Athenians more than Socrates.

His strong personal influence was due to his firm and upright character and his contagious spirit of inquiry. His integrity and his devotion to justice and high ideals were inflexible. Alone against the executive committee of the senate, he defended the generals at the Battle of Arginusae from unjust summary treatment. He risked his life in refusing to carry out a lawless order of the Thirty Tyrants. With brave endurance he could confront both danger and iniquity; his only concern was lest he himself be unfair in any way. His criticism of the conventional religious beliefs and practices resulted from his own deeper and more searching spirit of piety. In an age of moral looseness and perversities, Socrates was pure without prudery, and temperate without constraint. He usually did not drink, but he could show capacity on occasion. His companions around the banquet table, as related in the *Symposium*, might drop off to sleep as wine overcame them, or stagger away; but Socrates drank and discoursed all night, even until daybreak, urging the drowsy Agathon and Aristophanes to acknowledge the kinship of the tragic and the comic spirit. Even while he remained unsullied by any pollution of sensuality, he was versed in all the intimate insights of gallantry, and, like a religious mystic, used the language of erotic intensity to express spiritual devotion and aspiration.

As in his moral conduct, so in his intellectual activity Socrates was possessed by a spirit of consecration which only Pythagoras before him had manifested in any degree. Beyond his curiosity that led him to explore the nature of things, Socrates had a pious devotion to critical inquiry; it was his mission in life. Who ever lived more whole-heartedly than he—yet always and only on his own terms? Whereas the Sophists made a good living out of philosophy, to Socrates, philosophy was the meaning and the worth of life. When unprincipled demagogues charged him with impiety and corrupting the young and induced an Athenian court to condemn him to death, Socrates was more concerned to defend his cause than his life: "Men of Athens, I honour and love you; but I shall obey God rather than you, and while I have life and strength I shall never cease from the practice and teaching of philosophy. . . ."[3] As his death verdict was confirmed, Socrates used his last minutes with his fellow citizens to plead before them the truth of his cause:

Wherefore, O judges, be of good cheer about death, and know of a certainty, that no evil can happen to a good man, either in life or after death. . . . When my sons are grown up, . . . reprove them, as I have reproved you, for not caring about that for which they ought to care. . . . The hour of departure has arrived and we go our ways—I to die, and you to live. Which is better, God only knows.[4]

"The Socratic Problem" in Histories of Philosophy

The martyrdom of Socrates, like the destruction of the Pythagorean fraternity house in Crotona, was a departure from the usual freedom of thought and discussion which marked the Greek communities. The imprisonment of Anaxagoras for impiety and the later banishment of Aristotle from Athens by the anti-Macedonian party are the other notorious instances. In all four cases, the prejudices of the populace were exploited by enemies of philosophy whose own motives were those of partisan politics. It is not difficult to under-

[3] Plato, *Apology*, in *The Dialogues of Plato* (trans. B. Jowett), 3rd ed. (in 5 vols.), Oxford, Clarendon Press, 1892, Vol. II, p. 29. The paging in all the quotations from Plato is that indicated along the margins of the work.
[4] *Ibid.*, p. 41.

stand why the Socratic method of discussion aroused the hostility of bigots and demagogues. But, when we try to probe the teachings of Socrates, we find his influence acknowledged by many diverse followers, and the full recovery of the original doctrine raises some baffling problems.

Socrates left no writings; hence in our study of his philosophy we have to rely on secondary sources, the earliest and principal ones being the works of Plato, Xenophon, and Aristotle. These three versions of the master's doctrines are at variance, and the historians of philosophy have been perplexed by the so-called "Socratic problem": How to take due cognizance of the divergent accounts without being led to a one-sided interpretation? This problem cannot be evaded, either now or later, for it concerns our understanding, not only of Socrates' teaching, but also of Plato's. We shall outline briefly the main alternatives of historical criticism.

The chief divergence is between Plato and Xenophon, both of them devoted disciples of Socrates. In his *Memorabilia*, Xenophon portrays Socrates as a moral teacher of unblemished integrity, concerned with the problems and principles of the good and godly life rather than with metaphysical principles or abstruse speculations about the nature and structure of the cosmos. But, in his *Dialogues*, Plato uses Socrates as the chief spokesman in the discussion and exposition of profound philosophical theories, metaphysical as well as ethical, about the nature of the universe, mind and matter, knowledge, reality, and value. The traditional explanation of these two different interpretations was sought in the patently different quality of mind shown in the writings of Xenophon and Plato. Xenophon was a keen observer and a faithful chronicler, but he lacked philosophical insight. While he reported the actual teachings of Socrates, which were mainly moral and practical, he did not perceive their ultimate systematic implications to which Socrates may have alluded on occasion, without emphasizing or developing them. But Plato not only heard the master's words, he also contemplated their full range and purport; he thought Socrates' ideas through to their ultimate conclusions. It is this philosophy which is expounded in Plato's *Dialogues;* it is Socratic in its first inception, but decidedly Platonic in its systematic expression. Thus, although we may find in the *Dialogues* the fuller development of the Socratic philosophy in its implications, the master's actual teachings were reported more reliably by Xenophon. So the traditional historical accounts of the Socratic doctrine have emphasized its moral-practical character, and have cited Plato's *Dialogues* when they agreed with the reports of Xenophon. The profound metaphysics in the *Dialogues* is Platonic even though, in his favorite method of exposition, Plato uses Socrates as its spokesman.

This traditional interpretation has been challenged by able critics, notably in English by John Burnet and A. E. Taylor. According to them, Plato, not Xenophon, is our most reliable source for the study of the Socratic teachings. In his early *Dialogues* and to a certain extent in the works of his maturity, like *The Republic*, Plato is expounding the doctrine of his master. This view recognizes the systematic mastery of Plato, which reached its fruition and developed along independent lines, as may be seen in his later *Dialogues,* in which Socrates is not used as the chief spokesman. But it maintains that, beyond his moral-practical teachings, Socrates pursued metaphysical inquiries in which he went beyond the Pythagoreans and Parmenides, to doctrines such as the theory of Ideas which have usually been regarded as Platonic.

An explicit choice between these two interpretations seems to be neither imperative nor warranted by the evidence. Xenophon's characteristic quality of mind, as a chronicler and an apologist rather than a systematic interpreter, is patent; but evident also is Plato's creative intelligence which possessed and fructified every idea that it touched. The Socratic doctrine would most likely be recognized as somewhere between the chronicles of Xenophon and the metaphysics of Plato. Socrates, who discussed everything with everyone in Athens, could not have remained indifferent to the naturalistic inquiries and theories of the earlier philosophers. But, while he refused to follow the skeptical vein of the Sophists, he seems to have shared their distrust of the contending cosmologies. And his own preference for inquiries into self-understanding and the principles of knowledge and virtue may have been reinforced by his noncommitment in physics and metaphysics.

Along this line of interpretation, the divergence between Xenophon's *Memorabilia* and Plato's earlier *Dialogues* does not appear so baffling. Some critics may cite here the reports of Aristotle, himself a pioneer historian of philosophy. Aristotle's explicit distinction between Plato and Socrates, in the first book of the *Metaphysics,* should be kept in mind:

Socrates was busying himself about ethical matters and neglecting the world of nature as a whole but seeking the universal in these ethical matters, and fixed thought for the first time on definitions. Plato accepted his teaching, but held that the problem applied not to sensible things but to entities of another kind. . . . Things of this other sort, then, he called Ideas.[5]

The Method and Teachings of Socrates

Socrates resembled the Sophists in his multifarious discussions with his many followers, and we find him thus portrayed—or rather cartooned—in the *Clouds,* the comedy by Aristophanes. Socrates is shown suspended in a basket, floating in the air and airy in his dismissal of common beliefs and principles. He is reckoned one with the Sophists,

> Who can show pleaders how to twist a cause,
> So you'll but pay them for it, right or wrong.[6]

[5] Aristotle, *Metaphysics* (trans. W. D. Ross), in Richard McKeon (ed.), *The Basic Works of Aristotle,* New York, Random House, 1941, 987b. The paging is that indicated along the margins of the work.

[6] Aristophanes, *Clouds,* Scene 1 (trans. T. Mitchell), in *The Frogs and Three Other Plays of Aristophanes,* London, Dent, n.d., p. 116.

As a comedy about unprincipled speculation, the *Clouds* was irresistible, and Socrates is reported to have laughed with the rest of the audience. But, as an interpreter of Socrates, Aristophanes went astray; in important conclusions, Socrates differed radically from the Sophists. Like them, he exposed much alleged knowledge as spurious, empty opinion. Indeed, as reported by Plato in the *Apology*, Socrates was described by the oracle as the wisest man in Athens, yet he was deeply conscious of his ignorance. He had set out to seek someone wiser than himself, but he found the other Athenians blind in their vain conceit, unaware of their own ignorance. When he sought to show them the error and confusion of their opinions, he naturally aroused the hostility of many.

But Socrates did not then proceed, like the Sophists, to a skeptical dismissal of knowledge. He was convinced that knowledge was to be had, and that the way to it began with the exposure of error and the conviction of ignorance: the so-called "Socratic irony" his characteristic manner. Although deadly earnest as he was about the problems of life which he was exploring, he did not presume to know the answers. The reverse of stodgy pedantry was the saving grace of humor with which he regarded his criticism of others, for it might well be turned on himself. In exploring their bigoted opinions by his critical method, he was ever wary of bigotry in himself. This attitude was tactically advantageous, especially in dealing with the Sophists; it gave him the favored position of a questioner. But, beyond argumentative tactics, the Socratic irony expressed his searching intelligence. Knowledge could come from the interplay of ideas by which minds proceed to real understanding. This was the dialectical method, the method of critical discussion, in which he proved himself a past-master. By raising the right questions, a mind may be led, beyond random impressions of particular things, to a firm grasp of some universal law or meaning. We may recognize here two things that may be fairly accredited to Socrates: inductive arguments and universal definition. In dealing with the mass of particulars in daily experience, the uncritical mind readily jumps to unconsidered conclusions. Through dialectical inquiry, we may explore the general warrant for our opinions; we may seek out the basic purport and meaning of our experiences and of the terms by which we express them.

May we not say that Socrates in his own way was raising the old problem of the nature of things? But, in common judgments of conduct, he insisted on keeping to the reliable ground of people's daily experience. Or at least he felt bound to start with a critical study of men's choices and practices. Before undertaking to know the structure of the cosmos, he would first try to know himself. He had in his youth pursued cosmological inquiries with the various explorers of nature. He had found them disappointingly inconclusive, and worse, misleading and irrelevant. Anaxagoras taught in general that the world was ordered and directed by reason, but he tried to explain the daily course of nature mechanically and did not really recognize the nature and role of mind in human affairs. How could one explain human action—say, Socrates' refusal to escape from his prison cell—mechanically, by the various twists and frictions of his bones and muscles? Whether or not we can ever understand the nature of the world, certainly we shall never know it adequately, and relevantly to ourselves, until we have first understood ourselves. To this most important understanding Socrates devoted himself.

Socrates first of all sought universal principles in ethics. Men use common terms of approval or condemnation: *just, unjust, courageous, cowardly*. But what is the real meaning of these so-called "good" and "bad" qualities of human character? Socrates described himself as the "gadfly of Athens." With his questions, he stung the Athenians and roused them from their mental torpor to examine, understand, and to define their common notions. In various *Dialogues*, Plato recorded and developed the Socratic pursuit of universal definitions. The *Charmides* raises the question, What is Temperance? The *Laches* is similarly concerned with Courage; the *Lysis* with Friendship; and, in a more systematic philosophical criticism, the *Republic* explores the meaning and the nature of Justice. We find repeatedly that Socrates not only seeks a definition of the specific virtue that is being examined, but he reaches beyond it to consider what makes it a virtue and what is the basic meaning of Virtue. This pursuit of universal definition is the main Socratic contribution to the philosophical theory of knowledge. Socrates noted men's common tendency to draw general inferences from the particular data of daily experience. Most of these opinions, however, are unsound, for they do not rest upon adequate reflection. The dialectical method aimed to achieve, by thorough examination and analysis, a true statement of the universal concepts by which our knowledge of the essential character of things is expressed.

These dialectical inquiries do not reach final conclusive results, but they advance the search after truth by clearing up common errors. We may consider briefly the discussion of the nature of Virtue, in the *Meno*. The subject of conversation is that of moral education: Can Virtue be taught? But, Socrates remarks, surely we should first ask, What is Virtue? To this question Meno has a ready answer: There are all sorts of virtues, appropriate to different sorts and conditions of persons—husbands or wives, friends or enemies, young or old. "How fortunate I am, Meno," Socrates exclaims, "When I ask you for one virtue you present me with a swarm of them!"[7] But, following the analogy of the beehive, Socrates insists: Bees differ, but surely they differ as bees; so virtues differ as virtues. Now what is the common quality which they share, on the basis of which we distinguish them from each other? The further course of the discussion is a good sample of dialectical argument. Meno proposes examples of virtue, attempts to draw a list of them, ventures on some definitions, but repeatedly Socrates exposes his unsound understanding of his theme.

These inquiries are not futile. Throughout Plato's *Dialogues*, Socrates reaches the conclusion that the various virtues and perfections of human character are practical expressions of true self-knowledge and understanding.

---

[7] Plato, *Meno*, in *The Dialogues of Plato, op. cit.*, Vol. II, p. 72.

The genuinely courageous man is not the one who merely, as we say, acts bravely; his conduct expresses his insight into the laws and the role of courage in human nature. It is an evidence of self-understanding. Each virtue in its way is an expression of intelligence in action. This is the great teaching of Socrates: Virtue is knowledge. By *Virtue*, however defined in detail, he means man's fullest perfection and his highest good. And by knowledge he means more than reliable learning and information: it is intelligent and life-possessing conviction: true vital conviction of the good, and resolute will to pursue and attain it.

No man knowingly and intentionally proceeds to his ruin. In any situation, a man's choice expresses his opinion that he is reaching for the best, the best in the circumstances. But this judgment may be right or it may be mistaken. The gold which the evil man rushes to grasp in his blind desire is fool's gold. Vice is really ignorance; virtue springs from true insight. It is essentially wisdom. Applied to various fields of human experience, it expresses itself in different but related excellences of character. Justice expresses an understanding of what is or is not our right and our obligation. Temperance indicates true discrimination of real satisfaction from delusive indulgence and pleasure. Courage manifests clear-headed self-possession in the face of danger and evil, knowledge of what is really to be feared and resisted.

So Socrates reached his basic conclusion: The unexamined life is not worth human living. One must live up to the full capacities and perfection of human nature. The good life is the intelligent life, and that life alone yields true and abiding satisfaction. The happiness of such a life is more than pleasure, just as its intelligence is more than learning. Our true career in life is not the amassing of wealth, nor external mastery, nor the indulgence of our desires and passions. Each of us is a soul capable of perfection. A man's chief aim and highest good must be to recognize himself, to bring his soul to full fruition and to make it as perfect as possible. This realization includes external attainment and social effectiveness, but its consummation is spiritual, in the inner life of man. Beyond any outward success or security, a man must be at peace with himself. To a truly good man, no mishap or hurt can be a moral disaster; he has already mastered the real evils and is in serene possession of the good. We shall see what use the Stoics in a later age made of this Socratic concentration on the supreme values of the inner life.

This Socratic spirituality was not ascetic. It was never divorced from the liveliest participation in the daily business of living. But it revealed inner regions of the soul's self-consecration in which the philosophy and ethics of Socrates manifested a religious-mystical spirit. The sage of Athens had qualities of saintliness. We remarked earlier that Socrates in all his discussions and inquiries seemed to indicate a feeling of a mission in life. For him, living philosophically was living in the sight of God. Just as he could not understand his own human nature without recognizing the central role of intelligence, so he was bound to acknowledge the rational direction of the cosmos. In pursuing and achieving the perfection of his soul, the best and the highest in his life, he felt himself also in harmony with the divine purpose in the world. He was ever alert to the utterance of the divine in his soul; he called it his guiding spirit, and he listened to it with pious resolution. In his life it played the role of conscience or of inspiration. In his hour of crisis this basic conviction of his spirit was supreme and imperative. "This, dear Crito, is the voice which I seem to hear murmuring in my ears, like the sound of the flute in the ears of the mystic. . . . Leave me, then, Crito, to fulfil the will of God, and to follow whither he leads."[8]

The Lesser Disciples of Socrates

Great thinking aims at simplicity, but it is complex, and it may point various ways. These qualities, already noted in the thought of Socrates and complicating the interpretation of his philosophy, are manifest also in his influence on his followers. The master's teaching, as carried on by his disciples, is reflected differently according to differences in their temperaments or special interests or personal outlook. Their emphasis on some parts of the Socratic philosophy, because it neglects other parts, gives us a distorted view of the whole. Correct in some of the details, their accounts do not achieve truth, which requires balance and integrity. Three types of lesser or imperfect Socratic schools exhibit the same basic defect in various ways. Fortunately, the Socratic circle included a philosophic genius in whom creative and systematic powers vied for perfection. Plato not only grasped the teachings and the problems of Socrates in all their bearings, but also brought them to fuller fruition in his own philosophy.

THE MEGARIANS

Socrates' emphasis on universal definition and his pursuit of the principle of Unity in Virtue received one-sided development in the school which his disciple Euclides established in Megara. Euclides was interested in questions of logical analysis, and he had studied with the Eleatics. His use of the Socratic doctrine shows the persisting influence of his earlier teachers. He identified the Socratic unity of the Good with the Eleatic unity of Being. But he and his followers then asked, How can there be many virtues, and how can the unity of Being be reconciled with a plurality of attributes or qualities? How can a tree be both tall and green; and how can green be both of the tree and of sea water? The Socratic doctrine that Virtue is Knowledge became, in its Megarian statement, a view of the good philosophic life as a preoccupation with logic; but this in the course of time degenerated into hair-splitting subtleties and conundrums. Is a liar lying when he tells us that he always lies?

[8] Plato, *Crito*, in *ibid.*, p. 54.

THE CYRENAICS

On the north coast of Africa directly across the Mediterranean from Greece lay the prosperous colony of Cyrene, protected by a range of mountains from the hot desert of the interior, with a pleasant climate, fertile and well watered soil, and good harbors for commerce—a lush garden of prosperity. The rich ranchmen and traders of Cyrene raced their horses at Olympia, sent their sons to school in the mother country. Thus there came to Athens Aristippus, the Cyrenaic (c. 435–356), an affable, debonair man-about-town, an easygoing, boon companion with a penchant for philosophy, which he reckoned among his chief diversions. Before he joined the Socratic circle, he had paid high fees to Protagoras, and he never forgot the great Sophist's insistence that all alleged knowledge is only shifting opinion. We can never go beyond our passing impressions and feelings.

When Socrates declared that the good life was the life of understanding and that it alone yielded real happiness, Aristippus translated the master's wisdom to mean that the happy life, the life of the greatest pleasure is the really intelligent and worth-while life. The course of our experience may be smooth or rough or quite stagnant; wisdom consists in knowing how to crowd the most enjoyment into our life, in not missing the joys that are within our reach. Like a bee that can suck honey from the bitterest flower, the wise man is a connoisseur in delights. Was not this the true excellence of Socrates, this capacity to make his life a continual feast of good cheer in situations that baffled ordinary men? Aristippus was the pioneer in hedonism, the ethics of pleasure that gauges the worth of life in terms of the enjoyment it yields.

Even in his hedonism, a disciple of Socrates might have sought the universal definition and estimate of pleasure. But Aristippus, like Protagoras, clung to the passing sense impression and relished each drop or crumb of pleasure, moment by moment. Still he reflected, one should keep himself in condition to enjoy, and this is the virtue of temperance, or rather prudence—knowledge of how to avoid satiety. If a passion enslaves a man, it jeopardizes his full enjoyment. "I possess," Aristippus boasted of his lusts, "but I am not possessed."[9]

In sunny, opulent Cyrene this doctrine gained disciples. But suave hedonism soon drifted into sensuality; and its practice jaded and discredited the theory. Various Cyrenaics pursued the doctrine to different conclusions. Some of them welcomed any kind of pleasure, be it thieving or adultery. But many of these enjoyments are apt to get you into trouble, so on the score of pleasure in the long run, better avoid them. Other Cyrenaics advocated critical judgment in pleasure-seeking. Friendship and gratitude and filial piety and patriotism may cost us some passing indulgence, but in the end they yield more real happiness. Quite different from this genial outlook

9 Laertius, op. cit., p. 85.

was the gloomy view of life which earned Hegesias of Alexandria the epithet "Advocate of Death," because he started an epidemic of suicides during the reign of Ptolemy Soter. The highest good in life, he agreed, is pleasure; but pleasure is fleeting, unreliable, and disgusting in satiety. The life of pleasure-seeking is a cheat, so our only alternative is indifference to whatever happens, whether we live or die; and indeed we might as well be dead, for life affords no true satisfaction.

THE CYNICS

The very opposite of Aristippus in temperament and conviction was Antisthenes (c. 444–365), the founder of the Cynic school. He introduced in the Socratic concert a severe, jarring note. His mother had been a Thracian slave, and the slights or the more insulting suavity of the Athenian aristocrats roused him to churlish disdain. The highborn who gave themselves such airs were not any nobler than snails or locusts. They were thralls to conventional demands, pampered, ungenuine, weak. They should learn from Socrates. Antisthenes walked five miles daily from the Piraeus to Athens to see the really free man, who was frank, unpretentious, unworried—always his true self. Socrates' motto was, "Know thyself." Antisthenes declared, "Be thyself." Most men are only masks and actors, their lives futile and weary pretense. Let a man seek virtue and satisfaction where alone it can be found, in his own individuality, every moment freely himself. Let him understand that most of his alleged needs are imaginary, his proprieties artificial, his dignities and possessions only burdens. The wise man should shake himself free of all these trappings. This is the ethics of the simple life of spontaneous self-expression and self-sufficiency.

Even more famous than Antisthenes was his follower Diogenes of Sinope (412–323). Either he or his father had been banished for counterfeiting, and the son learned the lesson thoroughly. Everywhere he found human life to be only counterfeit, vain pretense. In full noonday, he set out with a lighted lantern looking for an honest man. He found only pretenders, even the best of them loaded with the conventional attachments. If one is a citizen of Athens, he may have to drink hemlock. If one marries, he may have to live with a shrew. If one acquires a house, its shelter is also a burden. From all these and other attachments, Diogenes would be free. So he lived in a tub, with his cloak for bedclothes, and his dinner, when he had a mind for it, he ate from his bag. Without envy, ambition, or any sense of obligation, in his own self-reliant candor, he was master of all. When Alexander the Great offered him any boon, he asked the king to step aside so that he could enjoy the sunlight.

Here was the Socratic emphasis on the supreme worth of the inner life, on tending and perfecting one's soul, but carried to excess and oddity. The forthright genuineness of the leading Cynics compelled admiration, but their scorn for the amenities of decent living aroused disgust. These philosophers who met at the Cynosarges (or the "agile dog," as the term has been translated) lived indeed a life without constraint; as the Greeks said, fit for the dogs. And wasn't their very disdain of the vanities of men a perverse vanity? When Diogenes tramped over Plato's fine rugs, exclaiming, "Thus do I trample on the empty pride of Plato," the wiser man remarked, "With greater pride you do it, O Diogenes!"[10]

SUGGESTED WORKS FOR FURTHER STUDY

CYNICS. Sayre, Farrand, *Diogenes of Sinope*.

PLATO. Plato, *Dialogues* (several translations are available).

XENOPHON. Xenophon, *Memorabilia and Apology* (trans. H. G. Dakyns).

BIOGRAPHIES AND CRITICAL STUDIES. Cornford, F. M., *Before and After Socrates;* Dawson, M. M., *The Ethics of Socrates;* Grote, George, *Plato and the Other Companions of Sokrates;* Rogers, A. K., *The Socratic Problem;* Taylor, A. E., *Socrates*.

[10] *Ibid.*, p. 226.

3. Plato: Idealistic Rationalism

Plato's Life and Career

Plato (427–347) came of an aristocratic family long identified with leadership in Athens. His father, Ariston, counted King Codrus among his ancestors; his mother, Perictione, claimed descent from Solon. The boy was named Aristocles, but he earned the epithet Plato on account of his broad build or forehead—perhaps both, for in his youth he won athletic as well as mental renown. His high social standing and connections, and his versatile genius, would have gained him dominance in any career he entered.

He lived in a critical period in Greek history. Pericles had died two years before Plato's birth, at the beginning of the Peloponnesian War, in which the naval empire of Athens was laid low. Plato's elder brothers, Adeimantus and Glaucon, familiar to us in *The Republic*, had fought bravely in this long war, as Plato himself may have done before its disastrous end in the year 404 B.C. This struggle between Athens and Sparta emphasized the issue which had also given rise to the struggle between the parties in the Athenian state: What are the sound principles of social-political order? Plato's reflection on this problem determined the course of his public career, and is manifest throughout his writings.

Plato's youth saw the decline and fall of Athenian power but not of Athenian genius. Phidias and Aeschylus, like Pericles, were great memories of the Golden Age; but, throughout the Peloponnesian War, Sophocles and Euripides continued to dominate the Greek theater in tragedy, and Aristophanes in comedy. The war situation itself provided the theme for the greatest Greek historian, Thucydides. Though Athenian arms were crushed by Sparta, the supremacy of Athens in Greek culture remained unchallenged.

In that age of social-political ferment and artistic achievement, two aims contended in young Plato's mind, until his meeting with Socrates decided his career. He chose the philosophic life of theory, but his mind did not abandon poetic creation and statesmanship. He had written poetry, perhaps composed a tragedy. After he witnessed the dramatic interplay of ideas in the Socratic discussions, he is said to have burned his poems. But his *Dialogues* show that the dramatist was not entirely submerged in the philosopher.

His intimacy with Socrates also convinced him that Athens offered him no choice in a political career that he could honorably accept. When the Athenian democracy was overthrown, at the close of the Peloponnesian War, the Thirty Tyrants who assumed power included kinsmen of Plato. But their government was sullied by bloodshed and corruption. They sought to implicate Socrates in their own tyranny by ordering him to take part in the lawless murder of a rich citizen whose property they wished to acquire. Socrates' firm refusal might have cost him his life had not the Thirty been overthrown in a democratic upheaval. But the rule of the populace proved no better than that of the Tyrants. After the trial and death of Socrates, under a democratic government, Plato turned away from Athenian politics in resolute disdain.

Forced for a while to leave Athens, along with other disciples of Socrates, he spent some time with Euclides in Megara. For a number of years thereafter he traveled widely. He probably visited Egypt, Crete, and Cyrene, and also the Pythagoreans in southern Italy. In Sicily he met Dion, brother-in-law of the tyrant Dionysius I of Syracuse. Dion, a young man of great ability and high principles, turned to Plato with deep devotion and urged him to reform the mind of Dionysius, but the tyrant dismissed him with scorn. On his homeward voyage, perhaps with the connivance of Dionysius, Plato was captured and sold into slavery, from which, happily, he was ransomed.

Returning to Athens, he established his school, the Academy, which became the first Greek university and lasted for some nine centuries. The second half of his life was spent in teaching and writing philosophy. Only two journeys interrupted these forty years in the Academy, both of them to Syracuse, where Plato tried in vain to educate Dionysius II as a philosopher-king. On both occasions, he risked his own life in interceding for his friend Dion, who was eventually assassinated. Though unsuccessful as a reformer of tyrants, Plato was active to the last in the realm of thought. As Cicero tells us, he died writing.

Plato's Dialogues and his Philosophical Development

Plato's complete writings have been better preserved than those of any other ancient philosopher. Classical literature, even the greatest, suffered badly from the ravages of time. Scarcely one tenth of the dramas of Aeschylus and Sophocles have come down to us. For our study of the earlier philosophers, we must rely on fragmentary remains or passages quoted by later writers. The philosophers who followed Plato fared much better than the pre-Socratics, but not nearly as well as Plato. There is no mention in antiquity of any Platonic dialogue which we do not possess.

Some of the dialogues have been recognized as spurious, and others—this is also true of the *Epistles*—have been regarded as debatable. Yet the student of Plato's philosophy can go to the original sources; these should give us a sounder basis for our conclusions than any expositor of his philosophy can provide. But the *Dialogues* are also our sources for the study of Socratic philosophy. In most of them Socrates is used as the main speaker. The problem is that of determining reliably when the disciple is reporting the master's teachings, when he is adopting Socratic ideas as the starting point in his own systematic development, and when his use of the name of Socrates is only an artistic device for the exposition of purely Platonic doctrines. As was noted in the last chapter, the interpretations of modern scholars do not agree on many important points.

The lesser disciples of Socrates had limited comprehension. They did not grasp the full purport of his philosophy and could not bring it to fruition. Like narrow sectarians, they bent the master's teaching to one side or another in distorted emphasis. But, in Plato's thought, the Socratic doctrine matured; its implications were revealed further than Socrates had developed them, and, in some directions, where he had not pursued them. More loyal than the other Socratics to the central truths of his teacher, Plato was never a mere disciple. Who reveals better than he the characteristic power of the Greek mind to assimilate and possess the ideas of others and to give them new life with original, creative power?

Plato's philosophy also reacted to other strains of Greek thought. Before he met Socrates, Plato had studied with Cratylus the Heraclitean, to whom he devotes one of his dialogues. He explored Eleatic speculation with Euclides in Megara, mathematics with Theodorus, the geometrician in Cyrene, the Pythagorean theory and practice with Archytas of Tarentum. His intimate knowledge of the Sophists is shown in the whole gallery of portraits of them in his *Dialogues*.

His use and criticism of all these doctrines were, of course, contributions to the systematic elaboration of his own philosophy, but the Socratic ideas were central and germinal in it. In the works of Plato's youth, the direct impress of his master's personality—his words and his deeds—was bound to find dramatic expression. Proceeding to fuller exposition, the dialogues of Plato's early maturity must have begun to express his own systematic philosophy, Socratic in its beginnings, but truly Platonic in its progressive realization. His system of principles raised its many problems; therefore, as we should expect, Plato in his later years pursued the various implications of his own doctrine in systematic exposition or in critical analysis of problems.

This view of the likely progressive development of Plato's philosophy is sustained by the record of it which we have in the *Dialogues*. Several modern Platonic scholars have undertaken to arrange the dialogues in the order of their composition by an analysis of their style. The appreciative estimate of the work of these stylistic experts by many competent critics has not been followed by unanimity in Platonic interpretation. We do not have, and can scarcely expect, complete or even substantial agreement among Platonists.

But, on some main points, the dissent is not as radical in principle as it may be emphatic in details.

The *Apology*, *The Republic*, and the *Laws* are, by fairly general accord, recognized as representing three main stages in Plato's philosophical activity. There is also broad agreement about three groups of his works. Belonging with the *Apology* are the so-called "Socratic dialogues": *Crito, Euthyphro, Charmides, Laches, Protagoras, Hippias Minor*, and probably *Gorgias*. In this period or a little later may be included the *Lysis, Ion, Meno*, and the beginning of *The Republic*. The unfolding maturity of Plato's thought may be studied in *Menexenus, Phaedo, Symposium, The Republic, Euthydemus, Cratylus*, and *Phaedrus. Theaetetus* and *Parmenides* seem to be transitional to his later dialogues, the *Sophist, Statesman, Critias, Timaeus, Philebus*, and finally the *Laws*, which, by common consent, is the last of Plato's works. Allowing for reasonable dissent regarding the grouping of some of the dialogues or the specific ordering of the works in each group, the above arrangement may enable us to follow the development of Plato's thought in outlook and penetration of problems.

The Beginnings of Plato's Philosophy

The early works of Plato may be read in two ways, both of which reveal his relation to Socrates. They may give us a reliable statement of the Socratic philosophy. But, in these dramatic colloquies, we can also trace the beginnings of Plato's progressive transformation of the master's doctrine. The early dialogues are called "Socratic," because they are memorials and eulogies of Socrates, as well as accounts of his philosophical method and teachings. The *Apology* and *Crito* portray the moral grandeur of Socrates during his trial and in prison, unwavering in his loyalty to justice and high principles. The "dialogues of search," as they have been called, trace the Socratic pursuit of universal definition in a number of specific inquiries.

These inquiries, as was noted in the preceding chapter, are concerned with the essential characteristics of the good life. The pre-Socratic philosophers had sought knowledge of the nature of things, the stuff and structure of the cosmos. The Sophists had dismissed these explorations as futile and had reached the skeptical conclusion that real knowledge is altogether beyond men's reach. Socrates maintained firmly that knowledge is attainable by the right method, the most important knowledge of oneself and of one's chief good, and he sought it in the rational grasp and universal definition of moral values. Plato began with this Socratic conviction, but proceeded to extend the range of available knowledge and thus achieved a metaphysics of reason.

We can trace, in the early dialogues, only the first steps of this Platonic advance. But we should also note that, while Plato reached forward, beyond the Socratic wisdom of self-knowledge and virtue to metaphysical insight into the nature of reality, he never lost his master's intense concentration on the principles of the good life. His last writings include a critique of the ethics of pleasure and further reflections on social philosophy.

The insistent Socratic demand for universal definition as the essence of knowledge in any field was in sharp contrast to the Sophistic skepticism and dismissal of all knowledge. Opposed as it was to the unprincipled doctrine of the Sophists, the Platonic teaching exposed their shallowness in dramatic portrayal in three early dialogues devoted to three leading Sophists. The least of these is *Hippias Minor*, a satire on the superficial versatility of a self-proclaimed master, who is shown to lack a real grasp of anything. Hippias claims to have invented a complete art of memory, but he cannot keep in mind the course of the argument.

Protagoras is a less satirical, but more thorough, exposure of the Sophistic position, and it also reveals some Socratic difficulties. Here, as in the *Meno*, the problem discussed is moral education and the nature of virtue. Protagoras is a famous and much advertised teacher of virtue. Others also have professed to teach it; but, as Socrates says, even statesmen have failed to impart it to their sons. Despite the variety of actions which we call virtuous, is there not a basic principle in them all, wherein all virtues are essentially one? Protagoras prefers expansive eloquence to searching analysis of ideas and is impatient with the Socratic dialectic. Although he is induced to concede the kinship of temperance, justice, holiness, and wisdom, he insists that courage is very different. In all this discussion of the nature of virtue, the Sophist is aiming at effective management of socially useful qualities; he is not seeking the rational knowledge of principles, which is precisely the guiding purpose of Socrates.

At this point, Plato's strategy in the argument takes a puzzling turn. Socrates expounds a hedonistic criterion of virtue defined as pleasurable activity. Is this an ironical advocacy of the Sophistic espousal of pleasure? Is it a genuine report of a hedonistic strain in the Socratic teaching, which Plato's later thought certainly rejected? Or is it a critical exploration of hedonism in a positive spirit to appraise whatever possible merits it may have? In any case its limitations as a standard are exposed. The good, or virtuous quality of pleasure requires due measure and balance, and this calls for knowledge, true insight. So again we are led to the basic demand for rationality.

In *Gorgias*, the Platonic Socrates is set in opposition to the unprincipled expediency of the Sophists. Gorgias is a professor of the art of rhetoric, which Socrates leads him to define as mastery in persuading law courts and public assemblies on matters of justice and injustice. Rhetoric should demand a firm grasp of justice and injustice. Gorgias candidly admits that his art of persuasion may be abused, yet protests that a good teacher should not be blamed if his pupil goes astray. Such abuse, however, may also disclose the unsound core of the doctrine.

Gorgias and Protagoras cannot be regarded as despicable. In their discussions with Socrates they do not manifest a socially disruptive temper. Plato himself could have used some of the ideas in Protagoras' eloquent myth, and Gorgias is fair-minded in his share of the inquiry. But neither of them is in quest of truth and probity, only of outward success and expediency.

Where no right principle is recognized, what can restrain the greed and insolence of lawless men? These evil consequences of unsound doctrine are shown in Polus and more flagrantly in Callicles, who take possession of the stage in the *Gorgias* and whose sophistry is exposed by Socrates with ruthless logic. It seems to them unthinkable that a mighty and successful tyrant should be deemed wretched. But Socrates leads them to face the truth that the unjust and evil man is indeed miserable, that true happiness is not in easygoing indulgence of pleasure or in unscrupulous power, but rests on justice and temperance and true knowledge of the good—even though a man of justice and integrity may fare badly in an unrighteous state. "He has the first place in the scale of happiness who has never had vice in his soul."[1] *Gorgias* records Socrates' premonition of his impending peril in Athens and the tragic serenity with which he is ready to confront it. "Renouncing the honours at which the world aims, I desire only to know the truth, and to live as well as I can, and, when I die, to die as well as I can."[2]

If the *Apology* is the earliest of the "Socratic dialogues," the *Gorgias* rightly concludes this first group of Plato's works. They portray the true philosopher in the supreme crisis of his life; they also show the high resolution of his will as rooted in the firm ground of his thinking, his sound philosophy of life.

These early dialogues do not reveal the detailed execution of the Platonic system of philosophy, or even some of its main principles of design. But many of the important beginnings and elements in its motivation may already be recognized. In opposition to any skeptical resignation to the random impressions of sense experience, here is the conviction that real knowledge is available through the rational grasp of universal principles. Socrates seeks to attain it in universal definitions in ethics and social philosophy, but these moral concepts point to principles of wider cosmic perspective. "Philosophers tell us . . . that communion and friendship and orderliness and temperance and justice bind together heaven and earth and gods and men, and that this universe is therefore called Cosmos or order, not disorder or misrule."[3] These words in the *Gorgias* clearly point to the metaphysical, as well as to the social-ethical, idealism of *The Republic*. In his systematic expansion of the Socratic convictions, Plato overcame much of the inconclusiveness of these early "dialogues of search," and achieved a system of rational principles. The tragic note of death in the prelude to Plato's philosophy was bound to accentuate the problem of human destiny. So Plato's mind, in which

---

[1] Plato, *Gorgias*, in *The Dialogues of Plato* (trans. B. Jowett), 3rd ed. (in 5 vols.), Oxford, Clarendon Press, 1892, Vol. II, p. 478. The paging in all the quotations from Plato is that indicated along the margins of the work.

[2] *Ibid.*, p. 526.

[3] *Ibid.*, p. 508.

systematic mastery and creative originality vied for perfection, was already on its way to philosophical maturity and fruition.

As we now proceed to an exposition of Plato's philosophical principles, an admonition must be heeded, which should be kept in mind consistently in interpreting other leading thinkers, but which is especially important in considering Plato. As we shall be noting presently, the Platonic philosophy is a contemplation of the eternal ideal realities, but the philosophy itself is not a set formulated system. What Plato gives us is not the finished abstract result of his thought, but his thinking in process. Is this Plato's development of the Socratic dialectic, the ongoing searching inquiry into problems from this and that alternate viewpoint? The seeming inconsistency of Plato as he shifts his view of his theme, the repeated elusiveness of his position that cannot be constricted in a definite concept, these are expressions of "something far more deeply interfused," which "the divine Plato," as he has been called, shares with his divine problem. Of course, we must try to report our understanding of Plato's philosophy in some definite statement, but we should remember that our abstract exposition cannot do full justice to his living thought. As Plato himself is believed to have written, his philosophy "requires long-continued intercourse between pupil and teacher in joint pursuit of the object they are seeking to apprehend; and then suddenly, just as light flashes forth when a fire is kindled, this knowledge is born in the soul and henceforth nourishes itself."[4] The best that any account of Platonism may hope to do is to catch perhaps some gleam of Plato's flame and to send some reader to its source of light.

Knowledge and Reality: The Theory of Ideas

The Socratic pursuit of knowledge through universal definition, in rational concepts, was radically opposed to the Sophistic preoccupation with the random particulars of sense experience. Failure to reach this Socratic insight was the defect of both the Cynics and the Cyrenaics. The former emphasized the spontaneous mood of the individual, unbound and uncommitted; the latter cherished the fortuitous pleasures of indulgence. Against them both, Plato built his philosophy on the Socratic conviction that Virtue is Knowledge, the knowledge of universal principles.

Plato extended his application of the method of rational analysis beyond ethical and social topics. He attained a general theory of knowledge in terms of reason. Sense perception, according to him, can give us only unstable impressions of particulars. But how can there be any truth on this basis? My impressions change from moment to moment and differ from yours. These impressions are in themselves neither true nor false; they are only our passing

[4] Plato, "Epistle VII":341, in *Studies in the Platonic Epistles* (trans. G. R. Morrow), Urbana, Univ. of Illinois Bulletin, 1935, p. 206.

opinions. False is our judgment of any of them as true, for no impression can have any such preferential validity, since perception in itself provides no standard by which such validity can be tested. If the resources of our minds were limited to sense experience, we should be driven to the skeptical views of Protagoras. Unless we seek—in or beyond the random course of changes—some law or principle of order, we can only resign ourselves to the meaningless flux of existence. But how can we believe that the world is like a leaky pot?

The opinions which men form on the data of sense experience may have a spurious generality, but they lack universal truth. At best, they are hints suggesting the real direction of knowledge, but they also confuse and mislead the mind. The real nature of things is not revealed to us in the variety and stir of material objects, in the changing reds and greens, the hots and colds of sensation. These are only phenomena—as Plato called them, "seemings." Reality is within and beyond these appearances and can be grasped only by reason.

Plato pursued his truth beyond the Socratic domain of morals in science and metaphysics. The words supposed to have been inscribed on the gate of the Academy are significant: "Let no one unversed in geometry enter here." Plato was scarcely thinking of the geometry of land measurement familiar to the Egyptian "knotters of ropes." With the Pythagoreans, he shared a conviction that knowledge was attainable in an understanding of mathematical forms and relations. The triangles of which we have real knowledge in geometry are not the triangles we draw and see. They are ideal figures conforming to certain rational definitions. No one has ever seen a really right triangle, yet of it alone is the Pythagorean theorem valid. The triangles of sense perception, like imperfect copies or shadows, only approximate or may serve to exemplify the realities of reason. In the same way, the actions we call just or temperate are only the possible but inadequate instances of the real principles of justice or temperance.

The famous Myth of the Cave, or Den, in the seventh book of *The Republic* is an imaginative version of this doctrine of knowledge, depicting the mind's advance from the particular impressions of sense experience to the universal principles of reason.

Behold! human beings living in an underground den, which has a mouth open towards the light and reaching all along the den; here they have been from their childhood, and have their legs and necks chained so that they cannot move, and can only see before them, being prevented by the chains from turning round their heads. Above and behind them a fire is blazing at a distance, and between the fire and the prisoners there is a raised way; and you will see, if you look, a low wall built along the way, like the screen which marionette players have in front of them, over which they show the puppets. . . . And do you see . . . men passing along the wall carrying all sorts of vessels, and statues and figures of animals made of wood and stone and various materials, which appear over the wall? Some of them are talking, others silent. . . . They see only their own shadows, or the shadows of one another, which the fire throws on the opposite wall of the cave.[5]

To them, the parade of their shadows would be the real world. "And now look again, and see what will naturally follow if the prisoners are released and disabused of their error." With poetic mastery, Plato portrays the arduous rise of the mind from uncritical opinion to scientific knowledge.

The reader of Plato's pages may at this point be struck by the analogy between his cave shadows and our motion pictures. We may propose an extension and a critical application of Plato's myth to the movie-made qualities of so much of the popular, spurious thinking in our own day, with its shallow generalizations, its artificial distortions of the basic realities and problems of life, its lack of really scientific insight. This living significance of Plato's thought is itself an instance of the truth on which he insists. When you rise above random opinion to universal knowledge, you grasp true principles that abide and are revealed in a variety of changing conditions—in ancient Athens and in Hollywood.

Plato extended this line of thought to cover the whole range of knowledge. Answers to the traditional problem of the nature of things was sought by him in rational terms. He contemplated the real nature of the universe as a cosmos, a system of universal forms, species and types of structure, norms, laws, principles, patterns, essential relations, meanings, ideals, and values. Plato called all these *Ideas;* when we use this term in interpreting Platonism, we should always capitalize it, lest we confuse it with our common modern word "idea," meaning any thought or item of experience. Plato's Ideas are the realities known by reason, not merely reasoned ideas or impressions of the mind. Not only are Ideas the valid formulas of science, they constitute the system of reality expressed in the rational formulas. Plato's Theory of Ideas is a doctrine of scientific knowledge and also a doctrine of reality, both conceived rationally.

Greater precision of statement is needed at this point. The Socratic definitions were intended to reach universal concepts like justice, virtue, beauty, knowledge. Such Ideas are universal principles, ideal meanings or criteria by which we may test the truth of specific judgments, "this action is just" or "that music is beautiful." These Ideas are concepts of the mind, and are themselves essentially mental. Here both our knowledge and the object of our knowledge are rational; we are exploring the range of self-knowledge, the mind's understanding of itself. Plato's idealism, first, is a philosophy that affirms the reality of reason and interprets the principal forms or universal expressions of its reality.

But Plato's theory goes further. His Ideas are also the universal laws, types of structure and systems of relations in nature. A triangle is such a structure and system, which geometry analyzes and formulates with logical thoroughness. In every realm of science reason attains valid knowledge as it contem-

5 Plato, *The Republic*, Bk. vii, in *The Dialogues of Plato, op. cit.,* Vol. III, pp. 514 f.

plates the patterns of cosmic order, the rhythms and interrelations of nature. So a Platonist might cite as modern instances of Ideas: gravitation, evolution, relativity, and the principal laws of the sciences in which the real order and universal system of relations in nature are manifested. Sense experience can, at best, only suggest these Ideas on occasion. They are Ideas of and for reason; in them the mind contemplates not merely itself and its own order but an objective cosmic system.

Ideas of this second class—patterns, relations, and laws—are objective, but they are scarcely objects in the sense of *things*. Are there not also Ideas of things, of kinds or classes of objects? Plato's answer to this question was affirmative, and it involved him in difficulties. Just as we ask universally what beauty or justice is, so we may seek a universal definition of *man* or *horse*. Beyond the particular men or horses which we can see or touch, our reason contemplates the universal Ideas of them, human or equine reality. Even if we do not share Plato's disregard of sense experience as a source of knowledge, we should still grant his claim that mere observation of this or that man or horse does not constitute understanding of human or equine nature. But do his universal Ideas, man and horse, have objective actuality as the particular men and horses of our sense experience have? That is, did Plato contemplate a cosmos which includes among its realities the universal man and the universal horse?

If, with Socratic insistence, we should press for a plain yes-or-no answer here, a Platonist would be reluctant to reply so simply, lest he be misunderstood. Certainly he would say that the universal man and horse are not material objects, but are two of the eternal realities which reason contemplates in nature. Plato himself was sometimes perplexed with this part of his doctrine. It clearly could be carried too far, but on what valid ground could he set a limit to its application? This problem is especially apparent in some of the later dialogues. In *Timaeus* he asked whether there is an Idea of Fire, and the *Parmenides* raised more embarrassing questions. Are there absolute Ideas of "such things as hair, mud, dirt, or anything else which is vile and paltry?"[6] "Certainly not," is the ready answer, but we might ask, and Plato seemed to be asking himself, Why not? The problem of the extent to which the Theory of Ideas should be applied realistically reveals a contest of motives in Plato's thought, which insisted on analysis and on evaluation. The reality of Plato's World of Ideas is rational and eternal; it is also ideal and perfect. The material objects of sense experience, in his judgment, fall short of expressing the full measure of reality, which is attuned to perfection.

Plato's system of Ideas is a hierarchy. Each law or principle or archetype of Being expresses the nature of reality, but not with equal adequacy. At the bottom of the scale of Being which Plato contemplated would be the "vile and paltry things"; at the summit, divine perfection. Plato's philosophy is the antithesis of any materialism. In his judgment the early explorers of

6 Plato, *Parmenides*, in *ibid.*, Vol. IV, p. 130.

nature who sought the basic stuff of which all things are composed investigated only one part of existence, and not the central and essential part. So in *Phaedo*, he criticized Anaxagoras for not grasping the importance of his principle that *Nous* (Reason), orders and directs all nature. Could we understand Socrates if we considered only his body—that is, his bones and muscles, flesh and skin, and their mechanical operation? Would they explain to us the character and life of Socrates; why he did not run away from prison, but remained loyal to Athens, even though unjustly condemned to death? Surely we do not and cannot know the real Socrates until we recognize his mind, his pursuit of knowledge, his judgment and choice of values.

So in the cosmos, as is true of Socrates, the higher range of reality is spiritual. The Ideas with which the physical sciences deal are of course real, but they represent, as it were, the framework of reality, the meaning and purport of which are ideal. The fuller understanding of rational activity, in a mind like Socrates', can lead us more truly to the center of reality than can knowledge of all the stars. For reason—which seeks truth and justice, and which is consecrated to the quest of perfection—reveals to us the highest Idea in the hierarchy of reality. Plato called it the Idea of Good or, as we may say, the Principle of Value and Dominant Perfection, "And this you will deem to be the cause of science, and of truth in so far as the latter becomes the subject of knowledge; beautiful too, as are both truth and knowledge. . . ."[7] Plato's Theory of Ideas proceeds to a metaphysics in which not dimension, matter, and force, but living mind and reason are supreme, and in which spiritual ideals and principles of value are the highest reality. These conclusions were cardinal in Plato's philosophical religion. They direct his ethical-social philosophy of life.

Plato's Ethics and Social Philosophy

Just as knowledge of reality proceeds beyond the unstable and confused impressions of sense experience to rational analysis and criticism, and to the grasp of universal principles in their hierarchical order, so the truly good life is the life of rational, critical appraisal of values. Casual indulgence of our desires cannot yield virtue and real happiness any more than random sense impressions can yield truth. Plato could not follow the Cyrenaic hedonism. The pleasures of the moment express no principle that can give order or meaning to life. In practice as in theory he demanded universal standards.

A man may act impulsively, urged or lured by some craving or passion, but such conduct, without any critical judgment, can lead to no real good. Impetuous lusts entice the man of indulgence this way or that, confused and unaccountable; or some stubborn hankering may drive him to ruin. Such

7 Plato, *The Republic*, Bk. vi, in *ibid.*, Vol. III, p. 508.

an unexamined life, as Socrates had said, is not worth human living. We need right judgment to discriminate between the tempting pleasures of the moment and the abiding good in life, to gauge the relative worth of contending interests or values, and to choose the best.

Plato's practical philosophy of life expressed a fundamentally aristocratic principle; that is, aristocratic in the true sense of the term, meaning the "dominance of the best." His basic conviction was that some aims and satisfactions in life are really better than others. A truly good man must recognize the things in life that matter most; he should give these major interests his chief attention; he will then keep the less important goods in their secondary place, and resist paltry or ignoble desires. This critical intelligence is self-knowledge manifested in choice and action.

So Plato undertook an analysis of human nature and of the complex organization of society as fundamental in his moral and political theory. In his thought, these two affect and reflect each other. The usual distinction of our higher and our lower nature—of intelligence as opposed to the passions— while important in ethical discussion and so used by Plato, was in his judgment incomplete. His examination portrayed the soul as tripartite. Three capacities or types of activity contend for dominance in human life, and virtue consists essentially in their right relation and cooperation. We are, in the common phrase, creatures of desire. Human nature includes a mass of appetites that crave gratification; our daily existence is a course of contention of manifold wants: hunger, thirst, lust, and the other cravings of sense. Plato distinguished from reason, not only this sensual nature of man, but also another, which he called *thymós*. We may translate it as "spiritedness" or "mettle," or perhaps better though less vividly, "will energy." It is the vital urge for action, the aggressive dynamic of our being. But we not only desire and press for action; we also think and judge. This is our rational faculty. Reason is our capacity to pursue and attain knowledge and practical understanding: analytic insight and discriminating judgment in choice.

That reason is the highest and noblest part of human nature, and that it alone is entitled to rule and direct our life, was evident to Plato from the very recognition of its characteristic, judging activity. It is best and rightfully dominant, for it alone can perceive and choose between the better and the worse. Reason is "the sacred and golden cord" of life, as Plato called it in the *Laws*. Desire and will energy have strength, but they lack judgment. Swept by the lure and abandon of our appetites, we plunge into a riot of dissolute pleasures; we waste ourselves yet find no abiding satisfaction. And our will energy may plunge us headlong into vigorous action; but, where right judgment is lacking, a man's mettle does not avail. He may drive furiously to disaster.

The good life is the life in which reason controls the desires and directs will energy. Thus, rightly ordered, human nature can achieve its characteristic virtues or perfections. When the appetites are controlled by reason, the indulgence or the restraint of any desire does not hang upon the random inclination of the moment. Our true enjoyment is based on balance and moderation, which lead to abiding satisfaction. Only thus can our life achieve the virtue of Temperance. Again, when will energy is directed by reason, our mettlesome spirit does not run away, reckless or ill tempered; our ardor becomes steady and resolute, sustained by rational insight, and—clearly aware of our resources and our perils—we exert our powers staunchly and hero-ically. This is the virtue of Courage. Reason itself, in its pursuit of truth and right principles, realizes its own characteristic fruition in the virtue of Wisdom.

These perfections of the three sides of human nature are interrelated; each of them in its own way expresses the essence of the good life, the virtue *par excellence*, which Plato called Justice. It is the character of rightness, or right judgment, in a man that gives due emphasis to every side and interest of his nature, and that conduces to the harmonious realization of human capacities, perfection, and real happiness. Plato called Justice—the proper virtue of man—"an honorable maiden,"[8] more precious than many pieces of gold.

This rational control and direction of life which achieves the cardinal virtues is the practical or active expression of self-knowledge. The good man knows what kind of man he is and in what kind of world he lives. Beyond the seeming rush and riot of existence, he contemplates the eternal system of universal principles. He recognizes his own nature as a manifestation and a symbol of the cosmic hierarchy, and by self-understanding and pursuit of the virtues he strives to play his true role in reality, to become fully what he is meant to be. This is aristocratic rationalism in ethics; the ideal of achieving man's characteristic perfection.

Plato applied the principles of his moral perfectionism in his social philos-ophy. His great dialogue, *The Republic*, in which his ethics finds its best statement, contains also his social-political theory, a philosophical vision of the perfect state and a critique of other forms of government. *The Republic* is Plato's richest texture of mature reflection on the whole range of philo-sophical problems. Here is a program of education, a criticism of art and religion, a theory of knowledge, and a system of metaphysics, and, through it all, a dramatic portrayal of human life in one of the greatest epochs of history.

According to Plato, the state is the individual writ large, with correspond-ing features of order and disorder. The tripartite nature of man is paralleled by the three classes in the organization of society. The so-called "class of artisans" includes not only wage earners and working men but all whose life is concerned with economic gain, with providing or amassing the mate-rial goods of life. These are the provisioners of society, be they rich or poor, the shipowner as well as the hired sailor or stevedore. This class corresponds to the appetites and desires of the individual. Like will energy in man's

8 Plato, *Laws*, Bk. xii, in *ibid.*, Vol. V, p. 943.

nature, so is the "class of warriors" in the state. Whether in peace or in war, the soldiers express and test the mettle of society. While the artisan class assures the provisionment of the state, the warriors maintain its security. But a third class is needed—as reason is in man—to form and to direct social policy, the principles and character of the state. This is the "class of guardians": the legislators, judges, and sage rulers of society. So Plato's ideal state is an aristocracy in which the best and wisest men have chief authority.

The abiding welfare of the state requires that each class of citizens perform its appropriate share in the work of society. Those fitted by their nature to be artisans should be artisans; the warriors should perform the military duties; the direction of the state should be entrusted only to those whose capacity to be guardians has been proved. Any looseness or disorder in this vital respect threatens to corrupt and to disrupt the state. Not only are the stability and welfare of society safeguarded by this strict distribution of offices, but in this way the right social order contributes to the perfection and real happiness of the various citizens. A man is a truly satisfied and loyal member of society only when he has found his own suitable place and role in it.

The high social station of the guardians carries grave responsibilities. Because the perfect welfare of the citizens depends upon the maintenance of the right social order, Plato deemed it all-important to insure the self-preservation of aristocratic prerogative in the rule of the state by its true sages. Their unwavering devotion to their duties as guardians should be assured, and plans for the education of youth and the selection for office should be devised to guarantee that the guardians would be succeeded by their worthy disciples. To realize these ends, Plato proposed that the guardians should own no property nor have any private family life. Marriages in the guardian class were to be controlled by solemn eugenic regulations, and all children were to be adopted and brought up by the state. Thus, he would avoid the risk that parental favoritism might put in high office unfit sons of noble fathers. Students of Plato through the ages have been disturbed because, despite his deep insight into human nature, he was willing to cripple thus the normal personal life of the state's best citizens. His proposals show us how resolved he was at all costs to preserve his chosen form of government. Plato's scheme has sometimes been described as a "communism of wives." This gives a misleading idea of his estimate of women. While he could not recognize that women had as high ability as men, he would admit them to participation in all the activities of the state, to the extent of their powers. Thus Plato might be reckoned as an ancient champion of women's rights.

The system of education outlined in *The Republic* has the same purpose, the perpetuation of state authority in the guardian class of sages. The program of studies is designed to discover, to elicit, and to develop superior ability, and, by a process of progressive selection, to assign the most intelligent persons to the highest offices. The youths begin with gymnastic and music, proceed to arithmetic, geometry, and astronomy, and then to dialectic—the science of first principles and "the coping-stone of the sciences"[9]—exhaustive rational analysis and philosophy. The students who have shown their excellence by the age of 35 are then subjected to further selection by assignment to various civil and military offices. Those who prove their highest worth are then chosen as guardian sages, to spend their remaining years in philosophical contemplation, in wise political direction, and in the education of youth. Plato could see hopes for the social progress of men only along this course of rational direction. He wrote in *The Republic:*

> Until philosophers are kings, or the kings and princes of this world have the spirit and power of philosophy, and political greatness and wisdom meet in one, and those commoner natures who pursue either to the exclusion of the other are compelled to stand aside, cities will never have rest from their evils—no, nor the human race, as I believe—and then only will this our State have a possibility of life and behold the light of day.[10]

Plato regarded his aristocracy as the ideal perfect state, "a pattern laid up in heaven,"[11] but he had no illusions that men had ever realized it on earth. He regarded the various existing forms of government as more or less corrupt. In the ideal aristocracy the ruling class represents man's highest faculty, reason. But as men often err in preferring a strong will to a wise one, so some states allow the chief authority to be assumed by generals and warriors famed for prowess. This is timocracy, a government of strenuous men of mettle. A further corruption of society is shown when a small class of wealthy men gain control of the state. This is oligarchy, in which persons are judged by their possessions, not by their personal worth. Where appetites and greed thus dominate men's lives, the poor multitudes may readily seize their chance to unseat the rich oligarchs and to establish a government of the masses in which no standard of better or worse, of higher or lower, is recognized, and only numbers and the prevailing wind of popular opinion decide everything. Plato called this rule by the masses "democracy." The term in its ancient Greek sense was derogatory. Where no standard of value is acknowledged, some crafty demagogues may sway the unthinking multitude by appeals to passion and greed and may with the people's blind support usurp power in the state. This is tyranny, the worst of all governments.

We may surmise that the social-political philosophy of *The Republic* must have been discussed critically for many years in the Academy. Plato's own sorry experiences with Dionysius II in Syracuse must have shocked his idealistic hopes about a philosopher-king. Two dialogues of his old age indicate the political trends of his later thinking. In the *Statesman*, Plato reviewed more realistically various lawful and lawless governments. Rule by one, if lawful (royalty) is the best of all; if lawless (tyranny) it is the worst. Government by the minority, if aristocratic, is not as good as royalty; if oligarchic, not as bad as tyranny. Popular rule is the least good of all lawful

---

[9] Plato, *The Republic*, Bk. vii, in *ibid*. Vol. III, p. 534.
[10] *Ibid.*, Bk. v, p. 473.
[11] *Ibid.*, Bk. ix, p. 592.

governments, but the least bad of the lawless. We shall be reminded of this when we consider the *Politics* of Aristotle.

The Republic expressed Plato's ideal vision of the one perfect state. Without renouncing this "heavenly pattern," and despite his grievous disappointments as a political reformer, Plato devoted his declining years to the formulation of a political and legislative program that could be adapted to the actual conditions of Greek society. This more realistic system of principles was presented in great detail in his last work, the *Laws*. The dramatic spirit of the earlier writings is almost lost here. Ostensibly a dialogue of a Cretan and a Spartan with an "Athenian Stranger," the *Laws* contain long expository essays by the Stranger. Plato undertook to frame a doctrine which, while exposing the defects of Athenian and Spartan legislation, would combine the merits of each in a reasonable spirit of concession. This long dialogue of Platonic practicality, in its patient disquisition of political and juridical policies, is too detailed to be discussed in a brief statement. There is evidence of its influence on Hellenistic and Roman jurisprudence.

Platonic Love, Beauty, and Art

Plato's ethics and social-political philosophy are guided throughout by the principle of aristocratic rationalism: the primacy of reason and its rightful dominance over the wants and impulses of our lower nature. We should not, however, misinterpret his philosophy of life as an edifice of cold reason. The original poet and dramatist in Plato was never eclipsed by the systematic analyst. The *Dialogues* show us continually how the philosopher's creative imagination turns the abstractions of reason into living realities.

The high spiritual nature of man, reason in its full meaning, is not only intellectual. It manifests itself also in its devotion and its creative activity. Here, as in cognition, our soul may crawl or it may soar. Plato's interpretation of love strikes some of the deepest notes in his philosophy. He is not an austere formal intellect spurning all emotion. Still less is he a romantic sentimentalist wafting celestial halos over sensual desires. Keenly aware of the dominant role of love in the drama of life, Plato reveals its action in different lives and at different levels of spiritual maturity. The corruption of character is traced to depraved strains of desire and the sham devotion of sensuality; and the rise of the soul to perfection is revealed as man's education in love. These problems engage Plato especially in the *Symposium* and *Phaedrus*, two of his most beautiful dialogues.

The *Symposium* is a series of after-dinner speeches in praise of love. Each of the speakers reveals, in his eulogy, his own spiritual range and tone. We should keep in mind the climate of Greek ideas and also practices in which these men move. Their speeches naturally tend to flow in mythical channels, for many are the myths of the earthly and the heavenly goddess of love,

Aphrodite, and of Eros who is Love deified, and a world-creating cosmic power. In the lives of men these speakers see the manifold expressions of love: the love of men and women, wedded or profligate; the slimy, homosexual craving that oozed out of Sparta and sullied many Greek communities including Athens; and men's professed and honored love of the good and perfection. In the speech of Phaedrus, love as a plainly sensual and pederastic passion seeks to justify itself by lofty rhetoric. Pausanias, who speaks after him, distinguishes earthly and heavenly love but does not escape the aberration of Phaedrus. Eryximachus, the physician, gives a medical-scientific discourse on the tensions of love in the human animal. Aristophanes, the comic poet, weaves a myth around love as a creature's yearning for completion. Human beings were first created double but deeming themselves strong, grew insolent; so Zeus split them in twain, and ever since the two halves have been seeking union with each other. Agathon, whose prize-winning tragedy is the occasion for the banquet, launches into high-flown praises of love, which he identifies with all the perfections in turn.

The speech of Socrates, by dialectical probing, brings the discourse on love from its rhetorical flutterings down to solid ground, and then grasping the truth, itself soars to spiritual heights. Love is the life-possessing quest for the beautiful with which the soul seeks union and through the union, a more perfect creative expression of itself. This attachment may be only sensual, or it may engage higher interests. The devotion may rise in the scale of spiritual capacities. Men crave to beget children; they may seek immortal fame by giving their high purposes living embodiment in noble deeds or great works; or, from fair practices, they may ascend to fair and great ideas. Thus, in higher and higher contemplation Socrates is led to his apotheosis of Love as sublime and transcendent, consecrated to "the true beauty—the divine beauty, . . . pure and clear and unalloyed, not clogged with the pollutions of mortality and all the colours and vanities of human life. . . ."[12]

In his vision of this expanding spiritual prospect, Plato combined the genius of the poet and of the saint. From this high vantage point, we can discern realms of religious consecration to the beauty of holiness and to the love of God, which passeth all understanding. Then, turning from divine to human perfection, we can understand better the creative activity of the mind in art and poetry, its hazards if it strays and the heights to which it can ascend. The problem of beauty continually engaged Plato's mind—its relation to love and to poetic-artistic expression, and its role in the well-ordered, rational life.

Plato's judgment of art and poetry impresses the student first on its negative side. Plato criticized the corrupting influence of art, depreciated it as a distorting imitation of reality, and proposed a censorship of the arts in his ideal society. This seeming hostility is not due to aesthetic unresponsiveness —quite the contrary. His criticism of poetry and the other arts is stern because he recognized their great power and the high function of true beauty:

12 Plato, *Symposium*, in *The Dialogues of Plato, op. cit.*, Vol. I, p. 211.

Musical training is a more potent instrument than any other, because rhythm and harmony find their way into the inward places of the soul, on which they mightily fasten, imparting grace, and making the soul of him who is rightly educated graceful, or of him who is ill-educated ungraceful.[13]

As with the dynamic of love, so with that of the arts: the spiritual level on which they move us is all-important. For, "everyone chooses his love from the ranks of beauty according to his character."[14] A man's perception and artistic expression of beauty indicate his spiritual growth and rank. Reason should on no account surrender these supreme enthusiasms of the soul to unworthy direction.

Beauty at all stages arouses devotion; it lures, charms, inspires. The contagious magic of enthusiasm may lead the poet, the rhapsodist, and their rapt listeners to mistake mighty speech for deep wisdom. No poet, not even Homer, is safe from this delusion. The artist in any field may go astray through lack of understanding and through low purposes and ideals. His thought and his will both need the guidance of reason. In his engrossment with the particular objects of sense, he may be painting only copies of shadows, instead of contemplating and giving concrete embodiment to the significant realities of life. Where philosophic insight is lacking, the artist may be even lower than the artisan. For example, the carpenter who constructs a bed gives us his own tangible impression of what a bed should be, his copy of the universal Idea of a bed; but the painter is content to copy the carpenter's handiwork; his picture is an imitation of an imitation!

It has been objected that this "mimetic" account does scant justice to the purpose of the artist. A work of art, we may say, is not intended as a copy of any particular thing. It is the disclosure of the artist's "theory," his way of looking at nature or human life. A Platonist might reply that the artist's contemplation seeks perceptual embodiment and, therefore, misses the full truth. But, in morals and social order, the rational ideal similarly must find expression in particular acts or institutions; yet Plato would not on that account spurn human justice as wholly astray. The artist's failure must be due, not to the radical inadequacy of his medium of expression, the language he uses, but to the shallowness of his mind. If he could attain to philosophical contemplation, his wisdom and insight should yield great artistic expression. Plato's criticism of art is thus rational and more especially moral.

In his infatuation with sensual desires and paltry ambitions, the bad artist betrays the ideal beauty. In *Phaedrus*, Plato described the human soul as a charioteer driving two horses. One of them is of a noble strain, clean and upright; "he needs no touch of the whip but is guided by word and admonition only." The other is a crooked, corrupt, and unruly beast, "hardly yielding to whip and spur."[15] These two steeds are the two strains in our nature which reason must curb and direct. The driving of life's chariot is never

---

[13] Plato, *The Republic*, Bk. iii, in *ibid.*, Vol. III, p. 401.
[14] Plato, *Phaedrus*, in *ibid.*, Vol. I, p. 252.
[15] *Ibid.*, p. 253.

more difficult than when shallow delusions entice us in the lovely forms of art, or when depraved lusts usurp the role of love in our souls.

Plato's aesthetics is moralistic in its insistence that poetry and music and all the arts should be responsive to man's highest spiritual demands and seek expression on these lofty levels. We should choose and cherish the noble utterances in art; we should detect and reject the rhythms which are "expressive of meanness, or insolence, or fury, or other unworthiness. [We should seek to] discover what rhythms are the expressions of a courageous and harmonious life; and when we have found them, . . . adapt the foot and the melody to words having a like spirit. . . ."[16]

Plato therefore would allow only two sorts of harmonies in his ideal state. They indicate the themes and dominant notes in the arts which he would accept and laud as worthy poetic utterances of ideal beauty:

I want to have one warlike, to sound the note or accent which a brave man utters in the hour of danger and stern resolve, or when his cause is failing, and he is going to wounds or death or is overtaken by some other evil, and at every such crisis meets the blows of fortune with firm step and a determination to endure; and another to be used by him in times of peace and freedom of action, when there is no pressure of necessity, and he is seeking to persuade God by prayer, or man by instruction and admonition, or on the other hand, when he is expressing his willingness to yield to persuasion or entreaty or admonition, and which represents him when by prudent conduct he has attained his end, not carried away by his success, but acting moderately and wisely under the circumstances, and acquiescing in the event. These two harmonies I ask you to leave; the strain of necessity and the strain of freedom, the strain of the unfortunate and the strain of the fortunate, the strain of courage, and the strain of temperance; these, I say, leave.[17]

The Platonic conviction that true beauty is wedded to moral-rational perfection never weakens; it is reaffirmed in the later dialogues. In *Timaeus* he wrote: "Nothing can be beautiful which is like any imperfect thing."[18] This conception of beauty and art may find not only individual utterance in a noble soul of poetic genius, but also social expression in the well ordered life of a people. So we read in the *Laws:*

We also according to our ability are tragic poets, and our tragedy is the best and noblest; for our whole state is an imitation of the best and noblest life, which we affirm to be indeed the very truth of tragedy, . . . the noblest of dramas, which true law can alone perfect, as our hope is.[19]

This vision of great art as the beautiful expression of sound thinking and noble living is the aesthetic-moral ideal which Plato had championed earlier, in *The Republic:*

[16] Plato, *The Republic*, Bk. iii, in *ibid.*, Vol. III, pp. 399 f.
[17] *Ibid.*
[18] Plato, *Timaeus*, in *ibid.*, Vol. III, p. 30.
[19] Plato, *Laws*, Bk. vii, in *ibid.*, Vol. V, p. 817.

Let our artists rather be those who are gifted to discern the true nature of the beautiful and graceful; then will our youth dwell in a land of health, amid fair sights and sounds, and receive the good in everything; and beauty, the effluence of fair works, shall flow into the eye and ear, like a health-giving breeze from a purer region, and insensibly draw the soul from earliest years into likeness and sympathy with the beauty of reason. . . . And when a beautiful soul harmonizes with a beautiful form, and the two are cast in one mould, that will be the fairest of sights to him who has an eye to see it.[20]

God, Evil, and Man's Destiny

The characteristic spirit and tone of Plato's philosophy, and also some of the unresolved problems of his reflections, are impressed on our minds by an examination of his religious ideas. What warrant did he find for belief in God? What were his ideas of God's character and attributes, of man's relation to God, of man's destiny under divine providence? And how did he reconcile our conviction of God's cosmic supremacy with a frank recognition of the evil, depraved strains in existence? These sublime themes and these abysmal problems were bound to engage Plato's mind in its pursuit of ultimate finalities in reality and value.

Plato was resolved to expose and to reject spurious ideas of the divine. Before the mind can reach true conviction or understanding of God, it must be emancipated from superstitions. This demand for religious enlightenment motivated his censure of the poets. Greater than his love of Homer was his love of the truth. The matchless poetic inspiration of the *Iliad* and the *Odyssey* should not blind our recognition of the unworthy ideas of Deity in the epics. The traditional myths which Homer, Hesiod, and other poets used in their works were full of lies about the gods. What falsehood could be more heinous than this sort of "deception . . . about the highest realities?"[21] Here are tales about divine lying and thieving, divine wrangling, vindictiveness, adulteries, and other abominations. How are men who entertain such foul ideas of the divine to recognize and pursue truth and virtue in their own lives? Thus Plato, like the great prophets of Israel, unmasked the crude and corrupt superstitions of religious tradition. The fables of the old mythology—from which the first explorers of nature had recoiled, and which men like Xenophanes had disdained as unworthy—were condemned by Plato as lies, vain delusions, and moreover as bad lies, low and corrupt. The religious problems which engrossed Aeschylus, Sophocles, and Euripides in their dramatic reenactment of the old myths were faced squarely by Plato. In opposition to error, however ancient and revered, he would seek and speak the truth about God.

[20] Plato, *The Republic*, Bk. iii, in *ibid.*, Vol. III, pp. 401, 402.
[21] *Ibid.*, Bk. ii, p. 382.

Plato's integrity and deep penetration in theology ruled out any easy certainty or precise formulation of doctrine. His arguments for God's existence and his interpretations of God's character reflected, but also complicated, each other. Sometimes metaphysical principles prevailed in his thinking, and sometimes moral-religious sentiments prevailed. God was considered as the ultimate supreme Reality, and also as the most perfect Author and Father of us all. This complex interplay of motives in Plato's thought is not exceptional or unfamiliar to theologians; but we should keep it in mind and not misinterpret the interfusion of Plato's religious ideas as confusion.

We have noted that Plato viewed the universe as a system of Ideas, universal and eternal laws, principles, patterns, relations, and ideals constituting real nature. The highest and supreme reality he recognized as the Idea of Good, the Principle of Value, or Dominant Perfection. The Idea of Good, ultimate in his metaphysics, has been interpreted as also supreme in his religion; that is, his deity. This identification of the Idea of Good with God has been criticized by some Platonic scholars. May we say that, although in his old age Plato gave a more definitely theological form to his metaphysics, during his middle years he sought a metaphysical version and foundation of religious conviction? In *The Republic* the Good is described as "not only the author of knowledge to all things known, but of their being and essence."[22] In the *Philebus*, Plato distinguishes between men's minds and "the divine mind," which alone is identical with the good. These two aspects of his thought were not dissociated; the change in his thinking was mainly one of emphasis.

The range of Plato's reflection may be indicated by the fact that many of the principal theological arguments for God's existence may be read in the *Dialogues*. The existence of things demands not merely finite, but really ultimate explanation. It points to a primal Cause, source and Author of all things. "How can a thing which is moved by another ever be the beginning of change? Impossible,"[23] Plato declared. Furthermore, the world is not a chaos of bare existence; it is a system of cosmic order that clearly manifests the directive power of a supreme intelligence. In its dedication to truth, virtue, and beauty, our own reason is evidence of these ideal realities in their infinite perfection. So we read in the *Sophist:* "O heavens, can we ever be made to believe that motion and life and soul and mind are not present with perfect being? Can we imagine that being is devoid of life and mind, and exists in awful unmeaningness, an everlasting fixture?"[24] This passage reaffirms Plato's conviction, voiced earlier in the *Phaedo*, "that beauty and goodness . . . have a most real and absolute existence."[25]

In the *Laws*, Plato's unwavering belief in God makes him intolerant of any denial; he would suppress it by statute. Not only atheism was to be outlawed, but any teaching that God is unconcerned about the justice or well-

---

[22] *Ibid.*, Bk. vi, p. 509.
[23] Plato, *Laws*, Bk. x, in *ibid.*, Vol. V, p. 894.
[24] Plato, *Sophist*, in *ibid.*, Vol. IV, p. 249.
[25] Plato, *Phaedo*, in *ibid.*, Vol. II, p. 77.

being of men. Even more culpable than the negation of divine providence was the pernicious notion that the favor of God can be procured by any flattery or offerings or incantations.

The characteristically Platonic Idea of God was that of infinite perfection, absolute truth, goodness, and beauty. But God's supreme ideal reality was also regarded as the creative source and Cause of the world. This theological cosmogony is unfolded in the *Timaeus*, a work of vast design and versatile mastery, rich in ancient science, obscure and subtle in myth and allegory. It is a preeminent example of the sort of work that requires a commentary much longer than itself. We can mention only one design in this complex texture. God is here portrayed as forming the world by an eternal pattern. Being perfectly good and nowise invidious, "God desired that all things should be good and nothing bad, so far as this was attainable."[26] He gave the primeval chaos life and form, a World Soul which in its turn was diversified into a multiplicity of cosmic powers—beings of lesser divinity, the earth and the stars—with their various kinds of life and systems of order.

This is not an absolute creation out of nothing. God was conceived by Plato as the creator of the cosmic order. The unformed material non-Being was thus fashioned into a universe. Corresponding to the dualism of sense impressions of phenomena and rational knowledge of the eternal Ideas, we may note an ultimate dualism of matter and God. "Matter," to Plato, seems to be the chaotic void or space—emptiness of all form or character of Being, the receptacle or matrix of all generation. Is this dualism absolute and irreducible? The impotence of empty matter to achieve form and order shows it to be alien to God's perfect nature. But does not its receptivity to the Creator's fashioning manifest it as not absolutely resistant to Deity?

Warily, Plato's thought picked its way along a narrow ledge between steep dilemmas of theodicy. The abysmal problem of evil confronted him as it has confronted anyone who views nature and man as defective works of the Absolute, the perfect Author. Note again the words in *Timaeus:* God desired that all things should be good and nothing bad "so far as this was atttainable." Plato taught the divinely appointed naturalness of man's rationality, his pursuit and attainment of perfection. But he also felt an undivine dark strain in man's nature, ingrained, ineradicable, and forever limiting the range of his rational ascent, setting its finite bounds. Fashioned we are in the image of absolute perfection, but made of the chaotic void. So our nature seeks to realize its perfect pattern, and always its ideal urge is checked by the lower, material drag which tends toward disorder, unprincipled, random non-Being.

Plato did not propose any easy solution of the problem of evil, but he was apparently resolved to resist two extremes, both of them intolerable to sound reason. One was a view of cosmic despair, impious in regarding nature as tainted to its core and summit. Plato rejected such blasphemy of supreme reality. God is essentially perfection, and only good can issue from His perfect Being. "Of the evils the causes are to be sought elsewhere, and not in

26 Plato, *Timaeus*, in *ibid.*, Vol. III, p. 30.

him."[27] Plato began and was determined to end with a morally acceptable Idea of God as unqualified perfection. The rest of his cosmology and philosophy had to meet this basic requirement.

But in his conviction of infinite perfection, Plato never ignored the ingrained imperfection of all finite existence. He never lapsed into the opposite extreme of uncritical optimism. He recognized forthrightly men's actual propensity to error, confusion, and manifold corruption and vice. He urged resolutely and confidently, against all manner of skepticism, men's striving to master their low greed and unruly impulses and to bend their energies to the pursuit of truth, virtue, and perfection. There is, however, a tragic strain in Plato's philosophy, darkening his rational resolution, though in nowise sapping it. It is a grim sense of a finally ineradicable defectiveness in our constitution and in nature itself.

Despite the most perfect design and fashioning of the divine Weaver, there is always in our texture, and likewise in all nature, the evil warp of matter. Plato wrote in the *Theaetetus:* "Evils can never pass away; for there must always remain something which is antagonistic to good. Having no place among the gods in heaven, of necessity they hover around the mortal nature, and this earthly sphere."[28] Only on these terms are human lives and finite beings at all possible. This is God's eternal choice in fashioning our nature. All this Plato recognized and admitted, but he did not accept it as the prevailing tone in his philosophy. Contemplating absolute divine perfection, he consecrated his mind and will to the fullest perfection attainable by man. His philosophy is the more deeply idealistic because of its tragic undertone.

The problem of human destiny in Plato's philosophy was an important part of his psychology and his religious outlook. It is raised or implied in many dialogues, but mainly in *Phaedo*, the beautiful and highly dramatic discussion between Socrates and his disciples on the last day of his life. Whether in every way Plato was here reporting the actual beliefs of his master, the reader of the *Phaedo* is not left in doubt regarding Plato's own firm conviction of man's eternal career. But the reflections on human destiny do not all point the same way. There are passages in the *Dialogues* which express Socratic balancing of judgment or invading doubts. In the *Apology*, Socrates, on trial for his life, calmly reckons his eventual lot, whether death be annihilation or not. Likewise, in the *Menexenus*, there is a venture of speculation whether the dead have any knowledge of the living. The belief in personal immortality is not convincingly a logical inference from the Platonic system, which recognized the eternity of the universal Ideas, of man, but which should have reckoned individual men and women among the passing phenomena. Despite these systematic objections, Plato's numerous arguments for personal immortality seem to express his deep conviction that the rational soul's career does not begin or end with the life of the body.

This Platonic belief in immortality does not rest on any specific proof, nor

[27] Plato, *The Republic*, Bk. ii, in *ibid.*, Vol. III, p. 379.
[28] Plato, *Theaetetus*, in *ibid.*, Vol. IV, p. 176.

on several. In the *Phaedrus*, the soul's immortality is inferred from its self-moving nature; but the stronger appeal is to man's rational character. The attainment of knowledge demands an advance from the particular impressions of sense experience to the universal principles of reason; so the recognition of man's true being goes beyond the perception of his mortal body. When Crito asks Socrates, "In what way shall we bury you?" the master's reply is revealing: "Catch me first."[29] Thus, Plato posed the problem: Is the real Socrates the body which has aged and which will soon be a corpse? Is it not rather he who has pursued eternal truth and lived in communion with God?

The several arguments for immortality in the *Phaedo* proceed from the analysis of the soul, its nature and its characteristic activity. Some of them are unconvincing sophisms; others are inferences from Plato's theory of knowledge; still others are the expressions of deep reflections on the essential worth of man. We are told that opposites generate opposites; since our life is followed by death, our death must proceed to another life. We assuredly have rational knowledge of the eternal Ideas; but this knowledge cannot be derived from the experience of our sense organs; it must be the recollection of our reason, which must have existed before birth and will not be dissolved at death. Besides, the soul is a simple entity, not a material compound; how then can it be destroyed by the death and disintegration of the body? The soul does not depend upon its body, like a harmony upon the lyre. It is prior to the body and it can control it. Nor is it likely, after wearing out several bodies, itself to pass away and be outlived by some body, as a weaver is outlived by some of his garments. This argument about the relation of the soul to generation, dissolution, and other bodily processes leads Socrates to reaffirm that his actions cannot be interpreted as due mainly to bones and muscles and "other eccentricities." His soul is moved by his beliefs and ideals. Its true life, now or hereafter, is beyond the hazards of bodily existence.

Plato believed in the eternal career of the soul, its preexistence, its survival, and its transmigration. In its bodily investment, the soul may pursue universal truths in the philosophic life, or it may yield to the enticements of sense. Divine judgment governs the cycle of rebirths, and each soul is reborn as it deserves, higher or lower in the scale of being. Plato expressed Pythagorean belief in metempsychosis, but the rebirth of the soul to a high or low station also signified to him man's range of alternative careers and the fateful judgment of preference which decides his lot and character. In the *Symposium* we are told of the various loves that rule the hearts of men and of the highest love of absolute beauty in the philosophic life, in which a man may "become the friend of God and be immortal, if mortal man may."[30] This "if" is not to be understood as Plato's skeptical proviso, but as his recognition of the spiritual ground of man's eternal worth.

[29] Plato, *Phaedo*, in *ibid.*, Vol. II, p. 115.
[30] Plato, *Symposium*, in *ibid.*, Vol. I, p. 212.

Plato had a pious faith in the eternal conservation of rational values. How could God allow the utter dissolution of a just person? So he wrote in the *Timaeus:* "All that is bound may be undone, but only an evil being would wish to undo that which is harmonious and happy."[31] Man's destiny was also conceived by Plato more gravely, in terms of moral choice and retribution. The myth of Er, the Pamphylian, in the last book of *The Republic*, portrays the souls as periodically selecting their future destinies. As the parable would say, a man's way of life here and in the hereafter reveals and depends on his choice of values. He may drift in the eddies of mortality or he may commit his soul to the divine immortal vision:

The tale has been saved, and has not perished, and will save us if we are obedient to the word spoken. . . . Wherefore my counsel is, that we hold fast ever to the heavenly way and follow after justice and virtue always, considering that the soul is immortal and able to endure every sort of good and every sort of evil.[32]

SUGGESTED WORKS FOR FURTHER STUDY

PLATO. Plato, *Dialogues* (several translations and many volumes of selections are available).

BIOGRAPHIES AND CRITICAL STUDIES. Burnet, John, *Platonism;* Cornford, F. M., *Before and After Socrates;* Demos, Raphael, *The Philosophy of Plato;* Dickinson, G. Lowes, *Plato and His Dialogues;* Field, G. C., *Plato and His Contemporaries;* Fite, Warner, *The Platonic Legend;* Grote, George, *Plato and the Other Companions of Sokrates;* Koyré, Alexander, *Discovering Plato;* Livingstone, Sir Richard, *Plato and Modern Education;* Lodge, R. C., *Plato's Theory of Ethics;* Lutoslawski, Wincenty, *The Origin and Growth of Plato's Logic;* More, P. L., *The Religion of Plato;* Morrow, G. R., *Studies in the Platonic Epistles;* Pater, Walter, *Plato and Platonism;* Ritchie, D. G., *Plato;* Ritter, Constantin, *The Essence of Plato's Philosophy;* Ross, Sir David, *Plato's Theory of Ideas;* Shorey, Paul, *What Plato Said;* Stewart, J. A., *Plato's Doctrine of Ideas;* Taylor, A. E., *Plato;* Wild, John, *Plato's Theory of Man;* Woodbridge, F. J. E., *The Son of Apollo;* Zeller, Eduard, *Plato and the Older Academy.*

---

[31] Plato, *Timaeus,* in *ibid.,* Vol. III, p. 41.
[32] Plato, *The Republic,* Bk. x, in *ibid.,* Vol. III, p. 621.

4. Aristotle: Realistic Rationalism

Aristotle and Plato

Coleridge distinguished two classes of thinking men: Platonists and Aristotelians. This classification is plainly incomplete, but it indicates a divergence in emphasis which may be noted repeatedly in the history of philosophy. On this issue, the Scholastic doctors of the Church divided during the Middle Ages, and it marks contending modern views of scientific and philosophical method.

Aristotle's thought branched off from the direction pursued by the Platonic Academy, but the starting point of his philosophy and many of his fundamental convictions were and remained Platonic. Here was a dramatic reenactment of Plato's own response to the teachings of Socrates. Through this incomparable confluence and divergence, classical philosophy probed the innermost truths of reality—those within the direct grasp of human experience, those of the summits of spiritual vision, and those dealing in broad survey and in searching investigation of nature and of man.

As we examine Aristotle's manifold relation to Plato, we should consider his temperament and the characteristic ways of thought in which this temperament found expression. Aristotle (384–322) had a predilection for natural history. His theoretic activity was always controlled by a direct awareness of specific facts. While contemplating reality, he was also engaged in dissecting it. When Plato committed his life to Socrates, he gave up his plan of becoming a tragic poet. If Aristotle had not turned to philosophy in the Platonic Academy, he would likely have followed his father's profession, medicine. He came of a family of physicians, and therefore belonged to the guild of Asclepiads, in which it was customary that boys should be trained early in clinical methods. His father, Nicomachus, was a native of Stagira near Mount Athos, in the Chalcidice south of Macedonia. Nicomachus was court physician to, and a personal friend of, the Macedonian king, Amyntas II, who was the father of Philip and the grandfather of Alexander the Great.

The young Aristotle's early impressions and memories were of a life lived in the shadow of the royal palace, and of the treatment of ailing bodies—an early introduction to his later work in social philosophy and in the biological sciences. But this influence and training did not last long, for the boy lost his parents, and his upbringing was then undertaken by a relative. The youth's distinguished family connections and his own high promise entitled him to the best education available, and so, at the age of 17, he was sent to the Platonic Academy.

It is interesting to know that, when Aristotle reached Athens in 367, Plato was away on his journey to Syracuse where he endeavored unsuccessfully to educate Dionysius II as a philosopher-king. Thus, young Aristotle's first impressions of Plato's teaching did not result from the direct personal sway of the master over a brilliant and plastic mind. His first direct contact with Plato's thought was in the master's library, reading his *Dialogues*. When the great man returned to the Academy, his own more direct influence on the youth from Macedonia was preeminent, but it was an influence on a mind already prepared both to learn and to question.

Of course we should not forget that Aristotle did not go to Athens as a young philosopher, but as a "freshman" pursuing his education. Unlike our colleges, the Academy was not a double society of professors and students. It included young men like Aristotle, more seasoned disciples or "graduate fellows," and also scientists and philosophers of greater or less distinction who were developing their theories in the creative interplay of ideas which Plato stimulated; they included cosmologists, mathematicians, and social philosophers. The Academy attracted productive minds from all Hellas, and it sent out to the various colonies not only educated public officials, but also systematic Platonists, who spread active philosophical thought. The Academy was a radiating center of ideas.

Aristotle remained in the Academy for twenty years, until Plato's death, first as a student and later as an associate and colleague—a more and more critical disciple who was bound eventually to develop his own systematic doctrine, but who was kept in the Academy by the powerful personal hold of Plato. The master thought very highly of him, but association through the years revealed the growing tension between their minds. Plato referred to the studious youth as "the reader," and "the mind of the school," but found in him a certain unplatonic worldliness. The royal physician's son was not only too preoccupied with observations of the material world, but too much concerned with worldly matters. He was regarded as showy in attire and too interested in his physical comforts, and he was reported to combine his high thinking with dissolute conduct. The latter charge seems baseless when we consider Aristotle's indefatigable and incredibly productive life. The long list of his extant works represents a bare fourth of his reputed writings.

Aristotle's main divergence from Plato was fundamental, for it concerned the doctrine of Ideas. Versed in this doctrine by his early study of the *Dialogues*, Aristotle also followed its critical discussion in the Academy, of which we get an echo in Plato's *Parmenides*. Aristotle's natural-scientific spirit increasingly reacted against the metaphysical view of the universal, ideal Forms and Principles which Plato held to be realities existing independently of the natural objects that the master depreciated as mere phenomena or as unstable appearances. Aristotle opposed especially a certain growing tendency in the Academy to regard the figures of geometry as realities. He was unresponsive to the Pythagorean strain in Platonism, its preoccupation with number symbolism. All these universal Ideas signified to Aristotle essential qualities, laws, and principles of the world of particular objects in nature. Surely the Ideas should not in and by themselves be viewed as substances. Thus, we might say, the universal law of falling bodies is the law *of falling bodies*. Aristotle thus resisted the dualistic trend in the Platonic cosmology. The real world of the universal Ideas of reason and the seeming world of particular phenomena of sense experience must somehow be recognized as related and, ultimately, as one.

Aristotle's especial interest in biological science accentuated his recognition of activity in nature, growth, and development. He found the Eleatic tendency in Plato uncongenial. Nature to him was an ongoing process, not a system of eternal entities. He distrusted also Plato's use of myths in place of scientific accounts. In the study and interpretation of nature, he preferred the prose of reliable description and analysis to the poetry of a sublime vision.

But in all these critical reactions to Plato, though manifested in the development of Aristotle's philosophy, certain basic Platonic principles remained firm, and they are evident in the Aristotelian system. They will be recognized by the reader in his examination of Aristotle's works; two or three may be mentioned here. Despite his revision of Plato's theory of knowledge, Aristotle relied finally on reason for systematic knowledge and truth. He was immersed in the world of particular facts, but he nowise considered nature as a mere mechanism of whirling clusters of atoms. His cosmology was as thoroughly teleological as Plato's. He criticized Plato's Idea of Good, but his own metaphysics found its consummation in God, the Principle of Creative, Rational Perfection.

As we consider the main Aristotelian doctrines, the divergences and agreements with Plato's will be recognized more clearly. The Academy tradition sometimes described Aristotle as a wayward disciple and a renegade. Diogenes Laertius speaks of his secession, and reports Plato as saying: "Aristotle has kicked us off just as chickens do their mother after they have been hatched."[1] As a commentary on these words, whether authentic or not, the modern judgment of Lange may be cited: "As often as we find an opposition between

[1] Diogenes Laertius, *The Lives and Opinions of Eminent Philosophers* (trans. C. D. Yonge), London, Bohn's Libraries, 1853, p. 181.

Aristotelian empiricism and Platonic idealism, we have also a point before us in which Aristotle contradicts himself."[2]

The various estimates of Aristotle's divergence from Plato—its thoroughness and critical advance, or its final inconsistency—will, of course, depend upon varying systematic interpretation. But his works repeatedly provide evidence that his disagreements with Platonism did not involve any personal hostility toward the Platonists or any lapse of his high regard for the master. He was reputed to have had a biting wit, but he does not show it in the *Metaphysics*—the long and continual criticism of the doctrine that Ideas and mathematical objects have substantial existence. In his social philosophy, he sternly criticizes Plato's communism of the guardian class, but it is without animosity. A passage in the *Nicomachean Ethics* is especially notable, in which Aristotle confesses that it is uphill work for him to criticize Plato's Idea of universal Good, "in view of our friendship for the authors of the doctrine of Ideas."[3] But though friends are dear, truth must be dearer still, and so he feels bound to proceed with his criticism. These passages are from later writings. Aristotle's early dialogues and other works seem to have been in substantial agreement with Plato and despite his various deviations, personal attachment to Plato kept him in the Academy.

After Plato's death in 347, when his nephew, Speusippus, became chief of the school, Aristotle left Athens and spent several years journeying in different parts of Aegean Greece. With his friend and fellow Academic, Xenocrates, he lent distinction to the philosophical group assembled by King Hermias of Atarneus, whose niece, Pythias, he married. He was also induced by his friend and later associate, Theophrastus, to pursue biological researches on the island of Lesbos.

About the year 343 he had his chance to emulate Plato's endeavors to educate a philosopher-king. Philip of Macedon, who had succeeded to the throne of his father Amyntas, heard from Hermias about the fame of Aristotle whom he had known in his youth, and called the philosopher to become the tutor of the crown prince, Alexander, then 13 years old. The education of the prince was bound to start with a study of Homer, but it also proceeded to scientific and philosophical ideas. Aristotle taught Alexander the principles of royal government, both domestic and colonial administration. The boy was attached to his tutor, but could not be dissuaded from his project to invade Asia, nor from his dream to fuse Greek and Asiatic cultures, a notion uncongenial to Aristotle's Hellenic outlook on life. When Alexander assumed power in 340, Aristotle left the Macedonian court and lived for some time in his old family home at Stagira. Less than twenty years of life remained to him, but they were to be years of incredible creative achievement.

[2] F. A. Lange, *History of Materialism* (trans. E. C. Thomas), 2nd ed., London, Kegan, Paul, 1892, Vol. I, p. 207.

[3] Aristotle, *Nicomachean Ethics* (trans. F. H. Peters), 10th ed., London, Kegan, Paul, 1906, Bk. I, sec. 6.

The Work of the Lyceum and Aristotle's Writings

In 335, following the death of Philip of Macedon and at the start of Alexander's campaign of world conquest, Aristotle returned to Athens and established his own school there, the Lyceum. This became the second Athenian university and before long rivaled the Academy. Aristotle habitually lectured and held discussions with his disciples while pacing up and down the covered walk or portico, *peripatos,* of the Lyceum; hence, the Aristotelians came to be known as Peripatetics. The new center of learning emphasized the investigation of nature and especially biological research. It included a zoological museum containing many specimens sent by Alexander from various countries. While the Lyceum did not emphasize mathematical studies, it probed the principles of rational analysis and achieved the science of formal logic. The dominantly human interest of the Socratic philosophy was not lost in the Lyceum, but it did not have the idealistic or utopian spirit of Plato's humanism. Aristotle studied man's soul and conduct, individual and social, with scientific objectivity. In pursuing his social-political philosophy he made a collection of the constitutions of Greek city-states, just as he collected biological specimens. All his special inquiries reflected his basic interpretation of the nature of things. Aristotle's thinking was marked by a keen sense of the historical stream of ideas. His own systematic construction was in continual interplay with his critical appraisal of his predecessors. He was the first historian of philosophy. Plato had called him "the reader"; he became a famous collector of manuscripts, and made his Lyceum a center of erudition as well as of research.

Notwithstanding this interest in the collection and study of books, the Lyceum did not preserve carefully the writings of its founder. Antiquity had lists of Aristotelian works which to us are only titles. During his twenty years in the Academy, Aristotle wrote a number of dialogues and other treatises mainly on Platonic lines, which seem to have been widely known in both Greece and Rome but are lost to us. During his twelve years of travel between leaving the Academy and founding the Lyceum, he probably began many of his works which, elaborated during the closing period of his life, have come down to us. The odyssey of our "Works of Aristotle" takes us from the library of the Lyceum to damp cellars in the Troad, then back to Athens. Sulla acquired the manuscripts in his conquest of the city and carried them as war booty to Rome. There they were finally reduced to order and edited in the time of Cicero, 250 years after Aristotle.

Any reader who turns from Plato's *Dialogues* to the works of Aristotle is bound to be impressed by the inferior form of the latter. This difference is not due merely to the literary excellence of Plato, supreme in the whole history of philosophy. Compared with the philosophical poetry of Plato's thinking, Aristotle's philosophy impresses us as prose, but even as prose his writings do not show mastery of style. The material is not always ordered with logical coherence; the reader is distracted by occasional shifts from one topic to another or by rehearsal and repetition. The exposition often impresses us as that of recorded oral discourse rather than that of a composed treatise. Many of these writings seem to have been series of lectures which Aristotle prepared and elaborated through the years he taught in the Lyceum. Thus, in serving the purposes of the school, they were in a state of continual revision, yet, some of them were given the more definite order and form which Aristotle must naturally have planned for all his works eventually.

A rude turn in the political course of events frustrated any such final editorial projects. A brief glance at the historical setting at this point will enable us to take our philosophical bearings more clearly. We should remember that the life of Aristotle coincided to the year with that of Demosthenes (384–322), and more broadly with the ineffective resistance of the Greek states to the expanding dominion of the Macedonian realm which finally subjugated them. When the brilliant son of the royal physician of Macedonia came to Athens in 367, Philip, the son of King Amyntas, was being held as hostage by the strong rulers of Thebes. Three years later, Philip returned to Macedonia, and eventually ended the bloody confusion of the interregnum by his successful struggle for his father's throne. The latter half of Aristotle's membership in the Academy was the decade of Philip's invasion of Greece. The Greek cities were torn by the struggle between the pro-Macedonian parties and the opponents to Philip's aggression; these latter were weakened by indecision and mutual suspicion. Aristotle's last years in the Academy were the years of Demosthenes' eloquent but futile appeals to the Greeks to resist the invader. The first *Philippic* was delivered in 351. Plato died in 347, the year in which Philip conquered and destroyed Olynthus, Athens' ally in the Chalcidice, and was ready to begin his definite struggle for the hegemony of Greece. The animosity aroused by the fall of Olynthus may have been a factor in Aristotle's decision to leave Athens after Plato's death. When he returned twelve years later, Aristotle had been the tutor of Philip's son, and was kinsman by marriage of Philip's ally, Hermias, in the Troad, and intimate friend of Antipater, whom Alexander appointed regent of Macedonia and ruler of Greece in 334 when he began his conquest of Asia. During these years of the rising fame of the Lyceum, we can understand readily the hostility with which Aristotle had to contend. There was the philosophical opposition to him among some members of the Academy. Its chief, Xenocrates, though an old personal friend, was actively anti-Macedonian. And popular enmity toward the Macedonian tyrant's teacher must have been seething, kept down only by the protective power of Antipater. The news of Alexander's death in Babylon in 323 inflamed Athenian resistance to Macedonia. During this struggle, Aristotle's enemies indicted him on the grave charge of impiety, because in his poem on the death of King Hermias he had virtually deified his friend. Aristotle realized the hatred behind this sort of accusation, and, remembering the fate of Socrates, is said to have declared that he wished to save the Athenians from committing a second crime against philosophy. He left Athens with some of his disciples and proceeded to Chalcis, in Euboea. There he died the next year, 322, at the age of 62.

Thus, Aristotle's works remained in their unfinished form. Despite their stylistic defects, they give an overwhelming impression of the encyclopedic range, the analytic mastery, and the systematic grasp of Aristotle's mind. We can readily understand his renown in ancient philosophy and science. More than fifteen centuries later, his fame revived during the Middle Ages, when St. Thomas Aquinas adopted his system as the intellectual framework of Catholic belief, and Dante called him "the Master of those who know."

The Aristotelian works covered the program of instruction and research at the Lyceum in science and the humanities. Aristotle distinguished all thought as theoretical, practical, and productive, and his writings may be classified accordingly. Under the theoretical are included all his contributions to the sciences: physics, astronomy, meteorology, biology, and his psychological treatise *On the Soul*. Aristotle called all these "second philosophy," the investigation of nature in detail, specific explanations of particular things and types of being. From these he distinguished his fundamental science of nature and first principles or, as he called it, "First Philosophy." His books dealing with his First Philosophy were placed, by the editor of his works, after those on physics, or *meta ta physica*, and so came to be called *Metaphysics*. Along with these theoretical works we should consider Aristotle's writings on philosophical method and theory of knowledge, especially his books on logic, which were assembled under the general title of the *Organon*, or the "instrument of thought." The works on his practical philosophy include his *Ethics* and *Politics*, and his productive or poetical treatises are two: the *Rhetoric* and the *Poetics*.

Our study of Aristotelianism cannot include detailed examination of any one of his treatises and must omit even passing allusion to some of them. It seems most advisable to survey here the range and the direction of Aristotle's thought, referring to a number of his works to illustrate statements of his doctrines.

Theory of Knowledge and Formal Logic

Aristotle regarded science and philosophy as fundamental human activities. The first sentence of the *Metaphysics* reads, "All men by nature desire to know." The problem of the right scientific—that is, the knowledge-yielding —method is thus paramount in Aristotle's way of life. We are reminded of Socrates's reflection that "an unexamined life is not worth human living."

But, *how* do we achieve reliable understanding of ourselves and of the world in which we live?

On this question of method Aristotle disagreed with Plato, although he shared Plato's conviction that real knowledge requires rational mastery of universal principles, and, like Plato, he discredited mere opinions based on passing sense impressions. Unlike Plato, however, he did not dismiss observation from his scientific procedure. Plato's exclusive emphasis was on rational analysis and rigorous deduction: a mathematical-logical ideal of science. Aristotle reaffirmed the importance of this deductive method as preeminent in certain departments of thought. In fact, as we shall presently see, it was Aristotle who gave us the first systematic exposition of deductive logic. But in other inquiries Aristotle recognized the important role of sense perceptions, to lead us to general concepts and laws from which rational inferences can be drawn. Aristotle recognized a limit to this logical procedure. The basic universal premises of knowledge in the field of inquiry cannot be attained inductively. The very possibility of science demands its reliance on self-evident initial, but undemonstrable, first principles.

While Aristotle thus resisted the dualistic trend in Platonism, and while he did not set sense perception in opposition to reason as unreliable, he nowise resigned himself, like Protagoras, to the particulars of sense. He included observation and experiment to provide the material data for his rational-scientific construction. But he recognized that the system of scientific knowledge thus achieved relied initially on self-evident first principles. Plato's view of science and philosophy was, all the way, that of purely rational analysis, theory and contemplation. Aristotle's account of knowledge would combine investigation of facts and theoretical procedure. Both Plato and Aristotle recognized, and had to explain, the mind's possession of the universal laws and principles from which it drew rational inferences. Plato's explanation was mythical: Since the mind could not derive its universal concepts from sense experience, it must have innate possession of them in the rational pre-existence of the soul. True scientific-philosophical reflection must be a process of progressive rational "reminiscence." This sort of doctrine was unacceptable to Aristotle. He did not regard the data of sense experience as merely random, transitory impressions. We retain in memory these sense data; in our reflection we compare and connect similar observations; we draw inferences from them and form expectations of certain characteristic behavior. We devise experimental conditions for testing the reliability of our general description or explanatory patterns; we proceed from tentative to more and more clearly defined concepts. Thus the mind explores and comprehends, in progressively larger generality, the classes and types of Being, the laws and principles and relations of nature which we are investigating. But the problem of self-evident, undemonstrable first principles still remained.

While Aristotle recognized the experimental method and, as far as he could, utilized it in his various scientific treatises, he did not subject the process of inductive reasoning to rigorous logical analysis or to a systematic treatise; he did not formulate the laws and methods of inductive logic. The renowned Aristotelian logic is formal logic, the analysis of deductive reasoning. Formal logic was said to have come from Aristotle's mind as Pallas Athene came from the head of Zeus, perfect and in full armor. While detailed additions to Aristotle's doctrine were made through the ages and modern criticism has subjected it to some fundamental revision (in many important respects it has replaced it), countless students in the past have been brought up on the logic of the Aristotelian Lyceum. Its formulas, its rules, and many of its class problems and exercises have been part of our educational tradition for over twenty centuries. We can scarcely presume to summarize a course in logic in a few pages, but we should indicate some of Aristotle's main principles here, for they are characteristic of his philosophical method and outlook.

The *Organon* expounds a logic of consistency and implication. Aristotle developed the method implied in the dialectic of Socrates and Plato, and gave it systematic formulation. He undertook to grasp in scientific principles the dialectical art of which Socrates was a past-master. Here we borrow our illustrations from Plato's *Dialogues* in order to recognize Aristotle's guiding principles. Let us recall the Socratic inquiry into the nature of Temperance as presented in the *Charmides*. The young Charmides first defined temperance as quietness; but, by a series of critical questions, Socrates led him to admit that his definition could not be maintained. Charmides then proposed another definition—that temperance is modesty—and yet a third, fourth, and fifth. In each case, he was brought to the same logical plight that showed his ignorance. He affirmed and then denied the same proposition. If we examine other Socratic discussions we see a similar logical pattern. The mind's ignorance and error are exposed in its self-contradiction. No statement is valid which, on further examination, is shown to require negation.

Real knowledge, therefore, must be based on a consistent system of thought. The objects and concepts with which our mind deals must be definable; that is, they should be viewed as having an essential character which we must recognize and which we must respect. The predicate we use to qualify any subject must express its nature significantly. And we may not both affirm and deny this predicate. "The same attribute cannot at the same time belong and not belong to the same subject and in the same respect."[4] This is the Law of Contradiction, or better, of Non-contradiction. Furthermore, "there cannot be an intermediate between contradictories, but of one subject we must either affirm or deny any one predicate."[5] A figure is either a triangle or not a triangle. This we call the Law of Excluded Middle. These basic laws of thought express the Principle of Consistency that is essential to logically valid thinking.

[4] Aristotle, *Metaphysics* (trans. W. D. Ross), in Richard McKeon (ed.), *The Basic Works of Aristotle*, New York, Random House, 1941, 1005b. The paging is that indicated along the margins of the work.
[5] *Ibid.*, 1011b.

Aristotle's logic is concerned with examining the valid and the invalid definition and organization of our thought: the various kinds of terms we use, the union of terms in propositions; and the combination of propositions as premises from which further inferences may be drawn. The last of these three, the procedure of combining ideas, the so-called "syllogism," is Aristotle's outstanding logical doctrine; but the first two are properly introductory to it.

The examination of logical terms is the theme of Aristotle's treatise, *Categories*. Consider any object, ox, man, or acorn: we express what it means to us by some appropriate term, be it adjective or verb. Thus, by a variety of predicates the nature of the object is indicated. Aristotle presented a table of ten categories, or the basic and most universal forms of predication: (1) *substance* (for instance, "man"); (2) *quality* ("white"); (3) *quantity* ("two cubits tall"); (4) *relation* ("twice or half as great"); (5) *place* ("in the Lyceum"); (6) *time* ("yesterday"); (7) *position* ("sitting"); (8) *state or condition* ("shod"); (9) *acting* ("lancing"); (10) *suffering* ("being lanced").

These categories may serve us in classifying the various terms of our daily discourse. The categories are not of equal importance. As might be expected, Aristotle gave special attention to quantity, relation, and quality. In another list, he omits position and state. However, for him, the outstanding category was substance; the others were clearly contributory and subsidiary to it.

Terms are combined in propositions, and, in his work *On Interpretation*, Aristotle classified the various kinds of statements that could be made about a term or its opposite, and examined their logical interrelation. The two terms, "man" and "just," may be related in four ways yielding a universal and a particular affirmation, "All men are just," "Some men are just"; and, likewise, a universal and a particular negation, "No men are just," "Some men are not just." What can be inferred from the truth or fallacy of any one of these four propositions regarding the truth or fallacy of the other three? How can we express the meaning of a negative proposition affirmatively or the meaning of an affirmative proposition negatively?

Aristotle also considered the process of conversion. On the basis of a given proposition, what statement can be made about its predicate: in each of the above cases what can we say about "just beings"? This question leads to others. In making a proposition about "men" and "just" the mind implies certain knowledge about "not-men" and "not-just." Aristotle thus undertook to explore the entire range of meaning of a proposition so as to determine its logical relation to all the other propositions using the same terms or their opposites in any combination: which of them were implied, excluded, or left uncertain by the original statement. In this study of the various processes of direct inference the mind could grasp fully and precisely the meaning of any proposition.

Beyond ascertaining the significance of a single proposition, the mind must combine it with other propositions. This is syllogistic reasoning, outlined by Aristotle in his *Prior Analytics*. A syllogism is a process of mediate reasoning. From two propositions (premises) having one term in common, a third proposition (conclusion) is deduced about the other two terms. If we know that "all B is C" and "all A is B," we can surely conclude that "All A is C." But the premises "All C is B" and "Some A is B" do not yield a certain conclusion; and the premises "No B is C" and "No B is A" do not warrant any conclusion. Aristotle undertook to draw up a list of all the ways in which the four types of propositions (universal or particular affirmations and universal or particular negations) could be combined as premises, and to ascertain what valid conclusions, if any, each pair of them yield. The syllogisms were seen to differ in their "figure," depending upon the position of the common, or middle, term in the premises; or in their "mood," depending upon the various combinations of propositions in each figure. Aristotle recognized only three figures, as illustrated above. The fourth figure (for instance, "All C is B," "All B is A," therefore "Some A is C") was proposed later by Galen, but Aristotle did not admit it, since it is a way of reasoning which can be formulated better in the first figure. By careful analysis, Aristotle established the valid syllogisms and the rules governing valid reasoning in each of his three figures.

An investigation of valid reasoning involves the exposure of fallacies. Analysis of the various syllogisms had shown fallacies due to our exceeding in the conclusion the knowledge of the terms afforded by the premises, or in our attempting to reason from insufficient mastery of the middle term. In his treatise, *On Sophistic Refutations*, Aristotle unmasked various other sources of erroneous reasoning. We may go astray by using our terms or propositions ambiguously; by misplacing emphasis or accent; by wrongly combining or separating terms; by confusing the essential attribute of a thing with one that is only accidentally applicable to it; by mistaking the qualities of some parts of a thing as characteristic of it as a whole; by begging the question and assuming what is to be proved; by not realizing what is required for refutation; or by presuming to have refuted more than we have. In pointing out these and other fallacies of direct inference or syllogistic reasoning, Aristotle clarified the entire territory of valid thinking.

In addition to exploring the varieties of valid and invalid reasoning, Aristotle inquired into the attainment and expansion of scientific knowledge. For a proposition about a thing may be correct but it may not be a true statement of its essential nature, and a conclusion may follow from its premises yet be only contingent on their validity and yield no real scientific knowledge. Aristotle thus considered, in the *Posterior Analytics*, the problems of adequate definition and scientific demonstration. The definition of a thing may be only verbal; it may not demonstrate its existence; only scientific demonstration can reveal the essential nature of things. An adequate definition must indicate clearly the specific attribute that differentiates the species being defined from the other members of its class or genus. In this procedure we grasp the character of a thing by definite classification.

But we can also understand the nature of a thing by recognizing the conditions of its existence. To this end, Aristotle proposed his doctrine of the four causes. How does my desk come to be what it is? Clearly, the material of which it is made is required—wood, pegs, glue, and varnish. This is the "material cause" of the desk. But a "formal cause" is essential: that into which the material is formed, a desk. Third, the material is formed into a desk by sawing, planing, joining, and finishing—the specific operations which Aristotle called "efficient cause." Furthermore, a thing is produced and explained by the purpose or end it is to serve, that for the sake of which it is made. This is its "final cause." This doctrine of the fourfold cause of things is central in Aristotle's philosophy; it leads us to his fundamental conception of nature. We may recognize that both efficient and final cause are really subsidiary to formal cause. Aristotle's basic distinction is between formal and material cause. His causal analysis thus leads us to the problem of Form and Matter, his critical revision of the Platonic doctrine of nature.

Aristotle's Metaphysics and Theology

Aristotle called his *Metaphysics*, "First Philosophy," and its fundamental principles are essential to his detailed account of the world. The philosophical quest of ultimate understanding is praised by him as the most divine and most honorable science. Knowledge of particular things and relations in nature is necessary in our daily activities, but our mind reaches toward a basic insight into the nature of reality itself. We are moved to wonder that things should be as they are; we search for the original causes of their being and activity.

Aristotle's fundamental account of nature criticizes Plato and relates him to the pre-Socratics. The early Ionian "physiologers" proposed a cosmology in terms of material stuffs or particles. But, how can water, earth, or fire, by themselves, explain the rational principles of truth, goodness, or beauty in the world? Yet reason which knows cannot be regarded as wholly above and beyond that which it knows. The nature of a thing is not its bare existence, but neither can it be apart from its existence. While the Platonic theory of Ideas was right in rejecting some earlier views of the cosmos as a fortuitous whirl of material particles, and, while it was right, too, in demanding universal formal principles of order and harmony in nature and a rational teleology, it erred in regarding this rational order as transcendent in the world of things. The correction of this error was a main purpose of Aristotle.

We come now to the Aristotelian doctrine of form-in-matter, and, first of all, a clear statement of his terms is important. Although Aristotle was revising the pre-Socratic and Platonic accounts of the material world, the word "matter" in his doctrine does not signify merely bodily-physical existence. Nor does the term "form," as he used it, mean merely shape or the set of qualities characterizing various kinds of being. Aristotle started with these ideas, but was led beyond them to a larger and more adequate view. He distinguished, but refused to separate, the bare existence of a thing from its real being. The real being is never bare; it manifests a certain character and a direction of activity which constitute its nature. Matter and form thus signified to Aristotle two fundamental aspects of any being, or two perspectives in which it can be regarded and understood. In the process of incubating and hatching, the egg matter manifests its chicken form. So may we distinguish the acorn from the oak, the sown field from the golden harvest.

But may we not go further? Analogous to these distinctions are others which the mind can make in its own processes. The rough material of our sensations and opinions may achieve form and logical order. The moist clay, the moulding, the glazing, and the firing, all together, find and show their form in the potter's vase. The Promethean myth and the creative struggle of Aeschylus with the problems of God and man provide the matter of the great tragedy. As Aristotle in his exposition reviewed and criticized the ideas of his predecessors, the whole course of previous reflection was to him so much matter, the material which he molded and organized, to achieve its fuller truth, character, and form in his own scientific and philosophical system.

Aristotle emphasized in his doctrine the immanence of form and matter. Form is *in* matter. The cosmos is not dual in nature, with eternal, universal, ideal forms and changing, particular matters of fact; nature is really cosmic, a harmonious order, in which we can distinguish, but may not separate, matter and form. Aristotle stated his doctrine of Form-in-Matter in another way to express the two aspects of nature which are manifested in the process of existence: in every activity he distinguished Potentiality and Actuality, or Realization. The nature of a being is shown in its present state and also in its future capacities, what it is now, and what it can attain. Here are two pebbly objects, this one is an acorn; it will normally grow into an oak. Here are two similar chicks, one is only a duckling, but the other is really a swan. Similarly, in the circle of his disciples, Socrates must have recognized that Plato, far above the others, had the potentialities of a great philosopher.

The formation of rocks or other substances, sprouting, hatching, scientific inquiry, and artistic production are all instances of the realization of potentiality. It is the drama or action of nature, things becoming actually what they are meant to be. Aristotle thus recognized an immanent teleology in nature. The behavior and specific operation of a thing may be said to subserve its characteristic end. But this end is not external or, as it were, assigned to it; such a view would be unacceptable mythology to Aristotle. He regarded the purpose or end of anything as its essential nature; actual realization of its potentialities is its natural fulfillment. Recalling Aristotle's fourfold causation, we see again that efficient cause and final cause are reducible to formal cause, and that this in turn is immanent in material cause.

The distinction of potentiality and actuality, or realization, enables us to recognize better another important principle in Aristotle's metaphysics, the relativity of form and matter. As we have seen, form and matter are distinguishable aspects of any being or any process in nature. But each thing or process is thus both matter and form. This realization of potentialities may itself be seen, in another perspective, as the potentiality of still further realization. This marble, we say, was the matter which found and realized its form in the Hermes of Praxiteles. But the marble block was also the suitable Form quarried from the mass of stone. The marble quarry of Paros, furthermore, was the form and realization of lower, elementary processes in nature. Looking now in the other direction, the statue before us, as we see and touch it, or can visualize it in its finished perfection, was the material embodiment or the matter of the Hermes and Child in the sculptor's ideal conception and purpose. Yet this higher form itself might manifest still higher potentialities of artistic vision.

So we may say that Aristotle contemplated nature as a scale or gradation, in which each being manifests the realization of certain potentialities, and the capacity of further, still unrealized actuality. In mounting a stairway, each step may be viewed as the completion of an arrival or as the beginning of a step forward. Any being which we try to understand may be viewed in two perspectives: either in its cosmic background of lower potentialities from which it has emerged, or in its prospect and vista of yet higher and fuller realization. Suppose we proceed in a descending course, so to say, "down the ladder of existence." We should then consider lower and lower types of being. The conceivable last rung of the ladder would be a thing that showed no emergence from anything lower or more elementary than itself. That would be Mere Matter without any form, utterly unrealized potentiality. Aristotle regarded such formless matter as only a notion in our minds. Nowhere in nature is there such bare potentiality; such a being without any quality or characteristic behavior or direction of activity, would in fact be nothing at all. Matter, according to Aristotle, always exists in relation to form, in some state of actuality or realization. "Matter is unknowable in itself."[6] This conclusion might well have been expected from his critique of Plato's dualism.

Must we reach a similar conclusion about form, that it, also, is "unknowable in itself," and so refuse a title to reality to Pure Form, as to Mere Matter? On this point, Aristotle's metaphysics has been charged with inconsistency, but also has been interpreted as manifesting a great advance through deeper interpretation. If we consider the universe as a hierarchy of beings, our ascending contemplation would reach its summit in the recognition of perfect and absolute realization, Pure Actuality, Pure Form with no material limitation or potentiality whatever. Aristotle did not call this a mere abstraction, like Mere Matter. On the contrary, he exalted Pure Form as the supreme

---

[6] *Ibid.*, 1036a.

reality, or God, and regarded theology as the essence and culmination of his First Philosophy.

Aristotle was led to his conviction of God's perfect and eternal reality by the analysis of potentiality and actuality, or realization, in the ongoing course of nature. Potentiality is implied in any growth and attainment, but potentiality alone cannot account for them. In the very process of realizing its capacities, a being reveals the reality of the higher actuality to which it attains. Unless the oak character were real, the acorn could not achieve it, and thus would not be an acorn. The realization of every potentiality countersigns in detail the actuality which is implied in it, which is real and logically prior to it. The hierarchy of nature exhibits the specific eliciting of the character and perfection which are eternally real and actual in God.

In the cardinal Book XII of the *Metaphysics*, as also in the concluding book of his *Physics*, Aristotle undertook to prove the reality of God. This is the First Mover, or First Cause, argument, also called cosmological, famous in a hundred treatises of philosophical theology. In his works, he reached his belief in God by other reasoning also, but the proof of God's reality, as Pure Form and First Cause is central in his philosophical system. Aristotle considered the whole world process of realizing potentialities kinetically, as a system of motions. How are these motions to be regarded and explained? The motions of particular beings point beyond themselves, and their movers are likewise moved by something else. But this whole series of motions must have their primary source in a first mover, which is either self-moving or wholly immovable. Aristotle regarded God as absolutely immovable, and related to the rest of nature only through the self-moving "first heaven." If we restate this argument in causal terms, we reach the conclusion that God, the First Cause, is the causeless basis of all finite causation.

Aristotle's God would not be properly described as the highest realization or the purest Form. Deity transcends the distinction between potentiality and actuality. The First Cause is not *a* cause. It transcends all individuality. Spatial and temporal references do not apply to God. If we speak of deity in personal terms, it is by a philosophical license which should not mislead us into anthropomorphism. God as the eternal, creative Reason is the highest object of our contemplation, but we are not objects of God's experience. Before St. Peter declared that God is "no respecter of persons," Aristotle believed that the divine thought is not of me or of thee; by its very character it can only be eternal self-contemplation. "It must be of itself that the divine thought thinks, . . . and its thinking is a thinking on thinking (*nóesis noéseos nóesis*)."[7]

So Aristotle viewed the hierarchy of beings in nature, a world of form-in-matter, realization of potentialities: from the utter unreality of formless Mere Matter to the absolute reality of Pure Form transcending all potentiality and all the distinctions of existent things. Aristotle needed God to

[7] *Ibid.*, 1074b.

explain the active hierarchy of nature, but he exalted Pure Form absolutely. It is the Prime Mover, but not of any moved thing, and the eternal, perfect Reason, but of a perfection which our reason can scarcely comprehend. Aristotle aimed to overcome Plato's dualism of the phenomena and the Ideas; at the culmination of his theory of reality, however, his pure Form is even more transcendent than Plato's Idea of Good. Aristotle also regarded God as "a living being, eternal, most good, so that life and duration continuous and eternal belong to God; for this *is* God."[8] On God do the heavens depend, and so does the world of nature. God is the final object of the world's desire and the highest goal of thought. In Aristotle's theology, the idea of God as the ultimate Reality, transcending all finite attributes and distinctions, seems to have contended with a more religious conception of God as the summit of all ideal aspiration.

The Physical and Biological Sciences

The reader of Aristotle's scientific works turns from surprise at his patent blunders and misjudgment to astonishment at his insight into the basic principles of structure and process in nature. The right appraisal of Aristotle as a man of science requires us to keep our historical perspective. We should remember his meager equipment for observation and experiment. He had no telescope or microscope; no watch, thermometer, or other devices for precise measurement and experimental control; no delicate instruments for dissection; and no electrical apparatus. He had mainly his own keenly observant and probing mind, the theoretical range and grasp of genius.

The physical sciences, or "second philosophy" of Artistole, explored, in detail the realization of form-in-matter in the various fields of nature. Thus, dependent upon the basic principles developed in his metaphysics, his physics requires the further consideration of certain basic aspects or modes of existence, the principal of which is motion. As we have noted, motion was regarded by Aristotle metaphysically as the realizing of potentialities, the attainment of form-in-matter. Nature is a vast process of manifold changes, of which Aristotle distinguished four kinds. Change may be substantial—in origin or decay; it may be quantitative—increase or decrease; it may be qualitative transformation; or it may be change of location.

Motion, we say, is in space and time, and Aristotle considered these two basic categories, or aspects, of Being. He rejected the Democritean doctrine of empty space—the void in which the atoms and masses of atoms move. Change of location does not require a vacuum; it may well be conceived as the rearrangement of bodies in a world of filled space. Space is not the material of which bodies are made, nor their enclosing shape or mold, nor the

[8] *Ibid.*, 1072b.

unoccupied interval between them. Aristotle defined space as "the boundary of the containing body at which it is in contact with the contained body."[9] The limits of space are thus the limits of the world, which are not definitely assignable.

Time was regarded by Aristotle as bound up with change and motion. It is the succession of changes, the measure or serial enumeration of movements. As motion is perpetual in nature, so likewise is time. Between the before and the after of time is the present moment, now. But these "nows" cannot be regarded as discrete parts of time that are joined together to yield its range of duration. Time is a flow, and not a whole, of sections. The idea of time is connected in our thought with our perception of movements. Aristotle considered, but did not quite answer, the question whether time is a wholly mental category. Would there be any time in a mindless world? He may be said to have inclined toward a negative answer. Without soul there would be no time but only that of which time is an attribute; there would still be motion, but no measure of it.

In his analysis of the composition and constitution of physical nature, Aristotle combined original views with stubborn adherence to traditional error. He adhered to the four elements of Empedocles, and added a fifth, unique and peculiar to the celestial bodies. His theory of the cosmic system is geocentric. The earth, a sphere, is the stationary center of a series of revolving spheres containing the various heavenly bodies, planets, stars, and the "first heaven." Aristotle's doctrine of the multiplicity of celestial spheres with their respective revolutions, a most complicated elaboration of a fundamentally erroneous idea, and its later development in the Ptolemaic theory, retarded the progress of astronomy until the sixteenth century, when Copernicus revived and perfected the heliocentric doctrine of the Pythagorean Aristarchus.

Aristotle's full stature as a scientist is shown in his biological works. The tribute to their fame is not merely that of uncritical tradition. Darwin's eulogy is well known: "Linnaeus and Cuvier have been my two gods, though in very different ways, but they were mere school boys to old Aristotle."[10] Aristotle's researches, in the fourth century B.C., were remarkably extensive, penetrating, and fertile in significant theoretical inferences. He examined and dissected hundreds of animals and showed right judgment in his zoological classification; he recognized whales and porpoises as mammals. He observed, and described carefully, fishes and other forms of marine life; he studied closely the hatching of chickens. But he also erroneously believed in spontaneous generation, and regarded worms and flies as produced from rotting bodies by the sun's heat, and, similarly, mice and frogs as emerging from slime in summer.

Darwin's praise does not mean that he regarded Aristotle as his predecessor

[9] Aristotle, *Physics*, in *ibid.*, 212a.
[10] Quoted in Francis Darwin (ed.), *The Life and Letters of Charles Darwin*, 2nd ed., London, Murray, 1887, Vol. III, p. 252.

in evolutionary biology. Aristotle taught the continuity of biological forms in the hierarchy of nature, but he did not teach the origin and evolution of species in different periods of time. Careful distinction is needed here to avoid misinterpretation. From the lowest and most elementary life to the highest and most complex species, the biological scale manifests no breaks. To be sure, he recognized certain broad and basic distinctions, as between plants, animals, and human beings. But sponges and apes seemed to be border organisms linking these main types in the chain or stream of living nature. Aristotle taught teleological fulfillment in nature, a scale of lower and higher forms of life. This was not like Darwin's evolution, conceived as the succession in time of simpler by more complex organisms. Aristotle regarded all species in the scale of nature as eternal, and as eternal, also, their relation to each other in the hierarchy. The structure and process of nature is one in which the potentiality of forms is eternally implicit in the lower forms of life, eternally realized in the higher, eternally revealing in detail the absolute perfection of creative reason in God.

Aristotle's Psychology

The treatise *On the Soul* (*De Anima*), presents a problem in the exposition of Aristotle's philosophy. He includes man with animals and plants in the continuous hierarchy of nature, hence the topic of this section would seem to be properly a part of the preceding one. Aristotle's psychology is a biological science. But his examination of the human soul leads him to recognize its unique character, which not only provides the basis for his ethics, but also points anew to the theological culmination of his metaphysics. Aristotle saw man as rooted in lower levels of nature but also soaring towards its summits. We should be aware of this twofold perspective in discussing the Aristotelian psychology; it may enable us to appraise both its merits and some of its ambiguities.

Aristotle's basic view of the soul was biological, not mental. In his judgment, the realization of the soul, or *psyche*, marks the distinction, not between thinking and unthinking beings, but between living organisms and inorganic bodies. He defined soul as the form of "the first entelechy of a natural body endowed with the capacity of life."[11] It is the principle of life, capacity for movement from within, or self-activity. This biological-organic view of the soul should not be confused with materialism. Aristotle rejects the Democritean account of the soul-atoms scattered through the body which, being round and smooth, are nimble, and easily stirred and hence "sensitive." As well might you think that you could animate a wooden Aphrodite by pouring quicksilver globules into it! The atomists neglected

11 Aristotle, *De Anima* (trans. W. A. Hammond), in *Aristotle's Psychology*, London, Sonnenschein, 1902, 412a.

the all-important teleology of the soul. An animate body seems to act intentionally. This teleology is manifested as adaptiveness in lower forms of life, as conscious purpose in the higher.

Aristotle's doctrine of the soul is in opposition to Plato's idealistic dualism of soul and body, and also in contrast to the atomism of Democritus. Soul and body, in his view, are one and integral. The soul is the form of the body. The soul form and the body matter can no more be separated than the concave and convex shape of a shell, or the impression and the wax in a seal. The soul is the essential and characteristic activity of a living organism, as vision is to the eye or cutting is to the axe.

The various grades or stages of living bodies in the hierarchy of nature manifest the various capacities of the soul, its expanding range of activities. Aristotle distinguished three main types of souls, those in plants, in animals, and in men. The plant soul is its vegetative activity; its growth and fruition through nourishment. A cabbage feeds, grows, and produces more cabbages. The animal soul adds to this nutritive power several other functions; an animal can move about; it senses, feels, and desires. Man is a living body with still higher capacities. Beyond the nutritive, locomotive, sensitive, and appetitive faculties of animals, the human soul excels in its distinctive rational power. Man is the rational animal.

Keeping in mind the solidarity of human life with that of animals and plants, we may now consider Aristotle's more distinctive analysis of man's soul. His insight is the more impressive in view of his many elementary errors. He had no knowledge of neural processes and, unlike his master, Plato, did not recognize the head as the seat of mental activity; instead he regarded the heart as the center of sensation and the seat of the common or central sense. Yet, both his keen observations of and his inferences concerning the conscious processes have evoked the high tributes of modern psychologists.

We share sensation with the animals, but in human life we can study its conscious manifestations. In sensation, we do not receive the matter of a body, as in nutrition, but apprehend its form in its various aspects: its color, sound, touch, taste, or odor, or its qualities common to several senses, like shape, size, motion, and rest. By the central sense, we become aware that we perceive, compare and relate our sensations. Although it is some form or power in the object that arouses our sense perception of it, the sensation is ours, and is determined by the character and capacity of our soul. Sensible qualities are thus both objective and subjective.

Besides the central common sense, Aristotle examined two other inner senses, memory and imagination. They are both after effects of sense perceptions. Memory is the retention by the soul of its former impressions and is concerned only with the past. It is either a passive and more or less random awareness of past experiences, or it is a recollection, the active recovery of our former sensations in our present consciousness. But we have also the capacity to stir up certain associated responses and apparitions. Dreaming, we may entertain these phantasms as sensations; in our waking life, likewise, these visions of the imagination may manifest a rich and lively transformation of our sense-perceived world.

The preeminently human faculty is rational intelligence. Aristotle agreed with Plato in regarding reason as the capacity to attain knowledge of universal, essential principles. These principles are essential to nature, and it is through our experience of nature that we grasp them in thought. The data of sense, however, cannot by themselves produce universal knowledge. It is by reason that we learn truth from them. The inductive attainment of general laws from the observation of things was, as we have noted, a primary tenet in Aristotle's theory of knowledge. And the combination of general ideas to yield further conclusions was the theme of his deductive logic.

Aristotle distinguished a passive and an active power in rational intelligence. Reason may be viewed as a capacity for universal knowledge, proceeding from not thinking to thinking, potentially boundless in its understanding of all things and principles which it has not yet possessed. This is the passive intellect—reason regarded as a progressively realized potentiality. It is intelligence as we know it in our own thinking, arduous, often baffled, achieving, and pursuing. But beyond the true conclusions of the passive intellect is the ultimate truth that is not a conclusion but eternally evident. At the basis of all demonstrative knowledge are the first principles which are not demonstrated. We must recognize the Active Intellect or Creative Reason, implied in the potential intelligence that is progressively achieved in experience and in reasoning.

The role of the active or poetic reason in the psychology of Aristotle is similar to that of God in his metaphysics. Nature is the process and system of realizing potentialities, form-in-matter. And Aristotle's philosophy of nature pointed to absolute reality, or Pure Form, eternal realization and plenitude of perfection. Similar is his account of human intelligence, the highest faculty of soul and our own consummation in nature. Here also—beyond the laborious rational mind, or passive intellect, which induces its general laws and deduces its inferences, and which turns from each solution to its next problem—Aristotle recognized the Active Reason, its perfect truth and eternal, unqualified finality. The Active Reason transcends the finite limitations of our daily knowledge; it possesses eternally the perfect universality to which our particular truths only tend.

The intelligence of the Active Reason, implied in the mind, is the ideal contemplation that is the eternal reality of God. We are confronted here by an ambiguity in Aristotle's philosophy that has given rise to animated controversies through long centuries. The ambiguity is exposed when we consider his doctrine of human destiny. Did Aristotle believe in personal immortality? As far as the nonrational faculties of the soul are concerned, his answer was, and could be, only a plain negative. Sensation and memory are bound up with the organism as vitally as nutrition and locomotion. Only if we consider rationality can there be any discussion of man's career beyond the death and dissolution of the body. In a general reference to mind or the power to think, Aristotle wrote: "In regard to reason and the speculative faculty, we have as yet no certain evidence, but it seems to be a generically distinct type of soul and it alone is capable of existing in a state of separation from the body, as the eternal is separable from the mortal."[12] But his further account of the potential intellect scarcely sustains this view.

Aristotle's exaltation of Active Reason was unwavering and emphatic. He called it "immortal and eternal." It is pure, it transcends all bodily limitations; it is passionless, and divinely perfect. But is this active reason the reason of Socrates and Plato? Did Aristotle maintain that each mind has this active rational character as an individual and is thus personally immortal? Or did he regard active rationality as an eternal principle in which individual persons participate for a season, according to the range and measure of their potential intelligence?

Aristotle considered active reason as ideally implied in human rational intelligence, but he also exalted it as eternally realized, pure and divine, as God, or as the ideal symbol of God's nature. Aristotle's psychology does not affirm personal immortality. The tenor and implications of the Aristotelian doctrine are rather in the other direction. A believer in immortality could find in Aristotle no more than the comfort of inconclusiveness. The master's successors in the Lyceum—Theophrastus, Dicearchus, Strato—erased the ambiguity and proceeded to denial. The Arabian Aristotelians in the Middle Ages faced the same perplexity that later confronted St. Thomas and his followers: how to reinterpret and revise Aristotle's doctrine so as to square it with the belief in personal immortality. The tangled arguments over this problem will engage our attention later in considering the medieval scholastic philosophers.

Rational Living: the Ethics of the Golden Mean

Aristotle's philosophy of human nature related theoretical with practical interpretations, and individual with social activity. His psychology provided a natural background for his ethics, and the ethics led to his political-social philosophy; these three comprise Aristotle's account of man.

Three ethical treatises of alleged Aristotelian authorship have come down to us. One of them—the *Magna Moralia*—however, is probably a post-Aristotelian work of the Lyceum. The *Eudemian Ethics* seems to represent a compilation of some early teachings of Aristotle and some later material, very likely edited by his pupil, Eudemus; three of its books are identical with the main Aristotelian work on morals, the *Nicomachean Ethics*.

Aristotle's ethical inquiry was distinctly teleological. All man's actions aim at some good. But some good is sought for the sake of another good that is

[12] *Ibid.*, 413b.

deemed better and more important. So the mind is naturally led to the problem of the chief or highest good that should serve us as guiding principle and standard in our choice and in the direction of our life. Men generally regard the chief good of life as happiness, but here we need some caution. Happiness is not to be defined simply as pleasure. Aristotle regarded hedonism as one-sided and inadequate. Pleasure is surely one of the values of life, but it is not the highest good and cannot serve as a standard. The really good life must be that which brings the fullest realization of our powers in the most satisfactory and worthiest activities. Our word *happiness* does not express the full meaning of Aristotle's *eudaimonia*, which is better translated as well-being or weal, doing and faring well, welfare.

We can see in this teleological appraisal a basically functional conception of value. Aristotle expressed it in his general definition of good as "that for the sake of which all else is done."[13] Anything is deemed good if it attains its proper end, if it performs its characteristic function well. So we may judge a knife or a boat, the work of a carpenter or a physician. The adequate judgment of a man's life as altogether good must therefore depend on our understanding of man's characteristic faculty. Aristotle at this point applied to ethics the conclusion of his analysis of the human soul, that man is the distinctively rational animal. Our unique and essential faculty is reason, and so the best life for man, his highest good, must be in the rational direction of his actions and the perfection of his rational powers. Thus Aristotle was led by his science of human nature to his realistic rationalism in practical philosophy. "Man's function then being . . . the exercise of his faculties and action of various kinds with reason—the good man's function is to do this thing well and beautifully."[14]

Aristotle's view of man's highest good as the rational direction of his life does not imply a strictly intellectual outlook in ethics. Aristotle exalted rationality as an ideal, but he required the direction of reason in all human activities whatever. He lauded the perfection of reason in its own preeminent domain, in the intellectual excellence of purely theoretical activities. But in the greater part of our life reason must contend with the drives and incitements of our lower nature. We need here not only true rational judgment but also the habitual inclination of our will in the right direction. Virtue is a habit of the will; repeated practice in reasonable conduct makes reasonableness more congenial to us and more reliable.

What is it that distinguishes rationally directed conduct from irrational behavior? When strong impulses prevail over the guidance of reason, a man's life loses balance. He acts on the spur of the moment. A random lure or incentive may plunge him into some excess; or a sudden misgiving may deter him unduly. Unreasoning impulsiveness leads us to extremes. The good life needs reason to achieve the right measure and balance in which our well-being can be realized. Aristotle regarded virtue as a rational balance or

---

13 Aristotle, *Nicomachean Ethics, op. cit.*, Bk. I, sec. 7.
14 *Ibid.*

"Golden Mean," between the opposite vices of excess and deficiency. His table of virtues is a survey of this rational balance as it is maintained or upset in the various activities and situations of our daily experience.

The detailed account of the moral virtues, to which the main part of the *Nicomachean Ethics* is devoted, is a careful examination of the broad range of human affairs. Aristotle gives us a very systematic examination of the moral scene in classical antiquity. In reviewing this examination, we may note first, as does he, two virtues which he shares with Plato: courage and temperance. Courage is the virtue manifested in fearful situations of danger or aggression. The impulsive man facing dire peril is apt to weaken cravenly, to break down or flee. Less frequently, a sudden attack may spur a rash man to reckless counterattack. Between the deficiency vice of cowardice and the excess vice of foolhardiness, the will may by rational direction achieve the virtue of courage. The courageous man is he who "endures and fears what he ought from the right motive, and in the right manner, and at the right time, and similarly feels confidence."[15] Likewise with regard to the pleasures and gratifications of our appetites. The impulsive man usually goes to extreme indulgence; this is the vice of intemperance, or profligacy. The opposite extreme is seen in the man so deficient in the normal enjoyment of pleasure that, like an insensible being, he eschews all satisfaction of desires. Between these two extremes, rational direction should enable us to pursue the path of moderate enjoyment, in temperance.

Aristotle's table of the virtues, below, shows the scope of his moral survey, and it may enable us to see more clearly further aspects and problems of his ethical analysis:[16]

VICE OF DEFICIENCY	VIRTUE AS THE RATIONAL OR GOLDEN MEAN	VICE OF EXCESS
Cowardice	Courage	Foolhardiness
Insensibility	Temperance	Intemperance
Meanness	Liberality	Prodigality
Niggardliness	Magnificence	Vulgarity
Humility	High-mindedness	Vain conceit
Lack of ambition	Right ambition	Ambitiousness
Spiritlessness	Good temper	Irascibility
Churlishness	Friendly civility	Obsequious flattery
Self-depreciation	Candid self-expression	Boastfulness
Boorishness	Wittiness	Buffoonery
Shamelessness	Modesty or shame	Bashfulness

Although this table is in three columns, Aristotle did not regard virtue in each case as exactly midway between the two vices. One or the other of the opposite unreasoning impulses may be so strong that rational balance may require our main resistance to it. Thus temperance consists chiefly in avoid-

[15] *Ibid.*, Bk. III, sec. 7.
[16] *Cf. Ibid.*, Bks. III and IV.

ing intemperance and profligacy. Courage is so radically opposed to coward-ice as sometimes to be confused with boldness; in fact, an accusation of rashness is sometimes accepted as a compliment.

The vices assigned to deficiency and excess indicate the characteristic Aristotelian valuation of the respective virtue. Thus, in the important virtue of high-mindedness or rational self-respect, as also in that of candid self-expression, we see clearly Aristotle's positive affirmation of personal worth. This differs from the Socratic irony, and even more from the later Christian sense of contrition and spiritual indigence: "Wretched man that I am!"[17]

The absence of justice from the table of the virtues needs explanation. In one sense, Aristotle agreed with Plato that justice is essential rightness, and he might have regarded it as the principle of rational emphasis expressed in his Golden Mean. But Aristotle also treated justice as fairness in social rela-tions: in correction of wrongs, in the distribution of goods, and in trade. Corrective justice requires restitution and retribution. In distributive justice, goods are allotted in proportion to deserts. Justice in trade demands an offi-cially recognized and stable medium of exchange, money, to assure fair trans-actions. The opposite of justice is always its deficiency, injustice. The equi-table man, exceedingly concerned to accord others their full right and even more, is admired above the man of strict justice.

Beyond the fair adjudication of contending claims, and beyond the nobility of equitable regard for others, is the more active mutual generosity of persons that finds expression in friendship. Aristotle dismissed the motives of utility and pleasure in true moral friendship. The best friends are those who are devoted to each other's perfection. In the attainment of this ideal, men may rise from lower to higher levels of personal communion.

In all these moral virtues, our human nature is realizing its rational poten-tialities, but always under some drag of our lower impulses. Matter is a condition for the attainment of Form, but not a medium for its perfect attainment. Even the best marble comes short of the sculptor's ideal, and even the Greek language sometimes baffled Euripides, as he once labored three days to perfect a single line in a tragedy. So the perfection of character finds only limited expression in the moral virtues. The consummation of man's distinctive faculty, reason, can be realized only in purely rational activ-ities. These are the intellectual virtues, which Aristotle regarded as the high-est. They are also the most godlike, for man is most like God when he emulates the activity of the Eternal Active Reason. We mention especially three of these contemplative virtues: science, or demonstrative knowledge, of necessity and of the eternal and imperishable; intuitive reason, or insight into the first principles that are the foundations of science; and philosophical wisdom, in which intuitive reason is combined with perfected scientific knowledge of the highest objects. Aristotle also recognized some minor intel-lectual virtues that are significant in conduct: a deliberative state of mind, practical understanding, and proper discriminating judgment. Hence his

17 Romans 7:24 (American Standard Version).

moral outlook reached its summit in a lofty note of pure philosophical
contemplation.

Aristotle's Social Philosophy

Aristotle regarded ethics as leading to social philosophy. He starts his
Nicomachean Ethics by declaring that the knowledge and mastery of the
highest good is the science and art of politics, and he returns to the same
point in his last sentence: "Let us begin, then," begin the inquiry into the
various political systems and their relative worth. The *Politics* thus continues
and completes the *Ethics*. In both his moral and his social philosophy, Aristotle emphasized man's pursuit of his characteristic values. In both, he drew
his guiding principle from his analysis of human nature. The rational view
of the good life was inferred from the recognition of man as a rational animal.
So in his *Politics*, Aristotle began with his characterization of man as a social
being.

This conception of human nature as essentially social is in opposition to
any doctrine of artificial formation of government by contract. Aristotle
declared: "It is evident that the state is a creation of nature, and that man
is by nature a political animal."[18] Rooted in the bare needs of living, the
state in its development provides the full fruition of human life. A state is
the union of families and communities, not merely living together but together aiming to live honorable lives under good laws. The citizens must
take an active part in legislation and administration. But they must also live
an actively individual life. Aristotle criticized Plato's denial of family life and
private property to the guardian class as being against the age-long experience
of mankind. Slaves and artisans who lack intelligence may live in a state, but
they are not members of it. Aristotle did not recognize the fundamental
rights and personal dignity of all men. He assumed that some men are capable of full citizenship; the rest are meant to serve their masters or to be ruled
by their betters.

As in his ethics, so in his social philosophy Aristotle sought a standard of
valuation. What form of state organization is the best? Authority in a state
may be vested in one chief person, in a few, or in the many. But any of these
forms of government will be good only if the rulers aim to govern justly
for the common welfare. Where the rulers exploit their office for their own
profit, the government is corrupt. Thus, we may have a good government
by one supreme ruler (royal monarchy), by a few choice leaders (aristocracy), or by the body of the people ruling for the good of all (commonwealth). Opposed to them are the three corrupt forms of government:
tyranny; oligarchy, in which the rich exploit and abuse the poor; or democracy, rule by a populace that spurns the rights of the minority.

[18] Aristotle, *Politics* (trans. B. Jowett), in McKeon, *op. cit.*, 1253a.

Aristotle had made a thorough examination of the constitutions of the Greek states, and he examines critically the various forms. Absolute monarchy may appear to be the best ideally, when a perfect man exercises all power for the promotion of the common welfare. But human nature is corruptible, and the king may turn into a tyrant or may be succeeded by an unworthy son. Government by a council of the select men is good, provided their title to office is moral nobility; but this form of rule runs the risk of becoming some form of exploiting oligarchy. Neither noble birth nor wealth can be accepted universally as a proper claim to public authority, nor yet the will of the majority. The few or the many are entitled to rule only when they pursue the true aim of the state, which is virtue and the common good.

That form of government would seem to be best which in the course of human affairs is likely to prove most abiding in its purity and beneficence. Some nations may thrive under a sovereign's authority, and in others an aristocratic council may prove worthy and reliable. But the best constitution for most states and the best life for most men, according to Aristotle, is constitutional government in which not the extremes of the society but the solid middle class prevails. A commonwealth of the moderate, reasonable body of the people, dedicated to law and respect for the common welfare, is most likely to prove incorruptible in the long run.

Aristotle was not moved by utopian zeal. It is true that he drew a picture of the ideal state: its territorial extent, population, and its facilities for trade and navigation. And, like Plato, he paid especial attention to the educational system, in order to assure the proper training of youth and the reliable preservation of worthy principles in the social system. But his attitude was more realistic than Plato's. He was less concerned to champion the supreme ideal than to discover the best practicable and least corruptible order of life that human societies were likely to attain.

The emphasis on stability as a standard of good government naturally inclined Aristotle to consider the causes and the prevention of revolutions. The history of the Greek states gave him abundant evidence. The disruption of states by revolutions is due especially to two strong urges in human nature: the desire for equality and the desire for superiority. The inferiors revolt to wipe out their disabilities and to gain equal status with their betters. But equality is intolerable to many, and they therefore rebel in order to gain exclusiveness and preeminence. In this way, aristocracies are debased into oligarchies by the arrogance of the rich; a commonwealth, on the other hand, may be degraded to lawless rule by the populace through the greed and envy of the poor.

A good state is likely to be protected against disruption by restricting the power exercised by public officials, by avoiding any abuse of legislation that may serve only special class interests and shake the people's confidence in the integrity of the state, and, above all, by educating the youth in a law-abiding spirit, in respect for the constitution. True liberty is possible and reliable only in a law-abiding society. "Men think . . . that freedom means the doing what a man likes. . . . But this is all wrong; men should not think it slavery to live according to the rule of the constitution; for it is their salvation."[19]

The Poetics of Aristotle

Aristotle, like Plato, did not achieve a systematic philosophy of art, but his short treatise, *Poetics*, gives us the outlines of his aesthetics. No other work, short or long, has had comparable influence in the whole history of literary, and especially dramatic, art and criticism. It is the preeminent statement of the classical tradition in poetry.

Aristotle followed Plato in regarding poetry as an imitation of nature or life, but his views of the aim and the effects of poetry are not Platonic. The poet's purpose is not to inform or to edify or to reform, but to please us. And the effect of poetry on the passions is not, as Plato believed, harmful excitement. The poet arouses our emotions in such a way as to purge and to refine them. Aristotle gave special attention in his *Poetics* to the critical interpretation of tragedy. The Aristotelian definition of tragedy is famous:

[A tragedy is] the imitation of an action that is serious and also, as having magnitude, complete in itself; in language with pleasurable accessories, each kind brought in separately in the parts of the work; in a dramatic, not a narrative form; with incidents arousing pity and fear, wherewith to accomplish its catharsis of such emotions.[20]

The term *imitation* is not used by Aristotle in a derogatory sense. If we remember that the Greek word *drama* meant "action," the dramatic imitation of life in tragedy may be properly called "reenactment." To be artistic, this reenactment must have a certain quality of noble dignity. Here we recognize the classical conception of the tragic hero, which Aristotle developed further in his doctrine. The tragic action must have a certain order and integrity; it must be a dramatic cosmos, not a random assemblage of incidents.

The analysis of a tragedy discloses six main constituents: plot, character, thought, diction, spectacle, and melody. The last three are evidently subsidiary; Aristotle was concerned with the critical appraisal of the first three elements. He regarded plot as the most important of all; for plot is, after all, the essence of the drama, which is action. A great plot is the prime achievement of the tragic poet. Next in importance are the characters. For the plot is a texture of actions, of persons acting. These two, plot and characters, should be discussed together. Aristotle considered the various plots, or situa-

[19] *Ibid.*, 1310a.
[20] Aristotle, *Poetics* (trans. I. Bywater), in *ibid.*, 1449b.

tions in life, to discover those most suitable for a great tragedy. He rejected several kinds of plot. A tragedy must not portray the ruination and misery of a thoroughly good man. This situation would be not tragically terrible or piteous, but simply odious. Nor should the tragic poet show us a bad man rising from misery to happiness. For this arouses neither pity nor fear in us, and is the most untragic situation possible. Nor again can we find tragic material in the downfall of an extremely bad man. A good tragic plot is one that engages "a man not preeminently virtuous and just, whose misfortune, however, is brought upon him not by vice or depravity, but by some error of judgment, of the number of those in the enjoyment of great reputation and prosperity."[21] Aristotle emphasized the dramatic importance of this tragic fault in the hero which proves his undoing. We are moved to fear and to pity by his ruin, for he is not unlike ourselves in his worth and in his tragic lapse.

The Aristotelian doctrine of the tragic *catharsis* has been the theme of long shelves of critical treatises. Aristotle stated that tragedy arouses pity and fear in order to accomplish the catharsis of such emotions. Did he mean that the tragic effect is one of emotional purging, or expiation, or refinement? Was he using the term here to suggest a medical analogy or religious-sacrificial purification and expiation, or yet a morally refining and perfecting action? Critics have followed each one of these lines of interpretation, and various modulations of them.

If we keep in mind the great tragedies of Greek genius with which Aristotle was concerned in his *Poetics*—especially his chosen masterpiece, Sophocles' *Oedipus the King*—we may suggest a possible interpretation of his doctrine. In arousing our pity and fear or terror, tragedy relieves these emotions of all that is merely painful and frightening in them when aroused by personal danger and suffering. We contemplate the purely pitiable and terrible for its own sake, very intently so that it moves us, but impersonally so that our contemplation of the tragic action is aesthetically satisfying. We experience a humane expansion of view and a quickened response, a pitying dread, without the grief and panic to which merely personal troubles may drive us. Tragedy thus effects in us, not moral refinement directly, but certainly a cherished spiritual enhancement and deepening insight.

SUGGESTED WORKS FOR FURTHER STUDY

ARISTOTLE.　Aristotle, *Works* (Oxford ed.); McKeon, Richard (ed.), *Basic Works of Aristotle.*

BIOGRAPHIES AND CRITICAL STUDIES.　Barker, Ernest, *The Politics of Aristotle;* Burnet, John, *Aristotle;* Butcher, S. H., *Aristotle's Theory of Poetry and Fine Art;* Cherniss, Harold, *Aristotle's Criticism of Plato and the Academy;* Davidson,

21 *Ibid.*, 1453a.

Thomas, *Aristotle and Ancient Educational Ideals;* Grant, Sir Alexander, *Aristotle;* Jaeger, W. W., *Aristotle;* Mure, G. R. G., *Aristotle;* Randall, J. H., Jr., *Aristotle;* Ross, W. D., *Aristotle;* Taylor, A. E., *Aristotle;* Zeller, Eduard, *Aristotle and the Early Peripatetics.*

5. Epicurus: Materialism and the Life of Pleasure

Hellenistic Culture and Post-Aristotelian Philosophy

Greek philosophy after Plato and Aristotle is like English poetry after Shakespeare and Milton. We have been on the summits, and the inevitable decline we experience in turning to lower grades of contemplation is liable to impress us as decay. That impression is scarcely warranted. Instead of belittling post-Aristotelian philosophy, we should try to understand its characteristic qualities and motives, and its relation to the complex and confused civilization of the aging classical world.

In 323 B.C. Alexander died suddenly in faraway Babylon; the following year Demosthenes committed suicide, and Aristotle, a refugee from Athens, died in Chalcis. The life purposes of the first two were frustrated in different ways, and the work of the third was cut short of its full fruition. The deliverance of the Greek city-states from the Macedonian yoke, and their free and vigorous development under Athenian leadership—to which Demosthenes had been dedicated—proved a futile hope. The Athenian revolt following the death of the world conqueror was speedily crushed, and though Sparta continued to resist, and late alliances recovered partial self-government for some city-states, the Greeks never regained real independence. In various degrees of subjugation, they had to pay tribute to their masters, until, in the middle of the second century, the spreading flood of Roman power finally swept over Macedonia and Greece, settling the fate of both as provinces of Rome.

Alexander, called "the Great," had visions not only of a world empire under his absolute sway, but also of a world culture, Hellenic in its dominant spirit and speech, yet integrating the many so-called "barbarian" strains in a more expansive civilization. It was a task demanding superhuman powers, and Alexander encouraged the popular adoration of his irresistible might. His mystical notions about himself, like his imperial plans, had no regional bounds.

He could confidently be the son of Apollo, and also of Amon in Egypt or of other divinities in other lands. But the absolute world monarchy and the universal cult of Alexander were both rudely shocked when the young Invincible was suddenly laid low by death.

The newly won universal empire lacked cohesion, and fell apart into contending realms ruled by Alexander's generals. Two principal military powers developed, besides the Macedonian. The Asiatic commanders moved their headquarters from Persia and Babylon to Syria, where the successors of Seleucus made Antioch a city of industrial might and a notable outpost of culture. Far more important for the progress of science and philosophy was the Egyptian monarchy of the Ptolemies. The city of Alexandria became the new world market of trade, industry, and ideas. By the mouth of the Nile, Alexander's dreams of a universal civilization approached realization. There Greek culture affected, and also reflected, the thought and the social and religious visions of Africa and the Middle East. There Greek science was advanced, in theoretical analysis and in experimental research, in which the minds of many races shared; witness Euclid's geometry, the geography of Eratosthenes, and Ptolemy's astronomy. There the greatest library of antiquity garnered the written knowledge, beauty, and worship of all mankind, making Greek wisdom native to former barbarians, translating into Greek the Holy Scriptures of the Jews.

Alexandria was the greatest but not the only center of this Hellenistic civilization. There was Antioch, already mentioned; Rhodes; and, on a more ambitious scale, Pergamum, whose kings vied with the Ptolemies as patrons of art and letters. Even after the imperial expansion of Rome overwhelmed the entire Mediterranean basin, Alexandria still remained, with Athens, a capital of world culture. As the Christian faith gradually spread and prevailed over Greek reason and Roman empire, Alexandria became at once the spawning pool of heresies and a nursery of orthodoxy.

In this new world of racial and cultural interfusion, thought leavened the culture of strange cities overseas, but in its homeland the Greek mind faced its own issues of alien incursion. The conglomerate realms into which Alexander's world empire split were unwieldy and continually rent by wars and revolts. But, while the Greek cities of the mainland and their former colonies thus changed masters, any hope for the real restoration of their self-government seemed futile. The old Greek city-state, *polis*, was gone; lost were the old social systems which Plato criticized in the *Republic*, also, the constitutions which Aristotle compared in his *Politics*. In the Greek philosophy of life, the former union of ethics and politics was now obsolete. Statesmanship was no longer an available career, political reform an issue, or social theory a problem.

The social-political upheaval did not overturn the established philosophical traditions. Just as in later ages the great universities of Europe survived wars and revolutions, so in Athens the Platonic Academy and the Aristotelian

Lyceum continued their activities. But in both schools the original rationalism of the masters was unsettled by their successors. The Platonic self-reliant rational analysis was disturbed by skepticism. The successors of Aristotle turned from his teleological metaphysics of form-in-matter and his theology to explain nature and human nature in increasingly materialistic terms. Intellectual, as well as social instability, turned philosophy to new directions or to radical reappraisal of the old convictions.

In their new life of subjection to alien masters, the Greeks might swerve from the principles and problems of free spirits to the pursuit of material profits. The more reflective minds might be thrown on themselves. They might seek in their own sense experience and in their private satisfactions the wisdom of life; or they might hold fast to reason and seek a way out in fortitude and resignation. The practical problem of coming to terms with life prevailed over the theoretical problem of basic understanding. The philosophy of the Hellenistic age was, in its motivation, a way of life, not one of mere contemplation and insight. These new sages differed only in their chief aims, all of them practical. The Stoics sought to reach rational peace by the full mastery of the passions. The Epicureans viewed philosophy as a daily business of speech and thought to secure a happy life. "If happiness is present, we have everything."[1]

The Life of Epicurus

Epicurus (342–270)—the third outstanding Athenian among the Greek philosophers (after Socrates and Plato)—was a typical product of an unsettled age, of its vicissitudes and its impulsions. It should be said at the outset that Epicurus and his doctrine aroused much controversy, in which both sides indulged in violent criticism and personal abuse. We do not need to learn about the Greek philosophers from Epicurus' often scurrilous comments. The accounts, Greek and Roman, of Epicurus and his disciples also need to be discounted. Even Diogenes Laertius, who relished philosophical gossip, after recounting some scandalous tales, brushed them off as all wrong. Modern Epicurean criticism has sifted out much of this chaff and gathered the grains of more reliable evidence about the man and his teaching.

Though of Athenian family, Epicurus was probably born in Samos, whither his father had moved from Athens in search of better fortune, and very likely he was brought up on the island. The boy seems to have grown up in unfavorable circumstances. His father was a poor schoolmaster, and his mother eked out the family income by going to people's houses to per-

[1] Quoted in Diogenes Laertius, *The Lives and Opinions of Eminent Philosophers* (trans. C. D. Yonge), London, Bohn's Libraries, 1853, p. 468.

form certain magic-religious rites and incantations. If it is true that she took her son as assistant in her ceremonial rigmarole, we can imagine how he must have learned the hatred of religious superstition, which was to become a first principle of his philosophy. Epicurus had shown his critical mettle early. When he read in school the words of Hesiod that in the beginning was Chaos, he wanted to know what was Chaos and whence it came.

In the year of Alexander's death, the 19-year-old Epicurus went to Athens to assume his citizenship and serve his term in the army. He may have heard Xenocrates lecture at the Academy, or Theophrastus, in Aristotle's place, at the Lyceum. But he did not stay long, for in 322, the year of Aristotle's death at Chalcis, Alexander's successor in Asia, Perdiccas, banished the Athenian settlers from the island of Samos, and Antipater, the Macedonian general, drove thousands of the landless poor from Athens. Epicurus had to return to his parents, refugees in Colophon on the coast of Asia Minor.

Regarding the next decade, his biographers are indefinite. His education was random, the very opposite of Plato's close attachment to Socrates, and Aristotle's twenty years in the Academy. Epicurus seems to have read variously, to have had some irregular instruction, and to have studied especially Democritean atomism. But Epicurus was averse to acknowledging any intellectual obligations. Aristotle's criticism of his predecessors was thoroughgoing, but he had always felt himself member and heir of a long tradition. Epicurus indulged the conceit of radical originality which often marks the unschooled—nothing like his wisdom had ever been thought before!

He started schools of his own, at Mitylene, in Lampsacus, and, about 306, he moved with some of his disciples to Athens, where he purchased a house and a garden that was to become famous in the memoirs of devotees and in the aspersions of scandal mongers. Here Epicurus spent the remaining half of his life in philosophical leisure and converse. The School of the Garden was coeducational, and, on that account, was bound to stir the Greek gossips, especially as the master counted among his pupils not only broad-minded matrons, but also some reflective courtesans. The charges of profligacy by the enemies of Epicureanism cannot besmirch the founder or the early teaching of the school. The society of the Garden was certainly not prim or stiffly virtuous; but neither was its doctrine nor its practice dissolute.

Among the chief joys of Epicurus was the writing of many books, but posterity did not preserve them at all. Diogenes Laertius mentioned more than 300 Epicurean treatises on all conceivable topics, not one of which has come down to us. For our study of the philosophy of Epicurus, we have to rely on the cited fragments of his teaching to be found in various works of antiquity. These need very cautious sifting. Three long letters by Epicurus and a list of his principal tenets were preserved by Diogenes Laertius. Another most important source for Epicurean study is a masterpiece of Latin literature, the poem in six books by Lucretius *On the Nature of Things* (*De Rerum Natura*).

The Epicurean Garden: Pleasure and Repose

Epicurean philosophy may be studied as a revival of pre-Socratic natural-ism, especially of the Democritean atoms, as contrasted with the metaphysics of Reason in the two dominant philosophies of Athens. Also, in opposition to Plato and Aristotle's more or less emphatic depreciation of hedonism, Epicurus espoused the teaching of Aristippus, that the chief good of life is pleasure. At the basis of Epicureanism was concentration on the data of im-mediate experience. Epicurus held fast to the phenomena, or "seemings," which Plato had spurned. The direct impressions of our senses were real and true to him, not the universal Ideas of reason.

Epicurus was a frank and positive empiricist. We know what we feel; seeing is believing. As a French disciple, La Mettrie, was to put it 2000 years after his master: "Trust the senses, they are my philosophers."[2] Turn aside from the vast but empty speculations of solemn reason, and incline to the reality close at hand, familiar to us all; its colors and tones, its savor and odor, and its feel tingling to your finger tips. Reason can argue against reason, but the senses cannot be gainsaid. Men have urged difficulties against this reliance on direct sense perception, but no other reliance avails us in the end.

For Epicurus, this concentration on the direct particulars of experience was the root of his philosophical theory and practice. But his interest in the root was for the sake of the fruitage, and his interest in theory, also, was for the sake of practice. We could, at this point in our exposition, pass log-ically from the Epicurean theory of knowledge to its atomistic cosmology. The world is a vast whirl of material particles, and man's body and soul are likewise. But we might then miss the prevailing motive in this philosophy, which accounted for its choice of its particular theory of nature. Epicurus seized and held to the atomism of Democritus because it assured him that the world was a self-operating mechanism that functions without the interference of divine providence or any other capitalized Reason in the processes of nature or in human lives. He needed and cherished repose as essential to his chief good, happiness. His views of nature and of human nature were dic-tated, first of all, by his concern for this main chance in life. We can enter into the spirit of Epicureanism if we first consider its ethics.

The Epicurean ethics revived, revised, and perfected the Cyrenaic hedon-ism of Aristippus. Like his predecessor, Epicurus declared that pleasure is the beginning and the end of the blessed life. But the idea of the highest good was no longer one of uncritical indulgence. The most abundant attainment

---

[2] Paraphrased from *Oeuvres philosophiques de M. de La Mettrie*, Berlin, 1775, Vol. I, p. 60.

of the chief good, according to Epicurus, requires cultivation of the art of living, both in its large design and in its detailed execution.

Epicurus judged his initial conviction to be in no need of proof. That pleasure is a good to be sought and pain an evil to be eschewed is as directly evident to us as that honey is sweet or that fire burns. Hedonism bases its doctrine upon the plain and incontestable data of sense experience. Pleasure is what we all seek and cherish, and the wisdom of life must consist in the most effective pursuit of it. In examining the quest for pleasure Epicurus reported its usual course and also undertook to appraise it critically. In the daily lives of men, the primary pleasures lie in the satisfaction of bodily appetites. The pleasures of the eye and the ear are common to us all; but stronger and more intense are the pleasures of taste and sexual passion. The Epicurean saying that primary pleasures are those of the stomach evoked harsh censure. Nineteen centuries before Carlyle, Cicero called hedonism an ethics of the pigsty. This blunt indication of the organic bedrock of pleasure, however, nowise expressed the wisdom of Epicurus or his moral aim and counsel. He is unswerving in his conviction that pleasure is the chief and final good in life. No ideals of rational worth or nobility command his devotion—he spurns them all—if they do not yield pleasure. But there are pleasures more lasting, more reliable, more fruitful than those of sensual indulgence. The good hedonist avoids profligacy, not because it is unworthy, but because its pleasures betray him in the end and bring him to grief. As a hedonist, he prefers some pleasures to others, because they assure him greater happiness. We should make this the daily strategy of our lives, to attain the maximum good with the least exposure to evil.

"Of our desires, some are natural and necessary; others are natural, but not necessary; others again, are neither natural nor necessary."[3] The first group of wants—those for food, clothing, shelter—cannot be neglected if men are to live well and comfortably. The sexual desires, natural but not necessary, may be indulged but may also be tempered. The third kind, the desires for luxuries, require good sense to spurn them rather than large means to gratify them. The wise man should not enslave himself to wasteful and debauched hankerings. The surest path to bodily comfort and mental ease is in the simple life—plain food and genial company. Eat barley porridge and drink water, your hunger and thirst are thus satisfied with the least toil and with no ill after effects. Be also merry with your friends, but without violent passions or envy, or vexing commitments or conflicts. Epicurus avoided excessive indulgence, not in a spirit of devotion to high principles, but as the sure way to the greatest happiness. "Nothing is enough for him to whom enough is too little."[4]

"Happiness and blessedness do not consort with extent of wealth or weight of responsibilities or public office or power, but with painlessness, with mild-

[3] Quoted in R. D. Hicks, *Stoic and Epicurean*, New York, Scribner, 1910, p. 189.
[4] *Ibid.*, p. 194.

ness of feeling, and that disposition of soul which defines what is according
to nature."[5] This is happiness in the emancipation from bodily aches, and
from the vexations, worries, and terrors of the mind. The Epicurean preferred the frugal, contented life of the Garden to the luxuries and the greed
of the rich, the ambitions and the anxieties of the mighty. He had no sense
of public duty nor a desire for honor and preeminence. He obeyed the laws,
but he was not concerned with legislation or social reform. Political ambition
was harassing and probably futile. Athens might be ruled by Antipater or
by Antigonus, what is that to you? Manage to evade their service, and risk
not their enmity; your own happiness is nearer at hand, without fame but
without fear, in the Garden of frugal joys. The avoidance of political offices
by the Epicureans did not signify an unsocial spirit; their social-mindedness
was personal, not public. They valued friendship highly as a condition of
human felicity, but in all intimate personal relations they never lost sight of
their own contentment.

This doctrine aroused various critical reactions. It may not be the highest
wisdom of life, but is it ignoble? This ethics of simple pleasures of body and
mind, genial repose and friendliness, quiet contentment of soul could be
translated into a life of blessed delight. The Epicurean wisdom, however, had
no convincing reply to the protests of sensual greed. The voluptuary in the
Garden could not share the philosophical pleasures of Epicurus, and was not
content with porridge and water. He knew the high cost of his own profligacy, but these other commended pleasures were not worth even their low
price—not to him. How could he rightly be admonished on the basis of a
strict Epicurean appeal to pleasure as the chief good of life? Hedonism here
exposed its essential incapacity to provide a convincing standard for judgments of moral preference and choice. These Epicurean sensualists multiplied, in Greece and in Rome, and they brought the School of the Garden
into ill repute.

The Atomistic Drive of Nature, Body and Soul

The Epicurean ideal of happiness and freedom from anxiety could not be
realized so long as men's sorest pang, the panic of the supernatural, harrowed
their minds. The chief value of scientific understanding must be to deliver
us from cringing piety, and this deliverance was the purpose that animated
Epicurus in his account of the nature of things. In his restatement of the
Democritean doctrine, atomism was more than a cosmological theory; it became a declaration of independence from the dark terrors of religious superstition. Epicurus undertook to extirpate the idea of the supernatural, root and
branch. The conception of the world as a self-propelled mechanism containing within itself all its causes and motive powers—a view that distinguished

[5] *Ibid.*, p. 193.

the emphatic atomism of Democritus from the inconclusive naturalism of Empedocles and Anaxagoras—was adopted in the Garden as the true insight into nature, and was essential to the Epicurean philosophy of life.

We cannot take seriously Epicurus' claims to originality. He might disavow his obligations to Democritus, but he did adopt the main outlines of the Democritean cosmology. On the other hand, we should err if we regarded Epicurus as a mere philosophical borrower. What he took he made thoroughly his own, and, in several important respects, he revised and strengthened the original doctrine with keen scientific perception. Modern criticism has pointed out three basic principles in his doctrine of nature. Epicurus maintained the all-including mechanism of nature; it admits of no increase, and everything in it is material and materially caused. In the mechanics of this universe of matter, furthermore, there can be only dissolution into parts or recombination, no extinction or utter destruction. Third, the changes in nature are changes of particulars, and do not alter its basic character. No radically new forces intrude into the universe or emerge from it. The world is, in detail, a stir of seeming instability; but its basic elements are eternally unaltered. As Clemenceau said of French coalition ministries, so Epicurus declared of the structures in nature: The more they change, the more they are the same. "All things are ever the same."[6]

The observable variety in the course of existence must, then, be due to a change in combinations; its basic persistence must be in a permanence of primary indivisible particles. In abstract theory, we could conceive of the infinite divisibility of matter. But Epicurus held to sensation, and, for him, the primary particles which we perceive as indivisible, and hence call atoms, may conceivably have their own respective least parts. They differ in size and shape; they are the *minima* of perception; whatever we perceive is some cluster or mass of them.

Nothing is more evident in our sense experience than the continual change of bodies. From this indisputable fact, Epicurus inferred that motion is inherent in atoms, and that they have a medium in which to move, a field of operations. So again, we get the Democritean description of nature as a world of atoms in motion in space. Space is the void; when it is filled by material particles, we have existent bodies.

At this point Epicurus diverged radically from Democritus. The naturalist from Abdera, as we have noted already, reasoned that the atoms, having magnitude, however little, have weight, and so he conceived their motion as initially downwards. In the world-wide rain of atoms, the larger ones, falling with greater velocity, caught up with the smaller, collided with them, and turned the rain into a dance of atoms swirling in every direction. Atoms in this manner hooked and joined onto each other, and formed the material clusters and masses of the world as we know it.

This explanation was inadequate for Epicurus. In the utter void of space, the larger atoms would not fall faster than the smaller. Weights and blows

[6] Translated from Lucretius, *De rerum natura*, iii:l. 945.

cannot by themselves account for the complicated stir of material combinations in nature. In order to explain this continual transformation, we must recognize an inherent power in each particle to swerve at any time from its downward course. This is the Epicurean doctrine of the declination of atoms, *clinamen:* "a tiny swerve . . . in no determined direction of place and at no determined time."[7] It has given rise to various interpretations. Did Epicurus require this fortuitous exception to the universal mechanism of nature in order to rule out fatalism and to allow for human free will? He declared himself just as firmly opposed to the doctrine of absolute fate as to the mythology of divine intervention in nature and human affairs. But was this not a precarious concession in a system of emphatic naturalism? Or did Epicurus use his theory of the swerve or "change of trend" to express his recognition of a certain baffling, but undeniable, contingency and chance in nature, the amazingly versatile and ever changing rhythm of existence? That would have been a witting or an unwitting admission of the shortcomings of an exclusively mechanistic cosmology. Or was he simply explaining the factual motion of bodies in all directions by his doctrine that atoms could swerve anywhere at any time? In that case, why did Epicurus have to postulate this swerving motion as the continual exception to the usual downward course of the atoms? The motion inherent in the atoms could have been recognized basically, as it is factually observed, as a motion in any direction. The problem of explaining this basic variation of motion might have been raised, but it would have been a problem no more perplexing than that of the swerve, and it would not have embarrassed the fundamental materialism by unsettling the universal mechanics of existence.

However we interpret the doctrine of the swerve of atoms, we can find no hesitation in the Epicurean inclusion of all existence in the atomic drive; stones and plants, beasts and men, bodies and souls—they are all swirling masses of atoms. The anthropology and psychology of Epicurus were explicitly materialistic. Man was described as a complicated system of moving particles. What a man calls his soul is an assortment of atoms scattered through his body. These atoms are the roundest and smoothest in existence; their shape makes them highly mobile, nimble, and readily stirred by the least flutter in the environment. This is their so-called "sensitivity." Our various sensations are the stirrings of these atoms in the eye, the ear, and the other bodily organs, in reaction to the motions of things around us. The soul particles are the finest conceivable. Like the flavor of wine or the fragrance of flowers which, swept by the breeze, leave them seemingly not a whit smaller, so it is with the soul atoms in the body.

The soul particles were declared to include the elemental nature of wind (or vapor), fire, air, and a certain nameless element, the nimblest and finest of all. Lucretius feels "the poverty of his country's tongue"[8] to express the

[7] Lucretius, *On the Nature of Things* (trans. C. Bailey), Oxford, Clarendon Press, 1910, Bk. ii, ll. 292 f.

[8] *Ibid.,* Bk. iii, l. 260.

nature and activity of these subtlest and most mobile particles. They first rebound in the impression of sense experience. The soul atoms are strewn all over the body. But there is a surging mass of them in the breast, which Epicurus regarded as the seat of thought and volition, and these atoms he called "the mind (*animus*)."

Subtle and superlatively fine though they be, the soul particles are all material. The whole career of the soul is bound up with the body. Without the soul the body becomes insensitive and lifeless; but the soul particles must be held together by the body in order to operate in sense experience. The soul can survive a partial bodily injury, but the total breakdown and separation which takes place at death is fatal to both soul and body.

On this point—the soul's mortality—the Epicurean was most positive. In the third book of his poem, Lucretius marshaled an imposing array of arguments against a belief in a future life. This chant of our mortality was probably a poetic version of some Epicurean discourses. No matter how we consider human nature and the facts of man's daily experience, always we are led to the same conclusion, that death is man's final end. The soul's structure precludes its survival outside the body. The soul atoms are sensitive only when held together by the bodily organs; their characteristic activity is possible only in and with the body; apart from it they are quickly dissipated. The soul shares the hale or ailing condition of the body, its shocks and injuries, and, in the end, it will be no more when the body is undone. Furthermore, the soul's activity is bound up with that of eye and nostril; how can we conceive of any kind of sensation in a disembodied soul? Lucretius finally passes from argument to irony, and, with tireless rhetoric, his hexameters proclaim the absurdity of the traditional beliefs in immortality.

We should not overlook a significant characteristic of all this argumentation, important to our understanding of the Epicurean philosophy of life. There is no suggestion of regret or renunciation of a cherished hope in this denial of immortality. Even the complacent submission to "the facts of science," which marks some modern materialists, is absent here. The Epicurean proclaimed the soul's mortality as a gospel of salvation—salvation from religion. Lucretius' poem is moved by hostility to the cringing terror of the supernatural. If there be gods, they, also, are natural beings, moving untroubled in the interstellar spaces. One of the surest ways to be freed from any fear of the gods is to realize that there is no hereafter to terrify us with its holy threats. Nothing can happen to us after we are dead, for we shall then be no more. "There is nothing terrible in living to a man who rightly comprehends that there is nothing terrible in ceasing to live."[9]

The Epicurean denial of immortality was the culmination of that concentration on the immediate scene of sense experience which found expression in his theory of knowledge and in his atomistic cosmology. In contrast to the

[9] Diogenes Laertius, *The Lives and Opinions of Eminent Philosophers* (trans. C. D. Yonge), London, Bohn's Libraries, 1853, p. 469.

imperturbable contentment of the sage, Lucretius portrayed the woeful state of the ignorant multitude:

Ah! miserable minds of men, blind hearts! in what darkness of life, in what great dangers ye spend this little span of years! to think that ye should not see that nature cries out aloud for nothing else but that pain may be kept far sundered from the body, and that, withdrawn from care and fear, the mind may enjoy the sense of pleasure![10]

To Lucretius, the conviction that this life is our only chance was a challenge to realize his one opportunity, "to dwell in the calm high places, firmly embattled on the heights by the teaching of the wise."[11] But to others—a growing number—the chant of mortality was a lure to sensual indulgence. In its view of human destiny, as in its ethics, Epicurean materialism could not find sound, reliable basis for commitment to the higher values of life.

SUGGESTED WORKS FOR FURTHER STUDY

EPICUREAN LITERATURE. Lucretius, *On the Nature of Things* (several translations are available); Oates, W. J. (ed.), *Stoic and Epicurean Philosophers: The Complete Extant Writings of Epicurus, Epictetus, Lucretius, Marcus Aurelius.*

CRITICAL STUDIES OF EPICUREANISM. Bailey, Cyril, *The Greek Atomists and Epicurus;* DeWitt, N. W., *Epicurus and His Philosophy;* Hicks, R. D., *Stoic and Epicurean;* Masson, John, *Lucretius, Epicurean and Poet;* Taylor, A. E., *Epicurus;* Zeller, Eduard, *The Stoics, Epicureans, and Sceptics.*

---

[10] Lucretius, *op. cit.*, Bk. ii, ll. 14 ff.
[11] *Ibid.*, ll. 7 f,

6. The Stoics of Greece and Rome: Materialism and Rational Control

The School of the Painted Colonnade

Stoicism was the first really Hellenistic philosophy: Hellenic in its principal systematic ideas, but expressing in characteristic tone and appeal the various contending strains in the world culture of the later classical age. Platonism and Aristotelianism were Greek to the core, and, although Epicureanism developed after the decline of the city-states of Greek tradition, it was, in its early stages, a school of Greeks, founded by a man of Athenian family. But, though Stoicism was established in Athens, it was not of Athens, and, though it combined in its system ideas from many Greek philosophers, its leadership, from the start, was cosmopolitan and mainly non-Hellenic. With scarcely a single distinguished Athenian adherent—its Greek representatives were mostly from the colonies—the Stoic movement drew its leaders from well-nigh every country in the ancient world, and it spread its influence through active centers overseas, notably in Rhodes, Alexandria, and Tarsus (where St. Paul had his early education). After its decline in Athens, it came to new life and power in imperial Rome. In the writings of its Roman period, Stoicism found its ethical and spiritual expression as a philosophical religion of the later classical world, and is of deep interest to the student of the moral foundations of our civilization. The roll of Roman Stoics is distinguished; suffice it to mention Cicero, Seneca, Epictetus, and Marcus Aurelius—all of them eminent in what is called the "wisdom literature" of mankind.

The founder of this fourth main philosophical tradition in classical antiquity was Zeno (c. 350–258), not to be confused with Zeno the Eleatic. The former was a native of Citium, a Greek settlement in Cyprus partly inhabited by Phoenicians; his own family probably had a Phoenician strain. At the age of 22, while sailing for Athens with a cargo of Tyrian purple, he was shipwrecked close to the Piraeus. The hope of learning, as well as the desire for gain, must have stirred in him, for when he trudged into Athens, he dried out his clothes and empty wallet in front of the first bookshop, while he pored over a manuscript. It was the second book of Xenophon's *Memorabilia* of Socrates. That day Zeno's life career was decided. "Mine was a prosperous shipwreck," he said, and asked the bookseller where he could find such men as were described in the roll, so that he could learn from them. At that moment Crates the Cynic passed by, and the bookseller said: "Follow that man."[1]

Zeno was impressed by the stern self-reliance of Crates, but found his intellectual diet thin; besides, he was too modest to bear with his master's bluff disregard for the customary decencies of life. This extreme Cynic lacked both the stimulating discourse and the personal dignity and charm of Socrates. While reading further about Socrates, Zeno changed several teachers, and, for some twenty years, explored the sources of Greek wisdom; then he set up his own school.

Despite Zeno's studies at the Academy, Socrates' influence on his thought came not through Plato but through Antisthenes and Diogenes. Unlike the latter, Zeno did not live in a tub. On the contrary, he chose for his classes with his disciples a beautiful colonnade, or porch, with paintings by Polygnotus, the *stoa poikíle*, by which the school got its name Stoic, or the "Philosophy of the Porch." It was said that he chose that place for his school, not on account of its beauty, but for the memories it preserved. Fourteen hundred Athenians had been murdered there by the Thirty Tyrants, and, as Zeno declared, he wished to make that spot tranquil by his teaching of virtue.

Disciples came to him from many lands. He dominated them as much by his upright character as by his teachings. King Antigonus sought him as a teacher, even as Dionysus II had sought Plato, but with happier results. Zeno sent the king one of his students and corresponded with him. Antigonus visited the school and retained a lasting respect for the sage who, as he said, was never elated and never humble.

Stoicism was, first and last, a philosophy of life. All of its inquiries and doctrines were oriented toward its principal aim, the right way of living. The Stoics spoke of philosophy as a fruitful field; logic is its wall, physics is its soil and planting, but its harvest and fruit are ethics. Because the fruitage is so vital to us, however, we are bound to understand the soil and the planting of the crops. This is the philosophical importance of natural science.

Stoic Cosmology and Theology: Materialistic Pantheism

The Stoic cosmology was a harvest gathered from many fields. Whether by way of adoption or of critical reaction, Zeno and his followers gleaned their ideas from various crops. We can recognize in them the influence of Heraclitus, the Pythagoreans, Hippocratic medicine, Platonic dialectic, Aristotelian metaphysics. But the dynamic heart and spirit of the Stoic philos-

[1] Diogenes Laertius, *The Lives and Opinions of Eminent Philosophers* (trans. C. D. Yonge), London, Bohn's Libraries, 1853, p. 259.

ophy was its own. It was a spirit of rational and upright concentration on the inner life, in which we can recognize the earnest candor of the Cynics, but without their stubborn oddities. It was a spirit of tension seeking resolution and peace, in quest of law, not for the sake of inquiry and understanding, but for guidance and loyal devotion. It was a spirit of truly natural piety, exploring the material stuff and roots of the noblest forms of existence, but discerning also in the lowest the evidence of rational direction and Divine Providence.

Thus Stoicism shared with the Epicureans their materialistic description of the world, but not their mechanistic view of it as a fortuitous swirl of atoms. The Stoics adapted to their own aims the Platonic and the Aristotelian rationalism, popularizing it in a more naturalistic statement but also in a more appealing religious version. As may readily be surmised, a philosophy of this sort, while it gained in practical interest and power, was likely to suffer in systematic coherence.

The Stoic doctrine of nature has been given a paradoxical label in the title of this section: materialistic pantheism. It drew both from the atomists and from classical Athenian rationalism, aiming to correct and to complete both. We may reach the Stoic's chosen truth by considering his criticisms of the errors he opposed. The Stoics described the world in material terms. Nature is a system of bodies and corporeal processes; matter is indestructible and eternal. Thus far, they agreed with the atomists. But they criticized the Epicurean failure to recognize qualitative grades of matter and real transformation in the corporeal world, and they rejected with scorn the Epicurean explanation of the complex nature of things in terms of fortuitous scrambling and unscrambling of particles. Matter is amazingly versatile in its forms and in its powers of metamorphosis; it reaches from the lowest, most rudimentary sort of being to the highest and most complex.

If we now turn from the Academy and the Lyceum to the Painted Colonnade, we shall follow an equally radical change in direction and emphasis. The Stoics followed Aristotle's criticism of the Platonic dualism of the rational Ideas and material processes—Form and Matter. But they did not regard his criticism as sufficient. The Aristotelian monistic cosmology, form-in-matter, required a more thoroughly naturalistic statement. To the Stoic, the Aristotelian hierarchy of form-in-matter was in truth a scale of the qualitative varieties of material existence. Form *is* matter. Metaphysics thus became simply physics, but physics in its turn required an explanation of the qualitative hierarchy of complex material existence, beyond the crudities of the atomic whirl.

The Stoic doctrine of tension, a distinctive contribution to cosmology, was probably advanced by Cleanthes, Zeno's successor in the direction of the school. The Aristotelian categories of activity and passivity are both important in the Stoic view of nature. Everything is continually acting and being acted upon. In this energetic conception, force is equally fundamental with matter in all existence. Various degrees of tension affect and transform bodies.

Thus, fire becomes air; air, water; and water, earth. A body maintains its qualitative identity only so long as it retains its inherent force; when that is subjected to overstrain or to a lag of tension in its interaction with other bodies, transformations result up and down the material scale. There is apparently no limit to this interaction and interfusion of bodies. With the requisite tension, a body may enter and permeate another and be both with the other and instead of the other in the same place: a perplexing inference in Stoic physics.

This account of nature in its detailed exposition had some familiar Heraclitean features: its insistence on continual change and transformation in nature, its view of the upward and downward movement, each thing becoming its opposite, the view of fire as the subtlest form of being. The Stoics conceived of cosmic fire, or World Soul, as the highest reality and everlasting dynamic in all existence. It is forever consuming the world, refining it more and more like unto itself. Likewise, things are forever, as it were, cooling off and stiffening into lower kinds of matter.

Heraclitus had seen nature as a universal flux, but a flux with a determinate character, proceeding through its changes according to order. This cosmic law of change he called the *logos*, which as he used it meant more nearly order and uniformity than reason. The Stoics however put into their doctrine of the germinating *logos* some aspects of Plato's Idea of Good and Aristotle's Creative Reason, but with the naturalistic vagueness of Anaxagoras' *Nous*, which Socrates had criticized. The logos is cosmic fire, dynamic in all existence; it is also divine providence directing all nature rationally. By calling God "cosmic fire," the Stoics reaffirmed their cosmological monism. God is not over and above matter; he is purest and subtlest matter. Our nearest approach to this subtlest nature is in our reason, which is a flaming spark of the divine fire in our body.

As may be noted, the Stoic metaphysics proceeded, like Aristotle's, toward a theology, but at the same time was intended to be firmly committed to its materialistic monism. The Stoic had no final provision for any transcendent deity or Pure Form. The divine, germinating logos is in and of the cosmic process itself, the rational dynamic and direction which makes it a cosmos. Nature is essentially a system of law, and there can be no chance. Causal necessity marks the entire world process. The Stoic cosmology is a thoroughgoing determinism. But the necessity in nature and in human life is not the blind necessity of mechanics. Like the logical necessity of sound reasoning, nature manifests an immanent teleology. The world of matter is itself the unfolding of a rational plan; divine providence directs and orders all wisely and for the best.

Continual balancing was needed to fuse and to hold together in one doctrine causal determinism and teleology, denial of any chance or free choice, and the affirmation of personal responsibility and creative activity. Here, as in some other philosophies of life, the unity was not logical, but dramatic; a harmony of characteristic tone drew together the contending strains.

We find that the Stoic held firmly to each one of these doctrines. Not a single leaf stirs in the forest, not a hair moves on our head nor any hint or feeling in the mind without an antecedent cause. A belief in chance or in free spontaneity is due to ignorance of the operating causes. No thing and no event can be truly understood apart from their respective causes and effects in which the nature and the natural role of each is manifested. Things go together as they belong together and have the same fate: the Stoics called them *confatalia*.

But though the Stoics insisted on inflexible necessity and even called it "fate," they did not proceed to fatalism. For fate is not blind; the cosmic system of necessity is rational at the core. It is the plan and teleology of Divine Providence. In seeming paradox, the Stoic's conviction of necessity was also his conviction that the world is not a fortuitous chaos, but a rational cosmos. He saw only two alternatives: universal rule of an all-wise providence, and a welter of blind atoms. Nature is necessary throughout; that is, it is reliably in God's directive power.

The evidences of teleology in nature were, in turn, used by the Stoics as grounds for belief in God. This is their argument from final causes, or argument from design. They dismissed as absurd the Epicurean speculation that plants and animals and men and all the intricate contrivances in nature were the eventual results of a fortuitous scrambling of particles, that finally happened to hit it off, say, in the framework of Epicurus, body and mind. The satirical eloquence of Cicero on this theme is familiar:

As well contend that words and verses come from the chance shifting of the twenty-one letters of the alphabet, and that the poems of Ennius could be produced by shaking together a sufficient quantity of these in a box, and then pouring them out on the ground! Chance would hardly produce a single verse.[2]

The Stoic's belief in God is more than a cosmological tenet. It is a genuinely religious assurance. As noted already, Stoicism was a philosophical religion in which men of a dozen different cultures, for whom their respective creeds had lost convincing power, united in a common rational faith. From their new vantage ground they could even find value in their former beliefs: like grown men speaking indulgently with children. This was their tolerance of enlightenment; so long as they thought with the wise, they might condescend to speak with the vulgar. There was no accommodating conformity to tradition, but rather an endeavor to recover for a higher religion the groping surmises of the populace. Some of this fusion of philosophical with traditional piety was confusing to both; but it could also attain to noble spiritual utterance, as in the Hymn by Cleanthes:

Most glorious of immortals, O Zeus of many names, almighty and everlasting, sovereign of nature, directing all in accordance with law, thee it is fitting that all mortals should address . . . so hast thou fitted all things together, the good

[2] Cicero, *De natura deorum*, ii:37, in P. Janet and G. Séailles, *A History of the Problems of Philosophy* (trans. A. Monahan), London, Macmillan, 1902, Vol. II, p. 265.

with the evil, that there might be one eternal law over all. . . . Deliver men from fell ignorance. Banish it, father, from their soul, and grant them to obtain wisdom, whereon relying thou rulest all things with justice.[3]

This duality of meaning, materialistic-pantheistic, characterized the Stoic philosophy of nature all the way through. The two aspects might be distinguished, as are line and color in a painting, but Stoic reflection was marked by its insistence on both. The Stoics' naturalistic description aimed at a pious appraisal, and their piety was a piety of nature. Even in Roman Stoicism, which concentrated increasingly on the moral-religious goal of philosophy, cosmology was outlined materialistically. So Seneca wrote:

It is fire which takes possession of the universe and transforms all things into itself. This fire dies down gradually, and when it is extinguished there is nothing else left in nature but moisture. In moisture lies hidden the promise of the world that is to be. Thus the world ends in fire and begins from moisture.[4]

The cosmogony of the Stoics—their view of the origin and succession of worlds—was among the boldest speculations of antiquity. The earlier followers of Zeno adopted and emphasized the doctrine of cosmic cycles which had already fascinated the Pythagoreans and which had been entertained also by Plato and by many imaginative minds across the ages. This seems to have been a world-wide notion from early times, for Babylonian, Brahmanic, and Buddhist versions of it have been cited. So Hebrew wisdom caught the recurring rhythm of nature in *Ecclesiastes:* "That which hath been is that which shall be; and that which hath been done is that which shall be done; and there is no new thing under the sun."[5] According to this sort of cosmogony, the world course is not linear but cyclic: it proceeds through its stages, but it eventually swings full circle, and then it starts its cosmic career anew. Heraclitus and Empedocles had been lured by this world rhythm, and the Pythagoreans extended their belief in transmigration of souls to include these visions of world dissolution and world refashionment. In Plato we read of a sort of oscillating process in the universe that determines a succession of world ages to be followed by eons in the opposite direction, moving forward and backward from harmony to disruption, from perfection to decay, worlds without end. The notion of a Golden Age in the past and others like it in the distant future, was instinct with nostalgic and utopian fascination.

The Greek Stoics believed that all things are produced by the World Soul —the creative fire—but are also permeated and so must be eventually consumed by it. The world thus courses through a succession of all the possible forms of existence and is finally brought back to its primary state of all fire. The Stoics called it the cosmic conflagration. After this consumption of all things by fire, fire itself, cooling, starts the formation of another eon of nature, destined to run its course to yet another conflagration. The sages of

[3] *Encyclopedia Britannica* (11th ed.), "Stoics," Cambridge, Cambridge Univ. Press, 1911, Vol. XXV, p. 947.
[4] Quoted in R. D. Hicks, *Stoic and Epicurean*, New York, Scribner, 1910, p. 31.
[5] Ecclesiastes 1:9 (American Standard Version).

the Painted Colonnade yielded to the full enchantment of this cosmogony. They regarded the cyclic formation and consumption of worlds as the universal rhythm of the divine fire or the germinal logos. The periodic rotation is not merely a general principle; it operates in detail to bring about the recurrence of each possible event. There will be again a Socrates, condemned to death, and again a Plato and his Academy, and all as before, not once but who knows how many times.

This vision may signify the promise and assurance of the return of the Golden Age. So Virgil, in his *Fourth Eclogue*, contemplated the revival of the vanished, heroic past, a classical nostalgic dream of progress in restitution:

> The last great age, foretold by sacred rhymes,
> Renews its finished course: Saturnian times
> Roll round again; and mighty years, begun
> From their first orb, in radiant circles run. . . .[6]

The Stoic looked forward confidently to the eventual recurrence of the great days of excellence. The eternal necessity of God's rational design predestined it. But the cyclic cosmogony included the repetition of the paltry along with the noble. This was the tragic note in his doctrine which dismayed the Stoics, as it was also to dismay Nietzsche. Panaetius, who introduced Stoicism to Rome, rejected the doctrine of world conflagration and eternal recurrence. But the old insistence that all things arise from God and to God return, from fire to fire, remained; it was now conceived as an unending course of universal process. Within the framework of this revised cosmogony, both the materialism and the pantheism of the Stoa persisted in its Roman versions.

Logic and Anthropology; the Nature, Activity, and Destiny of the Soul

The Stoic's anthropology conforms to his general account of nature. On the first reading, it seems to be materialistic like the Epicurean. Man's soul is not incorporeal but only composed of a subtler kind of matter, like flame in a log. Soul and body are interdependent in sickness and in health, in life and in death. Were the soul incorporeal, how could it be attached to the body, move it or act through it? Souls differ even as bodies, depending upon the stuff that is in them. Irascible men have an excess of fire in their make-up; scantiness of it would make their tempers frigid or dastard. The Stoic explanation of different temperaments recalled the doctrine of humors in the old Hippocratic medicine, according to which health or disease depended upon the proper or improper distribution of blood, phlegm, yellow bile, and black bile in the body. Galen, who revised and developed this teaching in the second century A.D., was trained in Stoicism; he explained man's distempers as due to the wrong mixture of the hot, cold, wet, and dry ele-

---

[6] Virgil, *Fourth Eclogue* (trans. J. Dryden). There are many editions available.

ments in the body. Across the centuries we can trace the persistent influence of this theory of humors and temperaments.

But we should misapprehend the Stoic view of the soul if we regard it as bluntly materialistic, like the Epicurean. Man's body and soul, though described as corporeal, exemplified preeminently to the Stoic the hierarchy of forms of matter which he maintained in his cosmology. The soul is a superlatively high form or type of matter, and correspondingly high are its capacities, its claims and its destiny. The Stoic world was material, but not merely a mechanical swirl of atoms. It was a drama of Divine Providence, the cosmic execution of a rational plot or design. So also in man's life; human nature is rooted in matter, but the higher capacities of the soul manifest rationality; they express, and must submit to, rational laws.

The Stoic analysis of the soul distinguished eight constituents in it: each of the five senses, the power of speech, self-reproduction, and a certain dominant rational factor. Like Aristotle, the Stoics located this factor, not in the head, but in the heart. As the World Soul is centrally directive in nature, so is the soul in man's body, and so is this dominant reason in the soul. Sensation, understanding, will energy—all finally refer to it; it sees, reasons, and decides. It knits soul and body together; through it the individual is one.

The Stoics' logic and theory of knowledge reflect their basic view of nature and, in accordance with it, their anthropology. In firm opposition to Plato's doctrine of Ideas, and—more radically opposed than was Aristotle—to his recognition of the sense data as providing the material which is organized by reason into a system of knowledge, the Stoics emphasized sense experience as the source of knowledge, its source and its test. There are no innate ideas; the infant's soul is as a clean slate; our ideas are the expanding stock of our sense impressions. As a seal imprints on the wax, so external events affect and form our consciousness. These perceptions are retained in memory; they are related to others; the mind is active in receiving and in organizing its impressions. There is always a certain judgment of acceptance in the mind's receptiveness; the Stoics called it "assent." Our judgment is the reflection of an increasing stock of experience on new data of perception. The reflective process, always resting on sense data, may yet produce ideas that are not reactions to specific external impressions. We may think of various objects of experience in groups, by considering some common aspect of them—this is the formation of concepts. More generally, the mind may entertain certain basic or common notions, such as justice or goodness. These general ideas carry their own immediate conviction, but the Stoics did not, like the Platonists, regard them as innate. They are not independent of sense experience, yet they seem to be fundamental expressions of intelligence.

Sense experience which is the source of our ideas also provides the test of their validity. An idea is true if it represents accurately the object or event to which it refers. The criterion of knowledge is perceptual self-evidence. In the operation of this standard, we test our perceptions by repeated observations, by making sure that our sense organs are normal and our sensations clear. We test our general inferences and ideas by checking the clarity of the comprehensive view which they present to the mind. Thus, perceptions and ideas sustain each other in the ongoing process of experience and thought. The mind has to rely continuously on general reasonableness and to be content with probability. But it proceeds, by the growing organization of its ideas, towards apprehension and systematic knowledge. Zeno told his disciples that sensation is like a hand with the fingers stretched out; in the judgment of assent the fingers close somewhat; in clear apprehension they are clenched in a fist; in systematic knowledge, one hand firmly grasps the other.

The main purport of the Stoic logic is its resolute direction of the mind to its natural ground in sense experience. Scientific knowledge differs from common untested opinion—not that it rises above the perceived data, but that it relates and organizes them more comprehensively. Should we ask how we judge rightly that the combination of perceived data in a certain concept is not sufficiently comprehensive, the answer in Stoic logic would be unclear. There is here a confidently proposed criterion of truth, but scarcely a definite theory of error.

The Stoic logicians reinterpreted syllogistic reasoning so as to express certain judged relations between perceived data. These judgments may express the dependence of perceived events on antecedent conditions—the specifically causal determination of certain processes, or the conjunction of various facts —or their disjunction which imposes a choice between alternatives. But, in all these judgments, we have no purely rational activity; the mind is always rooted in its direct perceptions.

The Stoics' doctrine of man's destiny was inferred from their account of human nature, body and soul. Just as one body is part of the world of bodies, so one's soul is part of the World Soul. This person or that is simply a particular and changing alliance of these two forms or grades of matter. Personal immortality would thus signify the eternal self-maintenance of a particular soul-body union. But this is precluded by the eventual world conflagration, and even in its nearer prospect it is doubtful. The earlier Stoics in Athens entertained some expectation of the soul's longevity, its outliving the coarser bodily texture, but not its immortality. Cleanthes ventured the belief that all souls survived until the cosmic conflagration; but Chrysippus, the third leader of the Stoic school, maintained that the coarser elements in the soul were bound to perish with the body, that only the higher rational powers in us—that is, only the wise souls—could survive death. There is no question of eternal life here; the utmost hope of the Greek Stoic was that men's souls, or at least the souls of sages, would persist until the world conflagration. The belief in personal immortality, which had always been qualified and very conjectural among the Stoics in Greece, was gradually and then definitely renounced by their Roman followers.

Seneca (3 B.C.–65 A.D.) was not clear in his attitude toward this problem. Some of his pages, addressed to souls bereaved and craving consolation, breathe assurance of a future life; the present life is dark misery, but in the hereafter a life of bright joy awaits the soul in the society of the gods. But these are scarcely philosophical arguments, nor are they characteristically Stoic. The writing of *consolationes* was a recognized literary activity in Rome. Seneca does not prove; he hints, hopes; at other times he hesitates, doubts, or is resigned: "Perhaps he whom we think we have lost has only been sent ahead.[7] . . . We mortals are lighted and extinguished."[8]

Epictetus (*c. 50–c. 125* A.D.) manifested not so much uncertainty as unconcern about any future life of the soul. He regarded man's life as having its history, its beginning and its end.

[God] gives the signal for retreat, opens the door, and says to you, Go. Go whither? To nothing terrible, but to the place from which you came, to your friends and kinsmen. [*Is this a promise of immortality?*] . . . to your friends and kinsmen, to the elements: what there was in you of fire, goes to fire; of earth, to earth; of air (spirit), to air; of water, to water.[9]

Epictetus was a teacher of wisdom, resolved to face things as they are. Moral resolution and commitment to the factual reflected and affected each other in his thought:

The ship is sinking—what then have I to do? I do the only thing that I can, not to be drowned full of fear, nor screaming, nor blaming God, but knowing that what has been produced must also perish: for I am not an immortal being but a man, a part of the whole, as an hour is a part of a day: I must be present like the hour, and pass like the hour.[10]

The earlier Stoics were led to the problem of human destiny by their account and analysis of the soul. But the prevailing tone and final purport of Stoicism were ethical; especially in Roman Stoicism the discussion of immortality became more and more an ethical problem. How can we reconcile the eventual extinction of rational persons with our confidence in the justice of divine providence? How could the gods allow the good, the wise, to perish? Marcus Aurelius (121–180) replied with a reaffirmation of unquestioning trust. Had it been better otherwise, Divine Providence would have so planned it. He was even enthusiastic in his resignation to his ultimate end: "Thou hast embarked, thou hast made the voyage, thou art come to shore; get out. . . . Depart then satisfied, for he also who releases thee is satisfied."[11] Stoic anthropology and psychology, as they raised the problem of man's cosmic role and scope and were led to the renunciation of any belief in personal immortality, reached in their final expression the same conclusion of resigned serenity to which the Stoic sage was committed by his moral outlook on life.

[7] Seneca, *Epistulae morales*, lxiii:16 (trans. R. M. Gummere), Cambridge, Mass., Harvard Univ. Press, Loeb Classical Library, 1917, Vol. I, p. 437.

[8] *Ibid.*, liv:5, p. 363.

[9] Epictetus, *Discourses*, iii:13 (trans. G. Long), New York, Burt, n.d., pp. 257 f.

[10] *Ibid.*, ii:5, p. 121.

[11] Marcus Aurelius, in *The Thoughts of the Emperor Marcus Aurelius Antoninus* (trans. G. Long), New York, Nelson, n.d., Bk. III, sec. 3; Bk. XII, sec. 36.

The Ethics of Rational Self-Mastery

The Socratic principle, Virtue is Knowledge, emphasized the problem of the conflict of reason and the passions in the pursuit of the good and happy life. Plato and Aristotle met this issue by advocating harmony and balance, moderate satisfaction of the desires and emotions, regulated by reason. The Stoic ethics was stricter, an uncompromising rationalism. It emphasized the conflict and insisted on the unqualified mastery of reason.

The Stoic sages were led to their moral judgments by their account of man's place in nature. They applied the Socratic wisdom in their cosmology and anthropology. Virtue is knowledge; that is, the good life is a life of understanding what sort of men we are, and in what sort of world we exist, how we are related to it, and how we are to live suitably in that relation. Determinism, the doctrine of universal necessity, was thus paramount in the Stoic ethics. Man's intelligent life in nature must be a life that conforms to nature, and nature is a rational system of law. So the Stoics interpreted virtue as living according to law. We cannot live unto ourselves; our life is woven into the texture of nature and has no meaning apart from its design. This is human perfection, to live fittingly in the world, a life duly appropriate, or "homologous," to nature. This suitable life is also the truly godly life, for God is the rational agency directing all cosmic order. Moral intelligence consists in our practical recognition of the universal law: that we choose and will the necessity which our reason knows in nature.

If man is to judge the purposes and values in which the worth of his daily life is expressed, he should have a true idea of his abilities and of what does and does not depend on him. The Stoics, therefore, applied their doctrine of cosmic necessity so as to refute the common belief in free will and spontaneous choice. This belief, according to them, stirs unreasonable expectations, leads to petulant demands and futile regrets. Man's arrogant illusion of independence in nature must be subdued before he can learn the acquiescence in law which leads to serenity.

The Stoic denial of free will was emphatic. Man's life is an interplay of his own nature and composition with the constitution of the world in which he moves, and necessity rules the process to the smallest detail. The eventual outcome in every case is determined, and serves to manifest the law operating in the circumstances. The difference between the wise man and the fool is that the former recognizes the necessary order and does not indulge in unreasonable hopes and complaints. The Stoics censured wishful thinking and living; they taught respect for the facts and the necessities of nature. There is a moral freedom in our lives, but it is not the freedom of doing as we will. It is the freedom of willing as we must—our rational compliance. Seneca summed up this ethical determinism in his epigram, "The fates lead the willing; the unwilling they drive."[12] Destiny was itself interpreted as the rational cosmic plan, the mind of God unswervingly directing all existence. Our true liberty lies in loyally acknowledging this divine necessity under which all of us have to live our lives.

We can thus understand the Stoic rigor in dealing with the issue between reason and the passions. The passions and desires lack understanding; men who yield to them seek their happiness in the wrong place, where it cannot be found. They cherish the wrong things, fear the wrong things; their whole life is oriented wrongly. They think that the good and the evil are things and external conditions, what they may acquire or lose, what may or may not happen to them. But, as Epictetus taught, "the essence of good and of evil lies in an attitude of the will."[13] Our well-being or frustration depends not upon external events, but upon the way in which our will confronts them. Tragedy emerges when a certain quality of will is brought to bear upon a certain tissue of conflicting events.

Foul words or blows in themselves are no outrage, but your judgment that they are so. . . . Keep before your eyes from day to day death and exile and all things that seem terrible, but death most of all, and then you will never set your thoughts on what is low and will never desire anything beyond measure.[14]

The Stoics could admit no possible compromise between reason and the passions. The least surrender to passion leads us astray, even as the least divergence from the straight path is crooked. The good life is the strictly rational life without any concession to desire or emotion. This moral ideal the Stoics called "apathy," impassive or passionless self-mastery of reason. They emphasized the ability of the sage to withstand the lures and incitements of sense and to endure the stings of passion and the blows of fortune. The wise man bears and forbears; he is continent among the profligate, calm among the violent, self-possessed and serene amid the tumults and fury of passionate lives.

As Aristotle's table of virtues portrayed the rational balance between extremes in the various circumstances of human experience, so the Stoic account of the virtues manifested the basic excellence of apathy in the daily course of life. Cleanthes regarded the rational subjugation of the passions as analogous to the great tension of fire which consumes the lower forms of matter. The virtues of the sage are the practical evidences of this higher tension. This strength of reason, "when it is displayed in endurance, where steadfastness is required, is self-control; when undergoing dangers, courage; when in matters where value is in question, justice; in cases of choice and giving way, temperance."[15] The cardinal virtues of the Academy and the Lyceum were

---

[12] Cleanthes quoted by Seneca, op. cit., cvii:11, Vol. III, p. 229.

[13] Epictetus, Discourses, i:29, in The Discourses and Manual (trans. P. E. Matheson), Oxford, Clarendon Press, 1916, Vol. I, p. 131.

[14] Epictetus, Manual, 20, 21, in ibid., Vol. II, p. 220.

[15] Cleanthes quoted by Plutarch, in Hilda D. Oakeley (ed.), Greek Ethical Thought from Homer to the Stoics, London, Dent, 1925, p. 207.

reinterpreted by the Stoics as species of apathy. Temperance was given a new slant as sobriety—not the moderate enjoyment of gratified desires, but self-control, continence and decorum in resisting sensual appetites. Courage was styled manliness, *virtus;* it was viewed no longer as vigor in aggression or resistance, but as power of endurance, fortitude—the inner strength of Socrates in the face of death, firm in his loyalty to his convictions. Wisdom, the characteristic perfection of reason, was regarded by the Stoics as practical prudence.

The Stoic's treatment of justice is of especial interest as a reflection of his social philosophy. Justice was called a political virtue; it consisted in rational, due regard for the rights and claims of others. Private property is not private by nature, but is established by custom and law in organized society. As members of the state, men must respect each other's claims as guaranteed by law. The system of laws is in the state as the order of necessary relations is in nature. Unlike the Epicurean, who avoided public commitments and cherished the private life of insouciance, the Stoic's conception of rational serenity did not preclude the fulfilment of his social duties. "That which is not good for the swarm," said the Stoic emperor, "neither is it good for the bee."[16]

Virtue was esteemed as worthy of man's utmost devotion for its own sake, not as a means to any ulterior advantage. He who looks beyond virtue for its rewards is a hired man who has never entered the mansion of morality. Zeno declared that virtue is a self-sufficient value of life, and this essential integrity of moral conduct was a dominant theme of Stoic ethics, the adequacy or autarchy of virtue. Virtue does not need happiness to crown it; virtue itself is the crown and happiness of life. For what is happiness but the calmly flowing life of the sage devoted to virtue? Chrysippus made here an expedient distinction: the virtuous man has use for everything but needs nothing. Epictetus and Marcus Aurelius never tire of declaring that virtue is good in and for itself, virtue *per se:* "Do you look for any greater reward for a good man than to do what is noble and right?"[17] Similarly, vice is its own punishment; "No harm but that of failing to do your duty: you will destroy the trustworthy, self-respecting, well-behaved man in you. Look not for any greater harm than this!"[18]

Thus, nothing really matters in life except virtue and vice. In this conviction the Stoics revived and perfected the truth in the teaching of Antisthenes, but without the oddities and the irresponsible individualism of the Cynics. They centered their attention on the inner life and disregarded externalities. "Dig within," wrote Marcus Aurelius, "Within is the fountain of good; ever dig, and it will ever well forth water."[19] The Stoic concentrated on right pur-

---

[16] Marcus Aurelius, *The Thoughts of the Emperor Marcus Aurelius Antoninus* (trans. G. Long), New York, Nelson, n.d., Bk. VI, sec. 54.
[17] Epictetus, *Discourses*, iii:24, in *The Discourses and Manual, op. cit.,* Vol. II, p. 92.
[18] *Ibid.,* iii:7, Vol. II, p. 28.
[19] Quoted in W. L. Davidson, *The Stoic Creed*, Edinburgh, Clark, 1907, p. 145.

pose, on truly self-representative action. How it comes out actually is in God's hands, not ours; but ours is the quality of the choice; our will should be unmistakable in our deed.

In this preeminence of the inner rational life, many of the things usually cherished or feared by men were declared of no real concern to the wise man, and indifferent to his main purpose; they were irrelevancies, *adiaphora*. These are not necessarily evil but not needfully good; a sage may use them or avoid them; they do not really matter to him one way or the other. Zeno cited a number of them: pain or pleasure, poverty or wealth, disease or health, shame or glory, and, when it comes to it, as it did to Socrates, death or life. One may be Hellene or barbarian, a Roman citizen or a provincial thrall. Epictetus grew up as a slave in the house of one of Nero's courtiers; Seneca was the tutor of the unspeakable emperor; Marcus Aurelius was himself emperor. These three sages differed only in the externals which did not matter; their essential kinship was in their rational self-mastery.

This depreciation of external differences found expression also in the cosmopolitan spirit of Stoicism. Platonic and Aristotelian ethics were Greek in their source and in their reference. But the Stoic was consciously a citizen of the world. Before the Christian vision of the communion of saints, Hellenistic culture achieved this spiritual republic of sages, all of them kinsmen and brothers in their firm devotion to reason.

The Stoic philosophy of life has evoked praise and criticism. Its emphasis on inner principles, beyond the external outcome of actions, has been judged an advance in ethical penetration. And another gain, in philanthropic range of outlook, led them to transcend Greek and Roman horizons in their universal view of rational, human brotherhood. Their ethics has been criticized chiefly on account of its austerity and its unresponsiveness to the inner worth of natural human feelings and sympathies. Was it a gain in morals to include personal love and devotion among the indifferent things in life? "His son is dead. What has happened? His son is dead. Nothing more? Nothing."[20] To be sure, the Stoic perfection is not always unfeeling. Though it never breathes the spirit of Christian love, it could contemplate the ideal of universal philanthropy. Cicero lauded love of mankind, "*caritas generis humani.*"[21] But the Stoic emphasis is mostly the other way, on rational self-mastery and apathy.

The doctrine of *adiaphora*, things that do not matter morally, and that are neither really good nor evil, might seem to settle the problem of evil, but only on the surface and in part. The problem of evil relates morality and religion by yawning abysmally before them both. The Stoics pointed out that many of men's complaints about life were unwarranted and due to mere petulance. Others could be regarded as tests of man's firmness of rational will, to meet adversity with fortitude and to rise the better for it. But still the basic quandary remained, the more perplexing in such a confidently rational-

[20] Epictetus, *Discourses*, iii:8, in H. Crossley (ed.), *The Golden Sayings of Epictetus*, London, Macmillan, 1920, p. 81.
[21] Cicero quoted in Janet and Séailles, *op. cit.*, Vol. II, p. 35.

istic philosophy. Why should this corruption of passion and this perversity of irrational impulse in man's nature be included in the presumably perfect rational plan of divine providence?

The Stoic sages have been criticized for their imperfect grasp of their problem. In their prevailing refrains, optimism and resignation colored each other. They were not reluctant to point out the common vices of men—their lusts, greeds, enmities, vanities, fears, and abject surrenders. But they never reached the tragic insight of Plato. Their philosophical piety permitted no question about the final perfection of the cosmic, rational plan. Their rational serenity in the midst of disaster was like the martyr's, unyielding in its immediate trust, but it was unclear in its ultimate grounds:

The immortal gods do not lose patience at having to bear age after age with the froward generations of men, but still show for them all manner of concern. Shall you, whose end is in a moment, lose heart?—you, who are one of the froward? . . . Do you not see that in hazarding such questions you arraign the justice of God?[22]

Such questioning was precisely what Marcus Aurelius could not for a moment entertain, and his own conclusion in perplexity was one of trustful resignation.

Natural Law in Roman Jurisprudence

The Roman mind did not manifest great creative power nor did it contribute preeminent, original principles to ancient philosophy. Even in its practical application of philosophical ideas, Roman thought achieved powerful moral appeal but scarcely a great system of ethics. The mastery of social organization, however, was a particular excellence of the people of empire, and in this field we may appraise a notable Roman application of the ideal of universal law. While it could scarcely be maintained that Roman jurisprudence was simply an inference from the Stoic principle of life according to law, it is a historical fact that Stoicism made distinguished contributions to Roman law and statesmanship. A number of the great jurists of the Empire learned their basic ideas from the Stoic sages.

This juridical development of philosophical principles involved a real contention of motives. The Stoic wisdom, as has been noted, was Hellenistically cosmopolitan in origin and development, and universal in its intention. It over-arched in its outlook all state boundaries and differences. But the Roman ideal of universality was the universality of the Roman imperium, *Pax Romana*. Even before the Empire, we may note this Roman reinterpretation in Cicero's use of the Stoic ideal of life according to law. The natural law gov-

[22] Marcus Aurelius, *Thoughts*, Bk. VII:70, XII:5, quoted in R. D. Hicks, *op. cit.*, pp. 52, 53.

erning human affairs arises out of the law of nature which is basic in human life, prior and superior to any statute. But this universal law signified to Cicero the normal expansion of essential Roman justice, freed of any of its peculiarities or corruptions. Not only Cicero himself, but also some of the older classical jurists studied Stoic wisdom. Their notion of equity expressed the principle of fairness basic in all law, which is formulated in legislation but which also may control it. Equity is natural and, in its normal prospect, universal.

· This universality of law was manifested in actuality and with definite limitations in its Roman historical development. The primary Roman law was the law of the Roman families, the patricians. The early patrician rights and sanctions were organized into the legal order of the Roman state, its civil law, *jus civile*. But with the spread of Roman power, the city of Rome and the provincial centers were filled with non-Romans—resident foreigners and traders with whom the Roman citizens had to deal, and to whom the old Roman laws and prerogatives did not apply. Self-regard and practical expediency required a system of laws reflecting this increasingly world-wide scope and complexity of the Roman social system. Practice and principle, custom and code, fused in the evolution of the law of nations, *jus gentium*, an expression which, in the thought of Cicero, led to the idea of universal law. The jurist, in his reflection, alternated between historical report and philosophical analysis. Sometimes the *jus gentium* was interpreted as synonymous with *jus naturale*, natural law, but more often as only a historical approximation to it. Slavery, for instance, was general and hence lawful among the nations; yet, by right, it was contrary to natural law. Historically, the law of nations expressed the effective sum and substance of the customs and sanctions acknowledged by the variety of racial stocks under Roman sway. Beyond this, it pointed to universally and essentially human principles of right—equitable social relations. Though the law of nations was at first admitted by the Roman citizen as a matter of necessary expediency, it was also regarded with some condescension—the way a real Roman had to deal with aliens, plebeians. But as the Roman state became the universal empire, the former expediency gained the dignity of lofty principle. The jurists first proceeded to expand and to supplement it; they then organized it into systems or codes, the most celebrated of which was the *Corpus Juris* of Justinian.

Thus, in the principle of *jus naturale*, natural law or natural right, Stoic rationalism found systematic expression in jurisprudence. And here the Roman mind, limited in theoretical grasp or depth of insight, showed itself highly gifted in practical application. The very confusion, or at any rate fusion, of historical and essential universality seemed advantageous in legal interpretation in its direct responsiveness to actual social conditions and demands in universal Roman law. Even within the limitations of actualities and expediency, the great Roman jurists recognized and expressed Stoic principles of the ideal higher justice. Ulpian spoke out that "all men, according to nat-

ural right, are born free and equal."[23] Five centuries before him, Zeno, the
first Stoic, had declared: "All men are by nature equal; virtue alone establishes a difference between them."[24]

As was the universality of Roman law, so was its eternity, both of them historical. The orientation of Roman legislation, and also its effectiveness, were
conditioned by the existing actuality of the universal imperium, the Eternal
City. But the essentially human universality of the principles outlasted the
Empire. So we may see today, for instance in Provence, the monumental
evidences of the Roman plan to build for eternity. Like the solid structures
of stone, the Roman principles of natural law, historical expressions of the
age that framed them, have maintained their power in the thought and in the
institutional order of European nations through the centuries.

SUGGESTED WORKS FOR FURTHER STUDY

STOICS. Seneca, *Moral Epistles* (trans. R. M. Gummere); Epictetus, *Discourses*
and *Manual* (several translations are available); Marcus Aurelius, *Meditations*
(several translations are available).

CRITICAL STUDIES OF STOICISM. Arnold, E. V., *Roman Stoicism;* Bussell, F. W.,
Marcus Aurelius and the Later Stoics; Davidson, W. L., *The Stoic Creed;*
Hicks, R. D., *Stoic and Epicurean;* Murray, Gilbert, *The Stoic Philosophy;*
Zeller, Eduard, *The Stoics, Epicureans, and Sceptics.*

[23] Quoted from E. Renan, *Marc-Aurèle*, in E. V. Arnold, *Roman Stoicism*, Cambridge,
Cambridge Univ. Press, 1911, p. 403.
[24] Quoted in W. E. H. Lecky, *History of European Morals from Augustus to Charlemagne*, London, Longmans, ed. of 1913, Vol. I, p. 306.

7.   Plotinus: The Emanation of God in Nature

The Decline of Classical Philosophy: Skeptical Unsettlement

Plotinus has been called the greatest philosopher in the almost twenty centuries between Aristotle and Descartes. His eminence can be recognized better if we view him across the foreground of lesser thinkers who spanned the closing stages of ancient civilization; in much the same way that, in a mountain range, our eye may finally rest on a lofty peak after following long ridges which describe the skyline but where no great height has dominated the vision. We may now note in later antiquity some lines of thought which are significant as indicating cultural directions, but which fail to reach preeminent expression, and then lift our spirit to a soaring consummation.

The first of these movements, skepticism, may be traced through several centuries as a discordant strain of doubt and negation in the schools of constructive Greek reflection. It was the persisting Sophistic challenge to self-reliant intelligence which Socrates and his followers had answered, but had not silenced. Just as the many contending doctrines of early Greek inquiry were spurned by Gorgias and Protagoras, so the rival schools of systematic philosophy, Athenian and Hellenistic, were challenged and invaded by the skeptical distrust in the foundations of knowledge.

The first of these skeptics was Pyrrho of Elis (*c.* 360–270 B.C.), contemporary of Aristotle and, after him, of Epicurus and Zeno. Pyrrho had turned from painting to philosophy, and had followed many masters. In the train of Alexander the Great, he had gone to India and had seen, if not understood, the dark sages of the East, absorbed in mystical meditation. His inference from all these teachings was one of general uncertainty. Man professed knowledge and wisdom, but he lacked stability and finality of conviction. Every alleged principle could be countered with its opposite, which was equally plausible and inconclusive. The mind oscillates between indeterminable alternatives, and vainly seeks refuge in dogmatic confidence. Equally futile and unwise is dismay in uncertainty. Wisdom consists in the genial suspense of judgment. Why fret about the mind's perplexities? If knowledge is beyond our reach, we should not set our heart on it. There is great relief in realizing that we do not have to understand anything. We can all relax together in our twilight, undisturbed by any empty controversy, but indulgently observing the varieties of human opinion. Here was a classical forebear of Montaigne.

The Pyrrhonic attitude of mind may be traced in a number of thinkers clear to the end of classical antiquity. It dismissed all reliance on the data of sense experience as unwarranted opinion. Like a skeptical contagion, it infected the Platonic Academy, as if it were a cloud of incertitude over the classical home of rational conviction. Some of these skeptics were consistent in professing complete suspense of judgment; they were not certain even about their uncertainty. Others, more systematic in their doctrine of ignorance, marshalled their lists of arguments to prove definitely that we could not prove anything.

A later skeptic, Carneades, carried the balancing of uncertainties to its extreme limits. Athens had sent him on a diplomatic mission to Rome. The Romans were enchanted by his eloquence, but were stunned by his skeptical dialectic. One day he moved them to moral fervor with his eulogy of justice, only to shatter their convictions the next day by his exposure of the vanity of justice and of all moral principles. He subjected to his agnostic scrutiny the eternal verities of rationalism and the alleged natural laws of the materialists; God, causal order, and ultimate atomic particles were all discredited as questionable presumptions of the mind. We should resign ourselves to our incapacity to reach any real knowledge.

Eclecticism and the Interfusion of Doctrines

The skeptical attack on systematic philosophy, and especially the unsettlement of rational confidence in the Platonic Academy, tended to turn many minds from the controversial issues which divided the philosophical schools to ideas about which there was some general agreement. This was a policy of compromise, but also a natural process of selection characteristic of Roman thought. Though Roman minds were not distinguished by originality in systematic theory, they had a genius for intellectual, as well as practical, strategy. They listened to the various Greek masters, chose whatever seemed reasonable and expedient in each doctrine, and fused their various impressions into a pattern of suitable wisdom. This selective philosophy of so-called "eclecticism" was sometimes shallow, but it could also achieve maturity of judgment, especially in dealing with practical issues. The creative imagination of Greek poetry, which had become only a great memory in the cultural decline of its native land, came to new life in the poetry of Virgil and Horace. The Roman sages revitalized the great ideas of the Athenian masters when these ideas were losing their power in Greece. The Epicurean poem by

Lucretius, *On the Nature of Things,* combined these two strains, the imaginative and the reflective.

CICERO

The outstanding eclectic in Roman philosophy was Cicero (106–43 B.C.). He knew by direct study the principal alternatives of Greek philosophy; he possessed the treasures of Greek literature and became the chief medium for the transfusion of Greek culture into the Roman system. His own distinctive qualities—which made him a great statesman, lawyer, and orator—were shown in his philosophy. It was not so much an exposition of a doctrine, as the advocacy of the principles which he had selected. His general position combined Platonic and Stoic ideas, some Aristotelian wisdom, and a contempt for Epicurean ideals. He was skeptical about the ultimate principles of metaphysics, but he believed that some general convictions of social tradition were innate and trustworthy: the belief in God, in divine providence, and in the immortality of the soul. In his accounts of nature and of human nature, he meditated, or vacillated, between the pure rationalism of Plato and the materialistic rationalism of the Stoics. As might be expected, his philosophy reached its summit in ethics. His moral discourses are enduring memorials of classical nobility, especially his treatise on the duties of men, *De Officiis.* Cicero's interpretation of the cardinal virtues and of the moral ideal manifested the urbanity and tact of the widely experienced man of the world, but it advocated no easygoing expediency. On the contrary, Cicero probed beneath the outward action in his quest of the right spirit and the genuine integrity of motives that mark the thoroughly good man.

HELLENISTIC-JEWISH PHILOSOPHY

Alexandria brought together in Egypt scientists, sages, and some saints—Greek, Jewish, Oriental. The doctrines and the ideals of classical antiquity were most influential, but they were colored by polyglot wisdom, both religious and social. Even before the spread of Christianity, Biblical ideas had been introduced into Alexandrian discussion by zealous Jewish teachers. The Hebrew Scriptures, in their Septuagint Greek version, were read by pagan students. Jewish scholars were seeking to achieve a synthesis of Greek and Hebrew wisdom, to harmonize Plato's reason, the Mosaic law, and the inspiration of the prophets. Here was a new variety of eclecticism. Convinced of his own divinely revealed and unquestionable truths, the Jewish philosopher declared that their expression in Scripture was symbolical, not doctrinal. In order to give these holy truths a systematic rational statement, he explored the treasury of Greek philosophy, to select and to combine the ideas that best served his purpose. But the Greek ideas were powerful ferments; they stirred some Jewish minds to non-Jewish speculation.

The chief representative of the Greco-Jewish philosophy was Philo—often called Philo Judaeus—who lived in the first century of the Christian era. His philosophical works contain an allegorical interpretation of the Hebrew

Scriptures in which Platonic, Aristotelian, and Stoic ideas are combined together with some original speculations that proved influential, both in the closing period of Hellenistic philosophy and in the theology of early Christianity.

Philo sought to reconcile two Hebrew convictions: that God transcends nature and human life, and that he creates and directs them. Rejecting all conceptions of God as cosmic fire or highest form of matter—or in any way a part of nature—Philo held that deity is above all forms of existence, and surpasses all our terms of definition. All definable existence is below God. But the Creator is not a craftsman; He produces the material world not directly, but through intermediaries. Here Philo combined several doctrines: the Platonic hierarchy of Ideas and the *Demiurge* world maker, the Aristotelian Creative Reason, the Stoic germinating logos, and the Jewish doctrine of the divine Spirit, or breath, infusing all existence. He conceived of God as creatively active through the Logos, or Word, the supreme agent in a hierarchy of beings between God and the material world. The Logos in turn operates through its highest potency, the cosmic Wisdom. The two may be distinguished as God's creative reason and its expression. Philo compared these two to the double breastplate of the Jewish high priest, a sample of the persistent allegory which complicated old philosophical speculation. In the scale of creation were distinguished the ideal man, or the first Adam, angelic beings and powers, the universal forms of being; and, at the lowest margin of reality, the material world of instability, corruption, and evil. As man's life and being are thus from God, so his true history is Godward. Philo advocated the ascetic suppression of sensual appetites, Stoic apathy, the mind's ascent from material engrossment to purely rational reflection, and above this, to mystical contemplation, or ecstasy, in which the godly soul attains union with God.

Philo's philosophy pointed toward a philosophical synthesis of theism and pantheism; a conception of the world as a manifestation of God, but also of God's perfect reality as transcending all possible manifestations.

The Religious Finale of Classical Wisdom: Neoplatonism

In the third century A.D., pagan philosophy was at its ebb and Christian theology had not yet reached high tide. Civilization seemed to stagnate in the ancient world, though the great Roman masters of jurisprudence added some intellectual luster to its general dullness, by expounding legal theory in a lawless world. The death of the philosopher king, Marcus Aurelius, in 180 was followed by the despotism of Commodus; the death of Septimius Severus, at York, in 211 exposed the hollowness of his plans for reorganized empire. The third century was also marked by civil wars, economic chaos, and cultural confusion. To the devout fathers of the expanding Christian Church, this collapse of the majestic pagan edifice signified God's judgment on a sinful world, which, in another century, St. Augustine was to proclaim in *The City of God*.

From a pagan perspective, the spread of Christianity was only one, the strongest, incursion of strange ideas from the East into classical life and thought; an incursion which naturally accompanied the influx into Rome of all sorts of aliens—slaves, traders, and the votaries of a dozen cults. This migration had continued for several centuries; Rome had become a museum of religions. The Hellenizing of Roman culture and religion had been followed by the introduction, during the Punic Wars, of the Phrygian lurid worship of the Great Mother of the Gods. Out of Egypt came the cult of Isis, in which Egyptian and Greek notions had been muddled with occult solemnity: "Isis is all the deities." The martial religion of Mithraism, the adoration of the Invincible Sun, spread from Persia into the Roman world, absorbed Greek myths of Helios, was carried by soldier votaries all over Europe, and, for a while, contended with Christianity for dominance. In the Roman system itself, the Imperial Cult—the deification, first of the deceased sovereigns, and then of the living emperors and empresses, some of them unspeakable persons—had corrupted the very idea of deity. Monsters of cruelty and profligacy signed themselves as gods. Religion became discredited in critical minds and was derided even by those who exploited it. Emperor Aurelian established the solar cult officially, and raised in his temple two statues of Helios and Baal to satisfy the popular homage of both classical and oriental divinities. In the first century, the dying Vespasian had viewed his impending imperial deification ironically, but in the third century, Caracalla murdered his brother Geta, and sneered that he had raised him to divinity.

This confusion of cults was itself the evidence of a spiritual unrest and an unsatisfied demand for convincing belief. Walter Pater's portrayal of the second century, in his *Marius the Epicurean*, is memorable. The third century was only more confused and more unsatisfied. The groping spirit which urged the superstitious populace from one shrine to another stirred many reflective minds to critical philosophical inquiry. The age had no great vision, but longed for it and awaited the great spirit who would reveal it. The neoplatonist, Plotinus, seemed to be this spirit.

PLOTINUS

There is a certain timelessness in the pages of Plotinus (204–270 A.D.); were not some personal knowledge of him provided by others, we should scarcely learn from his own writings to what time or land he belonged. Yet his thought was responsive to his age; he sought and trod the way of eternity out of the confusion and problems of his day. He is supposed to have been a native of Lycopolis in Egypt, though his name does not enable us to identify his origin. Body, birth, and mortal descent were disdained by him. Egyptian and Jew, Greek and Roman, were alike to him who lived in the Eternal.

His works reveal not only a well educated mind, but a mind thoroughly versed in all the philosophical and religious traditions of antiquity. In Alexandria, he seems to have heard advocates of every doctrine. He was attracted to the Pythagorean teachings; he knew Aristotelianism and made good use of it; he respected the Stoic's control of the passions, but discredited their materialism; the atomism and the sensuality of Epicureanism aroused his firm opposition. The classical fountain of truth, he felt, was in Plato, but the arid arguments and the skepticism of many Platonists unsettled his confidence in the doctrine of the Academy. While he was thus in quest of a convincing philosophy of life, Plotinus was advised by a friend to hear the discourses of Ammonius Saccas, who was teaching a religious reinterpretation of Platonism. Ammonius was a poor man who had served as a porter. He had been reared as a Christian but had turned to Greek philosophy. Avoiding written publication of his doctrines, he imparted them in intimate confidence to his disciples, among whom was Origen, the learned Christian theologian. Plotinus' response to Ammonius was immediate and decisive. "This is the man I was looking for!"[1] he declared, and studied with him for eleven years.

The hope of deepening his spiritual insight, through the study of Persian, and perhaps Indian, wisdom led Plotinus to join Emperor Gordian's expedition to Persia. But the assassination of the sovereign in Mesopotamia put an end to these plans. Plotinus returned to Antioch and thence, at the age of 40, proceeded to Rome, where he soon was teaching philosophy in Greek to a circle of devoted disciples gathered from many lands.

His method of instruction was thorough in the analysis of doctrines and intimate in imparting his spiritual message. Plotinus regarded his philosophy as basically Platonic. A great student of his philosophy, St. Augustine, described him as a second Plato. But his relation to Plato was not that of a disciple who reports and echoes his master's doctrine. Even when he expounded it, he transformed it. The Platonism of Plotinus shows not the fidelity of a reliable interpreter but the originality of creative reconstruction. What matters here is the power of the dominant principle, in the light of which the old ideas reveal new facets of meaning.

The writings of Plotinus were not intended as the studied exposition of a system; in their inception they were discourses on specific problems which he examined with his disciples. His earliest treatises were written about his fiftieth year. They were arranged in systematic order and published after the master's death by his follower, Porphyry. Fifty-four particular treatises were assembled in six groups of nine each, called the *Enneads,* or "Nines." The first of these six *Enneads* treats of human and moral problems; the second and third deal with the sensible world in which we move; the fourth explores the nature of the soul; the fifth is a study of rational intelligence; the sixth, and last, is devoted to the contemplation of the One Perfect Reality.

[1] Quoted in W. R. Inge, *The Philosophy of Plotinus,* 3rd ed., London, Longmans, 1929, Vol. I, p. 24.

In its order and direction the philosophy of Plotinus was intended to reveal man's true spiritual career: from the present scene of his daily activities to the realm of the eternal; from the random impressions and lures of the senses to the divine contemplation and consecration of the spirit; from this world to God. The Platonic nostalgia of spirit held captive in the body was expressed devoutly and with mystical intensity by Plotinus. As he lay dying, his last reported words were: "That which is divine in me departs to unite itself with the Divine in the universe."[2]

The World as the Emanation of Deity

Neoplatonism expressed the dual conviction of a religious philosophy. It was a conviction of ultimate unity; the world and all therein are from God, "in whom we live and move and have our being," as St. Paul had said. But the opposite conviction was equally strong, of the world's alienation from God and of a tragic conflict in human nature, the urge of the divine and the drag of corruption and sin. The prevailing motive in such a philosophy could not be the purely intellectual, Aristotelian "desire to know," nor even the practical "way of life" of the Stoic. It was a way of salvation, man's way to God.

Neoplatonic cosmology can be understood as the systematic expression or explanation of this twofold conviction. Both the merits and the difficulties of this philosophy should be appraised in terms of its basic motivation. Plotinus rejected or revised the earlier accounts of nature because they did not recognize adequately the spiritual source and destiny of all existence. And those to whom reality is essentially spiritual, and the understanding of it likewise spiritual, have found profound insight in Neoplatonism. But, in his consecration to spirituality, Plotinus described and explained the course of nature and human experience without due regard for the apparent facts. His religious intensity illumined his vision but dimmed his scientific perception. So we may go to Plotinus for his strength, but we must not forget his weakness.

Plotinus did not adopt any one of the traditional doctrines of God's relation to the world. Though, like the Jews or the Christians, he spoke of God's "creative activity," their doctrine of creationism, the idea of God as a personal world maker, was to him unphilosophical, anthropomorphic mythology. But the conception of God as the highest form of matter, the World Soul, was likewise unacceptable and indeed unworthy. The Epicurean atomism which recognized only matter and motion was downright "absurd" to Plotinus; its "disorderly swirl" could not explain even human intelligence and will; how could it comprehend divine perfection? The pantheistic theory that God is the universe was confused in its interpretation of nature.

[2] Quoted in *ibid.*, p. 121.

Plato seemed, to Plotinus, to have grasped the two essential principles: that God is infinite perfect reality, and that matter is actual, but essentially deficient in real being, and corrupt. In his firm adherence to his first principle, however, Plato felt bound to admit the bare existence of matter. God's creative act gives it such form, order, and relative perfection as it may allow. God is the Author, not of matter, but of the material cosmos. This dualism was resisted by Plotinus, and he must have avoided it the more because of certain extreme doctrines of two primal and conflicting creative agencies, such as the Ahura Mazda and Ahriman of the Zoroastrians.

In his opposition to ultimate cosmic dualism, Plotinus held fast to the conviction that the world is somehow the manifestation of God. But the sense of moral conflict and general finite imperfection also demanded recognition. God is manifested in nature, but not perfectly; yet this defectiveness could not be regarded as marring the divine creative plenitude. How could these requisites of a true doctrine be realized together? Plotinus answered: By the right understanding of what manifestation signifies. Any manifestation both reveals and qualifies that which is manifested. The world has character or significance because of that which it manifests; but being a manifestation, it is finite and limited. It is a version of infinite perfection, but no version can be infinitely perfect.

Repeatedly in the *Enneads* we can feel this dual demand which Plotinus undertook to meet in his doctrine. As Plato's deepest spiritual insight found utterance in his "myths," so Plotinus shows his genius for imaginative expression in the variety of metaphors by which he portrays the creative activity of God in nature. By its very plenitude of perfect Being, the divine reality flows out, diffuses itself, or radiates throughout. One of these sublime analogies has given his cosmology its name, *Emanationism*. To Plotinus emanation signified efflux, outflowing, or outpouring:

Imagine a spring that has no source outside itself; it gives itself to all the rivers, yet is never exhausted by what they take, but remains always integrally as it was; the tides that proceed from it are at one within it before they run their several ways. . . . [Or] think of the life coursing throughout some mighty tree. . . .[3]

Or again, we may consider fragrance that is diffused from its source and wafted farther and farther; or, yet again—and most revealingly—imagine sunlight that radiates from its flaming center in ever expanding circles, illuminating each zone, but less and less brightly, proceeding to dimmer and dimmer twilight.

In this cosmology of divine emanation, Plotinus undertook to relate and to perfect the Greek theories of the hierarchy of nature. The Platonic criterion of reality received preeminent emphasis in the Neoplatonic conception of God. God's absolute reality transcends all particularity or specific form

[3] Plotinus, *The Enneads*, III:viii:10 (trans. S. MacKenna), 3rd ed., New York, Pantheon, n.d., p. 249.

or character and is beyond the range of any definition. God is neither material nor mental, neither thinking nor unthinking. God is the source and ground of all existence, but surpasses space, time, and all the conditions of definite existence. God is the infinitely transcendent, the One and All. All issues from God, but essentially God is the absolute One, "the Alone." God is infinite perfection, the Good, but no specific perfection may be ascribed to God nor any characteristics of the perfection and values which we know, neither feeling nor reason nor will, neither personality nor impersonality. Neoplatonism proclaimed the supreme recognition, but disclaimed any cognition, of deity. It spoke of God in negatives—not the negatives of negation, but of utter transcendence of all finitude. If we are to approach the ultimate reality which we cannot really comprehend, it must be by surpassing the marks and distinctions of finitude. Plotinus recognized that God is ineffable; if we are to speak of God at all, it must be in metaphors:

> The vision floods the eyes with light, but it is not a light showing some other thing, the light is itself the vision. No longer is there object seen and light to show it, no longer Intellect and object of Intellection; this is the very Radiance that brought both into being.[4]

While Plotinus thus exalted the transcendent infinitude of God, he also regarded it as the creative source of all existence. The infinite plenitude is infinitely active, even as light that radiates, as fragrance that wafts, as a stream that flows out. Emanation attests itself as the basic principle of reality. "It is of the essence of things that each gives of its being to another; else the Good would not be Good. . . . The law is, some life after the Primal Life, a second where there is a first; all linked in an unbroken chain, all eternal."[5]

The first stage of the emanation of the divine reality would be the highest qualified Being, the most nearly absolute and eternal Being that still has *a* character and admits of definition, the least finite of finite realities. Plotinus called it *Nous*, a term which has been translated variously as "spirit," "mind," "universal intelligence," "divine mind," "intellectual-principle," or "impersonal reason." It is the supreme principle of rationality which both Plato and Aristotle had recognized. As it is the first and supreme emanation of God, so it expresses most perfectly the essential character of the world. It is the archetype of the cosmos. Nature, the existing world, is supremely rational-spiritual.

Spirit, or the principle of rationality, has a character of universality that surpasses any spatial or temporal bounds or qualities; it is eternal. Plotinus distinguished eternity from everlasting time. Things endure or pass away in time, but Spirit, rationality, is timeless; it has neither past nor future; it is "outside of all notion of time." It similarly transcends any plurality,

---

[4] Plotinus, *The Enneads*, VI:vii:36, in Grace H. Turnbull (ed.), *The Essence of Plotinus* (with selections from MacKenna's translation), New York, Oxford Univ. Press, 1934, p. 205.
[5] *Ibid.*, II:ix:3, p. 64.

and is nowise definite; it is not *a* spirit, a *certain* reason. Its unity is not the numerical unity of a sum or system. It has no consciousness of objects, of others; its knowledge is self-knowledge. Like Aristotle's Creative Reason, it eternally thinks itself. Without other finite marks or limitations, Spirit, or divine Mind, manifests the supreme principle of rationality, the summit in the cosmic hierarchy, the highest being this side of deity.

Even as Spirit, in the process of emanation, issues from deity, so Spirit in its turn is manifested in soul, or Psyche. The soul is, like Spirit, a universal principle; but in it the further and lower marks and distinctions of finite existence are beginning to be apparent. Its essence is spiritual activity, but it is involved in distinctions from and relations to its objects of consciousness. Soul itself is universal, but it differentiates within itself as individual souls, each with its distinguishable medium of activity. Soul is thus peculiarly transitional in the process of emanation. Lower than *Nous*, it is still like it, a type of spiritual reality, but already it points toward some embodiment or physical medium. Its sense activity, its life and growth reach over the peripheral zones of Being which mark the lowest range in the process of emanation, the material world.

Matter and Evil: The Theodicy of Plotinus

In a philosophy so thoroughly spiritual as Neoplatonism we could scarcely expect a plainly scientific account of the physical world. Plotinus combined in his cosmology ideas selected from his predecessors with interpolated religious explanations of his own. So the term "celestial system" had more than an astronomical connotation for him. The heavenly host is composed of flaming, luminous bodies, but they are also divine, as is the earth. He saw "no longer any absurdity or impossibility in the notion that the soul in the earth has vision . . . in fact, it is a god since certainly soul must be everywhere good."[6] Plotinus felt in all physical existence a contending activity. On the one hand bodies represented to him a deprivation of the spiritual character of the soul, which is what he meant by calling matter, as Plato did, "non-Being." On the other hand, even in physical nature he saw the radiance of the soul, however dimly reflected. Nature itself seemed to have a certain sensation or understanding. "All life is a kind of spiritual vision."[7]

Plotinus shared with the earlier Stoics the idea of eternal recurrence. Out of strict necessity, the cosmic system proceeds through its cycles of possible events, both on its vast astronomical scale and in the minimal detail of motion and configuration of the least grains of sand. When all possible alternatives

[6] Plotinus, *The Enneads*, IV:iv:26 (trans. S. MacKenna), 3rd ed., New York, Pantheon, n.d., p. 309.
[7] Plotinus, *The Enneads*, III:viii:8, in Inge, *op. cit.*, Vol. I, p. 161.

have been exhausted, the entire cycle is evolved again, and so on through eternity.

The soul's spiritual character was regarded by Plotinus as being beyond the vicissitudes of material existence, and he therefore believed in personal immortality. Against the Epicureans, he argued that mind can be produced by no atomic motions or bodily activity whatever. With the Aristotelians, he agreed that man's daily life is that of an embodied soul, or animated body, and that the material side of us is transitory. But he expressed a firm Platonic conviction that the intelligent soul has an eternal career. It existed before it assumed a certain bodily vesture as this or that man, and it will continue to exist after the dissolution of the body. Plotinus believed that the essential emanation of the universal soul principle into a material stage of existence recapitulates itself in the case of individual souls, not only once but repeatedly. In this way, he reaffirmed the Platonic doctrine of transmigration of souls.

The Neoplatonic account of the material world of sense—of causality, space, time, motion, life—can scarcely be subjected to analysis or criticism as a system of natural science. In all his reflections on physical matters, Plotinus manifests his basic view of matter as essential deprivation or barrenness of real being. Matter lacks perfection, is not good; it is the cause and the realm of evil. In assuming its bodily vesture the soul is swept along into unstable, disordered, and corrupt existence. Plotinus spurned all sensuality and surrender to the body as a betrayal of the soul. But in his ascetic withdrawal from all material attachment he did not regard the existence of corrupt matter as staining the infinite perfection of God. He resisted the cosmic pessimism of the Gnostics, their doctrine that, in creating the material world, God exposed a fatal taint in the divine reality itself.

The term *Gnosticism* designates a confused variety of doctrines which issued out of the Middle East during the second Christian century, both from a heretical movement within the Church, and from the opposition to Christianity. Ranging over the whole field of Hellenistic culture, the Gnostics raked together philosophical principles, religious insights, arrant superstitions—a profound esoteric muddle. Among their camp followers were mystery mongers and downright charlatans, but their leaders also included men of spiritual power and bold speculation. The conviction which many of them shared was a conviction of cosmic depravity. The world produced by God's creative activity was a swarm of powers, some divinely spiritual, others trammeled by corrupt matter. Within the church these Gnostics taught that true Christianity was purely spiritual, a gospel of salvation from the evil worship of the Jewish God who created the material world. Others, less emphatic in their condemnation of the Creator, regarded the creation of matter as evidence of a self-degradation or original "fall" of God. Still others inclined toward a Persian dualistic explanation of the strife of good and evil in human life—Matter is a dark, cosmic principle, evil and corrupt and everywhere at war with God.

In opposition to the Gnostics, Plotinus maintained with equal firmness two theses: the cause of corruption in the world and of evil in our nature is matter, but the production of matter in the process of emanation does not sully the perfection of God. If there is to be a world distinguishable from God, emanation must proceed to less and less divinely spiritual being. In this process there must needs be a "least" of the radiating perfection, an outermost zone, twilit, dim, and dark. This is the material world.

In calling matter "non-Being," Plotinus explicitly pointed out that he did not question its actual existence. Matter, bodies, the physical world exist, but they do not manifest the fullness of reality, which is spiritual. Failure to understand this spiritual core of Being caused the blindness of the Epicureans, who imagined, as Plotinus said, that "the onslaught of an atom striking downward or dashing in from any direction could force the Soul to reasonings, impulses or thoughts."[8] Epicureanism is a distorted philosophy; it mistakes the meager actuality of physical existence for abundant reality and true Being. Unversed in real harmony, it would make a cosmos of the disorderly atomic swirl. Its practice is astray even as its theory is. It seeks its blessedness in sensual indulgence, dull to the divine raptures of the soul.

In escaping the downfall of materialism, however, we should not plunge into the opposite, Gnostic abyss. Material existence is the lowest and the least in the process of emanation, but in that divine process it has its place. At each stage of its being, the world hierarchy manifests its characteristic degree of perfection. One is the perfection of Spirit, another is the World Soul or the individual soul's perfection, still another is the perfection of animals and plants. Perfection is commensurate with type or grade of being. If we do not lose our perspective and confuse the low with the sublime, we can, with a certain cosmic benignity, behold the lovely sights in the world of sense, not be lured or deceived by them, but laud in the spectacle of them the higher perfection of God that can manifest beauty even in matter.

Every string [of the lyre] is set in the precisely right position for the due production of the tones within its capacity. . . . The universe is good when everyone throws his own voice towards a total harmony, singing out a life—thin, harsh, imperfect though it be. The harmony is made of tones unequal, differing, but together they form the perfect consonance.[9]

In the book of Genesis, the first of the two Hebrew stories of creation concludes with the statement that "God saw everything that he had made and, behold, it was very good."[10] But right after this cosmic approval and blessing, we are told in another story of the serpent in paradise and of man's original sin and expulsion from Eden. The reader of Plotinus may get a similar impression as he turns from the theodicy to the ethics of the *Enneads*. The material world of sense was accepted serenely by Plotinus in his theodicy, as having its proper place and role and its own characteristic perfec-

[8] Plotinus, *The Enneads*, III:i:3, in Turnbull, *op. cit.*, p. 69.
[9] *Ibid.*, III:ii:17, p. 88.
[10] Genesis 1:31 (American Standard Version).

tion in the cosmic emanation of God. But Plotinus taught an ascetic morality: resistance to the evil lures and incitements of the sensual life, the soul's ascent from the corruption of matter to the purity of spirit.

The thought of Plotinus swung from one of these convictions to the other, or rather it sought a way of reconciling these two contending emphases in his philosophy. Plato faced a similar problem, and its perplexities have embroiled other philosophers through the centuries. When Plotinus tells us in his theodicy that "each member of the All contributes to that All in the degree of its kind and condition,"[11] even matter, we may be convinced that all is well in God's world. But how then are we to be aroused to the deadly peril of evil and to the moral struggle with it on which our salvation depends?

Plotinus' analysis seems to have explained emanation as proceeding metaphysically from the most to the least of being. The evil of material existence would be, as it were, its metaphysical indigence, its utter finitude. There should be no complaint of God, but how could there be condemnation of carnal man? When Plotinus proceeds to emphasize the moral antithesis of good and evil, carnal nature and material corruption seem to be defined morally as antiperfection, and not merely as metaphysical meagerness or finitude. But how, then, can we avoid viewing the process of emanation in a Gnostic perspective as an inverted hierarchy of degradation, imperiling theodicy? If the problem of vindicating God's creative activity arises at all, how can it be solved?

Beauty, Goodness, and the Mystical Ascent to God

The earliest writing of Plotinus deals with Beauty. For him, as for Plato, beauty concerned more than art; it expressed nobility worthy of loving devotion. Like "the divine beauty, pure and clear and unalloyed"[12] of Plato's *Symposium*, so the perfect beauty for Plotinus is "the Beauty of the Authentic Intellect."[13] The progress in spiritual mastery for both philosophers may be traced in the pursuit of beauty as in the quest of truth or goodness. These are three aspects of perfection in ideal interplay.

Aesthetic beauty is the beauty of *aisthesis*, or sensuous perception. The object beautiful to sight and the lovely harmony are not to be explained as merely shapely or symmetrical. We find an object of sense beautiful because in it we experience sensuously a certain adumbration of spiritual meaning: "The material thing becomes beautiful by communicating in the thought that

---

[11] Plotinus, *The Enneads*, IV:iv:45, in Turnbull, *op. cit.*, p. 138.
[12] Plato, *Symposium*, in B. Jowett (trans.), *The Dialogues of Plato*, 3rd ed., Oxford, Clarendon Press, 1892, Vol. I, marginal page 212.
[13] *Ibid.*, V:viii:1, p. 170.

flows from the Divine. . . . Harmonies unheard create the harmonies we hear and wake the soul to the consciousness of beauty."[14]

From this sensuous perception of beauty, the soul can rise to loftier admiration for ideal objects. It can look upon the face of Justice and Wisdom, "beautiful beyond the beauty of the evening and the dawn";[15] it can behold "the godlike splendor of virtue, . . . the perfect Goodness established in the stainless shrine."[16] But in order to have this vision of the First Beauty, the soul itself must be beautiful; for only spirit can commune with spirit. "We ourselves possess Beauty when we are true to our own being; ugliness is going over to another order; knowing ourselves, we are beautiful; in self-ignorance we are ugly. Thus beauty is of the Divine and comes thence only."[17]

Aesthetic contemplation, therefore, was no specific vision for Plotinus. Beauty, as he interpreted it, traverses art and enters morality, philosophy, and religion. It is one side of the pathway to Perfection. Moral activity is another. Plotinus saw men's daily lives as spurred by sensual desires, but spiritually dull and inert. He conceived of morality as the emancipation of the soul from the shackles of the body so that, no longer fettered, it could fly to itself, be cleansed of its dross and alloy, be purely itself, soul alone.

The evil souls are lost through misdirection, they have "deserted towards the abyss." The choice of direction is the crucial choice of life, for each of us is all that he chooses to be. In the soul that has made the right choice, and so long as it holds to it resolutely, the battling of lower impulses with higher is mastered by intelligence; the lower nature here stands in awe of reason. The soul that achieves virtue by intelligent self-possession rejects "unmeasure, excess and shortcoming"; it maintains balance and harmony; it comes up to its distinctive capacities in rational expression. This is achievement of spiritual character. It is, however, no definitely accomplished task; it rises to ever higher purposes. As the soul turns from the lower sensual scene to its own loftier realm, so through itself it looks above itself to Spirit, and aspires towards God. Its happiness is in fullness of life and the possession of the supreme good. This spiritual plenitude is prefigured in the cardinal virtues, but they are not its consummation. In all of his reflection on the details of the good life, Plotinus always looked through them and above them to their greater fulfillment. "It is to the gods, not to good men, that our likeness must look; to model ourselves upon good men is to produce the image of an image; we have to fix our gaze above the image and attain likeness to the Supreme Exemplar."[18]

This ethics, in the one word, *good*, expressed the ever finite achievement

[14] *Ibid.*, I:vi:23, p. 43.
[15] *Ibid.*, I:vi:4, p. 44.
[16] *Ibid.*, I:vi:9, p. 49.
[17] *Ibid.*, V:viii:13, p. 178.
[18] *Ibid.*, composited from sections I:ii:7, I:viii:4, and IV:iii:6, pp. 27, 55, 119.

of man and his truly infinite aspiration. Good, real good, is the prerogative of God; our so-called "goodness" is only a hint of it, and yet this real good is alone the true final purpose of any genuinely moral endeavor. Thus, in the Gospel, Jesus said to the man who had called him good, "Why callest thou me good? There is none good but one, that is, God."[19] But, in the Sermon on the Mount, we are urged: "Be ye therefore perfect, even as your Father which is in heaven is perfect."[20] So Plotinus wrote, as an epitome of his ethics—not with presumption at all but with the boundless aspiration of piety: "Our concern is not merely to be sinless but to be God."[21]

Beauty and goodness thus point to communion, and union, with God. This divine vision Plotinus regarded as the goal of philosophical contemplation. As is the progress from the life of sensuality to rational conduct and spiritual consecration, so is the advance from random opinion to rational knowledge, and to the still higher mystical vision in ecstasy. In this mystical intuition the soul does not comprehend its object but is one with it; it does not lift its object unto itself, but is itself lifted up and made one with God. Plotinus prized his several mystical experiences as the only real life of his soul in the arid expanse of mortal existence. "He who has *seen* knows what I say—that the soul takes on another life as it approaches God; thus restored, it feels that the Dispenser of true Life is There and that we must put aside all else and rest in This alone, This become, This alone. . . ."[22]

St. Augustine, of whom it has been said that he came to Christ by way of Plotinus, cites this lofty tribute to Neoplatonic ecstasy in *The City of God:* "That vision of God is the beauty of a vision so great, and is so infinitely desirable, that Plotinus does not hesitate to say that he who enjoys all other blessings in abundance, and has not this, is supremely miserable."[23] As will be noted in the next chapter, St. Augustine, in his writings against the Manichean heresy, continued in his Christian theology the philosophical opposition of Plotinus to Gnosticism. The transition from classical antiquity to medieval Christianity was in many ways a spiritual revolution, but we should not exaggerate the philosophical contrasts between the two, or ignore the continued influence of Greek ideas in the formation of Christian doctrine. As a parallel to St. Augustine's admiration for Plotinus, we have been reminded of the Prologue to the Fourth Gospel, which a pagan Platonist said should be written in letters of gold. No words can better connect the last wisdom of the classical age with the Gospel of the new Christian life: the vision of the Christ, the Logos, the Word of God, and the Neoplatonic vision of God's emanation in the world: "The light shineth in the darkness, and the darkness apprehended or overcame it not."

[19] Matthew 19:17 (Authorized Version).
[20] *Ibid.*, 5:48.
[21] Plotinus, *The Enneads*, I:ii:6, in Turnbull, *op. cit.*, p. 26.
[22] *Ibid.*, VI:ix:9, p. 220.
[23] Plotinus, *The Enneads*, I:vi:7, quoted in St. Augustine, *The City of God* (trans. M. Dods), Edinburgh, Clark, 1872, Vol. I, p. 404.

SUGGESTED WORKS FOR FURTHER STUDY

CRITICAL STUDIES OF SKEPTICISM AND ECLECTICISM.   Bevan, E. R., *Stoics and Sceptics;* Wolfsohn, H. A., *Philo;* Zeller, Eduard, *The Stoics, Epicureans, and Sceptics.*
PLOTINUS.   Plotinus, *Enneads* (trans. Stephen MacKenna); Katz, Joseph (trans.), *The Philosophy of Plotinus* (selections); Turnbull, Grace N. (ed.), *The Essence of Plotinus* (selections).
CRITICAL STUDIES OF PLOTINUS AND NEOPLATONISM.   Bigg, C., *Neoplatonism;* Fuller, B. A. G., *The Problem of Evil in Plotinus;* Inge, W. R., *The Philosophy of Plotinus;* Whittaker, Thomas, *The Neo-Platonists.*

II. THE DOCTORS AND SAINTS OF MEDIEVAL CHRISTIAN PHILOSOPHY

8.   St. Augustine and
the City of God

The Christian Philosophy of Salvation

The City of God is the title of St. Augustine's chief treatise; it also expressed a personal and social ideal in religion, which was epoch-making in its direction of medieval civilization, and which is still a basic factor and alternative in our modern outlook on life. St. Augustine's philosophy manifests his original insight and systematic power, but his work reveals him mainly as the minister of the City of God, proclaiming its charter of principles to the cities of earth. The medieval Christian philosophy, to which we now turn, is a philosophy of ministers, disciples, and apostles of God in Christ.

The Christianization of the Mediterranean world was a radical revolution in the history of philosophy which changed the direction of men's interests and purposes, the emphasis in their thinking and the problems which engrossed them, their sanctions and methods. The moving spirit in the early Church was not the classical spirit of critical inquiry. The writings of the New Testament were not philosophical treatises or systematic expositions of the nature of things; they were gospels and epistles, glad tidings of salvation and personal exhortations. The Christian convert was not a scientific or philosophical inquirer engaged in investigation or theory or in the pursuit of understanding. He was a sinner come to the throne of grace in humble hope of salvation. Both wisdom and virtue, the true insight and the right way of life, were to him centered in his certainty of redemption through Christ. Christ was the way, the truth, and the life.

This indifference toward science or philosophical reflection in the early Church was intensified by its so-called "eschatological" spirit: its expectation of the imminent end of the world, the return of Christ to judge the living and the dead. The all-important quest of salvation, which excluded all naturalistic interests, gained dramatic emphasis by its alertness to the speedily impending doom. "The fashion of this world passeth away."[1] We can thus readily understand the initial contrast which the Christian teaching presented to Greek philosophy, and to classical culture generally. St. Paul's Epistles reveal an attitude of mutual disregard between the learned Greeks and the early Christians. Very few of his converts were wise after the flesh, and his preaching of Christ crucified was foolishness to the gentiles; nonetheless, he never tired of repeating that the wisdom of this world was foolishness to God, and devoutly he declared: "We are fools for Christ's sake."[2]

But while proclaiming its divine Gospel of eternal life and the imminent end of the world, the Christian movement was itself in its own time in this world; it was influenced by the civilization which it transformed. St. Paul and the author of the Fourth Gospel show that, even in the first century, the Church included men of intellectual preeminence as well as religious genius. The Gospel that made its initial appeal to the weary and heavy laden gradually united in faith communities more and more representative of the various social and cultural classes. Growing numbers of educated men turned from their classical wisdom to the Christian Gospel of salvation.

The new Gospel was compared in a parable unto leaven which leavened three measures of meal. Without analysis or argument, it pierced through all surface details to the heart of moral and spiritual values. It declared the unique and inviolable worth of man—any man—in the sight of God. It centered all concern on the values of the inner life: "What is a man profited, if he gain the whole world, and lose or forfeit his own self?"[3] It depreciated outward success and mastery, and, in its Beatitudes, exalted the poor in spirit, those that mourn, the meek, the pure of heart, the merciful, the peacemakers, those that hunger and thirst after righteousness and are persecuted for righteousness' sake. Its spirit was one not of self-reliance, but of trusting faith—the faith of a sinner and a prodigal son returning home to his Father. The entire attitude and spiritual outlook of men were revolutionized as they turned from their present life of understanding and achievement to the new eternal life of humble repentance and blessedness, redemption by Christ's love, here and in the hereafter. The conviction of immortality dominated all Christian thinking, a hope and a solemn admonition.

The progressive expansion of Christianity among the educated classes brought into the Church the influence of classical ideas. Thinking men did not stop thinking. Accustomed to inquiry, they sought a clear understanding of their new faith. They were sure to reflect upon their new Christian experiences as compared with their former life. The contrast was one of humble piety and worldly sinfulness, but it was also a change in beliefs and ideas. It was a change from the *Nicomachean Ethics* to the Beatitudes, from the myths of Plato to the parables of the Gospel, from Aristotle's statement,

---

[1] I Corinthians 7:31 (American Standard Version).
[2] *Ibid.*, 4:10.
[3] Luke 9:25 (American Standard Version).

"Virtue is a habit of the will,"[4] and the ideal of the godly life as a life of rational contemplation, to the words of Jesus: "Except a man be born again, he cannot see the kingdom of God."[5] But it was also a change from various Greek metaphysics and cosmologies to the doctrines of St. Paul and St. John. The Christian Gospel as a way of life challenged and mastered pagan pride by the divine sublimity of its ideals. Let a modern classical spirit, Goethe, speak for a thousand Christians reared in Hellenistic culture: "However far the human mind will expand, it will never be able to surpass the majesty of the Christian gospel."[6]

It was in the region of their thinking, in their ideas, that the classical converts to Christianity were bound to be perplexed. From what to what had they been converted? They had perhaps been Stoics or Platonists; how were they now to regard their old doctrines—were they to reject, revise, or to reaffirm them—in the light of their new Christian truths? Instead of the unformulated, burning convictions of the early converts, a new spirit invaded the Church, in which men sought a convincing statement of their beliefs, were embroiled in manifold controversies, and hence imposed the demand for orthodoxy, an acknowledged true Christian doctrine.

In the Sermon on the Mount, Jesus expressed his spiritual principles and values in contrast to the rigid laws of the priestly Jewish tradition. He spiritualized men's relation to God. The Kingdom of God was not to be an external theocracy in Jerusalem but a spiritual state: "The kingdom of God is within you."[7] In place of the outward act of religious observance, obedience to God's law and justice toward men, Jesus emphasized love of God and love and brotherhood of all mankind.

The Christianization of the Mediterranean gentile world brought out a different, but equally significant, contrast between Christian and Greek philosophical ideals. The classical outlook on life was secular; the Christian was otherworldly. The Greek pursued an understanding of the nature of things and the harmonious consummation of human powers and capacities. His cardinal virtues—temperance, courage, justice, wisdom—were all expressions of rational human achievement. The Christian virtues were faith, hope, and love. The godly life was seen in humble piety, purity, mercy, and holiness, not seeking any worldly goods or mastery, but aspiring beyond this world and this life to everlasting blessedness in the hereafter. The Christian wisdom was the trusting faith of a child; the Christian temperance was continence and purity from any carnal taint; the Christian justice became loving nonresistance and the return of good for evil; the Christian courage was long-suffering patience, the martyr's firm loyalty unto death.

[4] Paraphrased from Aristotle, *Nicomachean Ethics* (trans. F. H. Peters), 10th ed., London, Kegan, Paul, 1906, Bk. II, sec. 1.

[5] John 3:3 (Authorized Version).

[6] Quoted in Robert Ulich, *History of Educational Thought*, New York, American Book, 1945, p. 71.

[7] Luke 17:21 (American Standard Version).

Though the Christian Gospel appealed mainly to the heart and the will, it was certain eventually to engage also the intellect. A religion that was primarily a devotion to God, a way of life according to God's will, a living hope of salvation by the grace of God in Christ, was bound to become also a doctrine about God, God's self-revelation in Christ, God's relation to the world and to men—a reasoned and formulated theology. In this development, this progressive engagement of the Christian reason, the leadership in the Church was naturally assumed by men of trained reason, and these were minds versed in Greek philosophy. Christian theology and philosophy issued from their endeavors to elaborate and to state systematically many deep but unformulated Christian convictions, and to reason out, consistently with prevailing Christian beliefs, a system of doctrines about nature and human nature which the early tradition of the Church had provided scarcely, if at all.

In the satisfaction of these intellectual needs the church, to be sure, used its Biblical resources and sought a Biblical formulation. But it had become increasingly a gentile Church. Even the interpretation and formulation of its Jewish traditions were being done mostly by minds that thought in Greek and Latin, or by manifold oriental minds with Hellenistic education. This interpenetration of ideas and ways of thought became a historical necessity for expanding Christianity. It had to make itself understood by Greco-Roman minds.

Naturally, the various theologians reflected in their Christian doctrines the influence of their respective philosophical beliefs. They might turn most resolutely against their own earlier philosophy, from which they had been converted to Christianity, or they might still adhere to it as a philosophy but seek to use it as an intellectual framework for the systematic formulation of their new Christian beliefs. In either case, their theology would show the influence of the earlier philosophy. We can recognize and distinguish many of these leading theologians as former Platonists, Aristotelians, Stoics, and later, as Neoplatonists.

Thus, Christianity—radically different though it was from, and indeed opposed to, the characteristic classical civilization—inherited, as it grew and developed, a great many of its systematic ideas from classical antiquity. In this cultural fusion, the Greek spirit repeated in Christendom its earlier achievement in Rome. Rome and Christianity both overcame Greek civilization, yet both became permeated by Greek ideas. This cultural interplay may be examined to advantage also in the relation of Christian to oriental thought. Actually, Christianity shared many of its leading ideas with one or another tradition in the Hellenistic-Roman world. With its Hebrew Prophetic inheritance it shared a monotheistic conviction and a belief in a personal God; with Greco-Jewish philosophy and with Neoplatonism it upheld the principle of the divine Logos, which influenced its central doctrine of Christ; with Stoicism it advocated cosmopolitanism, universal brotherhood, and suppression of the passions, but all three differently and for different reasons. With Plato, and with some oriental religions, it shared a faith in personal immortality.

Certain hazards lay in the correlation of Christian and non-Christian ideas, and there was definite opposition to this within the Church. Even while they themselves used philosophical ideas in their systematic reflections, many theologians were suspicious of those ideas when used by others, and would banish them altogether if they could. St. Jerome bewailed his own former devotion to classical literature: "What has Horace to do with the Psalter, Virgil with the Gospels, and Cicero with Paul?"[8] But, as early as the second century, Justin Martyr declared that all good teachings of any philosophers should be possessed by the Christians. And, almost three centuries later, St. Augustine wrote, "Let every good and true Christian understand that truth, wherever he finds it, belongs to *his* Lord."[9]

We noted at the close of the preceding chapter the importance of not ignoring the rapprochement of certain ideals in the declining classical antiquity with those of expanding Christianity. But a unique characteristic which should not be overlooked distinguished the Christian theologians. Even when they used Platonic or Stoic ideas, they did not use them as Platonists or Stoics. Their basic conviction was that the truth to which they had been converted was truth revealed to men by Christ, not merely a human attainment. Their Christian doctrine was to them not just another doctrine, better than others but like them admitting of criticism, revision, and development. It was *the* truth. Their problem was and could be only this: how to understand and to express this truth rightly.

In place of scientific investigation and philosophical inquiry, the Christian emphasized authoritative interpretation of the one and only Christian truth, orthodoxy. Any departure or variation from the one true way was now regarded, not merely as mistaken, but as heresy. This fundamental divine sanction, which Christian theology acknowledged, determined its method and its principles of dogmatic authoritarianism.

The basic character of medieval Christian philosophy is reflected in the history of its development. Its first period covers the formation of orthodoxy by the apologists and by the fathers of the Church; this is called "Patristic" philosophy. It reaches its culmination in the system of St. Augustine in the early fifth century. After the several centuries of intellectual stagnation which followed the fall of Rome, the second period of medieval philosophy begins with the revival of learning; this is called "Scholastic" philosophy. The great schoolmen started with the established principles of orthodoxy and elaborated them into systems of Christian philosophy. The main purpose of the philosophical theologian was and remained to give intellectual statement to his divinely revealed and indubitable Christian convictions.

---

[8] St. Jerome, "The Virgin's Profession," in F. A. Wright, *Fathers of the Church,* London, Routledge, 1928, p. 254.

[9] St. Augustine, *Epistle 166,* as quoted by A. E. Burn, "Creeds," *Encyclopedia Britannica,* 11th ed., Cambridge, Cambridge Univ. Press, 1911, Vol. VII, p. 392.

Scholastic philosophy has been called "faith seeking to understand (*fides quaerens intellectum*)."[10]

At this point is should be stated plainly and briefly that the present book is a history of philosophy, not a history of our civilization. We cannot undertake here by detailed discussion to do adequate justice to the role of Christianity in the historical life of the western world. Our task is a more special one. As we kept in broad view the classical setting of Greek and Hellenistic civilization, in which we studied more particularly the development of ancient philosophy, so now the outlines of the new Christian world will not escape our attention, but we shall mainly be concerned with philosophy in the Christian medieval culture, its intellectual, systematic expressions in method and in doctrinal conclusions.

The Formation of Christian Orthodoxy: the Logos Doctrine

The Christian religion began as a movement in Galilee and Jerusalem, but it soon spread from Damascus to Rome. It thus affected many faiths and had to distinguish itself, first from Judaism, and then from the various doctrines and cults of the Hellenistic world. The first issue for Christianity —and it was crucial—was decided by St. Paul: the way to the Christian life was not through prerequisite Jewish conformity. Christ's Gospel was for all mankind. St. Paul was "the Apostle to the gentiles," and he sealed the destiny of Christianity as a universal religion. But its meaning to its converts was bound to reflect their different backgrounds of tradition. The churches in Palestine inclined toward a Jewish interpretation; Jesus the Christ was, to them, the Messiah foretold by the prophets, son of David, born in Bethlehem. To the early gentile churches—Greek, Roman, and oriental—these Jewish traditions were unfamiliar, and could scarcely be vital. These gentiles would construe the new doctrine in the light of their own characteristic beliefs. Common to all, however, was their new faith in Christ, and their problem was to express clearly and convincingly this faith: "What think ye of Christ?"[11] The evolving theology of the churches was primarily a doctrine about Christ and Christ's relation to God.

The initial Jewish interpretation, the Messianic doctrine, served to preserve for Christianity its Biblical kinships—the ethical monotheism of the prophets, the worship of a personal God of righteousness, justice, and mercy. But the Messianic doctrine yielded in central importance to a Greek idea which had found various expressions in the religious-philosophical speculation of Hellenistic culture. This was the Logos doctrine, first introduced into Christian thinking by the author of the Fourth Gospel: "In the begin-

---

[10] Étienne Gilson, *The Spirit of Medieval Philosophy* (trans. A. H. C. Downes), London, Sheed and Ward, 1936, p. 5.
[11] Matthew 22:42 (Authorized Version).

ning was the Logos, and the Logos was with God, and the Logos was God."[12] Christian speech in the West rendered this term by the Latin, *Verbum*, the "Word," and so it has passed through the ages into every tongue of Christendom. But *logos* meant not only *word*, but also *thought;* not only *oratio* (expressed thinking), but also *ratio* (reason itself); and not reason only, but rationality, the rational-productive principle of cosmic order.

Throughout the history of ancient philosophy, as we have noted, this Logos principle was recognized in various ways: the Heraclitean logos, or world order, the everlasting law in all processes of change; the Platonic and Aristotelian interpretation of Logos as the rational power or principle; and the cardinal, but dual, Stoic doctrine of the logos as synonymous with deity, and signifying the vital seminal principle of active reason operating in all material existence. In the first Christian century, the Greco-Jewish philosopher, Philo, interpreted the Logos as the creatively self-manifested deity: God regarded as the productive power in the universe, God's uttered and rationally comprehensible perfection. Within the early Christian Church and outside of it, Gnostic speculation in many tongues expounded its ideas of the Logos in doctrines, which seem to be foregleams of Neoplatonism and also perversions of it: Logos as the first self-outpouring of deity in the world, Logos as the first lapse or downward step in the process of God's self-degrading series of finite manifestations.

These various logos doctrines influenced the philosophical training and thought of educated Christian theologians. They were topics of controversy in the churches, and convictions of aggressive sectaries. As they were in partial or radical disagreement, Christian wisdom was advised to suspect them as partly or wholly heretical. But then, it was bound to seek the one true orthodox interpretation of the Christ-Logos: Christ, the Word of God.

The Christian thinkers were thus involved in the ultimate problems of their theology—the relation of God to the world and to man's life and destiny; God's relation to Christ, the Savior of men; and the relation of the Son of God to the Son of Man, the divine to the human nature of Christ. A long column of theological terms would signalize to us the contending doctrines in the formulation of Christian orthodoxy. The theologians sought an acceptable synthesis of their basic monotheism with their central conviction of Christ's divine character and mission. The required orthodox doctrine should distinguish, but not separate, Christ from God. It should not so overemphasize God's unity as to leave Christ's personality in any way ambiguous, but neither should it conceive of the relation of Christ to God so as to imply either any ultimate duality and only vague monotheism, or any uncertainty that the Christ-Logos is God.

The monotheistic insistence on the essential unity of God was dominant. According to Harnack, the eminent historian of Church doctrine, the uni-

[12] John 1:1.

tarian view prevailed as late as the beginning of the third century. The firm resistance to any hint of polytheism led the so-called "Adoptionists" to maintain that Jesus was a man imbued with God's spirit, and so perfectly holy that he was adopted and divinized by God. A less unacceptable form of basic unitarianism was the doctrine that God's essential unity manifests itself in a plurality of phases, or roles. Thus, the one God is active as the creator or director of the world, as God the Father, but God is also the Savior of men, God the Son, and likewise, God is the life-giving Spirit in the Church—God the Holy Spirit. These are three phases, or *modes*, of God's self-manifestation, and, accordingly, this doctrine was called "Modalism." It was also called "Sabellianism," after Sabellius, the leader of the unitarians who acknowledged the divinity of Christ. The stricter champions of monotheism were also called "Monarchians," believers in a single sovereign principle. Some of them, as noted, inclined to Adoptionism. But those who regarded the Christ-Logos and God the Father as only different modes of the one deity seemed to their critics to imply that God the Father suffered on the cross, and hence were labeled "Patripassians." The human life and career of the Savior were described by some theologians as only apparent; Christ had only a phantom body and, in his divine essence, was unaffected by any material nature, and he did not really, but only seemingly, suffer on the cross. This doctrine was called "Docetism."

The development of the Logos doctrine in Christian theology was a major problem in Patristic philosophy. During the second century, able theologians like Justin Martyr and Irenaeus maintained firmly the divinity of the Christ-Logos, but distinguished it from unqualified deity. The Father of all is really beyond any definition. The Christ-Logos is God's only begotten Son, of one mind and will with God but still generated by God. Christ was the Anointed, but God was the Anointer. The Holy Spirit was likewise related hierarchically to God and the Christ-Logos. But Irenaeus firmly resisted the Gnostic dualism of God and matter as a faulty metaphysics and as an unthinkable position for Christians, since it questioned the omnipotent perfection of God. This doctrine was trinitarian in its intention, but some of its features were closer to later Neoplatonism than to orthodox Christian theology.

The Neoplatonic influence was especially notable in the theology of Origen (*c.*185–*c.*254), who had been a fellow student of Plotinus in the school of Ammonius Saccas, as well as a catechetical pupil of the Church father, Clement of Alexandria (*c.*150–*c.*215). These two men, Clement and Origen, had a thorough mastery of classical philosophy and culture, and they championed the liberal policy in the Church, that would appreciate and incorporate the best truths of Greek thought into the divine and perfect wisdom of Christianity. They were the most philosophical of the Greek Church fathers, and in their conception of the world mission of Christianity may be contrasted to their notable Latin contemporary, Tertullian (*c.*155–*c.*222).

Tertullian was the embodiment of militant Christianity, not of the Beatitude, "Blessed are the peace-makers,"[13] but of the saying attributed to Jesus: "I came not to send peace, but a sword."[14] A North African well trained in classical philosophy and eloquence, he turned from a legal career to become a pleader for the Christian cause. His service to his divine client recognized no compromise. His knowledge of classical philosophy was matched by his contempt for its pagan vanity in matters of religion. To him, Christ was all, and he admitted no possible dependence of Christian truth on classical wisdom. He opposed Greek philosophy even when he used it, as when he expounded a Stoic variety of materialism, blending it with the Biblical doctrine of the material world as created by God, and describing the human soul as subtly material and surviving the disintegration of coarse matter. His basic policy was firm: "What do Athens and Jerusalem have in common, or the Academy and the Church?"[15] In his warfare for Christ, as he understood it, he was not very scrupulous in his choice of weapons. He was a ruthless controversialist, marked neither by Christian love nor by ordinary pagan fairness; his flaming earnestness burned his convictions into the mind and life of the western Church. His single devotion lacked critical breadth of outlook, but its roots were deep. He did not depend on Greek or any other theory or reason for his Christian beliefs; Christian truth is not a dialectical conclusion, but an immediate intuition of faith. God in Christ is directly evident to the Christian conscience, but not by way of rational proof, and despite all possible objections by lame reason. We need neither analysis nor investigation, but only unwavering belief. Christian truth defies the pagan logic; "It is certain just because it is impossible. It is credible because it is inept."[16] Tradition has summed it up in the words, "I believe it because it is absurd (*credo quia absurdum*)."[17]

Radically different was the spirit of Clement of Alexandria. He opposed pagan corruption in the Church as firmly as did Tertullian, but to him truth was truth, irrespective of origin. He recognized it in Plato as well as in St. John. "Philosophy was a tutor to bring the Greek mind, as the law was to bring the Hebrews, to Christ."[18] Faith is an unfailing energy in Christian life, but it can attain maturity and fruition as it is sustained and expressed by reason.

Clement's interpretation of the Christ-Logos continued that of Justin Martyr. The divine perfection radiates universally, as the light of the sun.

[13] *Ibid.*, 5:9 (American Standard Version).

[14] *Ibid.*, 10:34.

[15] Translated from Tertullian, as quoted by Clemens Baeumker in his chapter "Die Patristische Philosophie," in *Allgemeine Geschichte der Philosophie* (multiple authorship), in the encyclopedic series *Die Kultur der Gegenwart*, I:v, 2nd ed., Leipzig, Teubner, 1913, p. 267.

[16] Translated from Tertullian, "De Carne Christi," in J. P. Migne (ed.), *Patrologiae Cursus Completus* (or *Patrologia Latina*), Paris, Migne, 1844, Vol. II, p. 761.

[17] Clemens Baeumker, in *op. cit.*, p. 268.

[18] Quoted from R. M. Jones (ed.), *Selections from the Writings of Clement of Alexandria*, London, Healey, n.d., pp. 15 f.

Christ is the consummation of all other partial truth; in him all holy hopes and strivings find their perfection; he is the eternal Reason in the world. For Clement, Christ was God made manifest and understood. The ultimate deity, God the Father, was to him ineffable. The metaphysical distinction between the Christ-Logos and Deity was unmistakable here; but the religious emphasis in Christian devotion was centered in Christ. "Yea, I say, the Word of God became man, that thou mayest learn from man how man may become God."[19]

Systematic theology and philosophy in the third Christian century reached their summit in the works of Origen, greatest of the Christian thinkers prior to St. Augustine. He was preeminently the intellect of the Patristic period. His merits as Church philosopher, as well as some of his lapses in orthodoxy, were due to his definitely rationalistic method. The Neoplatonic strain in his theology, mentioned above, is notable in his Logos doctrine. He regarded Christ as the essential and eternally generated divine Logos. This self-manifestation of God could not be regarded by Origen as a historical event in time, for the ultimate immutability of God was the central principle of his theology. The Christ-Logos is coeternal with God, of the same essence with the Father; but, while unquestionably divine, he is not Deity; he is a spiritual creation or expression of God. The Holy Spirit, likewise, Origen regarded as a sort of further emanation of the divine principle.

Origen not only regarded the Christ-Logos and the Holy Spirit as coeternal with God, but he also maintained that the world was created by God eternally, else we would have to conceive of God's creative activity as having a historical origin and determination. To Origen, eternal creation implied the eternity of individual souls; that is, their preexistence, as well as their immortality. Their imprisonment in the body is due to a prenatal carnal attachment. The cause of sin is not matter, but the misdirected choice of man's free will which brings ruinous consequences. From this deep-lying sinfulness we are delivered by Christ's love. And this salvation is not for some only, but for all. There is no finite evil that can eternally withstand the redeeming grace of Christ, who will finally draw all souls to himself and to eternal blessedness.

THE ARIAN CONTROVERSY AND THE CREEDS

In the fourth century, the Logos problem embroiled the Church in violent discord which required authoritative settlement—this was the Arian controversy which began at the church of Alexandria. Arius, a presbyter of the church, set out with the conviction that Deity is essentially one and self-existent. The Christ-Logos is the only begotten Son of God; he is our perfect and divine Savior, and so, in a moral sense, is to be worshiped; but still he is not deity, not really God, who alone is unbegotten. Condemned and

[19] *Ibid.*, p. 32.

excommunicated by his bishop, Alexander, whom he in turn accused of heretical denial of any essential distinction between God and Christ, Arius appealed to his sympathizers in Palestine and Syria.

The controversy split the Christian party, on which the Emperor Constantine relied for his support. Reasons of state, as well as demand for Church unity required a settlement of the dispute. The First Ecumenical Church Council was convened at Nicaea, in 325, mainly for the purpose of terminating this controversy. After extended argument, the majority of the assembled bishops and presbyters condemned the Arian doctrine and adopted the following creed as the orthodox belief of the Church:

We believe in one God, the Father Almighty, the maker of all things visible and invisible. And in one Lord, Jesus Christ, the son of God, begotten of the Father, only begotten, that is, of the substance of the Father, God of God, Light of Light, very God of very God, begotten, not made, of one substance with the Father, by whom all things were made both those in heaven and those on earth. Who for us men and for our salvation came down and was incarnate, was made man, and suffered, and rose the third day, ascended into heaven, and is coming to judge quick and dead. And [we believe] in the Holy Ghost.[20]

The leading opponent of Arius at the Nicene Council was Athanasius of Alexandria. He maintained resolutely that the Church creed should declare that Jesus Christ was *homoousios*, "of one substance with the Father," and repudiate the Arian sharp distinction between the Christ-Logos and Deity. But *homoousios* had been used to express the relation of a man to his own reason; moreover, to many bishops, it seemed heretical in ignoring the distinct personality of Christ.

The condemned Arians were not silenced. Through Bishop Eusebius of Nicomedia, who had influence over Emperor Constantine, they regained power. Ten years after the Nicene Council, the Arians were readmitted to communion, and Athanasius was exiled to Gaul. A later council sought an acceptable, though vague, compromise statement by avoiding the term *homoousios* and describing the relation of Christ to God to be such "as the Scriptures say."

In 361, Emperor Julian, called "the Apostate," ascended the throne in the East. Disdaining all Christian theologians, he undertook to establish pagan worship, probably a form of Neoplatonism, in the empire. But he lost his life in a Persian campaign. The words attributed to him—"Thou hast conquered, O Galilean!"—whether authentically his or not, were true.

The Second Ecumenical Council, held at Constantinople in 381, reaffirmed the Nicene creed, but amplified it, declaring that the Holy Ghost "proceedeth from the Father." Seventy years later, at the Third Ecumenical Council held at Chalcedon in 451, the Trinitarian doctrine commanded gen-

[20] Quoted in A. E. Burn, "Creeds," in *Encyclopedia Britannica*, 11th ed., Cambridge, Cambridge Univ. Press, 1911, Vol. VII, pp. 395 ff. See also G. F. Moore, *History of Religions*, New York, Scribner, 1919, Vol. II, p. 180.

eral support as the basis of Christian orthodoxy. Though repudiated by the leaders of Christian belief, Arianism continued its vigorous resistance for some time. Several Germanic tribes, among them the Goths and the Vandals, were converted to it.

In Rome the Athanasian doctrine was held firmly. Among the Eastern churches, nonconforming theologians sought to outflank the advancing orthodoxy by various modulating formulas. The Nicene Council expression, that Christ was *homoousios* (of one substance) with the Father, was revised by the insertion of an *i*: *homoiousios*, meaning that Christ was "of like nature" to God the Father. Furthermore, champions of "likeness" and "unlikeness," *Homoii* and *Anomoii*, contended with each other.

Is this section abstruse and confusing? It reports only a part of the controversial subtleties in which the early churches were embroiled. And it is essential to our understanding of the history of Christian thought that we recognize its early variety of contested alternative doctrines. Even after the Council of Chalcedon, the demand persisted to reaffirm the parity of Christ with God the Father beyond the possibility of any hint of reservation. This was the purpose which a council of western bishops, sitting at Toledo in 589, sought to accomplish. To the third article of the creed, which speaks of the Holy Ghost "who proceedeth from the Father," they added the phrase "and from the Son (*Filioque*)." This Roman addition was repudiated by the eastern churches as tampering with the creed. It precipitated the breach between them and the Church of Rome—a breach which was already imminent on account of other disruptive issues that do not enter into the history of philosophy.

Another controversy which stirred up the churches, especially in the East, concerned the relation of the human to the divine nature of Christ. How was the Church to think of the Savior as both man and God? The so-called "Monophysites," or single naturists, whose views had strong influence in the eastern imperial court, declared that Christ the God-man had only a single nature. They cultivated the popular adoration of the Virgin Mary, who was called "Mother of God (*Theotokos*)." The sharp opposition by Patriarch Nestorius of Constantinople to this teaching was pronounced heretical by a synod of bishops. The spread of the Nestorian Church in Syria will interest us later, for its scholars preserved Greek learning in the Middle East and transmitted it to Mohammedan civilization, especially by translating Aristotle's works into Arabic.

The formation of Christian orthodoxy, the basis of Christian medieval philosophy, was indeed an arduous process, involving extended and varied strife among doctrinal interpretations. To bring out this character of Patristic thought, our attention has been centered here on the genesis of one doctrine of orthodoxy. But this doctrine of the Trinity, though it be a cornerstone of Christianity, is not its whole structure. So we may now turn to consider the formation of Christian orthodoxy more comprehensively by examining the systematic philosophy of St. Augustine, in which Patristic thought found its culmination, and which has proved fundamental in Christian belief down through the centuries.

Augustine's Way to Christian Truth

Augustine (354–430) declared in his *Soliloquies:* "God and the soul, that is what I desire to know. Nothing more? Nothing whatever."[21] His philosophy and his interpretation of the world and of history turned on the one crucial issue: the soul without God—the soul with God. On this theme was played the stirring drama of his life.

His *Confessions* is one of the most revealing autobiographies. We shall not summarize it here, but shall only recall some of his experiences which shaped his philosophical development. He was a native of Tagaste in North Africa, the son of a pagan father and a devout Christian mother, Monica. His mother had reared him in the Christian faith from his childhood. He was to have been baptized during a sudden illness, but he recovered, and, since Monica was of the belief that sins committed after baptism were doubly grievous, she postponed the rite until after her son had sown his wild oats. Augustine reports that he sowed a large crop during his youth, and put aside all thought of the Christian life. Despite his dissoluteness, he was a brilliant student, and his father sent him to the best schools in Africa— Madaura and Carthage—hoping to prepare him for a distinguished and profitable career as a master of Latin eloquence.

At the age of 19 he was moved to higher purposes as the result of reading a book of philosophic exhortation by Cicero. But at that time he became attached also to the Manichean heresy, which held him for about ten years. The Manichean dualism, of perfect deity and matter with its inevitable corruptions, seemed to explain his profligacy, but, since it did not justify it to his higher nature, he finally abandoned the doctrine. Although he was a successful teacher and orator, he was keeping a mistress, and he was torn between devotion to his son, shame before his mother, and yet an unwillingness to heed her appeals to enter the narrow path of godly living. In this confusion of spirit, he moved to Rome where he continued his career.

Meanwhile, greater minds than Cicero were leading Augustine toward higher standards of thought and action. He read Plato and Plotinus. Plato's *Dialogues* turned him from the skepticism of the later Platonists, to which he had inclined for a time. Plotinus centered his thought upon the single creative source of all being and the spiritual direction of all things by God. In Milan, where he had accepted a position as city orator, he gradually came

---

[21] St. Augustine, *Soliloquies*, I:7, in W. J. Oates (ed.), *The Basic Writings of St. Augustine*, New York, Random House, 1948, p. 262.

under the influence of Bishop Ambrose, who, like himself, was a master of classical culture but unwavering in his Christian devotion. Ambrose guided him through, but also beyond, Plato and Plotinus to Christ.

Augustine's conversion in 386, described unforgettably in his *Confessions*, decided all his future life. His mother died in peace, her prayers for her son finally answered. For almost forty-five years, he served the Church as a presbyter, and later, as Bishop of Hippo in North Africa; but he made Christian history by his writings on systematic theology and philosophy. In this field he has been ranked as one of the great pillars of Roman Catholic orthodoxy; his rank in Patristic philosophy is as that of St. Thomas Aquinas in Scholasticism.

As might be surmised, a great deal of his work was controversial. His own soul had been torn by error and dissension, and, in the intensity of his new faith, he undertook to refute dangerous heresies in the Church, some of them partly ecclesiastic, like Donatism, but others vitally involving the Christian view of God, the world, and the Christian life, such as Manicheanism and Pelagianism. His own spirit, intense in advocacy and in opposition, responded in turn to contending alternatives in Christian conviction which he could not reconcile, and which have repeatedly stirred controversy in Christian thought, both Catholic and Protestant.

God, the Soul, and the World

Augustine's conversion to Christianity was a conversion of his mind from skepticism to complete certainty. His theory of knowledge and his theology sustained each other. The definite distinction between theology and philosophy is not recognized by him; neither Tertullian's opposition of the two nor the Christian synthesis of them, which had been contemplated by Clement of Alexandria, and which was later undertaken by St. Thomas Aquinas in the thirteenth century. For St. Augustine, true philosophy was the Christian truth. Christian truth demands faith, but not the abrogation of reason. One must believe in order to understand, but understanding deepens and strengthens the foundations of belief. Belief and understanding, first and last, are centered in God. Science—knowledge of nature—may lead us to recognize the Author of nature, otherwise it is idle and misleading. True knowledge must guide us to wisdom, and true wisdom is piety.

St. Augustine distinguished intelligence from sensible perception. The latter has at least subjective certainty. Probability itself, and even doubt or self-deception, are evidences of our own indubitable recognition of ourselves. "If I err, I am."[22] I may doubt whether I move, but not that I think or that I am. (We shall note that a similar immediate conviction inaugurated systematic modern rationalism with Descartes.) From our knowledge of

[22] Translated from St. Augustine, *The City of God*, XI:26.

sense experience, we may rise to an understanding of universal principles; and the self-understanding of the mind may also lead us to true insight and to God.

The supreme reality of God is more evident to St. Augustine than the objective existence of anything in the world. The intelligent design of nature reveals its divine Author. Our own recognition of the right bespeaks the perfect Exemplar of all rectitude. In all the change and imperfection of our thinking, our intelligence reaches toward the unchanging infinite truth. St. Augustine's conviction is still deeper. Not only does our reflection lead us to the certitude of God's reality; it is through God's illumination of our mind and heart that we are enabled to contemplate His reality and perfection. St. Paul had urged his converts: "Work out your own salvation with fear and trembling; for it is God who worketh in you both to will and to work."[23] Even so, for St. Augustine, the source and the ground of our primary and ultimate knowledge of the truth is in God's self-revelation to us. Without God, our rational activity and moral endeavor would lose their final significance.

The nature and the attributes of God were repeatedly expounded by the great theologian. Prerequisite to all theological exposition was the admission of its ultimate inadequacy. Like Plotinus and Clement of Alexandria, St. Augustine recognized that God is ineffable. Pious confession of our incapacity to grasp Him adequately is better than any formal definition. But our reason cannot renounce its goal even though it may not reach it. First and foremost, St. Augustine unreservedly rejected his earlier Manichean heresy of dualism. God is the one ultimate creative power. No being—matter or spirit—is coeternal or coordinate with God. Whatever problems in cosmology and theodicy this first principle may involve, they cannot be solved or avoided by an initial ruinous error. God is the one—eternal and perfect, infinite in power, wisdom, and goodness. He is unqualified Reality, creative Source and Author of all.

The doctrine of the Trinity was upheld by St. Augustine as a confession of Christian faith, but he also sought to clarify it by philosophical exposition. The analogies he uses do not always suit his intention. God, he declared, is triune, but not triple. God is not a universal class of three persons; but neither is God one person with three phases, as held by Modalism. Yet St. Augustine himself distinguished the persons of the Trinity as comparable to the being, knowledge, and will or love in our nature.

In considering God's relation to the world, St. Augustine rejected not only Manichean dualism, but also pantheism and the emanation doctrine of Plotinus. If God *is* nature, what would you understand by either perfection or imperfection, or by moral judgment? If you regard the soul and the world as manifestations coeternal with God—as being of the divine essence —how can you explain their corruption? So he was led conclusively to creationism, the true doctrine of the Church. The Creator is not merely a

[23] Philippians 2:12, 13 (American Standard Version).

world craftsman, but is its absolute Author. The world is created by God out of nothing, and the created world exists only by the divine fiat; unless God sustained it, it would perish. The creation is continuous creation.

In denying the eternity of the created world, St. Augustine was involved in the problem of a creation in time. Was there a change in God's will when He decided to create the world, and what was God's activity before He began His creation? According to St. Augustine, these ideas wrongly import finite temporal distinctions into our conception of God. He maintained that time itself was created; it has no reality apart from created existence. Past and future have no meaning in the timeless eternity of the divine. Before God created the world, there could not be any "before." Once more, this does not mean that the world is eternal, nor yet that it had a beginning in time. The world is *in* time, and time is *of* the world; but God is eternally timeless, beyond any temporal perspective.

St. Augustine regarded the soul as immaterial, but as acting in and through the body. Just how the union of the two is achieved was not expressed clearly. The soul animates and directs the body. Beyond the animal faculties, we have rational power; the animals have sensations, but not understanding. In his account of the distinctively human capacity of intelligence, St. Augustine emphasized especially the will. In his treatment of the problem of free will, he was involved in a balancing of judgment that was not due to mere theological tactics, but rather to his conception of the Christian religion which he was expounding, and which determined his whole philosophical position. Without free will divine punishment and reward would both be unjust. Therefore, God must have given man free will, and he must have given it to man for acting rightly. But this freedom of will, as it is ours by the gift of God, so its holy expression in the godly life is by divine grace. Left to our own devices, we misuse our freedom and drift into sin. This interpretation of free will is evidently involved in St. Augustine's treatment of the problem of evil, to which we shall turn directly.

Regarding the soul's origin, St. Augustine's thought was not settled definitely between alternative theories. He could not accept the Platonic doctrine of preexistence, and he did not wholly abandon the view that each soul is specifically created; he leaned somewhat toward traducianism, that all souls since Adam have been transmitted from parent to child. On the subject of the soul's destiny, however, there could be no hesitation. St. Augustine rejected any belief in transmigration and firmly maintained personal immortality. The principles of reason are imperishable; how could we believe that the rational soul is ever extinguished? The soul is immortal, for the truth and the other perfections and values that dwell in it are beyond the touch of death. Other arguments, some of them recalling Plato, proceed to the same conclusion. It should be noted that, for St. Augustine, the doctrine of immortality was not mainly a chapter in psychology or cosmology. He was concerned with the soul's destiny under divine providence, under God's justice and grace in Christ.

The Problem of Evil: Sin and Salvation

The Christian religion that St. Augustine expounded and championed is a religion of salvation. Apostles and theologians were dominated by a conviction of sin, spiritual indigence, and by a burning hope of redemption, of spiritual abundance by the grace of God in Christ. These two motives in the Christian experience demanded a mediation that would recognize both without espousing either. Such a mediation should not, in misguided self-reliance, lose sight of man's woeful sinfulness, nor should it interpret sin as a depravity in creation itself that taints the perfection of the Creator, nor as evidence of any ultimate dualism of good and evil powers in the universe.

All of these errors found their heretical votaries in the early Church. There were theologians of sturdy Stoic will, who interpreted Christian saintliness as man's active emulation of the Lord's perfection by rational insight and moral resolution. There were Gnostics of various stripes who regarded God's creation of the material world and of all carnal existence as a tragic self-degradation staining the perfection of the Creator. There were the Manichean dualists who in some ways inherited the Gnostic platform, and who ascribed the evil and corruption of the material world to a dark ultimate power throughout existence that contested the creative power and the sovereignty of God. St. Augustine faced the main issue between the conviction of essential corruption that compromised the Creator's infinite perfection or His omnipotence, and the placid, or resolute, self-reliance of the moral will. Between these two opposite heresies, he sought the middle path of orthodox Christian theodicy.

His first task was to confute the Manichean heresy which had enslaved him for almost a decade. Manicheanism represented the third wave of dualistic teaching which had swept out of Persia, home of the Zoroastrian religion of Ahura Mazda and Ahriman, contending creators of good and evil. Gnosticism was the first heresy and rival of Christianity which was influenced by Zoroastrian dualism. The second was Mithraism, a form of solar worship, a martial religion of the warriors of light fighting with the powers of darkness, which appealed especially to the soldiers in the Roman legions and which was spread by them from camp to camp throughout the Empire. As it gradually lost power during the fourth century, Manicheanism became for a time its residuary legatee.

This new faith of Mani, the Persian, combined the Zoroastrian dualism of good and evil with the Greek dualism of God and matter, adapting also some Biblical ideas. It declared that material existence is essentially corrupt and in conflict with spiritual deity, but it also described the struggle of good and evil in material terms, as between light and darkness. Adam was created not by God, but by Satan, in his own image. The dark, evil creator hid in his new creature some rays of divine light which he had stolen from heaven. But this made man's nature dual, and eventually contributed to his salvation. The godly life was conceived as ascetic suppression of carnal desires, but it was also described fantastically as lifelong labor to free the divine light which Satan was always stealing and imprisoning in the dark caverns of nature. While this new religion spread eastward toward India and Turkestan, in its westward advance it both resisted and sought to exploit Biblical ideas. It distinguished between a Jesus of darkness and a Jesus of light and truth and described its own founder as the Paraclete, the Holy Spirit or comforter promised in the Gospels. At its best, Manicheanism resisted sensuality, taught humble and loyal devotion to spiritual aims; at its worst it was a farrago of demonology and a mystery-mongering cult.

St. Augustine denounced the basic Manichean dualism as confused and pernicious. There can be no creative power in the world other than God. The sole Author of all nature and human nature is omnipotent, infinitely wise and good and perfect. Therefore, evil and sin cannot be imputed to God as essential blemishes in his work. Evil cannot be explained either as created by Satan nor as manifesting a fatal degradation in God's own nature; this latter would be an unthinkable blasphemy. Christian theodicy must deny the essential natural character of evil. Nothing in the world is evil in its proper nature, neither matter nor the flesh. St. Augustine held firm by God's reported approval of his creation in the Book of Genesis, "Behold, it was very good." All things are admirable in their own places, he said, excellent in their own natures, beautifully adjusted to the rest of creation, as it were to a commonwealth. "Even poisons, which are destructive when used injudiciously, become wholesome and medicinal when used in conformity with their qualities and design, [but on the other hand,] food, drink, and the light of the sun, are found to be hurtful when immoderately or unseasonably used."[24] Evil, then, can be only a deprivation of good, a misplacement or perversion.

This conception of evil was applied to morals and religion to describe the essential character of sin. The cause of wickedness is in the misdirected choice of our free will. The best statement of this conclusion is in *The City of God:*

When the will abandons the higher and turns to what is lower, it becomes evil—not because that is evil to which it turns, but because the turning itself is perverse. . . . For its defections are not to evil things, but are themselves evil; that is to say, are not towards things that are naturally and in themselves evil, but the defection of the will is evil, because it is contrary to the order of nature, and an abandonment of that which has supreme being for that which has less.[25]

The swinish life that was natural and appropriate for the swine was sinful for the prodigal son, and his repentance came when he turned upward, from

[24] St. Augustine, *The City of God*, XI:22 (trans. M. Dods), Edinburgh, Clark, 1872, Vol. I, p. 462.
[25] Revised from *ibid.*, XII:6, pp 488 f.

the pigsty to his father's house. Even "he who inordinately loves the good which any nature possesses, even though he obtain it, himself becomes evil in the good, and wretched because deprived of a greater good."[26]

While he thus vindicated God's creation from Manichean detractions, St. Augustine saw Christian truth threatened from the opposite side by the Pelagian heresy. Pelagius, a British monk of moral resolution, had denounced the loose living of churchmen who confessed their sinful helplessness and hoped for the gift of grace. God has given us all the power to choose the right, so He holds us responsible for our choice. Pelagianism rejected the doctrine of man's original taint and depravity as children of Adam. We have the moral capacity to turn from Adam's path of sin to the blessed path of Christ. In its more emphatic statements this doctrine savored of "Stoic pride" unseemly in a Christian, and St. Augustine branded it as false in ignoring the sinner's woeful helplessness and the solemnity of God's grace in Christ. If we could save ourselves, what need was there of the Savior? St. Augustine found evil in the perverse choice of man's will. But why should the will choose perversely, why was its first choice in Eden the choice of sin? Augustine reasoned that God had allowed Adam the possibility of choosing either good or evil, thus respecting his moral freedom and dignity. God did not compel Adam's choice, but, in His omniscience, He knew that it would be evil, and His justice foreordained the penalty for that evil choice. In Adam's guilt, all mankind was lost, and it can be saved only by God's loving grace through Christ.

St. Augustine regarded sinful man as without merit and without capacity for salvation. God's grace is a free gift, but whether to all or only to some was not definitely stated. Only some receive it, and not by their own endeavor but by God's grace. This theodicy has stirred constant controversy. The doctrine of free will seems to be affirmed here, to fix responsibility for Adam's evil choice on him and not on God; but free will is virtually denied to the rest of us, to show our own incapacity to choose the good without God's gift of grace. Augustine might reply that, by his evil choice, Adam lost his ability not to sin; so we children of Adam can choose, but only evil; only the saint's holy will, blessed by God's grace, has the perfect freedom to choose only the good, has the inability to sin. For perfect freedom of will is freedom from evil, even as perfect intelligence, wisdom, is freedom from error.

But surely, it has been urged, Adam's choice revealed the character of his will; it was his free self-expression. Was God nowise concerned in, or responsible for, the sort of person He had created? And, if all men are tainted with the consequences of that evil choice, so that no one is capable of choosing the good without God's saving grace, how is the eternal punishment of the unsaved justifiable? Twelve centuries after St. Augustine, these issues were embroiling Protestant as well as Catholic theologians: Calvinists, Jesuits, Jansenists.

[26] *Ibid.*, XII:8, p. 491.

Christian Philosophy of History: the Earthly City and the City of God

Our study of St. Augustine should reveal his dramatic spirit in thought and in action. As we have said, his life and his philosophy turned on the momentous issue of the soul without God vs. the soul with God. Peace and blessedness for man lie only in the godly life. St. Augustine wrote on the first page of his *Confessions:* "Thou hast formed us for Thyself, and our hearts are restless till they find rest in Thee."[27] But most people are prodigal sons; the same tragic contrast is shown in the life of most peoples. The portrayal of this contrast is the theme of St. Augustine's philosophy of history.

The City of God is, in the first place, a defense of the Christian religion against the pagan charge that it had caused the collapse of imperial Rome. The Romans had not been abandoned or punished by their old gods because they had forsaken their idolatry. Their gods were the figments of their corrupt fancies, and their road was the road that led to destruction. St. Augustine saw in the Roman Empire the most stupendous edifice of man's worldliness, a monument of wrong purposes and principles which was destined for ultimate ruin. It was the greatest Earthly City, which men had built in their vain pride, but it was not the City of God, and therefore it could not prevail against it.

The contrast and contest of these two "Cities," or ways of life, according to St. Augustine, have been the central meaning of history. Men's lives are directed by the love that moves their wills:

Two cities have been formed by two loves: the earthly by the love of self, even to the contempt of God; the heavenly by the love of God, even to the contempt of self. . . . In the one, the princes and the nations it subdues are ruled by the love of ruling; in the other, the princes and the subjects serve one another in love.[28]

The Earthly City is inflated with pride; it aims at mastery and oppression; the peace which it seeks through victorious wars is not the peace of concord, but the peace according to its own will and dominion. Its freedom is license, uncontrolled indulgence of its lusts, greeds, and ambitions. Augustine surveyed the spreading corruption of the Earthly City in the course of history: in the kingdoms and proud empires of the East and, in its summit of majesty, the Roman peace, the *Pax Romana;* peace that was no peace without God.

[27] St. Augustine, *Confessions* (trans. E. B. Pusey), 1838; ed. of 1909, Everyman's Library, London, Dent, p. 1.
[28] *Ibid.*, XIV:28, Vol. II, p. 47.

Against this fortified power of evil in the world, the Earthly City, Augustine portrayed the City of God. He viewed this, also, in its outward manifestation during six historical periods, from Adam and Noah to the establishment of the Church and to its ultimate consummation, when Christ will be Lord of All. But St. Augustine saw more than a historical contrast of states and institutions; Jerusalem against Babylon, the Church against pagan Rome. In the historical life of humanity he disclosed the counteraction of two ways of life; the love of God and the life of the spirit resisting, and finally confuting, the pride and greed and lust of the world. His philosophy of history is also his social ethics, each conceived in a Christian perspective.

Even the Earthly City, though it springs from pride and greed, needs law and order if it is to operate at all. In this merely human justice and institutional regime, men submit themselves to law for the general protection of their interests. The godly men who live in the Earthly City are themselves truly citizens of the City of God. They are in the world, but not of the world. Yet, in the Earthly City, Christians are law-abiding residents. They "render unto Caesar the things which are Caesar's,"[29] though while rendering unto Caesar, they serve and love God above all.

Augustine passed Christian judgment on several social institutions. Thus, the true Christian is not possessed by greed for material goods, but he respects property rights as sanctioned by law and makes good use of his own. Though he lauded the priestly celibate's self-dedication to God, St. Augustine respected the virtues of family life as natural and blessed by God. Because a Christian does not seek his own advantage willfully, he never violates the rights of others and is thus the most law-abiding man in the Earthly City. But when a wicked king or government demands disloyalty to his own higher law, disobedience to God, he refuses, without violence but unflinchingly, be it even to martyrdom.

It may be seen how this antithesis of the two Cities could, and did, develop into the issue between State and Church, temporal and spiritual authority, civil and canon law. St. Augustine himself did not intend his *City of God* to be a charter of ecclesiastic prerogatives, but neither did he explicitly and firmly preclude such an interpretation. His higher thought and vision were a contemplation of the communion of saints, who—in all ages, and in whatever realm—have lived, not unto themselves, but in consecration to God. As is the saintly soul on earth, so will be its blessed consummation: "delivered from all ill, filled with all good, enjoying indefeasibly the delights of eternal joys, oblivious of sins, oblivious of sufferings, and yet not so oblivious of its deliverance as to be ungrateful to its Deliverer.[30]

We are told that the Pelagians regarded the portrayal of the world-wide contest between the Earthly City and the City of God as evidence that Augustine had not emancipated himself completely from the Manichean

---

[29] Matthew 22:21 (American Standard Version).
[30] St. Augustine, *The City of God*, XXII:30, *op. cit.*, Vol. II, p. 542.

dualism of his youth. We may perhaps reflect that Augustine's spiritual life was experienced dramatically, as a struggle. One could imagine what an intense Zoroastrian he might have been a thousand years earlier in Persia. Both his Manichean attachment and his vision of the City of God expressed his martial devotion, which endured in the dark wilderness of his groping as well as in the full light of his understanding.

SUGGESTED WORKS FOR FURTHER STUDY

HISTORICAL AND CRITICAL STUDIES OF MEDIEVAL PHILOSOPHY. Gilson, É., *The Spirit of Mediaeval Philosophy;* Taylor, H. O., *The Medieval Mind;* Turner, William, *History of Philosophy;* De Wulf, Maurice, *History of Medieval Philosophy.*

WORKS OF ST. AUGUSTINE. Oates, W. J. (ed.), *Basic Writings of St. Augustine.*

BIOGRAPHIES AND CRITICAL STUDIES OF ST. AUGUSTINE. Gilson, É., *The Christian Philosophy of St. Augustine;* Glover, T. R., *Life and Letters in the Fourth Century;* McCabe, Joseph, *St. Augustine and His Age.*

9. Erigena, St. Anselm, and Abelard: The Scholastic Problem of Universals

Four Centuries after St. Augustine: the Carolingian Revival of Learning

The title of this section may suggest the intellectual condition of Europe after the collapse of classical Rome. The whole of modern science and philosophy since Copernicus covers only four centuries. But the similar 400 years between St. Augustine and Erigena did not produce a single creative thinker, and, after Erigena, two more centuries elapsed before systematic philosophical activity again engaged European minds. We shall have occasion to note how unwarranted is the loose description of the entire medieval period as "the Dark Ages." We cannot call a civilization "dark" which produced Dante and the Gothic cathedrals and St. Thomas Aquinas. But there was intellectual and cultural darkness, or twilight, in Europe during several centuries in which the new Christian civilization was being established on the ruins of the Roman world and among the barbarians in the north.

The fall of Rome in 476 was followed by complete cultural disintegration. On the throne previously occupied by Caesar Augustus and Marcus Aurelius sat men who could not even sign their names. The Germanic hordes that overran and devastated the classical world had no schooling of their own, and it was long before they acquired even the rudiments of Latin learning. Literacy became the exceptional distinction of the clergy, a fact of which the expression "a clerical error" reminds us, for it was an error which only a cleric could make in an utterly illiterate society. Yet even the clergy did not often go beyond literacy; that is, the ability to read the missal at church services. More extensive learning was cloistered in the monasteries. The organization of monastic life by St. Benedict's Rule (529) tended to replace the earlier hermit austerities—which had been socially unproductive—by a regulated communal life of physical and mental labor. The monks copied manuscripts and wrote devotional works, commentaries, and chronicles. Men of exceptional mental competence shared the higher Church offices with ecclesiastical barons; hence, as the power of the Church grew, its theology did not altogether languish. But there were no more Patristic systems of Christian philosophy like those of Origen and St. Augustine.

Two or three lines would suffice to list the names of the few intellectual leaders during these four centuries of general ignorance, and these leaders were notable as the guardians of learning rather than as productive thinkers. They expounded the seven liberal arts—grammar, rhetoric, dialectic, arithmetic, astronomy, and music. Some of them combined Christian devotion with cultivation of classical learning, but others dismissed Greek and Latin erudition as idle frivolity.

Different is the case of Boethius (c. 480–524), who has been called the last Neoplatonist, or Aristotelian, and the first precursor of Scholasticism. A minister of state in Ostrogoth Italy, he was unjustly accused of treason and put to death, but while he was in prison, he wrote his best known work, *On the Consolation of Philosophy*, which King Alfred translated into Anglo-Saxon, which Chaucer and Queen Elizabeth later translated into English, and which Gibbon judged not unworthy of the leisure of Plato or Cicero. Philosophy appears to the imprisoned Boethius as a lady of noble dignity who consoles him in his sorrow by turning his mind from the loss of his worldly fortune to the true happiness of man, which happiness lies in God. The discussion takes up the problems of evil, free will, and divine foreknowledge.

He translated several of Aristotle's logical treatises, and wrote commentaries on them which later started the Scholastic dispute over the problem of universals, to be discussed later in this chapter.

Boethius was almost alone in his thinking, and those who could read him were few in his century and fewer in the next. But the eighth century—though it has been called the "darkest in French culture"—saw at its close a revival of learning under the leadership of Charlemagne. Charlemagne's palace school set the pattern for monastic and cathedral schools throughout his realm. He is said to have understood Greek and to have spoken Latin, but he could not write. He brought Irish and English masters to teach Frankish youth. Ireland had been spared barbarian devastations; priests and monks had preserved there Latin and Greek learning; the island was called the Lamp of the North. England also had a tradition of scholarship; Canterbury and York were famous for their learning, and the library at York was rich, not only in Patristic but also in classical works. The Irish and English teachers in France found pupils and patrons. Thus, learning was not altogether extinct in Europe, and it soon began to flourish. Though it died again, later, under the opposition of the bigots—the Carolingian revival of learning was a dawn not to be followed by a sunrise, and Europe was to sink back into mental torpor for two more centuries—this age of glimmering intelligence did produce one unique thinker of creative power and systematic grasp: Erigena, alone, was the redeemer of 600 years of philosophical stagnation.

John Scotus Erigena

Of somewhat uncertain origin, John Scotus Erigena (*c.* 800–*c.* 877) was known by many names—Scotigena, Ierugena, Eriugena—and has been described at once as an Englishman, as a Scot from Ayr, and as a Scot from Ireland. Most probably he was an Irish scholar. In good medieval Irish manner, he combined Greek with Irish learning, in which he exceeded all men of his time. His first definite appearance on the European scene was at the court of Charles the Bald, who appointed him director of his palace school. King Charles admired learning, and did not stand on his dignity with the Irish scholar. When, in a bibulous moment, he glanced one day across the royal table and asked, "What separates a Scot from a sot?" John Scotus answered without a quiver, "Only this table."

Erigena's renown for his vast learning spread over Europe, but his doctrines were soon suspected of heretical tendencies. At the request of Archbishop Hincmar, of Reims, he wrote a treatise, *Divine Predestination*. The Archbishop had expected it to be a refutation of the bitterly controversial doctrine of Gottschalk, who had taught that God's predestination is double, that some men are predestined to saintliness and eternal bliss, while others must go to sin and damnation (the orthodox view held that, while God has foreknowledge of the sinner's evil life and doom, His predestination is only of the godly men to good). The Archbishop had erred in his expectations, however.

Erigena plunged into his problem by philosophical analysis, for, in his judgment, religious truth could be reached only by true philosophy. Although we distinguish God's various attributes—His will and His wisdom, His justice and His love—we should not forget that they are ultimately transcended in the divine essence, which is one. God's predestination is, therefore, only one of our ways of regarding Deity. And, because God is infinitely perfect, we cannot believe that He wills the evil and ruin of men in any way whatever. Evil is really negation and non-Being; it is good misdirected. Not God's will, but the sinner's perverse choice leads to damnation. Archbishop Hincmar was shocked by this method of refuting Gottschalk's heresy, and Erigena's doctrine was condemned by two councils. Erigena aroused further criticism by his translation of Pseudo-Dionysius, a writer of the fifth century using the name of Dionysius the Areopagite, and expounding a Christian version of Neoplatonism, which enjoyed a certain occult fame. The Pope declared that a man like Erigena should not have been asked by Charles the Bald to translate them.

The philosophical fame—or notoriety—of John Scotus, and also his final condemnation by the Church, however, rested on his main treatise, *On the Division of Nature*. This is a philosophical theology and a system of metaphysics written in the form of dialogues between a master and his disciple. Erigena's dominant principle is theocentric: God is the one ultimate reality; all existence is a theophany, a manifestation of God; all existence in its final destiny refers and returns to God. Combining the words of St. Paul, "In him we live and move and have our being,"[1] with the Pseudo-Dionysian, Neoplatonic vision of God as outflowing into all possible being, Erigena contemplated all being as from God, in God, and to God.

His philosophical exposition spreads over two or three hundred thousand words, but its essence can be indicated in four sentences which distinguish four fundamental views of nature, or reality. Uncreated, creative nature is the absolute essence of deity, and transcends any thought or definition. Created, creative nature is the divine Logos—God expressed as the primordial causal principle in all existence. Created, uncreative nature is this, our world of bodies and souls, of manifold objects and processes. Uncreated, uncreative nature is deity again as the final destiny, the end and solution of all things.

Even while maintaining this fourfold distinction as the framework of his philosophy, Erigena set down, as a precondition of true philosophy, that one must recognize its limitations. Not deity itself, but our mind's approach to deity is thus fourfold. Deity is ultimately ineffable. Erigena's first aspect of nature really expresses this basic recognition, that deity transcends any cognition. His philosophical theology is both affirmative and negative. In true Christian doctrine we can ascribe to God the various attributes of perfection —infinite power, wisdom, justice, and love. But even as we thus contemplate God's infinitude, we realize that God transcends all these attributes of our contemplation. Without wholly rejecting our affirmations, we also negate them. Our thought of deity demands expression, but also acknowledges its limitations. God is the source, ground, and destiny of all being, but being cannot ultimately be ascribed to deity; God transcends being, and is "superessential." So the Apostle writes of "the peace of God, which passeth all understanding."[2]

While we should always remember that the uncreated creator of all is beyond the categories of our thought, we must move toward this unattainable truth of God, and not away from it. This right direction of thought is true philosophy. Misguided reflection may confuse the reality of nature with the random changes and objects of the world of sense. But truer insight reveals to us that the highest creative manifestation of deity is the divine Logos. Erigena's metaphysics thus recalls the Neoplatonic. Reality is most truly recognized by our mind as a system of infinite, rational essences and principles. This system constitutes the conceivable nature of true reality as rational, eternal, and perfect. Just as Plato declared that the highest Idea of Reality is the Idea of Good, Erigena maintained that only good has

[1] Acts 17:28 (American Standard Version).
[2] Philippians 4:7 (American Standard Version).

ultimate Being. The Augustinian account of evil as misdirection of will or deprivation of good—which had guided Erigena's refutation of Gottschalk —was reaffirmed in the metaphysics of Erigena, which denied the ultimate reality of evil.

The third aspect of reality is created, uncreative nature, or the world of finite existence operating in space and time. Thus manifested, the primal divine unity is disclosed as a multiplicity of particular bodies and minds. Here we may distinguish the lower from the higher creatures, as more or less unlike the infinite perfection which each of them in its manner adumbrates. The radii of a circle are all united at the center but stretch away from each other as they move outwards. As our thought moves Godward, we also may proceed beyond the surface variety of particulars to the rational perception of the universal principles and laws which comprehend them, and to the supreme contemplation of their ultimate unity in God.

In uncreated, uncreative nature the world returns to its source, the manifestation moves to its eternal original. This is deity as the ultimate destiny of all Being. Thus the infinite circle is completed. Even as Christ's promise to draw all men unto himself—or as the sublime vision of the saints of the blessed consummation when God will be all in all—so is Erigena's contemplation of the cosmic climax in the *adunatio*, the universal divine restoration.

Viewed in different perspectives, the fourth aspect of nature expresses the culmination of this philosophy, but also exposes some difficult problems in it. Erigena regarded it metaphysically as the final reaffirmation of reality, which is one, universal, and infinite through the absorption and transcendence of all finite multiplicity and individuality: no more of this and that, of thee and me. In terms of cognitive experience, the culmination is mystical in tone, pointing beyond the sense experience of particular data, and also beyond the universal principles, or Ideas of rational analysis, beyond all definition, in the ecstatic contemplation of the union of all in the absolute One.

The moral-religious implications of Erigena's *adunatio* were disturbing to orthodoxy. He revived in it the vision of universal salvation which had been entertained in the third century by Origen, the fellow student of Plotinus. Evil, as Erigena had already argued, is a deprivation of reality, and it can have no final status in and for God. Erigena, like Origen, believed in the universal salvation of all misdirected sinful wills, and also of the fallen angels. Yet the propriety of the term *salvation* in Erigena's doctrine is questionable. The universal restoration is the absorption of all finite beings into the undifferentiated, infinite perfection. Furthermore, the metaphysical reduction of evil to mere perverse or misdirected finitude has grave implications in morals. If evil is not evil to God, not really and finally, will the moral struggle itself be ultimately viewed as indifferent to deity? Is our arduous moral good, good for God?

Some of the problems in which Erigena was implicated resulted from his Neoplatonic endeavor to maintain both the immanence and the transcendence of deity. This aim is basically Christian, but a too radical pursuit of it, like any one-sided emphasis, is liable to turn heretical. *The Division of Nature* cannot be described offhand as pantheistic. God is the one true reality in us all, but all our conceivable reality is still short of deity. God courses, flows through all existence, yet ever abides as ultimate and absolute; only as we keep both of these truths together, can we grasp Erigena's full meaning. It is as truly God's nature to be manifested as it is to transcend all manifestation. Yet, for Erigena, the final restoration—oneness with God, *adunatio*—is final, the ultimate culmination, and not a climactic act in the eternal drama of cyclic recurrence. Absolute unity does, and will, finally prevail over finite distinctions; likewise will mystical insight prevail over rational analysis, and unqualified good over all specific evils. His emphasis is unmistakable.

Erigena's doctrines were repeatedly condemned, both in his lifetime, and in the thirteenth century, when *The Division of Nature* was denounced as "swarming with worms of heretical perversity,"[3] and still later, by Pope Gregory XIII during the Renaissance. But his influence persisted and can be noted in some important modern philosophies: in Bruno, Spinoza, and Hegel. Even Catholicism does not seem to have disowned him altogether. His works were included in Migne's *Patrologia Latina*. Erigena's intellectual stature in his age was incomparable; he impresses us as the great solitary of medieval philosophy, in which he rises, so it has been said, like a monument of art out of the sands of the wilderness.

The Growth of Scholasticism After the Tenth Century: The Problem of Universals

Order and the conditions of civilization were slowly developing. The spread of feudalism provided a degree of personal safety, and stabilized social relations. When the firm rule of Charlemagne disintegrated under his successors, the nobility who had acted for the emperor in their districts increasingly assumed authority in their own names. The peasantry—the common people—yielded free service to their lords in exchange for their protection; and the lord in turn was a vassal bound to his liege. Thus, land tenure, and security in the use of it, provided the basis for elaborate systems of obligations and loyalties.

The inner reforms in the social and economic life of western Europe under the feudal system were undertaken, especially by monastic leaders, notably by the Benedictine order of Cluny, founded in 910, which spread from its home in France, establishing several hundred monasteries throughout Europe. As has been pointed out, "Cluny moulded the moral sense of chivalry, trans-

[3] *Encyclopedia Britannica*, 11th ed., "Erigena," Cambridge, Cambridge Univ. Press, 1911, Vol. IX, p. 743.

formed its ideals, and introduced religion into its ceremonies."[4] This moral sense of chivalry perfected feudal sentiments regarding the value and dignity of the individual man, a man's rights and responsibilities in his own domain, his institutional loyalty, the honor of his word and name, and courtesy, charity, and hospitality. In the progressive realization of these ideals, medieval education gained recognition. Monastic life set an example for external reform and inner cultivation. By their Christian treatment of their own serfs, the Cluny monks showed the rude barons the meaning of justice and charity in daily personal relations. While the feudal life of the laity was thus being humanized, monastic reform undertook also to raise the standards of intelligence and personal conduct of the clergy. The spreading demand for purer living and higher thinking that had moved Cluny, characterized also the later Cistercians. The lofty ideals of the Franciscan and the Dominican orders, founded in 1210 and 1215, respectively, soon yielded to them the leadership of medieval intelligence and Christian principles.

Scholasticism, the philosophy of the medieval schoolmen and doctors, was, like Patristic thought, the work of theologians. But the difference between the two periods of medieval philosophy is important. The Patristic problem was the formation of orthodoxy; the Scholastic problem was the analysis of orthodox doctrine and its elaboration into a system of philosophical principles. Scholasticism built on a recognized basis of orthodoxy. Not even the genius of an Erigena could deviate from the strictly prescribed path with impunity. The schoolman began with the fundamental doctrines of Christian belief; he analyzed them so as to elicit their logical implications for various topics of philosophical interest. What is the sound and consistent Christian teaching about the grounds for our belief in God, the attributes of deity, God's relation to the world and to man, the nature of the soul, human reason and free will, the destiny of man? Considerable latitude of reflection and variety of argument would be expected in this process, but there was one indubitable test of the soundness of his thinking. The schoolman's final conclusions must sustain his initial orthodox premises, and must in no way question them.

Where analysis of ideas and systematic deduction played so important a role, it was natural that the theory of knowledge should take the form of a critical discussion regarding the status of universal ideas and principles. This, to be sure, is a problem which confronts any philosophy, or any persistent reflection. Our knowledge seems to be of two sorts. We know the particular objects of sense experience: this moving body, this concord of two sounds. But we also have intellectual knowledge of universal qualities and laws that transcend any specific particulars, for example, the laws of motion, the nature of harmony. So we are bound to ask, What is the character of these universal ideas? Is our knowledge of them a knowledge of realities? Or is it only our convenient, but also questionable, way of ordering our

[4] Maurice de Wulf, *Philosophy and Civilization in the Middle Ages,* Princeton, Princeton Univ. Press, 1922, p. 27.

sense data of particular objects, and are these objects the only realities? As soon as we ask these questions, the various answers to them in ancient philosophy come to mind, alternative theories of knowledge, or Sophistic and skeptical dismissals of them.

This was the so-called "problem of universals," central in Scholastic philosophy. Its direct introduction into medieval discussion was made by Boethius, who translated and wrote commentaries on Porphyry's *Introduction to Aristotle's Categories*, which was used in the schools as a textbook in logic. The logician speaks of "genus," "species," "differentia," "property," and "accident." Do these terms designate realities, or are they just five convenient words in the logician's operations? Porphyry had raised three questions: (1) Are these so-called "universals" realities, or are they only expressions of the bare intellect? (2) If they have reality outside of our understanding, are they corporeal or incorporeal? (3) Do they exist apart from the objects of sense perception, or do they exist in these objects and in accord with them?

But Porphyry had not answered these questions. Boethius proposed answers which tended to mediate between the sharp alternatives: universals are both subsistent realities *and* ideas. A universal, like "man," is incorporeal in abstract thought, but not in nature. Universals are manifested in the objects of sense experience and apart from them in thought. This mediating procedure and the vagueness of Boethius served to arouse a demand for a more definite and convincing solution of the problem.

Using our modern terminology, we may say that the sharp issue here is between *rationalism*, the philosophy of the analysis and systematic organization of universal principles, and *empiricism*, the philosophy of reliance on the particular impressions of sense experience. In Greek philosophy, this contrast was represented by Plato's distrust of sense impressions, by his theory of knowledge and reality as a system of universal Ideas—or rational principles, and by the Epicurean doctrine that our knowledge comes through our sense impressions of the real specific motions of particular masses of atoms in space. The philosophy of Aristotle represented a mediate position combining analytical with empirical-experimental methods. Aristotle agreed with Plato that real knowledge is rational knowledge of universals, but maintained that the particular data of sense perception provide the material which reason organizes into a system of knowledge. The universal law is a law of the particular data. These universal principles can be further elaborated systematically by theoretical analysis.

In the historical development of the Scholastic problem of universals, the ancient Greek alternatives were reenacted. The respective appraisal in each case was motivated by the special orientation of Scholastic philosophy, which was theological and not natural-scientific. The Scholastic theory of knowledge proceeded from a predominantly Platonic view toward an Aristotelian position. An early version of Epicurean empiricism was promptly rejected. The reliance on sense perceptions and specific experiments was to wait until the fourteenth century, when a revived interest in the direct observation of nature marked the decline of Scholasticism and the transition to modern science.

The earliest Scholastic theories of knowledge affirmed the reality of universals. This position is called "realism," a term which, in medieval thought, had the opposite meaning from our use of it. The Scholastic realist was one who maintained that universals are realities, *universalia sunt realia*. Realism of this sort was to be expected from theologians whose convictions concerned universal ideas, of which theology itself is an elaborate system. The early Scholastic realists also manifested strong Platonic, Neoplatonic, and Augustinian influences, all of them emphasizing the reality of universals above the particulars of sense experience and without any reliance on them. We shall note presently the systematic formulation of this Platonic realism by St. Anselm. An outstanding exaltation of the reality of universals has already been discussed in the philosophy of Erigena. Some critics of Erigena's heresies might defend his realism despite his use of it. Others would tend to question his theory of universals along with his universal theophany.

The Nominalism of Roscelin

The objections to realism were brought into sharp relief by the French schoolman, Roscelin (*c.* 1050–*c.* 1122). This canon of Compiègne maintained that only the particular objects of our sense experience really exist. Universals are simple ideas in the mind by which we designate the various qualities or groups of similar things. We derive universal ideas from our knowledge of particular things. Universals come after things, *post res.* Tart and sweet apples are each real, but "apple," "tartness," and "sweetness" are mere terms or labels used by the mind. Thus, the empiricist Roscelin concluded that universals are names—*universalia sunt nomina*—whence this view was called "nominalism."

This doctrine was bound to trip its theological advocate. Roscelin might urge that the universal "humanity" was only our name for all the really existing men, and likewise with the universals "acidity," "felicity." But what about the Trinity; is it only an idea in our mind, the name by which we refer to the three real persons or divine substances, Father, Son, and Holy Spirit? This and similar implications of blunt nominalism seemed abhorrent to the orthodox schoolmen, and must surely have been pointed out to Roscelin by his critics. To be sure, he could have retorted by citing the heresies implied in the extreme realism of Erigena. It was generally believed that Roscelin himself applied his nominalism to a heretical interpretation of the Trinity, but this has been doubted by some modern students. He was condemned by a Council at Soissons and forced to recant. The angry populace menaced the accused heretic's life, so Roscelin fled to England, but roused opposition there also. Later in his life he apparently made his peace with the Church and resumed public teaching, but did not gain repute for his doctrine.

St. Anselm of Canterbury: Platonic Realism and Orthodox Analysis

St. Anselm (*c.* 1033–1109) may be regarded as the first real master of Scholasticism. His works expressed its characteristic purposes, to distinguish and to relate Christian faith and orthodox understanding. His first and final reliance was on faith; but, although steadfast in his faith, he undertook to analyze his beliefs, to search out their grounds, and to give them the most convincing rational statement.

A member of the Italian nobility of Piedmont, his pious mother turned his thoughts toward the devout life. But she died during his youth, and his father's surly refusal to let him enter a monastery caused Anselm's flight from home. He traveled to France, and, after attending several schools, was attracted by the fame of Lanfranc of Pavia, becoming his pupil at the Abbey of Bec in Normandy. When Lanfranc left Bec, Anselm took charge of the school, and soon made it the most famous in Europe. He became abbot, and later succeeded Lanfranc as archbishop of Canterbury. His struggle with two Norman kings for the recognition of papal authority is a notable chapter in the ecclesiastical history of England.

On the problem of universals Anselm was a Platonic, or, as a critic would say, an extreme realist. He denounced the nominalism of Roscelin as unchristian and philosophically unsound. The nominalists were so preoccupied with the particular objects of sense impression that they could not recognize the universal character of reality. Even a person's own identity through life embraces a variety of individual manifestations; why should Roscelin fail to recognize that the three persons of the Trinity are one God? Thus Anselm maintained that universals are realities. Furthermore the particular only exemplifies the universal, which is really prior to it. The reality of human nature, of justice, is presupposed in the recognition of anyone as man or any act as just. So Anselm held that the reality of universals is prior to particular things, *ante res*. Universality for Anselm is the criterion of reality. The basic truth and rightness of all true and right things is one and the same; and the most real being is the most universal. The implications of this position for St. Anselm's theology were clear, and he pointed them out.

Like St. Augustine, whose writings influenced him deeply, Anselm centered his philosophy on God and on man's soul under divine providence. He undertook to explore thoroughly the rational grounds for the belief in God. Theologians have sought to prove God's existence by reasoning from the existence of particular things, or from their order and design. But Anselm characteristically preferred to reason from God to finite beings. He felt bound to recognize the ultimate universal before he could understand the character or the very existence of any particulars. Finite things point beyond themselves to the ground of their existence; their being can be recognized ultimately only in relation to the infinite, self-existent Being, God. Again, as all truth and rightness are ultimately one, so true goodness is one in all good things, supreme and sovereign perfection, God. We must recognize this infinite perfection as presupposed in all the degrees of finite perfection; without perfect deity, what would be the meaning of calling anything more or less perfect?

St. Anselm's emphatic realism is manifested especially in his ontological argument for God's existence, presented in his treatise, *Proslogium*. The reasoning proceeds in the form of an imaginary argument of the Psalmist with the fool who "hath said in his heart, there is no God."[5] How is the fool to be convinced of his folly? Surely he understands that one being may be judged to be greater than another, and a third as still greater. So he can and does entertain the idea of a being than which nothing greater can be conceived. This is what Anselm means by God, that God is the greatest conceivable Being. The fool understands the idea of this Being, but does not understand it to exist. Anselm therefore inquires: Can the greatest conceivable Being be regarded as not existing? By its very nonexistence it would fail to qualify as the greatest conceivable Being. Rigorous analysis demonstrates that the idea of the greatest Being conceivable is and must be the idea of an existent Being. And the idea of God is the idea of the greatest Being conceivable. Therefore, St. Anselm concluded, God exists. But the manifest conclusion from his premises is that the idea of God is the idea of an existent Being. The readiness with which Anselm proceeded from the one to the other conclusion is a striking expression of his realism. The idea which he judged to be logically irrefutable demonstrated to his mind its existential reality. "So truly, therefore, dost thou exist, O Lord, my God, that thou canst not be conceived not to exist; and rightly."[6]

This ontological argument was questioned by the monk, Gaunilo, in his book *In Behalf of the Fool* (*Pro insipiente*). If Anselm considers the idea of God in the mind to be, by definition, such that it cannot be conceived as not also existing in reality, then he assumes what he has to prove, and he has no real argument with the fool. But, if the idea of the greatest Being conceivable is to be analyzed on its merits, the attribute of existence is not necessarily deduced. Suppose that we conceive the most beautiful of all islands, does it follow that such an island exists? In his reply, Anselm reaffirmed his argument and expanded his analysis, which in its original statement had been very brief. Yet, a greater one than Gaunilo, St. Thomas Aquinas, also criticized Anselm's argument for passing by the logical analysis from the implication of an idea to its existential reality. This, as will be noted later, was essentially Kant's criticism of Anselm. Before Kant, the

[5] Psalms 14:1 (as quoted by St. Anselm).
[6] St. Anselm, *Proslogium* (trans. S. N. Deane), Chicago, Open Court, 1903, p. 9.

systematic rationalists, Descartes, Spinoza, and Leibniz, revived the ontological argument.

We are told that, late in life, St. Anselm contemplated a treatise on the origin of the soul, but died before he wrote it. In some of his writings, he seems to alternate between Augustinian traducianism—that all men's souls are propagated along with the body, initially from Adam—and the doctrine that each man's rational soul is individually provided by God. But he was more positive in his analysis of the soul's activities, and unwavering in his view of its destiny. The soul is spiritual; though bound to the body, it is meant to know and to love its Creator. Our knowledge is knowledge of the good and the evil, and our true wisdom is our will to choose and to pursue the best. In choosing the godly life, we must choose it for its own sake, for it is blessed. Yet the sinful will perversely yields to lower impulses and leads us astray. The will becomes evil when it turns from its true end, which is justice and righteousness, when it deserts and loses a great thing and, instead, prefers something unworthy. Therein lies its ruin, for "the soul which despises the love of the supreme good will incur eternal misery."[7] Every human soul is destined by God to immortality, an eternity either of saintly bliss with God or of damnation.

In his reflections on the will's turning to good or to evil, and on sin and salvation, St. Anselm showed the influence of St. Augustine and faced some of his issues. The problem of free will engaged both thinkers. Anselm rejected the definition of freedom as ability to sin or not to sin. Neither God nor the blessed angels can sin, and by his inclination to do evil, man can enslave himself to sin and not be able to express and achieve his freedom. Freedom lies in the ability to realize our true end, to will as we ought, to pursue righteousness. Free will is given us by God to afford us this self-expression of our soul that our will may be genuinely upright. We are thus morally responsible for what we will.

But this upright will is God's gift, and it is a fact of moral experience that men lose their rectitude. If it is lost, St. Anselm declared, we cannot recover it by ourselves. Have we then lost our free will? Sin may be a corruption of our freedom, but is it the extinction of our will's capacity to choose? St. Anselm's treatment of this problem was more theological than philosophical. He was thinking throughout in the Christian perspective of sin and divine grace. He did not believe in man's utter corruption. God grants men a certain capacity for righteousness, and they need his grace to bring this righteousness to fruition. But the will of countless men can on its own initiative refuse or abuse righteousness. How are we to explain this perversity of will in human nature? This remained a problem for Anselm as it did for Augustine.

[7] *Ibid.*, p. 137.

Peter Abelard: Critical Scholasticism

The Platonic realism of St. Anselm prevailed against extreme nominalism, but the Platonic emphasis on the reality of universals was carried to untenable extremes by William of Champeaux (1070–1121). Between the rejection and the exaggeration of rational knowledge, critical reflection sought a more acceptable doctrine. This criticism was undertaken by Peter Abelard (1079–1142). William and Abelard had both been students of Roscelin and had turned against him, but in different directions. William gained fame rapidly as a master of Scholastic wisdom. At the age of 33, he was professor at the cathedral school of Notre Dame in Paris; ten years later he was made Bishop of Châlons. His faithful disciples hailed him as "the pillar of doctors."

Among the specific doctrines of William of Champeaux, his account of the soul's origin may be mentioned. He rejected traducianism and maintained that each soul is created by God. This creationist psychology was to be revived by the great schoolmen of the thirteenth century in their adaptation of Aristotelianism to the needs of Catholic orthodoxy.

William's great renown was gained in his treatment of the problem of universals. On this issue Abelard contested, and finally discredited, his authority. William's position was one of very exaggerated realism; he went far beyond St. Anselm in reaffirming the reality of universals. He adopted the idea that the universal substance is real and identical in each individual member; thus, the essence of man, humanity, is identically present in each man. What is truly real in Socrates is the same as what is truly real in Plato.

Peter Abelard, a Breton of noble descent who had renounced a military career and had left his father's castle to pursue Scholastic wisdom, came from Roscelin's classroom to that of William at Notre Dame when he was not quite twenty. By nature a contentious man, he soon found himself even more vigorously opposed to William's exaggerated realism than he had been to the nominalism of Roscelin. William's doctrine impressed him as absurd in its implications, which he did not tarry to elicit in open dispute with his master. If the universal humanity is wholly and essentially present in each man, it must always be wherever Socrates is, and also wherever Plato is; how, then, could the real Socrates and the real Plato ever be apart? If we are to believe Master William, though it may seem that he is lecturing from his pulpit and I, Abelard, am humbly seated among his pupils, yet, in reality, he is always in my place and I in his. Abelard was resolved to make such a transposition of the two of them an actual fact. The shafts of his dialectic shook the pillar of doctors and eventually forced William down. He modified his doctrine, only to have it discredited once more by Abelard. The universal, as William explained, is in the individual, not wholly and essentially, but "indifferently" as to the reality of particular things. Beyond their specific individual differences, all individual members share in a common universal essence.

Abelard's own solution of the problem of universals lay between the position of Roscelin and that of Anselm, and his dialectic revealed an Aristotelian direction. Though the body of Aristotle's works was not available to him, his keen mind discerned from the *Organon* the further implications of the Aristotelian criticism of Plato. He had rejected Roscelin's teaching that the universal is a mere name, a sound of man's voice; and yet universals are words, words that are used to signify things. Universals are not wholly and essentially real in any one individual; nor are they really existent apart from the individuals they signify. Their reality is exemplified in the individuals whose nature they express. Apart from the individuals of which they are predicated, the universals are concepts. Thus Abelard sought a mediating truth between the two errors which he resisted. Universals are realities, but their reality is manifested in individual existent things, as humanity is in Socrates and Plato. The same holds true with universals expressing character or condition. We can imagine Abelard arguing in the lecture hall of Notre Dame that surely dullness is a reality, but it does not walk by itself; it abides in the minds of Master William and his ilk. While thus real in the dullards, dullness is a concept in the minds of the rest of us.

This position of conceptualism may have been nearer Roscelin's than William's, yet the doctrine of Abelard preserved an important element of realism. He affirmed the reality of the universals of reason as signifying the nature which the existing individuals share and by which their essential character is known. This essential character of universals is eternally known to God's mind, prior to the existence of particular things, but our minds are led from the perception of individuals to the understanding of universals. Abelard thus approached, though he did not develop fully, the moderate realism of the later thirteenth century Aristotelians.

Abelard's career in the schools of the twelfth century was unparalleled. After breaking with William of Champeaux, he started his own school, first at Melun, then nearer Paris at Corbeil, and eventually in Paris, where for a while his classes at Sainte Genevieve gained great renown. Before long, he was lecturing from William's old pulpit at Notre Dame. His success was astounding. His logical mastery in analysis and criticism seemed irresistible; his irony pierced through solemn arguments to expose their shabby texture. His eloquence has been described as sublime; it commanded the treasures of Latin literature, and, in particular, it owed its power to his creative imagination that could charge abstract discussions with dynamic human appeal. Alongside William, he was as a wasp to a buffalo. Cleric and laity, plain and noble vied in crowding his lectures. His thousands of pupils at one course of lectures are reckoned to have included a future pope, nineteen cardinals, and over fifty bishops or archbishops.

His brilliant lectures won him admirers and disciples, and also opponents. His devotion to orthodox theology was genuine but his treatment of theologians could be as harsh as the strategy of his dialectic required. With renowned use of *sic et non* (yes and no), in dealing with any doctrine or problem, he reviewed the conflicting positions of theological authorities and induced his students and readers to undertake a critical judgment. This method was stimulating to active minds, but it led to the disturbing inference that Christian truth was like pagan philosophy, variously formulated and variously subject to criticism and revision. It was this intellectual reliance on a logic ever in process which turned the leaders of orthodoxy against him and led to his condemnation by the Church. Even if, with his eloquence, he could persuade them that he was sincerely seeking Christian truth, they could not pardon him for pursuing it along pagan paths.

Abelard's method of critical reconstruction may be seen in his treatment of several important problems. Two examples will illustrate this method and the genuinely constructive spirit and orthodox aim in his critical dialectic. In his treatise *Ethics, or Know Thyself* he undertook an analysis of the nature of sin. A man's sin is not merely human infirmity—the natural inclination to evil—but the consent of his own will to it. Sin lies essentially in wrong motive; it is in the will's expressed contempt for God. The evil action to which this contempt leads is the external result of the sin rather than the sin itself. Abelard thus centered the moral career of man, Christian godliness, in the activity of conscience. The decisive thing for each man is to will and to choose rightly. Saintliness is not motivated by a longing for the blessings of Paradise, nor by horror of God's punitive justice, but is found in the utter harmony of our will with the divine; "Thy will be done." Abelard thus anticipated Kant's ethics of duty and the upright will.

Our second example illustrates Abelard's critical method in theology. In his reinterpretation of the Doctrine of the Atonement, he disagreed with both St. Augustine and St. Anselm, and developed the idea attributed to St. John, which had been advocated by Origen. How did Christ's death atone for our sins? St. Augustine, following some Pauline ideas, held that Adam's original sin put all children of Adam in the power of Satan. But by causing the death of the sinless Son of God, over whom he had no claim, Satan forfeited his hold on men; thus are we ransomed by Christ's death. St. Anselm rejected the idea that Satan had any claims on men which God recognized. In place of the ransom doctrine, Anselm maintained that Adam's original sin, which stained us all, was a violation of God's eternal justice that demanded satisfaction. Men could not possibly satisfy this demand of justice; their utmost righteousness would only be, as it were, their current obligation to God and could nowise expiate the original guilt. Man's salvation was possible only if sinless God-become-Man could satisfy God's justice. Thus, God's love through Christ's death atones for man in his utter need. This explanation was on a higher moral plane than the ransom doctrine, but it still proceeded on the legalistic principle of substitutionary expiation.

In distinction from both of these doctrines, Abelard interpreted Christ's atonement as a manifestation of God's infinite love, a love unto death, which redeems us by arousing us to love of God. Before the divine grace that shines from the Cross, we are literally born anew, roused to genuine devotion, illumined to see the true way, and strengthened and resolved to pursue it.

In philosophy, as in theology, Abelard was marked by critical rationalism. The Scholastic "faith seeking to understand" found in him a vigorous intellectual expression. Careful readers of his works have failed to find in them the explicit statement "I understand so that I may believe (*Intelligo ut credam*)."[8] But, in dealing with any problem, his mind was always bent on critical understanding. This aggressive rationalism won him wide renown, but also led to his condemnation by the Church. It was natural that he should be opposed by William of Champeaux, whom he had ridiculed and discredited publicly. But the implacable, and finally crushing, antagonism of St. Bernard of Clairvaux (1091–1153) was not personal. It sprang from a radically opposite view of Christian truth and life. St. Bernard demanded the dominance of unquestioning faith, for he relied not on logic and valid reasons, but on the soul's direct communion with God in mystical ecstasy. The mysticism of St. Bernard cannot be dismissed with a brief remark here; it will be considered in Chapter 11. But Bernard, a mystical opponent of Abelard's rationalism, was also an astute and powerful ecclesiastical statesman against whom Abelard's dialectic proved ineffective, at the Church council and at the Vatican.

In the long run, however, despite Bernard's victory, Abelard's principles were the ones that prevailed in philosophy, and, to some degree, in theology also. The Church canonized Bernard, but systematic Scholasticism, without honoring Abelard, used and developed his dialectical procedure. The success of critical Scholasticism required champions whose personal Christian character was above reproach and whose spirit and attitude had more convincing orthodox piety. Among the leaders the thirteenth century produced, the chief was St. Thomas Aquinas.

One long chapter of Abelard's life, that can only be mentioned here, is recounted in his *History of Calamities:* his love for the young and brilliant Heloïse, and its dire course, which was disastrous for them both. Their famous letters, written many years later, reveal a tragic devotion, the ardor of which is still glowing under the ashes of long monastic repression.

SUGGESTED WORKS FOR FURTHER STUDY

STUDIES OF ERIGENA. Bett, Henry, *Johannes Scotus Erigena;* Gardner, Alice, *Studies in John the Scot (Erigena).*

WORKS BY ST. ANSELM. St. Anselm, *Proslogium, Monologium and Cur Deus Homo* (trans. S. N. Deane).

[8] Quoted in J. G. Sikes, *Peter Abailard*, Cambridge, Cambridge Univ. Press, 1922, p. 31.

BIOGRAPHIES AND CRITICAL STUDIES OF ST. ANSELM.   Church, R. W., *Saint Anselm;* Rigg, J. M., *St. Anselm of Canterbury.*

WORKS BY ABELARD.   Abelard, *Ethics* (trans. J. R. McCallum).

BIOGRAPHIES AND CRITICAL STUDIES OF ABELARD.   Compayré, G., *Abelard and the Origin and Early Histories of Universities;* McCabe, Joseph, *Peter Abélard;* Sikes, J. G., *Peter Abailard.*

10. St. Thomas Aquinas: Christian Aristotelianism

The Arabian and the Jewish Aristotelians

The branching development of the problem of universals manifested Scholastic emphasis on rationalism and a critical revision of it. The sharp condemnation of Roscelin's nominalism excluded any Epicurean or other empiricist theory of knowledge based on sense experience. The doctors of the Church pursued mainly rational analysis and exposition. The earlier direction of Scholasticism had been Augustinian-Platonic. It sometimes took a Neoplatonic turn and manifested suspected pantheistic leanings, as in Erigena, but, more authoritatively, as in St. Anselm, Scholasticism had expressed mainly a Platonic emphasis on the reality of universals. This emphasis was carried to excess, and so produced a critical reaction, notably by Abelard, toward an Aristotelian position.

The terms "Platonic" and "Aristotelian" should be used with caution here. The schoolmen whom we have considered so far had very limited knowledge of Plato's *Dialogues* and Aristotle's works; they knew Plato's *Timaeus* and parts of the *Organon*. The systematic achievements of the thirteenth-century doctors, to whom we are now turning, were made possible by the expansion of the Scholastic library of classical philosophers and chiefly by the translation and interpretation of Aristotle's writings. In this expanding work of the Catholic schoolmen, Jewish and Arabian philosophers served as intermediaries.

The medieval Odyssey of Aristotle, from Athens to Rome and Paris, is a stirring epic in the adventures of ideas. Caliph Omar is said to have burned the classical treasures of the Alexandrian library, but his successors soon became patrons of learning and zealous collectors of ancient manuscripts. Bagdad in the east and, later, Cordova in Moorish Spain were centers of classical erudition, interpretation, and systematic philosophy. The knowledge of Aristotle which Mohammedan scholarship was to give to the orthodox doctors of the Church was first brought to the Arabs in Bagdad by Christian heretics, the Nestorians of Syria. Banished from Constantinople during the

Monophysite controversy of the fifth century, these followers of Patriarch Nestorius had preserved Greek scholarship and had translated classical works into Syriac. During the eighth and ninth centuries, Syrian scholars filled the Bagdad libraries with Arabic translations of Greek philosophy, mathematics, medicine, and natural science, which were made either from their Syriac versions or directly from the originals.

Aristotle's works were known much more extensively than Plato's. Three or four centuries earlier than in the Christian West, Aristotle was read and interpreted by Arabian thinkers. These Arabic translations of his writings spread throughout the Mohammedan world, from Bagdad and Persia to Damascus, Alexandria, and Moorish Spain.

Even a brief statement will suggest the importance of this medieval Arabian revival of learning. As might be expected, rigid Mohammedan orthodoxy imposed problems and limitations on these philosophers which were analogous to those of Catholic schoolmen. Unbending orthodox zealots in Islam were suspicious of any philosophical speculation. Dissidents and sectaries explored new religious directions. The "professors of the word" were confident that Koran orthodoxy could be expounded more convincingly by the logic of Greek rationalism. Mystics distrusted this alien reason and put their faith in intimate, ecstatic communion with Allah. The more systematic philosophers, while not breaking with Mohammed, concentrated in the main on Aristotle, but also took up Platonic and Neoplatonic ideas.

An early distinguished Arabian student of Aristotle was Alfarabi of Bagdad and, later, of Damascus—a tenth-century Aristotelian commentator who also knew Plato and who compared the two. He used Aristotle's cosmological argument to prove the existence of Allah. The fame of his treatises on Aristotle was widespread. Avicenna declared that he had read Aristotle's *Metaphysics* forty times, but still did not understand some things in it until they were explained to him in Alfarabi's commentary.

AVICENNA, OR IBN-SINA

Avicenna (980–1037), the greatest of Arabian philosophers in the East, was renowned also for his medical and scientific knowledge. In Bokhara and Khiva, and later in Persia, his fame as a physician and a philosopher was unrivaled, and it soon spread to the Christian world. About one hundred works were ascribed to him, and for five centuries his treatises were authoritative in European medical schools. His philosophy followed Aristotelianism closely, yet retained some Neoplatonic elements. According to Avicenna, God—the supreme intelligence and perfection—generates the active reason, which then manifests itself as a soul, and the soul in turn manifests itself as a material body. Avicenna reinterpreted Aristotle's psychology so as to reach the requisite Mohammedan proof of immortality.

Of special interest is Avicenna's solution of the problem of universals. During his youth in Bokhara, he had read the *Isagoge* of Porphyry, and, like the Christian schoolmen who studied Boethius' translation of that work, had pondered on the nature of universal ideas. His own position, influenced by Alfarabi, developed into an Aristotelian moderate realism similar to that developed later by the Scholastic doctors. In nature, universal ideas are immanent in particular things, through which they express their essence. The idea of "humanity" is manifested in men and expresses their nature. This universal essence, or nature, of men is conceived by man's intellect through abstraction from a number of perceived human beings. But all universals are eternally real in the infinite mind of God, contemplated before the existence of any particular things, even as an artist contemplates the idea of his work before he creates it.

AVERROËS, OR IBN ROSHD

The list of centers of learning mentioned here will suggest the wide spread of philosophical and scientific culture in the Mohammedan Middle East, from Alexandria to Bagdad, to Khiva and Bokhara. It reminds us of the extensive diffusion of Stoic teaching in the Hellenistic age. This Arabian wave of learning rolled westward; during the twelfth century, Moorish Spain witnessed a revival of classical learning in which Mohammedans and Jews, and later, Christians cooperated. Toledo, Seville, and especially, Cordova became centers of philosophical and scientific-medical inquiry. The lesser minds would attract more notice if they were not eclipsed by two outstanding men, an Arab and a Jew.

The greatest Arabian philosopher was Averroës of Cordova (1126–1198). His fame as an Aristotelian commentator surpassed even Avicenna's. Dante put these two among the illustrious pagans in Limbo, with Socrates, Plato, Euclid, and Ptolemy. Jewish scholars in Spain translated the work of Averroës into Hebrew and into Latin, and although Averroës' ideas proved objectionable to Mohammedan, Jewish, and Christian orthodoxy, his Aristotelian authority was paramount; for some time it contested that of St. Thomas, even in Christendom. Church doctors who denounced his infidelity continued to learn their Aristotle from his pages.

The great Arabian commentator regarded Aristotle as the fount of wisdom, but showed original thought of his own in his critical reinterpretation of the Greek master. His solution of the problem of universals was similar to Avicenna's moderate realism. He adopted and developed Aristotle's doctrine of Form and Matter; he maintained the eternity of matter, and regarded God's creative activity which forms the nature of things as operating through the celestial intelligences. He moderated, but did not exclude, the Neoplatonic tone of the earlier Arabian versions of Aristotle's cosmology. His philosophy intensified the antagonism of the zealots and mystics of the Koran who had charged him with heresy. These were partly responsible for his banishment to Morocco.

The critical originality of Averroës, and also the resistance he aroused in Islam and in Christendom, is seen more clearly by a discussion of his important doctrine of the nature and destiny of the soul. Immortality is a fundamental conviction in both Christianity and Mohammedanism, and Aristotle's psychology presented a crucial problem to his medieval commentators. In his interpretation, Averroës distinguished the active intellect from the nonrational faculties of the soul which men share with plants or with animals: nutritive, locomotive, appetitive, and sensitive. These all perish with the body. Any question of immortal destiny can only concern our rational intelligence. But whether such immortal destiny is yours or mine will depend on the character of reason, whether it is individual or universal.

Averroës held that reason is not individual, the form of an individual body. It deals with pure, eternal ideas, and it is itself immaterial and universal. Yet we individual men are rational because of our capacity for conceptual knowledge, which is our potential reason. This is only a disposition in us which is activated by the universal intellect. Shall we say, then, that the universal principle of rationality is actively manifested in the individual passive intellects of Socrates or Plato? If so, in each rational mind there would be a certain capacity for an immortal career beyond the decay of the body. Averroës seemed to have maintained the universality of the passive as well as of the active intellect. But, if rational intelligence is nowise individual, all human minds would seem to be one mind.

This Averroist doctrine of the eternal unity of the intellect aroused great controversy among medieval thinkers, and it still embroils modern expositors. The contending interpretations cover a wide range. Could Averroës possibly have denied the individuality of reasoning persons and retained his sanity? Did he not mean to emphasize the universality of rational principles and intelligent nature in which we all share? Surely he must have intended to maintain the universal perpetuity of humanity, of civilization. Perhaps his vague statement is due not to unclear thinking, but to caution, or else to compunction in his expression. His philosophical ambiguity saved him from rejecting, as an Aristotelian, belief in personal immortality, which, as a Mohammedan, he was bound to retain. Whatever his intended or logically available inferences may have been, Averroës was generally regarded and criticized by his medieval students as a denier of personal immortality. Humanity abides, but not the individual human mind. Against this doctrine—as a proposed statement of the truth and as an interpretation of Aristotle—St. Thomas Aquinas disputed with the Scholastic Averroists at the University of Paris. And, in his *Purgatorio*, Dante, while reserving a choice place in Limbo for Averroës, denounced his doctrine for its separation of the intellect from the soul.

MOSES MAIMONIDES

The philosophical importance of Philo's fusion of Jewish and Greek ideas, at the beginning of the Christian era, has already been noted. This fusion influenced the direction of Alexandrian, Hellenistic, and Christian thought. During the medieval revival of learning, Jewish scholars, physicians, and philosophers once more played a mediating role, especially in translating and transmitting the Arabian versions and interpretations of Aristotle for the use of the Christian schoolmen. Jewish learning flourished under Moorish tolerance in Spain. The Moorish caliphs used Jewish as well as Arabian physicians, and Jewish sages as their counsellors. Both Jewish and Arabian philosophers had to contend with the opposition of orthodox traditionalists, who were suspicious of all philosophy and science.

Moses Maimonides (1135–1204), the greatest of Jewish Aristotelians, was, like Averroës, a Cordovan; like Averroës also, he was the victim of religious antagonism, for the earlier Moorish era of tolerance had been replaced by a regime of bigotry. Moroccan zealots in Cordova offered Jew and Christian alike their choice of the Koran, exile, or death. After much wandering—including some perilous times in Morocco—Maimonides' family finally went to Egypt, where the future philosopher settled for life, enjoying the protection which Sultan Saladin offered to the persecuted Jews.

His major treatise, *Guide for the Perplexed*, which deals with problems of physics, metaphysics, cosmogony, and theosophy, is really a sustained essay on Jewish-Aristotelian ideas. The only philosophy worth studying according to Maimonides, is the Aristotelian, and it should provide a suitable philosophical version of the truths of Judaism. Let the inquiring mind first state clearly the truths of Jewish tradition; then search out the rational philosophical basis of these truths; and lastly, apply these reasoned convictions to the guidance of daily conduct.

Maimonides undertook a thorough-going repudiation of all anthropomorphic ideas of deity. God is one, eternal and spiritual, without any finite human characteristics admitting of definition. When the man of understanding reads in the Bible human-personal terms describing God, he should know that they are to be taken allegorically. No word of ours can do justice to the infinite nature of God. Only by negation of our finite qualities do we approach insight into deity.

Maimonides relied mainly on Aristotelian causal arguments for his proof of God's existence. He disagreed with Aristotle about the eternity of the universe and preferred, in this area, to retain Jewish creationism. In considering the nature of the soul and its moral career, he believed in freedom of the will, and he rejected any astrological or other type of fatalism. Omniscient God knows, but does not predetermine, our choices; for them, we alone are responsible. Divine providence governs all existence and all human life, but this does not make God accountable for our wickedness or for the evils in life. Evil lies in our finite shortcomings, and in the absence or the misdirection of good.

The proposed harmony of reason and faith in *The Guide for the Perplexed* and the other works of Maimonides had a profound effect on Jewish thought. The advocates and the opponents of Maimonides became, in fact, the advocates and the opponents of philosophy. Beyond Jewish circles, his interpretation of Aristotle in support of orthodox belief influenced also Mohammedan and Christian reflection.

The Expanding Outlook of Thirteenth-Century Scholasticism

Scholasticism reached its culmination in the thirteenth century, during which the doctors of the Church achieved their greatest systems of thought. Philosophically, this period was marked chiefly by the adaptation and adoption of Aristotelianism as the intellectual framework of Catholic belief. But this synthesis of ideas was itself a systematic expression of many important cultural contacts of medieval Christendom.

The twelfth and thirteenth centuries are known to historians as the age of the Crusades. When St. Anselm began his career as Archbishop of Canterbury, Pope Urban II and Peter the Hermit were preaching the first Crusade. Pope Gregory X made the last notable effort to call the Crusaders to arms in 1274, the year in which St. Thomas Aquinas died. These eight Crusades stirred Europe's multitudes into motion and brought Christians face to face with their Moslem foes, men as brave and able as themselves and, in many ways, better versed and more cultured. Though Christian arms were zealous for war with the Arab infidels, Christian minds knew that much was to be learned from them. In medicine, as in scholarship, Europe was in a receptive mood.

Western Europe had always had its explorers of Greek and eastern wisdom, and their zeal now spread widely and gained many devotees. We may recall the mystical works by Pseudo-Dionysius which a Byzantine emperor sent as a gift to King Louis the Pious, and which Erigena was asked to translate. In the centuries following Erigena, the pursuit of classical learning gained momentum, and advanced from reliance on Arabic translations to direct study of the Greek texts. The earliest immediate source of this learning was found in Moorish Spain, where Jewish doctors collaborated. Some of the Latin versions were made from Hebrew translations from the Arabic. At Toledo, Christian scholars were learning to read their texts at a college of translators. Thus Renan writes that Averroës' commentaries on Aristotle, as they were first read by Christian scholars were "a Latin translation of a Hebrew translation of a commentary made upon an Arabic translation of a Syriac translation of a Greek text."[1]

But the Christian schoolmen did not delay long in gaining access to the original Greek works. Sixty years after the death of Averroës, not only the *Organon*, but all the works of Aristotle had been translated from the Greek texts by learned men. Though Aristotle had first been brought to Christian Europe by infidel hands, he was now known directly. Many objectionable interpretations by Arabian commentators could now be rejected by the Christian Aristotelians—but, to be sure, only after long controversy among conflicting experts.

[1] Translated from E. Renan, *Averroès et L'Averroïsme*, Paris, Calmann-Lévy, n.d., p. 52.

The chief center of all this productive Scholasticism was the University of Paris. Here men of various national groups assembled in multitudes to study with the learned doctors of every land in western Europe. Overarching all nationalities in that age of universal learning was the Church, which they all served, and whose language was their common communication medium. It was mainly at Paris that Aristotle was suspected, resisted, argued, and adopted. In 1209, the reading of his natural philosophy and of the commentaries on it was forbidden by the Paris city council, and in 1215, this prohibition was extended by the University of Paris to the *Metaphysics*. But, in 1254, the same Aristotelian writings were included in the university's curriculum; a dozen years later, however, controversies over Aristotle were still filling Parisian lecture halls. The leaders in this expanding, Scholastic activity were the doctors of the Franciscan and the Dominican orders, established in 1210 and 1215, respectively. The systematic Christian Aristotelianism of the Scholastic culmination was preeminently a Dominican achievement.

Scholasticism was exploring the full resources of classical philosophy, and also its own theological and philosophical alternative doctrines. The thirteenth century led Scholastic thought from the earlier Platonic-Augustinian views toward a mainly Aristotelian position. We may note first an interest in Aristotle, but with a prevailing adherence to Plato, then an attempted harmony as a tentative transition, and finally an increasingly positive Aristotelian alignment.

ALEXANDER OF HALES

An Englishman from Gloucestershire, Alexander of Hales (d. 1245) was called "the Irrefragable Doctor." He was a Franciscan professor at the University of Paris and the first Scholastic master who lectured on the basis of the complete works of Aristotle. As a moderate realist, he regarded universals as *in rebus*, the forms of things in nature; but, as a Platonist, he also maintained that universal principles are the eternal archetypes in God's infinite mind, prior to the existence of particular things. With Aristotle, he regarded God alone as Pure Form; all other existence is composed of form and matter.

In his Aristotelianism, Alexander of Hales rejected the admixture of pantheistic elements and Neoplatonic doctrines of emanations which had marked some Arabian and Jewish commentators. While his interpretation thus made Aristotle's philosophy more acceptable to Christian minds, Alexander influenced Scholastic philosophy technically by perfecting its method. His *Summa*, or system of theology, was developed by topical discussions in which contending positions on each question were examined in critical order —a procedure followed and perfected by St. Thomas Aquinas.

ALBERT THE GREAT

Albertus Magnus (d. 1280), beatified in 1622 and canonized in 1932, was a member of the Suabian noble family of Bollstädt. The year of his birth, usually given as 1193, may actually have been about 1206. He was the first great schoolman of the Dominican order; in Paris and Cologne, he gained preeminence as a commentator on Aristotle and as a master of all available knowledge, whence his epithet, "the Universal Doctor." St. Albert is known mainly as the teacher and elder colleague of St. Thomas Aquinas. The philosophies of the two men were largely the same, but St. Thomas' was far more systematically developed; hence, historians of philosophy have been content to deal briefly with St. Albert. However, St. Albert must have certain unique claims on our attention if we are to do full justice to the Scholastic period of culmination.

St. Albert was also called "the ape of Aristotle" by his detractors, as he possessed certain Aristotelian characteristics: an encyclopedic range of knowledge, and deep and varied scientific interests, all uncommon in a medieval mind. The mere listing of the sciences in which this Dominican theologian was a reputed expert indicates the radical difference of his intellectual outlook from that of his predecessors: astronomy, geography, climatology, physics, mechanics, alchemy, mineralogy, botany, zoology, and physiology. In addition to his Aristotelian erudition, he shared Aristotle's versatile naturalistic spirit of inquiry, but a respect for fact led him to disagree with the Greek master on various matters in which his observations or experimental evidence did not sustain the Peripatetic doctrines.

Albert's botanical and zoological researches have earned him high praise from modern scientists. He wrote his theology in his cell, his botany in the fields. His alchemy was not a crude belief in the "philosopher's stone" by which base metals could be changed into gold; he held that various metals are compounds of more elementary substances which could be recomposed, and that the transmutation of metals was thus possible.

All these investigations Albert pursued in a spirit of natural piety—as he told his Dominican brothers, he studied beasts and plants to the "glory of Almighty God." As a Christian and an Aristotelian, his mind proceeded from physics to metaphysics, from the "second philosophy" of detailed facts and laws, to the "first philosophy" of supreme reality and first principles. His solution of the problem of knowledge seems to have been an expression of his own intellectual experience. The universal principles—highest in reality—are the ultimate attainments of our minds. We reach toward them from our more immediate experience of particular things. But natural science shows us that universals are inherent in things and manifested through the particulars. In God's infinite intelligence, universals are eternally prior to all finite existence. This solution of the problem of universals recalls Avicenna's; it combines the partial truths of Roscelin, Abelard, and St. Anselm into the doctrine of moderate realism, which St. Thomas shared and established as firm Scholastic conviction. Universals are *post res* in our minds; *in rebus* in nature, *ante res* in God's intelligence.

Albert not only distinguished recognition of fact from respect for authority, but also classified his authorities according to their respective competence, a critical distinction far-reaching in its implication for a Scholastic mind. "In matters of faith and morals, Augustine is our greatest authority; in medicine, Galen and Hippocrates; in natural science, Aristotle."[2] Accordingly, he signalized certain problems, like those of the Trinity and the Incarnation, as topics of revealed theology which were beyond philosophical analysis. On the other hand, he examined the problem of God's existence as a pure metaphysician. He found St. Anselm's ontological argument unconvincing, and followed, instead, the cosmological, or first cause, argument of Aristotle's *Metaphysics*.

A number of other doctrines which St. Albert shared with St. Thomas Aquinas will be considered in the latter's statement of them. But Albert's ethics will be noted here more specifically; it is characteristic Christian Aristotelianism; the substantive here is genuine, but the adjective is decisive. Albert followed the *Nicomachean Ethics* in recognizing the initiative of the active will, the normal rationality, and the moral capacity of man. But, although he expounded the civic virtues, and, with Aristotle, found the full fruition of individual character in the life of the state, in the end the ideal life for him is monastic retirement and intimate communion with God. We are told that Albert was so strict in his Dominican renunciation of worldly goods that he waived any claim to his own writings. Above all the virtues of the Aristotelian ethics, he exalted Christian *caritas:* pure love without any thought of reward or any fear of punishment, utter devotion to God and charity toward men. Albert praised monastic humility, submission, and longsuffering patience. This distribution of emphasis is important, for it indicates the intense spirit of medieval piety which marked even this most scientific Aristotelian. We may speak significantly of the philosophical renaissance of the thirteenth century, but we should not fail to note certain Scholastic, theologically pious limits which it never transgressed.

As has already been indicated, the preeminent systematic philosophy of the Scholastic culmination was that of St. Thomas. But more impressively than St. Thomas, Albert served his age by the surpassing breadth and variety of his knowledge, by his expansive intellectual range that made his works an encyclopedic treasure house. His unrivaled erudition, to be sure, was not impeccable; he was apt to write of the Epicureans as influencing Plato; he confused the Eleatic with the Stoic Zeno. But it would be dull to make capital of such slips in a writer of a generation to which the classical library was first being made available in its fuller extent. Remarkable are not Albert's errors, but his mastery of the vast new knowledge which he explored and assembled, and which his illustrious student and colleague organized into a system.

[2] Quoted in P. Hieronymus Wilms, *Albert der Grosse*, Munich, Kösel, 1929, p. 42.

The Philosophical Principles of St. Thomas Aquinas

The life and career of St. Thomas (1225–1274) were drawn into many crosscurrents of his age. He was born near Aquino, between Rome and Naples, in his ancestral castle of Roccasecca. The worldly honor of his family outranked that of any other philosopher since Plato and Marcus Aurelius. His mother was of high-born Norman lineage; his father, Count of Aquino, was a nephew of Frederick Barbarossa, Holy Roman Emperor. In his childhood, he was sent as an oblate to the nearby monastery of Monte Cassino. This great center of the Benedictine order not only controlled several bishoprics, but also held vast estates. A kinsman of Thomas' father and Barbarossa's grandson, Frederick II, who was Roman emperor and king of Sicily and Naples, had been plundering the rich monastery in his struggles with the papacy. Count Landolfo of Aquino planned to set up his studious son some day as abbot of Monte Cassino, to protect the holy house from Frederick and also to swell his own influence and prosperity. But young Thomas was won to monastic devotion rather than to his father's diplomacy.

Thomas was sent later to the University of Naples, which Frederick II had established to spread the new Arabian learning. Naples followed the pattern of worldliness which the Emperor had set at his Sicilian court, and where the Emperor had not only assembled learned Arabists and Jewish and Mohammedan Aristotelians, but spun the radical projects of a more genial and amenable church, practiced Saracen polygamy, and maintained an imperial harem. Thus early was Thomas confronted with the confusion of learning un-Christian beliefs and practices from which he was to rescue the Aristotelian philosophy.

The most decisive step of his Neapolitan years was his attachment to the Dominican order, with whose ideals he became firmly identified. His family were enraged at this frustration of their plans for him of the abbacy of Monte Cassino, and went to great lengths to dissuade the young mendicant friar from his chosen course. In vain, Pope Innocent IV offered to let the young man wear his Dominican habit as an abbot of Benedictine Monte Cassino; in vain, his family held him in virtual imprisonment in the castle to break his resolution. Thomas was determined to be a preaching friar, and was finally allowed to proceed with his theological and philosophical education.

He went to Paris where he entered the classroom of Albert the Great, and thus began the lifelong collaboration of the two greatest Dominicans. Albert soon perceived the commanding intelligence of the deliberate and plodding Neapolitan. "You call him 'the dumb ox,' " the master told his students, "but one of these days the bellowing of this ox will be heard round the world."[3] Later, the two went to Cologne to help organize the newly established university there, after which they returned to Paris. Here Albert's universal erudition and knowledge, and Thomas' mastery of logical analysis and systematic exposition, gradually spread an understanding of the Aristotelian doctrines, adapted to the needs of Catholic orthodoxy. The two men defended them against Averroist and other un-Christian interpretations. The victory was strongly contested in Paris and Rome, but, when finally won, it set the prevailing position of Scholasticism, and later, Catholic philosophy. Thomas interrupted his strenuous university career with long lecture tours for his order or in compliance with papal appointment. He died while on his way to the Council of Lyons, where he had been summoned as a counselor for Pope Gregory X. Scholasticism lauded him as "the Angelic Doctor," and he was proclaimed a saint within fifty years after his death.

St. Thomas was an indefatigable writer of systematic treatises; especially important for the study of his philosophy are his *Summa Theologica*, the *Summa contra Gentiles*, and his commentaries on Aristotle's doctrines.

The *Summa Theologica* opens with a discussion of the nature and domain of sacred doctrine; an important introduction to the philosophy of St. Thomas is his clear statement of the relation of philosophy to theology. All truths are eternally in God, but God may reveal them to us by inspiration, or he may endow us with the ability to pursue and attain them ourselves. There are truths of philosophical science, knowledge of the facts and laws of the world of nature, which we are to pursue and attain through investigation and rational analysis. There are the blessed truths of divine revelation: the Trinity, the Incarnation, and the Sacraments. These are beyond the reach of philosophical reason to analyze and prove; they are certainties of faith which are accorded to us by divine grace. And, thirdly, there are the fundamental truths and doctrines of Christian belief, which are also conclusions attainable by philosophical reasoning. Such philosophical-theological truths are, for instance, the truths of God's existence and the immortality of the soul.

Christian wisdom needs the understanding of the proper relation of philosophy to theology. We should accord human reason its fullest rights within its proper domain, but we should also recognize its limitations. As far as it takes us, sound reason is in the right direction—toward God—but it does not take us the whole way. For the consummation of divine truth we need also the guidance of faith. True philosophy thus guides us to knowledge of God; it is a handmaid to theology, *ancilla theologiae*.

It is important to keep the respective domains of truth in their right correlation. We err when we demand rational proof of revealed truths; we err also when we fail to achieve the rational knowledge within our reach. We may also err when we do not recognize in certain philosophical-theological truths the inconclusiveness of philosophical reasoning and the necessary re-

[3] Quoted in W. J. Townsend, *The Great Schoolmen of the Middle Ages*, New York, Stechert, 1920, p. 201.

vealed faith as ground of assurance. For example, in regard to the doctrine of creation, St. Thomas was severely criticized for not rejecting, philosophically, the theory of the possible eternity of the world as refuted by philosophical reasoning. But he maintained that reason could not prove the universe to be either eternal or created. From this indecisiveness of reason we proceed to the revealed certainty of God's creation.

St. Thomas was ready to "render unto Caesar the things that are Caesar's" because he had already reserved for God the things that are God's. He shared Albert's advocacy of scientific investigation and systematic philosophical reflection. Here he recognized the preeminent mastery of Aristotle, to whom he referred as "the Philosopher." But his ultimate loyalty was always to God. He proceeded resolutely with philosophy, but he was always on his way to theology, and he was ready to turn from reason to faith whenever reason—his own or Aristotle's—was unsteady in directing him to his faith. He followed Aristotle, but always in the service of Christ. This was his method and his life-possessing conviction. His last words as he lay dying sound this deep note of his whole philosophy: "For love of Thee have I studied and kept vigil, toiled, preached, and taught. Never have I said word against Thee."[4]

We should therefore recognize the thoroughness of Thomist rationalism, but we should not mistake its dominant spirit. The dialectical procedure of Aquinas resembled Abelard's "Yes and No" only superficially. The Angelic Doctor had no zest for the impressive counter-array of authorities, argument against argument. He was not mainly concerned with his effect on his students and readers; he was neither eager to stimulate their argumentative inclinations nor heedless how he might unsettle their piety. He was, first of all, with God pursuing God's truth. Through the conflict of opposed doctrines, he sought the growing conviction of the more reasonable conclusion. His aim was not criticism, but orthodox construction through criticism: a reasoned piety and the consummation of reason in faith.

Although we must not lose sight of the primacy of theology in the thought of St. Thomas, we can here deal only with his main philosophical ideas. Regarding the problem of universals, St. Thomas shared the position of moderate realism adopted by Albert the Great. All principles and types of being are eternally real in the mind of God. Finite existence exemplifies in detail this eternally contemplated reality. But our minds proceed to these universals from the experience of particular things. With Aristotle, St. Thomas held that the senses supply the data which the intellect organizes into a system of knowledge. Whereas the operation of the intellect has its origin in sense perception, its manner of operation—in abstraction, definition, analysis, judgment, and inference—reveals the rational powers of the mind that really achieve knowledge. The philosophical emphasis here is unmistakably rationalistic, but the rationalism of St. Thomas rules out any doctrine of innate ideas.

[4] Quoted in M. C. D'Arcy, *Thomas Aquinas*, London, Benn, 1930, p. 48.

We now consider the Thomist view of reality—of God, of the world, of man, and of the nature and career of the soul. Knowledge of God is the first principle of our intelligence and its ultimate attainment; in God all our desires and purposes find their final rest. In the beginning of the *Summa Theologica*, St. Thomas outlined five arguments to prove God's existence. In the first three, he developed and completed the cosmological argument presented in Aristotle's *Metaphysics*. First, the explanation of motion requires us to recognize the reality of an unmoved first mover. Second, the explanation of the course of existence by efficient causation implies the existence of a first cause, which we call God. Third, reasoning from possibility and necessity, we find that things in nature are contingent; they would not exist except for that on which they depend, which, in turn, is contingent on something else. But a universe of merely contingent things would lack an adequate ultimate ground for being. We must therefore recognize the reality of an eternally real and self-dependent Being, God. St. Thomas' fourth argument for God's existence is based on the gradation, or hierarchy, of perfections in things. Any judgment that one being is more or less perfect, wise, or nobler than another implies their greater or lesser resemblance to an infinite maximum of perfection, which we call God. And fifth, reasoning from the governance of the world, we see that all beings which act for an end must be guided by intelligence, as the arrow is directed by the archer, and this universal teleology implies an infinite divine mind that governs all.

The arguments by which St. Thomas undertook to prove God's existence also express his interpretation of the nature of God. Our finite mind is led irresistibly to the conviction of God's Being, but it cannot comprehend the divine through a definition. God is the ultimate necessary ground of all being, but He transcends our limitations, and we can speak of Him only by negating our finite qualities. We must beware of conceiving Him by misleading analogies. Thus, man's soul is the form of his body, but we cannot think of God as the World Soul, the form of universal matter. In God all such relations are surpassed; He is pure form, pure actuality, infinite perfection. His essence implies His existence, and comprehends it. God's infinitude embraces the universe but is not reducible to it; the world of creatures does not add to the reality of God. The universe is distinguishable from God, but the universe plus God is not more than God.

We should not apply limiting attributes to God, and St. Thomas opposed any crude anthropomorphism. But there are spiritual attributes which, when predicated of men, suffer characteristic human limitations; these attributes manifest their essential infinitude when applied to God. In this sense, we can speak of the divine intelligence, or will, the justice, love, and perfection of God. Aristotle conceived of God as infinite thought eternally thinking itself. St. Thomas thought of God as knowing us all, every one, as individual beings and in our universal essence.

As is God's knowledge, so is His will, perfect and all-comprehending, self-determined and free. St. Thomas distinguished the antecedent from the consequent will of God. Antecedently or on principle, God wills the salvation of all men; but consequently, or in just retribution, He wills the punishment of the sinners. In interpreting God's power and His love, St. Thomas avoided misleading exaltation. God's omnipotence cannot signify anything that contradicts His other attributes. It means that God's power is without any limitation in all that is divine. "God can do nothing that is not in accord with His wisdom and goodness."[5]

The cosmology of St. Thomas rests on his doctrine of God's relation to the world, as creator and directing providence. As noted already, Aquinas was not convinced of Aristotle's doctrine of the eternity of the world, but he saw no conclusive rational proof to the contrary; he adopted creationism as a doctrine of Christian faith. His scientific exposition was broadly that of the Aristotelian physics and the Ptolemaic astronomy. The detailed investigation of nature did not engage St. Thomas as actively as it did Albert the Great. Only the main outlines of the Thomist cosmology need be indicated here. Every creature manifests a potentiality and an actuality; that is, is composed of matter and form. At each level of existence, form is the principle of a being's characteristic nature: of the physical and mechanical properties of objects, of the vitality and growth of plants and animals, and of the essential attributes and faculties of human nature. The cosmic system of St. Thomas is geocentric; from the earth as the center, in a series of celestial zones, the various planets, including the moon and the sun and the stars, extend outward in their orbits of motion. This is the system of worlds contemplated poetically in Dante's *Divine Comedy*.

Man's Nature and Destiny: Moral and Social Philosophy

The Thomist account of living beings, like the Aristotelian, prepares us for the doctrine of man's soul and career. The teleology of nature is manifested on the biological level in progressive degrees of immanence or integrity of behavior. Life, as Aristotle defined it, is the power of self-movement, and we may trace the perfection and increasing complexity of this power in plants, animals, and human beings. St. Thomas traced this process in the gradation of life in his *Summa contra Gentiles*. On the mechanical level, one body acts on another; but a plant draws moisture and nourishment, and it uses light to unfold its powers into leaves, blossoms, and fruits. More immanent is animal activity; in sensation and desire, the response is externally aroused, but expresses itself from within. It is only in the human soul that this integrity is fully achieved, in the activity of self-consciousness—intelligence understanding itself and reflecting upon its own ideas.

The recognition of this progressive manifestation of immanence and in-

[5] St. Thomas Aquinas, *Summa Theologica*, Ia:21:4, in A. C. Pegis (ed.), *Basic Writings of St. Thomas Aquinas*, New York, Random House, 1945, Vol. I, p. 227.

tegrity led St. Thomas, against considerable medieval criticism, to maintain the living unity of form. A person is not a multiplicity of forms; he has an essential unity of character. We may distinguish, but we should not separate, the various aspects of Socrates, for he is one living soul, the one real Socrates —an Athenian and a man, the husband of Xanthippe and Plato's teacher.

As Aquinas, on the one hand, rejected the doctrine of the plurality of forms, so, on the other, he insisted on the genuine individuality of intelligence in each man's soul. He repudiated the Averroist doctrine of the unity of intellect in Socrates and Plato. This dispute is crucial in any system of Christian Aristotelianism, for it concerns the doctrine of personal immortality and involves a basic interpretation of human character and personality. The psychology of St. Thomas was therefore fundamental in his Scholastic undertaking.

Aristotle's psychology was ambiguous regarding personal immortality, but no such ambiguity was possible for the Christian Aristotelianism of the Angelic Doctor. How could Aristotle's doctrine of the soul be interpreted or revised so as to yield the required Christian conclusion? Unlike his treatment of the issue between an eternal and a created world, St. Thomas proceeded here on the conviction that personal immortality can be proved by philosophical reasoning.

With Aristotle, Aquinas regarded the soul as the form of the body, and he followed Aristotle in his biological treatment of the faculties which man's soul shares with plants and animals. Thus far, it would seem, the Thomist account, like the Aristotelian, would have to be an essay on man's mortality. The problem of immortal destiny can arise only in considering the distinctive human faculty of reason. Aristotle defined man as a rational animal; he recognized the eternity of rationality and rational principles; but, did he —and could he—maintain that reason is immortal in its individual manifestations, as, for example, the rational souls of Socrates and Plato? In a Christian Aristotelianism, this question required an affirmative answer.

Aquinas regarded the soul generally as the form of the body, but he maintained that the rational powers of the soul cannot be explained as having their origin in the bodily processes of nature. The intellect is not like smell, the soul's reaction through a bodily organ to bodily changes. Intelligence has no particular organ; it knows objects corporeal or incorporeal; it knows universal and necessary ideas; and, in its activity, it manifests its immaterial character. It cannot, therefore, be produced by the body, nor can it perish with it. St. Thomas reasoned that the rational soul, while it is the form of the body, cannot be caused by natural generation. In each man it "cannot come to be except by creation."[6] So, as the form of the body, the soul, in its rational faculty, is a soul superadded by God.

This doctrine was defended by St. Thomas and his followers as sound Christian Aristotelianism. Dante gave it a poetic version in the twenty-fifth canto of his *Purgatorio*. The production and growth of the human embryo

6 *Ibid.*, Ia:90:2, Vol. I, p. 866.

which begin in the process of conception follows, at first, a purely natural course of generation. But, at the proper time, God intervenes and infuses a rational faculty into the child that is to be born. The rational soul organizes all activities and gives them this integral human character. It is one with the body, its form and directive principle; but it is not a bodily product or subject to bodily corruption.

From the origin and character of the rational soul, St. Thomas next considered its destiny. Death, the destruction of the body, must necessarily be a radically transforming experience for the rational soul, after which the soul could no longer continue those of its activities which require a bodily medium. But its purely intellectual activities would be enhanced and perfected. In its pure contemplation, it would no longer see as through a glass darkly, but face to face. "Dwelling as it were on the horizon of time and eternity, it approaches the highest by receding from the lowest."[7]

This conclusion shows the Christian fusion of Platonic and Aristotelian emphases in their analyses of the soul, and provided for the required Christian implications and corollaries: the ultimate restoration of the soul to its full scope of activities, through the resurrection of the body and its final reunion with the soul; and the soul's eternal career in the hereafter under God's rewarding or punitive justice.

The ethical and social aspects of the philosophy of St. Thomas were guided by his view of man's career as being under divine Providence. The harmony of Thomist and Aristotelian doctrines, and also their differences in fundamental spirit and tone may be seen by reading the second part of the *Summa Theologica* side by side with the *Nicomachean Ethics*—the spirit of medieval godliness compared with the spirit of the classical pursuit of perfection. Aristotle expounded the virtues as the high qualities of rational mastery in the various fields of human conduct; St. Thomas traced moral progress as man's pathway to God. To Aristotle, the highest virtues were those of philosophical contemplation; the summit to which St. Thomas aspired was the beatific vision of God.

The essential principle in the ethics of Aquinas is the rational direction and order of man's voluntary activities. Good conduct is the active expression of right insight. We realize what we ought to do as we recognize what we really are. The moral life is the full and rightly ordered consummation of ourselves. This can be achieved when rational intelligence prevails over our lower and undisciplined impulses and passions. Our desires impel us toward random, perishable values: riches, pleasures, and honors. But our highest good cannot be in any of these, for they neither abide nor reach and satisfy our highest nature. The essential good cannot be in happiness itself; the moral worth of any satisfaction depends on the worth of the ends or purposes which it satisfies. The life of sensual pleasure or gratified ambition must be judged by the low moral rank of the desires indulged. Failure to

---

[7] St. Thomas Aquinas, *Summa contra Gentiles*, II:81, in D'Arcy, *op. cit.*, p. 213.

grasp this truth is the shortcoming of hedonism and any other ethics of worldly pursuits.

Our final and sovereign aim cannot be anything finite. Created by God, in God's image, we are made for God. Our highest wisdom, happiness, and perfection can only be in the godly life, in emulating divine perfection. This is the free choice of the supreme law of our being. Our inner conviction that we ought to prefer and choose the higher value is our conscience. In all our deliberations and actions, our conscience admonishes, directs, and commends or condemns us—our God-given rational insight in conduct. It is reliable and authoritative, but not all-sufficient. We may advance toward godliness partly through the exercise of our rational will, but, for the full attainment of Christian blessedness, we need divine grace. At this point, the Thomist ethics makes a distinction in a relation analogous to that already noted in the treatment of reason and faith, philosophy and revealed theology. We shall see this relation again presently in the social philosophy of St. Thomas, in the subordination of the state to the Church.

St. Thomas' guiding ethical principle is shown in the treatment of the cardinal virtues: *virtue* is defined by St. Thomas as the stable disposition of a rational will to act rightly and to do well. In his exposition, he did not cover the whole Aristotelian tabulation in order, but selected the cardinal virtues shared with Plato or the Stoics: temperance, prudence, fortitude, and justice; in relation to these, he discussed the other moral perfections. It will be recalled that St. Augustine, agreeing with St. Ambrose, interpreted all these virtues as expressions of Christian love. St. Thomas followed Aristotle and distinguished the moral virtues of human achievement from the intellectual perfections of the contemplative life—intellectual intuition, science, and wisdom. But proceeding, as a Christian, beyond Aristotle, he subordinated all these rational attainments to the higher theological virtues, the Pauline triad of faith, hope, and love.

St. Thomas' discussion of the cardinal virtues expanded their scope. *Temperance* he interpreted as control of sensual appetites so as to emphasize abstinence, sobriety, chastity, modesty, decorum, meekness, clemency, and humility. Likewise, in explaining *courage* as fortitude, he emphasized the control of our irascible and aggressive impulses—not fiery daring, but firm endurance, long-suffering forbearance, perseverance in righteousness, and unwavering martyrdom. *Prudence*—or wisdom in practice, or intelligent direction of the will—was seen to include right counsel and judgment, a circumspect and deliberate state of mind, and a certain rational concern or solicitude. *Justice* was defined by Aquinas as "a habit whereby with a standing and abiding will one gives everyone his due."[8] Justice is essentially social, and concerns our dealings with others. While St. Thomas restated Aristotle's distinction of retributive and distributive justice, he also explored further the scope of justice, and noted its kinship to obedience, gratitude, filial piety,

[8] Quoted in Joseph Rickaby, *Aquinas Ethicus*, London, Burns and Oates, 1896, Vol. II, p. 11.

and veracity—each of which we owe to men in various relations, and the worship and devotion which we owe to God.

The higher, theological virtues of divine grace reach their summit in Christian love, *caritas*. This is our friendship with God our Father, that leads us to brotherly love for our fellowmen and to charitable relief of their distress and destitution. Beyond any particular expression, pious or philanthropic, love is the supreme expression of Christian perfection, and the consummation of spiritual life.

The Thomist moral philosophy has been examined here on its positive side; but it recognized and emphasized man's sinful perversion of his spiritual ends. *Sin* was defined by St. Thomas as our willful turning away from the divine, imperishable good to the pursuit of lower goods that do perish. The turning away, *aversio*, according to Aquinas, as also according to St. Augustine, is the essential evil; what the perverse will turns *to* determines the specific kind of sinfulness, be it avarice or lust or worldly ambition.

Sin perverts and negates our true human nature; yet human life is generally corrupt and sinful. How can we explain this common depravity without imputing the blame for it to the Creator? The theodicy of Aquinas, like his interpretation of sin, recalls the doctrines of St. Augustine. No appeal to Manichean or any other cosmic dualism was to be admitted. This conclusion was decided one day, when, lost in meditation at the table of King Louis of France, amidst the gay chatter of the courtiers, Thomas suddenly startled everyone by striking the royal table with his fist: "That will settle the Manicheans once for all."[9] The evils in this world do not tarnish the Creator's perfection. Our misdirected will is responsible for them. Our nature is the nature of a created being; its perfection is finite and has its limitations, but within its finitude we are to realize it in godlike activity. When, in our choice, we refuse this high career, we will our own undoing, and this nonbeing of our true selves is our ruin.

The social-political doctrine of St. Thomas develops some of the principles of Aristotle's *Politics*, but subordinates secular to spiritual authority. Recognizing man's nature as a social being, he conceived of the state as the natural institutional medium for the full fruition and well-being of the people. A good government is thus one which uses its authority to promote the common welfare. A virtuous sovereign is the devoted father of his people, and loyal obedience to his laws is his people's bounden duty. In the exercise of his authority, the king may well be advised by good counselors or he may seek the direct expression of his people's will. Priest and bishop should admonish the people to law-abiding service. But, if lord or king misuse his legitimate power to defeat the true end of law, to plunder and oppress the people, the duty of the Church is plainly to succor the people in their need, to warn, judge, and condemn the tyrannical ruler, and to absolve the people from their loyalty to him. The Church must take an even

[9] Quoted in Townsend, *op. cit.,* p. 206.

firmer stand, and excommunicate the iniquitous king when he abuses his temporal power in strife with the higher ecclesiastic authority. "The eternal law is the exemplar of the divine government,"[10] and by this divine standard all human law is to be judged and accepted or rejected.

SUGGESTED WORKS FOR FURTHER STUDY

GENERAL.   Husik, Isaac, *A History of Medieval Jewish Philosophy;* Maimonides, *The Guide for the Perplexed* (trans. M. Friedländer); Baron, S. W. (ed.), *Essays on Maimonides.*

WORKS OF ST. THOMAS AQUINAS.   Pegis, A. C. (ed.), *The Basic Writings of St. Thomas Aquinas;* D'Arcy, M. C. (ed.), *Thomas Aquinas: Selected Writings;* Rickaby, Joseph (ed.), *Aquinas Ethicus: or, The Moral Teaching of St. Thomas.*

BIOGRAPHIES AND CRITICAL STUDIES OF ST. THOMAS.   D'Arcy, M. C., *Thomas Aquinas;* Maritain, Jacques, *Saint Thomas and the Problem of Evil;* Wicksteed, P. H., *Dante and Aquinas.*

---

[10] St. Thomas Aquinas, *Summa Theologica,* Ia:93:4, in Pegis, *op. cit.,* Vol. I, p. 767.

11. St. Bonaventura and Meister Eckehart: Philosophers of Mystical Insight

The Mystical Resistance to Rationalism

Scholastic philosophy issued from the demand of Christian minds to comprehend what they believed: to analyze their convictions, to point out the grounds and the evidence for these convictions, and to pursue their implications. It was faith seeking to understand. The schoolmen asked: What are the true Christian ideas of God, of nature and human nature, and how can these ideas be presented most convincingly to reason? Medieval philosophy was not a process of exploration to discover the truth; it was mainly an expository undertaking aimed at an intellectual version of the truths of faith.

This character of Scholasticism was shown also in its sanctions. A doctor of the Church must start with orthodox premises and end with orthodox conclusions; otherwise, his systematic reflections would be manifestly unsound. Either your formulation of doctrine, or your dialectic, or both, must be wrong if you reach a pantheistic conclusion, or are led to skepticism about personal immortality. Thus Scholastic systems might be judged and refuted, or they might contend with each other, reason vying with reason —St. Anselm with Roscelin, St. Thomas against the Averroists.

But beyond this contest of dialecticians was a more radical reaction, which was not against any specific conclusion or doctrine, but against the reliance on reason, a distrust of the dialectical activity itself. This reaction was manifold. It might have been due to the rigid traditionalism of orthodox theologians who were suspicious of any systematic inquiry. It often expressed a subordination of reason to will, or to mystical intimacy of feeling as more decisive religiously. This strain of mysticism is notable throughout the history of ideas, and is of special importance in medieval culture.

Mystical devotion was congenial to the medieval mind, even to the most systematic and logical. In his ontological argument, St. Anselm undertook a purely analytic proof of God's existence, but on the page preceding his statement of it is a rapturous paragraph of devotion. The *Summa Theologica* is the greatest achievement of Scholastic reason, but when St. Thomas lay dying at the monastery of Fossanuova, he asked the monks to read to him the ecstatic sermons of St. Bernard. The mystics to whom we turn here were those in whom this appeal was predominant. Yet, despite their refusal to commit their faith to reason, they were also schoolmen; they argued their mysticism. Some of them championed the mystical way to Christian truth; others, like St. Bonaventura, undertook a synthesis of orthodox belief and devout ecstasy; and Meister Eckehart probed the abysses of mystical speculation, beyond the reach of dogmatic tradition.

Bernard of Clairvaux (*c.* 1090–1153), "the Mellifluous Doctor" was the most eloquent medieval preacher and the acknowledged Christian leader of his age, irresistible in devout appeal, in ecclesiastic statesmanship, in convincing power of Christian character. He healed a papal schism which threatened to split the Church; he preached the second Crusade; he championed a reform in medieval monasticism. Within thirty years after he founded the Cistercian Abbey of Clairvaux, almost 100 monasteries branched from it in various countries. The age had more learned and more profound minds, but Bernard expressed the medieval idea of saintly wisdom. Dante, in his *Paradiso*, chose him as his guide through the sublime altitudes of Heaven.

St. Bernard's importance in medieval philosophy is as a fervent and effective advocate of a way of Christian believing, rather than as an exponent of important doctrines. In his resolute contest with Abelard, he cited the latter's specific heresies; but the real heresy which he sought to confute was Abelard's heretical state of mind, the self-confident dialectic that dismembered the articles of faith. To St. Bernard, Abelard's use of reason seemed heedless and arrogant. But he distrusted any reliance on reason, even when it did not impress him as offensive in tone. According to Bernard, the way of rational inquiry cannot lead us to God, for this way is inconclusive, and does not point toward the very center. Reason weaves cold proofs, but faith demands burning assurance and springs from loving devotion and a longing after God. What can be more fatal to faith than for it to commit itself to arguments and to refuse to believe what reason cannot formulate or demonstrate? God is truly known, not by logical definition or conclusive inference, but by intimate communion and rapture, indefinable but indubitable. The way to God begins with devout humility and the longing of love seeking its holy consummation. St. Bernard's contemporaries called him "the man of love." This emphasis on love as the true way to Christian insight was shared by the medieval mystics. To the agelong problem concerning the priority of belief or understanding, they proposed their solution that love of God is a prerequisite to any Christian understanding: "I love in order that I may understand (*Amo ut intelligam*)."[1] Love impels the pilgrim to God's presence, and love illumines his path. The saintly soul sheds all that hampers its absorbed meditation; by God's grace it rises to the contemplative summit and experiences the supreme ecstatic communion.

The famous Abbey of St. Victor in Paris was, during the twelfth century, a center of mystical devotion which became less and less systematic, and increasingly hostile to philosophical inquiry. The founder of this school, Hugh of St. Victor (d. 1141), was as famous for his learning as for his mysticism. He did not disdain knowledge or logic, but he would not put his final trust in them. Reason cannot give us the communion with God for which our soul longs; reason by itself cannot probe the true reality of things in nature. Reason can only begin to approach these aims; the consummation is not rational, but mystical. In the Christian ascent to God, Hugh distinguished the soul's threefold eye, or three stages of insight: *cogitation*, by which we study God's works in nature; *meditation*, in which the soul seeks God's presence in its own spiritual depths; and finally *contemplation*, the mystical communion and union with God. Hugh's mysticism was explicitly orthodox in spirit. His reasoned philosophy avoided the unorthodox and thus also avoided the unsound conclusions of Roscelin and Abelard. He distrusted their dialectic because it was not rightly motivated. Reason is trustworthy only when it is submissive to faith, only as the preparation of the mind for its final mystical assurance.

Hugh's successors, in emphasizing mystical ardor, became increasingly hostile to Scholastic inquiry. Even when they recognized a legitimate field of scientific investigation or philosophical analysis, they depreciated the value of the knowledge yielded by such secular inquiries. They even stigmatized the dialectical method as an art of the devil to trap the unwary.

Franciscan Mysticism: St. Bonaventura

During the thirteenth century, the two mendicant orders—the Franciscans and the Dominicans—provided most of the leaders in Scholastic philosophy. The two greatest Aristotelians were Dominicans, and the emphasis on reason has usually been regarded as a Dominican characteristic. The Franciscans were distinguished by their more intimate faith and devotion. They had great scholars and dialecticians, but they put their final trust in the loving heart, not in the learned head. This distinction should not be pressed unduly. Of the schoolmen whom we have yet to consider, only Meister Eckehart was a Dominican, and he was a mystic to the core. Roger Bacon, Duns Scotus, and William of Occam were all Franciscans, and surely they cannot be grouped as mystics. Despite their various doctrines, however, what marked them all was a certain distrust of rational system.

[1] Quoted in W. Turner, *History of Philosophy*, Boston, Ginn, 1903, p. 305.

The Franciscans concentrated on intimate spiritual experience. St. Francis sought to bring his followers to Christ in purely Christlike living, divested of all externalities of worldly possessions or ecclesiastical forms or doctrinal learning. They were to own neither money nor houses nor books. Their naked souls were to come directly to Christ. Though the followers of St. Francis eventually relaxed his initial vow of utter poverty and renunciation of all worldliness, they did not altogether lose their early spirit of devout faith and mystical intimacy.

The most eminent Franciscan mystic was "the Seraphic Doctor," St. Bonaventura (1221–1274), who, in boyhood, was called John Fidanza, and who came from a distinguished Tuscan family. He was a student of Alexander of Hales, in Paris, and he himself lectured there later as a colleague of St. Thomas. He became general of the Franciscan order, refused the Archbishopric of York, but was later appointed a cardinal by Pope Gregory X.

Bonaventura's philosophy was prevailingly Platonic-Augustinian, but he knew and used Aristotle's doctrines in the development of his own system of ideas. Like St. Thomas, he distinguished revealed theology from the philosophical study of nature, but he agreed with Hugh of St. Victor that even in its limited field philosophy requires divine grace and guidance if it is not to go astray. He did not, like St. Thomas, merely subordinate reason to faith. He did not recognize any strictly secular field of philosophical-scientific inquiry. The entire scope and career of intelligence were regarded by him in the light of faith. Thus, he entitled one of his major works, *The Mind's Pathway to God*. Bonaventura contemplated Christian wisdom as integral, ascending in its enlightenment toward its mystical summit. This enlightenment is of four kinds: (1) the exterior light of mechanical arts; (2) the inferior light of sense knowledge; (3) the interior light of philosophical knowledge; and (4) the superior light of grace and holy Scripture. Even at the lower stages of knowledge, the truly enlightened mind must dimly, and then more clearly, reach toward the divine zenith. The difference between Bonaventura and Aquinas here is important. The Franciscan's philosophy is comprehended by his theology, which directed the entire career of the mind. He reckoned his learning as merely incidental to his insight, which was God's gift to him in prayer. When St. Thomas asked to see his friend's library, the source of his erudition, St. Bonaventura humbly pointed to a crucifix.

Judging great philosophers by his chosen standard, Bonaventura esteemed Plato's contemplation of the divine Idea of Good as higher than the systematic naturalism of Aristotle. Hence, although he knew Aristotle's causal arguments for God's existence, he emphasized the proofs which proceed from the depths of our own spirit: God self-evident to our intelligence. Our minds recognize truth, and all truths imply the eternal Truth and First Principle that can only be in God's mind. St. Bonaventura also developed and perfected St. Anselm's ontological argument. Bonaventura followed Augustine in firmly maintaining the doctrine of creationism. St. Thomas

regarded the issue between the doctrines of a created and an eternal world
as not settled by rational argument, and he insisted on the Christian belief
as an article of faith. But in conformity with his principle of our unitary
and continuous enlightenment from natural to supernatural wisdom, St.
Bonaventura held that true philosophy points definitely toward the orthodox
conclusion, and he advanced several proofs to refute the doctrine of an
eternal universe.

Within the framework of a creationist cosmology, Franciscan and Dominican doctors reinterpreted Aristotle's doctrine of form and matter. St.
Bonaventura interpreted matter as potentiality, and form as actuality or
realization. Therefore, as God alone is Pure Form, all created existence includes both form and matter. But we should not be betrayed by a word and
speak of incorporeal beings, spirits or angels, as immaterial, that is, as pure
form. From the lowest to the highest range of form in finite beings, corporeal and spiritual alike, matter or the element of potentiality is universally
present.

At this point, a disputed position developed which was contested by
Franciscans and Dominicans. The question was raised: How are the various
substances and kinds of nature produced? St. Thomas maintained that there
is a general capacity in matter, a capacity to receive certain forms and to
realize certain types of being. But St. Bonaventura followed Alexander of
Hales in teaching a plurality of forms. The general potentiality of being,
materia prima, is not a bare indeterminateness, not a mere indefinite potentiality. God created it as a fertile matrix of various potentialities. This is
the doctrine of *rationes seminales*, a plurality of productive principles infused by God in the creation of the world. These seminal forms are manifested in the various fields of existence, and through them finite being is
enabled to attain its various types and characteristics. Nature is like a nursery
garden or seed bed, *seminarium*, in which the Creator has implanted the
diverse seeds which, by his blessed direction in the course of existence, mature and attain their respective forms.

The mystic's ideal of direct communion and union with God might lead
his critics to charge him with a belief in ontologism. The ontologist was
alleged to hold that he possessed a direct, intuitive knowledge of God, and
that all his other knowledge was derived from his assured idea of the
supreme Being. St. Bonaventura cannot be interpreted rightly as an ontologist. To be sure, his philosophy and theology alike issued from his faith in
God, and his final hope was to attain the vision of the divine. But he never
forgot God's surpassing perfection, beyond the reach of any mind in this
mortal career. In this life we can only reach toward the spiritual consummation.

St. Bonaventura exemplified better than any medieval mind the harmony
of systematic reflection and mystical intensity, both directed by orthodox
commitment. When he distinguished rational demonstration from mystical
intuition, he viewed them as lower and higher degrees or stages in the process

of contemplation. His contemplation was unwavering in its orthodoxy. Just as his initial act of reason was the acknowledgment of his Christian faith, so in his mystical ascent he did not forget himself or lose sight of his abiding certainties. His philosophy, his theology, his rapture were all in tune with the indubitable truths of Catholic orthodoxy.

Meister Eckehart

Eckehart, or Eckhart (*c.* 1260–*c.* 1327), has been called the "peak of the mystical range." His contemplation reached beyond the bounds of orthodox doctrine, and did not draw back from heretical abysses. His Scholastic learning and dialectical mastery were renowned, but in the heart of his thought he was not like the doctors of the Church. His meditation did not proceed on the basis and in the direction indicated by Church authority. He did not think or speak as committed to a certain orthodox tradition. He explored religious experience directly, as a modern scientist investigates nature. His mysticism yielded creative speculation.

While his precise dates are uncertain, we do know that he was born near Gotha; that he was the son of a Thuringian castle steward; that he joined the Dominicans and gained distinction in the order, eventually becoming Vicar of Bohemia and Superior of the German Province; and that he lectured in Paris, wrote *The Book of Divine Comfort* for the queen of Hungary, and preached his famous sermons to the clergy and to the common people. Toward the close of his life, he was accused of heresy, and, after his death, many of his teachings were condemned. Knowing these details of time and place we find in his words a note beyond space and time. As when climbing a mountain summit, there is no one and nothing around, so was Eckehart, in his spiritual ascent, alone with God.

The dominant note in his mysticism is utter absorption in the ultimate. Man's engrossment in the random mass of particulars and his indulgence of each passing appetite drives him, distracted, away from the truth. For the truth is in unity, in the final single reality of God. We never really know anyone so long as we know him as another; nor can we know God unless we are lost to ourselves and find our true being in God. God alone exists, really. Priest, layman, and the least gnat—each has a certain nature or essence, but their real existence is not theirs; it is in and of God. "God flows in all creatures and yet remains unmoved throughout."[2] Even so, in a spinning wheel, the center is on all the whirling spokes, but itself does not stir. Eckehart wrote: "This depth is a simple stillness, that in itself is moveless; but from this movelessness all things are moved, and all things have their life that live in reason and possess themselves."[3]

[2] Translated from Franz Pfeiffer, *Deutsche Mystiker des vierzehnten Jahrhunderts*, Vol. II, *Meister Eckhart*, Leipzig, Göschen, 1857, p. 81.
[3] Quoted in Josiah Royce, *Studies in Good and Evil*, New York, Appleton, 1898, p. 282.

Many a page of Meister Eckehart reminds us of the Brahmanic *Upanishads*, with their pantheistic wisdom, that Atman, the inmost reality of each soul and of everything whatever, is one with the ultimate reality of Brahman. The seers of the *Upanishads* concentrated on this conviction as on a holy refrain; and whatever else they expounded, they returned to it, to fix the one sovereign truth in their minds: *"Tat twam asi* (that thou art)." Meister Eckehart had many wise thoughts, but they were all ultimately this one wisdom. Without it, all the rest is naught. So he criticized the learned masters and theologians of Paris: "With all their science, those people . . . are not able to discern what God is in the least of creatures, not even in a fly!"[4]

As the true being of ourselves is beyond thee and me and transcends distinctions, so God's true being is beyond this and that; it transcends definition. "Four and twenty masters came together and would tell what God is, and could not do it."[5] To describe God is to fence him in; each predicate we apply to him limits and negates him. God is not a certain kind or class of god; this way of speaking of God is only our weak speech of ignorance. "In God there is naught but God."[6]

Plotinus spoke of his amazement at finding himself again among others after having been in God, "alone with the Alone." St. Paul before him wrote: "I live, yet not I, but Christ liveth in me."[7] Thus, Meister Eckehart thought, acted, and lived on two levels, or zones. He performed his duties as a high Dominican official; he kept his daily schedule of Christian service; he pursued his Scholastic studies; but, within this stirring periphery of externalities was always the stillness of his inmost being, in which he was absorbed and extinguished in God. He did not neglect or disdain the externalities; he only bewared of putting his trust in them. They may not be spurned, but they do not suffice. In all his details of godly living, Meister Eckehart was ever aiming to live in God. His whole theology and philosophy was, as it were, a sermon on St. Paul's words to the Athenians about God: "In him we live, and move, and have our being."[8] But in his mystical *élan*, he expanded this conviction of divine immanence into a metaphysics of cosmotheism.

SUGGESTED WORKS FOR FURTHER STUDY

st. bonaventura.   St. Bonaventura, *The Life of St. Francis* (published with *The Little Flowers of St. Francis* in Everyman's Library).

meister eckehart.   *Meister Eckhart* (selected works, trans. R. B. Blakney).

[4] Quoted in R. B. Blakney, *Meister Eckhart: A Modern Translation*, New York, Harper, 1941, p. xviii.
[5] Quoted in J. Bach, *Meister Eckhart, der Vater der deutschen Speculation*, Wien, Braumüller, 1864, p. 66.
[6] Quoted in Royce, *op. cit.*, p. 297.
[7] Galatians 2:20 (Authorized Version).
[8] Acts 17:28 (American Standard Version).

12.　The Decline of Scholasticism: Roger Bacon, Duns Scotus, and William of Occam

Promotion of Scientific Research: Roger Bacon

We have noted the fruitful interplay of Christian, Arabian, and Jewish minds in thirteenth-century Scholasticism. The medieval fund of available knowledge was expanded in many directions. The schoolmen studied Latin versions of the Arabic translations of Aristotle's works and of systematic commentaries on them; they also learned Arabian and Jewish science, mathematics, astronomy, and medicine. The western mind could not remain passively receptive; it pursued the new knowledge, but it also criticized and revised this knowledge. It did not waver in its firm conviction of its own Christian truth, and it did not accept the work of the Arabs as final. Not satisfied with second- and third-hand, unreliable versions of Aristotle, the schoolmen made their own translations directly from the Greek. They studied the great commentaries of Avicenna and Averroës, but they proceeded to make their own critical reinterpretations. Arabian and Jewish scientists or physicians instructed western intelligence, but they also challenged it to achieve its own reconstruction.

These strains of productive thinking were all characteristic of the thirteenth-century Renaissance. In positive achievement, they marked the culmination of Scholasticism as manifested preeminently in the *Summa Theologica* of St. Thomas. But the actively and consciously critical-original spirit was also a challenge to the Scholastic method, and it threatened to disrupt the whole medieval edifice. This challenge was not an ungodly incursion from without, but stemmed from an inner unrest. It jeopardized not Christian faith, but Christian philosophy. Firm in its own Christian convictions, the new spirit questioned their alleged logical foundations and systematic superstructure.

The emphasis on mystical intuition had some of these unsettling implications; for, while mysticism might never swerve some minds from the straight and orthodox path, it could plunge others into heretical abysses. From another angle, the critical exploration of sources and primary evidence, in erudition and in investigation, was, in principle, a menace to the spirit of authoritarianism. It might not be hostile in intent, but it was sure to arouse the hostility of dogmatists, and it led, eventually, to a demand for wholly undogmatic science and philosophy. This critical appeal from traditional authority to direct evidence marked the pioneering work of the Franciscan friar Roger Bacon (c. 1214–c. 1294), "the Marvelous Doctor."

Bacon studied at Oxford, where he learned from Robert Grosseteste how first to master the Aristotelian commentators and then to go directly to Aristotle's original text. But he went beyond Bishop Robert's scholarship; he not only read Aristotle for himself, but, like Aristotle, he investigated nature by observation and experiment. This searching spirit of inquiry made his erudition and his investigations exhaustive, and led him to condemn severely many authoritative treatises. Only men ignorant of Aristotle's original works could continue to expound the corrupt manuscripts bearing his name; rather they should use them to start their own fires. And, along with many spurious commentaries, the erroneous accounts of nature must be discarded, even Aristotle's errors, which sixteen centuries of repetition might confirm in men's minds but could not establish as true.

In Oxford and in Paris, this intrepid demand on traditional authority to produce its credentials stirred much opposition, and not alone from rigid dogmatists. Bonaventura, general of the Franciscan order, forbade Bacon to lecture at Oxford, and, in 1257, ordered him to Paris, where, for many years, he was under strict surveillance and was prohibited from publishing his ideas. But, in 1266, Pope Clement IV, whose interest had been aroused by Bacon's work, asked him for copies of his treatises. This papal command stimulated Bacon to record and to send to Rome his *Opus Majus* and some other works. Clement died in 1268, but before his death, he secured Bacon's release from Paris and his return to Oxford. Ten years later, the bold friar was again charged with disobedience and opposition to the Church, and he was imprisoned for fourteen years; he regained his liberty shortly before his death.

In his *Opus Majus*, Bacon stated the purpose of true philosophy, exposed the chief obstacles in grasping truth, explored several fields of inquiry, especially those of philology, mathematics, and optics; he outlined the experimental methods of investigation, and proceeded to moral philosophy which he held as the culmination and fruit of all science.

Friar Bacon opposed the dogmatism of godly men, not their godliness. His own aim was theological. Theology for him was the mistress of the sciences: "The whole aim of philosophy is that the Creator may be known through the knowledge of the creature."[1] For this purpose mere belief does

[1] Roger Bacon, *Opus Majus*, in R. B. Burke, *The Opus Majus of Roger Bacon*, Philadelphia, Univ. of Pennsylvania Press, 1928, Vol. I, p. 40.

not suffice if it is not true. We should, therefore, surmount the obstacles to truth, and they are mainly four: "submission to faulty and unworthy authority, influence of custom, popular prejudice, and concealment of our own ignorance accompanied by an ostentatious display of our knowledge."[2] Like a medieval Socrates, Bacon proceeded to expose the unsoundness of self-confident traditionalism; he appealed to thorough reasoning and to tested, factual evidence for his principles of knowledge. The truth of an idea is not guaranteed by its antiquity; more recent thinking may be more accurate. Nor is general consent a test of validity; on the contrary, what is commonly believed is liable to be false.

If we are to judge traditional authority aright, we must have reliable knowledge of it, in its original sources. So Bacon advocated the study of ancient languages, not only of Greek, but also of Hebrew, Arabic, and Chaldaic. The master of these tongues would have direct access to ancient wisdom, and the long experience and culture of the East would be open to him, thus expanding his understanding.

Our critical judgment of traditional authority requires right standards of validity. A chief introduction to these standards and foundations is mathematics. The translation of Euclid in the twelfth century spread the interest in geometry, and that interest extended to astronomy, optics, and to other fields of inquiry. Bacon valued mathematics both as a basis for other sciences, and as a reliable mental discipline that enables men to diagnose their specific errors in bad inference, to reach demonstrated conclusions, and to achieve a coherent system of truth.

Bacon made notable applications of his mathematical methods to astronomy, cosmography, and, especially, to optics. He proposed needed corrections to the Julian calendar, he calculated the earth's circumference to be 20,428 miles, and he entertained the possibility of circumnavigating the globe. A fifteenth-century writer, who quoted Bacon without acknowledgment, is said to have influenced Columbus in his epochal project. Bacon's work in optics not only was an exposition of Greek and Arabian works, but also included original research in the anatomy of the eye and in various problems of perspective.

Bacon devoted more than half of his treatise to mathematics and optics, but he placed his chief emphasis on experimental science. Mere argument and reasoning do not suffice; for conclusive certainty we need confirmation by experience. Bacon satirized the futile dialectic expended on venerable errors, which the most fleeting appeal to the facts should have dispelled. Long disquisitions had been written about the old theory that goat's milk could dissolve diamonds; but this notion needed only one comment: "experimentally verified as false." The experimental method has three prerogatives or chief merits: (1) It can test the factual validity of scientific surmises or conclusions obtained by reason; (2) it yields knowledge of facts and laws which cannot be gained in any other way; and (3) it opens up new regions

2 *Ibid.*, p. 4.

of investigation and thereby expands the domain of science.

As Bacon began with theology, knowledge of God, so he concluded with moral philosophy, insight into godly living. This for him was the fruition of the speculative sciences, better and nobler than they. The omission of this concluding part from the first printed edition of the *Opus Majus* left Bacon's philosophy in a wrong perspective which more recent study of it has been correcting. Bacon distinguished man's three basic duties, to God, to others, and to himself. The second and third are subsidiary to the first, and should lead to it. Indeed, Bacon was suspicious of any merely secular discipline of conduct. All virtues must point to righteousness and holy living. His early instruction in Aristotelian ethics is apparent in his moral exposition; but even more evident in his repeated and extensive citation is the influence of Seneca's Stoicism. The medieval-monastic outlook on life is shown in this, that, unlike the Aristotelian examination of the virtues, Bacon's ethics exposes the manifold vices of sinful men.

Bacon's thought was a foregleam of modern ideas, but in many ways it was still medieval in tone. He castigated the Scholastic submission to authority, but he never failed to cite the authorities on his side. He advocated direct scientific investigation of nature, but was convinced that it would sustain the truths of Scripture; he would abhor it if it proved hostile to Christ. If it is without Christian conscience, he wrote, "philosophy in itself leads to the blindness of hell."[3] He was not completely emancipated from the errors of tradition, as witness his reactions to astrology and alchemy; yet he not only resisted the cruder speculations regarding the latter, but he also rejected its basic conception of a primary matter. He maintained the distinct characteristics of various substances, but recognized certain productive and transforming processes in nature to which he would not assign rigid limits.

In many ways, Roger Bacon anticipated by three and a half centuries the promotion of experimental science by the more famous Francis Bacon. But the thirteenth century was not ripe for his ideas, or rather, it was not ready for his way of promoting them. Albert the Great showed what real advancement of scientific investigation was possible within the Scholastic edifice. Bacon's procedure compromised the immediate success of his undertaking. He was an aggressive protagonist, and he aroused the hostility of men who were as able as himself and who were more powerful in their day. In the exposure of old errors, he sometimes proceeded to counter errors of overstatement—and even to boasts which exposed him to the charge of charlatanism, as when he claimed that he could teach a pupil Greek or Hebrew in a few days.

Despite many persisting medieval ideas and ways of thought, Roger Bacon was an outstanding expression of the spirit of scientific investigation, which was bound erelong to challenge many basic principles of Scholastic philosophy. He expected that his investigation of nature would provide firmer

---

[3] *Ibid.*, p. 74.

proofs of the Christian truths and would clear up many errors of dogmatic tradition. But after him came men in increasing numbers, who, like him, were bent on investigating nature, but who, unlike him, were aiming solely at the knowledge of facts, whether or not it sustained theology.

The Unsettling of Scholastic Reason by the Logic and the Voluntarism of Duns Scotus

Few philosophers have received such discrepant and problematical interpretations as John Duns Scotus (c. 1265–1308). Since the title of this section indicates one sort of appraisal, we are bound to mention others; the difference between them is due, in part, to the difference in interpreters, but due also, in part, to the acceptance or rejection of certain works of debated Scotist authenticity. Duns Scotus has been treated as the opponent of the Scholastic system, but also as one of its greatest masters. The most extensive English study of his thought reaches the conclusion that "it is in Scotus rather than in Thomas that Scholasticism reaches its maturest development."[4] Some historians of philosophy have sought safety in a broad balancing of judgment, and this procedure may seem unavoidable in dealing with some of the problems on which the intention of Duns Scotus was undecided or perhaps shifted.

The biographer faces perplexity; the disputes about Duns Scotus's nationality recall the ancient controversies over Homer's birthplace. Duns Scotus was perhaps Irish, but, more probably, was British, or perhaps Scottish. He joined the Franciscan order and studied at Oxford, where he has been regarded as a famous son of Merton College. Oxford was then marked by its opposition to the philosophy of Thomas Aquinas; it was also a center of mathematical studies eminently represented by Roger Bacon.

Duns Scotus gained fame through his mastery of rigorous analysis and abstract reasoning which he used in criticizing the doctrines of his predecessors, especially those of Aquinas. No one before him had exploited more perfectly the resources of Scholastic logic, but the Scotist victories were more polemical than constructive, and they raised doubts about the stability of any rational system built on Scholastic foundations. In the days when the dialectic of the schools was still renowned, his surpassing mastery of it brought him great fame, first at Oxford and, later, in Paris. His admirers called him "the Subtle Doctor." Thousands crowded his lectures, as they had for Abelard. But a later age came to regard his endless parades of syllogisms as formal displays which lacked sense. It was the irony of a radical change in intellectual outlook that used the name of the Subtle Doctor of Scholasticism to produce the word "dunce."

The systematic philosophy of Albert the Great and St. Thomas Aquinas

---

[4] R. S. Harris, *Duns Scotus*, Oxford, Clarendon Press, 1927, Vol. I, p. 122.

had turned Scholastic thought from an Augustinian-Platonic to an Aristotelian perspective. This mainly Dominican direction was resisted by many Franciscans who had Aristotelian learning, but who retained a mainly Augustinian emphasis. The critique of Duns Scotus was more original and proceeded to his own radical conclusions. Repeatedly, in his opposition to Aquinas, he passed by the Augustinians to take his stand on new ground. His radicalism was not always in the explicit statement, but in the available implications of his doctrines. His own philosophy was not worked out systematically; it could only be surmised from the multitude of critical analyses to which he subjected every conceivable thesis of his predecessors. Only a few of his many important arguments have been selected for mention here.

On the problem of universals, his formal position was one of moderate realism, but the emphasis in his exposition differed from that of Aquinas. While the universal concepts are ideas in the mind, they also express the nature of things, our knowledge of their nature. Duns Scotus contemplated the universal in two "intentions," or perspectives: as the absolute "quiddity," the essence or nature of a thing which we know; and as the universal idea or concept of it, which is, of course, only in the intellect. In a primary intention, he was prepared to contemplate the original infinite essences as universal principles prior to particular things; that is, *ante res*. This doctrine of universal forms tended toward a revival of Platonic realism. But more important in its implications was Duns Scotus' insistence that the actually existing beings are individual things. We might say that, while on the whole he maintained moderate realism, an important accent in his exposition might lead some of his readers toward nominalism—as, in fact, it did lead William of Occam.

The Scotist emphasis on individual things may have reflected the influence of Roger Bacon's concentration on the direct study of factual, particular nature. Duns Scotus bent his subtle mind on solving the basic problem of individuality. We know both Socrates and Plato as Athenians, as philosophers, as men, and as rational animals; but what is it that constitutes *Socrates* as a real individual distinct from *Plato?* Can we follow Thomas and his master Aristotle and regard the difference between individuals as not in the essential formal principle, which is immanent in them all, but in the material, detailed variations which differentiate them? The distinction between Plato and Socrates is not merely that of two bodies, like two barrels of water. If, in their rational nature—which really interests us—they are the same, will we not be heading for the Averroism which Thomas combated? The Augustinian solution of the problem of individuality was in terms of the unique self-consciousness, but it did not acknowledge the material factors in individuation.

Duns Scotus advanced the thesis that the basic character of individuality is as real in the constitution of things as is the universal character of essence, or nature. We cannot recognize Socrates adequately if we regard him as a member or instance of this or that universal type—philosopher, man, etc. We must acknowledge him, also, as real and irreducible Socrates, this one unique Socrates, and no other. Duns Scotus applied his principle of *haecceitas* (might we say, "thisness"?) more generally to emphasize in his account of nature the unique, ultimate individuality.

A basic issue between Duns Scotus and Thomas Aquinas concerned their doctrines of reason and will. Against the rationalism of St. Thomas, Duns Scotus championed the primacy of the will. The will is not subject to rational necessity; it is free and sovereign. Choice is not merely the active completion of rational deliberation. It is an act of absolute and unaccountable decision. To be sure, our specific volition expresses our intellect's view and estimate of things and motives, but the tenor of our understanding is ultimately determined by our will.

This primacy of will is not characteristic of us only; its recognition is fundamental in our interpretation of God. At this point, Duns Scotus intends to cut deepest into the doctrine of St. Thomas. The exaltation of reason in Thomism might lead us to regard God's creation of the world as the necessary expression of his perfect rationality; that is, God being what He is, did create and could create this world and no other. But this is all vain presumption, according to Duns Scotus. No determining reason can be assigned for God's creative activity. The world was created and is what it is, simply and ultimately because God so willed it. The necessity of the laws of nature derives ultimately from God's absolute will. They are its edicts.

This is not a mystic's derogation of reason. No one could be more expert or resolute in minute rational analysis than Duns Scotus. But he saw a peril to Christian faith in Thomist rationalism. Reason cannot be accorded the final authority even in our human life: how can we rely on it in theology? St. Thomas subordinated reason to faith, but he recognized a large domain of philosophical-theological truths within which he trusted in reason. Duns Scotus so limited the field of reliable rational theology as to make his emphasis on faith radically different from that of St. Thomas. To be sure, reason has formulated all these arguments for God's existence, all these proofs of man's immortal destiny under Divine Providence. But our real possession of the Christian verities is shown in our voluntary act of faith.

The doctrine of the primacy of the will over reason has ethical and social-political implications which Duns Scotus did not make explicit, but which his successors drew out. If the world is the creation of God's absolute and unaccountable will, and the laws of nature are divine edicts, shall we regard the moral law likewise, and hold that justice and love and the other cardinal virtues are good simply because God's will has chosen to exalt them above their opposites? Duns Scotus was mainly a speculative rather than a practical theologian; despite his exaltation of will, he did not devote much attention to ethics. We can follow his occasional exposition of Christian morals as the realization of man's true end, but then we are not following the ethical completion of the Scotist doctrine. It is hard to see how he could have developed a moral philosophy integral with the rest of his system in the same way that the second part of Thomas' *Summa Theologica* is integral with the first. When the extreme corollaries of Scotism were reasoned out, as they were by Occam, they compromised the basic doctrine.

As we noted earlier, Roger Bacon advocated direct investigation of nature, confident that it would provide new and solid foundations for Christian truth. But the promotion of science after his time actually pursued its own secular course. In an opposite way, Duns Scotus also weakened the theological edifice which he labored to fortify. He distrusted the Thomist rationalism in theology. According to him, the Christian truths cannot be mastered in rational proofs, and they do not have to be proved. They are the certainties of faith. But a new spirit of naturalism was arising. Men in increasing numbers were becoming interested in things that could be investigated and proved. What these men learned from Duns Scotus was that such knowledge and proof were unavailable in theology, and so they turned toward the scientific field. Thus, despite his devotion to the cause of Christian truth, Duns Scotus became a factor in undermining the Scholastic philosophy of faith seeking to understand.

William of Occam

The Christian Aristotelianism of Aquinas withstood the strong opposition in which even leading Dominicans took part. Thomas was proclaimed a saint in 1323. But the fourteenth century did not continue systematic work on the level set by Aquinas and Albert the Great. It was a period of abstract formalism, acuteness, and radical audacity.

William of Occam, or Ockham (d. 1349), called "the Invincible Doctor," was the most famous British schoolman of the fourteenth century. The date of his birth has been put at between 1270 and 1300, and so it is not certain whether, as a young Franciscan, he attended the lectures of Duns Scotus during his studies in Oxford and Paris. Occam certainly studied the works of Scotus, and he carried some of the Subtle Doctor's ideas to great lengths.

The Scotist theory of knowledge balanced the doctrine of the objective reality of universals with an insistence on the strict individuality of actually existent things. Some followers of Duns Scotus emphasized the former aspect of his theory, and proceeded to exaggerated realism. Occam took the opposite course. Starting with the irreducible individuality of existent things, he proceeded to a nominalistic theory of general concepts. Never in experience do we find anything but particular things. Universals, he maintained, are the terms which we use in our propositions about particulars. The actual objects are individual. This position has been called "terminism"; the universals are terms, their general meanings are intended by the mind, but they are not in themselves realities. The mind derives these terms from the data of sense experience, the initial source of our ideas. Universals do not exist in nature; to believe the opposite is "simply false and absurd." A term is a *supponens;* that is, "it stands for" the individual things which alone are real and "stood for," *supposita*. We should not confuse the organization or classification of our mental concepts or categories, which are subjective words and to which the existent individual objects are and must be prior. Abstraction in logic presupposes, and depends on, perception. Occam's entire procedure is empiricist. He is suspicious of any intellectual concepts that are not evidently derived from direct experience. He set it down as a principal rule that men should not introduce such vain superfluous notions. This is the famous "Occam's razor": "Entities should not be multiplied beyond necessity." Since he thus began with the concentration on particulars, he saw no meaning in the agelong problem of the principle of individuation. We should not regard the things which we perceive as universal realities specifically "individuated" by matter. The real individual is always this or that existent perceptible thing. This nominalism was proscribed in Paris, but made its way in some of the new universities in the fourteenth century.

Occam's doctrine would incline secular minds toward observation and experiment, the direct investigation of particular facts. It confirmed his pious Franciscan soul in his distrust of theological rationalism. Christian truths are not achieved by reason; they are evident to faith. God's existence cannot be really proved, nor can we adequately analyze God's nature. So piety needs not logical acumen, but the grace of revelation.

Occam carried the voluntarism of Duns Scotus to its extreme implications, interpreting all laws whatever as laws by fiat, decrees. The ultimate ground of the moral law is its promulgation by God's will. To call actions "good" or "evil" can mean only that they are commanded or forbidden by God. Presumably hatred of God would have been a virtue, if God's will had commanded us not to love, but to hate Him! To Occam's piety, this doctrine signified humble devotion to God's laws; but ethical Scotism could also be given a secular version in a doctrine that reduced morality to legality. Moral duty would then be obligation to a statute for as long as the statute remained an effective statute. This comes perilously close to referring authoritative sanction to prevailing force. While Occam's Christian ethics scarcely went to these lengths, his ecclesiastical and political theory and practice at times moved in adjacent regions.

Occam's career is of more than strictly philosophical interest, for it concerns the general history of the period. He was personally involved in the contest for dominance between Church and State. Boniface VIII opened his papal jubilee of 1300 with bold declarations of theocracy. But though he might proclaim "I am Caesar!" his words came too late. They were ignored by the French king, Philip the Fair, who had no intention of submitting to mere words without the power to sustain them. Philip later settled Pope Clement V in Avignon under his surveillance. Thus began the Babylonian Captivity of the papacy, during which two popes, and sometimes three, pronounced judgment in the name of God.

William of Occam was a man of intense human sympathies and Franciscan piety. His boldness in thinking was matched by dauntless practice. Outraged by the venality and corrupt luxury of the papacy, he denounced its pretensions to secular power. He was thus embroiled in the struggle between Pope John XXII of Avignon and King Louis of Bavaria. Occam took the line of religious censure. Popes and bishops should return to the true Christian life of holy poverty; they should speak the sovereign word of God's holy will as spiritual guides to men, and they should not aspire to worldly power and possessions. For this radical outburst, Occam was summoned to judgment and imprisoned in Avignon. But he escaped and fled to Louis of Bavaria, to whom he is said to have declared frankly, "You defend me with your sword, and I shall defend you with my pen."[5] Even Occam's piety could thus proceed from an unquestionable recognition of God's sovereign will to a practical reckoning with actual prevailing power. The transition from the denial of a rational basis of authority to achnowledgment of operative absolutism in practice found expression three centuries later, during the struggle between the English king and Parliament, in Thomas Hobbes' *Leviathan*.

Occamism thus in many ways expressed the decline and disintegration of the Scholastic foundations. The age was marked by increasing political and social instability, and by conflicts and bloody wars which ravaged European culture. Occam, who had been swept into the struggle between Pope John and King Louis, lived to see the beginning of the Hundred Years' War between England and France, after which England was again torn for thirty years by the Wars of the Roses.

During this age of unrest and strife, the spirit of critical thinking and direct investigation of nature was spreading in Europe and leading men to a new view of the world and to a new outlook on life. As in the transition from classical antiquity to Christian-medieval culture, so in this transition to modern philosophy the change was radical, but it was not abrupt. The period of the Renaissance, to which we now turn, was marked by the struggle of persistent medieval ways of thought and life with the new ideas and ideals. The gradual emergence of modern philosophy, with its principles and its problems—especially in its early period—must be viewed in this broad historical setting.

SUGGESTED WORKS FOR FURTHER STUDY

ROGER BACON. Bacon, Roger, *Opus Majus* (trans. R. B. Burke); Bridges, J. H., *The Life and Work of Roger Bacon;* Little, A. G., *Roger Bacon;* Newbold, W. R., *The Cipher of Roger Bacon.*
DUNS SCOTUS. Harris, C. R. S., *Duns Scotus.*

[5] Quoted in Maurice De Wulf, *History of Medieval Philosophy* (trans. E. S. Messenger), New York, Longmans, 1926, Vol. II, p. 178.

III.   THE EARLIER
MODERN PHILOSOPHERS

13. The Philosophers of the Renaissance

The Expanding Modern World Outlook

The Renaissance was a period of revival, discovery, and awakening—an age of expanding outlook in every direction of human experience. Men discovered new treasures in the past, new interests and problems in the present, and vast prospects for the future. The sense of boundless unexplored nature, and of unsounded depths in the inner life, roused a spirit of investigation, but it also baffled conservative minds. We who have just crossed the threshold of "the atomic age" can understand both the adventurous quest and the perplexed qualms of the Renaissance. The first chapters of modern civilization were an early version of a philosophical drama that is being reenacted today on a new and vaster stage.

The expanding modern world and life are also characterized by their accelerated rhythm of creative activity. The course of western civilization extends over some twenty-five centuries. Still to be discussed is the last fifth of this time span, but it will require almost two-thirds of our historical review—a striking contrast to the intellectual wilderness of the 500 years after St. Augustine. Once again we are brought to our own time, to its stunning rapidity of epoch-making changes; a new world of achievement—or of disaster—flashes before our bewildered minds.

The radical turn from medieval to modern culture was not abrupt or without preparation. The Renaissance was, in many ways, the fruition of Scholastic ideas and tendencies, even though it developed counter to Scholastic intentions. In its basic theme—faith seeking to understand—medieval philosophy sometimes made the transition from devout to secular reflection. Scholastic reason could not be limited to the tasks assigned to it by orthodoxy. Its theological culmination, in the thirteenth century, was also the beginning of its definite turn toward scientific inquiries.

During the almost two centuries from Anselm to Aquinas, the Crusades had brought European multitudes to war, but also into contact with Mohammedan civilization, and, in the latter half of that period, Scholastic libraries had been vastly enriched with translations of Greek science and philosophy, especially those of Aristotle and his Arabian and Jewish commentators. The schoolmen explored this learning in quest of a better philosophical understanding of their Christian faith. But Aristotelian interpretation was bound to pass from a theological to a more philosophical perspective. Medieval minds also turned from Aristotle and Plato to other classical thinkers. Going beyond erudition and expert interpretation, the Scholastic doctors undertook their own systematic construction. Albert the Great, in his scientific inquiries, showed an Aristotelian breadth of comprehension. Roger Bacon used Seneca in developing his own moral philosophy, and, at Oxford, he went beyond Aristotelian interpretation to explore nature directly as Aristotle had explored it in Athens. The Greek leaven was slowly but surely permeating medieval minds, and in two ways, both characteristic of the Renaissance: first, a revival of classical learning, enthusiasm for the cultural treasures of Greek and Roman antiquity; and second, a revival of the classical spirit of humanism and naturalism that inspired new creative activity in all directions.

Humanism: The Revival of Classical Learning and Philosophy

How early the new spirit manifested itself may be judged from the fact that Petrarch, who has been called "the first modern man," was a young contemporary of William of Occam. He died in 1374, only one century after St. Thomas. To Petrarch, Scholastic Aristotelian mastery was insufficient; was not Plato a far greater writer than the Stagirite, and, in some respects, a greater thinker? Petrarch was not a Greek scholar, but he possessed the treasures of Latin literature as no one else had for almost a thousand years. Petrarch's ideal was to emulate Virgil's perfection in poetry and Cicero's in prose, and, in both verse and prose, to express his own spirit. He wrote his disciple, Boccaccio, that a modern work should not be like a copy of a classical original, but should show a child's resemblance to his father.

The mastery of classical Latin was followed by enthusiasm for Greek. Florence became the first center of this Hellenism—about 1400. After the arrival of Chrysoloras, Lionardo Bruni wrote of him: "I gave myself to his teaching with such ardour, that my dreams at night were filled with what I had learned from him by day."[1] The first half of the fifteenth century saw a rapprochement of Greek and Latin Christianity. The Eastern Roman Empire sought Italy's help against the Turks; its Church sent her scholars to Florence and Rome; the Italians formed no permanent alliances, military or ecclesiastical, and sent no troops, but they kept the scholars. After the fall of Constantinople in 1453, Greek teachers in increasing numbers streamed into the cities of Italy, where they were received with acclaim.

[1] Quoted in Sir R. C. Jebb, The Cambridge Modern History, Cambridge, Cambridge Univ. Press, 1931, Vol. I, p. 542.

The flourishing study of Greek found an important philosophical, as well as literary, expression in the establishment of a Platonic Academy in Florence by Cosimo de' Medici. Its Platonism was actually a blend of the *Dialogues* and the *Enneads*. Its first head, Marsilio Ficino (1433–1499), translated Plato and Plotinus into Latin, and contemplated the idea of a world religion for enlightened modern men which would unite classical insight and aesthetic vision with Christian mystical devotion. Ficino's disciple, Giovanni Pico della Mirandola (1463–1494), in his short life astonished Italy with his versatile learning and speculative genius; he explored Greek wisdom, Christian saintliness, and Moslem and Jewish-Cabalistic mysteries in his quest for the principles of a spiritual philosophy.

The Renaissance cult of Platonism and Neoplatonism, which had devotees in high places even in the Church, was resisted by Greek Aristotelians who supported the Thomistic Christian Aristotelianism, but who also stimulated the direct, objective study of Aristotle's works, without any theological commitments. Every school of Greek philosophy had its champions in the Renaissance. Stoicism had never lost its hold on moralists, and, during the Renaissance, it gained new disciples—not only among philosophers, but also among literary men and classical scholars who emulated the style of Cicero and Seneca.

The preeminent Italian master of classical Latin, Lorenzo Valla (*c*. 1406–1457), became a resourceful opponent of dogmatic tradition. In his strategy, philological expertness, erudition, historical method, and philosophical speculation were all aimed at undermining venerable errors. He exposed the blunders in the Vulgate translation of the Bible made by St. Jerome. He proved that the "Donation of Constantine" was an ecclesiastical forgery, by analyzing the Latin used in that document on which the papacy based its claims to temporal power. As his classical scholarship thus unseated spurious dignities, so in his philosophy of life, he smote what he regarded as the holiest error, the Christian ascetic denial of pleasure. Valla espoused Epicurean hedonism. His treatise, *On Pleasure and the True Good*, was a bold tract of radical defiance. Behind the screen of an ostensible dialogue between a Stoic and an Epicurean, Valla urged the worldly pursuit of pleasure as the frank philosophy for men who want to get the most out of life.

Valla's Epicureanism expounded in doctrine a way of life to which increasing multitudes of Renaissance men of the world inclined without systematic exposition. Lorenzo de' Medici (1449–1492) was a patron of the Platonic Academy who cultivated lofty philosophical contemplation as well as classical scholarship and style. But Lorenzo had a genius for versatile indulgence, and, in his own life, enjoyed the whole scale of beauties described by Socrates in Plato's *Symposium:* he reached toward the highest ones in aspiration, but he did not miss any of them on his way up or down. His Tuscan poems, like his own life, bespoke his insatiate zest for unbound living.

Humanism thus expressed a wide variety of demands and satisfactions, all of them characteristic of the Renaissance. Its leaders were cultured men of the world. But it also affected the schools and the Church. To cite only one instance, the school established at the court of Mantua by Vittorino da Feltre (1378–1446) was an educational expression of the best humanist ideals. By classical instruction in Latin and Greek, the pupils were taught to appreciate perfection of style and various excellences of mankind. Cultivation of body, mind, and character was to prepare the youths for the duties and the fruits of distinguised careers in private life or public office. One of Vittorino's pupils was Lorenzo Valla.

The Medici spirit of humanism, already noted in Cosimo and in Lorenzo, possessed the Vatican during the period when Giovanni de' Medici was Pope Leo X (1513–1521). This holy father cultivated classical literature, art, and philosophy. His secretary, Cardinal Pietro Bembo, excelled in Italian prose style and in Ciceronian Latinity, and he criticized both St. Jerome's Latin and St. Paul's Greek. Pope Leo X was resolved to "enjoy the Papacy." To provide the funds for his lavish enjoyment, he proclaimed the widespread sale of indulgences which aroused the opposition of Martin Luther and gave rise to the Protestant Reformation in Germany.

The expanded Renaissance outlook on life found expression also in the fine arts. Medieval art, like Scholastic philosophy, was a handmaid of religion; it served the Church. Renaissance art did not renounce this office; in architecture, sculpture, and painting the Church remained the chief patron of artistic genius, a point which the single example of Pope Julius II would doubtless illustrate. But the Renaissance also expressed in its art its new-found human vitality and its zest for living here and now. Just as the men who pored excitedly over newly discovered classical manuscripts also sought direct self-expression in noble speech, so the anthropomorphism of the classical gods and goddesses inspired Renaissance artists to more concrete human expression, and gave even their religious images a new spirit of life. Renaissance art responded thus to the classical inspiration because it was already moved by the impetus to more concrete human utterance.

This spirit may be seen in the fourteenth century in the general piety and emotional intimacy of Giotto's paintings; they remind us of St. Francis of Assisi, who preached to the birds and was on friendly terms with "Brother Wind" and "Sister Water." But, in the course of the Renaissance, the fine arts found expression analogous to the "more humane letters (*literae humaniores*)" of secular enjoyment. Artists chose classical subjects for their works, and the new spirit was reflected even in the religious art, in Brunelleschi's Dome of the Florence cathedral, which Alberti called "an abode of delight, devised for joy and good cheer."[2] We have only to imagine such a comment about a medieval Gothic church to realize the radical change in the outlook on life.

In considering the philosophical significance of the Renaissance tendencies

[2] Translated from the quotation in O. Dittrich, *Geschichte der Ethik*, Leipzig, Meiner, 1926, Vol. III, p. 347.

in art, we should keep in mind the versatility of Renaissance genius. The philosophers were also poets; the classical scholars were also lawyers or statesmen; the physicians pursued mathematics or dabbled in alchemy. What man of this or of any other age manifested universality of creative powers comparable to the genius of Leonardo da Vinci (1452–1519)? He was painter, sculptor, musician, anatomist, engineer, and mathematician. The versatility of his mind and the perfection of his achievement rivaled each other, and, in both respects, he ranks among the supreme few. In the history of modern thought, his long-neglected manuscript notes represent a treasury of brilliant ideas which anticipated later science and philosophy. Especially important is his clear conception of scientific method, which combined direct observation and experiment with the rational interpretation of material by mathematical analysis.

Our survey of the Renaissance has been concentrated on its development in Italy, for there it had its beginnings. But neither the classical revival nor the new life that it nourished was limited to Italy. We should not forget that while Italy certainly produced her full share of Scholastic doctors, the great centers of medieval philosophy were north of the Alps. Classical scholarship and the creative spirit of humanism, criticism, and original thought had distinguished representatives throughout western Europe. No one voiced more powerfully the demand of the Renaissance for the full release of human energies and desires, without any scruples, than did Rabelais in his *Gargantua and Pantagruel*—not even Benvenuto Cellini (1500–1571) in his *Autobiography*. The first great modern vision of the perfect society was the *Utopia* of Sir Thomas More (1478–1535). While the songs of Lorenzo de' Medici still charm us with their carefree joy of living, they do not move the heart as do the ballads of the blighted Francois Villon (1431–*c*. 1463). Comparisons are invidious; we have yielded to some of them only in order to give due, though brief, recognition to the transalpine spread and penetration of the new culture.

ERASMUS OF ROTTERDAM

Outstanding for his classical scholarship, Erasmus (*c*. 1466–1536) is even more important as the foe of all bigotry and as the notable pleader for tolerance during the Renaissance. His was a spirit of urbanity, sane balanced judgment, and ironic disdain of all partisan extremes. He could not afford the cardinal's hat which Pope Paul III thought of offering to him, and he would not side with the Lutherans, for he considered one orthodoxy burden enough for free minds. He condemned learned pedantry as severely as he did rigid dogmatism. Classical mastery, the goal of so many humanists, was to him only a means to the mind's emancipation from arrogant superstitions. His regard for religious truth, however, was genuine, and his theological studies were extensive. His Greek edition and his new Latin version of the New Testament exposed traditional blunders and strengthened the cause of freer criticism.

Erasmus opened doors and windows to new truth and provided fresh insight into human values and purposes. His *Adages* were compiled as a treasury of mankind's sage counsels in all ages and cultures to lead men from a parochial to a more universal outlook on life. His *Colloquies* became a manual of tolerant and reasonable evaluation of customs, laws, and doctrines of authority. Its motto might have been taken from the Gospel: "The Sabbath was made for man, and not man for the Sabbath."[3] With imagination and irony, he took up the many obligations and scruples of individual conduct and social-institutional order, testing them all in their bearing on men's happiness and well-being.

The powerful influence of Erasmus was reflected in the wide sale of his books. His career as an author is, in fact, an important chapter in the first period of printing. The early printers considered themselves only one degree removed from the manuscript copyists. The first Vatican press brought out editions of two and three hundred copies. But the *Colloquies of Erasmus* went through sixty editions during his life, and one of them ran to 24,000 copies. This increasingly wide dissemination of ideas was characteristic of the Renaissance.

The Protestant Reformation

The Reformation manifested both analogies and contrasts to the Renaissance. Like the Renaissance, it was a movement of resistance to discredited authority and a demand for direct self-expression of man's spirit. But the reformers opposed the worldliness of Renaissance men, their self-reliance of intellect and will, their vanities and passions. The Protestant turned away from the Catholic Church, not in order to go his secular way, but to reach God more directly, and to do God's will more fully. This personal intensity of devotion was not altogether unprecedented. Repeatedly, during the Middle Ages, ecclesiastical worldliness and corruption had roused godly men to rededicate themselves to Christ in humble monastic poverty. The history of the Benedictines and Franciscans provides notable examples of this process of reform from within.

The sharp, critical reactions of the laity to priestly and monastic depravity may be read in the literature of every European country. Dante's *Inferno* had a pouch in the Malebolge for the simoniac dealers in holy offices. When the poet reached that spot in hell, the venal ecclesiastics there mistook him for Pope Boniface VIII. During Dante's youth, a French poet, known as Jean de Meun (*c.* 1250–*c.* 1305), sang an undivine comedy in his *Roman de la Rose*. With Gallic satire, he derided staid traditions, unmasked priestly and monastic hypocrisy, and released scruples and inhibitions. A century later, William Langland, in his *Vision of Piers the Plowman*, portrayed more

[3] Mark 2:27 (Authorized Version).

sternly the oppression of the peasantry by barons and bishops alike. Another 100 years later—during the high Renaissance, when Julius II was pope—Michelangelo, who was creating his masterpieces for the Church, exposed in two lines the corruption under its outward splendor:

> Here helms and swords are made of chalices:
> The blood of Christ is sold so much the quart.[4]

In Italy, the worldly spirit of humanism and the entrenched authority of Rome were both dominant. A Protestant Reformation in Italy lacked the motivation needed for any chance of success. The Italians of the Renaissance who did not remain in the Church went their own worldly way. But, in the North, opposition to Rome found organized religious expression. In Britain, the Lollards—as John Wycliffe's followers during the fourteenth century were called—preached a gospel of plain Christian service to the peasants, without ecclesiastical pomp or extortion, and combined holy living with social reform. Religious and social-political motives eventually combined to free the Church of England from papal domination. Social reform, as well as religious rededication, found expression in the Bohemian Protestant movement led by John Huss (1369–1415). The Swiss leader, Huldreich Zwingli (1484–1531), perceived clearly that the new Christian reform must include the establishment of free political institutions and social-economic reconstruction.

MARTIN LUTHER AND JOHN CALVIN

The economic and political factors in the resistance of the northern nations to the extortionate Roman hierarchy should be neither overlooked nor overemphasized. The Reformation was a reaction to the pressing needs and problems of men's daily lives, but it was primarily a religious reaction. The Lutheran struggle with Rome engaged princes, nobles, and common people. It transformed the traditional medieval pattern of life, and, if it was to succeed, it had to recognize—and even to exploit—social and political demands and opportunities. But the initial deep motive that impelled and sustained Martin Luther (1483–1546) in his revolt was his unwavering dedication to God's will, his vision of a true union with God in faith, and his own soul in free communion with Jesus Christ, with all ecclesiastical barriers and instrumentalities swept away. Christian salvation could not be secured through any good works or external performance, nor could it be procured through priest or bishop; it could be obtained only by the grace of Christ in the sinner's repentance and loving faith.

Luther's opposition to the popish sale of indulgences was not merely resistance to an unholy traffic in the name of Christ. It expressed his basic conception of religion as man's own intimate relation to God. This personal communion must be the source of any true Christian living, and, in this inner

---

[4] Michelangelo Buonarroti, "Qui si far elmi," in *The Sonnets of Michael Angelo Buonarroti* (trans. J. A. Symonds), 3rd ed., London, Murray, 1912, p. 7.

godliness, priest and layman are alike. The farmer at his plow and the housewife at her daily tasks can serve God as truly as can the priest at the altar. Service to God does not require external priestly or monastic separation from the normal life of men and women. Hence, Luther would abolish priestly celibacy and monastic seclusion. The clergy and the laity were to lead active lives in home, field and trade, and in all their work to serve and glorify God. Luther was not an intellectual but a religious and social reformer. His writings manifest an indifference to the humanism and to the scientific-philosophical strivings of the Renaissance. When he advocated the establishment of schools for the people, his aim was to enable everyone to read the Bible and to learn God's will directly for himself.

The mental outlook of the Renaissance in the Lutheran movement was represented by the reformer's chief associate, Philipp Melanchthon (1497–1560), a distinguished humanist, who was called to teach Greek at the University of Wittenberg, where Luther's dynamic spirit changed his career. He became the formal expositor of Lutheran theology, though he could not always agree with Luther. He shared with Erasmus a conviction of free will: We are saved by God's grace, but our will is also needed to accept it. Resolute moral endeavor was thus emphasized by Melanchthon in his doctrine of the Christian life. Moral education, the culture of the mind and the discipline of character, should include the best that classical antiquity can teach regarding nobility and integrity. We are thus enlightened in our moral outlook, strengthened in our virtuous resolution, and confirmed in Christian piety as we see the transcendent excellence of the Gospel over any pagan ideal. So we also realize our final insufficiency and our need of divine grace. Melanchthon sought a reasonable middle course between those taken by St. Augustine and Pelagius. A persistent classical view of the life of active moral realization affected but did not transform his Lutheran ideas of sin and righteousness.

In doctrinal interpretation, Calvinism may be viewed as an emphatic version of Augustinian principles. Like Luther, John Calvin (1509–1564) rejected priestly sacramentalism, external observance, and good works as instruments of salvation. But he proceeded to the conclusion that we are wholly dependent on God's grace and that our will cannot contribute to our salvation in any way whatever. We are born in sin, and there is no health in us. Our trust can be only in God, and therefore we cannot have any fear or indecision. By God's grace we are charged to do God's work, and so we go unwavering—not by our power, but by God's spirit. Thus, Calvinism became the religion of the unflinching instruments of God's will on earth. The doctrine of predestination that might have been supposed to yield fatalistic resignation expressed itself in strenuous moral activity. The doctrine of human depravity viewed all men as equally in need of grace. If all alike are dependent on God, rank and dignities are of no avail. Calvinism reaffirmed that God is no respecter of persons. The inference of a democratic social order thus could find religious premises.

The Protestant Reformation sought to realize a thoroughly personal conception and expression of religion, even as the Renaissance mind turned to the direct study of nature and of its own inner life and activity. By putting priest and laymen in the same direct and intimate relation to God, the Reformation became a religious secularism. But, unlike the Renaissance worldliness, the Protestant ideal was to imbue the entire daily life of man with spiritual meaning.

The Catholic Church replied to the Protestant movement with vigorous, and even violent, opposition, but it also carried out its own ecclesiastical, moral, and social reforms. During the so-called "Counter Reformation," an outstanding role was played by the Jesuit order, with its great missionary zeal, rigid organization, and devotional-mystical intensity. These were combined with its astute statesmanship and urbane accommodation to the world, which was to be won for Christ and for Rome.

As the reformed churches established their organization, they developed their own respective orthodoxies, in some ways as rigid and unyielding as the doctrines of Rome. The modern spirit of free investigation in science and philosophy proceeded on its own critical way.

Reinterpretation and Rejection of Aristotle: Pomponazzi, Vives, and Ramus

In their attack on the Thomistic Aristotelianism of the Church, Renaissance thinkers sometimes appealed to Aristotle's original doctrine, sometimes rejected both him and his Scholastic interpreters.

Pietro Pomponazzi (1462–1525) used strict Aristotelian argument to reject both the Averroist and the Thomist doctrines of the nature and destiny of the soul. While thus renouncing personal immortality, he insisted firmly on the imperative character of the moral laws. His fame at the University of Padua gained popularity for his writings, which increased when they were condemned by the Church.

On the burning question of Aristotelian controversy—the immortality of the soul—Pomponazzi sustained St. Thomas against Averroës, but opposed to them both a critical reinterpretation of Aristotle's text. Aquinas was right in rejecting the Averroist doctrine that the intellect is universal and essentially one in all men. But, in opposition to the Thomist doctrine that each person's rational soul is infused or superadded by God before birth and is capable of disembodied existence, Pomponazzi maintained, as the straightforward doctrine of Aristotle, that the human soul is a natural form of the body. The soul in its intellectual career on earth is capable of entertaining universal principles; it "partakes of immortality" in its rational contemplation, but cannot achieve it personally. The claims for individual immortality are unconvincing and cannot be sustained by good Aristotelian arguments. Our thought and our outlook on life should be kept—without presumption

—on our human scale, here and now. Eternal verities are beyond the span of our finite experience; we cannot unlock the portals of the hereafter. Surrounding our dimly lighted mortal horizon is the vast night of the unknown.

Shall we then, in cherishing our little scrap of life and its passing pleasures, renounce virtue, honor, and glory as vain phantoms? By no means, answered Pomponazzi. The moral order is real and imperative, without regard to any hereafter. It does not depend on promised rewards or on threats of damnation. Virtue is its own reward, and it vindicates itself; vice is likewise its own condemnation. Only when a man realizes that he has no immortal prospect can his true devotion to virtue be really tested. In this vein of Stoic resolution, Pomponazzi advocated a life of serene rationality. Our moral task is to realize our place and our role in the world, and honorably to acquit ourselves as men. Our scope and our career do not transcend mortal limits; but, within our present life span, it is within our power to realize our utmost suitable perfection by achieving rational mastery over our lower impulses and passions. In this pursuit of virtue, we find our highest good and our true felicity during the brief day that is ours.

The Aristotelian authoritarianism of Scholastic tradition encountered strong opposition from Ludovicus Vives (1492–1540). This Spanish humanist studied in Paris, was a friend of Erasmus, lectured at Oxford, and served Henry VIII as tutor to Princess Mary. He advocated educational reforms and the replacement of dialectic and disputation by the direct study of nature. The sciences, he declared, have stagnated because men have been content to reason from authority instead of investigating the facts. The experimental method, which Vives espoused, is shown in his treatise on the soul. To him, this method is not a metaphysical inquiry, but a direct examination of the actual course of our experience—our sensations, ideas, feelings, and other mental processes.

Petrus Ramus, or Pierre de la Ramée (1515–1572), was a most outspoken, and even violent, critic of Aristotelianism. Of noble descent but born in poverty, he was the son of a charcoal burner. He went to Paris as a servant and studied at night, his energy and his brilliant mind winning him great distinction. Even in his student days, he took his stand aggressively with the radicals, choosing for his first dissertation the thesis, "Everything that Aristotle taught is false." He followed his general attack with a specific and exhaustive criticism of the Aristotelian logic and with his own radical treatises on dialectic. His bold lectures split the university. The conservatives demanded and secured from Francis I the suspension of his teaching, but the influence of his friends prevailed with Henry II, and Ramus returned to Paris as Professor of Philosophy at the Collège de France, where he is said to have lectured to audiences numbering 2000. His great fame and influence, and his strong official support, were upset by his conversion to Calvinism, and he was forced to flee Paris. During his absence, his enemies burned his library, and on his return, he lost his life in the massacre of the Protestants on St. Bartholomew's Eve.

The antagonism of Ramus to Aristotelianism should not be misunderstood. He rejected Aristotle's doctrine as unsound, but what he really combated was the Scholastic servility to "the Philosopher." Ramus was a humanist in his admiration for classical antiquity; but he would emulate, not merely repeat the classics. Antiquity was great because of its genius for self-expression, and the modern mind can achieve great truth only in the same way, by understanding itself and its world. We should respect only tested evidence and sound reason, which are above any authority. In this spirit, Ramus revised the Scholastic logic and dialectic. For the discovery of new facts, he advocated the inductive procedure; but he did not neglect rational analysis and systematic coherence, and he emphasized mathematical methods. He hailed with admiration the new astronomy of Copernicus as superseding that of Aristotle and Ptolemy. More important than his specific doctrines, were his conception and vigorous advocacy of the true role of modern philosophy: to free the mind from subservience to authority and from impulsive, spurious opinion; and, by direct investigation, to discover and organize the materials and the formal system of knowledge. Like Vives, Ramus was a champion of radical educational reforms, and his importance in this field was outstanding.

The Scientific Age of Discoveries and Inventions

The transition from medieval to modern civilization was, as has been noted, a gradual process. No date can be accepted as indicating a definite turning point between the two. But some events stand out conspicuously as marking important aspects of the epochal change. Thus, the westward streaming of Greek scholars after the fall of Constantinople in 1453 was a cardinal event in the humanism of the Renaissance, for it marked rediscovery of the treasures of classical culture. Correspondingly significant in the Renaissance discovery of nature was the voyage of Columbus in 1492. With these two dates, a third should be included, 1543, the year when the astronomy of Copernicus and the anatomy of Vesalius were published, introducing modern scientific methods in two domains of investigation. The period embraced by these dates—1450–1550—represented a thorough-going reorientation of men's ideas. The historian of philosophy must take note of the discoveries and inventions which inaugurated modern civilization, for they altered men's views of the world and of their own nature quite as effectively as learned arguments.

The parochial, earth-centered universe of medieval minds was radically changed—in two opposite directions—by Columbus and by Copernicus. The geographical discoveries revealed a larger earth than the schoolmen had surveyed, but the new astronomy unfolded so vast an expansion of cosmic outlook that in the infinite modern universe things terrestrial shrank to minimal extent and importance. Both of these slants in world perspective influenced modern thought.

The early Greeks had pictured their world as surrounded by the cosmic ocean, and medieval minds viewed the earth hardly more extensively. The very name "Mediterranean Sea" suggests their standpoint; they lived at the earth's middle. The near-eastern periphery had been made familiar to them by the Crusades; Marco Polo and Franciscan missionaries had brought marvelous reports of kingdoms farther east. The profits of the Asiatic trade lured adventurous navigators to dreams of a sea route to India. Vasco da Gama reached his goal by sailing around Africa; Columbus thought he had reached it by his voyage across the Atlantic. The circumnavigation of the globe by Magellan in 1521 made the sphericity of the earth no longer a theoretical inference, but an ascertained fact. These geographical discoveries not only expanded the terrestrial horizon, but led men of adventure to take it all naturally as a matter of course, to enter and to possess it. In place of the imagined eastern, earthly Paradise, and the sunset regions of the descent into hell, here were simply more lands like their own, extending in all directions. Columbus and Magellan were educating modern naturalists.

We may recall the Pythagorean Aristarchus' advocacy of a heliocentric astronomy in the third century, B.C. That theory had to wait eighteen centuries for its due recognition, by Nicolaus Copernicus (1473–1543). In an age of new discoveries and of emancipation from traditional ways of thought, Copernicus reconsidered the old astronomical calculations from a new standpoint. Where motion is perceived, what is moving—the perceived object, or the observer himself, or both? Copernicus proceeded on the hypothesis that the sun does not revolve around the earth, but that on the contrary, the earth is one of a system of planets revolving in their respective orbits around the sun. This heliocentric theory had the merit of simpler verification. But its implications were boundless and epoch-making. The philosophical and theological significance of a cosmology in which the earth was no longer the center of the universe but only a planet in one of possibly countless world systems was perceived and brought out by Giordano Bruno. The further mathematical and physical development of the Copernican ideas led to the new astronomy inaugurated by Kepler and Galileo.

Johannes Kepler (1571–1630) entertained an aesthetic view of the world as a system of harmony. He regarded adequate mathematical formulation as the best demonstration of the harmonic relations which, to him, were the essence of reality. We understand nature, not as we perceive the qualities of things, but as we attain a quantitative explanation of their operation. Kepler emphasized geometrical analysis as essential to physical science. Where matter is, there is geometry. But the right scientific method combines theoretical construction with direct observation and verification of hypotheses. In this spirit, he accepted and developed the Copernican theory. It would be verified, in his judgment, if it could be demonstrated to be the simplest and the mathematically most perfect formulation of the observable astronomical data.

Tycho Brahe had dismissed the Copernican theory as mere *a priori* speculation, but, as Tycho Brahe's successor at the Prague observatory, Kepler used
Tycho's observations and his own to sustain the theories of Copernicus. Kepler proved that the plane of each planet's orbit passed through the sun's
center. By more searching inquiry, he undertook to perfect the new theory;
if records of astronomical observations failed to sustain the Copernican supposition that the planetary orbits are circular, he would try a new hypothesis
that would correct the error. So he reviewed his data about Mars on the hypothesis that its orbit is an ellipse with the sun as one focus, and demonstrated
the validity of his theory as a law. His further calculations led to the formulation of his second law: the radius vector of a planet—the line joining its
center with the center of the sun—revolves over equal areas of its ellipse in
equal times. His third law stated that the square of the time in which a
planet's revolution is completed is proportional to the cube of its mean distance from the sun. These laws not only provided sound basis for the new
astronomy, but also prepared the way for Newton's law of gravitation.

Galileo Galilei (1564–1642) advanced the new science by his theoretical
mastery and by his inventions and perfection of experimental procedure. At
the University of Padua, when he turned his perfected telescope on Jupiter,
even the dogmatic Professor Cremonini saw the planet's satellites with his
own eyes, although he vowed that he would never again look through that
anti-Aristotelian glass!

Especially important was Galileo's interpretation and use of the true scientific method. He did begin with a Neoplatonic faith that the universe is a
harmony and that the course of nature is a system of relations admitting of
mathematical formulation; but he advanced to a truly modern approach to
his problem, by combining observation and experiment with mathematical
demonstration. Instead of starting with an authoritative doctrine and trying
to fit his data into the preconceived conceptual molds, and instead of appealing to august principles of complete unity and harmony in Nature, Galileo
resolved to proceed step by step, testing his facts, checking them against
previous general doctrines, and, if he found discrepancies, seeking more adequate patterns of explanation. Always the data needed systematic elaboration;
always the systematic theory must be sustained by the available evidence.
Truly scientific work, in his judgment, involved the use of two methods
which he called *metodo compositivo* and *metodo risolutivo:* that is, science
must combine observation and experiment with theoretical analysis. For a
century and a half after Galileo, as we shall note, philosophers tended to
concentrate upon the one or the other of these two methods, until Kant, in
his critique of both empiricism and rationalism, reaffirmed Galileo's principle
in further systematic development.

All his life, Galileo worked under the threat of persecution by the guardians of orthodox tradition. The new science was a new outlook on life, a
new state of mind. In his great *Dialogue on the Two Great World Systems*
(1632), which led to his condemnation by the Holy Inquisition, Galileo

dramatically portrayed the clash of the old and new ideas as a contest between supine conformity to dogmatic tradition, the bold adventure of radical speculation, and the critical and fruitful spirit of investigation, cautious in its regard for facts, not in its respect for tradition.

Scientific progress during the sixteenth and seventeenth centuries was made in every direction. The period has been called the "age of physical science," and notable in this field were Gilbert's work in magnetism and the discovery of air pressure by Torricelli and Pascal. But important scientific advances took place also in other fields. Vesalius' anatomical researches were followed by physiological and biological discoveries—Harvey's proof of the circulation of the blood, and the investigation of microscopic life by Leeuwenhoek.

Invention and discovery stimulated each other, as the perfecting of the telescope and the microscope indicated. Once more we must mention the great importance of the invention of printing. At the very time when new ideas were opening new worlds to modern minds, Gutenberg made possible their rapid and unlimited circulation. Knowledge was no longer confined to the few; it was made available for anyone who could read. The new ideas reached a growing public, and the process of enlightenment was spread; an outstanding example of the accelerated rhythm of modern civilization.

New Speculative Ventures: Nicolas of Cusa, Telesio, Campanella

A transitional thinker who combined Scholastic loyalties with a modern critical temper, was Nicolaus Chrypffs (1401–1464), or Krebs ("Crabbe") —more commonly called Nicolas of Cusa, after his native town. During his school days at Deventer, he was influenced by the mysticism of his teachers, the "Brethren of the Common Life." At the University of Padua he concentrated on mathematics, law, and philosophy. Wavering in his choice of career, he finally became an ecclesiastic, and rose to the ranks of bishop and cardinal. His legal training served him well, for he was sent on papal diplomatic missions. On his return from one such mission, he conceived the fundamental ideas which provided the title of his major work, On Learned Ignorance (De Docta Ignorantia).

According to Nicolas of Cusa, man's mind is an organizing process aiming at unity. Higher than sense perception and imagination is the power, or rational faculty, of analysis and discrimination, and still higher is the speculative intelligence which organizes differences into systematic unities. While the mind aims at unity, it requires distinctions. In approaching its goal, it must, perforce, both transcend and annul itself. Only in mystical ecstasy is the perfect union consummated, and, in that rapture, strict thinking is no more. This supreme mystical insight is learned or instructed ignorance;

knowledge seeking to realize itself yet transcending and negating itself, resolving all contrasts by surmounting them in ultimate harmony. This is the godlike blessedness of intuition, for, in God, all differences are comprehended and absorbed, in the "coincidence of opposites." God is both the infinite, including all, and the infinitesimal, present in the smallest particle. In Him are absolute necessity and perfect freedom, yet neither necessity nor freedom defines Him, for He transcends all definition.

While one phase of his doctrine thus connects him with Erigena and Meister Eckehart, Nicolas of Cusa also entertained ideas that had modern scientific import. He faced the antinomy of atomism which Kant was to analyze more than three centuries later. Abstractly considered, there can be no limit to division, but in our investigation of nature we come, in fact, to simple indivisible particles. A similarly variable view and principle of relativity led him somewhat in the direction taken by Copernicus. We cannot speak of the earth as the center of the universe, for center and periphery are relative in the All. Nor can we regard the earth as at rest. Its motion in regard to other moving bodies may be surmised, but the nature and laws of this motion may transcend our knowledge.

Bernardino Telesio (1508–1588) showed his modern outlook, not so much by his actual as by his intended originality. His major work, *On the Nature of Things (De Rerum Natura)*, shared more than its title with the poem by Lucretius and with the pre-Socratic treatises. But it was meant to be a new cosmology.

His opposition to Aristotle expressed his antipathy to all rationalism. He proposed the complete demolition of the Scholastic system and a new scientific construction on the plain basis of sense experience. Reason yields empty abstractions; real knowledge can be supplied only by the data of perception. From such a resolute empiricist we should expect reluctance for metaphysical theory. But Telesio actually promoted a cosmological system which in its speculative abandon reminds us of the pre-Socratic "physiologers." It has been called a meteorological theory of nature. Like Heraclitus and Empedocles, Telesio saw in all existence a tension, or counteraction, of two opposite forces. One of them is an expanding principle of action: it is dryness and heat, and it reaches its highest intensity in the sun. The other force is contracting; it is wetness and cold, and its greatest saturation is at the center of the earth. The hot-dry principle is the moving, volatile force of ceaseless action; the cold-wet principle is the static factor. Between these two extremes of material existence all nature oscillates, in strife and prevalence one way or the other, which may be observed in the different objects or conditions of our experience.

This doctrine of tension recalls Stoic cosmology, but Telesio's materialism was Epicurean rather than Stoic, in its dismissal of rational essence and in its insistence on the plain mechanics of existence. Man is material stuff, soul and body alike; he differs from the other animals only in being more agile, more receptive, more flexible. Sensation and consciousness simply transmit the heat, which is essentially motion in all its forms—impulse, growth, and perception.

While Telesio thus advanced a materialistic theory of the soul and of sense perception, he also supported hylozoism in describing all matter as capable of some sort of feeling. At this crossroad of cosmological speculation, he took a traditional by-path; he appended to his theory of the soul the Scholastic doctrine of an immaterial principle specially infused into each embryo by God. This higher faculty of the soul he called its "superadded form"; it contemplates the eternal design of God, and its destiny is immortal under divine providence. This doctrine, plainly inconsequent in Telesio's system, was either a way of recognizing the higher intelligence of mind, or his compromise with the theologians. If it was the latter, it proved insufficient, for after his death his books were condemned by the Church.

In appraising the philosophy of Tommaso Campanella (1568–1639), we should remember that he outlived Bruno by almost forty years and was a contemporary of Galileo. He lived in the new age, dreamed utopian dreams of the future, and grasped the new ideas, but he also was bound by traditional loyalties that he could not renounce. A Dominican from Calabria, he pursued, in his youth, Telesian studies and learned to despise Dominican Aristotelianism. Charged with conspiring against the Spanish government in Naples, he was imprisoned for twenty-seven years, and later for three more years by the Roman Inquisition. During the last five years of his life, he enjoyed freedom and some dignity in Paris.

Campanella proclaimed that God has revealed himself in holy Scripture, but also in the book of nature. Theology interprets one of these revelations; philosophy should study the other. The truth must be the same in both; thus, Campanella was confident that a sound knowledge of nature cannot lead us astray from faith. But we must be sure of our knowledge; it comes from two sources: from sense experience and from reasoning. Campanella would follow Telesio in proceeding from the data of sense perception, but doubts about their validity must first be cleared up. So he reasoned: I know only my impressions of things, but they may be misleading. My direct basis of certainty is my own immediate consciousness of myself. I am indubitably aware of myself as acting, knowing, willing. In God these qualities must be perfect, but in me they are limited—limited by something that is not myself, in relation to which I act, know, or will. So I can reliably infer the reality of an objective world because I am immediately certain of my own reality.

The best known of Campanella's works is his vision of the perfect society, *The City of the Sun*, published in 1623. The ideal republic of enlightenment was to be free of all the evils of injustice, exploitation, and oppression. Campanella would establish economic and family communism; he would abolish slavery and poverty along with luxury, overwork, and idleness. The City of the Sun would be a state in which all cooperate for the common good, without exclusive profits or privileges. Knowledge would be within the reach of all, and nature would be investigated and its forces harnessed to increase man's power and to perfect his way of living. But in its government Campanella's state was to be a theocracy, a monarchy under papal authority.

The Philosophy of Giordano Bruno

The outstanding philosopher of the Renaissance, Giordano Bruno (1548–1600) is also the most characteristic representative of the period's many tendencies and conflicts. His career of wandering throughout Europe was in the futile quest for tolerant reception of his radical ideas. His inner life also was an epic of an exploring spirit, soaring in its aspiration, but tragic in its destiny. Like Telesio and Campanella, Bruno was a southern Italian, from Nola near Naples. His family were gentlefolk of reduced circumstances who were relieved when, at 15, Bruno joined the Dominican order. He exchanged his baptismal name, Filippo, for Giordano. The triple monastic vow affected him in various ways. Poverty he had already; chastity he sought, hoping to find in his cell refuge from his intense passions. But obedience proved an insurmountable barrier, for his mind was bent on going its own way, and he was soon involved in conflict with his superiors. He studied the Thomist Aristotelianism and rejected it, then ranged through ancient philosophy. He examined for himself the old theological heresies and was fascinated by the radical new cosmologies.

Bruno answered stern warnings with firm resistance, and when he saw himself threatened with a prison cell in the monastery, he ran away to Rome. The Dominicans' order for his arrest followed him there, and he fled to the north. Discarding his monastic habit, he crossed the Alps into Geneva, but found the Calvinists no less hostile to his ideas than were the Dominicans. He went to Toulouse and, for two years, lectured at the university there, but again aroused antagonism. He then proceeded to Paris, where his brilliant controversies with the Aristotelians and his lectures on the new scientific ideas finally won him fame. He gained the interest of Henry III, and was offered a professorship at the university, but he could not accept it because he refused to attend Mass.

Two years in England proved most productive. At Oxford, his violent opposition to Aristotle received scant sympathy, but in London he found distinguished friends; even Queen Elizabeth seems to have been kind to him. Here Bruno perfected his ideas and wrote some of his best Italian works, especially those developing the philosophical implications of the Copernican astronomy. He returned to Paris, and proceeded to Germany; failing to find academic welcome on his own terms in Marburg, Wittenberg, or Prague, he settled in Frankfort as an independent scholar.

A Venetian aristocrat, Giovanni Mocenigo, who had heard of Bruno's radical ideas and who had hoped that they included a knowledge of magic, invited him to be his guest and tutor. Bruno's longing to see his native Italy again prevailed over his fears of the Inquisition, but the fears were soon realized. Learning that there were no black arts in Bruno's repertory, and weary of geometry and cosmology, Mocenigo consulted his confessor, looked over his guest's papers in his absence, and betrayed him to the holy fathers in 1592. Bruno's first defense against the charges of heresy was an appeal to the double-truth doctrine. Averroës had sought the same way out in his struggle with Mohammedan orthodoxy. Bruno acknowledged his doctrines as his scientific and philosophical conclusions; but speaking as a Catholic, he declared that he trusted only in Christian faith and submitted to the Church.

His appeal was not accepted, and he was taken for more thorough judgment to Rome, which was no longer the Rome of classical-pagan enthusiasm. The Church had turned against the new scientific and philosophical spirit, and was resolved to suppress it. Bruno's trial dragged on for years, and as he realized its meaning, his resistance grew more and more resolute. The Inquisition demanded his recantation of specific doctrines, but beyond his adherence to the Copernican astronomy, beyond any of his specific teachings, the Church was, through him, condemning the free spirit of direct investigation of nature. When Bruno finally refused to yield, he was condemned to death, and he was burned at the stake in 1600, twenty centuries after Socrates drank the hemlock in 399 B.C. On the spot of his martyrdom, a statue was erected in 1889, made possible by men of liberal spirit throughout the world.

Bruno's philosophy typified Renaissance thought most characteristically in its brilliant anticipation of important ideas that found more thorough development in later philosophical systems. While his thinking was thus a forecast of the future, it had its many roots in the past. He told the Inquisition how thoroughly he had studied St. Thomas, Averroës, and Aristotle before turning away from them. In ancient philosophy, he was especially well read in Platonic and Neoplatonic works, and in Lucretius. These two tendencies were reflected in his own philosophy, which sought a spiritual meaning in naturalistic views.

Among his nearer predecessors, besides Telesio, Nicolas of Cusa should be mentioned, but most important of all was Bruno's relation to Copernicus, of whom he wrote in superlative terms, "There is more understanding in two of his chapters than in the whole philosophy of nature of Aristotle and all the Peripatetics."[5]

The Copernican astronomy satisfied Bruno's conception of the process and the field of human knowledge, and he used it as the scientific basis for his philosophical system. Like Nicolas of Cusa, Bruno held that, while man's mind aims at ultimate unity, it can never attain knowledge of it but may only contemplate it in faith. Bruno centered his thought on the attainable, but he always felt the appeal of the transcendent ideal. Our knowledge pro-

[5] Quoted in J. L. McIntyre, *Giordano Bruno*, London, Macmillan, 1903, p. 151.

ceeds from differences toward unities in which progressive analysis reveals
further differences; beyond them we seek a higher synthesis. The sense data
of direct observation are relative to the observing mind, and, while they
indicate universal patterns of order and relation, they vary and only approximate the ideal nature expressed in the law. Reason is thus dependent
upon the data of sense, but it must allow for their specific disparities in
formulating their basic uniformities. Bruno pointed out that nature in its different manifestations requires different methods of measurement and explanation. What is an adequate account of a mechanical process may not be
satisfactory in explaining a work of art. Yet these different sciences are not
unrelated; they form a hierarchical order. The science of mind, or of life,
depends upon the mechanical sciences, but it goes beyond them.

This relativity of scientific procedure demands recognition of a relativity in our basic principles of space, time, and motion. Any description of
the world is relative to the observer's location and point of view, and should
be qualified accordingly. Spatial terms such as "above" and "below" have no
absolute status. There is no absolute here or there in the universe, no central
or outermost point. These are all relative terms. Relative also are motion and
rest, and likewise all time references. We have to use these qualifying terms,
but we should always allow for their relativity.

From this general perspective, the Copernican theory became, for Bruno,
the starting point for a thoroughgoing cosmological reconstruction. He rejected with equal scorn the popular parochial view of a Rome-centered
world and the more abstruse, but no more defensible, view held by Ptolemy
and Aristotle. He followed the logic of the Copernican doctrine beyond its
initial statement. Not only is the earth a small planet in the solar system, but
the so-called "fixed" stars are also suns in their respective planetary systems.
The universe is a boundless system of systems sweeping through infinite
space; it is eternal, without origin or termination, without center or periphery. The numberless planetary systems may be reasonably supposed to have
many worlds like ours, inhabited by beings more or less intelligent like ourselves. In the infinite universe, terrestrial events and affairs cannot be regarded as central. How could we think of God as picking out our earthly
speck for his single Mesopotamian Eden and his one Palestinian incarnation?
The judges of the Inquisition were aware of these heretical implications.
Yet Bruno intended no atheistic world but a world permeated by one
eternal, infinitely perfect Being: "One matter, one power, one space, one
efficient cause, God and Nature, everywhere equally, and everywhere
powerful."[6]

The passage just quoted seems to forecast Spinoza's "God or Nature."
Sometimes Bruno also tried the geometrical method of philosophical proof
which was to be perfected in Spinoza's *Ethics*. But his first cosmology was
more nearly Neoplatonic. He seems to have viewed the vast cosmic system
of systems as an emanation of God. In the second stage of its development,

[6] *Ibid.*, p. 184.

Bruno's metaphysics, like Spinoza's, definitely advocated pantheism, or rather, cosmotheism. The world we know is a world of particulars and of distinguishable attributes. But in its ultimate reality this world of definite manifold beings is the manifestation of Deity: God beyond any qualities and definitions, all-comprehensive and all-absorbing, recognized, if not cognized, by our intelligence.

This cosmology did not satisfy Bruno finally, for it did not give due recognition to the unique reality of individuals or to the active character of all Being. He conceived of the triple minimum: mathematically, it is the point; physically, it is the atom; metaphysically and ultimately, it is the monad. The monads are miniature worlds, each one of them a unique, active self-expression of deity. God is the Monad of monads, the infinite active system of all unique, active individuals. In this stage of his philosophy Bruno anticipated Leibniz.

This rich fertility of thought expressed also the many clashing strains in Bruno's philosophy, all of which demanded recognition. Plotinus and Epicurus, commonly reckoned as antipodes, sought reconciliation in his cosmology. He replaced Dante's Aristotelian "Ten Heavens" by the Copernican mechanics of planets in their orbits; but his cosmic mechanism was pervaded by the divine World Soul. He wrote Lucretian descriptions of the atomic swirl, but also contemplated all nature as a manifestation of God. As in his own life spiritual aspiration was ever contending with sensuality and violent passions, so in his philosophy ideal principles and material forces vied for dominance.

Bruno planned to formulate a moral philosophy of life suitable for men with a Copernican world outlook. Two books which he wrote in England indicate its probably leading ideas. Their titles are characteristic: *The Expulsion of the Triumphant Beast* and *On the Heroic Enthusiasms*. The first of these is an allegorical tract or an expanded parable. Zeus is represented as proposing to rename all the stars, so that they will no longer remind men of the shameful deeds of the Olympians, but will bear the names of the various virtues for the edification of all who behold them. The brightest stars in heaven should be named after the cardinal virtues. But right here the lively discussion starts: What are the highest virtues? With this device Bruno began a critical examination of the traditional moral values. The triumphant beasts which he would expel are the ruinous vices, and also many reputed virtues of dull, supine conformity to tradition. The ethics of dogmatic authority—an ethics of rigid intolerance and superstition, cruel inhumanity, stupid inertia—must be replaced by the ethics of free minds dedicated to the pursuit of truth. Bruno exalted truth as the brightest star in man's heaven. Besides truth, his list of cardinal virtues included prudence, wisdom, law, judgment, courage, culture, repentance, simplicity, solicitude, and philanthropy. Bruno's satire was also a confident appeal for the reform of human life by the radical revision of acknowledged moral values.

On the Heroic Enthusiasms is a work of tragic motivation. As in his theory of knowledge Bruno regarded as unattainable the final unity at which man's thought aims, so in his ethics he declared that the ideal consummation which will ennoble human life is beyond man's reach. The sensualist obtains his low pleasures, but the heroic soul's pursuit of the ideal perfection is futile and tragic in its failure. Bruno's moral philosophy in this work echoed his cosmology. He contemplated not only a universe boundless in space and time, an infinite system of systems, but also an infinite universe of values, a hierarchy of boundless perfections. In this infinite hierarchy of values, man is a beholder and also an active participant. The ideal drama is the only one which man would choose honorably, yet to act his full part in it transcends his powers. In this work Bruno's philosophy touched some deep notes of modern reflection.

Theories of Law and Government: Machiavelli, Bodin, and Grotius

The radical reinterpretation of nature and of human nature expressed itself also in new conceptions of the state. As in cosmology and psychology or ethics, so also in politics Renaissance minds were undertaking to replace dogmatic pronouncement by knowledge and practice based on factual evidence. The medieval ideal of the state was that of a universal Christian community in which political government and social order acknowledged the higher spiritual authority of the Church: the laws of men subserving the Law of God. This ideal of the subordination of the lower to the higher principle, of the royal power to ecclesiastical authority, was expounded by St. Thomas Aquinas. In his treatise *On Monarchy*, Dante championed the imperial cause as a necessary basis for effective law and peace, and while he resisted the political ambitions of the Church, he also contemplated a universal, law-abiding state of godly men. But the actualities of life, medieval and modern, were different and changing: feudal stratification of society, clashing ambitions of suzerains and vassals, dynastic wars for expansion of power, conflicts between kings and popes, the emergence of national consciousness as the ground for political cohesion.

The Renaissance, rejecting dogmatic authority, required a new and secular basis of law and social-political sanction. This secular upsurge gained in scope and extended to fundamentals. The most radical step would be the rejection of any principle of authority and the assertion that, in human affairs as in the mechanics of nature, prevailing force was the only operative factor. But, dismayed by the consequences of such a doctrine, modern minds sought a rational basis of law and political order.

The shift from lawful authority to prevailing power found expression in *The Prince*, by Niccolò Machiavelli (1469–1527), humanist secretary of the Florentine republic, diplomat, and a realistic and cynical student of human character. Machiavelli saw organized national states rise to power in Spain and England, he saw France decline after her loss of the centralized royal power which she enjoyed under Philip the Fair. He saw Italy weak through disunion. Italians were Venetians, Genoese, Milanese, Florentines, Neapolitans—prosperous but insecure, and the prey of native adventurer or foreign invader. Machiavelli hated the papacy for obstructing a united Italian State. Rejecting the superstitious submission to a corrupt Church, and disillusioned about the effectiveness of any principles of sovereign law or justice, he put his political trust in effective mastery, and explored its strategy in his manual for successful despots. We can understand and judge his works, *The Prince* and his *Discourses on the First Ten Books of Titus Livius,* if we remember that he wrote both books after the fall of the Florentine Republic in 1512. In the *Discourses,* he studied the expansion of the Roman republic. But popular rule had collapsed in Florence through its inability to retain power under existing conditions in Italy. Italian security required absolute monarchical government, and, in *The Prince,* Machiavelli undertook to show how it could be attained and maintained.

In selecting for his princely model a man like Cesare Borgia, Machiavelli did not express approval either of Cesare's tyrannical aims or of his vicious methods and practices. But he admired Borgia's realistic consistency, his unwavering pursuit of his goal without any confusion of motives because of moral scruples. The security and expanding power of a state require effective rule, and to rule his people well, a prince must know their weaknesses and vices, and he must exploit them to his advantage. He may seem generous and devoted to the people's well-being if it suits his tactics to win their love, or ruthless and cruel if he must cow them into submission. He may keep his word, or break it without hesitation—whichever advances his interests. He may advocate high principles to others, but he should never compromise his own success by consulting his conscience when he is reckoning his chances.

This proposed divorce of politics from morals was an undisguised challenge, and it has aroused various reactions. Its strategy has been followed by many rulers who have been loftily indignant about the policies it advocates. It has had a shocking effect in exposing the deep roots of despotism in actual human affairs. And it has led more reflective political minds to reexamine the grounds of law and obligation in human nature.

The most systematic work of sixteenth-century political philosophy was *The Republic* by Jean Bodin (1530–1596). Among the multitude of partisan books and radical or conservative tracts of the period, this treatise was impressive in its dispassionate criticism. Bodin combined thorough knowledge of classical and Scholastic doctrine with a direct investigation of social conditions in his day. His modern political outlook was paralleled by his genuine religious tolerance; his *The Republic* was published four years after the massacre of the Protestants on St. Bartholomew's Eve. But he was not entirely emancipated from traditional beliefs and superstitions. He was unable to understand the meaning of the Copernican astronomy, and he showed rank bigotry in his writings on witchcraft.

In opposition to Machiavelli, but with Aristotle, Bodin regarded social-political philosophy as dependent on ethics and as completing it. Society is a tissue of institutions, and the most important knots that strengthen its texture are its families. He defined the state as "a lawful government of several households, and of their common possessions, with sovereign power."[7] Domestic relations are therefore of social, not merely individual, concern. He upheld the stability of the home and condemned divorce, but he would not prohibit divorce lest wretched persons be driven to lawlessness. The same reasonable spirit marked his treatment of economic problems in the state. He opposed peasant servitude, but advocated a gradual reform of the existing oppressive system to prepare the serfs for the fair livelihood which he regarded as their due.

Bodin devoted much attention to the problem of sovereignty. Basically, he distinguished sovereignty from power in government. Power may be shared, transferred, or delegated, but sovereignty is indivisible, inherent, and supreme. The form of government in a country depends upon the factor of sovereignty. Where the king is supreme and the members of parliament are only his clerks or advisers, the sovereignty is monarchical. If a king rules by a compact with the council of nobles to which he is responsible, there is an aristocracy. Where the king is elected by the people, there may be a monarchical government, but democratic sovereignty. Bodin inclined to this last, for he would maintain the king's responsibility to the people, but he distrusted direct popular government. He wanted a strong, but nowise irresponsible, royal regime based on respect for constitutional guarantees. His balancing of emphasis between these two aspects of his thought affected the consistency of his doctrine.

The treatise, *On Law in War and Peace* (1625), by Hugo Grotius (1583–1645), was the outstanding early modern work on the science of international law. Grotius undertook to establish law on a strictly nontheological basis, and to distinguish, in his secular philosophy, the basic and unalterable principle of law from the various statutes enacted in specific countries and under specific conditions. Grotius was led to his search for a universally valid basis of law by the strife and disorders in his native Holland, many of them due directly to religious bigotry. The premier infant prodigy of his day, he realized his early promise of great learning, deep insight, and high statesmanship. A theological controversy at the University of Leyden flamed into a civil war that rent Dutch national unity. Grotius was imprisoned, he escaped, and he wrote his treatise as a refugee in France.

What must be the basis of a universal law governing the relations of individuals and nations, by which all men can live in peace, but which will

[7] Quoted in G. H. Sabine, *A History of Political Theory*, New York, Holt, 1937, p. 402.

also retain authority over them in their conflicts and wars? This law cannot rest on a theological basis, for it must be valid for societies of different religions. Grotius maintained that there is a natural law derived from the basic character of man. Itself an expression of human nature, it is valid for men generally. This law is the expression of man's social nature; in this, too, Aristotle had found the motive and foundation of the state. From it are derived the commonly acknowledged rights and obligations: the right to respect for what is one's own; the duty to keep one's promises and agreements; the necessity of suffering the due hardships and penalties for one's wrongdoing. This law of essential rightness does not depend on any specific promulgation, nor can it be abrogated by any judge or sovereign. God Himself cannot annul it. A nation may be forced into war when its natural rights are menaced by another nation or ruler. But such hostilities cannot negate all rights and obligations. The essential laws must still control the conduct of the war.

In seeking proofs for his system of law, Grotius proceeded, by rational analysis, from his basic idea of man's social nature, but he also appealed to factual, universal validity as expressed in the universal consent, or the general acceptance of certain laws by all nations or by all enlightened peoples. He thus combined a rationalistic with a historical-empirical procedure. We are reminded of the tendency of the Roman Stoic jurists to identify the natural law of philosophical jurisprudence, *jus naturale*, with the law of nations, *jus gentium*, which developed historically in the administration of justice by Imperial Rome.

Occultism, Mysticism, and Skepticism: Paracelsus, Boehme, and Montaigne

Mocenigo's invitation to Bruno was inspired by the hope of learning the black arts from him. The Renaissance mind combined with its scientific interest a hankering for the marvelous and the occult. In going from the traditional theology to philosophy, speculation often turned aside into the mysterious bypaths of theosophy. On a general Neoplatonic pattern of emanation, the devotees of the occult wove half-comprehended, alleged secret doctrines from the Jewish cabala, and from the lore of the alchemists and wonder healers.

The leading hierophant of the age was a Swiss, Theophrastus Bombastus von Hohenheim, who called himself "Paracelsus" (1493–1541). In his philosophical investigation, he opposed, and also paralleled, the macrocosm of nature and the microcosm or man's soul and being. Each is a mirror of the other, to be understood through the other. Throughout nature runs the World Soul, the "Vulcanus," and a presiding genius, "Archeus," directs the career of each being, each man. But this living principle in mankind is harassed by demonic forces. Alchemy and magic are needed to banish them and thus to cure diseases. This healing art of which Paracelsus was the professed master required expert knowledge of alchemy, of the correct quintessential tinctures and salves; it actually combined some attested skill with a considerable amount of quackery.

The metaphysics of Paracelsus is as occult as is his medicine. The world has sprouted from the primary matter through the interaction of three basic principles which he called mercury (the liquid factor), salt (the solid), and sulphur (the fiery or combustible). Through these three are formed the four elements, fire, air, water, and earth; and each of these four has its ruling spirits: salamanders, sylphs, undines, and gnomes, in that order. Paracelsus' wide renown is reflected in the many portraits of him by such great artists as Tintoretto, Baldung, and, perhaps, Dürer or Rubens. The numerous cartoons of him also indicate his notoriety.

Meister Eckehart's Christian pantheism in the thirteenth century was the fountainhead of a stream of mystical devotion that coursed through Germany and the Low Countries during the next two centuries. That it reached deep levels of spiritual experience may be seen from its upspringing in Protestant as well as in Catholic ground; one major exponent of this sort of mysticism was Boehme.

Jacob Boehme (1575–1624) was a cobbler of Görlitz, who had no formal education and who was unfamiliar with classical or Scholastic philosophy, but who was steeped in the Bible and widely read in mystical and theosophical writings. His profound meditation throughout many years found its consummation in several mystical experiences or illuminations in which, he felt certain, the inmost nature of God and all the mysteries of the world were revealed to him with blinding clarity. Boehme's basic struggle was with the problem of evil, and, in accounting for it, he advanced the principle of opposition, from which both his cosmology and his moral philosophy were derived. Opposition, or conflicting duality, is the basic fact of all existence; there can be no light without darkness. Opposition is ultimate in God's nature also. Through it God is revealed to Himself, and through it the world is generated. Boehme taught that the primal Godhead is indefinable, without attributes. Like Eckehart, he used everyday German speech, but he packed subtle meaning into his words, as when he called the ultimate, *Ungrund*, groundlessness, to express its fathomless and reasonless abyss, without basic nature or explanation. To reveal and recognize itself, deity must project itself. So God the Father contemplates Himself in the Son, and this divine procession is the Holy Spirit.

Boehme's cosmology reads sometimes like a religious version of that of Paracelsus. Within the dark potency of God stirs the will to manifest divine perfection in undivine material being. In the creation of the world, two agencies operate: the desire of life and the will to achieve perfection. These two contend with each other. From desire, as unassuaged want and pain, emerge solidity and heat, the salt of alchemy. Then a flowing, spreading activity manifests itself in water, the mercury of Paracelsus. These two clash, yielding a shudder of restless awareness, which is sensibility. Out of this contest of agencies, cosmic fright bursts forth like lightning. It is the tension between dark nature and emergent spirit. But now the will to perfection begins to prevail over this realm of shuddering wrath. Light and love irradiate creation. Spirit utters itself in the audible word, intelligent sound. And all these factors—conflicting, but also kin—are related in the cosmic order and the harmony of nature. Nature is God's body, or His garment, revealing and concealing divine perfection.

Thus, Boehme is faced with the problem of evil. Evil as the opposition of the dark glow of wrath and the light glow of love is in the very tissue of existence, in God's own creative activity. But this evil is not *bad*, for it is itself a condition of good. This opposition, or tension, leads to righteousness when the soul rises from wrath to love. But it sinks in sin when it turns in the other direction.

In Boehme's cosmology may be noted Neoplatonic ingredients seasoned with alchemy and brewing with Gnostic fumes, but his moral philosophy of life is insistently Biblical-Christian. It is man's blessed destiny to pass from struggle into peace, and, in overcoming negation, to cast his will into God's will and to become one with God. "Thou art dead indeed as to thyself, but art alive unto God."[8]

The rejection of dogmatic authority by the early modern minds was bound to raise the problem of a reliable standard of knowledge. This fundamental emphasis on method, as will be noted presently, characterized the systematic philosophy of the seventeenth and eighteenth centuries. But the collapse of authoritarianism also resulted in a general unsettlement of ideas and the invasion of doubt. These tendencies may be noted in many thinkers who do not yield to them; sometimes, however, they prevail and lead to outright skeptical doctrines. Mysticism has been characterized as an alternative to skepticism; both spring from a distrust of knowledge and reason. The mystic has a way out of his uncertainty; but the skeptic resigns himself to his entangling doubts. In this middle region of uncertainty and intuition, many Renaissance minds move in various directions. Here is Nicolas of Cusa's "learned ignorance," and his "negative theology." Here is the tragic strain in Bruno's ethics. Here also is Pomponazzi, refusing the mystical ascent and resolutely fulfilling his transitory tasks.

In the *Essays* of Michel de Montaigne (1533–1592) skepticism produces a philosophy of genial reflection on the varieties of human experience. Montaigne's motto was "*Que sçai-je?* (What do I know?)"[9] Skepticism was not his doctrine, but his renunciation of doctrine. What really marked Montaigne was his fresh and unprejudiced approach to the ongoing drama of human life. He had read too many versions of it to accept any one of them as the

---

[8] Boehme, "Of the Supersensual Life," in *The Signature of All Things*, London, Dent, Everyman's Library, 1926, p. 255.
[9] Quoted in G. Saintsbury, "Montaigne," in *Encyclopedia Britannica*, 11th ed., Cambridge, Cambridge Univ. Press, 1911, Vol. XVIII, p. 749.

original and authoritative one. He himself had witnessed too many different scenes of that drama to presume to write any final commentary on the whole. Classical erudition and direct experience, both, had taught him the wisdom of uncommitted reflection. The ancients that lined the walls of his library expanded his experience with men; his daily experience with men confirmed or revised ancient wisdom. But wisdom, ancient or of the moment, was for him always in solution; it must never stiffen into doctrine.

Montaigne's *Essays* are characterized by a lyrical spirit of direct self-exploration and self-expression. He says frankly that he himself is the subject of his book. He is most interesting to himself; he "listens to himself" and tells us his own ever unfolding and unending story. What impresses him is his own protean character, ever shifting and varying, and belying every formula. His own experience teaches him the strategy of indecision, alertness to the unexpected, serene readiness for the fortuities of life.

This genial skepticism expresses itself in ready tolerance, in moderation of judgment and emotion, without enthusiasm, devotion, or indignation, and free of any fanaticism. But Montaigne seems to lack the heroic touch and the note of moral dignity which requires conviction and devotion. In reading all his brilliant comments and reflections on the human scene, we somehow feel that his intelligence is uncommitted because it has not been fully engaged. How could he so genially record the failure of the mind to attain truth, failure in its essential role, and confusion about its ultimate nature and destiny? Thus was Montaigne judged by Pascal, who, like Montaigne, admitted the skeptical plight of reason, but who, unlike him, refused to accept it. Pascal's struggle with the problem of knowledge will be considered in Chapter 16, which deals with Cartesian rationalism. Modern philosophy required a critical view of the scope and the true method of seeking knowledge before it could proceed to systematic construction. In confronting thought with this essential problem, skepticism served intellectual progress in the Renaissance, even as the buoyant spirit served it when it plunged confidently into scientific and philosophical inquiry.

SUGGESTED WORKS FOR FURTHER STUDY

HISTORIES OF MODERN PHILOSOPHY.   Adamson, Robert, *The Development of Modern Philosophy;* Boas, George, *The Dominant Themes of Modern Philosophy;* Falckenberg, Richard, *History of Modern Philosophy;* Höffding, Harald, *A History of Modern Philosophy;* Randall, J. H., *The Career of Philosophy from the Middle Ages to the Enlightenment;* Wright, W. K., *A History of Modern Philosophy.*

HISTORIES OF AMERICAN PHILOSOPHY.   Riley, I. W., *American Philosophy;* Schneider, H. W., *A History of American Philosophy;* Townsend, H. G., *Philosophical Ideas in the United States;* Werkmeister, W. H., *A History of Philosophical Ideas in America.*

HISTORIES OF ENGLISH PHILOSOPHY. Forsyth, Thomas, *English Philosophy*; Seth, James, *English Philosophers and Schools of Philosophy*; Sorley, W. R., *A History of English Philosophy*.

HISTORY OF FRENCH PHILOSOPHY. Lévy-Bruhl, L., *History of Modern Philosophy in France*.

THE RENAISSANCE. Burckhardt, J. C., *The Civilization of the Renaissance in Italy*; Cassirer, Ernst, Kristeller, P. O., and Randall, J. H., *The Renaissance Philosophy of Man*; Fletcher, J. B., *Literature of the Italian Renaissance*; Owen, John, *The Skeptics of the Italian Renaissance*; Pater, Walter, *The Renaissance*; Santillana, Giorgio de, *The Age of Adventure: The Renaissance Philosophers*; Symonds, J. A., *The Renaissance in Italy*.

THE REFORMATION. Lindsay, T. M., *A History of the Reformation*; Smith, Preserved, *The Age of the Reformation*.

SCIENTIFIC DEVELOPMENT. Burtt, E. A., *The Metaphysical Foundations of Modern Physical Science*; Santillana, Giorgio de, *The Crime of Galileo*.

RENAISSANCE PHILOSOPHERS. Böhme, Jacob, *The Signature of All Things* (C. Bax, ed.); Boulting, William, *Giordano Bruno*; Bruno, Giordano, *Ths Heroic Enthusiasts* (trans. L. Williams); Campanella, Tommaso, *The City of the Sun*, in Morley, H. (ed.), *Ideal Commonwealths*; Da Vinci, Leonardo, *Note Books* (trans. E. McCurdy); Erasmus, *Colloquies* (trans. N. Bailey) and *The Praise of Folly* (trans. H. H. Hudson); Galilei, Galileo, *Dialogues Concerning Two New Sciences* (trans. H. Crew and A. de Salvio) and *Dialogue on the Great World Systems* (trans. Saulsbury as rev. by G. de Santillana); Grotius, Hugo, *The Rights of War and Peace* (trans. A. C. Campbell); Machiavelli, Niccolò, *The Prince* (trans. A. H. Gilbert, and L. Ricci); McIntyre, J. L., *Giordano Bruno*; Montaigne, Michel de, *Essays* (several translations are available); Nicolas of Cusa, in Bett, Henry, *Nicolas of Cusa*; Pomponazzi, Pietro, in Douglas, A. H., *The Philosophy and Psychology of Pietro Pomponazzi*; Ramus, Petrus, in Graves, F. P., *Petrus Ramus and the Educational Reformation of the Sixteenth Century*; Vives, Ludovicus, *On Education* (trans. F. Watson).

14. Francis Bacon: Champion of Inductive Science

The Problem of Philosophical Method

The Renaissance mind was alert, adventurous, independent, and fertile, but it was not systematic. Its new secular interests in the investigation of nature and human nature weaned it from submission to theological authority, but left it in need of another reliable guide. Undogmatic thinking required its own test of validity. Hence, the problem of method imposed itself on modern philosophy. This problem marks the advance from the exuberant speculations of the Renaissance to the systematic philosophical achievements of the seventeenth century.

The main alternatives in method and theory of knowledge were suggested to critical minds even before the Renaissance. In his resistance to sterile authoritarianism, Roger Bacon had championed both rigorous mathematical analysis and the experimental method. Instead of the medieval citing of traditional authorities, the modern age needed a new procedure to serve truly inquiring minds that did not, like lawyers and theologians, begin their inquiry with their conclusions. Men needed to learn how to discover facts and to ascertain truths, not merely how to argue a case or to secure acceptance of a thesis. Whether by analyzing the system of reasoning, or by examining the processes of mental activity in reaction to nature, the modern mind required a clearly enunciated, undogmatic procedure. This method did not have to be invented by philosophers. Actually, the right procedures in dealing with different problems were both discovered and vindicated in the course of scientific inquiry. What scientists learned in the course of their investigation, philosophers had to understand and to formulate systematically. Modern science could progress prior to the formal enunciation of its method, but modern philosophy could not.

Systematic modern philosophy was thus begun with discourses on method. They raised the two basic problems in the theory of knowledge: What are the sources of our ideas, and what is the test of their validity? How do we get our knowledge, and how do we know truth when we have it? Two proposed methods dominated the philosophical field. One called for rigorous deduction from axiomatic first principles—the mathematically minded rationalism of Descartes and his successors, notably, Spinoza and Leibniz. The other method was the experimental, involving the reliance on carefully organized data of experience—the philosophy of the British empiricists, Bacon, Locke, Berkeley, and Hume. The period from the death of Francis Bacon to that of David Hume was exactly 150 years (1626–1776). Then came Kant, who subjected both rationalism and empiricism to a thorough-going revision in his Critical philosophy of intelligible experience.

Francis Bacon's Career and His Vast Project

Francis Bacon (1561–1626) took an early leading part in the formulation of philosophical method. In mapping out the field which modern minds essayed to explore and master, his trumpet call to great endeavor was far reaching. Bacon's work has been variously appraised, and we shall be less likely to misjudge him if, from the outset, we recognize him, not as a productive scientist, but as a promoter of science. He regarded himself as a herald of modern research; "I only sound the clarion, but I enter not into the battle."[1]

The details of his life are well known. His father kept the great seal under Queen Elizabeth. After his education at Cambridge, Francis Bacon went with an embassy to Paris. His father's premature death left him, a younger son, to his own devices, for his uncle, Prime Minister Burghley, would not help him. Two great purposes motivated him: to rise high in government and to achieve leadership in modern science and philosophy. Though his first aim could not be realized during Queen Elizabeth's reign, he did rise high under James I, who made him Lord Chancellor. But he was charged with and condemned for bribery by Parliament, and his last five years were spent in retirement, which he turned to account by producing his philosophical treatises.

Pope's characterization of Bacon—"the wisest, brightest, meanest of mankind"[2]—of which Macaulay's famous essay is a brilliant elaboration, has confused modern judgment. And it must be confessed that the student of Bacon is confronted with puzzling contrasts. For one who recognizes in philosophy the compass of life and a deep expression of the human spirit, it is disconcerting to find, in Bacon, a loyal devotion to philosophical ideals side by side with lax fidelity in personal relations; integrity in scientific method, combined with decidedly furtive moral standards. Was Socrates right in his dictum that virtue is knowledge, or was Macaulay right when he said that mental and moral genius nowise imply and condition each other?

[1] Quoted in R. W. Church, *Bacon*, London, Macmillan, 1908, p. 179.
[2] Alexander Pope, *An Essay on Man*, IV, l. 282.

Embarrassment has led some writers, who hold fast to Socrates, to mitigate Bacon's moral vices or to depreciate his intellectual virtues.

When we turn to Bacon's philosophy, we find intellectual expressions of his character, its merits and its defects. His mind tended to breadth and expansiveness, not to depth and penetration. He declared that he had "taken all knowledge for his province."[3] Although his works surveyed all the sciences and criticized their entire cosmic sweep, they have aptly been described as a series of magnificent and impressive introductions. To do justice to Bacon's philosophical achievement, we should keep his limitations in mind, else we impose on him standards which he will fail to meet. He made no considerable contribution to scientific knowledge in detail. Does his just claim to honor in the history of thought rest on his encyclopedic grasp of knowledge, on his advocacy of the proper method for attaining this knowledge, on his prospectus of work to be done by others, or on his enthusiastic call to work in the vineyard of science?

Bacon was convinced that scientific and philosophical inquiry required a radically new start and a new method. With firm faith in the human mind, he mapped out his "Great Instauration," a program of intellectual revival and reconstruction for the modern age, which would enable it to investigate nature and to apply the knowledge of its laws to the advantage and progress of mankind. In its final form, his vast project was supposed to comprise six parts: the partition or classification of the sciences; the interpretation of nature; natural and experimental history; the scale or hierarchy of intelligence; the forerunners or anticipators of the new philosophy; and, finally, the principles and substance of this philosophy which were to be achieved progressively in the future.

Bacon's projected "Instauration" was really a fourfold undertaking. The first was a topical survey of existing knowledge, an inquiry into the unpromising condition of the sciences, and a diagnosis of the causes of their stagnation. This is broadly, though not precisely or adequately, covered in his treatise on the *Dignity and Advancement of the Sciences*. The second involved the detailed elaboration of a new method for scientific and philosophical inquiry. This new logic, which is in explicit opposition to the Aristotelian, is found in the *Novum Organum*. The third comprised a natural history in the fullest and most encyclopedic sense of the term, an immense undertaking of which only fragmentary suggestions are given in his writings. A list of some 130 of these natural histories which Bacon had in mind suggests the broad range of his enterprise, and explains his pressing demand for means to undertake his grand intellectual exploration on a vast scale, with a large corps of assistants. The fourth and crowning part, to which the other three were regarded as introductory, was to be the true interpretation of nature, an empirical philosophy solidly based on scientific fact. This part, of course, Bacon was not able to execute in full; to prepare for it was the object of his other inquiries. In comparison with his vast proj-

[3] Quoted in John Nichol, *Francis Bacon*, Edinburgh, Blackwood, 1907, Pt. I, p. 1.

ect, the career of courtier and statesman seemed to him narrow and impermanent. The work of an inventor, though less imposing, lasts forever.

Bacon's Exposure of Dogmatism and Its Errors

First of all, Bacon distinguished sharply between science and theology. The confusion of these two, he insisted, had been ruinous to both. He was not irreligious; he was prepared to give to God the things that are God's, and to Caesar what is Caesar's. He wrote in his essay, "Of Atheism": "I had rather believe all the fables in the Legend, and the Talmud, and the Alcoran, than that this universal frame is without a mind. . . . It is true, that a little philosophy inclineth man's mind to atheism; but depth in philosophy bringeth men's minds about to religion."[4] But in the next essay, "Of Superstition," he went on to say: "It were better to have no opinion of God at all, than such an opinion as is unworthy of him."[5] In theology you proceed on faith. Theology is like a game of chess; if you wish to play at all, you must follow the rules. There is thus a fundamental antithesis in method and attitude between the scientist and the theologian. The pendulum of thought swings between skepticism and unquestioning faith; reason does not answer the questions of religion and cannot accept the answers of theology.

Bacon attributed the stagnation in science of fifteen centuries to the adoption of theological methods. Theology begins with its indubitable dogmas, but true science must proceed by inquiry, pure and simple; it must not anticipate its conclusions, it must not anticipate nature at all, but it must seek to interpret the facts of nature as it finds them. Having thus sharply distinguished between science and theology, Bacon applied himself to the former. He treated science in three categories in accordance with the three faculties of man (memory, fancy, reason): history, poesy, philosophy. History he divided into natural and civil; poesy into epic, dramatic, and didactic or parabolic, regarding the last as the greatest—a hint to the well-meaning people with ample leisure who consider Bacon as the author of Shakespeare's plays. Philosophy he classified under three heads as dealing with God, with nature, and with man. By the philosophy of God, Bacon understood the doctrine of first principles. The philosophy of nature was divided into mechanical and teleological science. The first examines the actual working of nature; the latter deals with final causes or purposive determination, and exhausts itself in empty abstractions. Bacon regarded it as inclined to dogmatism, as the obedient handmaiden of theology, and he called it a virgin, consecrated to God, but barren. He classified philosophy of man in a variety

[4] Francis Bacon, *Essays*, in J. M. Robertson (ed.), *The Philosophical Works of Francis Bacon*, London, Routledge, 1905, p. 754.
[5] *Ibid.*, p. 755.

of categories, which were grouped together under two heads: man as an individual and man as a citizen.

Bacon considered correct method as more essential than genius to intellectual achievement. Science has decayed because men have had no clear view of the path and the goal, and they have wandered into futile by-paths. Even a cripple keeping steadily on the right road can outstrip a fast runner who is forever wandering off the road and losing his way. Dogmatism, confusion, and false philosophy have been the sources of error and decay. The adoption of the right procedure is the sovereign remedy.

The first obstacles in the way of scientific inquiry are the prejudices with which we are beset, and which Bacon called the "idols of the mind." He classified these under four heads. Some of our preconceptions are artificial; Bacon called them the "idols of the theater": for they are the intellectual conventions and fashions. They set the tone and determine the initial course of our thinking. Thus misguided at the outset, the farther we go on, the more we wander from the truth. Like plays upon the stage, they succeed each other, and what is accepted unquestionably by one generation may be out of the question for the next. The other three "idols" are more natural sources of error, prejudices native to every one of us. We can never eradicate them utterly, but can only recognize them, make allowances for them, and seek to check them as much as possible. Thus, all thought requires expression in words, but words are elastic and protean, unstable bearers of confused meanings. These are the "idols of the forum" or the "market place," the most troublesome of all. On the mart of ideas, the medium of exchange is language; counterfeit here passes undetected for true coin. Besides buying and selling with mere counters, men barter in words, all the while thinking that they are dealing in real goods; word mongering passes for thinking, and monstrous and meaningless errors are thus begotten. In addition to the error caused by the confused use of words, each of us has prejudices of his own, individual prepossessions, partialities, and peculiarities. These are the "idols of the cave" or "den." Underlying all these are prejudices and erroneous ways of thought which seem ingrained in human nature, in the tribe or race of men. Bacon called them "idols of the tribe." We mistake the mere succession of two events for a causal relation between them, from whence arise superstitions without end, about thirteen at table, traveling on Friday, looking over one's left shoulder. We notice instances which bear out our special prejudices, and completely overlook instances to the contrary. We generalize hastily from insufficient data, leaping at conclusions based on random similarities, mistaking the odd and striking for the characteristic.

Before fruitful scientific work can be assured, the mind must be rid as much as possible of the confusing influence of these "idols." The "idols of the theater," our intellectual conventions, should be disciplined or repudiated. The "idols of the market place," the confusion of words, are to be checked and corrected by keeping as close as possible to concrete things, by perfecting the precision of our terms, and by avoiding abstractions which are merely empty shells. We must ever be clearly aware of our racial prejudices and individual prepossessions, being on our guard lest they mislead us. The scientific mind should be an open mind, a blank tablet or clean slate on which nature may write its own story. The mind must be made an unbiased recorder of facts.

The New Logic of Induction

Unprejudiced scientific investigation is to use a new logic of induction from particular observations to general conclusions. This Bacon proposed to formulate in the second book of the *Novum Organum*. The richer our collection of data, of course, the better prepared we are; but Bacon warned against depending on the mere counting of instances:

The induction which proceeds by simple enumeration is childish, its conclusions are precarious, and exposed to peril from a contradictory instance; and it generally decides on too small a number of facts, and on those only which are at hand. But the induction which is to be available for the discovery and demonstration of sciences and arts, must analyze nature by proper rejections and exclusions; and then, after a sufficient number of negatives, come to a conclusion on the affirmative instances.[6]

Uncritical induction is like the work done by the ant which only collects and drags materials together. The dogmatist is like the spider that spins cobwebs out of its inner cosmos. But the true scientist is like the bee which "gathers its material from the flowers of the garden and of the field, but transforms and digests it by a power of its own."[7] True induction does not merely enumerate; it also eliminates.

In more specific detail, Baconian investigation must begin with a clean slate, observing nature without any preconceptions. Before long, looking over our data, we may note the recurrence of certain reactions or forms of behavior in a variety of conditions. In seeking their causal explanation, we inquire whether there is any single common factor or instance in them all. Bacon called this the "Table of Essence" or "Presence." If we find one, our inference that it has a causal relation to the shared reaction or behavior may be further confirmed if we were to find two sets of conditions, identical in every respect except in this one factor previously noted, in the absence of which the noted reaction is also absent ("Table of Deviation" or "Absence in Proximity"). But again, we may observe the different degrees of this reaction in different cases, when the factor in question is also seen to vary, by comparing increase or decrease. This was called by Bacon the "Table of Degrees" or of "Comparison." A general conclusion is thus drawn, like the

[6] Francis Bacon, *Novum Organum*, I:cv, in *op. cit.*, p. 291.
[7] *Ibid.*, I:xcv, p. 288.

first vintage in the interpretation of nature. This is followed in Bacon's plan by a series of inquiries calculated to perfect the completeness and to test the accuracy and adequacy of the induction. Bacon gave particular and extended treatment to what he called "prerogative instances": solitary, clandestine, constitutive, and twenty-four others, most notably "instances of the finger-post" or "crucial instances." These last are decisive experiments which sway the balance between contending views of the understanding. These "afford very great light, and are of high authority, the course of interpretation sometimes ending in them and being completed."[8]

Bacon's logic of induction has been variously estimated; it has aroused the highest praise, but also negligence and disdain. In his defense of the positive merit of the *Novum Organum*, Fowler has called attention to seven points in particular: Bacon's constant emphasis on the necessity of a thorough ac-quaintance with the facts of nature as a guard against prejudice and dogma-tism; his advocacy of artificial experiments to supplement the usual ob-servation of nature; his distinction between scientific induction and the mere counting of instances; his recognition of the relation between induction and deduction; his distinct perception of the fact that the real object of science is causal knowledge; his insistence on the unity of nature and of science; and his classification of fallacies, the doctrine of the "idols." But Church criticized Bacon because he

. . . never adequately realized that no promiscuous assemblage of even the most certain facts could ever lead to knowledge, could ever suggest their own inter-pretation, without the action on them of the living mind, without the initiative of an idea. [Bacon had] one conspicuous and strange defect for a man who under-took what he did. He was not a mathematician.[9]

This lack accounts in a measure for his inability to understand, to appreciate, and to share in the scientific work of a mathematically minded age. It indi-cates a still more fundamental flaw: his inadequate estimate of the importance of hypothesis in all scientific work, his suspicion of system in his over-emphasis on inventory of data.

In opposing the deductive formalism of Scholastic logic, Bacon, for all his protestations to the contrary, inclined too much to the side of pure induc-tion. Scientific experiment involves the use of hypotheses. The investigator makes no fetish of them; he is ready to abandon them the moment experience shows them to be untenable, but he cannot move without them. In studying nature, we cannot proceed with our minds utterly blank; we must be looking for something. We may not find it, of course, or we may find something radically different. Like Saul, we may be looking for mules and asses, and discover a kingdom, or our fortune may be just the reverse. Nature speaks to us in different languages according to our different problems and in-quiries. But to him who lacks a problem nature is dumb because he is deaf.

[8] *Ibid.*, II:xxxvi, p. 343.
[9] Church, *op. cit.*, pp. 193, 195.

Every fruitful inquiry involves both induction and deduction. Of this truth, Bacon was by no means entirely unaware. Had his grasp of it been sufficiently thorough, however, the *Novum Organum* would have been a different book, different also the entire Baconian philosophy.

Bacon maintained to the end a sublime confidence in ingenious contrivances, mechanical or logical, that would make all minds equal, keys that would unlock any door for any man. Although he engaged in wholesale prosecution of truth and proclaimed himself generalissimo in the mapping out of a campaign for all the sciences, he was insufficiently acquainted with the work of the soldiers and captains of science in his own day. He complained that no formulas for the abridgment of arithmetical computations had been discovered, yet he made no mention of Napier's logarithms. He disparaged the work of Gilbert, his contemporary who was advancing science with his studies of magnetism. The Copernican astronomy he rejected with increasing decision, and, apparently, he was unaware of Kepler's work. In mechanics, he took no notice of Archimedes, nor was he sufficiently appreciative of his own great contemporary Galileo. And, as has been wittily stated, "he depreciates Roger Bacon, who invented gunpowder, whereas Francis thought the courage of soldiers might be increased by eating it."[10] Most amazing is his ignorance or his ignoring of Harvey's work on the circulation of the blood. Harvey was Bacon's own physician as well as the favorite doctor of the king. It is true that his great work did not appear until two years after Bacon's death, but in 1615 Harvey was teaching anatomy and surgery in London. Is it conceivable that Bacon, who was loudly trumpeting to the world the need for combined effort on the part of many investigators to wrest from nature its many secrets, took no occasion to find out what his own physician was investigating? An ardent advocate of experimental methods, Bacon himself was no direct investigator of any note. One of his experiments, which caused his last illness, was to stuff a fowl with snow to determine if it would retard putrefaction.

Social Organization of Scientific Research

Bacon's principal merits as a philosopher were his effective stimulus to scientific inquiry, his promotion of inductive methods, and his expansion of the scope and application of scientific work. He had boundless confidence in the mind's productive capacities, not only to discover the laws of nature but also to exploit its resources for man's use. Knowledge is power. The full realization of these purposes required organized social cooperation.

Bacon promoted this project with utopian zeal in his *New Atlantis*. In the ideal society which he portrayed, he emphasized the work of a government research institution called "Salomon's House." Its aim was "the knowledge

[10] John Nichol, *op. cit.*, Vol. II, p. 196.

of Causes, and secret motions of things; and the enlarging of the bounds of Human Empire, to the effecting of all things possible."[11] Salomon's House differed from the specialized research foundations of today in its typically Baconian all-comprehensiveness; it was unlimited in the scope of its investigations. Its lower regions—caves three miles deep—were laboratories for the artificial production of metals and the preservation of bodies at low temperature (recall Bacon's snow-stuffed fowl). Its upper regions—towers half a mile high and located on high mountains—were weather bureaus. It harnessed the power of violent streams and cataracts, and built engines for the control and direction of winds. It used medicinal waters and the regulation of temperature and humidity for the cure of diseases. It had chemical and biological laboratories and botanical gardens for the testing and production of new substances of animal and plant foods. It carried on experiments in mechanical and industrial production. While some members of its staff were field workers, others were sent abroad on traveling fellowships to learn about scientific advances being made elsewhere. The reports of all researches were continually appraised by the leading experts, and its own projects were extended or revised accordingly.

Bacon opened up large vistas of applied science, but we should not misjudge him as a mere exploiter of knowledge. The end of knowledge is not the mere satisfaction of curiosity, private gain, fame, or controversial skill. It is for the glory of God and the relief of man's estate that the scientist must ever be laboring. Science may not look loftily on this everyday world as if she had no part and lot in it. On life's stage only God and angels may be onlookers. But this does not mean that scientific inquiry is to aim at immediate practical profit and utility. Bacon distinguished "experiments of light (experimenta lucifera)," and prefers them to the "experiments of fruit (experimenta fructifera)"[12] for the former are designed to understand nature. Although perhaps of no immediate use, in the end they serve to reveal the vaster sources of human advantage. Here is clear recognition that applied science must rest on pure science.

Confident that his methods would advance natural science, Bacon was hopeful, also, that inductive inquiries would promote real knowledge in the field of morals. In ethics, as in physical science, he demanded emancipation from theological authority. He paid his respects to godliness, but concentrated on the good life that man can achieve by his own intelligent will. Scholastic tradition called moral philosophy the "handmaid of theology," but Bacon commented that doubtless much could be left to the discretion of the handmaid. Thus, humbly or astutely, Bacon would secure a place for a definitely secular ethics. Before formulating universal principles of conduct or prescribing how men ought to act, Bacon said that we should first investigate widely and thoroughly how men do act; that is, we should study the customs and practices of different societies. Descriptive ethics he ad-

---

[11] Francis Bacon, *The New Atlantis*, in Robertson, *op. cit.*, p. 727.
[12] Francis Bacon, *Novum Organum*, I:xcix, in *ibid.*, p. 289.

vocated as a proper introduction to any systematic theory of morals. We should investigate human nature in the same spirit of direct inquiry that has proved effective in physical science. We must study and watch our fellowmen so as to know how best to treat them and to use them. This wisdom has a sour Machiavellian aftertaste, and reflects the mind of Bacon the courtier and the everlasting suitor of preferment. But his demand for the thorough, direct investigation of the development of moral ideas and practices has proved very fruitful in modern ethical science. As in natural science, Bacon's work in ethics is important, not so much as a systematic contribution, but as a stimulating proposal of useful inquiry.

His ethical doctrine emphasized man's social character. The radical opponent of Aristotle's *Organon* followed here in Aristotle's steps. Nature and human nature disclose their kinship, for in both we may observe the dominance of the greater magnitude. The part submits to the whole. In spite of magnetic attraction, a heavy bar of iron in the presence of a loadstone moves to the earth; so man, while attached to his own interests, yields dutifully to larger social obligations. Individual virtues are completed in the institutional order of the good society.

It would be difficult to overestimate the extent of Bacon's influence on his contemporaries and immediate successors. It must be granted that many people have mistakenly given him the tribute that is properly Galileo's or John Locke's. But the fact remains that Bacon's name adorns the cornerstone of some of the noblest edifices of scientific and philosophical inquiry. In pursuing this spreading renown, we should note the wide expansion of organized scientific activity throughout Europe. Isaac Walton called Bacon "the great secretary of nature and science," and he spoke for a distinguished multitude. When Bishop Sprat published the first history of the Royal Society of London, he said that his book required one of Bacon's writings as a preface. Wallis, Hooke, Boyle, Evelyn all recognized in Bacon their master; his vision of Salomon's House in the *New Atlantis* was the inspiration of the Royal Society. And not only in Britain did Bacon's work bear fruit; in 1666, the Academy of Sciences was organized in Paris, and its first secretary put Bacon's induction on a par with Aristotle's syllogism. At the inaugural session of the Berlin Society, in 1711, Bishop Jablonski called Bacon by the name which Dante had applied to Aristotle, "the Master of those who know." In Galileo's Italy, in 1714, Count Masigli founded an institute at Bologna, and placed it under the auspices of the great Lord Chancellor of England.

The later course of Bacon's fame was not uniform. The French Encyclopedists swelled his renown during the eighteenth century. It has been pointed out that d'Alembert, in the *Preliminary Discourse to the Encyclopedia*, listed Bacon with Descartes, Newton, and Locke as the four masters of modern philosophy. To Leibniz, d'Alembert gave only a few phrases, to Galileo two lines, to Spinoza not even one; but, for him, Bacon was "the greatest, the most universal, the most eloquent of philosophers." The nineteenth century, however, was unsteady in its appreciation of Bacon. Macaulay laid bare the unlovely sides of his character, and the chemist, Liebig, turned on him with undisguised hostility. But Charles Darwin recorded, in his *Autobiography*, that, in beginning his evolutionary inquiries, he "worked on true Baconian principles, and, without theory, collected facts on a wholesale scale."[13]

When we turn from Bacon's wide renown to his more definite philosophical influence, we find that the systematic development of British empiricism gained headway seventy years after Bacon, and that it was actually initiated by the work of John Locke. But, as we trace this development later, we should keep in mind that, by his vigorous promotion of experimental science, Bacon prepared the way for Locke's more systematic philosophy of experience.

SUGGESTED WORKS FOR FURTHER STUDY

WORKS BY FRANCIS BACON. McClure, M. T. (ed.), *Selections;* Robertson, J. M. (ed.), *Philosophical Works.*

BIOGRAPHICAL AND CRITICAL STUDIES. Church, R. W., *Bacon;* Fowler, Thomas, *Bacon;* Nichol, John, *Francis Bacon.*

[13] Quoted in Francis Darwin (ed.), *The Life and Letters of Charles Darwin,* 2nd ed., London, Murray, 1887, Vol. I, p. 83.

15. Thomas Hobbes' Materialism: The Mechanics of Human Nature and Social Order

Natural and Social Laws in the Seventeenth Century

The seventeenth century was the age of systematic physical science that links the names of Galileo, Descartes, and Newton. It drew up the main principles of the cosmic mechanism which have guided the modern scientific interpretation of nature. But, while physical science was formulating its basic laws of causal necessity, the laws of human conduct and of social order were in a precarious condition. The century was a period of partisan strife and conflict of ideas in well-nigh every field of human activity. Bruno's martyrdom at the stake in 1600, and the condemnation and imprisonment of Galileo, marked the struggle of the new science with ecclesiastical bigotry. Theological differences flamed into bitter disputes, as in the Catholic-Jansenist controversy over the doctrine of divine grace and salvation, and the similar debate in Protestant Holland which rent the country in a bloody combat between liberals and conservatives. Religious and political animosities in France, which had stained the previous century with the massacre of St. Bartholomew's Eve, devastated Germany in the Thirty Years' War (1618–1648). Overlapping this conflict was the English Civil War, which began in 1642, and which was a struggle of King and Parliament, Church and State. The voyage of the *Mayflower* was the first step of resolute pilgrims toward "a new heaven and a new earth" of godly social order overseas. In all these struggles, the basic issue was that of sovereign laws of human life in various fields of individual activity and social relations.

The principles of law and authority, acknowledged or sought by the contending parties in each conflict, expressed their respective views of the nature, role, and destiny of man. This struggle did not begin in the seventeenth century; it was waged during the long transition from Scholastic to modern scientific culture in the Renaissance. These views were, at times, stubbornly medieval in their resistance to modern secularism; at other times, they expressed the frank release of passions and impulses which flared in the unbound worldliness of the Renaissance. On the one hand, they undertook to apply the mechanical interpretation of nature to include all human affairs; on the other, they sought to safeguard, within the new naturalism, a truer humanism of genuine spiritual values. The wide span of contending alternatives may be indicated by the social theories of Machiavelli, Bodin, and Grotius. Hobbes is significant for his resolute proposal to erect a doctrine of human nature and social-political order upon a strictly materialistic foundation, the mechanics of motion.

The Life and Career of Hobbes

Thomas Hobbes (1588–1679) was involved throughout his long life in the tensions and conflicts of his age. He and fear were twins, he said, alluding to his premature birth which was caused by his mother's fright at the terrible rumors about the Spanish Armada. The boy's father has been described as an ignorant vicar who "could only read the prayers of the church, and the homilies; and valued not learning, as not knowing the sweetness of it."[1] The vicar had a choleric temper; coming out of church one Sunday, he was provoked by another cleric into a wrangle during which he struck him with his cane. He was forced to flee his parish, leaving his family to the care of his brother, who was a prosperous glover of Malmesbury. Thomas received a good schooling, and, in due time, went to Magdalen Hall, Oxford. His conservative university training he held in lifelong contempt on account of its neglect of modern science and its continued servility to the Scholastic doctrines of "egregious blockheads." But Thomas valued and perfected his knowledge of the classics. His first literary labor was a translation of Thucydides; his last works were English versions of the *Iliad* and the *Odyssey*.

His employment as tutor in the family of Sir William Cavendish, first Earl of Devonshire, gave him opportunities to travel in France, where he was introduced to the scientific Cartesian circle, and in Italy where he met Galileo. His studies and reflections made him a confirmed champion of the mechanistic explanation of nature. His own scientific development came late; an Oxford graduate, he was over 40 before he first saw a copy of Euclid, which was lying open to the Pythagorean theorem in a gentleman's library. He read it and swore out loud that the proposition was impossible. But it referred him to other theorems, which he also studied, and so he was brought back step by step to the first definitions and axioms. Thus, at last convinced of the rational coherence and validity of geometry, he pursued it with zeal. But he had the confidence of the self-taught, and it later betrayed him, for

[1] John Aubrey, "The Life of Mr. Thomas Hobbes," in F. J. E. Woodbridge (ed.), *The Philosophy of Hobbes*, Minneapolis, Wilson, 1903, p. xi.

his claims to have squared the circle involved him in lamentable disputes with the mathematician John Wallis.

Social-political philosophy vied with mechanics and geometry in dominating his thought. The inferences from his developing doctrine of human nature, as well as his own social judgments, pointed toward political absolutism. The course of events in the strife between king and parliament and the resultant civil war in England led him to seek refuge in France. But his opposition to papal imperialism exposed him to French Catholic hostility. Hobbes combined a passion for controversy with a definite distaste for martyrdom. His defense of absolute, royal sovereignty set him against the parliamentary party; his later submissive acknowledgment of the strong revolutionary government estranged confirmed royalists. After the restoration of the Stuarts, his monarchical preferences found readier expression. When King Charles returned to his throne in London, he welcomed his old tutor, and Hobbes, with his ready wit in any argument, was often at court. "Here comes the bear to be baited,"[2] Charles would say to his courtiers. The old, zealous disputant took good care of his position in any debate.

Materialistic Principles of Nature and Human Nature

Hobbes translated some of Francis Bacon's essays into Latin, and Bacon admired his quick firm grasp and clear expression of ideas. But Hobbes did not share Bacon's devotion to inductive procedure. Experience was his field, as it was Bacon's, but he did not trust its exploration by mere observation and experiment. "Experience concludeth nothing universally."[3] Hobbes, like Bacon, demanded the fullest survey of the facts in order to apprehend their basic characteristics, but he sought demonstrative conclusions by strict deductions from evident principles.

He admired Galileo for his grasp of fundamental principles in the explanation of nature. Galileo, according to Hobbes, was the "first that opened to us the gate of natural knowledge universal, which is the knowledge of the nature of motion."[4] This principle, notably vindicated in astronomy and physics by the great Italian, was applied universally by Hobbes, especially in the explanation of human nature and conduct. His initial philosophical project was the writing of a three-part, mechanistic treatise which deals with body or matter, man, and society. He wrote the last part first, De Cive (On the State), but the other two followed in their turn.

Geometric procedure impressed Hobbes as expanding knowledge by rigorous deduction from primary definitions. Philosophy, according to him, is

[2] Quoted in ibid., p. xix.

[3] Thomas Hobbes, Human Nature, in Sir Willam Molesworth (ed.), The English Works of Thomas Hobbes, London, Bohn, Vol. IV, 1840, p. 18.

[4] Quoted in Sir Leslie Stephen, Thomas Hobbes, London, Macmillan, 1904, pp. 77 f.

concerned with the causal explanation of things. As we understand and express clearly the nature of a thing, we can infer its various qualities and consequences. Thus we move from proposition to proposition in formulating our system of knowledge. In committing philosophy and science to a causal account of nature, Hobbes took a mechanistic view of all existence. Every event involves some sort of motion, and its cause must be some other motion that stirred and produced it. Motion is in space, and all existence of which we can have any knowledge is material.

This view of the world, as bodies in motion in space, was expanded by Hobbes to include all nature and human nature, and all bodily and mental processes. He paid great tribute to Harvey for discovering the circulation of the blood, and not only physiology, but psychology, too, demanded a mechanistic statement in terms of the interaction of motions. It should be mentioned, however, that, for all his eulogy of Harvey, Hobbes's physiology sometimes went back to Galen and the ancients. Hobbes described the nerves as carriers of the animal spirits, and regarded the heart as the controlling organ in mental as well as in organic reactions.

Hobbes viewed mind as a certain kind of complex mechanical activity in the body. Sensations are motions in the organism stirred by other moving bodies. The various bodily organs should be seen as diverse mechanisms. The heart is a spring, the joints are wheels, and life itself is a motion of limbs. So with our sense organs. When we say that we see, hear, touch, taste, or smell, in each case some part of our body is receiving the pressure of an outside moving body: "which pressure, by the mediation of nerves, and other strings and membranes of the body, continued inwards to the brain and heart, causeth there a resistance, or counter-pressure, or endeavour of the heart to deliver itself."[5] Our ideas of things are literally our impressions of them. We are, as we say, aware of changes: more properly, our perceptions and ideas are themselves changes from rest to motion, from one motion to another. Without change or motion, in an immobile existence, there would be no consciousness.

We should mention a problem here. Though sensations and thought are, in Hobbes' opinion, bodily motions, pressures and counter-pressures, we are not aware of them as motions. Hobbes called them our "phantasms," our ideas, what we mean or signify by the respective motions. We can use these phantasms, add and subtract them, compute or draw a sum or balance. This is reasoning. We combine names, terms, or definitions and infer valid conclusions. Our reasoning is the more reliable the more closely it keeps to the names or marks of specific motions. Hobbes criticized the excessively abstract Scholastic procedure of the medieval doctors, and also the algebraic symbolism of Wallis, whose formula-ridden pages, it seemed to him, were "as if a hen had been scratching."[6]

[5] Thomas Hobbes, *Leviathan*, in Molesworth, *op. cit.*, Vol. III, 1839, p. 2.
[6] Thomas Hobbes, *Leviathan* (W. G. Pogson Smith, ed.), Oxford, Clarendon Press, 1909, p. 7.

Emotions also are, according to Hobbes, due to interior motions in the heart, in reaction to its strong arousal by some sense perception or idea. Each passion in the heart springs from a motion stirred by an idea in the brain, and it expresses itself in an outward motion or action, either in desire toward, or in aversion from, something. This motion may be impulsive and precipitate, or it may waver, because it is countered by opposite motions due to other conceptions. Eventually, in this seesaw of motives, one or the other will have its way, and the resulting motion is what we call the action of our will.

This cosmology recalls the atomism of the Epicureans. As did Lucretius, in his poem *On the Nature of Things*, so Hobbes, in his vivid prose, portrays the world and men's lives as a stirring immensity of moving bodies. Every event is either an impact or a rebound of some sort. Our so-called "memories" are like gradually subsiding tremors; our so-called "purposes" are drives persisting in certain set directions, and so also with the other activities of the mind. Accordingly, Hobbes once illustrated the association of ideas or trains of thought as a series of mechanical processes in which one motion stirs others in an adjacent area:

In a discourse of our present civil war, what could seem more impertinent, than to ask, as one did, what was the value of a Roman penny? Yet the coherence to me was manifest enough. For the thought of the war, introduced the thought of the delivering up the king to his enemies; the thought of that, brought in the thought of the delivering up of Christ; and that again the thought of the thirty pence, which was the price of that treason; and thence easily followed that malicious question, and all this in a moment of time; for thought is quick.[7]

This general comparison of Hobbes with the Epicureans may be pursued further in considering his theology and his doctrine of human destiny. Epicureanism unreservedly rejected the belief in divine providence and was, in effect, atheistic, even though it entertained the notion of some otiose material deities, relaxing somewhere in interstellar space. For Hobbes, also, God, like any other being, must be some kind of material substance. Though Hobbes had a great deal to say about Christianity and Scripture in his works, and devoted the entire second half of his *Leviathan* to the discussion "Of a Christian Commonwealth" and "Of the Kingdom of Darkness," Hobbes did not require God in his mechanistic cosmology, in which all teleology or final causes are rejected.

In his doctrine of human destiny, however, Hobbes felt either the need or the advisability of having recourse to divine assistance. His doctrine of man's state after death was signally different from the Epicurean view. In his hexameters, Lucretius arrayed twenty-eight arguments against the immortality of the soul, and, without the slightest concession, rejected the traditional beliefs in a future life. But Hobbes contrived to tie a doctrine of

---

[7] Thomas Hobbes, *Leviathan*, in Molesworth, *op. cit.*, Vol. III, pp. 12 f.

immortality and the resurrection of the body onto his materialistic account of human nature; and not as a mechanistic-causal consequence, this time, but as a pure gift of God's grace! Man is strictly material; his body is subject to death and dissolution; it is not, by nature, capable of immortality. But God is omnipotent, and on the day of judgment he will give new life to the righteous man. He will reassemble his ashes, "renew his inanimate, and rotten carcase into a glorious, spiritual, and immortal body."[8] But the unrighteous and unrepentant souls will suffer a second and everlasting death. What did Hobbes mean here by righteous and unrighteous bodies, and how could all this divine judgment and transformation be accomplished within the framework of a strictly mechanistic cosmology? Perhaps the most reasonable explanation is that Hobbes was carried away by controversial zeal to show that he could quote Scripture as effectively as the bishops, and to prove the Christian doctrine of the resurrection of the body in his materialistic way. His venture into apologetics cannot be ignored, and now that we have mentioned it, we should return to his systematic cosmology.

In this vast concourse of motions, everything proceeds out of strict mechanical necessity. Hobbes rejected all teleology and all spontaneity in nature; he taught determination of the strictest mechanics. In his protracted controversy with Bishop Bramhall, Hobbes defended the unqualified necessity of every event in nature against any doctrine of chance, and the necessity of every human action against any freedom of will. The scientific study of human nature and conduct can recognize the operation of no arbitrary, inexplicable agents, but only the same causal production and explanation of events as is true everywhere else in nature. In each case, our so-called "choice" involves the expression of the motive which prevails in our view or expectation of the situation that confronts us. Our will is not some unaccountable spirit or agent inside of us; it is simply our active nature.

Determinism is not to be understood as disowning personal responsibility for one's actions. A person acts in accordance with his nature; he is what he is, and he is judged for what he is and does. If he is harmful to us, we oppose him and demand his punishment. Hobbes said that he did not wish a murderer to plead, as his defense, "Mr. Hobbes tells me that I couldn't help it." But, with this doctrine of determinism, we may remark, the murderer would not seem to be blamed differently from his bullet. In condemning the manslayer as doing wrong, we cannot mean that in the state and order of nature he is as he ought not to be. We can and must understand and explain both man and bullet, physically. Only when we consider the social order and the system of laws, and a sovereign power to enforce them effectively, can we conceive of the murderer as a law-breaker, as punishable and wrong. The implications of Hobbes' determinism in ethics and in legal-social philosophy are thus evident.

In interpreting all nature and human nature in terms of bodies in motion,

[8] *Ibid.*, p. 631. See also pp. 614 f.

Hobbes emphasized, throughout, the dynamics of existence. Like the Epicurean swirl of atomic clusters, his world is in continual unrest and drive, each object impelled and impelling. The seeming quiescence of anything is not really static; it is only a latently inclined or diverted motion, alert to some impulsion and ever ready to go. Human felicity lies in the active experience of prospering, not in the state of having prospered. All our actions, and the intervals between them, must be viewed in this dynamic perspective to which Hobbes referred by the term "endeavour."

Hobbes was led by his deterministic interpretation of free will and of necessity to the same conclusion that followed from his doctrines of perception and emotion. The natural drive or "endeavor" in each man, as in every other thing, is a restless assertion of power, of striving to persist and to prevail. This desire to dominate, and our pleasure in its gratification, color all our experiences. Neither our feelings nor our reflections are disinterested. Science itself, in its way, aims at mastery, for "the end of knowledge is power."[9]

An acid will corrode the metals it touches as much as it can; this is its nature, just as it is the nature of gold to resist this corrosion effectively in most cases. In human relations we call this assertive behavior "selfishness," but we must understand its plainly natural character. Men being what they are, we can only expect them to vie with each other. Egoistic exploitation or oppression is the natural inclination of each, and this universal contention of selfish wills marks human life in the state of nature as a continual race, as impending or overt war. Each man strives to prevail over his rivals and to circumvent their efforts to prevail over him.

Hobbes developed his idea of human life as a competitive race to encompass the whole range of man's affections and passions in one conclusive survey:

[In this race for mastery] to endeavour, is appetite. To be remiss, is sensuality. To consider them behind, is glory. To consider them before, is humility. To lose ground with looking back, vain glory. To be holden, hatred. To turn back, repentance. To be in breath, hope. To be weary, despair. To endeavour to overtake the next, emulation. To supplant or overthrow, envy. To resolve to break through a stop foreseen, courage. To break through a sudden stop, anger. To break through with ease, magnanimity. To lose ground by little hindrances, pusillanimity. To fall on the sudden, is disposition to weep. To see another fall, is disposition to laugh. To see one out-gone whom we would not, is pity. To see one out-go whom we would not, is indignation. To hold fast by another, is to love. To carry him on that so holdeth, is charity. To hurt one's self for haste, is shame. Continually to be out-gone, is misery. Continually to out-go the next before, is felicity. And to forsake the course, is to die.[10]

---

[9] Thomas Hobbes, *Elements of Philosophy*, in Woodbridge, *op. cit.*, p. 7.
[10] Thomas Hobbes, *Human Nature*, in Molesworth, *op. cit.*, Vol. IV, p. 53.

The Leviathan: the Social Contract and Lawful Order under Absolute Sovereignty

Hobbes was resolute in pursuing his principles to their final conclusions. His greatness as a philosopher is evident in the consistent thoroughness of his deductions. His vigorous system comprehensively brings out the strength of his materialism and also discloses some of its shortcomings as an account of human nature and conduct. Both its merits and its defects are manifest in Hobbes' main treatise, the *Leviathan* (1651).

The mechanical explanation of human behavior does not warrant any moral judgments. Inherent in the natural state of man, according to Hobbes, there can be no justice or injustice, no right and wrong. In common speech, the words "good" and "evil" signify what we like and hate, what pleases and displeases us; either in their prospect (fair or foul), or in their effect (delightful or unpleasant), or in the means used to attain (useful or hurtful). But these are all judgments of what suits or disturbs, delights or vexes us; they nowise signify moral approval or disapproval. Nor are there any fundamental rights in human nature inherently entitled to respect. In the natural course of human existence, all men equally desire preeminence over others. This race and strife are always in favor of the fleet and strong; the winners do not owe the losers any show of consideration.

We must recognize the ruthless exploitation and hostility which mark the natural state of man, and also the lack of any scientific basis for a condemnatory judgment of it. The hostile state of nature is anarchic—a contention of powers—which recognizes no sanctions or scruples. It is a condition of universal conflict, a war of all against all. The strong oppress and trample the weak; the weak yield but are alert to any chance for escape or counterblow. Greed, fear, and "gloriation" incite men to war; they fight for booty, for protection, for the vanity of power. Even in our organized society the persisting effects of our hostile suspicion of each other are to be noted. We lock our chests and our doors; we demand bonds and sureties; we seek guards when we go on a journey, but we do not trust them, so we arm ourselves as well. How much more is this true in the natural state, without any law or authority to control or to protect men in their dealings with each other! How can we, then, accuse or condemn men for their selfish behavior? "The desires, and other passions of man, are in themselves no sin. No more are the actions, that proceed from those passions, till they know a law that forbids them: which till laws be made they cannot know: nor can any law be made, till they have agreed upon the person that shall make it."[11]

In his problem of accounting for moral sanctions, the only ethical theory Hobbes could deduce from his materialistic view of human nature is legalism.

[11] Thomas Hobbes, *Leviathan*, in *ibid.*, Vol. III, p. 114.

Before we consider this implication of his mechanistic cosmology, we should examine his explanation of the incentives which lead men to form their social contract. No real social-mindedness motivates the organization of the social order, but only the same natural selfishness that spurs men to conflict. Men are moved by greed and the desire for power, but also by anxious concern for security. The rampant strife which promises boundless loot assures them no safety. The life of internecine war, in prospect so bountiful, is actually a cramped, terrible, and ruinous existence.

In such condition, there is no place for industry; because the fruit thereof is uncertain: and consequently no culture of the earth; no navigation, nor use of the commodities that may be imported by sea; no commodious building; no instruments of moving, and removing, such things as require much force; no knowledge of the face of the earth; no account of time; no arts, no letters; no society; and which is worst of all, continual fear, and danger of violent death; and the life of man, solitary, poor, nasty, brutish, and short.[12]

The natural demand for self-preservation motivates men to seek escape from this precarious existence. If this desire for security is to be reliably satisfied in any one's life, it must operate effectively in all of us. We can be securely protected from the selfish greed and hostility of others only as they are similarly protected from us. This can be assured solely by a universally established system for the mutual suppression of the naturally selfish drive, by the common agreement of all to submit their anarchic will to the authority and laws of one sovereign will. This is the social contract which replaces the natural state of war by peace under the absolute dominion of Leviathan.

We should note that Hobbes did not intend his account of the establishment of the social order to be a historical narrative. His Leviathan is not a historical person, nor is his social contract a historical document. On the basis of his cosmology and anthropology, Hobbes undertook to point out the impelling conditions and the fundamental laws of nature which account for the organization of effective government. In several works, he compiled various lists of these laws, and presumably he did not intend to give a definitive tabulation of them. The basic law—in the common phrase, the "first law of nature"—is that of self-preservation. Man seeks by every means to preserve himself. As he is ready to go to war to promote or to protect his interests, it is only for more assured self-preservation that he can submit his will to another. Here reason infers and urges a second law: to surrender one's boundless claims and, in self-limitation, to "be contented with so much liberty against other men as he would allow other men against himself."[13] This second law was a sort of negative golden rule for natural egoists. To make this law effective, a third one is required, an inviolable contract for all. Their covenant must be irrevocable, subject only to the first law of self-

12 *Ibid.*, p. 113.
13 *Ibid.*, p. 118.

preservation; that is, the sovereign authority cannot require a man's self-destruction. The other laws—sixteen or more, which Hobbes derived from these three fundamental principles—were intended to comprehend in greater detail the sanctions of organized, law-abiding society. In his third law, Hobbes indicated his unwavering commitment to political absolutism. The social contract by which men renounce their anarchic will in universal submission to their sovereign must be an inviolable covenant. The authority of Leviathan is not subject to their periodic consent or repudiation, or to control by any other power in the state. It is irrevocable and indivisible authority. It should be noted that the social contract is of the people, with each other; it is not a contract with the sovereign. The people are Leviathan's subjects and they owe him obedience, but, strictly speaking, he has no obligation to them. His will is their law and the basis of all obligation.

In conceiving the absolute sovereignty as indivisible, Hobbes did not necessarily reject all governments other than monarchy. On principle, he recognized democracy and aristocracy as alternative regimes. In fact, the basic social contract is a sort of democratic enactment, whereas an aristocratic council of rulers might be expected in a society of men with different capacities for leadership. Hobbes actually inclined toward monarchy, and referred to Leviathan as a single person. But his main point was that the ruler must be truly sovereign and must rule absolutely. From the civil war in England he drew the inference that divided authority is a political inconsistency. Either the king is the employed agent of Parliament, or its members are his clerks. Where each claims some control over the other, there is no really supreme power in the state, and dissension and eventual anarchy threaten. The greater hazard of such dissension in a democratic assembly or in an aristocratic council as compared with that under the sovereignty of a single will seemed to Hobbes sound reason for advocating absolute monarchy.

Leviathan's authority is unlimited in covering all men's affairs and relations—not only in strictly political matters, but also in domestic, economic, social, and religious activities. Here again, Hobbes' doctrine reflected the issues and conflicts of his age with regard to the struggle between Church and State. He rejected all ecclesiastical pretensions to temporal authority. The sovereign's will must be supreme in the Church as well as in all other human institutions; the clergy are the ruler's agents and must obey his laws. According to Hobbes, this plan, while safeguarding the State from churchly cabals, nowise disturbs the truly religious life of the people. The essence of the Christian religion is the simple belief that Jesus is the Christ; it does not include subservience to the ambitions of bishop or pope.

If Leviathan cannot acknowledge the pretensions of lofty prelates, much less can he tolerate the crotchets of sectaries and the sundry scruples of individual conscience. In rejecting all pleas for freedom of conscience, Hobbes pointed out that he was referring to overt action. A man's beliefs are his own and cannot be controlled, any more than his sensations can. They all depend on the way in which his particular bodily organs react to other moving bodies. But all men, whatever their particular beliefs, must be moved in their actions by the controlling power of Leviathan's promulgated laws.

According to Hobbes, the true moral philosophy is the science of the basic laws of human nature within the absolute sovereignty of Leviathan. Justice and injustice have no real meaning apart from the performance or transgression of his laws. But if the covenant which establishes Leviathan's government institutes morals, right and wrong, what did Hobbes really mean by calling this covenant "inviolable"? Did he mean only that it could not be violated, or could he mean that it ought not to be violated; that it would be wrong to violate it? As with the basic contract, so with any specific law: if the laws rest simply on Leviathan's sovereign will, all we could say is that there are the laws to be obeyed. Within the social order, they have a necessity analogous to that of the laws of nature.

But if the people's co-called "moral obligation" to obey the laws is constituted by Leviathan's sovereign will, does it not also depend upon his effective sovereignty? The people have surrendered their will to him in order better to insure their self-preservation, which depends upon unchallenged, operative authority. If, through domestic or foreign compulsion, the sovereign is swept away and is no longer actually dominant, what ground remains for his subjects' continued loyal devotion to him, and for how long? Shall we seek our answer in Hobbes' own public conduct? During the strife between king and parliament, he and other royalists sought refuge in France, where he later was tutor to Charles in exile. But, when the stable power of the revolutionary government proved convincing to him, he returned to England and acknowledged its authority. When, however, King Charles afterward returned to his throne, Hobbes was once more loyal to the actual sovereign.

Hobbes' political career seems consistent with his doctrine. His social contract, in effect, expressed his conviction that only an absolute sovereign's control of men's lives can insure their peace and protection from each other. But Hobbes was criticized for recognizing only a sovereignty *de facto*, not an authority *de jure*, since in his basic account of human nature he could find only conflicting powers, not contending principles of right and wrong. His government might demand and secure submissive obedience of subjects, but not the genuine loyalty of citizens. And in a social order that rested solely on overwhelming power, moral conduct would not be possible any more than it was in Hobbes' state of nature. The mechanics of human behavior are not altered by the institution of Leviathan's overmastering might. The laws may be actually effective ordinances; but real morality requires principles of rightful authority, *de jure*, that rest on the recognition of higher and lower values in human life and not only of the mechanics of conflicting forces and motions.

Critical Reactions to Hobbes' Politics and Ethics

Hobbes' philosophy aroused criticism and vigorous opposition that engaged British minds for almost a century. A radical alternative to Hobbes' materialism, and also to Baconian induction and empiricism, was represented in the rationalistic philosophy of a group of Cambridge philosophical theologians—or Cambridge Platonists, as they are called—chief among whom were Henry More and Ralph Cudworth. Both were free from sectarianism, and both criticized Puritan intolerance as well as Roman Catholic rigidity. Loyal to the central truths of Christianity, but also genuine humanists in their appreciation of the spiritual values of ancient classical philosophy, they sought a truly rational synthesis. Like St. Thomas, they were confident that sound reason leads the mind reliably toward the truths of faith; with Plato, they were convinced that the essential character of reality was rational-spiritual; and, unlike Francis Bacon, with his assemblage of sense data, they trusted to universal convictions, rational verities evident to normal intelligence. In moral, as in theoretical, reflection, they sought to organize these ideas into a reasonable system.

Before the Cambridge Platonists, this confident intellectualism had been advocated by a younger contemporary of Bacon, Lord Herbert of Cherbury (1583–1648), in his work De Veritate (On Truth). The mind neither is, nor ought to be, a clean state, a tabula rasa; nor does it receive and gather its sense data passively. We have not only a basic rational capacity but we also have certain convictions of normal intelligence, which, like the Stoics, Lord Herbert called "common notions." They are innate and not derived from sense experience or observation, although the mature experience of reasonable men has sustained and vindicated them. Our conviction of them finds expression in the general consensus of intelligent men.

This general consensus Herbert of Cherbury undertook to trace and to report in morals and religion. Beyond the desire for pleasure or for worldly goods, he pointed out a general recognition of the higher values that ennoble life. Men's minds are turned to justice, to love and true felicity. He listed five common notions on which he believed that men are agreed as essential to religion—that there is a God; that He should be worshiped; that divine worship is, in the main, virtue and piety; that the godly life demands repentance and rejection of our sins; and that God rewards and punishes us for our acts, in this life and in the hereafter. In his work on The Religion of the Gentiles, he was a pioneer in the comparative study of religious beliefs and practices.

Henry More (1614–1687) from an early age found his highest satisfaction in rational reflection. Morals and Christian piety, alike, were, in his view, the fruits of sound reason in our lives. In proving God's existence, he used the teleological and cosmological arguments, but emphasized St. Anselm's ontological argument. All our thought points to the divine spiritual substance, eternal and infinitely perfect. Divine providence directs nature and rules human lives in wisdom, justice, and goodness. On this moral assurance, More relied for his conviction of human immortality. His doctrine was the very reverse of that held by Hobbes. Whereas Hobbes sought to comprehend all nature and human life and conduct in a mechanistic doctrine, More did not admit any finality in mechanistic description. According to More, the ultimate character of everything is spiritual. His resistance to Hobbes' "belluine," or warlike, account of the natural life of man, as an unprincipled and insatiate selfish drive, was expressed, not in direct attack, but in urbane advocacy of the nobility and loveliness of virtue. Hobbes had spoken of men's lust for power; More also spoke of virtue as a power, but it was "an intellectual power of the soul, by which it over-rules the animal impressions or bodily passions; so as in every action it easily pursues what is absolutely and simply the best."[14]

Moral insight, according to More, finds expression in certain universal rational principles, or *noemata*. He expounded a list of twenty-three such ethical intuitions; their application in practice marks the general framework of morality. His *Enchiridion Ethicum*, or *Ethical Manual*, shared more than its title with the Stoic work by Epictetus, but More did not follow the Stoics in advocating apathy. He would engage both emotion and rational intelligence in the moral pursuit of the blessed life. He distinguished three basic virtues—prudence, sincerity, and patience—and, corresponding to them, three derivative virtues—justice, fortitude, and temperance. With these, he associated certain external goods of the blessed life after the manner of Cicero: not only mental, but bodily skill and vigor, and also such advantages as health and wealth. In contrast to Hobbes' reduction of human motivation to the mechanics of egoistic impulses, More portrayed the moral guidance of our lives by what he called the "*boniform faculty*," a capacity for active goodness: "By this the soul relisheth what is simply the best; thither it tends, and in that alone it has its joy and triumph."[15]

The Cambridge Platonists objected strongly to Hobbes' doctrine that morality has no status in nature, that justice and injustice, right and wrong, signify simply obedience or resistance to Leviathan's laws. Was not this a flagrant example of the error made by Scotist theologians in referring virtue and moral goodness to the fiat of God's will? Against both versions of this ethical confusion, that God's or Leviathan's ordinance constitutes any action good or evil, the Cambridge Platonists maintained the essential and rational validity of morals. This conviction found vigorous systematic exposition in the *Treatise Concerning Eternal and Immutable Morality*, by Ralph Cud-

---

[14] Henry More, *Enchiridion Ethicum* (trans. E. Southwell), in *An Account of Virtue: or Dr. Henry More's Abridgment of Morals*, New York Facsimile Society, 1930, p. 11.
[15] *Ibid.*, p. 156.

worth (1617–1688). This work was published forty-three years after its author's death, but its main principles were anticipated in his larger volume, *The True Intellectual System of the Universe*. Cudworth's fundamental position is an unwavering affirmation of the eternal and fundamental validity of rational principles:

> . . . that all things do not float without a head and governor, but there is an omnipotent understanding Being presiding over all; that this God hath an essential goodness and justice; and that the differences of good and evil moral, honest and dishonest, are not by mere will and law only, but by nature; . . .[16]

Cudworth applied this principle thoroughly, in theology as well as in ethics and politics. Against all Scotism, he maintained that man's basic assurance of God's existence is an expression of his confidence in the eternal and prevailing reality of rectitude: God is essentially that which ought to be. How can we then countenance Hobbes' notion that justice and virtue hang upon the edicts of Leviathan? Why should we obey Leviathan's law? Is it because we have so covenanted, and it is a law of nature that covenants are inviolable? But Hobbes could not mean that it is unjust to violate them; his human mechanics excludes any natural principle of justice or injustice. He could only mean that it is ineffective in nature, and forbidden by Leviathan, to violate covenants. We can never derive any real principle of justice or morality unless we recognize its fundamental reality in man and in nature, and, if this is so conceived, it is right and natural to express it.

Cudworth directed his criticism of Hobbes' ethics and politics to undermine Hobbes' entire mechanistic cosmology. Mind, intelligence, art, law, and morality are, in his judgment, basic realities, which are more essential than physical processes and qualities. The merits of Cudworth's philosophy are those of rigorous rationalism; its defects are those of a too rigid formalism. His moral philosophy lacked the direct examination of human conduct and values which distinguished the ethics of Henry More. But he championed a Platonic conviction of the eternal reality of spiritual principles which contended in British thought with the empiricist concentration on sense experience and inductive methods.

The systematic importance of Hobbes' philosophy was its thorough exposition of a materialistic cosmology. His ethical and political theories owe their importance to the same ruthless consistency with which he pursued his inferences. His conclusions shocked his theological and philosophical contemporaries. However, in undertaking to repudiate him, they were led to reexamine their own positions. The criticisms of Hobbes from these different points of view stimulated systematic reflection in ethics and social philosophy, which was a distinguished characteristic of British thought during the late seventeenth and early eighteenth centuries.

---

[16] Ralph Cudworth, *Treatise Concerning Eternal and Immutable Morality*, in *The True Intellectual System of the Universe*, Andover, 1837–1838, Vol. I, pp. 34 f.

SUGGESTED WORKS FOR FURTHER STUDY

HOBBES.   Hobbes, Thomas, *Leviathan* (several editions are available) and *The English Works of Thomas Hobbes* (W. Molesworth, ed.); Laird, John, *Hobbes;* Robertson, G. C., *Hobbes;* Stephen, Sir Leslie, *Hobbes;* Taylor, A. E., *Thomas Hobbes;* Woodbridge, F. J. E., *The Philosophy of Hobbes.*

THE CAMBRIDGE PLATONISTS.   Campagnac, E. T., *The Cambridge Platonists;* Cudworth, Ralph, *The True Intellectual System of the Universe* and *Treatise Concerning Eternal and Immutable Morality;* More, Henry, *Enchiridion Ethicum* (trans. F. Southwell), and *The Philosophical Writings of Henry More* (Mackinnon, F. I., ed.).

16. Descartes and Systematic Rationalism

Descartes' Life and Works

René Descartes (1596–1650) has been called the "father (or the founder) of modern philosophy," and his claims to this title outrank those of any other thinker. Descartes was also a leader in modern science. Just as in the beginnings of Greek thought, so during the early modern period, philosophical and scientific activity stimulated each other. Experimental research and theoretical reflection expanded the resources and the outlook of modern minds, and defined their problems.

We can readily understand why the seventeenth century, notable for its advance in systematic science—from the work of Kepler and Galileo, to that of Newton—was also the century when several great systems of philosophy were formulated. The achievements of systematic modern philosophy depended upon substantial progress in the organization of scientific knowledge, and also upon a recognized demand for the principles of a fundamental integrating method. The earlier thinkers of the Renaissance were epoch-making in their rejection of Scholastic authoritarianism, alert in their response to alternative doctrines of ancient thought, and original and fertile in their own speculation, but they lacked the coherence and stability of systematic procedure. Bruno's expansion of the Copernican astronomy into a philosophy of nature showed, in its three successive versions, both the cosmic sweep of his fertile mind and his need of methodical scientific discipline. Francis Bacon and Thomas Hobbes were notable champions of the use of scientific method in philosophy, but neither of them had any real mastery of productive science or a full insight into its systematic principles. Bacon's inductive method could not express adequately the logic of modern science. Hobbes adopted and promoted geometrical procedure, but he lacked the mathematical training and competence required for its reliable application in philosophy. Systematic intellectual progress in the seventeenth century demanded a philosophical outlook in scientific work, and a scientific method in philosophy. Descartes met this twofold need by his unique combination of

277

qualities. An original scientist, he was possessed by the philosophical problem of the principles of a fundamental method, and he had the mathematical, rigorous logic required for the thorough exploration of his problem. His theory of the structure of nature was involved in difficulties which his successors tried to overcome, but his formulation of philosophical method had vital influence on the entire development of modern philosophy.

René Descartes (he disliked the Latin form of his name, *Cartesius*) came from a family long established as country officials in central France. His father and elder brother were councilors of provincial parliaments, and they might have expected him to follow them in their careers. But young René showed early his keen inquiring intelligence; his continual questions led his father to call him his "little philosopher." His mother had died of consumption soon after his birth, and the boy's own health was precarious. To take care of both his frail body and his brilliant mind, his father sent the boy to study from his eighth to his sixteenth year at the College of La Flèche, in Maine. This school had been established with generous endowments by Henry IV, to provide for the Jesuit teachers whom the monarch had readmitted to France after their banishment by the Parliament of Paris. The course of studies naturally emphasized Scholastic doctrine, but also included the reading of ancient classical literature and instruction in mathematics. The considerate Jesuit teachers allowed the frail boy to room by himself and to lie in bed mornings, for, while his body in this way got its needed rest, his active mind, through study and reflection, mastered all class assignments. His teachers were alert to the new advances in knowledge. When Galileo's telescope at the University of Padua identified the satellites of Jupiter, a sonnet celebrating the discovery was composed and read to the student body at La Flèche. Descartes' training in mathematics was sufficient to start him on his own reflections, which led to his work in analytic geometry. Despite his later radical departure from Jesuit Scholasticism, he retained a lifelong personal appreciation of La Flèche. Mersenne, one of his school acquaintances who was eight years his senior, became his intimate friend and the active promoter of his ideas.

After his eight years of schooling, Descartes was sent by his father to Paris for an extended visit. With only a valet to look after him, René entered into the gay life of the capital; but fencing, card-playing, and the other diversions of titled frivolous youth soon palled on him. His friend Mersenne, and the mathematician Mydorge to whom he had been introduced, reawakened his intellectual interests. Hiding away from his boon companions, he lived for a while in studious seclusion, and then left Paris to study law at Poitiers.

Returning to the capital, he was drawn again into its whirl; once more he fled from it, and he resolved to devote his life to the pursuit of truth. But he was not sure of his intellectual principles. The study of ancient doctrine had failed to convince him; it merely filled him with distrust of all traditional learning. The new knowledge of mathematics did not by itself satisfy him; beyond the specific conclusions, which he was able to formulate, he was seeking the more universal principles to which it pointed. Already he felt the philosophical zeal for the ultimate, to which he later gave systematic expression. Since abstract geometry, by itself, was not enough for him, he sought a geometry that would explain the structure and processes of nature.

In this state of mind, he decided to see more of the world and, particularly, of men in military service, and, in 1617, he joined the garrison of Prince Maurice of Nassau, a noted military engineer who had attracted a number of scientists to his camp. Descartes' solution of difficult mathematical problems earned him the admiration of experts such as Isaac Beeckman, but his mind—remaining unsatisfied with special accomplishments—sought the center and foundation of knowledge. His inner mental conflicts moved him toward a crisis.

The crisis came on November 10, 1619, and Descartes has given us a vividly dramatic, though not altogether definite, account of it. He was then in winter quarters at Neuburg on the Danube. Confined all day to his warm room by the bitter cold—which also kept any visitors from disturbing him —he was absorbed in deep meditation. Full of enthusiasm, as he wrote, he had found the basis of a marvelous science. Was not this science more than merely analytic geometry—the application of algebraic analysis to geometrical problems—did it not encompass a universal rational system, in which algebra and geometry and mechanics were to be integrated, and the secrets of nature and of mathematics "unlocked with the same key"?[1] His new idea possessed him awake and asleep. He had three dreams which he interpreted as the challenge and choice of his destiny: "What road shall I pursue in life?"[2] He was at the turning point of his career. In a spirit of consecration to his recognized mission, he vowed that, in gratitude to the Blessed Virgin for his divine inspiration, he would make a pilgrimage on foot to her shrine at Loretto. When we consider the logical rigor of Descartes' philosophy, we should also remember this mystical fervor that marked its inception.

Descartes did not proceed from basic certainty to an assured and extensive exposition of his ideas. He seems to have prepared a preliminary outline of them, but could not decide to publish it. He continued his travels and military service. His rational self-concentration, his reliance on his own logical analysis, made him not only indifferent to traditional learning, but unresponsive even to the scientific advances of other men in his own time. Yet his interest seems to have strayed for a while into occult inquiries, seeking the alleged universal science of the Rosicrucians, but he found nothing ascertainable. In Prague, he examined the astronomical instruments in Tycho Brahe's observatory. A whole decade passed while he was developing his ideas. Meanwhile, his return to France and several years' residence in Paris con-

[1] J. P. Mahaffy, *Descartes*, Edinburgh, Blackwood, 1880, p. 27.
[2] Quoted in Elizabeth S. Haldane, *Descartes, His Life and Times*, London, Murray, 1905, p. 51.

vinced him that he could not find, in his native land, the intellectual tolerance he required for the development of his ideas. So he sought freedom of thought in Holland. He was to learn before long that Protestant dogmatism could be as rigid as the Catholic. Descartes' *Treatise of the World* was ready for the printer when he heard of the condemnation and imprisonment of Galileo, in 1633. Descartes' own work was in such agreement with Galileo's main conclusions, that he ordered Father Mersenne to halt all plans for publishing the book, for he would not bring himself into a clash with the Church. Continually, during his life, he reaffirmed this practical loyalty to the orthodoxy when his own conclusions did not square with it.

His ideas, even unpublished, were gaining wide currency, and, urged by his friends, he released some of his works for publication. The most important are the *Discourse on Method* (1637), *Meditations on First Philosophy* (1641), *The Principles of Philosophy* (1644), and *The Passions of the Soul* (1649). Of special philosophical interest is Descartes' correspondence with Princess Elizabeth of Bohemia and Queen Christina of Sweden. Christina's invitation brought him finally to Stockholm, and to the rigors of an arctic winter, during which the queen chose the hour of five in the morning for her philosophical conferences. Descartes' lungs did not last out the first season, and he died six months after his arrival in Stockholm, in 1650.

The Cartesian Method

Descartes' mind was dominated by a rational demand for clear and certain understanding, and by the recognition that many of our ideas are only vague opinions, on which, nevertheless, we have to act. From tentative precepts of practice, we have to move toward final and indubitable principles of theory. In the third part of his *Discourse on Method*, Descartes stated four maxims of provisional conduct for one who is in pursuit of the truth. First, he would obey established laws, conform to the social and religious practices in which he had been brought up, and avoid any radical excesses. Second, he would act resolutely on his chosen views, even though he lacked clear certainty about them. Third, he would try to control himself and his desires, rather than petulantly seek a change in the world order. And fourth, he would consider various careers and resolve to choose the best, and, since the best lies in cultivating his reason in the pursuit of truth, he would proceed steadfastly in that course. Descartes' own life and career exemplified this combination of a reasonably traditional conformity in practice with the self-reliant and rigorous pursuit of the truth, wherever it might point.

Nine years before the publication of his *Discourse on Method*, Descartes had formulated his *Rules for the Direction of the Mind*, which included thirty-one principles of rational procedure. Some of these are detailed rules of intellectual operation, but others are fundamental articles of the Cartesian philosophy. Thus, the second rule may lead to the unfolding of the rationalistic method. Descartes proposed to give attention only to those objects about which sure and indubitable knowledge is attainable. His basic purpose was to reach real certainty. True knowledge is clear, self-evident, or thoroughly grounded; its certainty is either axiomatic or conclusively demonstrated. He wrote in the *Discourse* that he would accept nothing as true unless, or until, it was indubitably clear and distinct. Strict analysis was required to resolve whatever was complex and difficult into its simplest parts for clearer examination. After thus mastering the simplest elements of a topic, he would proceed reliably to the more and more complex. He would not be content until the entire problem had been thoroughly mastered.

In applying this method to any specific object or problem, we always come short of finality, for our idea refers us to others on which it depends. It is a conclusion or inference of some sort, no more valid than the premises on which it rests. Beyond this relative deductive firmness, Descartes demanded an ultimately certain foundation for his rational system of ideas. Its first principle must have the self-evidence of a mathematical axiom.

As we need an unquestionable first principle, there can be only one starting point in strict philosophy, namely, questioning, and Descartes gave its simple formula: *I doubt*. This initial skepticism is only the preface to systematic construction. Subject every principle, every doctrine to the test of doubt until you find an indubitable idea. Now, Descartes reminds us, if, like Socrates, he says that he doubts everything, surely, at least he knows that he doubts. The one point that is unshaken by his doubt is the fact of doubt itself. And what does doubting imply? It is a process of thinking. I doubt, that is to say, I think. At this point Descartes took his great decisive step of analysis: "I think, therefore I am (*cogito ergo sum*)."[3]

Is this a direct analytical explication, or an inference, or a logical leap? Descartes did not intend it as an inference or as a conclusion; he regarded it as axiomatic, a self-evident first principle. Strictly speaking, he should not have used the term *ergo*, "therefore." In proceeding from "I think" to "I am," he meant only to complete his analysis and interpretation. In recognizing that I think, I acknowledge myself to be a thinking being. There would be an unwarranted leap in the analysis if I affirmed here my existence as such and such a self, mind and body, thus or otherwise related to others. This Descartes did not do as yet. He simply asserted the axiomatic self-certainty of a thinking being. The Latin text of one passage in *De Methodo* reads: "*Ego cogito, ergo sum, sive existo.*"[4] Descartes used a firm Latin statement. In all my doubting, he intended to say, surely I must acknowledge at least this, that I who think, I exist. We are reminded of St. Augustine's reflection twelve centuries earlier: "If I err, I am." Descartes began his philosophy with the fundamental self-attestation of the thinking self.

[3] Descartes, *Discourse on the Method*, in E. S. Haldane and G. R. T. Ross (eds.), *The Philosophical Works of Descartes*, Cambridge, Cambridge Univ. Press, 1911, Vol. I, p. 101.

[4] Descartes, *Oeuvres* (C. Adam and P. Tannery, eds.), Paris, Cerf, Vol. VI, 1902, p. 558.

Can we proceed directly from the clear and distinct certainty of the first principle to other clear and distinct conceptions? Specific ideas about external objects of thought may be derived from sense experience, which is not reliable. Even when attained by reflection, they are not directly recognized as beyond doubt. Once again, Descartes considered the implications of doubting. I think, I have ideas which I doubt; hence as a thinking being, I fall short of perfection. But I do entertain the idea of a perfect Being, infinite, omniscient, and omnipotent. This idea cannot have its origin merely in my thought. My imperfect mind cannot have produced this idea, nor can it have been derived from any other finite and limited source. The only adequate explanation of this idea of infinite perfection is the infinitely perfect reality of God.

In thus proceeding from his first principle of the indubitable thinking self to the necessary inference of infinitely perfect deity, Descartes was convinced of having discovered a reliable foundation, an objective, intelligible order of nature. By ascertaining the real nature of God through rational analysis, he would find the logical warrant for his further philosophical deductions. Already he could contemplate the realization of his rationalistic ideal of knowledge: a system of valid and consistent deductions, all derived from an indubitable self-evident first principle.

The Existence and the Attributes of God

In his first argument, just cited, Descartes deduced that the existence of God is required to explain the conception of an infinitely perfect Being by an imperfect mind. He expanded this reasoning in another argument, in which he considered God's existence in relation to his own. Again he began with himself and his idea of the infinitely perfect Being. If there were no God, how could he account for his own existence? If he had created himself, he should have bestowed on himself the infinite perfection of which he has the idea, and should therefore himself be divine. Clearly, then, he owed his existence to another author. But that author could not have been imperfect; neither his parents nor any other finite cause could adequately account for him and his idea of infinite perfection. That idea not only implies God's reality but also explains man's own existence as created by God.

Descartes analyzed further the idea of an infinitely perfect Being, by reformulating St. Anselm's ontological argument. Whereas in his other reasonings he had proceeded from the fact that he entertained the idea of deity, here he explored the implications of the idea itself. Various ideas are seen to imply certain properties without which they cannot be conceived. I cannot think of a triangle without entertaining its essential attributes of lines and angles; nor can I have the idea of a mountain without implying the idea of a valley. In conceiving of valleys or mountains or triangles, their existence is not necessarily implied; but it is otherwise with my idea of an infinitely perfect Being. If I considered this Being as nonexistent, surely my idea of it would be enhanced if I were to recognize it as also existent. But I should then be illogical, for, by definition, I maintained it as the idea of infinite perfection, not admitting of enhancement. Existence is thus seen to be a necessary attribute of infinite perfection; hence Descartes concluded that God, the infinitely perfect Being, exists.

This Cartesian version of the ontological argument aroused sharp criticism, notably by Pierre Gassendi in his published objections to the *Meditations*, to which Descartes replied. Like the monk, Gaunilo, in his criticism of St. Anselm, Gassendi challenged the major premise of the ontological argument, that the idea of an infinitely perfect Being implies its existence. Existence, according to Gassendi, is not a necessary attribute of perfection. A nonexistent thing is not said to be imperfect but to lack reality. In beginning with the idea of infinite perfection, Descartes exposed his argument to Gassendi's objection. It should be recalled that Anselm had reasoned from the idea of the greatest Being conceivable. The reformulation of the argument in later rationalism, as by Spinoza, emphasized the conception of God as the ultimate reality. This was also Descartes' view of deity in the exposition of his cosmology. But here, at the gateway to his account of nature, Descartes' method required a convincing warrant for his reliance on rational analysis. This warrant, as will be seen directly, required an emphasis on the infinite perfection of God. Thus we are necessarily led to Descartes' analysis of God's attributes.

Descartes formulated his conception of God as supreme, "eternal, infinite, immutable, omniscient, omnipotent, and Creator of all things which are outside of Himself."[5] God's infinity signifies a boundless reality without any limitation or defects. Deity is without source or destination, self-caused and self-active. All things depend on God, who includes them in His creative supremacy. His own activity is not undetermined; its cause is His own essence or nature.

In our analysis of God's nature we may contemplate it from certain fundamental perspectives, but we should recognize that God transcends their respective limitations. In conceiving of God's eternity, Descartes realized—as St. Augustine had before him—that time and its distinctions apply only to finite existence, and are transcended in Deity. Likewise with space; God's omnipresence does not signify His elastic spatial ubiquity. Instead of explaining how God can be everywhere, we should rather understand that strictly speaking He is not anywhere. Or, we might better say that date and location concern finite beings and do not qualify deity.

Descartes' conception of God's creative omnipotence is far reaching. The Creator's activity, it may be repeated, is without date or location. All things are created by God in the sense that all find their ultimate source and ex-

---

[5] Descartes, *Meditations*, in *The Philosophical Works of Descartes* (trans. E. S. Haldane and G. R. T. Ross), *op. cit.*, Vol. I, p. 162.

planation in His infinite nature. And this dependence of all things on God is continuous. We should keep in mind this doctrine of continuous creation when we consider Descartes' physical doctrine of the cosmic mechanism. The causal necessity, which connects the operation of all things in accordance with the laws of motion, itself finds its basic and perennial explanation ultimately in the creative activity of God. Or, should we not rather say that, by God, Descartes signified ultimately the basic cosmic reality? The Cartesian doctrine may be interpreted in both of these perspectives; the second one will eventually require more critical consideration.

Descartes recognized no necessity, no Moira or Nemesis, to which God's will is subject, but only God's own perfect nature; so his reasoning admitted no logical principles or laws that do not ultimately issue from God. For Descartes, God is the Creator, not only of all things, but also of all essences, the Author of all eternal truths. In creating the world, God creates the conditions, the nature, and properties of all things, as well as their respective principles, laws, and truths.

This analysis of God's attributes has suggested some of the outlines of Descartes' account of the structure of nature. One other attribute, though it is mentioned last, is primal to the Cartesian method. This is God's eternal veracity as the warrant for our reliance on rational analysis. Descartes had already resolved not to accept any ideas that were not clear and distinct. But how could he be sure of the reliability of this rational test? Its warrant was in God's infinite perfection. God would never deceive us; of that we can be certain. Therefore, the more we contemplate the necessary inference of God's existence from the idea of the infinitely perfect Being, and the more thoroughly we analyze the nature and attributes of deity, the more solidly is the rationalistic method of inquiry established. Reason can now proceed with confidence to examine the variety and essential properties of things and go on to systematic knowledge of their nature.

The Structure of Nature: the Dualism of Bodies and Minds

The Cartesian method emphasized rational analysis and deduction from self-evident first principles, or, in the words of Descartes, "intuition and deduction." In this way, the Cartesian method is in opposition to the inductive method of Bacon. But Bacon recognized the rational factor in experimental procedure, even though he neglected to develop it. Likewise, Descartes' preoccupation with rational analysis expressed the main emphasis in his philosophical method, but this should not be understood to signify his dismissal of direct observation and experiment. When he was writing his treatise on animals in Holland, Descartes was asked what his most valued sources and authorities were. Descartes pointed to a gallery which adjoined his house where a calf was being dissected. "There is my library," he said, "and that is the study to which I now attend the most."[6] We may recall that, when St. Bonaventura was asked a similar question, he pointed to a crucifix above his desk. These are all different emphases; by keeping them duly distinguished, we can understand the leading characteristics of various philosophers and of the different periods of our civilization.

Descartes' axiomatic first principle had already yielded him insight into the nature of reality. I exist, a thinking being; God exists, infinitely perfect, creative Author of all being and primary ground of my rational self-reliance. Systematic inquiry into the nature and structure of existence leads me to recognize other minds. The world is seen to include thinking substances. But my mind's experience also discloses another sort of being, unthinking substances which we call material bodies. What is their essential character, just as thinking is the essential attribute of mind? Descartes noted that many of the perceived qualities of bodies are only variables of our sense experience of them. Thus, beeswax has its own taste, fragrance, color, and hardness or softness; but these properties would alter in time, or even immediately, if it is heated. What remains throughout all these changes is that beeswax is a certain extended thing, having length, breadth, and depth, and being in a certain state of motion or rest.

The essential attribute of bodies or material substances is extension. Descartes pursued the implications of this conclusion in his scientific analysis. Bodies and extension involve each other, and, therefore, the notion of empty space, of extension which is not body, must be rejected. He also opposed the doctrine that the world of bodies is finite, that it has limits in space. (When Queen Christina expressed concern about the likely heresy in the theory that the material universe is infinite, Descartes replied that Cardinal Nicolas of Cusa had taught it without being condemned.) Descartes also held that there could be no limit to the spatial divisibility of bodies whose essence is extension, and thus he denied the doctrine of indivisible particles or atoms.

This view of material existence indicates what Descartes meant when he sought a geometry that would explain the structure of the world. He applied these principles of his geometrical physics in his explanation of motion, but it became necessary to expand his interpretation of them. The mechanics of nature could not be reduced to a geometrical-extensional statement. The common idea of motion as change of location, the passing of a body from one place to another, was revised by Descartes in his *Principles of Philosophy* to accord with his analysis of a body as an extension, and with his denial of empty space. Motion is the transference, or transposition, of bodies or parts of bodies in their relation to each other. This change in the mutual relation of bodies is not occasional. Motion is essential to the material world; what we call rest is not a static condition of existence, but only another

[6] Quoted in Haldane, *op. cit.*, p. 280.

phase of bodies in motion. Rest is impeded or checked motion. The "first cause," or ultimate explanation, of motion, in Descartes' words, cannot be other than God. Omnipotent Deity has created matter with its processes of motion and rest. But Descartes did not expound a simply extensional or geometrical view of motion. In his cosmic mechanics, motion implies also a type of force by which the spatial interrelations of bodies are effected: God's primary endowment of matter. God being immutable, the totality of moving force in the world remains constant; its particular distributions are variable. These "secondary causes" were formulated by Descartes in his several laws of motion.

The first law, that of inertia, holds that everything remains in the state in which it is in motion or at rest unless it is altered by an outside cause. According to the second law of Cartesian mechanics, every moving body tends to maintain its movement in a straight line, and, if given a circular course, it tends to move away from its center. The third law states that a moving body which comes in contact with another stronger than itself loses nothing of its movement, but alters its direction; if it meets one less strong than itself, it loses as much motion as it imparts to the other body.

Even though the first principle of Descartes' philosophy concerns the self-evident reality of the thinking mind, most of his account of the world is concerned with bodies, with the mechanics of material existence. Everything in nature is included in this mechanical view except the rational thought of the mind. Descartes extended this strictly physical interpretation to all biological processes and to human physiology. He praised Harvey for his discovery of the circulation of the blood, because it replaced the earlier teleological and vitalistic accounts with a mechanical explanation in terms of motion. To Descartes animals were merely mechanisms.

But this very insistence on excluding all teleology, or "final causes," from his account of the physical world—because it emphasized sharply the contrast of bodies in space to thinking minds—confronted him with the problem of their ultimate, metaphysical synthesis. Body and mind are the two finite substances in the Cartesian dualism, but, in calling them "finite," Descartes raised the question of their relation to each other. Both are distinguished from God, the infinite Substance. God comprehends and transcends body and mind; these find their ultimate source and ground in deity, but the idea of deity cannot be analyzed in terms of either of them. Strictly speaking, God, the infinite substance, is the only really ultimate Substance. Body and mind are substances after a fashion, finitely considered.

These issues involving the problem of mind and body were fundamental in the Cartesian system, and their alternative interpretations marked the development of modern rationalism. Descartes was confronted with them in his psychology, for human experience disclosed the apparent daily interaction of two substances, which, according to Cartesian metaphysics, could have no causal connection whatever.

Human Nature and Conduct: Descartes' Psychology and Ethics

In considering Descartes' account of human nature, we should recognize at the outset its implied challenge to his rationalistic method. His rational analysis, guaranteed by the eternal trustworthiness of God, yielded a dualistic cosmology. Bodies and minds are substances of radically different and unrelated nature. But the evidence of our daily experience seems to indicate the active connection of our mind with our body. Was he then to question his experience, or his rational analysis, and so his whole metaphysics?

The gravity of this problem is emphasized by the thoroughness with which he developed his dualistic cosmology. All bodies operate in strictly mechanical terms, as extended magnitudes in states of motion or rest. Not only animal, but also human, physiology must be treated as chapters in physics. Our organisms function through the agencies of impact, heat, and other analogous mechanical factors. When we consider the human mind, we recognize a fundamentally different sort of nature. Mind is not spatially extended, and none of our laws of motion or any mechanical categories apply to it. Mind is a thinking substance. Strictly speaking, no bodily changes can move it, nor can it in any way move bodies.

But both of these processes of interaction, ruled out in the Cartesian metaphysics, were admitted by Descartes as psychological data. In every sense perception, bodily changes apparently have mental effects. In every voluntary action, our ideas apparently cause bodily changes. How are we to explain this interaction of body and mind if we regard the one as strictly mechanical and the other as purely rational and immaterial? This question Descartes did not answer satisfactorily. He ventured the opinion that the chief seat of the soul, through which it is united to the rest of the body, is the pineal gland in the brain. But this gland is a bodily organ, in space; how could it contain, or affect, or be affected by, the immaterial mind? The whole problem was still unresolved.

These difficulties are seen sharply in the Cartesian account of the emotions. In his treatise, *The Passions of the Soul*, Descartes stated his aim explicitly; he would explain the passions "not as an orator, nor even as a moral philosopher, but only as a physicist."[7] And so he proposed a reinterpretation of the moral situation. In deliberation and choice, the conflict is not between the higher and the lower interests of the soul. It is a counteraction of tendencies, one set by the animal spirits, the other by the will. A purely immaterial being would have no passions, any more than mindless animals have them. The passions arise from the mind's opposition to bodily impulses.

Pascal expressed the mind's plight in dealing with a bodily shock: "The

[7] Translated from Descartes, *Oeuvres, op. cit.*, Vol. XI, 1909, p. 326.

greatest philosopher in the world, on a plank wider than necessary, if there is an abyss below, . . . would grow pale and wince, . . . even though his reason convinced him of his safety."[8] In such emergencies of passion, Descartes could find reliance only in the rational guidance of our will. The action of the will on the body is not direct, but it can be effective. Mere resolution does not suffice, but, when sustained by convincing reasons, its motivating power may prove decisive in a crisis. Our will needs wise and persistent practice in the use of its proper means—firm judgments and true insight into good and evil—to achieve the control and direction of the passions in virtuous conduct.

Descartes' ethics combined Stoic and Epicurean elements. With the Stoic, Descartes emphasized rational discipline and guidance, but he did not include Stoic apathy. He shared the Epicurean pursuit of happiness; but true happiness, or blessedness, according to him, is found only in the pursuit of virtue, in the perfection and expression of the soul's nature. Our well-being consists in a true understanding of ourselves that leads us to pursue the most suitable aims and satisfactions. This supreme excellence of the soul Descartes called "generosity," an ideal which recalls and develops the Aristotelian virtue of high-mindedness, or rational self-esteem.

Descartes' ethics are not clearly consistent with his cosmology, and, in fact, serve to expose unresolved issues in his rationalism. Our will manifests the free activity of our mind, but not its effective freedom of action on the body. We are thus responsible, essentially, for the way we think and will. To think and will rationally is to achieve a godlike mind, and therein lies our true perfection, for truth, justice, and the other ideal values are constituted good by God's eternal choice of them. But against this ideal and rational province of the mind's characteristic activity is the strictly mechanical nature of our bodily processes, which our mind should contol and direct, but with which it has been shown to have essentially nothing in common. How can human nature, thus split in the Cartesian dualistic cosmology, be seen in its active integrity of conduct and still yield unambiguously the basis of an ethical interpretation of human purposes and actions? This problem confronted rationalistic philosophy in its several alternative versions after Descartes.

Critics and Followers of Descartes: Pascal, Geulincx

The Cartesian philosophy gained speedy and wide renown, acquiring opponents along with its adherents. In France and in the Low Countries, Catholic and Protestant clerics combated the new teaching. The theological passions aroused by the Jansenist-Augustinian controversy over the doctrine

---

[8] Quoted by Henri Chamard, "Three French Moralists of the Seventeenth Century," in *The Rice Institute Pamphlet*, Houston, 1931, Vol. XVIII:1, pp. 24 f.

of divine grace and salvation affected also philosophical discussions. Some of the leading minds in Jansenism were regarded as sympathetic toward Cartesianism, despite their criticism of some of its doctrines. In their onslaught on the Jansenist camp, the Jesuits extended their hostility to their supposed Cartesian allies.

The preeminent champion of the Jansenists was Blaise Pascal (1623–1662). His attack on the worldliness and duplicity of the Jesuit casuistical morality produced one of the masterpieces of controversial literature, *The Provincial Letters*. His *Thoughts* (*Pensées*) contained the intimate and tragic diary of a mind consecrated to certain and indubitable truth, seeking it above all in religion, but unwilling to accept it with only half-proofs, and so struggling with its own inconclusiveness.

Pascal shared Descartes' high estimate of the method of rational analysis. He called it "the geometrical method," and esteemed it as the most perfect that our mind affords. He himself had achieved distinguished success with its scientific use, in mathematics and physics. What the geometric method could do at all, it could do superlatively well. But it had its limitations. Unlike Descartes, Pascal did not regard the rational method as capable of yielding the primary and ultimate certainties that our spirit demands. Reason must begin with primary concepts which it cannot define and with axiomatic first principles which it cannot prove. Reason cannot demonstrate the ultimate verities of religion, the existence of God, the immortality of the soul. The more we reflect on our logical powers, the more limited and unstable our intelligence appears.

Pascal's skeptical vein expressed the critical reserve of his rigorous, logical mind. But skepticism did not remain his final attitude, and therein he differed from Montaigne. The genial reflections on human incertitude which inspired Montaigne's *Essays* were intolerable to Pascal. He admitted skepticism, but he would not accept it; he struggled with it tragically. Man's state of inconclusiveness and doubt reveals his misery, but his very misery in uncertainty reveals also his grandeur. He is lashed to incertitude and finitude; he knows it, and yet he reaches after infinite truth. His reach exceeds his grasp. "Man is but a reed, the weakest in nature; but he is a thinking reed."[9] In the world of bodies, he is an insignificant fly, a speck in the vast universe; but greater than the worlds in space is the thinking mind, and above bodies and minds is the spiritual realm of values, of love, *charité*. Man cannot write the formulas of this highest reality, but he can identify himself with it. He cannot know whether God does or does not exist, but he can take his stand and stake his life on God's side. This is not the rational solution, but the mystical resolution of the problem. "The heart has its reasons, which reason does not know at all."[10]

Descartes' preoccupation with cosmic mechanism, and his announced re-

[9] Translated from B. Pascal, *Pensées*, 347, in L. Brunschvicg (ed.), *Oeuvres de Blaise Pascal*, Paris, Hachette, Vol. XIII, 1904, pp. 261 f.
[10] *Ibid.*, 277, p. 201.

solve to study human passions as a physicist, led many of his readers to interpret his philosophy as essentially materialistic. Despite the recognition of
the self-evident thinking mind in his first principle, and his arguments for
God's existence, most of his account of nature was concerned with bodies.
The strengthening of the rational-spiritual side of Cartesianism, and its unambiguous alliance with Christian truth, was undertaken by several of his successors. The first notable step in this direction was made by Arnold Geulincx
(1625–1669), a professor at Louvain and Leyden. He undertook, in particular, to deal with the Cartesian problem of the relation of mind and body,
and the relation of these two finite substances to the infinite substance, God.

Philosophy, according to Geulincx, includes three main inquiries. It seeks
knowledge of oneself, knowledge of the physical world of bodies, and
knowledge of God, and, therefore, it also seeks clear understanding of the
relations of these to each other. Like Descartes, Geulincx began with self-
knowledge, the mind's intuitive self-recognition; Cogito, ergo sum. But, to
Geulincx, the mind is convincingly revealed to itself in action. I know myself as thinking. Thinking constitutes me; that is, it expresses and represents
my nature. Whatever is caused or produced by my mind must be a thought
which I can understand. But if I do not understand clearly the cause or explanation of something of which I am aware, then my mind is not its cause.
Hence, my mind can derive a conclusion from its premises or can analyze
it and elicit its further implications. This I can understand as my mind's activity. But, when I have visual or auditory perceptions of bodily changes, I
cannot explain how certain motions can produce certain ideas in my mind.
Likewise, my mind cannot understand the connection between certain of
my ideas and my so-called "voluntary" actions. I think of the word terra
(earth), and my tongue is moved to roll the sound of it, but this cannot be
understood any more than could my moving the earth itself by my will.

Neither perception nor voluntary action can be explained by the causal
interaction of minds and bodies. Descartes admitted this interaction as a fact
of experience, even though he could not reconcile it with the dualism of
finite substances in his metaphysics. Geulincx reaffirmed the dualism. Minds
are completely immaterial, and are not in space; bodies are strictly material
things in space. There is not, and there cannot be, any causal connection between them. And yet, when the dinner bell sounds, I hear it, my mind understands its meaning. It tells me to stop my work and go to dinner, and my
body proceeds to act accordingly. How are these correlations to be explained? It can be in only one way, Geulincx said, through the activity of
God, who is neither body nor mind, but who embraces both in His infinite
Being. On the occasion of certain bodily changes, He causes my mind to
have certain ideas, and on the occasion of certain ideas in my mind He
causes certain actions to be performed. This is the doctrine of occasional
causes, or occasionalism.

Geulincx drew a strict inference from this doctrine in his moral philosophy. Since I am the real author only of what I think and will, my conduct

should be concentrated not on external accomplishment, but on my inner rational activity. Will only what you can achieve. In this development of the Cartesian ethics, the high-minded *générosité* of Descartes becomes humility, appropriate self-esteem. With humility as the fundamental moral value, Geulincx advocated the cardinal virtues of justice, diligence, and obedience. The pursuit of outward mastery and power, all pleasure seeking and worldly striving are vain and futile. We should seek perfection in the mind's own rational activity, in directing our will to the pursuit of truth that leads us to God. Dante's great line should be recalled here: "His will is our peace."[11]

The Occasionalism of Nicolas Malebranche

The revision of the Cartesian philosophy in terms of occasionalism was carried on in France by Malebranche independently of Geulincx. Nicolas Malebranche (1638–1715), who has been called "France's second metaphysician," reinterpreted the new rationalism so as to emphasize its kinship with the doctrines of St. Augustine, and to proceed toward a Christian Platonism. A person of frail health as was Descartes, but, unlike him, inclined to contemplative solitude, Malebranche had no interest in military life or travel. At the age of 22, he left the secular world to spend his life in a cell of the Congregation of the Oratory, a religious community of men devoted to the systematic perfection of Christian doctrine in its relation to philosophy and science. Its theology emphasized the influence of Augustinian ideas; its philosophy manifested a positive response to Cartesian rationalism.

Malebranche's earlier studies had been mainly Biblical and ecclesiastic. But his whole intellectual career was altered four years after he entered the Oratory, when, by chance, he came across Descartes' *Treatise on Man*. He mastered the Cartesian method, but, instead of pursuing the physical doctrines of the cosmic mechanism, he used the new rationalism as the basis of a more convincing system of Christian truth. His two principal works are *The Search after Truth* and *Dialogues on Metaphysics and on Religion*.

The Cartesian emphasis on clear and distinct ideas was reaffirmed by Malebranche, but he applied it in his criticism of Descartes' own cosmology, to the doctrine of the alleged causal interaction between minds and bodies. The idea of such an interaction is confused and untenable. Bodies are rightly conceived as extended and moving magnitudes, and minds are distinctively thinking and willing activities. "The soul thinks and is nowise extended; the body is extended and does not think."[12] There is no finite medium in which either of them could causally affect the other. Yet our experience

---

[11] Dante, "Paradise," iii:85, in *The Divine Comedy*.

[12] Translated from Malebranche, *Traité de la morale*, I:x:13; discussed in Jules Simon, *Oeuvres de Malebranche*, Paris, Charpentier, 1842, p. v.

assures us of a mutual correspondence between certain ideas and feelings and certain bodily movements. Prick the body, and the soul feels it; think of an approaching object as dangerous, and the body moves to avoid it. The only admissible explanation of this apparent connection must be sought in the efficacy of the divine will. The relation between mind and body is through God.

Malebranche pressed this conclusion of Occasionalism further than Geulincx had done. For Malebranche, causality cannot be strictly predicated by finite beings. The true and only real cause is God. Not merely the seeming interaction of minds and bodies, but the mind's thinking and willing, and also all bodily movements and the entire process of whatever exists have their primal and basic explanation in God, in the divinely established system of modalities. In his philosophy, Malebranche would repeat and expand the words of St. Paul: In God we think and live, and in him all things have their being.

While Malebranche thus derived all finite existence and process from the divine creative activity, he was cautious not to conceive of God in terms of any finite attribute. The infinite cause determines the finite effect, but it is not limited or qualified by this effect. Unlike some traditional idealism, his doctrine did not define God as infinite reason. God is infinite in every respect, and in every respect transcends finite categories. He comprehends the activity of bodies and minds but He cannot be defined either as extended body or as thinking mind. While it is less ambiguous to conceive of God's infinite intelligence than of His "intelligible extension," we should realize that neither one of these concepts can adequately represent His nature. Malebranche resisted any interpretation of his theocentric cosmology as pantheism; he would in no way ally his philosophy with that of "the miserable Spinoza," as he called his pantheist contemporary, whom he felt bound to regard with pious detestation.

As he did in his theory of reality, Malebranche, in his practical philosophy, proceeded from his conviction of our ultimate dependence on God. Our mind must pursue the true ideas, and our will must choose the true values, and in both we must seek and find our true being in God. We may trust our senses and our imagination to preserve our body in its contacts with others, but not to yield to us real knowledge. This comes from reason alone, from contemplating our relation to God and the principles of God's eternal order of reality.

This rational enlightenment is essential to the good life, for, while our will is committed to the pursuit of the good, its choice is guided by its true or mistaken idea of the good. The problem of evil, of error and sin, which confronts us here, was treated by Malebranche in his mainly Augustinian theodicy. God moves invincibly toward the good, but His will demands our free moral choice, and thus allows the possibility and actuality of error and sin, and their just consequences. God has created us that we may rightly recognize and cherish His perfection, in truth and in love. But our attainment of this blessedness is impeded by our confused perceptions and misguided passions. Rational direction and control are required to grade our devotion and our love for contending goods according to their true relative degree of perfection, and, in all our preferences and choices, to make God's will our own final aim, our highest good and supreme law. Ascetic withdrawal from the sensual distractions and vanities of the world can prepare the soul for its single-minded devotion to the godly life. Thus, Malebranche turned Cartesian rationalism from its scientific-philosophical goal—true insight into the structure of nature—toward the mind's devout meditation on God and the godly life.

SUGGESTED WORKS FOR FURTHER STUDY

DESCARTES. Descartes, René, *Philosophical Works* (trans. E. S. Haldane and G. R. T. Ross) and *Selections* (R. M. Eaton, ed.).

BIOGRAPHIES AND CRITICAL STUDIES OF DESCARTES. Fischer, Kuno, *History of Modern Philosophy; Descartes and His School;* Gibson, A. B., *The Philosophy of Descartes;* Haldane, E. S., *Descartes, His Life and Times;* Iverach, James, *Descartes, Spinoza, and the New Philosophy;* Keeling, S. V., *Descartes;* Mahaffy, J. P., *Descartes;* Maritain, Jacques, *The Dream of Descartes;* Smith, Norman Kemp, *Studies in the Cartesian Philosophy.*

PASCAL. Pascal, Blaise, *Provincial Letters* (trans. T. M'Crie) and *Thoughts* (trans. C. K. Paul, and W. F. Trotter); Bishop, Morris, *Pascal;* Webb, C. C. J., *Pascal's Philosophy of Religion.*

MALEBRANCHE. Malebranche, Nicolas, *The Search After Truth* (trans. J. Taylor) and *Dialogues on Metaphysics and Religion* (trans. M. Ginsberg); Church, Ralph W., *A Study in the Philosophy of Malebranche.*

17. Spinoza: Monistic Determinism and Moral Values

The Life, Character, and Kinships of Spinoza

In *The Republic*, Plato compares a certain type of philosopher to "one who, in the storm of dust and sleet which the driving wind hurries along, retires under the shelter of a wall; and seeing the rest of mankind full of wickedness, he is content, if only he can live his own life and be pure of evil."[1] Better than any other thinker of his age, Spinoza expressed this philosophic spirit in his thought and in his life. Amid the tumult of new ideas and old bigotries which surged in every field of human activity during the seventeenth century, his philosophical career avoided both partisanship and cold neutrality, and achieved the steady serenity of reason. Students of his philosophy have sought to trace its sources in Descartes or Bruno, in Scholastic or medieval Jewish speculation. But Spinoza's thought is distinguished by a universal, eternal quality of contemplation.

Spinoza and his philosophy have aroused both bigoted animosity and romantic adulation. The advance of modern study, however, has tended toward a more balanced understanding and appreciation. Recognition of his philosophical rank nowise rules out criticism of the ambiguities and other defects in his doctrine. The greatness of a philosopher depends not so much on the conclusiveness of his answers as on the significance of his problems and his thorough grasp of them. With a thoroughness that discloses both its merits and its limitations, Spinoza's philosophy expresses one of the fundamental ways in which nature and human nature may be contemplated.

Baruch (Benedict) Spinoza, or de Spinoza (1632–1677), came from a family of Jews who had escaped from Portugal or Spain to seek freedom of worship in Holland about the end of the sixteenth century. In Amsterdam —the chief center for Jewish refugees—the Spinozas attained leadership; both the grandfather and the father of the philosopher held the office of warden

[1] Plato, *The Republic*, Bk. vi, in *The Dialogues of Plato* (trans. B. Jowett), 3rd ed. (in 5 vols.), Oxford, Clarendon Press, 1892, Vol. III, p. 496. The paging is that indicated along the margins of the work.

in the synagogue. Michael Spinoza was also warden of the Jewish school in which his boy was trained in the Hebrew language and in the faith of Judaism. As his brilliant mind unfolded through the years, the youth first won the admiration of his teachers, but later aroused their alarm. While he mastered Jewish doctrine, he was also ready with his searching criticisms of it. He perfected his knowledge of Hebrew, but he wanted also to learn Latin in order to read the new works in science and philosophy. He joined a Latin class taught by a former Jesuit and an alleged atheist. His studies became less and less rabbinical, and his expressed ideas indicated not only his nonconformity to Jewish orthodoxy, but a radical and growing alienation from it.

The leaders of the Amsterdam Synagogue were deeply concerned about the brilliant young man who was going astray. Spinoza's father had died, and the son had to plan more definitely for his own livelihood. The rabbis called him to their council and offered him an annuity of 1000 florins to enable him to pursue his studies, on condition that he abandon his erring ways. Spinoza refused the rabbinical "fellowship" and its terms. He was then promptly subjected to stern public censure, with a warning of worse to come. He was almost resolved to withdraw from the synagogue, when his decision was confirmed by the attempt of an orthodox fanatic to assassinate him. He left the Jewish community and the city of Amsterdam and retired to a secluded house in the country with some Remonstrants who had been excommunicated by the Protestant Synod of Dort.

In 1656, the synagogue proceeded to anathematize him as a heretic. Thirteen years earlier, the works of Descartes had been condemned and burned publicly by the Calvinist authorities of Utrecht. Ten years before that, in 1633, Galileo's *System* had been burned by the Holy Inquisition as contrary to God's truth. In all three cases, Galileo's comment held true; his surest way of conforming to God's truth was to make his own doctrines as true as possible. So Spinoza was to write in his first treatise: "God or . . . Truth . . . The Truth is God himself."[2]

After several changes of residence, Spinoza finally settled at The Hague. He supported himself by grinding lenses, an expert trade by which he also advanced his inquiries in optics. By living frugally, he could afford much time for his studies and meditations, and his philosophical ideas were gradually organized into a system. Some of his writings were circulating in manuscript as early as 1663. His correspondence and other intellectual contacts brought him favorable response and criticism, not only from young students and disciples, but also from some of the leading minds of his day, including Oldenburg and Boyle of the Royal Society of London, and, toward the end of his life, from Leibniz. Some of Spinoza's friends urged on him large sums for his support; but in his sturdy independence, he refused to take ad-

---

[2] B. Spinoza, in A. Wolf, *Spinoza's Short Treatise on God, Man, and His Well-Being*, London, Black, 1910, pp. 78, 103.

vantage of these offers; he would accept only some aid toward the purchase of books required for his studies.

The Elector Palatine—and brother of the philosophical Princess Elizabeth, with whom Descartes had corresponded—Karl Ludwig, offered him a professorship at the University of Heidelberg, promising him full freedom of speech in philosophy, and expressing confidence that he would not misuse it to disturb the established religion. Spinoza declined the appointment on the grounds of his resolve to persist in the reflections of unconstrained solitude. The Elector Palatine's tolerant attitude was in contrast to the treatment Spinoza had received from the conservative authorities in Holland. The anonymous publication of Spinoza's *Theologico-Political Treatise*, in 1670, had aroused strong opposition, and when his authorship of the book became known, the animosity shown by the Calvinist divines was like that of the Amsterdam rabbis fifteen years earlier. The projected publication of his *Ethics*, in 1675, created such an uproar that Spinoza withdrew the manuscript. This work, together with some other writings, was published by Spinoza's friends in a volume bearing only his initials and entitled *Opera Posthuma*, several months after his death in 1677. The following year, the book was condemned by the Dutch government as atheistic and blasphemous.

For 100 years, Spinoza's name was held in infamy by bigots. Then Lessing, the German champion of tolerance and free critical thought during the period of the Enlightenment, revived the study of Spinoza with contagious enthusiasm, in which he was followed by Jacobi, Schleiermacher, and Goethe. The man who had been cursed as godless came to be eulogized by poets and philosophers as "the God-intoxicated man." Two centuries after Spinoza's death, a statue of him—made possible by the contributions of thinking men all over the world—was unveiled at The Hague. About the same time, the Italian people were planning the erection of a monument to Giordano Bruno.

Critical interpretation of a philosopher's system of ideas requires reliable knowledge of his sources, the course of his development, and his historical affiliations. In the case of Spinoza, this reliable knowledge is not readily available. The history of philosophy repeatedly reveals a logical order and succession of ideas which do not quite correspond to the chronological order and history of the philosophers themselves. So the historian of Greek philosophy rightly examines the atomism of Democritus before considering the Sophists Gorgias and Protagoras and before proceeding to Socrates, even though Democritus outlived the other three. In the logical development of modern rationalism from Descartes to Leibniz, the doctrine of occasionalism raises problems that point to Spinoza's more thorough analysis. But this logical connection does not warrant our regarding it as an actual historical succession and dependence. Spinoza's early outline of his philosophy, made in 1661, antedated Geulincx's works and Malebranche's first look at a book by Descartes.

Spinoza's close relation to Descartes is evident throughout his works, but it is not that of a disciple to a master. Cartesianism provided a good systematic starting point for Spinoza's exposition of his philosophy. The roots of his system of ideas are ramified, and tracing them has led to many explanatory surmises. The origins of Spinozism have been sought in the fertile speculations of Renaissance thinkers, especially in its most stimulating philosopher of nature, Giordano Bruno. Historians of ideas have also explored Spinoza's likely dependence on Maimonides, and, more generally, on medieval rabbinical doctrines. But critical inquiry here must always recognize Spinoza's originality in his use of the ideas of others. He may share some ideas with Bruno; as Spinoza used them, however, these ideas are not brilliant cosmological speculations, but probed systematic principles. He begins with the Cartesian doctrine of Substance, but he at once transforms it through rigorous analysis.

This original and self-rooted quality of Spinoza's thought is a characteristic expression of his philosophical mastery, and comprises one of the elements of its vitality, but it also accounts for some of its limitations. In going his own way with his ideas, Spinoza did not explicitly compare his position and principles with those of his predecessors. The clearer exposition of Spinozism, which such a critical comparison and appraisal would have yielded, might also have led to significant revision of it.

Theory of Knowledge: Spinoza's Geometrical Method

Certain, systematic knowledge was, to Spinoza, not merely an intellectual requirement. He regarded it as the perfection and chief good of life, and made the pursuit of it his principal aim. Above all things, he would seek "knowledge of the union existing between the mind and the whole of nature."[3] The problem of the sources and the test of knowledge was therefore primal in his thought. He needed, first of all, reliable principles of method.

Convinced that truth reveals itself as it discloses error, Spinoza examined critically the various sources of men's ideas and men's judgments of things. His account may be read in his unfinished work, On the Improvement of the Understanding, and also very concisely in a "Note to Proposition XL," which appears in the second part of the Ethics. People commonly get their opinions from hearsay, the authority of custom, the routine ascription of certain meanings to certain words, or else from vague, unexamined sense experience. Ideas derived from these sources provide the large stock of men's beliefs. They may be impulsive or variable, or they may be held stubbornly, but they are not sound knowledge. Neither the grounds on which they rest

[3] B. Spinoza, Improvement of the Understanding, in R. H. Elwes, Spinoza's Chief Works, London, Bohn's Libraries, 1912, Vol. II, p. 6.

nor the inferences which they warrant are clear to the mind. They are mere opinions, and no system of truths can be based on them.

True knowledge of anything requires understanding of its essential nature and of its fundamental connections with other things. It is systematic knowledge, the knowledge of things in their necessary settings and relations. This is attained by reason—by inferring one thing from comprehension of another—and by adequate analysis and definition of a thing—by perceiving its essential properties and its relations to other things, and its distinction from others in its field and system.

This rational method, emphasizing rigorous analysis and deduction, had shown its excellence preeminently in mathematics, and had been designated more especially as the geometrical method. Pascal called it the most perfect method of the mind, because it defines its terms and proves its propositions. But, as was noted in the last chapter, he ultimately found this method to be insufficient, for it had to begin with certain primary indefinable terms, with unprovable, axiomatic first principles, and, more importantly for him, because it could not answer our ultimate questions in morality and religion.

Spinoza's rationalism was not unsettled by Pascalian doubts, but he also could look, beyond rational deduction, to a more immediately evident knowledge. Unlike Pascal's appeal from reason to the heart, Spinoza's highest knowledge may be called the consummation of rational insight, or the transcendent excellence of rational genius. As rational intelligence attains its perfect mastery of the order and connection of things, it may come to know things, not only as it infers them step by step in ordered explanation, but also directly, recognizing them as they are in their essential reality. This highest achievement of the mind Spinoza called intuitive knowledge or intuitive science. We shall note his discussion of it in the concluding part of his *Ethics*. He contemplated this culmination of intelligence, but he did not examine or interpret it as extensively as we might expect from so thorough an analyst as was Spinoza. In his philosophical system, he proceeded mainly by the geometrical method, showing the attainment of knowledge and truth as the mind advances from its common and uncritical opinions, to a rationally grounded and ordered system of ideas.

Spinoza not only adopted the geometrical method in principle, he applied it in the actual exposition of his philosophy. Descartes had made a start in this direction. In connection with his *Responses* to the second series of *Objections* to his *Meditations*, Descartes used a geometrical procedure to prove the existence of God and the essential distinction between our minds and our bodies. Spinoza used this geometrical procedure—with its definitions, axioms, theorems, corollaries, and scholia—in his critical exposition of Descartes' *Principles of Philosophy*, and, preeminently, in his *Ethics, Demonstrated in Geometrical Order*. This chosen method of philosophical exposition may often seem to constrict the full development of Spinoza's thought into a formal framework, but it also perfects and evinces its closely reasoned and ordered connection of ideas.

Fundamental Principles in Spinoza's Account of Nature

The following exposition of Spinoza's system of philosophy is based mainly on the *Ethics*, but occasionally it utilizes the earlier outline of his ideas—written in his late 20s—entitled *Short Treatise on God, Man, and His Well-Being*. The *Ethics* is in five parts, which have been compared to the five acts of a drama. The first part is entitled "Concerning God," and presents Spinoza's metaphysical doctrine of Nature, or Substance, or ultimate reality. The second part deals with the "Nature and Origin of the Mind." The third part is "On the Origin and Nature of the Emotions." The last two parts present in dramatic contrast "Human Bondage, or the Strength of the Emotions" and "The Power of the Understanding, or Human Freedom."

Descartes based his account of the structure of nature upon his conviction of the eternal veracity of God, whose existence he inferred directly from his initial axiom and first principle: his own reality self-evident in the act of thought. Spinoza began his metaphysics by analysis and demonstration of the ultimate reality of the infinite Substance. His first definition is of the self-caused Being, and it is an analytical statement of the ontological proof of God's existence. Self-caused Being is "that of which the essence involves existence, or that the nature of which is only conceivable as existent."[4] We can recognize here the ultimate rational conviction on which Spinoza was to base his cosmology. Real knowledge in science and philosophy is knowledge about the essential nature and cause of things. But our knowledge of the whole system of things which are causally determined by others presupposes our rational certainty of the ultimate, self-caused Substance. At the foundation of Spinoza's rationalism we can thus also recognize the central conviction of the cosmological proof of God's existence. In the *Short Treatise*, he began explicitly with proofs of God; in the *Ethics*, his first propositions present his analysis of Substance, or God, the ultimate reality. All finite existence implies and depends upon the infinite Being. If anything whatever is real, the ultimate Substance is real; it cannot be conceived as nonexistent.

Spinoza therefore undertakes, first of all, to grasp through rigorous and thorough analysis this idea of the infinite Substance, the ultimate reality. And he is directly led to disagree with Descartes' cosmological dualism, the doctrine of two finite substances. "By Substance," Spinoza wrote, "I mean that which is in itself, and is conceived through itself."[5] Substance, rightly analyzed and understood, cannot be conceived as finite, as dual and limited. Strict rational analysis here points to unqualified monism. The ultimate Substance, self-caused Being, is and can be only one. It is infinite, self-existent,

---

[4] B. Spinoza, *Ethics*, I:i, in Elwes, *op. cit.*, Vol. II, p. 45.
[5] *Ibid.*, I:iii, p. 45.

self-determined, and eternal. Spinoza spoke of it as "God or Nature (*Deus seu natura*)."[6]

The expression "God or Nature" is noteworthy at this point. Spinoza began with proofs of God's existence, but he was engaged in metaphysical, not theological, reasoning. To him, "God" signified the infinite reality, the ultimate Nature of all being. Spinozism may rightly be described as pantheistic, if we recognize that the pantheism is intended to emphasize a cosmological, not a religious, monism. God is Nature. This initially naturalistic perspective did not rule out for Spinoza a later interpretation more relevant to religion. But he must begin with Nature, with infinite Substance. His philosophy aims to achieve a rational ethics, but, as he said, ethics must be based on physics and metaphysics. The framework of Spinoza's philosophy is that of monistic naturalism.

The infinite Substance is the fundamental ground of whatever other things we consider as existing. All things must be regarded in their relation to God or Nature, as aspects or states of the infinite Substance. Thus Spinoza proceeded to his doctrine of Attributes. He defined *Attribute* as "that which the intellect perceives as constituting the essence of Substance."[7] The infinite Substance must be regarded as having an infinitude of attributes, or aspects of self-manifestation. Our understanding recognizes two of them, body and mind. Body, or material existence, was defined by Spinoza as extended Being, existing in space. Mind, on the other hand, expressed the essentially thinking aspect of Substance. Unlike Descartes, then, Spinoza regarded body and mind, not as two finite substances distinguishable from the one infinite Substance, God, but as two essential attributes, or aspects, of God or Nature. Thought is an attribute of God, and so is extension. They are, as it were, two versions of reality, two ways in which we view and can know and interpret Nature, as a material-extended and a mental-thinking system.

Spinoza's definition of attributes has given rise to conflicting interpretations of his doctrine. According to J. E. Erdmann, the attributes body and mind express the essence of Substance as our intellect perceives it. The attributes represent our intellect's two views and versions of reality; we think of Substance as extended and as thinking. This interpretation underscores the first half of Spinoza's definition of attribute. Kuno Fischer takes an opposite view; he emphasizes the second half of Spinoza's definition; the attributes constitute the essence of Substance, which the intellect perceives truly and necessarily. This issue does not allow of explicit settlement, but the textual evidence in Spinoza's works and correspondence inclines our judgment toward the latter view. Spinoza regarded reason as yielding real knowledge; the rationally necessary analysis of essence showed him the certainty of existence. To be sure, he distinguished existence from the mind's understanding of existence; but for him this distinction was not one between

---

[6] *Ibid.*, IV:Preface, Vol. II, p. 188.
[7] *Ibid.*, I:iv, Vol. II, p. 45.

reality and mere appearance. On the other hand, Spinoza seems to have regarded the distinction between the attributes as men's intellectual view and perspective. Our reason sees Substance as extended or as thinking; but infinite Substance comprehends its attributes. Substance must be recognized as both extended and thinking, yet it cannot be defined in either of these ways. Between the two very definite, but also somewhat one-sided, alternative interpretations mentioned above, Spinoza's thought seems to pursue a deeper insight, which, however, is not free from ambiguity.

In his *Short Treatise*, Spinoza distinguished two views of Nature: as the self-acting cause of all existence, and as the self-caused, necessary consequence of its essential Being. The former he called *natura naturans;* that is, Substance and its attributes. The latter, *natura naturata,* comprehends all the particular existent things, states, and conditions. Spinoza called them the "modes of Substance." These modes may be infinite, expressing the essential modifications of the material or the mental attribute of Substance, or they may be finite modifications of the attributes in particular things. The infinite modes of bodily existence are motion and rest; those of thinking being are intellect and will. Finite modes are particular motions or conditions of rest, particular mental states of intellect and will.

The world in its boundless variety of things and events was thus contemplated by Spinoza in a monistic perspective. Everything in the universe—a planet or a grain of sand, a mind or a hatchet—must be seen and can be understood only as a modification of the one infinite, eternal Substance. All finite things are like waves of the boundless sea. In our sense experience, we may be engrossed by the particular wave or ripple, its beginning and end. But, if our reason leads us to probe and to recognize its real nature and explanation, we see it in its cosmic relations.

Spinoza's doctrine of attributes led him to explain the interrelation of bodies and minds by his double-aspect theory. Material existence, with its modes of motion and rest, is a manifestation of the essence of nature; and so, likewise, is mental existence, with its modes of intellect and will. Substance can be interpreted in terms of each of these. They are like two versions of the same epic. Therefore, their relation to each other must be one of parallelism or correspondence. Each event in nature must be conceivable in one and also in the other perspective. In each case, these perspectives will involve two views of existence, radically distinguishable, but mutually correspondent. For example, consider the present case of my writing this chapter, or the reader's perusal of it. A bodily account of each of these actions is available in terms of mechanics and physiology, but there is also a mental account, in terms of understanding, agreement, and criticism. These two accounts must not be confused, but recognition of their parallelism is essential to an adequate understanding of the writer's or reader's activity.

Hence, Spinoza concluded, "The order and connection of ideas is the same as the order and connection of things." And again, "Substance thinking and substance extended are one and the same substance, comprehended now through one attribute, now through the other."[8] Are we to understand only the fundamental correspondence of these aspects of nature in their ultimate relation to Substance, or also the mutual correspondence of specific bodily and mental states? The latter interpretation will rouse objections. Psycho-physical parallelism may insist that each perception, or idea, corresponds to some bodily process. But can we also maintain the converse, that every specific material event in the universe corresponds to some specific mental experience? The implications of this ambiguity in Spinoza's cosmology may be far reaching.

Spinoza's philosophy has been called a geometry of the cosmos. From his viewpoint of body as extension, and its infinite modes as motion and rest, his account of nature emphasized space, and space relations. This cosmology has been criticized for its failure to give due recognition to the dynamic aspects of reality, to ongoing process and activity. In reply to such criticisms, advocates of Spinozism have cited chapter and verse in support of a more dynamic interpretation. Did Spinoza not describe both extension and thought as "powers"? Did he not correlate the essence or the reality of things with their degree of activity? Yet his emphasis is scarcely on dynamism. In his contemplation of the eternal system of relations, he may be said to exemplify Plato's description of the philosopher as "the spectator of all time and all existence";[9] but time is not central in his view of reality. In our day, Samuel Alexander, after calling "the discovery of Time" the most characteristic feature of our modern thought, raised the problem: "What changes are produced in Spinoza's doctrine if we regard Time itself as an attribute of the ultimate reality?"[10]

The principle of causal necessity is fundamental in Spinoza's cosmology. Reason attains real knowledge of anything as it recognizes its essential nature, which is manifested in its necessary relations to other things. This strict determinism excludes any doctrine of arbitrary chance or spontaneity or freedom in nature. All such suppositions of the imagination must be rejected by reason as unwarranted. The infinite self-determination of God or Nature necessarily establishes in detail the specific nature and causally determined character and behavior of all things. If we ascribe chance arbitrariness to some things, this can only signify our ignorance of their determining conditions. Spinoza similarly criticized the belief in the freedom of the will. No unaccountable spontaneity decides our choice and action, but all our thoughts, desires, and acts are expressions and effects of our being what we are.

Spinoza's determinism ruled out teleology as a principle of explanation. Like Bacon and Hobbes, he rejected in his cosmology Aristotle's "final causes." There is no "design in nature," no preference, no choice; nor can

[8] *Ibid.*, II:vii, Vol. II, p. 86.
[9] Plato, *The Republic*, Bk. vi, *op. cit.*, Vol. III, p. 486.
[10] S. Alexander, *Spinoza and Time*, London, Allen, 1921, p. 36.

we properly apply to nature our judgments of value. Thus, he wrote in the *Short Treatise:* "All things are necessarily what they are. . . . In Nature there is no good and no evil."[11] Spinoza would apply this doctrine, not only in physics, but in theology. God's manifestation as mind, in the modes of will and intellect, is no less thoroughly self-determined than his manifestation as body, in the modes of motion and rest. Properly speaking, purpose and choice, good and evil, have significance in an account of human conduct, but are rightly understood only when we consider them in their human perspective, as necessary determinations of human nature. "Nature's laws and ordinances, whereby all things come to pass and change from one form to another, are everywhere and always the same. . . . Thus the passions of hatred, anger, envy, and so on . . . answer to certain definite causes, through which they are understood. . . ."[12]

Is this, and can this be, Spinoza's conclusive dismissal of all teleology and finalism in his philosophy? Spinoza explored the origin and nature of the emotions, man's servitude in the grip of passion, and the emancipation and perfection of human nature by the power of intelligence. In a philosophical system like Spinoza's, which insists throughout on rational consistency, the latter half of the *Ethics* cannot be accepted gratefully as an encouraging moral postlude to the strict geometry of nature which preceded it. We are bound to ask how Spinoza's moral philosophy is related to his doctrine of nature and human nature. Does his naturalistic framework require reconstruction, in order to provide a basis for genuinely moral judgments; or does he—by maintaining his naturalism in dealing with human conduct—indicate the radical redefinition of the moral problem which is essential to a rigidly scientific ethics?

Spinoza's Psychology and Doctrine of the Passions

True knowledge of human nature, as of any other thing in the world, cannot be derived purely from sense experience and imagination, for these yield only unclear and unwarranted opinions. We require rational understanding of ourselves, and of our role in and relations with nature. We seem to have ideas that are induced by various changes in our body, and we seem able voluntarily to produce certain change and motions of our body. But how all this does, or could, take place we cannot explain.

By truly understanding the parallelism of the attributes in nature, according to Spinoza, we are enabled to perceive the basic confusion in the doctrine of causal interaction between our mind and our body. These two are not separate and interacting objects; they are distinguishable but correlated aspects of human nature. The correlation is not causal; it is a cor-

---

[11] B. Spinoza, in A. Wolf, *op. cit.,* p. 75.
[12] B. Spinoza, *Ethics,* III: Introduction, in Elwes, *op. cit.,* Vol. II, p. 129.

respondence of different phases of the same activity. As with mind and body generally, so with any mental or bodily state. When I hear a clap of thunder, feel the sudden downpour of rain, and run for shelter, I seem to distinguish two concurrent series of processes. But it is really one and the same process, now seen under the bodily aspect of extension and now under the mental aspect of thought. The order and connection of ideas in our experience correspond to the order and connection of our bodily changes. We should not confuse these two versions of what takes place; ultimately they must be seen as different but parallel phases of the same reality.

Spinoza was equally rigorous in applying his determinism to human nature and human activities. No unaccountable spontaneity or free choice can be admitted in human conduct. A running man is no less determined than a rolling stone; in each case, the nature of a being is manifested in its necessary operation under certain specific conditions. If we are truly to understand the course of human life, we must examine it as objectively as we examine any other process in nature. Thus, Spinoza declared in the "Introduction" to his *Political Treatise:*

I have laboured carefully, not to mock, lament, or execrate, but to understand human actions; and to this end I have looked upon passions, such as love, hatred, anger, envy, ambition, pity, and the other perturbations of the mind, not in the light of vices of human nature, but as properties, just as pertinent to it as are heat, cold, storm, thunder, and the like to the nature of the atmosphere. . . .[13]

A similar passage at the beginning of Part III of the *Ethics* introduces his doctrine of the passions. It recalls the Cartesian doctrine, but surpasses it; it has been praised in the highest terms by physiologists and psychologists alike.

Human life exemplifies the principle that self-preservation is the first law of nature. Like all other things, man endeavors to persist and to maintain his being. This endeavor, called *conatus* by Spinoza, is not a mysterious urge; it is simply the essential operation of human nature as of everything else. It is therefore neither exceptional nor occasional, but is characteristic of man throughout his existence. His will is, in fact, this endeavor mentally regarded. When referred to mind and body conjointly, it is called appetite; desire is appetite aware of itself. Our judgments of value—approval or disapproval—do not determine our desires, but follow from them; because we desire something, we deem it to be good.

Any human experience represents either an effective power of self-maintenance, or a checked and frustrated endeavor; it makes for either enhancement or loss of vitality. The first of these states is called pleasure; the latter, pain. In the life of endeavor and desire, these two provide the medium in which the great variety of emotions may be distinguished. Pleasure and pain, when referred to their external cause, arouse the emotions of love and hate. These emotions express themselves in corresponding judgments of good or evil. We cherish what we love, that is, we approve it and seek to preserve it; contrariwise, we detest, and try to avert, the hateful.

[13] B. Spinoza, *Political Treatise*, Introduction:4, in *ibid.*, 1909, Vol. I, pp. 288 f.

Desire, pleasure, and pain, expressed in love and hate, yield a great variety of manifestations in the various situations of life. Spinoza undertook to distinguish and to analyze the subtle currents of love and hate in the life of desire, and to define the various passions. The citation of two or three of the forty-eight definitions should suffice to indicate his keen insight into the nature of the passions:

. . . [regret is] the desire or appetite to possess something, kept alive by the remembrance of the said thing, and at the same time constrained by the remembrance of other things which exclude the existence of it.[14] [Cowardice is] attributed to one, whose desire is checked by the fear of some danger which his equals dare to encounter.[15] [Disparagement is] thinking too meanly of anyone, because we hate him.[16]

Likewise Spinoza also defined wonder, devotion, hope and fear, joy, pity, indignation, humility and pride, envy, honor, anger, revenge, gratitude, ambition, avarice, and many other emotions.

The nature of any passion manifests our self-maintenance or our reaction to the object of our attention, the way it moves or affects us. We may become so possessed by our idea of something that it distorts our entire outlook. In our outburst of wrath or jealousy, we are blind to everything else. We feel and act on the idea that engrosses our mind, and that idea may be utterly misleading and drive us to ruinous passion. Poets and sages have voiced man's tragic confusion and sought a way out of this calamity. In morals and in art man faces the same peril of distorted vision.

The problem is how to overcome the enslaving power of passion. The most drastic proposal was that of the Stoic moralist who would repress emotion altogether and live the impassive life of reason in serene, untroubled apathy. Some Stoic influences on Spinoza have been pointed out, but his proposed treatment of the passions is radically different from that of the Stoic. The essential nature of emotion rules out its suppression in a life of apathy. Emotions arise in the correlation of mental and bodily states. Whatever idea we have of anything is manifested in the way we feel toward it. Complete extinction of the emotions would thus signify cessation of mental activity. In each case, the real problem is to control or to suppress a particular passion. This can be done only in the mind's own province, by a revision of our ideas. Change your idea of anything, and you will feel differently toward it; your former passion will be replaced by another emotion. A passion arising from a confused and mistaken idea of anything "ceases to be a passion, as soon as we form a clear and distinct idea thereof."[17] But the resulting mental state is not impassivity; it now has the emotional tone of the new prevailing idea. An emotion can be controlled only by a stronger opposite emotion.

[14] B. Spinoza, *Ethics*, III:xxxii, in *ibid.*, Vol. II, p. 181.
[15] *Ibid.*, III:xli, Vol. II, pp. 182 f.
[16] *Ibid.*, III:xxii, Vol. II, p. 178.
[17] *Ibid.*, V:iii, Vol. II, p. 248.

Ethics and Social-Political Philosophy

This examination of the contending emotions in human life may be pursued in a naturalistic spirit. Spinoza's doctrine of the passions is an important chapter in the modern science of man. The range and course of the passions show men's mental outlook and direction, rising from narrow and rash bigotry to balanced enlightenment, or, again, distracted and swept by some unreasonable notion.

But Spinoza's aim was not merely anthropological. His resolutely naturalistic inquiry seems to have been motivated by his search for a sound moral philosophy. He sought the true facts of human nature, for he needed the right principle of human conduct. His rationalism is geometrical-analytic in method, but its goal is ethical. Pascal's great words might have been also Spinoza's: "Let us therefore strive to think well; such is the foundation of moral life."[18] Spinoza stated how he had spurned other alleged good things in life to center his entire quest on his greatest need "as a sick man struggling with a deadly disease, when he sees that death will surely be upon him unless a remedy be found, is compelled to seek such a remedy with all his strength, inasmuch as his whole hope lies therein."[19]

The nobility of Spinoza's ethics and social philosophy becomes evident to any fair-minded reader, but, to some critics, this has seemed to emphasize the crucial problem in Spinozism. Ethics, he was convinced, must rest on physics and metaphysics. Did his cosmology and anthropology actually provide this required foundation for his moral philosophy, or is there a discrepancy between his theoretical and his practical philosophy? Does this indicate an obvious incongruity and a surrender of Spinoza's thoroughly naturalistic rationalism; or does it reveal an expansion of his philosophical outlook, higher and deeper reaches in his perception of ultimate reality? These questions should be kept in mind as we consider Spinoza's account of man's servitude and emancipation, the rise to perfection in the life of reason.

The terms "passion" and "affection" suggest men's subjection to external lures and influences. When men are moved by random sense impressions or fancies, without rational judgment, they are at the mercy of any impulse of the moment. They are swept by partisan opinion, unstable, or stubbornly bigoted; they are victims of their ignorant feelings. We may call these affections "passive" emotions, and, subjection to them, "human bondage," or "servitude." When they are present, the mind has not reacted to its impressions with its full reflective power. We are moved, we know not why or how, by things and toward ends which we do not comprehend.

[18] Translated from L. Brunschvicg (ed.), *Oeuvres de Blaise Pascal*, Vol. XIII, pp. 262 f.
[19] B. Spinoza, *Improvement of the Understanding*, in *ibid.*, Vol. II, p. 5.

It is quite otherwise when the mind attains a rational grasp of its ideas. As a man perceives each thing or experience which engages his attention in its true relation to himself and to other things, he is no longer under misapprehension. His feelings and his conduct are rational, appropriate to the situation. His mind is integrally expressed in it, and its experience may be called "active" emotion. In the life of understanding, the mind has realized itself and it can freely play its proper role. The deterministic Spinoza called this experience "mental freedom," or "blessedness."

Spinoza's ethics and social philosophy may be viewed in the light of this contrast of "passive" and "active" emotions. True reason makes no demands which are contrary to nature, and the virtuous or fully rational life is a life of intelligent self-maintenance and perfect expression of man's nature. The mastery of reason is not only the surest way toward perfection, but is itself man's perfect self-realization. Spinoza generally considered virtue to be a power; its summit, the utmost of human power, must be perfect rationality. A man who thus attains plenitude of harmonious self-expression finds no grounds for discontent, nor is he beset by worries or upset by fears. His reasonable life is its own justification and he welcomes it on its own terms. He serenely accepts the prospect of its eventual, natural termination. "A free man thinks of death least of all things; and his wisdom is a meditation not of death but of life."[20] This rational life itself has the seal of eternity, but not in the traditional sense of survival after death, immortality. It is the eternal nature of the rational truth and of the principles by possession of which the mind realizes its perfection.

Reason is always marked by its knowledge of the essential nature and necessary relations of things. With the full power of intelligence, we may be enabled to respond suitably to everyone and everything and to attain emotional harmony. We shall then see and feel everything in a universal setting or, as Spinoza expressed it, "*sub specie aeternitatis*"—in an eternal perspective or under the pattern of eternity. Beyond our concern with particular things, our mind may be dominated by their interrelation and their role in the infinite reality of God, or Nature. Our virtue, the realized power of reason, also manifests our highest satisfaction and happiness. This virtue is itself the blessedness of a sage. "The mind's highest good is the knowledge of God, and the mind's highest virtue is to know God."[21] This is *amor Dei intellectualis*; that is, the intelligent or understanding love of God.

We may call this doctrine pantheistic ethics, corresponding to the metaphysics of the one infinite Substance—God or Nature. The highest good is "the knowledge of the mind's union with the whole of nature."[22] The expression "love of God (*amor Dei*)," even in an intellectual version, cannot be accidental in Spinoza's philosophy. This pantheism has also its religious im-

---

[20] B. Spinoza, *Ethics*, IV:lvii, in *ibid.*, Vol. II, p. 232.
[21] *Ibid.*, IV:xxviii, Vol. II, p. 205.
[22] Paraphrased from B. Spinoza, *Improvement of the Understanding*, in *ibid.*, Vol. II, p. 6.

plications. But we should first consider the social philosophy of Spinoza's rationalism.

As rational knowledge is integrating knowledge, which sees everything in its systematic relationships, so the rational life of virtue is an intellectual integration of individual and social values. "Men who are governed by reason . . . desire for themselves nothing, which they do not also desire for the rest of mankind, and consequently, are just, faithful, and honourable in their conduct."[23] The intelligent love of God precludes jealousy and strife. The rational life of truth and justice is a life of active cooperation, in which true sages are never rivals, but always colleagues. The values of rational perfection are, in their essence, fruits of social participation; the more they are attained by others, the more attainable they are by us. The highest good is thus the most shareable value, or as Spinoza said, it is "common to all, and therefore all can equally rejoice therein."[24]

Spinoza developed this principle of generous reasonableness not only in his social ethics of personal relations, but also as the basis of his political theory. This is presented in the second part of his *Theologico-Political Treatise* and also in his unfinished *Political Treatise*. The guiding thesis of the former is stated explicitly on the title page: "Freedom of thought and speech not only may, without prejudice to piety and the public peace, be granted; but also may not, without danger to piety and the public peace, be withheld." This thesis is also expressed in Spinoza's conclusion: "That state is the freest whose laws are founded on sound reason, so that every member of it may, if he will, be free; that is, live with full consent under the entire guidance of reason."[25]

Spinoza undertook to establish political theory on a strictly scientific basis. As in ethics, so in social philosophy he would consider human conduct and institutions as objectively as though he were concerned with lines, planes, and solids. The method of geometrical-scientific analysis prevailed in principle even when it was not strictly employed in his exposition. In every social situation, according to Spinoza, men's actions are determined by their state of mind and the conditions under which they live. In a life of unenlightened passions, men are driven by blind desire to greedy strife with one another. When thus spurred by anger, envy, or hatred, "men are naturally enemies."[26] But these words are not to be taken as a quotation from the *Leviathan*, nor did Spinoza proceed to Hobbes' rigid conclusion that a lawabiding society can be attained only by absolute sovereignty and control of the individual's will. A state in which people are "led like sheep . . . may more properly be called a desert than a commonwealth."[27] More natural, because it is a fuller realization and expression of human nature, is the social

[23] B. Spinoza, *Ethics*, IV:xviii, in *ibid.*, Vol. II, p. 202.
[24] *Ibid.*, IV:xxxvi, Vol. II, p. 211.
[25] B. Spinoza, *Theologico-Political Treatise*, in *ibid.*, Vol. I, p. 206.
[26] B. Spinoza, *Political Treatise*, ii:14, in *ibid.*, Vol. I, p. 296.
[27] *Ibid.*, v:4, Vol. I, p. 314.

order in which men can live and realize their purposes freely in accordance with the laws of reason.

The social contract, as Spinoza understood it, is motivated by high expediency. "A compact is only made valid by its utility, without which it becomes null and void."[28] *Salus populi suprema lex;* men organize, maintain, and perfect their systems of government in order to attain greater security and fuller scope for self-fulfilment. When these expectations are frustrated, the natural basis of conformity to law is undermined; men resist ruinous dominion and seek their well-being under more beneficent authority. Spinoza did not follow Aristotle's teleology, but he came near to agreeing with him regarding political sanctions; he held that the state arises that men may live, and develops that men may live well. Though a good system of laws safeguards the citizen's security and yields him reliable freedom of action, it also regulates and limits that freedom. But the citizen submits to the political controls because they enhance the available range of human activities and hence allow greater individual development. And this indeed must be the true aim of government "to enable men to develope their minds and bodies in security and to employ their reason unshackled."[29]

The policy of high expediency, which guided Spinoza's reflections on law and political obligation, was maintained in his views of foreign policy and international relations. On a lower level of statesmanship, governments regard each other as potential enemies and seek safeguards for every eventuality. A treaty should be made when needed, and kept in force as long as interests of state demand it. This doctrine has been criticized as Machiavellian, but Machiavelli's expediency differs basically from Spinoza's in its motivation. In the one case, the devices for effective, prevailing tyrannical dominance are explored; the other is concerned with the resources of flexible policy required for the fullest security and rational activity of the citizens.

Spinoza's comparative analysis of the various forms of government reflect his political liberalism. He indicated that monarchies usually include an admixture of aristocratic elements, and that aristocracy requires for its stability a system of checks on the dominion of the nobility. He chose democracy as "of all forms of government the most natural, and the most consonant with individual liberty."[30] Unfortunately, in the unfinished and posthumously published *Political Treatise*, he did not get beyond the first four paragraphs of the chapter on democratic government.

The emphasis on freedom of thought and speech, mentioned on the title page of the *Theologico-Political Treatise*, was essential in Spinoza's liberalism. The connection of politics with theology in that book was not accidental. His own life and career were disrupted by religious bigotry. Sectarian strife was aggravated into civil war even in the Netherlands, where

[28] B. Spinoza, *Theologico-Political Treatise*, in *ibid.*, Vol. I, p. 204.
[29] *Ibid.*, Vol. I, p. 259.
[30] *Ibid.*, Vol. I, p. 207.

persecuted men from many countries had sought refuge. During Spinoza's youth all central Europe was upset, and Germany was being reduced to a state of savagery by religious wars. On a broader scale, the entire course of modern civilization—scientific, social, and spiritual progress—depended on safeguarding the principles of tolerance.

The first part of the *Theologico-Political Treatise* is a classic in the early history of modern Biblical criticism. Spinoza treated his subject without evasions, but he knew how disturbing his treatment would be to popular convictions. He wrote as a scholar for men of critical understanding, and he asked others not to read his book. His exposure of the unsound traditional belief in the Mosaic authorship of the Pentateuch directed free minds toward a rational interpretation of the Bible. His equally searching examination of the belief in miracles and of divine law and authority probed ultimate problems concerning the bases of faith in relation to reason. While in these ways Spinoza himself inaugurated a new age of religious tolerance, he championed the freedom of men's minds in every field and direction of thought. Priests and theologians should never be allowed to control and to restrict people's beliefs. Let all men be free within the bounds of law and also under its protection; let the state be the one to decide what is lawful and unlawful conduct. Thus, in living and thinking in a free land, man will the more surely reach the highest truth, which can come only from the free interplay of ideas. For true science and true religion each require a sound basis in reason, which yields to evidence, but not to dictation.

The Ultimate Nature of Spiritual Values

As Spinoza's philosophy reaches its climax in Part V of the *Ethics*, it is confronted with its crucial problem, an interpretation of ultimate reality. This problem is indicated in the title of this chapter; it has been mentioned in our discussion; and it should now be considered more directly. It concerns the ultimate status and role of values, of good, evil, and perfection, in Spinoza's naturalism.

In his exposition of the structure and operation of nature, Spinoza's rejection of teleology is plain and firm. The infinite Substance is self-caused, and all existent things, bodies and minds, are its necessary manifestations. They are what they are, and they act as they act. They must be explained in terms of their cause or ground, not in terms of any ultimate purpose. Purpose and the evaluation it implies do not concern nature, which is eternally as it is. Ideals have no metaphysical status. Good and evil are only relative in a human-rational way of regarding things. Their reality is not as the reality of bodies and minds. There is no good and evil ultimately, nothing that ought and ought not to be; ultimately, there is only what there is, actuality, nature. This is the naturalistic tenor of Spinoza's cosmology.

In this firm naturalism, Spinoza's philosophy expresses the basic tone and outlook of modern science, its strict concentration on factual description and explanation. Science also relies on the logical principles and validations which it requires in its systematic development. It leaves the field of values, norms, and ideals to the humanities. But philosophy demands a cosmic synthesis, and this demand becomes emphatic in Spinoza's thought because of its insistent ethical aim. Spinoza's naturalism seems to be as firm in precluding a real basis for ethics as the rest of his philosophy is firm in requiring it.

The direction of thought by which Spinoza's ethical aim is progressively vindicated in his philosophy may be surmised from the unfolding of the ethical theory itself, as it reaches the level of his third, or highest, form of knowledge—intuitive insight. Here the concluding part of the *Ethics* gives us some clues. We note some contending motives in his meditation on ultimate reality; at times, naturalistic convictions seem to prevail, at others a higher note of spiritual finalism may be recognized. Thus Spinoza declared: "He who loves God, cannot endeavour that God should love him in return."[31] To expect this would be to entertain a wrong idea of God or Nature, the infinite Substance. Yet, in man's intellectual love of God, Spinoza recognized a quality of eternal insight that expresses the mind's essential harmony with the infinite. Corresponding to man's intellectual love of God is the infinite intellectual love with which God loves Himself. Furthermore:

> The intellectual love of the mind towards God is that very love of God whereby God loves himself, not in so far as he is infinite, but in so far as he can be explained through the essence of the human mind regarded under the form of eternity; in other words, the intellectual love of the mind towards God is part of the infinite love wherewith God loves himself.[32]

The explicit beginning of this proposition, reaffirming the one preceding it, and the subsequent qualifying clauses, are very significant. Together they express the interplay of the two ground notes of Spinoza's thought. Even within the indicated qualifications, the ethical ideal view of God's nature— that is, of ultimate reality—was judged by Spinoza in this proposition as a true and warranted contemplation of the human mind, as sound philosophy. In a corollary, he went further when he maintained that "God, in so far as he loves himself, loves man."[33]

In his monistic naturalism, Spinoza emphasized causal necessity. He identified God with Nature, *God or Nature*. But his ethical contemplation leads him to or toward a view which may be expressed in the principle, *Nature or God*. This latter expression of his philosophy is not developed with any such thoroughness as the former, nor are the two adequately harmonized.

[31] B. Spinoza, *Ethics*, V:xix, in *ibid.*, Vol. II, p. 256.
[32] *Ibid.*, V:xxxvi, Vol. II, pp. 264 f.
[33] *Ibid.*, V:xxxvi, Corollary, Vol. II, p. 265.

The interplay of the two in the last part of the *Ethics*, reveals the depths, and some difficulties, of Spinoza's philosophy. We are moved to repeat his concluding words: "All things excellent are as difficult as they are rare."[34]

SUGGESTED WORKS FOR FURTHER STUDY

WORKS BY SPINOZA. B. Spinoza, *Chief Works* (trans. R. H. M. Elwes), *Ethics* (trans. R. M. Elwes, A. Boyle, H. White and A. Stirling), *Short Treatise* and *Correspondence* (trans. A. Wolf), *The Principles of Descartes' Philosophy* (trans. H. H. Britan), and *Selections* (John Wild, ed.).

BIOGRAPHIES AND CRITICAL STUDIES. Alexander, S., *Spinoza and Time;* Browne, Lewis, *Blesséd Spinoza;* Caird, John, *Spinoza;* Duff, R. A., *Spinoza's Political and Ethical Philosophy;* Joachim, H. H., *A Study of the Ethics of Spinoza;* McKeon, Richard, *The Philosophy of Spinoza;* Martineau, James, *A Study of Spinoza;* Pollock, Sir Frederick, *Spinoza;* Powell, E. E., *Spinoza and Religion;* Roth, Leon, *Spinoza;* Wolfsohn, H. A., *The Philosophy of Spinoza.*

---

[34] *Ibid.*, V:xlii, Vol. II, p. 271.

18.   Leibniz: Monadology and Theodicy

Leibniz's Versatility and Originality

In psychological studies of the early development of men of genius, Gott-fried Wilhelm Leibniz (1646–1716) heads the lists with the half-dozen most precocious minds of great eminence. Like Pascal, young Leibniz was not driven to his amazing intellectual attainments by intensive parental discipline, but by his own boundless urge for mental activity. When he was 6, he lost his father—a lawyer and a professor of moral philosophy at the University of Leipzig. His mother, deeply pious, guided the child in religious principles, but allowed his gifted intellect full range. The boy was taken away from a dull teacher and given the run of his father's large library. Never was free-dom from school discipline better deserved. By the age of 15, young Leibniz was not only prepared for the university, but he had already read classical and modern literature—especially philosophy and jurisprudence—more widely than many mature scholars. He had gained mastery of a good Latin style; he had studied the principal philosophers of his day, and had also read with care the Scholastic doctors whom many of his contemporaries were dismiss-ing without previous study.

His five years at the university expanded and ripened his powers; his doctor's thesis was on the relation of jurisprudence to philosophy. The Leip-zig professors were wary of his mere 20 years, but the University of Altdorf not only accepted his brilliant dissertation for the doctorate in law, but also offered him a professorship. Leibniz declined the honor; instead, he soon ac-cepted another appointment as secretary to Boineburg, minister of the very powerful Elector and Archbishop of Mainz. This decision was characteristic of his personality and his whole career. He had walked out of the classroom as a pupil; he would not enter it as a professor. His reluctance was due to his widely ranging intelligence that would not be tethered to any professional specialty or schedule. But his unwillingness to enter an academic career also revealed the practical diplomatic strain in his character. Allied with his purely intellectual quest of knowledge was an ambition to apply his beliefs and purposes in public affairs. In Leibniz's program of life, as in Francis Bacon's, statesmanship contended with science. As might be expected, it often diverted both of them from contemplation to the vanities of court life.

In his new post at Mainz, young Leibniz enjoyed great latitude for the exercise of his many talents. He utilized and expanded his erudition in historical and theological research. He also ventured into high diplomacy. He hoped to check the spreading power of France, which imperiled the German states, by persuading Louis XIV to lead an all-European war against the Turks. Victory in the Middle East, he argued, would give France the rich prize of Egypt. This scheme did not succeed, but its promotion was only the first of many efforts, futile at the time, to realize a purpose which was dominant in Leibniz's mind. He aspired to achieve a reconciliation of political and religious enmities in Europe, so as to unite the spiritual energies of western civilization in leading mankind to a higher level of peace and Christian culture. He was undiscouraged and indefatigable in trying one path after another to this goal. Leibniz had been in the cradle when the Peace of Westphalia was signed; he grew up amid the ravages of the Thirty Years' War into which religious conflicts had plunged his Germany. He aspired to pacify Europe by reuniting Protestants and Roman Catholics, and his correspondence with Bishop Bossuet reveals his skill, though not his success, in ecclesiastic diplomacy. Failing in this, he tried to bring the various Protestant churches into closer cooperation. His contacts with Peter the Great were aimed at the establishment of an Academy of Sciences at Saint Petersburg which should promote the Tsar's plans to bring the Russian people into the circle of western civilization. He conferred with Jesuit missionaries regarding the spread of the Christian faith and of European ideas in China. Throughout his life, Leibniz pursued the ideal of a world society of nations guided by modern science and culture, and by Christian principles. His age did not respond to this ideal; even today, it is still uncertain of realization.

His extended visit to Paris, and later to London, brought Leibniz into direct contact with many of the leading thinkers and men of letters. Especially fruitful for his intellectual career was his friendship with Huyghens, which stimulated his interest and great advance in mathematics, realized before long in his discovery of the calculus. Newton's similar achievement, probably of an earlier date, was soon to give rise to a deplorable controversy.

Another highly important event in Leibniz's philosophical development was his contact with Spinoza, whom he visited in 1676. Spinoza, at first, was wary of the young courtier-savant and of his negotiations with the French monarchy, but later he became more confident and loaned him a manuscript copy of his *Ethics*. Examination of Spinoza's cosmology helped to confirm Leibniz in his rejection of the Cartesian dualism, but he could not adopt Spinoza's unqualified monism. The cosmic outlooks of these two men were as different as were their personalities. Unlike Spinoza's unwavering analysis and single-minded systematic construction, was the many-sided responsiveness and resilience of Leibniz; unlike Spinoza's uncompromising integrity, was Leibniz's diplomatic pliancy in action and thought. But, while Leibniz was not firm in his endeavor to satisfy seemingly opposite demands, his creative intelligence led him to original and brilliant reconstruction.

Meanwhile his close relations with the court of Mainz were terminated by the death of the Archbishop Elector and of his minister, Boineburg. Leibniz thenceforth was mainly in the service of the House of Brunswick at Hanover, as councilor, historian, and librarian. His official duties and his philosophical-scientific interests involved him in extensive correspondence with hundreds of persons. Needless to say, a great deal of this activity was high bureaucratic routine. But his versatile fertility took him into many channels of productive work, for, as said, his mind could not be filled by one single interest. Throughout his life he explored the many provinces of his vast realm of ideas. He developed the mining, industries, and educational system of the province. He invented and perfected calculating machines. He would devise a world language and a system of universal and applicable symbolism. His historical research comprised jurisprudence and theology as well as the history of the House of Brunswick.

Even his life at court was by no means intellectually sterile. His brilliant ideas engaged, and sometimes disturbed, titled and crowned heads. For Prince Ernst of Hesse-Rheinfels, he wrote the *Discourse on Metaphysics;* later in life he sent Prince Eugene of Savoy a brief statement of his philosophy, either *The Principles of Nature and Grace* or *The Monadology.* His correspondence with Bossuet was stimulated by the Duchess of Hanover and her sister. At Hanover, Leibniz had influenced the mind of the Duke's daughter, Princess Sophie Charlotte—a niece of Descartes' Princess Elizabeth and of Elector Karl Ludwig, who had invited Spinoza to the University of Heidelberg—who later became Queen of Brandenburg-Prussia. It was mainly for her instruction that he wrote the *Theodicy*. Leibniz was active in organizing the Berlin Academy of Sciences, and he became its first president. Toward the end of his life, his friend, Caroline of Anspach, later Queen of England, induced him to engage in an important correspondence with the philosophical theologian, Samuel Clarke. We should keep in mind these public aspects of Leibniz's intellectual career, for they reflect the wide spread of philosophical interests in aristocratic circles prior to the period of the eighteenth-century Enlightenment. Leibniz's biography is a chronicle of the intellectual history of his age.

Court intrigues brought Leibniz bitterness in his last days, and impeded the direct exercise of his full influence on the thought of his time. A large part of his philosophical and scientific work appeared in his unpublished manuscripts and his voluminous correspondence, which were mixed with his official papers. Since it might be indiscreet to examine and to publish them, the Hanover Court put all his manuscripts and letters under lock and key. The publication of his writings and the full scope for his philosophical and scientific influence were thus impeded for many years. In fact, it is only in our time that a complete edition of his works is being undertaken.

This adventurous course of Leibniz's ideas and influence has perplexed historians of philosophy in deciding where to include most suitably their discussion of his thought. Few of his philosophical writings appeared prior to Locke's *Essay Concerning Human Understanding*. Leibniz's own *New Essays Concerning Human Understanding*—very important for a full grasp of his philosophy—was intended as a criticism of Locke's theory of knowledge. The book was completed about 1704, but Locke died that year; hence, Leibniz decided not to publish his philosophical polemic, especially in view of the unfortunate arousal of English public opinion by his contention with Newton regarding the discovery of the calculus. Leibniz's *New Essays* finally appeared in 1765, after Locke's empiricism had run its course in the works of Berkeley and Hume, and in the philosophy of the French empiricists and skeptics. The philosophical influence of the *New Essays* was first manifest in the critical development of Kant's thought. Thus, some historians of philosophy have placed their chapter on Leibniz after their examination of British empiricism and the French Enlightenment, and just before Kant. This order of exposition seems inadvisable because it shifts unduly the actual historical setting. Leibniz's doctrines are systematically related to the other theories of seventeenth-century rationalism. When he criticized Locke, Berkeley had not published a word, and Hume, Voltaire, Rousseau, and Kant had not yet been born. Notwithstanding Kant's central importance in the history of modern philosophy, Leibniz's doctrine, even his theory of knowledge in the *New Essays*, can be understood and appraised better if it is examined as the third major system of seventeenth-century rationalism, than if it is considered mainly in its bearings on the later German Enlightenment, as an important background of Kant's critical philosophy.

The traditional order, whereby Leibniz is placed after Spinoza and before Locke, is advisable also in view of the fact that so many of Leibniz's writings are definitely dated, being letters, polemics, or other works of specific criticism that related him to the thinkers of his own day: Arnauld, Spinoza, Bayle, Locke, Newton, and Clarke.

Activism: Monadology and Preestablished Harmony

The principle of harmony was dominant in Leibniz's thought. His versatile mind, confronted with a variety of contending views of reality, would not accept a one-sided solution; instead it sought some original standpoint from which they could all be reconciled and unified, an original synthesis. Unlike Descartes, who wanted to proceed on his own, wholly independent of earlier philosophy, Leibniz was critically alert and also responsive to all available theoretical alternatives. He said that, like Socrates, he was ready to learn from everyone.

From his early youth in his father's library, his precocious erudition had filled his mind with the principal doctrines of nature—had filled, but had not satisfied it. Scholastic Aristotelianism impressed him by its recognition of a hierarchy in nature and a teleological order pointing to deity, but its dogmatic procedure clashed with the methods of modern science. The materialism of Hobbes proclaimed its strict adherence to the mechanics of existence, but it was discredited by the inferences which its author drew from it, and which he boldly applied to ethics and politics. The Cartesian dualism of minds and bodies included both rationality and mechanics, but it could not relate them in nature. Their alleged connection through the pineal gland was confusing, and their ultimately common ground in God was ambiguous. Leibniz did not value highly Descartes' contribution to science, despite his own profit from the Cartesian analytic geometry. He wrote to Malebranche: "Nothing useful has come from Descartes to compare with the experiments of Galileo."[1]

Leibniz explored the alternative cosmologies of his time which were stimulated by Descartes. Both the occasionalism of Malebranche and Spinoza's monism were significant advances beyond Descartes' dualism in their rejection of a causal interaction of body and mind, and their alternative theories of correspondence and parallelism. But Malebranche made no real provision for natural science, and Spinoza's theory afforded no recognition of the unique reality of individuals. In the reconciliation and synthesis of these alternative views of nature which Leibniz sought, he was partly guided by his mathematical-logical principles. His work also revealed his many-sided personality in which scientific, humanistic, and religious motives vied for recognition. His philosophy is logically reasoned out, but it is also enacted —a dramatic expression of the ideas contending in his mind.

Leibniz gave a concise statement of his basic problems in the preface to the *Theodicy:*

There are two famous labyrinths, in which our reason often goes astray: the one involves the great question of *liberty* and *necessity*, especially concerning the production and origin of *evil;* the other consists in the discussion of *continuity* and of the *indivisible points* which appear to be its elements, and this question involves the consideration of the *infinite*. The former of these perplexes almost all mankind, the latter engrosses only the philosophers.[2]

Leibniz struggled with the first issue in his *Theodicy;* the second one was fundamental in his whole philosophical system. Throughout the history of philosophy, this latter problem has engaged abstract monism and pluralism. It may be expressed in a variety of ways. How can we recognize the permanence of substances and also admit their changing states? How can a real whole include real and distinguishable parts? How can we think of a growing person as self-identical through all the stages of his development? Leibniz

[1] Quoted in H. W. Carr, *Leibniz*, Boston, Little, Brown, 1929, p. 23.
[2] Paraphrased from G. W. Leibniz, *Theodicy*, in *The Monadology and Other Philosophical Writings* (trans. R. Latta), Oxford, Clarendon Press, 1898, p. 21.

met this problem in his logic and in his cosmology, and in both he was led toward his doctrine of monads.

We shall first consider the logical approach. In a proposition, a predicate is attributed to a subject; when the subject is a substance, its predicates are numerous, and by recognizing these predicates we come to know the substance. These qualities of a thing may be manifested or absent at different times, yet somehow all characterize it throughout. If we really understood and knew it, we should recognize its self-identical, persistent character with all its variety of predicates. We should then see it as a unique miniature system of reality. Though, in judging on the basis of any one of its predicates, we may be able to draw only contingent inferences about the others, we should know that it necessarily implies them all. We may not know the specific causes of the particular qualities or actions of a thing, but we do know that none of them lacks explanation. "No fact can be real or existent, and no statement true, unless it have a sufficient reason why it should be thus and not otherwise."[3] This is Leibniz's Law of Sufficient Reason.

Now it may be seen that full knowledge of a thing will reveal its universal involvement and its peculiar manifestation of all being. Leibniz formulated his view for Arnauld as follows: "Every individual substance expresses the whole universe in its own manner, and in its full concept it includes all its experiences together with all the attendant circumstances and the whole sequence of exterior events."[4] The important phrase here is "in its own manner." We can conceive of a vast number of individual substances, each expressing the whole universe, if we regard them as so many distinguishable centers of activity, or roles, in the drama of reality, but not if we regard them as different parts or segments of the total area of existence. And we can see how the cosmic drama may include all the various roles, and each of them be truly individual and unique. Leibniz was turning from a geometrical-spatial cosmology toward a dynamic system. This was the fundamental activism of his doctrine of Substance.

Cartesianism was more adequate in its analysis of mind than in the analysis of body. Descartes recognized mind as thinking activity—*Cogito, ergo sum* —that is, thinking constitutes me. But in considering body, Descartes, Malebranche, and Spinoza all identified it with extension. This spatial or dimensional view of material existence was criticized by Leibniz. The real nature of a body cannot be understood as so much occupied space, nor can motion be conceived adequately in merely spatial terms.

Leibniz subjected traditional doctrines of space to a radical criticism. According to him, space and time are neither substances nor attributes of things. They are always relative to things and processes, two patterns or

[3] G. W. Leibniz, *Monadology* (trans. H. W. Carr), Los Angeles, Univ. of Southern California, 1930, p. 71.

[4] Paraphrased from G. W. Leibniz, *Discourse on Metaphysics, Correspondence with Arnauld, and Monadology* (trans. G. R. Montgomery), Chicago, Open Court, 1902, p. 69.

ways in which coexistent and successive things and events are ordered. Thus, Leibniz insisted in his correspondence with Clarke that the notion of absolute space is an untenable abstraction. Without things in it, how does one point of space differ from another? Against the doctrine of absolute space that includes an infinitude of real points, and against the doctrine of time as a reality in itself, Leibniz firmly maintained the sole reality of active monads, of things and events. The individuality of each monad puts it in a unique spatial-temporal relation to others: the order is relative to the perspective. While it could scarcely be said that Leibniz anticipated the modern theories of relativity, his thought inclined in that direction.

His cosmology advanced from a spatial to a dynamic interpretation of motion. Motion fundamentally implies force; even at rest a body has a certain capacity to act. It is itself a center of activity, a way of existing, unique and distinguishable from other centers of activity, but like them, "in its own manner," reflecting the universe. The real differences or similarities between an oval stone, a walnut, and an egg cannot be grasped in extensional terms. They are to be understood essentially in their respective activities. "The very substance of things consists in their power of acting and suffering."[5]

By this dynamic cosmology, or activism, Leibniz proposed to find a way out of his so-called "labyrinth"—the problem of reconciling cosmic unity with real individuality—by his Laws of Continuity and of the Identity of Indiscernibles. He had already pursued the idea of continuity in mathematics; it had led him to his differential calculus. He expressed his astonishment that no one had as yet thought of it and realized its far-reaching implications. Resolved to elicit them in cosmology, he came to regard the Law of Continuity as "among the most completely verified," and the Law of the Identity of Indiscernibles as its logical completion. "Nature never makes leaps";[6] it is infinitely variable, and there cannot be two perfectly similar, individual things. We may think of the universe as of a curve—that every position on the curve is filled and filled uniquely—or else, as of a drama, that every role in it is being played without duplication.

Leibniz was advocating a view of material existence analogous to the Cartesian dynamic view of mind as thinking substance. Conceive of body as you conceive of mind, in terms of force and action, dynamically. He, at first, called his individual, active substances, "souls," and described his universe as a "world of souls." This expression suggested an interpretation of his philosophy as "spiritual pluralism," which some of his commentators adopted, to which Leibniz himself also was often inclined, but to which he was not logically committed. His reasoning permitted an analogical use of the phrase "world of souls," but scarcely required or warranted a descriptive use of it.

---

[5] G. W. Leibniz, *On Nature in Itself*, in G. M. Duncan, *The Philosophical Works of Leibnitz*, New Haven, Tuttle, Morehouse, and Taylor, 1908, p. 124.

[6] G. W. Leibniz, *New Essays on the Human Understanding*, in Latta, *op. cit.*, p. 376.

In his later writings, after 1695, he referred to the individual centers of activity by the term "monads." How far he was influenced by Bruno in his doctrine of monads is conjectural.

Spinoza had written in his *Ethics:* "The endeavour wherewith everything endeavors to persist in its own being, is nothing else but the actual essence of the thing in question."[7] While reading Spinoza's manuscript and copying extensive parts of it, Leibniz must have wondered why its author had failed to follow this principle to the conclusion he himself had reached. Equally evident to him was the light his doctrine threw on the problem of the relation of mind and body. As in a hierarchical series of active centers, the monads represent different levels or grades of existence. Minds are related to bodies as more perfect, self-conscious centers of activity are related to less perfect, unconscious centers. Leibniz distinguished three kinds or grades of monads, unconscious, conscious, and self-conscious or rational. Each monad has its own unique, realized perfection and its own characteristic responsiveness; nevertheless, he described his three classes of monads more definitely as entelechies, souls, and rational intelligences or spirits.

Leibniz rejected Cartesian interactionism and Malebranche's divine intervention. The correlation of the monads, according to Leibniz, is due to their eternally preestablished *harmony*. He first used this term, as well as the word *monad*, about 1696; as late as 1704, he described himself, in the *New Essays,* as "the author of the system of preestablished harmony." The principle of preestablished harmony served to correlate the Law of Continuity and the theory of monads, for these two, in turn, gave full systematic expression to the earlier principle. Each monad is a unique expression of the universe, and so, in a real sense, it is free and self-determined. It cannot reach out to touch or to affect causally any other monad, but, in its nature and activity, it corresponds to the nature and activity of all other monads. "The soul follows its own peculiar laws and the body also follows its own laws, and they agree in virtue of the preestablished harmony between all substances, since they are all representations of one and the same universe."[8]

Leibniz used various terms and analogies to express his idea of preestablished harmony. He called it the hypothesis of accords. He compared it to synchronized clocks or watches which keep time together. He used the less mechanical illustration of several different bands of musicians or choirs who, while quite independent of each other, may be in perfect unison—in perfect unison, but nowise identical, for, although in harmony with the others, each choir or band and each voice and instrument would have its own timbre or tone color. The harmony must be the concord of unique individuals.

The harmony of the monads recalls the parallelism of Spinoza's attributes. Conceive of Spinoza's infinitude of possible attributes as unique activities,

---

[7] B. Spinoza, *Ethics,* III:vii, in R. H. M. Elwes, *Spinoza's Chief Works,* London, Bohn's Libraries, 1912, Vol. II, p. 136.

[8] G. W. Leibniz, *Monadology,* in Duncan, *op. cit.,* p. 321.

each in its own way constituting the essence of Substance or Nature; their mutual correspondence of behavior might then be called a preestablished harmony. But Leibniz required an unambiguously theistic explanation of nature. The harmony of the monads expresses the perfect divine order of existence. God is its Author and it is God's masterpiece. The universal republic of minds is the City of God. Leibniz's monadology and preestablished harmony lead to his theology and theodicy. But before turning to these ultimate perspectives, we should consider his account of human life and the nature and experience of minds, the thinking monads.

Psychology and Theory of Knowledge

The specific modern problem of knowledge which divided empiricists and rationalists does not seem to have been an early problem in Leibniz's philosophical reflection. He proceeded to reach his principles by rational analysis; he assumed that knowledge of ultimate reality was available, and he reasoned it out in his metaphysics. He was faced with the problem of the sources and process of knowledge when he read John Locke's *Essay Concerning Human Understanding*. Finding himself at variance with Locke on psychological and epistemological issues, he wrote his *New Essays Concerning Human Understanding*. As already noted, this treatise was completed in 1704, the year of Locke's death, but it did not appear until 1765, when Lockian empiricism had already run its course of development. Though late, the book was still in good season to influence Kant. The *New Essays* should be considered here first as developing and clarifying some parts of Leibniz's cosmology, especially his interpretation of minds, the thinking monads.

Without anticipating the discussion of Locke's theory of knowledge, which will engage us in the next chapter, we may cite Leibniz's own concise statement in the Preface, concerning his major disagreement with his English contemporary:

Our differences are upon subjects of some importance. The question is to know whether the soul in itself is entirely empty as a tablet upon which as yet nothing has been written (*tabula rasa*), . . . and whether all that is traced thereon comes solely from the senses and from experience; or whether the soul contains originally the principles of many ideas and doctrines which external objects merely call up on occasion. . . .[9]

The empiricist doctrine that the mind is initially like a clean slate, without ideas, and that it gets its knowledge from sense impressions made by external objects, was unacceptable to Leibniz for at least two reasons, both important to him. It was contrary to his doctrine that the monads act in harmony, but

[9] G. W. Leibniz, *New Essays Concerning Human Understanding* (trans. A. G. Langley), New York, Macmillan, 1896, p. 42.

do not interact causally, or, as he put it, "have no windows by which anything can enter in or go out."[10] Knowledge cannot be a process in which ideas are imported into the mind; like all other activities of the monads, it must "depend on an inner principle."[11] Furthermore, the empiricist doctrine was at variance with Leibniz's Law of Continuity. The mind's own career as a thinking monad, like its relation to other monads, must be viewed as continuous throughout, without any clefts in its being, unbridged or bridged, such as a change from a clean slate to a mind stocked with sense perceptions would represent.

When the empiricist criticized the doctrine of innate ideas, Leibniz agreed with him that the mind does not start with any inborn explicit, formulated principles. But this nowise implies that the mind is initially blank. It is in its nature a thinking activity, and this activity finds in the process of experience its characteristic manifestation in specific ideas. There are no specific innate ideas. But the endowment or capacity to entertain ideas is what makes the mind a mind, and this capacity is not imparted to it from without. Even in its lowest and darkest recesses, beneath the level of clear consciousness, this process, tendency, or power of intelligence lies latent, ready to express itself on suitable occasions. And even in its broadest expanse of experience, the mind in its more perfect contemplation is reflective, that is, it mirrors nature in its characteristic system of intelligence.

Leibniz defined his position clearly by revising a famous Scholastic formula: "Nothing is in the understanding which was not previously in sense." To this he added, "except understanding itself (*nisi ipse intellectus*)."[12] So he supported Locke against Descartes that there are no specific innate ideas, self-evident axioms, or other first principles; but he maintained the unacquired and fundamentally characteristic power of intelligence in the mind. We shall see the development of this idea in Kant's theory of knowledge. Leibniz's view of mental activity as reaching below the levels of clear consciousness also adumbrated modern views of the mind which are receiving fuller recognition only in contemporary psychology. His own doctrine of knowledge, as it were, exemplified itself. It was latent and implicit in his monadology. Locke's *Essay* served to bring it clearly into his consciousness —in Leibniz's words, it "aroused it on occasion."

Moral Philosophy

In the perspective from which Leibniz viewed mental activity, we could consider all specific knowledge and understanding as the progressive self-realization of intelligence, the self-manifestation of the thinking monad. This

---

[10] G. W. Leibniz, *Monadology*, in Carr, *op. cit.*, pp. 38 f.
[11] *Ibid.*, p. 45.
[12] G. W. Leibniz, *New Essays Concerning Human Understanding*, in Langley, *op. cit.*, p. 111.

activity reveals itself also in the moral life, in the recognition and achievement of purposes and values. This teleological process indicated to Leibniz an ideal strain in reality, a principle of dominant perfection. Here he reaffirmed ancient Platonic convictions, and anticipated modern idealism.

Leibniz recognized a teleological order in nature, even below the levels of conscious existence. He called the unconscious monads "bare," to indicate their lack of awareness, but he saw in them a certain adaptiveness analogous to purposive tendency; hence he named them "entelechies," realized potentialities. Individual forces may so correspond to each other that, like a swarm of bees, they cooperate and serve a common end, though without any clear, conscious idea of it. But on the level of rational intelligence, people not only express reality in their careers and capacities, but understand what they express and can make it their deliberate purpose in life. In the perspective of intelligence nature manifests its plenitude with vastly greater clarity than it does in the bare, unconscious monads. "A single spirit is worth a whole world."[13] We might say that, in the universal drama of reality, rational minds are the chief characters, expressing its central meaning.

As we recognize cosmic role and rank of persons, we can understand their true purpose and responsibility. A truly intelligent act is one in which the will is clearly self-determined, deliberate and conscientious, identified with the choice and action, recognizing them as in line with its own role in relation to others. We attain perfection as we thus realize ourselves; that is, as we attain self-understanding and self-fulfilment. This progressive self-realization reveals both self-regard and benevolence. Moral intelligence is social in its outlook. It recognizes the interrelatedness of human needs and satisfactions, it respects in others the same right to happiness which it claims for itself, and it pursues a course of rational philanthropy.

While thus outlining the rational ideal in life, Leibniz did not forget that human beings are not pure intelligences. As he recognized the latent stirrings of purposive activity even in unconscious monads, so in human beings he saw the persistence of lower drives. Our desires are marked by impulses and appetites in which our conscious nature reaches toward lower levels of being; desires also point to our more distinctive rational will. But Leibniz did not probe or expose the life of human servitude as Spinoza had portrayed it in his doctrine of the passions. His ethical discussion is more suave; like More, the Cambridge Platonist, he concentrated on the reasonableness and nobility of virtue.

Leibniz's interpretation of moral responsibility and freedom follows from his monadology. The activity of a monad is not causally affected by that of any other monad but always expresses its own character as a unique version of the universe. Accordingly, Leibniz rejected both the arbitrary freedom of indifference and also any mechanical necessity of human conduct. The intelligent will is free of any external determination; the intelligent will is

[13] G. W. Leibniz, *Discourse on Metaphysics, Correspondence with Arnauld, and Monadology, op. cit.,* p. 61.

determined in its own unique self-expression. Of this self-determination, man's intelligence may become progressively convinced as it matures. Moral freedom is thus relative to self-understanding and rationality in conduct.

Individual life and social-institutional activity reveal the boundless range of perfectibility. In his conception of values as in his doctrine of substances, Leibniz emphasized the dynamic principle, activism. The perfect world is the eternally perfectible world, a world always in the process of creation. Human self-realization and happiness, in ever being achieved, are ever in prospect. Neither individually nor socially nor cosmically can there be an assignable limit to spiritual progress. This conviction implied the immortality of rational souls: "All the changes of matter cannot make them lose the moral qualities of their personality."[14] And this spiritual life finds social expression in the expansive range of civilization. Throughout his life, Leibniz pursued this ideal of a world society of nations actively cooperating and, in peace and goodwill, promoting the values and satisfactions of the human spirit. He called this the "Republic of Minds" or the "City of God," the divine masterpiece, "a moral world in the natural world."[15]

To Leibniz, this was more than a human-social ideal; it had cosmic prospects and ultimate religious implications. It signified God's self-realization in human lives. For God is not only the Architect of nature, but also the ideal director of the moral order; he is, to rational minds, "not as an inventor to his machine, . . . but as a Prince to his subjects, and even as a Father to his children."[16] Leibniz's ethics and social philosophy, like his monadology and preestablished harmony, were conceived finally in theological perspectives. He demanded these theological finalities, but they involved his philosophy in grave perplexities.

Theology and Theodicy

In his philosophy, Leibniz required deity to account for the activity essential in the nature of things. God also was needed to assure cosmic unity to his multitude of monads, and infinite reality to the ideal values of the rational life. Leibniz's thought arrived naturally at the idea of God, and he used it without any doubt. In formulating his arguments for God's existence, he wrote not as an inquirer but as a believer, to instruct others.

His theology followed, but also revised, the two standard proofs, the cosmological and the ontological. In this connection, it is important to note his distinction between necessary and contingent truths. A proposition affirming the existence of anything is contingent and depends for its truth upon a proposition about some other thing. More generally, a world of con-

---

[14] G. W. Leibniz, *Monadology*, in Latta, *op. cit.*, p. 307.
[15] Leibniz, *Monadology*, in Carr, *op. cit.*, p. 137.
[16] *Ibid.*, p. 135.

tingent existence does not contain in itself the ultimate cause and ground of its being. Thus, the final reason of things must be in a necessary substance, and this sufficient reason of all existence is God. This is Leibniz's form of the cosmological argument. He reasoned further, in the argument from the eternal truths, that God is the source, not only of existences, but also of essences. The region of eternal truths, or of the ideas on which they depend, is God's understanding, and thus, Leibniz continued, if there is a reality of eternal truths, this reality must be founded on the existence of an absolutely necessary Being. He also advocated the ontological argument of St. Anselm, but amended his statement of it. Leibniz reaffirmed that God's existence could be validly concluded from the idea of the greatest and most perfect Being, but only if that idea is possible and without contradiction. This he undertook to prove. "God alone (or the necessary Being) has this prerogative that he must exist, if he is possible. And since nothing can hinder the possibility of that which has no limitations, no negation and consequently no contradiction, this alone is sufficient to establish the existence of God *a priori.*"[17]

Leibniz's conviction of the preestablished harmony of the monads assured him of its divine authorship. His thought seemed to point in two ways. The monads are the creations or "fulgurations" (emanations) of God, and God's perfection is manifested in their harmonius correlation. Or, reasoning in the other direction, from the harmony of the monads, Leibniz inferred its divine composer.

He pursued the idea of God by both causal and teleological reasoning. God is the creator and also the architect or designer of the world, and He is likewise divine providence, cosmic judge, prince, and "a Father to his children." By definition He must be a perfect Father, and hence, all should be well with His children. But is all well? And if, in many ways, it is not well but ill, how are we to explain the evils? How are we then to think of God, and of His infinite justice and His other perfections? To this problem of the origin and explanation of evil, Leibniz devoted his *Theodicy* (1710).

✦

BAYLE'S SKEPTICAL IRONY

Leibniz wrote the *Theodicy* at the request of the "divine princess," Sophie Charlotte, whose Christian faith had been disturbed by reading the *Historical-Critical Dictionary* of Pierre Bayle (1647–1706). Bayle's life, like his thought, was embroiled in the religious conflicts of the seventeenth century. His father and brother were Huguenot pastors in the south of France, where the Albigensian sectarians had been persecuted during the thirteenth century. Bayle learned his Latin and Greek, and his Protestant doctrine, in his father's study, but was converted to Catholicism by the Jesuits in Toulouse. Rome, however, held him for only seventeen months. His return to his Protestant communion exposed him to persecution in France as a religious renegade, and he fared no better in Holland in his relations with the Calvin-

---

[17] Paraphrased from G. W. Leibniz, *Monadology,* in Duncan, *op. ct.,* p. 315.

ist theologians. An omnivorous reader who never forgot anything that he could turn to his account, he especially explored the theological controversies of the past, in order to continue them in his own critical writings. His works were read and discussed throughout Europe; Voltaire called them the library of nations. They reopened old debates, raised new issues, and unsettled orthodox conformity in religion and the reliance on reason in philosophy.

Bayle reasoned that philosophy demands the universal validity of its principles, but it cannot demonstrate it. Religion exacts a firm faith which it cannot sustain by sound reasons. Bayle was never tired of exposing these two quandaries of the human spirit. The first one perplexes moral philosophy. Bayle was rigorous in his ethical principles. Virtue and godliness should not be motivated by farsighted expediency, nor are the pleasures of the worldly life to be dismissed as spurious. Vice has its satisfactions, and virtue should be preferred to it, not because in some way or in the long run it is more enjoyable, but solely because it is nobler. Our moral choice should express our devotion to God's perfect will, not our calculating prudence. Furthermore, the moral worth of our actions is determined by what we will to do, not by the actual results. Decisiveness in morals is the integrity of the good conscience. It must recognize the universal laws of right and wrong, and loyally identify itself with God's will as expressed in them. This is what Bayle regarded and respected as genuine morality, but when he inquired into its warrant, he was dismayed to find it so questionable. The principles which command our devotion cannot certify themselves to our reason. Moral and religious convictions rely on our faith in the eternal justice, wisdom, and love of God, but how is this faith to be sustained against the incursions of doubt?

Bayle's skeptical reflections were particularly engrossed by the problem of evil. This problem is fundamental in the Christian religion of salvation, and, through the centuries, scores of theologians have sought to overcome its perplexities when formulating their doctrines of divine grace. The Jansenist controversy in Catholic France, and the Arminian in Protestant Holland, reopened tangled issues which St. Augustine had not settled, and which Bayle explored ironically in the ample columns of his *Dictionary*. Manicheans, Pelagians, Paulicians, and other heretics presented their arguments, which Bayle found logically cogent, though quite unacceptable to orthodox faith.

According to Augustinian orthodoxy, evil was brought into the world by Adam's free choice, which God, respecting Adam's moral dignity, did not prevent, but which, by divine justice, implicated the whole human race in its dire consequences. Bayle asked, did Adam's moral perfection require this free capacity to choose evil? Furthermore did he not show his real character in actually choosing evil, and, was God wholly unconcerned in creating him with such a character? Bayle pursued one line of argument after another and repeatedly reached the disturbing conclusion that the truths of faith do not rest on solid ground. Reason can unsettle belief, but cannot yield positive assurance. Bayle's further thought took a decidedly ambiguous course. Sometimes he expressed a Pascalian reaffirmation of faith, a defiant will to believe. But more often he concluded, or rather terminated, on a note of skeptical irony. Reason has been exposed as inconclusive and unavailable as a basis of orthodoxy, but without reason we can only cling to our faith, not lay claim to truth.

LEIBNIZ'S OPTIMISM: THE BEST OF ALL POSSIBLE WORLDS

Leibniz's *Theodicy* was intended not merely to justify the ways of God to man, but also to vindicate reason as a basis of religious conviction. His piety and his rationalism were both directed against the skeptical inroads of Bayle's dialectic.

In dealing with the ultimate problems of theodicy, rash judgment based on limited impressions would be misleading. We must view things in their cosmic perspective, or, as Spinoza said, in the light of eternity. Leibniz exposed two sources of likely error, both due to defective breadth of outlook. We should not judge the divine plan by our brief span of experience, and condemn it because of blind impatience; nor should we draw conclusions about the vast universe from the meager range of our life on earth. God's justice operates on an infinite scale, eternal and cosmic.

The second source of error in theodicy arises from a one-sided interpretation of God's nature, a preoccupation with some one attribute of divine perfection. Leibniz insisted on the principle of the "compossibility" of God's attributes: infinite wisdom, infinite goodness, infinite power, all creatively active in perfect harmony. God's goodness and love will the creation of all possible good. When the skeptic asks, why should there be any evil in the world, he fails to learn from God's wisdom. No created world could be without some imperfections, for these are the marks of finite existence. Absolute perfection is for God alone. The infinite wisdom of God eternally knows this. Of all the possible worlds, God, in His grace, has chosen the least imperfect, and His infinite power has created it, the best of all possible worlds.

Leibniz undertook to strengthen this cosmic reassurance in his theodicy by a closer analysis of the nature of evil. He distinguished three kinds of evil: physical, moral, and metaphysical. Physical evil is suffering; moral evil is sin; metaphysical evil is the imperfect character of finite being. Leibniz's account of physical evil reflects his optimistic temper. Bodily frailties and ailments are not as common or as grievous as complaining men believe, and a great part of them can be blamed on our own sins. Sin, or moral evil, presented great perplexity to Leibniz. He could not tone it down as he did physical evil, for the gravity of sin must be a central conviction in any Christian theodicy. He could not recognize it explicitly as antiperfection, a real factor in human nature antagonistic to the perfect Creator, without conceding a point to Bayle's dualistic heretics. Could he, while reaffirming

God's condemnation of it, finally reduce it to a variety of metaphysical evil, the imperfection of finite beings? This is what Leibniz did, but it produced moral ambiguity in his theodicy.

If both physical and moral evil are explained ultimately as metaphysical evils, imperfections essential to finite beings, we see them as obviously natural conditions in a created world and we can have no reasonable complaint against God. But should not God, likewise, be expected to regard the sinner with the same reasonable benignity? If sin is ultimately mere finitude, how are we to view it as abhorrent to God? To achieve his theodicy, Leibniz reduced the moral antithesis good-evil to the metaphysical, infinite-finite. But in so doing, did he not unsettle the foundations of a real ethics? Moreover, he made the gravity of sin too tenuous and the meaning of God's infinite goodness too vague for an acceptable Christian theodicy.

SUGGESTED WORKS FOR FURTHER STUDY

WORKS BY LEIBNIZ. Leibniz, G. W., *Philosophical Works* (selected and trans. G. M. Duncan), *The Monadology and Other Philosophical Writings* (trans. R. Latta), *Discourse on Metaphysics, Correspondence with Arnauld, and Monadology* (trans. G. R. Montgomery), *New Essays Concerning Human Understanding* (trans. A. G. Langley), and *The Monadology* (trans. H. W. Carr), *Philosophical Papers and Letters* (trans. L. E. Loemker, *Theodicy* (trans. E. M. Huggard); Wiener, P. P. (ed.), *Leibniz; Selections.*

BIOGRAPHIES AND CRITICAL STUDIES. Carr, H. W., *Leibniz;* Joseph, H. W. B., *Lectures on the Philosophy of Leibniz;* Merz, J. T., *Leibniz;* Russell, Bertrand, *The Philosophy of Leibniz.*

BAYLE. Robinson, Howard, *Bayle the Sceptic.*

19. John Locke and the Philosophy of Experience

Locke's Career in English Thought and History

John Locke (1632–1704) may be considered the most widely influential philosopher of English speech. Like Descartes before him, and Kant after him, Locke signalized an epoch. From these three minds streamed the main philosophical currents of the three modern centuries. Beyond his strictly intellectual importance, Locke was a leader in the liberal movement that was to reconstruct social-political order on both sides of the Atlantic. His method and his outlook on life stirred French thinkers to new activity in new directions for a whole century. We shall first briefly consider his work in its British setting.

Locke grew up in the vicinity of Bristol; his father was a country attorney with some property. Young Locke's education at Westminster School was rigorously classical. At Christ Church College, Oxford—where as student and fellow he was at home for some thirty years—he grew dissatisfied with Scholastic doctrines and turned to the natural sciences and medicine, thus learning to value experiments above erudition. A careful study of Descartes' works aroused his interest in systematic philosophy, but, despite many agreements, he felt himself a critic, not a disciple of Cartesianism.

His work as a tutor at Oxford did not draw him into an academic career, and he was reluctant to take holy orders, preferring his secular freedom. But he committed himself politically and socially when, in 1666, he became physician and counsellor to Lord Ashley, later Earl of Shaftesbury, the leader of the liberals in the English struggle with royal encroachment on the people's rights. Shaftesbury came to depend on Locke personally and in public office. Locke's surgery saved the statesman's life; Locke found a wife for Lord Ashley's invalid son, and later directed the education of his grandson, the future philosopher Shaftesbury. Locke's own fortunes fluctuated with Shaftesbury's. He rose to high public office when Shaftesbury was made Lord Chancellor, was swept out with the overthrow of his chief, and returned to office when Parliament forced King Charles to release Shaftesbury from prison and to restore him to power. When Shaftesbury—once again out of office—had to flee to Holland (where he died), Locke also hid there from the English king's agents. Locke became the sage counsellor of the Englishmen who prepared and carried through the Revolution of 1688. On his return to the new England under King William, he declined high diplomatic appointments, preferring to devote himself to his philosophical career. He published his most important *Essay Concerning Human Understanding* (1690), the first of his *Letters on Tolerance*, and *Two Treatises on Government*. His later books, on *Education* and on *The Reasonableness of Christianity*, broadened the scope of his philosophical activity. He was the acknowledged voice of philosophical and social liberalism as long as he lived, and the eighteenth century expanded greatly the range and power of his influence.

Locke's Account of the Origin and Nature of Ideas

Locke's philosophical mind matured slowly; he did not undertake systematic construction until he was almost 40. During a discussion with his friends, he was perplexed by their common inability to determine the bounds of human understanding and effective inquiry. Locke stated his purpose very modestly; unlike the master builders in the history of philosophy, he meant to be only a laborer engaged in "clearing the ground a little, and removing some of the rubbish that lies in the way to knowledge."[1] Although unpretentious himself, he did not undervalue his task. Before we can appraise any system of philosophical ideas, we must have reliable criticism of the sources and tests of knowledge. His plain purpose was "to inquire into the original, certainty, and extent of human knowledge, together with the grounds and degrees of belief, opinion, and assent."[2] These problems were bound to manifest their implications in metaphysics, but Locke was reluctant to pursue them there. His inquiry was primarily epistemological, a theory of knowledge. The recent discovery of two partial drafts of the *Essay*, dating from 1671, enables us to trace the long and steady development of his thought for almost two decades prior to the publication of this work.

Locke's use of the term "idea" should not be confused with Plato's. By an idea, Locke meant "whatsoever is the object of the understanding when a man thinks."[3] An idea is any perception or concept of thought, anything whatever which the mind entertains. In undertaking to trace the origin of ideas, Locke was confronted at the outset by the doctrine of innate ideas

[1] John Locke, *An Essay Concerning Human Understanding* (A. C. Fraser. ed.). Oxford, Clarendon Press, 1894, Vol. I, p. 14.
[2] *Ibid.*, p. 26.
[3] *Ibid.*, Vol. I, p. 32.

held by some Cartesians, if not always definitely by Descartes himself; more especially, by the Cambridge Platonists; and by rationalists, like Lord Herbert of Cherbury. In Book I of the *Essay*, Locke argued that neither principles nor ideas are innate. No principle, speculative or practical, can be cited which all minds recognize at birth. To infer the innateness of certain so-called "common notions" from their universal acceptance by men is unwarranted, for they may have been generally acquired in the common course of experience. But, as a matter of fact, there are no such universally held ideas or principles. Neither the laws of identity and contradiction, nor the principle of justice, nor the idea of God can be said to have such universal and innate character.

If men had been endowed by the Creator with certain truths, these would surely have included knowledge of God and of the good and godly life. Yet there is evidence of the greatest diversity of moral and religious ideas throughout history. "The saints who are canonized among the Turks, lead lives which one cannot with modesty relate."[4] The transgression of a moral principle may not signify that it is unknown; "but the *generally allowed* breach of it anywhere . . . is a proof that it is not innate."[5] Furthermore, if it be argued that these are innate ideas, but that they have been effaced or distorted by misleading influences in life, we should expect to find them in their pristine clarity in the cradle. Such a statement about the insight of children would require no discussion, unless it were argued further that the mind may have ideas without being conscious of them, an opinion which seemed "hardly intelligible" to Locke.[6]

If ideas are regarded as innate because reason can obtain certain grasp and general acceptance of them, all mathematical propositions and other scientific truths, "all the certain truths which reason ever teaches us"[7] must be considered innate. We may recall here the difference between Locke's position and that taken by Leibniz. While admitting that there are no specific innate ideas, Leibniz emphasized his conviction of the mind's inherent rational capacity which is realized in the actual process of knowledge. Locke, of course, did not deny that the mind is capable of acquiring ideas by sense perception, intuition, and demonstration. But he insisted that ideas are and must be acquired. He rejected the doctrine of innate ideas as without warrant or merit. It has "eased the lazy from the pains of search" and has confirmed dogmatists in their demand *"that principles must not be questioned."*[8] But the mind that seeks real truth must set this empty notion aside; it must explore the sources of its ideas so as to inquire further into the extent and the adequacy of human knowledge.

Having thus "cleared the ground of some of the rubbish," Locke proposed his own explanation of the way the mind gets its ideas. Bacon had urged us

[4] *Ibid.*, Vol. I, p. 73.
[5] *Ibid.*, p. 75.
[6] *Ibid.*, p. 40.
[7] *Ibid.*, p. 43.
[8] *Ibid.*, p. 116.

to be rid of all our idols or preconceived ideas, and to come to nature with our mind a *tabula rasa*. Locke maintained that the mind is precisely that at the outset of its activity, a clean slate, "white paper, void of all characters."[9] All ideas are derived from experience. Experience was analyzed by Locke into two processes: first, the reception of impressions through the various senses, and second, "the operations of our mind within us, as it is employed about the ideas it has got."[10] These two, sensation and reflection, are the only sources of our ideas.

In tracing the origin of various ideas more particularly, Locke distinguished several kinds. Some ideas are received through one sense—such as colors, sounds, tastes, smells, cold, heat—together with their respective degrees or mixtures—such as blue-green or tart-sweet. Others are experienced by more than one sense—by sight and touch, as in ideas of extension, figure, motion, and rest. Ideas of reflection include two main groups: perception, or thinking, and volition, or willing. In the first belong the ideas of retention, or memory, discerning or distinguishing, and comparison, composition, and abstraction. When sensation and reflection operate jointly, the mind experiences such ideas as pleasure or delight and pain or uneasiness, power, existence, and unity.

This classification of ideas may be regarded as a plain survey of experience, without commitment to any specific cosmological doctrine. But it cannot be thus regarded for very long. On the first page of the *Essay*, Locke wrote:

> I shall not at present meddle with the physical consideration of the mind; or trouble myself to examine wherein its essence consists; or by what motions of our spirits or alterations of our bodies we come to have any sensation by our organs or any ideas in our understandings; and whether those ideas do in their formation, any or all of them, depend on matter or not.[11]

Actually, and despite his reluctance to consider metaphysics, Locke did take a certain view of the structure and operation of nature which should be kept in mind, for it affected the further development of his theory of knowledge. He could not give an entirely clear statement of his ideas of sensation without considering the relation of his mind to his body and to other bodies. Nor was he altogether satisfied with his definition of sensation. He sought to improve it:

> When I say the senses convey into the mind, I mean, they from external objects convey into the mind what produces there those perceptions. . . . Sensation . . . is such an impression or motion made in some part of the body, as produces some perception (makes it be taken notice of) in the understanding.[12]

Apparently Locke proceeded on the assumption that "external objects" exist, that they produce certain motions or impressions in our bodies which induce

[9] *Ibid.*, p. 121.
[10] *Ibid.*, p. 123.
[11] *Ibid.*, p. 26.
[12] *Ibid.*, pp. 123, 141.

a certain awareness in the mind, and that ideas originate in this interaction of minds and bodies. There is no extended definite exposition or proof of these views in the *Essay*. Their kinship with the cosmology of Descartes is evident. Unlike the Cartesians, Locke was not mainly interested in explaining the relation of mind and body; he was examining the course of ideas in the process of experience. But the Cartesian dualism of substances is reflected in his analysis of the qualities of bodies which we perceive, and also in his account of substance.

Locke's doctrine of the qualities of bodies plays a role in the development of British empiricism which corresponds to that of the Cartesian doctrine of substance in seventeenth-century rationalism. It will be noted that the successive revisions of this doctrine involved a radical reconstruction of the Lockian cosmology. By the quality of a body Locke understood its power to produce an idea in the mind. He distinguished two kinds of qualities: (1) primary or original qualities, which we perceive but which inhere in bodies, whether perceived or not, as for instance solidity, extension, motion or rest, and number; (2) secondary qualities, which are manifested only in our ideas of objects, only as bodies are perceived, such as colors, sounds, tastes, smells, and similar qualities of sense. An apple really has a certain size and shape and consistency, but its redness and tartness and fragrance are only in my experience and enjoyment of it.

In modern terminology, these two kinds of qualities may be called objective and subjective. "The ideas of primary qualities of bodies are resemblances of them, and their patterns do really exist in the bodies themselves, but the ideas produced in us by these secondary qualities have no resemblance of them at all."[13] Recalling Locke's doctrine that all our ideas are derived from experience, we might ask how he could derive this just-quoted idea from experience. How could he know from experience what does and what does not exist outside of experience? But it would be better to let George Berkeley ask him this question. We should remark here that, despite his sharp distinction of qualities, Locke did compare the power of a burning object to produce an idea of heat in a person with its power to change the solidity or consistency of wax or clay. Without expounding a system of nature, he regarded the world dualistically: minds receiving ideas of the qualities of bodies.

In his further examination of ideas, Locke classified them as simple and complex. He was not settled in his mind about this classification. He distinguished three kinds of complex ideas: modes, substances, and relations. By modes he meant combinations of simple ideas: either variations of the same simple idea (simple modes) or combinations of various kinds of simple ideas (mixed modes). Thus there may be simple modes of space such as distance, capacity, immensity; or of time, such as hours, succession, eternity; simple modes of colors, sounds, tastes. Mixed modes vary with custom or interest shown by the mind in the compounding of ideas, such as obligation, drunk-

13 *Ibid.*, p. 173.

enness, dishonesty, or, more generally, virtue and vice, appeal or triumph, sacrilege or veneration. As may be seen, they cover a wide range of mental activity, and Locke was content with a brief reference to them. In an earlier draft of his *Essay* (1671), he had discussed both space (place) and time more at length as relations. He did not present a definite theory regarding the nature of space. He was not satisfied with a merely relational view of it. He was probably inclined toward the view that space is the capacity of bodies to exist. He would not identify space or extension with body, for empty space or a vacuum is conceivable. But he did not countenance the doctrine of absolute real space. Our ideas of space originate in our sensations and are developed more fully in our understanding.

Locke's account of the complex ideas of substances involved him in the cosmological perplexity already noted. With his typical candor, he admitted that he had no other idea of pure substance in general, but "only a supposition of he knows not what *support* of such qualities which are capable of producing simple ideas in us";[14] he cited the Indian's notion that the world rests on an elephant, and the elephant on a tortoise, and the broad-backed tortoise on "*something, he knew not what.*"[15] But Locke was as ready to classify his substances as he was candid in confessing his perplexity about the basic idea of substance. In discussing substances, he usually had bodies or corporeal things in mind. But he also recognized spiritual substances, spirits, or minds. Can mind be conceived as a substance that supports or comprises the stock of ideas? Is this what is meant by the self-conscious mind? Locke wavered somewhat regarding this distinction. Toward the end of the second book of the *Essay* he stated: "*Self* is that conscious thinking thing—whatever substance made up of (whether spiritual or material, simple or compounded, it matters not)."[16] From corporeal and mental substances, Locke, like Descartes, distinguished the infinite Substance, God, "an eternal, most powerful, and most knowing Being."[17]

Unlike the ideas of substances, which always point beyond themselves, the complex ideas of relations are free products of the mind, to which no specific objective reality corresponds. They arise from our comparison of one idea with another. The idea of Caius as a man considers the individual Caius. But if we think of him as a husband or a parent, we suggest his relation to some other person or persons. Language expresses the great variety of relations in which an individual may be compared with another or others; thus we get correlative terms like husband-wife, parent-child, larger-smaller, near-remote, above-below, earlier-later, similar-dissimilar, identical-different, cause-effect. The last mentioned idea is "the most comprehensive relation, wherein all things that do, or can exist, are concerned."[18] Locke's examination of it anticipates in part Hume's later more thoroughgoing analysis. In

14 *Ibid.*, p. 391.
15 *Ibid.*, p. 392.
16 *Ibid.*, pp. 458 f.
17 *Ibid.*, Vol. II, p. 309.
18 *Ibid.*, Vol. I, p. 432.

his discussion of the idea of power Locke noted the uniform succession of changes in the past which leads us to expect a future repetition of like uniformities, and from which we infer a certain power or capacity in some things to affect or to be affected by others. His explanation of the idea of causal relation somehow included both of these considerations. The cause of a thing is that which uniformly precedes it and which in some way makes it begin to exist or act. But the complex idea of cause and effect seemed to him finally reducible to simple ideas, of the observed beginning of something, after the observed existence or activity of some other thing. The problem of the objectivity and necessity of this succession and connection was not explored by Locke.

The first two books of the *Essay* deal with the origin and nature of ideas. While they involve questions of the validity and adequacy of knowledge, these problems are not considered explicitly until the end of the second book; they receive their main treatment in the fourth book. Locke devoted the third book to the critical examination of words as the signs of general ideas. By a process of abstraction, men enable themselves to consider groups or classes of simple ideas, "as it were in bundles," and so can improve their use and communication of them. These general ideas of this or that sort of thing do not correspond to real, universal entities such as some rationalists entertain. "When we quit particulars, the generals that rest are only creatures of our own making."[19] Locke's words often suggest a nominalistic interpretation. But he also recognized the universal element in experience, the meaning or essence of the particular existents.

The mind's convenience in its use of words to preserve and to share its ideas also involves the hazard of misapprehension. Words are naturally imperfect signs of the ideas they represent, particularly so in the case of mixed modes and ideas of substances. To clear general terms of confusion, we should reduce and refer them to the simple particulars from which they are derived; we should keep as close as possible to direct experience. We should be clear and constant in our definition of terms, and, when departing from uniformity or commonly accepted usage, we should not fail to explain our deviation. Like Francis Bacon in his discussion of "Idols of the Forum" or "Market-Place," Locke was concerned to clear up "the errors and obscurity, the mistakes and confusion, that are spread in the world by an ill use of words."[20]

Critical Estimate of Knowledge, Opinion and Faith

After his exploration of the origin and varieties of ideas, Locke inquired into their validity, "the certainty and extent of human knowledge." Again

[19] *Ibid.*, pp. 21 f.
[20] *Ibid.*, p. 149.

he classified ideas, this time by standards of evaluation. Some ideas are clear and others obscure; some are distinct and others confused. Their obscurity may be due to the dullness of sense organs or to very slight and transient impressions or to weakness of memory in retaining them. A distinct idea stands out definitely apart from any other, and so, in fact, it does in direct sensation, but confusion arises from too hasty formation of complex ideas in the mind, jumbling disorder in the use of names, indefiniteness and un-steadiness in combining simple ideas.

Locke also distinguished ideas as real and fantastical, and adequate or in-adequate, depending upon their agreement with the real existence of things or with their archetypes. A fantastical idea, such as that of a centaur, has no foundation in nature. The extent to which a real idea conforms to its archetype determines its adequacy. Thus, all our simple ideas are adequate. Of the complex ideas, those of modes and relations represent the mind's variation and combination of simple ideas, and since they conform to the mind's intention and archetype, they are adequate. But our ideas of sub-stances refer to real beings and come short of adequate conformity. Though, in progressive investigation, a scientist's idea of iron may come to include more and more real properties of that metal, it can never reach a fully ade-quate comprehension of its nature.

Our knowledge of the nature of things, therefore, may approximate but cannot completely attain truth. We may speak of true and false ideas, but actually, truth and falsehood belong to propositions in which ideas are re-lated. The mind expresses truth or is in error in the way it judges its ideas, affirms or denies something of them. It may relate them to the ideas of others as intended by the use of various terms, or regard them as conforming to some real existence or to the real constitution and essence of something to which it refers. The mind's likelihood of reaching adequate and true ideas is limited when it is concerned with external objects or substances, and must rely on the data of sense experience; but it can proceed to universal cer-tainty when it is interrelating its own ideas, as it does preeminently in mathe-matics.

It is evident that Locke, mainly an empiricist in his account of the sources of ideas in the process of experience, showed a definite rationalistic tendency in his critical appraisal of human knowledge. This tendency is especially ap-parent in the fourth book of the *Essay*. Locke regarded knowledge as "the perception of the connexion of and agreement, or disagreement and repug-nancy of any of our ideas."[21] This agreement or disagreement may be of four kinds: (1) of each idea with itself, as "blue is not yellow;" (2) in its abstract relation to other ideas, as "two triangles upon equal bases between two parallels are equal;" (3) in its necessary connection with other ideas of qualities coexisting in certain substances, as "iron is susceptible of magnetic impressions;" and (4) in its disclosure of actual, real existence, as "God is."

[21] *Ibid.*, p. 167.

How far does our knowledge extend in these four varieties of mental activity?

In examining the certainty and limits of knowledge, Locke distinguished several varieties, or degrees, of knowledge: intuitive, demonstrative, sensitive. Intuition is direct and unwavering insight, certain and irresistible; the immediate conviction that an idea is as we perceive it, and different from another idea precisely as entertained by the mind. Demonstrative knowledge does not have this direct certainty; it proceeds mediately and concludes by rational inferences from combinations of ideas. Sensitive knowledge—namely, of the existence of things perceived in sense experience—though it commonly passes under the name of knowledge, should more properly be called faith or opinion. We have a certain intuition of our perception itself, but whether it is a bare idea or really represents an existent thing is a conjecture, and possibly doubtful.

Locke was convinced of the self-evidence of ideas and the immediate certainty of his own existence. Here he agreed with Descartes in both principle and detail: "If I doubt of all other things, that very doubt makes me perceive my own existence, and will not suffer me to doubt of that."[22] Like Descartes again, from his intuitive conviction that he exists, an actual something, Locke inferred directly and certainly the existence of an infinite, ultimate source of his being and of all existence whatever—eternal, most powerful, and most knowing deity. That God is omniscient, Locke was convinced when he reflected that minds or cogitative beings could not have been produced by an incogitative first cause. His own thinking mind assured him that there must be thought and intelligence at the source of existence.

Certain of his own mind's existence and convinced of God's reality, Locke was also assured that there were other finite beings besides himself. In our experience, he reasoned, we have sensations of something. But this assurance nowise signifies that we have certain knowledge of the nature of things perceived by sense. Locke pointed out his inadequate knowledge of substances. Our knowledge of the primary qualities of bodies is imperfect, and we have no means of ascertaining beyond mere probability what necessary connections may exist between their primary and their secondary qualities: "what figure, size, or motion of parts produce a yellow colour, a sweet taste, or a sharp sound."[23] Although physical science inclines the mind to belief, it falls short of certain knowledge in so far as it rests on the data of sense experience.

The basic distinction between corporeal and spiritual substances, according to Locke, may be conjectural and permit an alternative view. He reaffirmed his conviction of a real and infinite mind, God; but unlike Descartes, he was not invariably positive about the ultimate distinction of minds and bodies. "Matter, *incogitative* matter and motion, whatever changes it might

22 *Ibid.*, p. 305.
23 *Ibid.*, p. 202.

produce of figure and bulk, could never produce thought."[24] But might there not be cogitative matter? In his controversy with the Bishop of Worcester, Locke entertained as a possible theory that, for all he knew, omnipotent Deity might have endowed certain kinds of matter with the capacity to think. His mind might then be his thinking body, and mental processes might be so much complicated physiology. But was not the counter alternative view also possible: that since our immediate knowledge is of the experience of minds, our so-called "material existence" may also be interpreted in terms of mental activity? Locke's view thus opened up further prospects of cosmological speculation, but with an alternative skeptical slant that disturbed the empiricist. We shall see the pursuit of these three lines of reflection in eighteenth-century philosophy.

In sharp contrast to the inconclusiveness of our ideas of substances, and hence, of our knowledge of the nature of things which affects the certainty of physical science, Locke insisted that the mind can be certain in its use of ideas of relation. Here the mind does not depend upon sense data, but organizes its ideas in accordance with strict definitions from which reason can infer universally valid propositions. The preeminent field of this certain knowledge is, of course, mathematics. Locke reduced mathematics to a system of analytical judgments. The series of theorems about a right triangle represent the progressive rational explication of what the mind understands by a triangle, its comprehensive definition. As will be noted presently, Locke believed that, if ideas of moral relations were rigorously defined, analyzed, and elaborated deductively, they could yield a rational system of ethics that would be as valid as mathematics.

The systematic conclusions of Locke's theory of knowledge seem to point at least two ways. On the one hand there is his empiricism. It rejects the rationalist's claim to innate ideas and would trace all knowledge to its sources in experience. But, for Locke, these sources are not only sense data; they include reflection, the mind's response to its ideas and its use of them. From the outset of his inquiry, his empiricism is never mere sensationalism, and his theory of knowledge turns somewhat toward rationalism. Not only did he recognize reflection; in the end he found real, adequate knowledge in the domain of reflective reason, in its organization of abstract, universal ideas.

In his view of mathematics and of ethics, Locke seemed to reduce valid knowledge to analytical demonstration. Our minds can excogitate, can reason out clearly and validly the implication of our abstract ideas. We can state systematically and certainly what we mean by *A* and *B*. But we cannot state with equal certainty whether *A* and *B* really exist at all, or objectively are as we conceive them to be, or whether future experience may not require us to redefine them. The proposition "all gold is malleable" would be as universally valid as a geometrical proposition about a right triangle, if we included malleableness in our definition of gold. But if this quality is not

[24] *Ibid.*, p. 313.

thus included, but is regarded as an experimentally attested predicate, we cannot claim certainty for it. For all we know, unmalleable gold may yet be discovered, which would lead us to qualify or entirely revise our proposition.

Locke's theory of knowledge thus cannot be interpreted as strict empiricism. He did not share Bacon's boundless confidence in induction, but held that observation and experiments do not yield universal and certain knowledge such as is obtained by mathematical analysis and rational deduction. On the other hand, the prevailing empiricism in Locke's thought, while admitting the inconclusiveness of experimental science, also maintained that the universals of reason lack objective reality. His rationalism did not include any Platonic conviction of the real world of Ideas, the objective laws or principles or essences of reason. This interplay of empiricism and rationalism in Locke's philosophy must be kept in mind if we are to interpret rightly his treatment of the complex problem of knowledge. Preoccupation with the empiricist strain in his theory led his successors to more rigorous development of its implications.

A theory of knowledge which finds only various degrees of probability in experimental science can scarcely be expected to guarantee the doctrines of theology. In Locke's religious criticism, his affirmations are as important as his negations and his tolerant suspense of judgment. He sought to "lay down *the measures and boundaries between faith and reason;*"[25] he rejected only what is counter to reason, and allowed faith to venture beyond the reach of definite evidence. He defined faith as "the assent to any proposition, not thus made out by the deductions of reason, but upon the credit of the proposer, as coming from God, in some extraordinary way of communication. This way of discovering truths to men, we call *revelation.*"[26] Thus, miracles disagree with our uniform experience of nature; but, in considering them, we may recognize God's will as comprehending nature and as being superior to it; thus considered, and, if well attested, they may be believed. Likewise, the belief in a future life does not accord with our customary ideas of the soul's sense experience; but when we regard God's omnipotence, our trust in his promise and prevailing will should confirm our faith in immortality. On the other hand, polytheism must be rejected as irrational superstition, for the very idea of deity contradicts belief in a multiplicity of gods.

In the *Essay*, in his *Letters on Tolerance*, and in *The Reasonableness of Christianity*, Locke maintained his conviction of the existence of God. He accepted the Bible as God's revelation of his will to men, and therefore claimed for himself and for others the right to study it directly, without having any dogmatic interpretation imposed on him. His conception of the essence of Christianity was simple: faith in Christ and his Gospel is the way to blessedness and life eternal. This simple faith may be interpreted and de-

25 *Ibid.*, p. 415.
26 *Ibid.*, p. 416.

veloped variously by sundry sects, but all are entitled to tolerance under a good government, which should not interfere with the religious beliefs of men, so long as they are law-abiding and do not endanger social order.

Locke's religious tolerance, to be sure, had its limits. Citizens should be free and unmolested by the state in their speculative opinions and matters of faith. But it may well be otherwise in practical matters which directly affect the lives of others. Obviously, our state would not tolerate religious sects that include human sacrifice in their worship, or that practice bigamy. But Locke would enjoin state control of papists who teach that faith is not to be kept with heretics; he would also restrict atheists who reject the basic acknowledgment of God and the sanctity of an oath. Locke's prevailing emphasis was upon religious tolerance. He would deprive ecclesiastical leaders of their political authority and would give all law-abiding men the protection of the law to worship God according to their faith and conscience.

While he thus championed the rights of nonconformists, he had distaste for any doctrinal or emotional vagaries in religion, preferring the dignity of the established Church. Within the Church of England, however, he advocated the latitudinarian ideal that welcomed a variety of genuine and reasonable convictions. His own religious views inclined toward a rational, liberal interpretation of theological doctrines. He has been ranked with Lord Herbert of Cherbury as a pioneer leader of English deism. Unlike the acknowledged deists of that age, he did not reject or neglect religious revelation, nor did he reduce worship to simple moral conduct. Just as, in his theory of knowledge, he did not definitely side with either of the two opposing schools of thought, so in his religious views he did not commit himself with sectarian rigor. His writings on religion are impressive because of their genuine Christian piety and their desire to give his faith as reasonable expression as possible.

Locke's Practical Philosophy: Morals, Education, Government

Locke's philosophical reflections began when he discussed moral and religious topics with some friends. His *Essay* closes on a reasonable note of practical guidance. In directing our life, where we do not have the certain light of truth, we should seek and follow the likeliest lead offered by probability. Still, Locke had absolute certainty of God's existence, and a sustaining assurance of the revelation of God's will in Scripture. He was also confident that rational moral demonstration and a universal science of ethics were available.

Probably no part of Locke's philosophy requires a more carefully balanced interpretation of contending ideas than his ethics. The familiar connection of the empiricist theory of knowledge with hedonism is manifested in Locke's general definition of good and evil in terms of pleasure and pain, and in his view of "man's proper business, to seek happiness and avoid misery."[27] But this definition does not satisfy Locke. Dominating his hedonism, though not entirely rejecting it, is a second and prevailing conviction, that morality requires acknowledgment of law and universal sanctions, recognition of authority. *Moral* good or evil, he reasoned, must be conceived as espousal or transgression of laws of conduct. Locke listed three kinds of laws, or sanctions, whereby our acts are judged as duties or as sins: the civil law, the law of social prestige or reputation, and the divine law.

Locke admitted that men's conformity to these rules and sanctions may be only calculating expediency in view of the eventual advantages or penalties. But the laws of right and wrong themselves have ultimate and inalienable worth. Neither prudential hedonism, nor circumspect obedience to a human or divine Leviathan, can express the true moral motive as Locke conceived it. In its essential character, virtue is entitled to our choice. Justice is ultimately God's law, and so will prevail, but God's will has chosen and established it because of its inherent worth, and, God being God, He "cannot choose what is not good."[28] Locke would trace the ultimate meaning of good and of God to the same rational idea of essential perfection.

Along this line of fundamental analysis, Locke considered the formulation of a universal science of ethics. In such a science, as in mathematics, reason would start with certain universal and clearly defined principles, and would proceed to a fuller and fuller logical explication and application of these principles.

The idea of a supreme Being, infinite in power, goodness, and wisdom, whose workmanship we are, and on whom we depend; and the idea of ourselves, as understanding, rational creatures, being such as are clear in us, would, I suppose, if duly considered and pursued, afford such foundations of our duty and rules of action as might place morality among the sciences capable of demonstration: wherein I doubt not but from self-evident propositions, by necessary consequences, as incontestible as those in mathematics, the measures of right and wrong might be made out.[29]

Locke's friend Molyneux of Dublin urged him to perfect such a science of morals. The plan was not carried out, perhaps owing to the empiricist strain in Locke's ethical reflections, which inclined him toward hedonism. A more likely reason for his reluctance was plainly stated by him; he did not conceive effective morality in a merely secular perspective. His final law and sanction in conduct were the divine. For his fully authoritative guidance in practice, he was bound, and also content, to go to Christ's words in the Gospels. "Here morality has a sure standard, that revelation vouches, and reason cannot gainsay, nor question; but both together witness to come from

---

[27] Quoted in Lord King (ed.), *The Life and Letters of John Locke*, London, Bohn's Libraries, 1858, p. 306.
[28] John Locke, *An Essay Concerning Human Understanding, op. cit.*, Vol. I, p. 347.
[29] *Ibid.*, Vol. II, p. 208.

God the great law-maker."[30] When reading Christ's words in the Gospels, was Locke hesitant to add words of his own, or was he less assured regarding an incontestable rational ethics? "He that shall collect all the moral rules of the philosophers, and compare them with those contained in the New Testament, will find them to come short of the morality delivered by our Saviour, and taught by his apostles; a college made up, for the most part, of ignorant, but inspired fishermen."[31]

Related to his moral philosophy, as well as to his general theory of experience, are his views on education, which were radical in his day. Locke set himself in firm opposition to the formal, classical training of the schools. He had only scorn for his language drills, at Westminster School, in Latin and Greek, and even in Hebrew and Arabic. Beyond some reading knowledge of Latin, he would sweep out the grammarian pedantry and train the boys for their life as gentlemen. This training should aim to form character, in which virtue is chief, sustained by wisdom, and refined by good breeding. In this training, learning has its part, but only as subservient to the other three. Locke emphasized the importance of physical discipline to harden the young constitution through vigorous exercise and simple, abstemious diet.

Moral self-control and mastery of one's desires were stressed by Locke as a "great principle: . . . that a man is able to deny himself his own desires, cross his own inclinations, and purely follow what reason directs as best."[32] Locke advocated self-control as a means to fuller self-expression. Education should develop the natural capacities of the individual and prepare him, not for the university, but for life; not for further studies, but for worthy action in his social station.

Although he was mainly concerned with the schooling of young gentlemen, Locke turned his attention also to the education of the masses. He advocated public support of working schools in which the children of the poor might be saved from vagabondage or delinquency, and receive training for the trades or crafts of their later humble employment. This proposal fell far short of modern democratic projects and practices, but it expressed his liberal views of the role of education in an extensive program of social reform.

Locke's active part in the preparation for the Revolution of 1688 gave his political theories timely interest and significance. He explicitly proposed to vindicate King William, "to make good his title in the consent of the people; which being our only one of all lawful governments, he has more fully and clearly than any prince in Christendom."[33] Of his two *Treatises of Government*, the first was a refutation of the theory of absolute monarchy; in the second, *Of Civil Government*, Locke maintained that political authority is

[30] John Locke, *Works,* London, 1812, Vol. VII, p. 143.
[31] *Ibid.,* p. 140.
[32] *Ibid.,* Vol. IX, p. 27.
[33] *Ibid.,* Vol. V, p. 209.

delegated to the ruler by the people only for the sake of the common welfare. The contract, basic in all lawful government, establishes the will of the majority as law. The people's will gives legislative enactments their validity and effectiveness to be enforced, amended, or abrogated. Locke subordinated the executive power in government to the legislative, the king to parliament. "The legislative power . . . has a right to direct how the force of the commonwealth shall be employed for preserving the community and the members of it."[34] The king and other executive officers must be subject to its restraints, as required by the public interest. Nor may parliament legislate contrary to the people's will and basic rights, nor should judges sustain such acts. Finally, if king, judge, and legislator proceed contrary to the people's trust and well-being, "the people have a right to act as supreme, and continue the legislative in themselves; or erect a new form, or under the old form place it in new hands, as they think good."[35] With this concluding sentence of his treatise, Locke took his stand resolutely on the principles of a government that rules by consent of the people and which is responsible to their will. These ideas matured and bore fruit in the expanding liberalism of English parliamentary rule. They inspired the American and French Revolutions, and, in other lands, they found expression in various forms of constitutional government.

In another of his political doctrines, Locke, without any radical intention on his part, raised a radical issue. According to him, government was bound to defend men in their property rights. For surely, everyone has a right to secure his livelihood from his own estate, nor may it be rightly taken from him without his consent. But Locke held that "labour, in the beginning, gave a right to property."[36] Man makes a piece of land his own by combining his labor with it. While Locke himself was not an economic radical, his views on the origin of property rights anticipated the labor theory of value in the modern social-economic struggle.

Newton's Philosophy of Nature

The development of the Lockian philosophy of experience will be traced in the revisions of it by his two eminent successors, and we shall also note its major influence in France and on American shores. In their initial sharp turn from Cartesian rationalism, the French *philosophes* of the eighteenth century advocated Locke's philosophical method along with Newtonian scientific procedure. It may be appropriate, at this point, to consider the latter briefly. It is beyond the range of our inquiry or our competence to examine here the great works in mathematics, optics, and general physics of

34 *Ibid.*, p. 424.
35 *Ibid.*, p. 485.
36 *Ibid.*, p. 364.

Sir Isaac Newton (1642–1727). Dominant in the development of modern science because of his exact formulation of its fundamental principles, Newton is also significant for his influence on the philosophical temper of his age; he aroused men's interest in the direct investigation of nature, confirmed critical minds in their recognition of the cosmic mechanism, and, at the same time, advocated a liberal, but positive, spirit in religion. The deism toward which Locke's inquiry into the origin and extent of human knowledge had inclined was interpreted by Newton with an unmistakably genuine piety that was as convincing to devout minds as his scientific eminence was to the more critical. The logical coherence of his science and his theology, however, has been questioned.

The modern history of ideas records some interesting coincidences. Galileo's famous *Dialogue*, which led to his condemnation and imprisonment by the Inquisition, was published in 1632, the year that saw the birth of Spinoza and Locke, two leaders in the resolute pursuit of truth. Isaac Newton was born in the year of Galileo's death, and he continued and perfected Galileo's synthesis of experimental and theoretical science. Galileo, not content with experimental reports, sought, also, rational demonstration of his conclusion. Newton was wary of abstract speculation without available factual warrant. "I frame no hypotheses,"[37] he declared, meaning that he would restrict his theoretical reasoning to ascertainable inferences from observed phenomena. His epoch-making work in physical science realized a fruitful union of Baconian induction and the Cartesian method of rational analysis. Bacon had promoted the direct interpretation of nature, and Hobbes had championed a universal science of mechanics, but neither of them possessed, as Newton did, the mathematical apparatus needed for the scientific realization of their aims.

In his *Mathematical Principles of Natural Philosophy*, Newton undertook to present the entire system of nature in all of its details—from the fall of an apple to the revolutions of the planets in their orbits—as manifesting the operation of the same universal laws of mechanics. In his principle of gravitation, he assumed no occult qualities or causes in nature. The force of attraction meant to him simply that a larger body causes a smaller body to move toward it. He was careful to note the factual data of experience and to organize them into a valid theoretical pattern. The astronomical conclusions of his modern predecessors and the formulated laws of mechanics were integrated by him in one universal summation. Newtonian gravitation thus came to signalize in men's minds the all-comprehensive mechanism of nature. Nature was disclosed as a cosmos, that is, every condition and change of material existence in it was shown to be causally necessitated by the same fundamental mechanism.

Although Newton formulated a thoroughly mechanical theory of nature,

---

[37] Sir Isaac Newton, *Mathematical Principles of Natural Philosophy and System of the World* (trans. A. Motte, revised by Florian Cajori), Berkeley, Univ. of California Press, 1946, p. 547.

he was also prepared to draw religious inferences from his cosmic synthesis. Nature impressed him with its harmonious, systematic order; his mind felt impelled to conclude that the world has an intelligent Author and Director. So he wrote at the end of his chief work, "this most beautiful system of the sun, planets, and comets, could only proceed from the counsel and dominion of an intelligent and powerful Being."[38] In this advocacy of the teleological argument for God's existence, Newton resembled Locke. Both of them kept within the bounds of ascertainable evidence, in their detailed scientific and philosophical exposition of ideas. Both had unwavering assurance of God's reality and perfection in their more ultimate outlook on reality.

SUGGESTED WORKS FOR FURTHER STUDY

WORKS BY LOCKE. Locke, John, *Works* (in 10 volumes, 1812), *Philosophical Works* (J. A. St. John, ed.), *An Essay Concerning Human Understanding* (A. C. Fraser, ed.), and *Selections* (S. P. Lamprecht, ed.).

BIOGRAPHICAL AND CRITICAL STUDIES. Aaron, R. I., *John Locke;* Alexander, S., *Locke;* Fox Bourne, H. R., *The Life of John Locke;* Fowler, Thomas, *Locke;* Fraser, A. C., *Locke;* Gibson, James, *John Locke;* King, Lord, *The Life and Letters of John Locke.*

NEWTON. Newton, I., *Mathematical Principles of Natural Philosophy and System of the World* (trans. A. Motte, Florian Cajori, ed.).

---

[38] *Ibid.,* p. 544.

20. George Berkeley: Empiricism and Idealism

Locke's philosophy of experience, which traced the origin of our ideas to sensation and reflection, was marked by a certain metaphysical reluctance to consider the ultimate nature of reality, and by distrust of our competence to know it. His own inconclusiveness influenced his successors variously. His definition of substance as "something he knew not what" might incline his readers to skeptical inferences regarding science and human knowledge generally. (David Hume's pursuit of this alternative will be considered in the next chapter.) Locke's tentative speculation, that mind may be a special kind of body endowed by God with the capacity to think, allowed mental activity to be interpreted as a physiological process, and so placed the new theory of experience at the service of materialism. It was thus used by some of his English successors and later, and far more thoroughly, by the French empiricists. But Locke's dualism of material and mental substances admitted also of reduction to a spiritualistic monism. A more radically empiricist concentration on the process of experience might disclose nothing real except minds and their ideas. This sort of idealism, mentalism, was championed by George Berkeley (1685–1753).

We should see Berkeley's philosophy in too restricted a perspective if we regarded it merely as an idealistic offshoot of Locke's theory. Berkeley was more than a critical and original reader of Locke's *Essay;* he was also a zealous student of Malebranche's *Search After Truth*, and, like both of his masters, he had struggled with the problems of Descartes. Earnestly pious, like Father Malebranche, he noted with deep concern the materialistic and skeptical conclusions to which both the Cartesian and the Lockian philosophy were pressed by mechanists and freethinkers. Like Plato, whose dialogue style of philosophical exposition he emulated more successfully than

346

any other modern thinker, Berkeley was a champion of ideal realities and values. The materialists and infidels of his day were, to Berkeley, like the Sophists of Plato's *Dialogues*, to be exposed and overcome by self-reliant intelligence.

Berkeley's remarkable precocity, in his studies and in his original reflection, steeped him early in the modern ferment of ideas. He raced through the fine schooling of Kilkenny, "the Eton of Ireland," and entered Trinity College in Dublin at the age of 15. Trinity provided ample fare for his avid mind. He studied in class or read for himself the classical and modern philosophers and scientists—not only Descartes and Malebranche, but also Hobbes, Spinoza, and Newton. Locke's *Essay* was used as a textbook. Berkeley was, in his way, a radical empiricist. Once he tried on himself an experiment in order to observe the course of ideas in a man who is being hanged, and his friend Conterini was almost too late in freeing him from the rope. His mind proceeded directly to original construction. He was convinced that he had a philosophical principle which perfected the truth expressed by Malebranche, corrected the basic error made by Descartes, completed Locke's philosophy by radical revision, refuted atheists and skeptics, and confirmed the truths of religion—a widespreading assurance.

As a young man in his 20s, Berkeley astonished British thinkers with his bold metaphysical speculations, published in three volumes within a span of four years. On his visit to London, he captivated men by his brilliant style and his fine personal qualities. "My Lord," said Jonathan Swift to Lord Berkeley when he introduced the young philosopher, "here is a fine young gentleman of your family. I can assure your Lordship, it is a much greater honor to you to be related to him, than it is to him to be related to you."[1] In trips between London and Dublin, and tours to Italy and France, young Berkeley expanded his acquaintance and knowledge of the world. Resolved to serve God and mankind, and distressed by the effete and corrupt civilization of his day, he conceived a plan to establish a college in Bermuda to train American Indians as Christian ministers to their people. Although this project eventually failed of realization, it brought Berkeley to America, where he influenced the leaders of thought and education in New England. On his return to Ireland, as Bishop of Cloyne, he continued his philosophical struggle with the forces of moral and religious decay. He was tireless in his efforts to better the condition of the Irish peasantry—Protestant and Roman Catholic alike. His last years marked his rise to great public eminence. He had the opportunity of becoming primate of Ireland, but he refused to be considered for the high post, preferring instead to spend his last days in meditation at Oxford, like the philosopher of Plato's ideal vision in *The Republic*.

[1] Quoted in J. M. Hone and M. M. Rossi, *Bishop Berkeley: His Life, Writings and Philosophy*, London, Faber, 1931, p. 89.

Berkeley's Empiricist Theory of Knowledge and Reality

The *Essay toward a New Theory of Vision*, which Berkeley published at the age of 24, was an empirical exploration of the idea of space. The Cartesians treated space, or extension, as the essential attribute of material substance. Young Berkeley, on his way to disposing of materialism, examined this alleged attribute of bodies. Our actual experience of space—that is, of distance, magnitude, and situation—does not disclose to us anything objective of which we have a direct idea. This perception involves an interplay of visual sensations with sensations of eye movements or, as Berkeley considered them, of touch. Distance is suggested to us by a combination of these two kinds of sensation. Our past experiences of direct, prompt, or delayed contact are related to certain respective ideas of sight and eye strain; thus we obtain corresponding ideas of the so-called "distance" and "magnitude" of whatever we perceive. Space, therefore, is not perceived, but rather is suggested to the mind. Not distance nor size nor situation nor spatial relation has any objective status in direct simple sensation. Beyond their compound origin as indicated, they are mere words. Instead of regarding space in Cartesian terms as an ultimate attribute of real bodies, Berkeley reduced the experience of it to a habitual result of the association of ideas.

The *New Theory of Vision* was intended as preparation for a more thorough exposition of Berkeley's philosophy. Its broad outlines had been foreshadowed in numerous passages of his early *Commonplace Book*. If space, the alleged essential attribute of bodies, proved on direct examination to be reducible to a habitual compound of sensations, what might the evidence from experience show regarding material substance itself? Berkeley turned his attention to the cosmological dualism which Locke shared with the Cartesians, and extended his criticism of the idea of space to the other qualities of objects which Locke had called "primary." The Lockian doctrine of primary and secondary qualities was subjected by Berkeley to radical criticism that aimed to unsettle any materialistic inferences that might be drawn from it, and that itself proceeded to an idealistic empiricism, or mentalism. This was Berkeley's undertaking in his *Principles of Human Knowledge* (1710) and *Three Dialogues between Hylas and Philonous* (1713).

The empiricist method used in examining the idea of space was applied by Berkeley in his investigation of the perception of bodies. His critical reconstruction of Locke's doctrine will be followed more clearly if his conclusion is stated in advance, as he himself expressed it at the beginning of his *Principles:* "A certain colour, taste, smell, figure and consistence having been observed to go together, are accounted one distinct thing, signified by the name apple; other collections of ideas constitute a stone, a tree, a book, and the like sensible things."[2]

In proceeding toward this reduction of material substances to the content of experience, and toward his further cosmological inferences, Berkeley pursued Locke's method of empiricist analysis, but more rigorously than Locke. In the "Introduction" to his *Principles*, he criticized Locke's doctrine of abstract ideas, which held that we form abstract ideas by considering some attributes common to several particular ideas, and by ignoring the aspects wherein they differ. Thus, words become general by being made the signs of general ideas. We remark the red color of an apple, a berry, a brick, a cockscomb, and by attending to this quality alone we get the idea of redness, or, by further similar abstraction, the idea of color in general, or else, of figure or solidity. Berkeley agreed that we have words to connote such common features of the perceived individuals, and he agreed that we form general ideas by attending to selected qualities of particular objects; but he denied that we can entertain new ideas of strictly abstract content. He could consider a figure merely as triangular without noting its other more specific qualities. But, try as he might, he could not frame a definite idea of a triangle abstractly without any of these qualities. What we really do in experience, he maintained, is to use ideas of particular reference to represent other ideas that are similar in certain respects. The ideas are, in fact, particular, but, by our words and terms, we may give them a generalized or abstract meaning. This distinction was important to Berkeley, for it implied a revised use of the word "idea." To Locke the term signified not only all perceptions, but any concept or thought whatever, every mental content. But, when Berkeley said that he could frame no abstract idea, he meant that abstractions cannot be presented to the mind as images. He restricted the term idea to denote perception and imagery. This revision of empiricist terminology and theory is further reflected in Berkeley's consideration of the empirical warrant of any idea, whether it is perceptible or represented in imagination.

By more vigorous empiricism, we could clear up many traditional difficulties in philosophy. "We have first raised a dust, and then complain we cannot see."[3] Our recourse must be to direct experience in order to expose our empty dogmatisms. Thus, Berkeley turned to Locke's doctrine of primary and secondary qualities. He reaffirmed Locke's arguments for the latter as convincing, but he could not see why Locke had failed to apply them to the so-called "primary" qualities. My ideas of the figure and size of an object, like my ideas of its color and taste, are derived from experience, attestable only in experience and having no real warrant beyond it. Any quality whatever has objectivity only as it is experienced; otherwise the idea of it is open to suspicion as an empty notion.

[2] G. Berkeley, in A. C. Fraser (ed.), *The Works of George Berkeley*, Oxford, Clarendon Press, 1901, Vol. I, p. 258.
[3] *Ibid.*, p. 238.

In developing his theory, Berkeley used the method of interpreting any particular quality in dealing with the objects of perception. For objects were disclosed to be empirical collections of qualities. As was said above, for him, the idea of an apple is the mind's way of designating a certain experienced combination of qualities, such as round, red, tart, and so forth. The apple exists in the same way as these qualities exist, in the process of experience. Berkeley regarded perceptibility not only as providing the sole warrant of objectivity, but as constituting its meaning. Thus, he formulated his central principle: "To be is to be perceived (*Esse est percipi*)."[4]

Berkeley was aware of the misinterpretations to which his principal conclusion was liable. He himself was partly responsible for being misunderstood as denying the existence of objects in nature. Thus, he wrote:

It is indeed an opinion strangely prevailing amongst men, that houses, mountains, rivers, and in a word all sensible objects, have an existence, natural or real, distinct from their being perceived by the understanding. . . . For what are the forementioned objects but the things we perceive by sense? and what do we perceive besides our own ideas or sensations? and is it not plainly repugnant that any one of these, or any combination of them, should exist unperceived?[5]

The readers were forewarned not to judge the new theory by "some passages that, taken by themselves, are very liable . . . to be charged with most absurd consequences."[6] Berkeley protested that he nowise denied the existence of the objects of our experience. In denying Locke's distinction between primary and secondary qualities, he rejected the alleged reality of the primary qualities entirely apart from experience, but he affirmed the real objectivity of the secondary qualities, as well as the primary, within the scope of experience. "That the colours are really in the tulip which I see is manifest."[7] He repeatedly defended his theory from the imputation that it doubted the reality of nature. What he did doubt and deny was the existence of a supposed material substance that transcended any perceptible qualities or any content of experience. He objected to being confused with Father Malebranche. The latter's influence on his thought was important, but, early in his *Commonplace Book*, Berkeley recorded his strong, critical reactions: "Malbranch . . . differs widely from me. He doubts of the existence of bodies. I doubt not in the least of this."[8] This remark is not so valuable in interpreting Malebranche's doctrine as in suggesting Berkeley's line of thought.

Berkeley's theory was aimed against materialism. He rejected the doctrine of material substance as unwarranted by direct experience, not required for scientific explanation of nature, and wholly inconceivable in sound reasoning. He was insistent on drawing a sharp distinction between the reality of bodies

[4] *Ibid.*, p. 259.
[5] *Ibid.*
[6] *Ibid.*, p. 235.
[7] *Ibid.*, p. 406.
[8] *Ibid.*, p. 50.

in our experience and material substances. His conclusion, *esse est percipi*, should not be misunderstood to mean that our ideas are mere figments of our imagination. When Dr. Johnson, on being asked to refute Berkeley, replied by kicking a stone, the Doctor might have been advised to read his source more thoroughly. Berkeley did not question the existence of the stone as available for Dr. Johnson's argumentative, tactual experience. "Whatever we see, feel, hear, or anywise conceive or understand, remains as secure as ever, and is as real as ever. There is a *rerum natura*, and the distinction between realities and chimeras retains its full force."[9] But this recognition of our experience of real things does not require us to entertain the notion of material substances x and y, occult and apart from any perceptual content.

Material substance was rejected by Berkeley as unwarranted in strict empiricism. The only real bodies a philosophy of experience may recognize are the bodies we perceive, not bodies divested of all perceptible qualities. The notion of indeterminate material substance is a mere notion without substance, a nonentity, an empty concept of reason. It denotes nothing ascertainable in actual experience, and is as useless as it is unwarranted. It gains concrete meaning only as it acquires content in experience, in specific perceived qualities.

Thus Berkeley reasoned by direct appeal to actual experience. But his argument led further. In its examination of ideas, his mind also was self-revealed, a spiritual substance. His theory of knowledge proceeded from immaterialism to metaphysical idealism. The self-inference of the mind required fuller justification. Berkeley was less axiomatic than Descartes, but not tentative like Locke, in his affirmation of the reality of the thinking mind. In his early philosophical reflection, he had sometimes regarded the mind simply as a compound or stock of ideas, "a congeries of perceptions."[10] But, in developing his thought, he affirmed the reality of mind as spiritual substance. Even in his *Commonplace Book*, he warned himself not to identify the understanding with the particular ideas, or the will with the particular volitions. Later, he came to the definite conclusion that "there is not any other substance than *spirit*, or that which perceives."[11]

Rejecting material substances, Berkeley reaffirmed the reality of spiritual substance. He defined spirit as "one simple, undivided, active being—as it perceives ideas it is called the understanding, and as it produces or otherwise operates about them it is called the will."[12] In brief statement, his real world is a world of minds and their ideas.

Berkeley might be asked, at this point, by what warrant he spoke of minds in the plural. How was he aware and assured of the reality of other minds? In direct experience his only knowledge of other minds could be

[9] *Ibid.*, p. 276.
[10] *Ibid.*, p. 27.
[11] *Ibid.*, p. 261.
[12] *Ibid.*, p. 272.

by their operation, by the ideas they excited in him. Thus, indirectly he was led to recognize other thinking agents whose ideas he could share, yet he could surmise in them also certain unparticipated individuality, and he could suppose that they likewise surmise it in him. In this way, he distinguished minds—thinking substances—from ideas, unthinking things that are perceived by minds.

This experienced world of many minds, partly overlapping and agreeing, partly unshared, but always manifesting available expansion, incompleteness, and limitations, led Berkeley to acknowledge the reality of an infinite Mind in whose eternal and all-comprehensive experience all finite minds share in varying degrees. Thus he arrived at his philosophical conviction of God as the ground and the summit, the alpha and omega, of his empiricism. His philosophy was announced on his title pages as directed against atheism and irreligion. His empiricist argument for God's existence should be considered more closely. His reasoning in part reaffirmed the teleological argument which may be read in Plato's *Dialogues* and on the last pages of Newton's *Principia:*

The constant regularity, order, and concatenation of natural things, the surprising magnificence, beauty and perfection of the larger, and the exquisite contrivance of the smaller parts of the creation, together with the exact harmony and correspondence of the whole [led him to a conviction of the] One, Eternal, Infinitely Wise, Good, and Perfect . . . Spirit, "who works all in all," and "by whom all things consist."[13]

These last cited clauses are important for Berkeley's cosmology. As his real world is the world experienced by his mind, likewise is the real world for any other mind, so also is the universe the world of God's eternal and infinite experience. In his version of the cosmological argument, the infinite reality of God was seen as the ultimate cause and basis of any objective reality for our minds. Berkeley saw a twofold merit in his doctrine—confirmation of scientific knowledge, and religious reassurance. In its tradition of dogmatic materialism, physical science had interpreted its laws in reference to its material substances. But experimental science could proceed with much stricter conformity to the direct evidence of experience, and from there it would move not toward, but away from religious skepticism. The laws of nature are the ascertained uniformities in the process of experience. They are the uniform ways in which God connects ideas in our minds. The consistency and evident necessity of their operation reveal to us the reliability of the universal language of nature, the experience of omniscient Deity. In science—that is, in our perception of the uniformity of nature—God speaks directly to our eyes and ears, to our minds; He is not far from every one of us; in Him we live and move and have our being. At this point, Berkeley's theory shows a kinship with that of Malebranche; both were led to the great words of St. Paul; but Berkeley expressed his view in terms of empiricism.

[13] *Ibid.*, p. 340.

Berkeley's empiricist writings manifested unwavering certainty of his theory and its central principle. "I wonder not at my sagacity in discovering the obvious and amazing truth. I rather wonder at my stupid inadvertency in not finding it out before—'tis no witchcraft to see."[14] But, since Berkeley claimed the warrant of direct experience for his theory, the strictness of his empiricism seems to demand inspection. His doctrine of spiritual substances may be questioned; do we have any better evidence for spiritual substances in experience than we have for material substances? Could not a still more rigorous empiricism reduce mind precisely to the "congeries of perceptions" considered in Berkeley's *Commonplace Book*, even as his apple was reduced to its constituent color, taste, or shape? Berkeley anticipated this objection to his theory, and he endeavored to dispose of it. David Hume argued this point to its radical conclusion. Hume, as we shall see in the next chapter, also subjected to empiricist criticism the conviction of the necessary connection of our experiences and the causal uniformity of nature, from which Berkeley had derived both scientific and religious reassurance against skepticism. May not this necessary connection and uniformity be shown to lack objective warrant in experience? Along these two lines of thought the prospects for Berkeley's empiricism appeared precarious.

Pious Prudence in the Pursuit of Happiness

Berkeley combined speculative zeal and originality in his theories of knowledge and cosmology, with deep religious convictions and devotion to moral and social reform. His published writings do not include a systematic ethical treatise, but he seems to have planned such a work and to have written it during his Italian travels. His manuscript unfortunately was lost, and he "never had leisure to do so disagreeable a thing as writing twice on the same subject."[15] It seems advisable to note the ethical views expressed in his various works, in view of his avowed use of Lockian principles in opposing infidelity and license in conduct.

Young Berkeley's mind was engaged by Locke's ideal of a deductive ethical science as incontestable as mathematics. He would examine human actions and motives, and analyze moral judgments, in which certain abstract terms like "just" and "temperate" gain general significance, even though they are not themselves universal ideas expressing any perceptions or images. By careful definition and faithful use of these terms or signs, a system of valid inferences from them would become available. "To demonstrate morality, it seems one need only make a dictionary of words, and see which included which."[16]

---

[14] *Ibid.*, p. xxvii.
[15] A. C. Fraser, *Berkeley*, Edinburgh, Blackwood, 1912, p. 112.
[16] Berkeley, *Works*, in Fraser, *op. cit.*, Vol. I, p. 39.

Later, Berkeley turned from this project of formulating a moral lexicon and a sort of ethical algebra, to advocate a theological utilitarianism by which he intended to confute more effectively the skeptics and libertines of his day. He refused to dissociate the moral pursuit of happiness from a pious regard for God's law; he satirized "men of fashion . . . bullies in morality, who disdain to have it thought they are afraid of conscience."[17] In his sermons on "Passive Obedience," and in the polemical dialogues of his *Alciphron,* he advocated, against the blind selfish indulgence of sinful men, the true self-regard of the man of conscience. The righteous man recognizes moral principles on which he can rely—they are God's laws, universal and authoritative. In obeying them, we realize our own blessedness and we promote the common welfare. But even when we do not see any immediate advantage, private or public, we are admonished to fulfill loyally God's will. The duty not to transgress the divine law must prevail in our motives over the so-called "first" law of nature, self-preservation. We should be willing to endure loss and pain in passive obedience rather than defy the divinely established authorities.

But Berkeley was no mere worshiper of statutes, civil or ethical, nor was he without substantial promises to the purely dutiful will. He was convinced that God will do his part in his own good season. Divine providence will finally crown the work of the righteous. They who, in serving the Lord, loyally forgo present indulgence will enjoy eternal blessedness in the hereafter. When Berkeley was off his guard, he might allow this thought to assume a morally impious expression: "It should even seem that a man who believes no future state, would act a foolish part in being thoroughly honest."[18] But his fuller and better judgment was different. He was as certain of the higher worth of moral satisfactions over the low pleasures of sinful indulgence, as of the blessedness which will ultimately justify the righteous man's present tribulations. His theological hedonism would combine a genuinely dutiful Christian spirit with unwavering trust in divine providence. Great is truth—and it shall prevail.

Panacea and Neoplatonic Contemplation

Berkeley's last important work, the *Siris,* has been appraised in more ways than has any other of his books. It has been lauded as the consummation of his thought; it has also been dismissed as a confused hodgepodge of unassimilated learning—medical, mystical, mantical—the very antithesis of the limpid style and thought of his earlier writings. A more reasonable interpretation of this work of Berkeley's old age may disclose, not its strict logical coherence, or its plain inconsistency with his empiricist immaterialism, but,

[17] *Ibid.,* Vol. II, p. 124.
[18] *Ibid.,* Vol. IV, p. 161.

rather, its joint expression of several characteristic demands of his mind. In the empiricism of his youth, he was confirmed in his recognition of deity by the uniformity and harmony of nature manifested in his experience. During his entire career in the Church, his worship of God's perfection reflected itself in devoted ministration to the needs of poor humanity. These motives did not conflict in his richly endowed character, but in his last work, they found a strange, but significant and dramatic expression.

Siris signifies "a chain," and the book is described thus in the long subtitle: "A Chain of Philosophical Reflexions and Inquiries Concerning the Virtues of Tar-Water and Divers Other Subjects Connected Together and Arising One from Another."[19] *Siris* was published in 1744 when Berkeley was almost 60. The reflections which ended in a cosmic vision arose from very simple, but pressing, inquiries. For several years, Ireland had been laid low by famine and a pestilence of a sort of dysentery which depopulated entire districts. Bishop Berkeley had always been concerned over the hardships and degradation of the peasants. In *The Querist*, he had asked several hundred questions concerning the social reforms needed in Ireland. The pestilence left the poor people in a hopeless state, without sufficient medical care, and without any cure that they could afford. Berkeley remembered the medicinal use of tar-water by the American Indians; he administered the remedy to his sick villagers, and was elated by its remarkable curative virtues. The bishop filled his shelves with medical and pharmaceutical treatises; he answered the criticisms of physicians by citing his cures: "I do not say that it is a panacea; I only expect it to be so: time and trial will show. . . . I would cry out to all the valetudinarians on earth: 'Drink Tar-water!' "[20]

For almost three hundred pages, *Siris* explores this panacea, the preparation and varieties of tar-water, its medicinal use in gout, gangrene, erysipelas, scurvy, and hypochondriac maladies, and its value in preserving teeth and gums. Berkeley proceeded from prescription to description, from medicine to metaphysics. Tar, pitch, and resin led him to speculate about the peculiar subtle spirit, a thin, volatile oil, in all vegetable juices. It is breathed into the air, the vivifying nursery of all sublunary forms. Subtler than air is the ether, the pure invisible fire pervading the whole universe. This fire, diffused especially in the native balsam of pines and firs, is benign and suitable to the human constitution, to alleviate its ills; "to warm without heating, to cheer but not inebriate, and to produce a calm and steady joy like the effect of good news."[21]

Berkeley's explorations convinced him of a fundamental truth, toward which his thought moved in progressive reaffirmation. Beneath the seeming random diversity of things, he saw the evidence of an all-embracing, harmonious order. In the scale of existence, "each lower faculty is a step that

[19] *Ibid.*, Vol. III, p. 115.
[20] Quoted in Hone and Rossi, *op. cit.*, p. 213.
[21] Berkeley, in Fraser, *op. cit.*, Vol. III, p. 225.

leads to one above it. And the uppermost naturally leads to the Deity. . . . There runs a Chain throughout the whole system of beings. In this Chain one link drags another. The meanest things are connected with the highest."[22] The virtue of tar-water is, in its essence, a diffusion of the divine perfection which impregnates all being. In his *Monadology*, Leibniz had quoted Hippocrates: "All things conspire, breathe together."[23] The lowliest thing is symptomatic of the whole course of nature. This fundamental principle of the Great Chain of Being, which in our day has been traced by Professor Lovejoy through its many expressions in the history of ideas, led Berkeley toward a Christian Neoplatonism as his final word in philosophy.

Jonathan Edwards

As mentioned earlier, Berkeley came to America with pious plans for reforming the manners of the colonists, and for converting and educating the Indians. He lived mostly in Rhode Island (he left his books to Yale), and stimulated philosophical thinking in New England. He could have found both response and stimulus in Jonathan Edwards (1703–1758), a young American contemporary and the most eminent thinker in colonial America. Edwards is best known for his burning sermons on God's holy wrath and the punishment of the wicked. But his spiritual range and penetration require fuller recognition, for he combined logical subtlety, metaphysical range, and mystical vision.

His theology, as revealed in his sermons and practical expressions, was, and remained, Calvinistic. His church theology and his pastoral devotion to admonishing, to saving souls from damnation, and his active part in the religious revival of the colonies, are familiar and need no mention in a history of philosophy. But his speculative mind went beyond Calvinistic theology and confronted theological problems of deep metaphysical significance. His meditations, the first real philosophy formulated in America, were set forth in the *Freedom of the Will*, the *Nature of True Virtue*, and the *End for Which God Created the World*. In these three treatises, Edwards developed three parts of his philosophy and theodicy.

His general philosophical outlook had already, and independently of Berkeley, proceeded from Locke's empiricism and Newton's experimental philosophy toward mentalism. Reliance on experience led him to a spiritual view of the world as a system of minds participating in various degrees in the infinite experience of God. His Calvinism and his conviction of God's omniscience led him to reject any human spontaneity or free will. Our actions are strictly determined by our nature, even as all physical events are causally necessary. In Edwards' judgment, determinism does not preclude

---

[22] *Ibid.*, Vol. III, pp. 269 f.
[23] G. W. Leibniz, *Monadology*, Sec. 61 (trans. by the present author).

responsibility. Our good or evil character renders us liable to God's retributive justice. The excellent is praiseworthy, the wicked and depraved deserve condemnation no matter how necessary they may be. "It is impossible but that offences will come, but woe unto him through whom they come!"[24] Edwards regarded virtue as marked by beauty or excellence in conduct. It is distinguished by its reflection, in a human perspective, of the universal divine exemplar of beauty and excellence. This is love of God, pursuit of divine perfection, the concord of our will with the divine will. True virtue and piety reflect our thinking and living in the direct presence of God, contemplating and emulating His perfection.

In this universal view of all being as centered in, and radiating from, God, what explanation is there for the sin and damnation, that loomed so awesome in the Calvinist outlook? Edwards' treatment of the problem of evil sought reassurance in theodicy by advocating a variety of Christian Neoplatonism. A created world manifests God's perfection, but it can manifest it only imperfectly. Edwards recognized "a disposition in God, as an original property of his nature, to an emanation of his own infinite fulness."[25] This world is the radiation of the divine light, but it is radiation in different degrees. Corruption and sin are the outer darkness in which glows the light of God's punishing justice. We are reminded of the words Dante read on the gates of Hell:

> Justice incited my sublime Creator;
> Created me divine Omnipotence,
> The highest Wisdom and the primal Love.[26]

SUGGESTED WORKS FOR FURTHER STUDY

WORKS BY BERKELEY. Berkeley, G., *Complete Works* (A. C. Fraser or A. A. Luce editions), and *Selections* (Mary W. Calkins or A. C. Fraser editions).
BIOGRAPHIES AND CRITICAL STUDIES. Fraser, A. C., *Berkeley;* Hicks, G. Dawes, *Berkeley;* Hone, J. M. and Rossi, M. M., *Bishop Berkeley;* Luce, A. A., *The Life of George Berkeley;* Wild, John, *George Berkeley.*
EDWARDS. Jonathan Edwards, *Works.*

[24] Luke 17:1 (Authorized Version).
[25] Jonathan Edwards, *God's Chief End in Creation*, in E. Hickman (ed.), *The Works of Jonathan Edwards*, 12th ed., London, Tegg, 1879, Vol. I, p. 100.
[26] Dante, "Inferno," iii:4 ff., in *The Divine Comedy of Dante Alighieri* (trans. H. W. Longfellow), Boston, Houghton Mifflin, n.d., Vol. I, p. 34.

21.   David Hume: A Skeptical Outlook

Hume: Philosopher and Man of the World

By fairly general consent, David Hume (1711–1776) is accounted the greatest British philosopher. Though not so widely stimulating and influential as Locke, nor so brilliant in metaphysical speculation as Berkeley, he excelled both of his immediate predecessors in the logical rigor and thoroughness with which he pursued the final inferences of the philosophy of immediate experience, without making it less rigorous or confusing it with rationalistic provisions. In Hume's works, empiricism was revealed unambiguously in its merits and in its limitations. He shared with Spinoza the authentic quality of philosophical greatness. Each of them explored a fundamental pathway to knowledge of nature with the originality and penetration of genius.

Hume came of a Scottish family of landed gentry—related to the earls of Hume, or Home—and from comfortable, if not affluent, circumstances. His father, a retired lawyer and laird of Ninewells, died when David was a child, leaving David's mother to devote herself to the education of her children. The indifference of her second son to her plans for his practical success in life, and his ceaseless and disturbing questions which she could not answer, led her to describe David as "a fine, good-natured creature, but uncommon weakminded."[1] He matriculated at Edinburgh at the age of 12 and he was barely 16 when he left college. With knowledge "extending little further than the languages,"[2] he returned home to the family library at Ninewells. His mother intended him to read his father's law books, but he preferred Virgil and Cicero.

The youth was seized with a fever for literary fame, but he was also beset with philosophical problems and religious doubts. A passion for great expression contended in his mind with the unsettlement of his convictions—a positive urge in a negative direction. "It began with an anxious search after

---

[1] Quoted in William Knight, *Hume*, Edinburgh, Blackwood, 1914, p. 5.
[2] Henry Calderwood, *David Hume*, Edinburgh, Anderson and Ferrier, n.d., p. 17.

arguments to confirm the common opinion; doubts stole in, dispelled, returned; were again dissipated, returned again; and it was a perpetual struggle of a restless imagination against inclination—perhaps against reason."[3] The necessity of choosing a career oppressed him; he would not be a lawyer, and, after a short trial, he decided against any commercial occupation. A work on philosophy had been taking shape in his mind for several years, and he went to France to write it. First at Reims, and then at the Jesuit College of La Flèche—where Descartes had studied more than a century earlier—Hume worked on his *Treatise of Human Nature*, completing it at the age of 25.

The book came stillborn from the press, and this first literary failure dampened Hume's ambitions in systematic philosophy, but not in literary work. His felicity in essay writing encouraged him to rewrite the three parts of his *Treatise* in more popular form, as three *Enquiries*. He disavowed his early work as juvenile, an estimate in which philosophical posterity has not followed him, for it has preferred the thoroughness and searching insight of the *Treatise* to the polished reflections of the *Enquiries*. It should be noted, however, that the *Enquiries* manifest not only a literary, but also a philosophical revision. While Hume did not abandon the skeptical inferences to which his examination of human knowledge had led him in the *Treatise*, he endeavored in the *Enquiries* to mitigate their baffling effects on the reader's mind. The revised argument does not alter the verdict, but states it more elegantly.

Meanwhile, Hume's spreading literary renown, and his rare social qualities, gained him a succession of appointments which perfected him as an accomplished man of the world, and as an able member of missions to Vienna and Turin. Yet his native Scotland was not consistently responsive to his merits. Although his friends included the outstanding Scottish thinkers and men of letters, he had opponents who were suspicious of his skeptical tendencies. They defeated his hopes of getting a professorship at Edinburgh or Glasgow; nevertheless, he was successful in being chosen as Librarian of the Edinburgh Advocates' Library, which post gave him the opportunity to write his *History of England*. This treatise brought him more criticism but it also spread his fame. When he went to Paris as secretary to the British ambassador, Lord Hertford, he was received with the greatest acclaim. On his return, he served as undersecretary of state, and, finally, he retired to his native Edinburgh to spend his last years in leisure, friendly converse, and reflection.

Hume combined the purest intellectual integrity with a certain social-practical adaptation. Having made his point clearly to his own satisfaction, he did not press it unduly; after thinking with the wise, he was willing to speak with the vulgar; yet he was not averse to stirring up the zealots. In his complex personality, he combined the single-mindedness of Spinoza and the diplomatic qualities of Leibniz. He said, regarding his *History of Eng-*

[3] Knight, *op. cit.*, p. 24.

land, that, while his estimate of the personalities in it was largely that of a Tory, the principles it expressed were apt to be Whig, liberal. He drew an ironical sketch of his own character in a letter to a friend whom he asked to find him lodgings in London: "a room in a sober, discreet family, who would not be averse to admit a sober, discreet, virtuous, regular, quiet, good-natured man of a bad character."[4]

Hume's Radical Empiricism

Hume described his major work as "an attempt to introduce the experimental method of reasoning into moral subjects."[5] This did not qualify his theory of knowledge as mainly an introduction to ethics. For any reliable moral principles, he depended on the direct evidence of experience, but he also regarded all knowledge as derived from the data of consciousness. The sciences of nature reflect the processes of human nature; by observing and understanding these characteristic human activities, the framework and patterns of scientific knowledge can be both explained and appraised. The *Treatise of Human Nature* was not intended as a system of metaphysics, but it explored the credentials of both metaphysics and physics in light of the evidence of experience which could sanction them.

The explicit commitment to direct experience ruled out any initial doctrines of substance. Locke had followed the Cartesian dualism; Berkeley, while rejecting corporeal substances, had reaffirmed the reality of mental substance. Hume rejected both doctrines as unwarranted in a strict philosophy of experience. We know neither the essence of the mind nor the essence of bodies. We have knowledge only of the course of our experience, and we should keep close to it. Just as for Berkeley a so-called "body" was actually the experienced compound of various qualities or ideas, so for Hume a so-called "mind" was the experienced compound or content of impressions and ideas. In distinguishing these two, at the outset of the *Treatise*, Hume disagreed with Locke. Locke's two primary sources of knowledge, sensations and reflections, implied his initial duality—the mind reacting to its sense impressions of objects. Hume assumed no such duality of substances, and he observed only the direct process of experience. When he distinguished sensation from reflection, he ascribed sensation to an original experience "from unknown causes," and treated reflection as derived from ideas in their further reappearance and combination in experience. Hume was intent on the process of experience itself. The initial and immediate perceptions of the greatest force and liveliness he called "impressions," and he applied the term "ideas" to the faint images of the impressions in thinking and reasoning. The proper

---

[4] Quoted in T. H. Huxley, *Hume*, London, Macmillan, 1902, p. 35.
[5] David Hume, *A Treatise of Human Nature* (L. A. Selby-Bigge, ed.), Oxford, Clarendon Press, 1888, p. ix.

exploration of the process of experience involves tracing every idea to the impression or impressions from which it is derived. Hume's general thesis is *"that all our simple ideas in their first appearance are derived from simple impressions, which are correspondent to them, and which they exactly represent."*[6]

Less lively than the impressions of direct initial experience are the ideas of them when they are retained and recalled in memory. Still less lively and weaker copies are the ideas of the imagination, which according to Hume are "faint and languid" perceptions that also lack steadiness and uniformity. The imagination connects, separates, and recombines ideas. We are apt to associate any idea with another one which has resembled it or has been experienced proximately to it in space and time. By this process of association of ideas, complex ideas are formed; these Hume, like Locke, classified as relations, modes, and substances. He disposed of modes briefly; substances, as was said above, he rejected outright. "We have . . . no idea of substance, distinct from that of a collection of particular qualities, nor have we any other meaning when we either talk or reason concerning it."[7]

Hume's unqualified denial of any doctrine of substance, material or mental, involved him in the problem of explaining selfhood or personal identity in terms of his theory of experience. Pursuing his chosen procedure with complex ideas, he sought the sense impression from which the idea of self could be derived. No single impression can give rise to the idea of self, or account for the alleged continuous self-identity which we associate with persons. All that we find in inspecting our so-called "selves" is a bundle of sensations, a collection of different perceptions. As in a kind of theatre, they pass, re-pass, glide away, and mingle in boundless variety. But we have a propensity to confuse the succession of our perceptions with their continued existence, and so run into the notion of a persistent self, or personal identity. In another and an important way, we associate and connect ideas as expressive of some common end or purpose, adding a sympathy of parts to confirm the bond.

Hume regarded the alleged personal identity, which is ascribed to the mind of man, as fictitious. That identity does not belong to the different perceptions, but is a quality which we ascribed to the ongoing sequence of our ideas by their union in our imagination. The subtle notions of a self-identical personality are our verbal ways of expressing the easy transitions of ideas in our experience.

The crux of Hume's empiricism is in his treatment of the complex ideas of relation. In considering the ways in which the reflecting mind sees fit to combine ideas, he listed seven "philosophical relations": resemblance, identity, space and time, quantity or number, degrees of quality, contrariety in existence and nonexistence, and causality. Some of these complex ideas— space and time, and causal relation—are selected for special examination.

[6] *Ibid.*, p. 4.
[7] *Ibid.*, p. 16.

Hume derived the ideas of space and time wholly from our experience of ideas; he rejected any doctrine of absolute space and time. He denied the notion that time and space are infinitely divisible. A mathematical point, without extension, and a moment of time, without duration, are both non-entities. The only points and moments that we really know have a perceptual content, and the space and time of experience are composed of such real parts.

If the idea of extension really can exist, as we are conscious it does, its parts must also exist; and in order to that, must be considered as colored or tangible. . . . The same reasoning will prove, that the indivisible moments of time must be filled with some real object or existence, whose succession forms the duration, and makes it be conceivable by the mind.[8]

Our idea of space is derived from the perceived contiguity of ideas. Our idea of time is our idea of the succession of perceptions. This empirical analysis of space and time prepared the way for the examination of the still more complex idea of cause and effect. Hume undertook to trace this idea to its simple components in sense experience. What relations between two perceptions do we intend to denote when we call one of them "cause" and the other "effect"? In the first place, Hume found that a cause and its effect are experienced as contiguous in space. Distant objects may sometimes seem to be productive of each other, but only through intermediate links; and, even when we do not directly ascertain these links, we surmise them so long as we continue to entertain the idea of causal relation. The second element in causality is succession in time, the perception regarded as the cause being prior to the so-called "effect." The view of these two events as perfectly simultaneous was discounted by Hume.

Contiguity in space, and the temporal priority of the cause, do not exhaust the connotation of the idea of causal relation. According to Hume:

. . . there is a NECESSARY CONNEXION to be taken into consideration; and that relation is of much greater importance than any of the other two above-mentioned. . . . *Why we conclude, that such particular causes must necessarily have such particular effects, and why we form an inference from one to another?*[9]

The crux of Hume's entire argument is here; that is, how experience gives rise to this idea of necessary connection. Hume would accept an answer to his question only from direct experience. And, in experience, he found a third type of relation between causes and effects; it is the relation of uniformity in the spatial contiguity and the temporal succession. Hume called it their "constant conjunction." Although our repeated past experience of this conjunction of two events does not yield objective certainty of their future and ultimate connection, we draw this inference. Hume asked again, "Why from this experience we form any conclusion beyond those past in-

[8] *Ibid.*, p. 39.
[9] *Ibid.*, pp. 77, 82.

stances of which we have had experience?"[10] He could see no convincing answer to this question that could establish the objective validity of the idea of necessary connection. He derived this idea from the idea of the experienced constant conjunction, through the process of the association of ideas, which forms a habit of belief.

Hume's more definite explanation of the process of experience was that, when two ideas have been experienced repeatedly as contiguous in space, with one of them uniformly prior to the other, this constant conjunction leads us to form a habitual association of the two ideas. When we again experience one of them, we believe in and expect the conjoint presence of the other. This belief, "A LIVELY IDEA RELATED TO OR ASSOCIATED WITH A PRESENT IMPRESSION,"[11] is a subjective inclination or demand of the mind to which we give objective interpretation. The experience of the cause, we believe, is bound to be followed by the experience of the effect.

Hume pursued this line of interpretation at length, considering the influence of belief and the probability of chances and causes. He reached the conclusion that the alleged objective necessity of causal relation is really a subjectively impelling association of ideas. "Upon the whole, necessity is something that exists in the mind, not in objects. . . . Either we have no idea of necessity, or necessity is nothing but that determination of the thought to pass from causes to effects and from effects to causes, according to their experienced union."[12]

The general conclusion—Hume called it "my hypothesis"—is that *all our reasonings concerning causes and effects are derived from nothing but custom.*"[13] In place of the causal necessity and uniformity in nature on which physical science insists and proceeds, Hume recognized only the strong, customary propensity of our minds to associate ideas which have been constantly conjoined in our experience. The philosophical inference is skepticism regarding the objective validity of any alleged universal law in science.

The denial of objective causal necessity was connected in Hume's thought with his rejection of any doctrine of substances. All that the senses yield is a mass of perceptions; the idea of externally existent bodies as alleged objects of perception is a notion of ours and can nowise be attested by experience, for the senses "cannot operate beyond the extent, in which they really operate."[14] We infer the existence of external bodies from the coherence and constancy of our impressions, but the alleged identity of the perceived object is a fiction, and the notion of its continued existence is unwarranted. We have in experience only the data of experience, a congeries of impressions and ideas. Hume's radical empiricism, while confirming the denial of corporeal substance, went beyond Berkeley's theory, and rejected mental substances. Men habitually speak of their minds, and Hume was not averse

[10] *Ibid.*, p. 91.
[11] *Ibid.*, p. 96.
[12] *Ibid.*, pp. 165, 166.
[13] *Ibid.*, p. 183.
[14] *Ibid.*, p. 191.

to using the customary term, but he made it plain that it was only a customary fiction. In his own view, "the mind is a kind of theatre, where several perceptions successively make their appearance; pass, re-pass, glide away, and mingle in an infinite variety of postures and situations."[15] The process of experience does not point reliably beyond itself to any substantial medium or objective basis whatever.

The question might be raised at this point whether Hume was really emancipated from the substantialism which he criticized so vigorously. He was led to his skeptical conclusions because he failed to find a warrant in experience for an external objectivity; that is, for such objectivity as was entertained by the cosmological dualists. But, in failing to ascertain any objective basis for a necessary connection outside the process of experience, was Hume bound to conclude *skeptically* that our ideas of causal order are merely subjective, our own customary propensities and beliefs? The objectivity might be sought in the process of experience itself. That would have required a reinterpretation of experience as a system, evidenced by the scientific mind in its fulfilled predictions—inferred uniformities leading to expectations of reactions which nature verifies in the process of experience. This further development of the theory of knowledge was pursued by Kant.

Reflections on Morals

Hume's principal influence in the history of philosophy has arisen from the radical empiricism of his theory of knowledge, especially in the reaction it evoked from Kant. But his skeptical views aroused immediate and wide resistance when he applied them in the field of religious beliefs. We should recall that he described his *Treatise* as an introduction of the experimental method of reasoning into moral subjects. He regarded his revised version of its third part, the *Enquiry Concerning the Principles of Morals*, as incomparably the best of all his writings. Did he propose to complete the work of his empiricist predecessors by writing the ethics of "the new philosophy"?

The second part of the *Treatise*, "Of the Passions," may be regarded as a psychological transition to the theory of morals. Hume pruned it ruthlessly in the second version, "A Dissertation on the Passions," reducing it to less than one-fifth its original length. His account of the emotions did not deserve this drastic abridgment. While it cannot vie with Spinoza's classical doctrine in its systematic exposition, it is likely to be more concrete in its direct report of experience, and more stimulating than the treatises of Descartes or Malebranche. Only a brief mention of it is possible here.

As Hume planned his approach to ethics, he might have been comparing his design for the *Treatise* with Newton's method in physical science. Traditional moral philosophy, in his judgment, needed the discovery and ap-

[15] *Ibid.*, p. 253.

plication of some simple principles of human nature to provide insight into experience and conduct. Such a basic principle Hume believed he had in his association of ideas, "by which we make an easy transition from one idea to another . . . to what resembles it, is contiguous to it, or produced by it."[16] He was as confident of applying this principle in the examination of the passions, as he was reassured by its confirmation of his conclusions about the understanding. The analogy of the two in revealing the same principle impressed him as very remarkable. "Grief and disappointment give rise to anger, anger to envy, envy to malice, and malice to grief again."[17] Hume agreed with Spinoza regarding "the double relations of sentiments and ideas." Our passion toward anything expresses our idea of it. Our love or hatred of it would correspond to our view or interpretation of it, but our judgment of approval or disapproval reflects the sentiment thus aroused, rather than any inference of reason.

This conclusion was important for Hume's ethical theory. Resolved as he was to proceed always as a strict empiricist, on the direct evidence of experience, he rejected not only the theological or metaphysical criteria in ethics, but also the proposals to grasp the essence of virtue and vice through logical analysis. Although, in the Enquiry Concerning Human Understanding, Hume followed Locke in regarding mathematical reasoning as demonstrative, he disagreed with Locke in ethics by refusing to make any concessions to rationalism. Moral good and evil cannot be defined in terms of any condition or relation from which rational inferences may be drawn. No matter how we may analyze or account for a certain act, our judgment of it lacks a moral tone so long as we limit ourselves to an intellectual statement. This failure of reason is the same whether we undertake to define good as obedience to a divine law, or in terms of an a priori principle, or by reference to certain objective relations. No such analysis suffices in morals. In judging any act as morally good or bad, a person signifies simply that, in considering the action, he feels a sentiment of approval or of blame. This view of Hume has been espoused in our time by some logical positivists and by advocates of the so-called "emotive theory" which regards moral propositions as not admitting of objective analysis or validation, as emotional reactions rather than intellectual conclusions.

Hume's ethics, at this point, requires a clearer and fuller account of the sentiments of approval and blame; how, for instance, are they distinguished from liking or disliking, from pleasure or displeasure; what evokes or motivates this characteristic moral feeling? Hume is sometimes disposed not to raise these problems, but to rest content with citing his moral sentiment. "The very feeling constitutes our praise or admiration. We go no farther; nor do we enquire into the cause of the satisfaction."[18] When Cicero de-

---

[16] David Hume, Essays Moral, Political, and Literary (T. H. Green and T. H. Grose, eds.), London, Longmans, 1912, Vol. II, pp. 144 f.
[17] Ibid., p. 145.
[18] David Hume, A Treatise of Human Nature, in Selby-Bigge, op. cit., p. 471.

scribes the crimes of Catiline, unless you feel indignation in your breast directly, the orator will vainly try to clarify or to complete his analysis.

In other ethical theories, the grounds of moral judgment had been indicated, and, in distinguishing his own view, Hume explored to some extent the specific character and motivation of the moral sentiment. Of particular interest here are his comments on egoistic accounts of morals, like that of Hobbes, and the relation of his theory to the utilitarian ethics of pleasure.

Hume's reaction to egoistic ethics seems to have ranged from partial admission to basic disagreement, and toward emphatic resistance. In the *Treatise*, we may note a certain balancing of judgment. Hume repudiated the extreme conclusions of the misanthropes; yet, he conceded a certain modicum of truth to their disparise of men. He judged it "rare to meet with one, in whom all the kind affections, taken together, do not over-balance all the selfish."[19] But, he also found "no such passion in human minds, as the love of mankind, merely as such, independent of personal qualities, of services, or of relation to ourself."[20] In the *Enquiry*, however, he took a more definitely altruistic position and stigmatized those who malign human character as though "all *benevolence* is mere hypocrisy, friendship a cheat, public spirit a farce, fidelity a snare."[21]

Hume did not explain the primary origin of kindly feelings, but he noted their genuine and frequent expression in human life, and he emphasized this element of sympathy in his account of the moral sentiment. "The voice of nature and experience seems plainly to oppose the selfish theory."[22] If we observe the process of moral approval and disapproval, we find a certain satisfaction or uneasiness. The feeling which determines moral judgment is one of kindly humanity, benevolent interest in the well-being of others, and sympathy. Hume even recognized a sentiment of "disinterested benevolence, distinct from self-love."[23]

The advance in sympathy from self-regard to social-mindedness was traced by Hume more specifically in his account of justice and benevolence. Our submission to justice often runs counter to our direct inclinations and desires, and, therefore, it must be motivated by strong considerations. Justice arises out of conflicts of private interests in a social system where such interests can be allotted fairly and rights maintained effectively. We support and submit to the system of laws because, under it, our estates and our lives are secured. But, by a process analogous to the association of ideas, our approval of the laws in which we recognize our own protection is extended to the system and principle of justice generally—even when our own interests are not involved. Injustice may rouse our disapproval when it does

[19] *Ibid.*, p. 487.
[20] *Ibid.*, p. 481.
[21] David Hume, *Enquiries Concerning the Human Understanding and Concerning the Principles of Morals* (L. A. Selby-Bigge, ed.), 2nd ed., Oxford, Clarendon Press, 1902, p. 295.
[22] *Ibid.*, p. 215.
[23] *Ibid.*, p. 301.

not even distantly concern us; we are disinterestedly indignant. By a sort of sympathetic contagion of sentiments, our submissive acceptance of the control of law, which we feel is eventually advantageous to us, is transformed into a benevolent and humanitarian loyalty to the justice that sustains the common welfare. *"Thus self-interest is the original motive to the* establishment *of justice; but a sympathy with public interest is the source of the* moral approbation *which attends that virtue."*[24] In comparing the earlier and the later versions of Hume's ethics, we may note a shift of emphasis, from justice to benevolence.

In his ethics, sympathy is correlative to his principle of the association of ideas. But, while he related his account of morals to his theory of knowledge, he did not recognize sufficiently that his ethics turned on the relation and on the distinction between self and not-self. The transition from selfish to altruistic feelings and acts, ruthless self-love and disapproval of it, justice, sympathy, benevolence, and the approval of them—these all imply the reality, or, at least, a clear idea of self-identity. But Hume's account of human experience made no provision for this idea of self. All that is disclosed in his empiricism is a sequence of impressions. To be sure, it may be said that in his moral reflections Hume was speaking more conventionally of our own selves and other selves as Galileo and Newton might have spoken of sunrise and sunset. But if, in less rigorous discourse, this way of speaking of self and self-consciousness had seemed plain, which in the careful investigation of the understanding had appeared so little credible, then, surely, either the reasonableness of the one or the adequacy of the other might well have been reconsidered by a keen mind like Hume's.

Hume's reaction to the utilitarian ethics of pleasure has been interpreted variously. His ethics has been pronounced as unmistakably utilitarian, but this judgment has been criticized on careful examination of his exposition. Hume often wrote as a hedonist, but not often without qualification: "Pain and pleasure, if not the causes of vice and virtue, are at least inseparable from them."[25] Locke had likewise described good and evil generally in terms of pleasure and pain, but he proceeded to define *moral* good and evil in terms of conformity or disagreement of our voluntary actions to some law. Hume qualified his general hedonistic statement in his ethics differently. Even his emphatically utilitarian statements about virtue are scarcely proposed as definitions of this quality. Let us consider a passage in which Hume expressed his view more fully, but with a vaguely fair recognition of the several aspects of his moral judgment: "Every quality of the mind, which is *useful* or *agreeable* to the *person himself* or to *others,* communicates a pleasure to the spectator, engages his esteem, and is admitted under the honourable denomination of virtue or merit."[26] Does this statement signify that an action

[24] David Hume, *A Treatise of Human Nature,* in Selby-Bigge, *op. cit.,* pp. 499 f.
[25] *Ibid.,* p. 296.
[26] David Hume, *Enquiries Concerning the Human Understanding and Concerning the Principles of Morals,* in Selby-Bigge, *op. cit.,* p. 277. See also *Treatise,* p. 601.

useful or pleasurable to oneself or to others is virtuous, and, therefore, rightly approved by our moral judgment? Or does it mean that our idea of its utility and agreeableness involves our ideas of esteem and approval, that the former ideas naturally lead to the latter? Or, does it mean simply that the actions we esteem and approve morally may be seen to be useful or pleasurable to oneself or to others, without any analytical or causal reduction of the former to the latter? Hume's account of morals seems to incline toward the last of these views; it scarcely allows of the first interpretation, and it does not seem very clear about the second. While he recognized familiar utilitarian features of moral good and evil, he referred moral judgment to a sentiment, and moral good and evil to the approval or disapproval of this sentiment.

Religious Perplexities

The application of empiricist methods to the examination of religion led Hume to disturbing conclusions, or rather to perplexed inconclusiveness. His problems in this inquiry were essentially the same as in those concerning the understanding and morals. He undertook to trace the actual sources of religion in the history of human experience. And, as in his earlier exploration of the scientific idea of causal relation, he proceeded to explore the alleged rational grounds of religious beliefs, relying for his appraisal on the direct or presumptive evidence of experience.

The Natural History of Religion, published in 1757, was, in effect, an extension of the *Treatise* and the revised *Enquiries.* Here the term "history" signified to Hume not only a record of religious beliefs, but a probing of their empirical sources and motivation. The philosophical theologian might deduce his idea of Deity from the systematic order of nature—Hume nowise scorned this sort of reasoning—but religion did not originate in any such rational reflections. It was far more likely that people's feelings of religious awe and their belief in supernatural powers arose from their observation of the seemingly miraculous and inexplicable events in the world. This occult waywardness in nature, analogous to certain mysterious and startling actions of men, led the ignorant multitude toward "some groveling and familiar notion of superior powers,"[27] conceived anthropomorphically as operating in the many zones of nature, and finding "no better expedient than to represent them as intelligent voluntary agents, like ourselves. . . ."[28] Polytheistic idolatry was thus regarded by Hume as the early form of religion, and men's worship was motivated by their dark fears and blind hopes, in a world of occult hazards and possible refuge.

Hume subjected the belief in miracles to radical criticism in a section of

[27] David Hume, *Essays Moral, Political, and Literary,* in Green and Grose, *op. cit.,* Vol. II, p. 311.
[28] *Ibid.,* p. 328.

his *Enquiry Concerning Human Understanding*. While his empiricism ruled out any doctrine of objective causal necessity in nature, he nowise denied that our experience records the constant conjunction of causes and effects. As good empiricists, we may not go beyond the evidence of experience and affirm a universal necessary connection of events; but neither are we warranted in rejecting our natural explanation of occurrences whose causes are not disclosed to us.

The uniform experience of men is as firm a basis for belief as our minds have, and whatever runs counter to it is naturally open to suspicion:

A miracle is a violation of the laws of nature; and as a firm and unalterable experience has established these laws, the proof against a miracle, from the very nature of the fact, is as entire as any argument from experience can possibly be imagined. [Therefore,] no testimony is sufficient to establish a miracle, unless the testimony be of such a kind, that its falsehood would be more miraculous, than the fact which it endeavors to establish.[29]

Hume held that no reported miracle was ever established on such full evidence. In support of his declaration he exposed the various confusions, prejudicial inferences, superstitions, and impostures which should discredit the idea of the miraculous in the judgment of reasonable men.

From superstitious polytheistic idolatry—with all its marvels, prodigies, and portents—religious belief advances to higher conceptions of the divine powers, of their character, their scope, and their majesty, and rises toward the ideal of a universal, all-wise, and perfect deity. Yet, even in the most sublime forms of religion, the majority of worshipers still seek God's favor by superstitious zeal and practices rather than "by virtue and good morals, which alone can be acceptable to a perfect being."[30]

The Natural History of Religion concluded on a skeptical note. "The whole is a riddle, an aenigma, an inexplicable mystery. Doubt, uncertainty, suspense of judgment appear the only result of our most accurate scrutiny concerning this subject."[31] We seek refuge in faith because we lack knowledge. The same inclination of thought marked Hume's essay "Of the Immortality of the Soul," which he himself did not publish. He saw no prospect of assurance about a future life "by the mere light of reason." If the metaphysical arguments for immortality deny the soul's disintegration, they would also establish its preexistence: "What is incorruptible must also be ingenerable."[32] The moral arguments from justice and retribution are unconvincing and inapplicable to human beings as we know them. "Heaven and hell suppose two distinct species of men, the good and the bad. But the greatest part of mankind float betwixt vice and virtue."[33] As to the physical

[29] David Hume, *Enquiries Concerning the Human Understanding and Concerning the Principles of Morals*, in Selby-Bigge, *op. cit.*, pp. 114, 115 f.

[30] David Hume, *Essays Moral, Political, and Literary*, in Green and Grose, *op. cit.*, Vol. II, p. 357.

[31] *Ibid.*, p. 363.

[32] *Ibid.*, p. 400.

[33] *Ibid.*, p. 402.

arguments, from the analogy of nature, the presumption seems decidedly against immortality. We are left groping in uncertainty about our destiny, and our sole gleam of hope is in faith. "It is the gospel, and the gospel alone, that has brought life and immortality to light,"[34] a pious venture for an empiricist like Hume, with an undertone of irony.

In his more constructive seasons of reflection, Hume was not disposed to reject the theologian's inference of Deity from the uniform order and design in our experience. Thus *The Natural History of Religion* raised a problem for discussion but did not settle it. Hume surmised that it did not admit of a solution, but it nevertheless engrossed his mind. The course of his reflection evinced a continual interplay of contending views, which his candor led him to cast into dramatic form in his *Dialogues Concerning Natural Religion.* The controversies which his writings on religious topics had already aroused made him unwilling to publish this work during his lifetime, yet he felt it should be presented to the judgment of men. The work appeared posthumously in 1779.

The three speakers in the *Dialogues* represent three attitudes toward religion. Demea is an orthodox believer who combines firm rational arguments with recourse to mystical assurance. Philo is a declared skeptic who exposes men's limited understanding in discussing the ultimate problems of nature. Cleanthes is a rationalist whose conviction of an evident design in nature leads him to a liberal philosophical deism, but makes him willing to consider any doubt or criticism. Although Hume intended Cleanthes to be the hero of the dialogue, Philo's objections concerned him deeply, and he gave them full expression. These objections cut deep into Cleanthes' deism which Hume wanted to maintain, and they unsettled Demea's theology even as Hume had unsettled it in his previous works.

As may be surmised, Demea mainly provided occasions for the critical exposure of the unsoundness of orthodoxy, although Hume really endeavored, not merely pretended, to keep the argument on a fair plane. Without antipathy toward the orthodox believer, he was also without confidence in his alleged certainties. The mystical refuge in unreasoning faith is a virtual though unwitting confession of doubt, and Philo's skeptical comments serve only to reveal to the unyielding devotee his actual incertitude.

Newton had concluded his *Principia* with a teleological conviction of deity. So Cleanthes reasons from the universal evidence of design in nature which assures us of its direction by the infinite and perfect intelligence of God. He is less concerned with establishing God's existence, which appears to him beyond question, than to interpret the nature and attributes of deity. It is precisely here that Philo's skeptical questions prove most disturbing. Why should he conceive of an infinite Author of a nature which we always experience as a finite series of processes? And how can we infer the omnipotence and omniscience of the divine mind, when limitation characterizes the only mental activity of which we have any knowledge? The ideal of God's

[34] *Ibid.*, p. 399.

infinite perfection perplexes the dialogue toward the end. How can the perfection of God be squared with the evils and miseries of a world created by his almighty will:

[with] the curious artifices of Nature, . . . to embitter the life of every living being? . . . Why is there any misery at all in the world? Not by chance surely. From some cause then. Is it from the intention of Deity? But he is perfectly benevolent. Is it contrary to his intention? But he is almighty. Nothing can shake the solidity of this reasoning, so short, so clear, so decisive; except we assert, that these subjects exceed all human capacity, and that our common measures of truth and falsehood are not applicable to them.[35]

This had been the conjecture of Voltaire, but its implications sapped the basis of ultimate moral principles. The balance of his argument Hume inclined toward teleological deism. Yet, he could not overcome the skeptical reflections; they contended in his mind with every reasonable approach to a belief in God. Religious conviction, like scientific objective certainty or universal moral value, was beyond his reach.

Hume did not relish the skeptical outcome of his empiricism; but he was not acquiescent, evasive, nor tragic about it. In daily practice, he might adhere to the common human beliefs in a reliable world order and in divine providence. His critical reflections exposed the unsoundness of these customary notions, and then, a general upheaval of his reasoning baffled him. How could he be sure that in leaving all established opinions he was following truth? In this mental quandary Hume's temperament seemed to mediate between Montaigne's geniality of indecision and Pascal's tragic uncertainty. Montaigne had been absorbed in surveying the groping inconclusiveness of human intelligence, and, never dismayed, was content "loyally to enjoy his being." Pascal had refused to surrender his mind to skepticism; he sought a way out by self-affirmation of pious will; yet, he realized therein the tragic humiliation of reason: Going to mass, and taking holy water "will make you believe, and will stultify you (*cela vous abêtira*)."[36] Hume saw no real way out of his doubts, and sought refuge in distraction. On this note of literal suspense of judgment regarding causal necessity, he concluded his *Treatise of Human Nature*, and his words might be cited also in connection with his religious perplexities: "I dine, I play a game of back-gammon, I converse, and am merry with my friends; and when after three or four hours' amusement, I would return to these speculations, they appear so cold, and strained, and ridiculous, that I cannot find in my heart to enter into them any farther."[37]

[35] David Hume, *Dialogues Concerning Natural Religion*, Part X, in N. K. Smith (ed.), *Hume's Dialogues Concerning Natural Religion*, 2nd ed., London, Nelson, 1947, pp. 194, 201.

[36] Translated from B. Pascal, *Pensées*, 233 in L. Brunschvicg (ed.), *Oeuvres de Blaise Pascal*, Paris, Hachette, Vol. XIII, 1904, p. 154.

[37] David Hume, *A Treatise of Human Nature*, in Selby-Bigge, *op. cit.*, p. 269.

SUGGESTED WORKS FOR FURTHER STUDY

WORKS BY HUME. Hume, D., *Works* (T. H. Green and T. H. Grose, eds.), *Treatise of Human Nature* (L. A. Selby-Bigge or A. D. Lindsay editions), *Enquiries* (L. A. Selby-Bigge, ed.), *Dialogues Concerning Natural Religion* (H. D. Aiken or N. K. Smith editions), and *Selections* (C. W. Hendel, ed.).

BIOGRAPHIES AND CRITICAL STUDIES. Burton, J. H., *Life and Correspondence of David Hume;* Calderwood, Henry, *David Hume;* Church, R. W., *Hume's Theory of the Understanding;* Hendel, C. W., *Studies in the Philosophy of David Hume;* Huxley, T. H., *Hume;* Knight, William, *Hume;* Laing, B. M., *David Hume;* Laird, John, *Hume's Philosophy of Human Nature;* Mossner, E. C., *The Forgotten Hume;* Orr, James, *David Hume and His Influence on Philosophy and Theology;* Shearer, E. A., *Hume's Place in Ethics;* Smith, Norman Kemp, *The Philosophy of David Hume.*

22. British Moralists of the Eighteenth Century

Shaftesbury: Moral Sense, Optimism, and Universal Harmony

A number of British philosophers during the eighteenth century emphasized ethical problems. Some of them invite comparison with the French *moralistes*, but the difference between the two is real. The British moralists were more systematic; they went beyond witty and sage comments on human nature and conduct, and sought to grasp and to formulate the principles of morality.

Constructive thought in ethics was aroused by the challenge to moral values in Hobbes' *Leviathan*. The description of human life in the state of nature as the insatiate, selfish pursuit of pleasure and power, of social order as merely submission to absolute sovereignty, and of moral conduct as only obedience to the sovercign's laws—this conception of man was criticized in a whole library of discourses and treatises. The controversies with Hobbism, which, for a century, engaged respectable British moralists, expanded to include also the doctrines of Locke. Aside from the criticisms of his theory of knowledge, Locke's ethics was resisted as a subtler variety of Hobbism. Instead of treating virtue as submission to the irresistible will of Leviathan, Locke interpreted it as regard for civil and social sanctions, and, ultimately, as obedience to the laws of God. This reduction of morality to decent conformity and pious expediency seemed to Locke's critics to be less offensive than the ethics of the *Leviathan*, but still inadequate as an account of true morality and the life of conscience.

The resistance to Hobbes and Locke may be noted in the writings of Anthony Ashley Cooper, third Earl of Shaftesbury (1671–1713). Shaftesbury's ethical thought matured early, and found its first statement in his *Inquiry Concerning Virtue or Merit*. This essay, first published without the author's consent, was reissued by him with a later work, *The Moralists*, in *Characteristics of Men, Manners, Opinions, Times, etc.*, Shaftesbury's best-known book.

It may be recalled that Locke, friend and family physician of the first Earl of Shaftesbury, directed the education of his little grandson. The youth had high personal regard for his teacher, but could not adopt his moral philosophy. If virtue were conceived as obedience to law, with expectation of rewards for compliance, morality would seem to be tainted with a mercenary motive. "If virtue be not really estimable in itself, I can see nothing estimable in following it for the sake of a bargain."[1] Young Shaftesbury had not recognized in Locke's ethics the insistence on the essential merit of virtue along with the provision for effective divine legislation and government in human lives. Thus, reacting sharply against one aspect of Locke's teaching, and seeking an ethics of inherent worth, he derived his ideals from Plato and the Stoic sages.

Shaftesbury criticized the Christian hope of divine rewards and punishments after death. Against the spirit of high expediency, he advocated a morality in which virtue is the fullest expression of human nature here and now, and its own self-rewarding satisfaction. "The excellence of the object, not the reward or punishment, should be our motive."[2] He also rejected the hedonist's appraisal of a good act on the basis of the pleasure that it yields. True morality is concerned with the right choice of pleasures. The mere fact of gratified desire does not make the act good. The real question in morals is whether we are rightly pleased; whether a certain experienced satisfaction is or is not to our credit. "Man may be virtuous, and by being so, is happy. His merit is reward; by virtue he deserves, and in virtue only can meet his happinesss deserved."[3]

Shaftesbury tests moral judgment by appeal to the moral sense. We perceive virtue and vice as directly as we perceive blue and brown, sour and sweet. The direct response of our moral sense may be dulled or refined, just as the response of our senses of sight or hearing. What a morally sensitive person judges directly without hesitation, he may also reason out and be convinced of; this conviction may be driven home by sound and vigorous reasoning even into a corrupted mind.

Virtue and moral worth are conceived by Shaftesbury in terms of a harmonious expression of man's nature: generous, benign, tranquil, benevolent. His judgment of moral value has an aesthetic tone, an appeal similar to those of beauty and fine harmony. In his detailed description of the good life, Shaftesbury used different tactics against Hobbes than did the professed rationalists. He did not revive the Stoic proposal that reason suppress the passions and bring about a life of apathy; like Spinoza, he advocated a life of enlightened emotions. In this enlightenment, however, he did not rely on reason alone, but optimistically trusted to the natural development of uncorrupted feelings. Man's well-being is to be sought in emotional harmony, and this harmony is attainable by the emotions themselves.

[1] Earl of Shaftesbury, *Characteristics of Men, Manners, Opinions, Times, etc.* (J. M. Robertson, ed.), London, Richards, 1900, Vol. I, p. 66.
[2] *Ibid.*, Vol. II, p. 56.
[3] *Ibid.*, p. 67.

He examined the feelings, or affections, and classified them under three heads: natural, or beneficial to society; private, or advantageous only to oneself; and unnatural, or harmful to oneself and others. He observed that any emotion, if carried to excess, becomes undesirable. But the absence or dullness of certain emotional responses was also condemned by him: "Overgreat concern for self-preservation, meanness and cowardice; too little, rashness; and none at all, . . . a mad and desperate depravity."[4] His problem, thus, was to determine the proper emphasis to be given his three kinds of affections in the good and satisfactory life.

Shaftesbury's solution of this problem emphasizes benevolence, moderates self-regard, and resists any destructive emotions; thus, his three conclusions:

(1) "That to have the natural, kindly, or generous affections strong and powerful towards the good of the public, is to have the chief means and power of self-enjoyment"; and "that to want them, is certain misery and ill." (2) "That to have the private or self affections too strong, or beyond their degree of subordinacy to the kindly and natural, is also miserable." (3) And "that to have the unnatural affections (viz. such as are neither founded on the interest of the kind or public, nor of the private persons or creature himself) is to be miserable in the highest degree."[5]

This moral ideal may be viewed in a social-political perspective. Since man is essentially a social being, the standard that determines a just measure and a true harmony of care for oneself and regard for others must be the general good of all. On this principle of the common welfare rest sound ethics and politics alike; "Morality and good government go together. There is no real love of virtue, without the knowledge of public good."[6] As long as a benevolent affection contributes to the good of all, it does not exceed the bounds of virtue; when it invades and interferes with the good of all, it sinks into vice. The ideal life is thus one of far-reaching philanthropy.

Shaftesbury may be said to have applied Plato's ideal of justice (right distribution of emphasis) in an emotional version. As, in his own way, he advocated a Platonic principle of harmony, so he followed Stoic wisdom in regarding the morally harmonious life as a life according to nature. Here Shaftesbury's ethics pointed toward his cosmic outlook. Nature itself reveals its essential character as a system of universal harmony. In his cosmology, aesthetic contemplation—decidedly teleological and optimistic—inclined him toward natural piety. The worship of the universal harmony made a powerful appeal to many minds, for it offered them an alternative to abandoned traditional religious beliefs and sentiments.

Shaftesbury was highly regarded during the eighteenth-century Enlightenment, especially on the Continent. Montesquieu ranked him with Plato, Malebranche, and Montaigne—a strange grouping! But his initial widespread

---

[4] *Ibid.*, Vol. I, p. 250.
[5] *Ibid.*, pp. 292 f.
[6] *Ibid.*, p. 72.

fame was followed by decided and increasing oblivion. His optimistic sentiment of cosmic harmony did not prove to be a lasting basis for a sound
philosophy of life.

Samuel Clarke and Richard Price: Advocates of Rational Moral Principles

Shaftesbury, expounding the naturalness of morality, criticized Locke
along with Hobbes as advocating a morality of decrees; indeed, he considered Locke's ethics as the more insidiously wrong. Samuel Clarke (1675–
1729) was a theological moralist who welcomed Locke's final ethical conclusions and his tribute to the moral teachings of the Gospels. But he was
opposed to Locke's empiricism, and so preferred to repudiate the Hobbist
strain in Locke's morals by a rationalistic attack on the *Leviathan*. He would
confirm Locke's conclusion regarding pious obedience to God's laws, but
he would reach it by universal, rational analysis of moral principles.

Clarke deemed it evident and incontrovertible that something must have
existed from eternity—some one unchangeable, self-existent Being, intelligent
and freely self-determined. God rules the universe with His infinite power,
wisdom, goodness, justice, and truth. The system of nature under divine
providence is thus bound to manifest principles of order and right relation,
which our reason can recognize and formulate. Science organizes these laws
in its examination of the physical universe, as in Newton's *Mathematical
Principles of Natural Philosophy*. Samuel Clarke's aim was to achieve a corresponding system of moral philosophy.

Systematic ethics requires the utter rejection of Hobbes' doctrine that
moral right and duty derive from submission to overwhelming power. Unless the so-called social contract were inherently right, conformity to it
could not be made right regardless of the strength of the compulsion. Civil
laws may formulate moral obligations, but they do not create or constitute
them. So incapable is Leviathan of inaugurating morality, that not even God
could act ethically in the role that Hobbes assigned to his autocrat. Suppose
a being of diabolical character, but of boundless power which it used to the
utter corruption, misery, and ruin of mankind; would the decrees of such
an infernal omnipotence carry any conceivable moral obligation?

Morality must rest on laws of inherent fitness and worth. For his universal
basis in morals, Clarke advanced the principle of righteousness: render to
each and to all their due. His interpretation of it recalls Plato's Idea of Justice. Consider righteousness as the essential fitness of thought and action in
the main relations of our life, and the cardinal virtues become clearly and
conclusively evident to sound reason. Righteousness in our relation to God
is piety; we may be confirmed in it the more deeply, the more we reflect on
God's attributes. Righteousness in our dealings with our fellowmen is manifested as justice and benevolence, that is to say, as essential fairness or equity

in the social adjustment of all claims and expectations, an active and expansive spirit of goodwill, and a promotion of the common welfare. Moral progress, individual and social, is marked by an advance from strict justice to generous benevolence. With respect to oneself, righteousness, or fitness of conduct, is sobriety. It manifests itself in various fields of experience as temperance, industry, moderation, and contentment.

In this rationalistic ethics, Clarke undertook to formulate the basic principles of morality by rational analysis. But his rationalism was theological; the perspective for his ethical reflection was that of the Christian dispensation. Though he rejected any reference to divine retribution in his definitions of virtue and vice, he regarded the Christian doctrine of rewards and punishments as a strong incentive to moral resolution in the actual daily lives of men. The conviction of our eventual moral prospects serves to strengthen our moral principles. Just because we recognize moral good and evil as inherently worthy and unworthy, we can be sure that God's perfect will unquestionably espouses the one and confutes the other. Divine providence is essentially on the side of the right, and it insures its consummation.

In his practical advocacy of the good life, Clarke undertook to combine his two convictions in a dual appeal: cleave to righteousness and true virtue, with a firm belief in the being and government of God. This implicit trust in divine providence may be shaken by a seeming maldistribution of justice in our daily lives. Clarke did not ignore the problem of evil, but he found a bulwark for his theodicy in the hope of immortality. The Christian assurance of a future life is a conviction of the full vindication of righteousness, and of punishment of sin under divine providence. So Clarke's ethics, which began on the plane of rational analysis, was consummated on the plane of pious Christian confidence.

The rationalism of Clarke, and that of Cudworth, was developed and found effective expression in Richard Price's *Review of the Principal Questions in Morals*. First published in 1758, this book appeared in the definitive edition in 1787, one year before Kant's *Critique of Practical Reason*. The kinship of Price's and Kant's ethics will readily be apparent to the reader of the two books. Richard Price (1723–1791) maintained the inherent imperativeness of right and of the rational and objective, not merely of the emotional and empirical sanction of moral judgments. His personal pretensions about his work were modest, but his principal aim was as ambitious as Cudworth's: "to trace the obligations of virtue up to the truth and the nature of things, and these to the Deity."[7] Price insisted that our ideas of moral right and wrong are far more than subjective feelings; they express our acknowledgment of universal principles and relations in reality. We may call them Ideas in the old Platonic sense, not intending merely the Humian reflected impressions. In refusing to emphasize sentiment, Price did not exclude it. He recognized that, in contemplating an action morally, "we have

[7] R. Price, *A Review of the Principal Questions in Morals*, London, T. Cadell, 1787, p. 5.

both a perception of the understanding, and a feeling of the heart."[8] But the foundation of our moral judgment is the rational recognition of right and authoritative principle. Like Clarke, Price acknowledged the retributive justice of divine providence, but upheld the worthiness of virtue apart from any rewards. Virtue is rewardable because of its inherent rectitude: it is not worth pursuing simply because it eventually proves advantageous.

Thus Price emphasized in his ethics the principle of universal and obligatory rectitude. Moral goodness consists in our dutiful pursuit of the right. Virtue is fidelity to a rational conscience. No amount of actually beneficent results of an action will atone for the absence of a conscientious spirit. On the contrary, a man may perform an actually disastrous act and still deserve praise if he acted conscientiously on his best available recognition of the right. For Price, and, as will be noted, for Kant, mere conformity to the moral law does not suffice. We must not only do the right, but we must do it because it is the right. Good inclinations are not enough for moral worth; we should be virtuous on principle. Price even used the same disturbing example as Kant did to illustrate this point. "A fond mother exposing her life to save her child"[9] would have the lower moral value the more it sprang from natural tenderness and lacked the explicit respect for duty. "The ultimate spring of virtuous practice in reasonable beings, is the reasonable faculty itself, the *consideration of duty*, or the *perception of right*."[10]

Price contemplated man's upright devotion to the law of rectitude as the revelation of an eternal, spiritual principle in human conduct, and he taxed his eloquence to laud its cosmic perfection and dominance. "It is self-valid and self-originated, . . . coeval with eternity; as unalterable as necessary, everlasting truth; as independent as the existence of God; and as sacred and awful as his nature and perfections. . . ."[11]

This single-minded commitment to duty did not remain for Price only a formal principle of his ethical system. He applied it to social and political problems, both in theory and in practice. His active and public support in England of the cause of the American Revolution was one instance of his conscience in operation.

Joseph Butler: Self-Realization through Conscience

The philosophy formulated by Bishop Butler (1692–1752) combined reliance on theological probability with a reasonable quest of the moral foundations of piety in the constitution of human nature. The evidence of daily experience is not sufficient to convince us fully of God's just providence, but

---

[8] *Ibid.*, p. 96.
[9] *Ibid.*, p. 324.
[10] *Ibid.*, p. 339.
[11] *Ibid.*, p. 179.

it does yield a real presumption of the moral scheme—of divine government —and it warrants our confidence that it will be perfected in the hereafter. In his *Analogy of Religion, Natural and Revealed, to the Constitution and Course of Nature*, Butler was concerned with showing that our minds do not attain certainty, but act with various degrees of probability. Science is a system of more or less reasonable inferences; we should not expect greater certainty regarding the ultimate problems of religion. Sufficient for effective belief would be a decisive balance of probability, especially when the opposite alternative is unreasonable and untenable.

Thus Butler sought to confirm his Christian hope of immortality. He began by undermining the arguments of negation. None of them really disprove the belief in a future life; they only raise objections to it. There are more serious objections to the negative view, and the believing mind is left disturbed, but not defeated. It returns to reaffirmed hope when it considers the moral grounds for its belief. The whole course of human life operates under laws of just retribution, but in no one's life does this operation appear to be complete. This moral inconclusiveness of our present life is our strongest natural ground for refusing to accept the finality of death. God does not begin his government of our lives in order to abandon us in mid-career. He will surely complete it for us all in the hereafter.

Butler's moral theory was presented in his *Sermons upon Human Nature* and the *Dissertation of the Nature of Virtue*. These are marked by neither elegance of style nor erudite scholarship. The careful reader, however, will recognize that their author has thoroughly examined and criticized the doctrines of many thinkers who are not cited, and he may also come to appreciate the plain grace and clear reasonableness of a style that seems to need no embellishment. Like Berkeley, Butler combated the easygoing impertinence of boasted infidels, and the detractors of character who would reduce all our motives to selfishness. But he opposed also the sentimental advocates of benevolence for their one-sided account of human motivation. He inclined toward Shaftesbury's view of the good life as a harmony, but he was not content with a harmony of the emotions nor with Shaftesbury's complacent optimism. He undertook a more comprehensive survey of men's incentives to action, and sought a more thoroughgoing principle of moral order as rooted in the constitution of human nature.

Human motivation is complex; it cannot be described in terms of egoism, nor does any hedonistic statement of it suffice. Regarding the latter, Butler exposed the unsoundness of psychological hedonism, which regards the desire for pleasure as the real incentive to every action. He showed that, while we experience pleasure in the satisfaction of our desires, the desire itself is always for an objective end. The hedonist confuses the object of desire with the emotional tone of its satisfaction.

In his criticism of egoistic ethics, Butler called attention to two aspects of human character, self-regard and benevolence. Our high esteem of benevolence in others should not be interpreted as covert selfishness; it is an expression of genuine social-mindedness. We are pleaders for approval by others; callousness to reputation evokes our contempt. We live with others, and our thought is with and of others. Yet, in all our sympathetic regard, we are also ever-conscious of our own interests and purposes.

These two, benevolence and self-regard, are normal expressions of our nature. Virtue and well-being depend upon their most suitable correlation, and, thus, require a directive faculty of order. This legislative role in conduct is assigned to reason in some theories of ethics. Butler called it "conscience," and viewed it as the authoritative voice of our character. Because he interpreted it as the expression of the basic constitution of our nature, he regarded it as rightfully dominant over any particular impulse, desire, or demand. Passions are intense, but conscience alone is imperative. "It is by this faculty, natural to man, that he is a moral agent, that he is a law unto himself."[12]

Not only does this imperative character of conscience normally prevail as does the whole spirit of a man over a passing inclination; it is rightfully authoritative, and entitled to obedience and loyal respect. If we defy its behests, we act against the law and order of our very being, we defeat our own true interest, and we set ourselves against the will of God who created us reasonable. Butler was not very explicit or detailed in his account of the good conscientious life. He did not accept a hedonistic description of it. Although he emphasized pious devotion to God's will and trust in divine providence, he sought a natural basis of moral principles. The most nearly adequate statement of his moral ideal is expressed by a life in which, by a normal interplay of benevolence and reasonable self-regard, the harmonious perfection of human nature is achieved, under the imperative and authoritative direction of conscience. Butler's ethics thus seem to combine ancient perfectionism with the ethics of conscience, both sustained by theological motives. At its best his doctrine gives promise of the modern ethical theory of self-realization.

Adam Smith: Moral Sentiments and Laissez Faire

Adam Smith (1723–1790) had a broad view of the Scottish, English, and French intellectual climate of his age. He was familiar with the moral-sense doctrine, but also with the strict empiricism of David Hume, to whom he was attached by very intimate ties of friendship, but whose accounts of the moral sentiments of approval and disapproval did not satisfy him. In his judgment, moral philosophy needed a more thorough inquiry into the psychology of sympathy, and into the social outlook and operation of conscience. He would use the experimental method of reasoning in moral sub-

[12] Joseph Butler, in W. E. Gladstone (ed.), *The Works of Joseph Butler*, Oxford, Clarendon Press, 1897, Vol. II, p. 51.

jects more searchingly than Hume, and therein utilize and improve the interpretations of sympathy and conscience by other moralists.

Adam Smith was marked by a liberal, but unmistakably respectable, spirit that is reassuring to the general reader. We do not know his definite views on controversial problems in religion, for he would not publish his theological papers, but, instead, had them burnt; he refused his friend's request to undertake their publication. In his judgment, Hume should have done likewise with his *Dialogues Concerning Natural Religion*. Adam Smith impressed his contemporaries with his reasonableness and fair moderation in both his ideas and his exposition. He sought to achieve convincing power by his style as well as by his substance. His elegant rhetoric, however, which gained him immediate and wide popularity, later aroused critical distrust in more exacting students of his work. But even the critics of his systematic reasoning acknowledge his urbanity, his generous view of human character, unwarped and sane in both his approval and his condemnation of it. If he erred on the side of complacency, he did not go astray through morbid reflection.

In his *Theory of Moral Sentiments,* Smith first considered the nature of virtuous actions, and second, the process of our judgment of moral approval. He examined virtue in the range of the emotions, and attributed it either to some dominant feeling or to the right ordering of our emotional life. Feelings are either selfish or philanthropic; by emphasizing one or the other of these, moralists have espoused ethics of self-regarding prudence or benevolence. In considering the orderly control and direction of the emotions, the principle of propriety becomes central in ethical theory.

Turning next to the judgment of moral approval, Adam Smith traced it to three possible motives: self-love, reason, or sentiment. His analysis led him to adopt sentiment as the characteristic moral incentive, and he proceeded to derive this moral sentiment from sympathy. It is the sympathetic consciousness of the propriety or social fitness or seemliness of certain feelings and reactions which yield generous and social-minded approval. He emphasized the element of justice in both prudential and benevolent feelings, in terms of the directing principle of propriety.

Smith explained sympathy, or feeling for our fellows, not as the actual sharing of another's emotion, but as the judgment of another's emotion by what ours would be were we in his place. We use our idea of propriety in passing judgment on his feelings under certain circumstances. He may not realize his woeful state or his shameful conduct; yet we weep for him, are ashamed for him. But he in turn may be dismayed by our misapprehension in prejudging him, and blush for us. In both situations, the moral judgment depends upon the estimate of the propriety, the suitable or unsuitable character and degree of a person's feelings and actions. In judging one's own conduct, sympathy operates similarly. A person considers himself as another person, examines and appraises himself. This is the spectator within our breast, our conscience, which is not deluded by undeserved praise or daunted by unmerited condemnation, but which imposes its own verdict. Its august sanction requires that it be kept enlightened and expressive of our really best insight and sentiments of propriety.

Adam Smith's detailed exposition of the moral life expounded the cardinal virtues of prudence and beneficence, as well as the appropriate self-control needed for their suitable realization. Between the eulogies of altruism and the arguments of the egoistic school, he sought a reasonable middle ground of propriety. His theory contemplated an expanding vista of moral fruition of character—from a largely self-regarding, but decent performance of one's just obligations to others, to a progressively more equitable and generous fellow feeling, beneficent sympathy in the judgments and in the conduct of a thoroughly social-minded personality.

The economics and social philosophy of Smith's famous work, *The Wealth of Nations*, may impress the reader as discordant in spirit with his ethical theory. Instead of sympathy, Smith seemed to emphasize the selfish desire for gain. The discrepancy is on the surface. In the two theories, he observed two different incentives, or sides, of human character, but each arrived at the same destination. As his ethics revised lofty altruism by integrating beneficence with prudence, so his economics pursued the normal fruition of intelligent self-regard in a social system calling for equitable trading that will be advantageous to everyone concerned. In the production and trading of goods, men are moved by a desire for profit. But, though the motive be self-regard, it operates in social relations and cannot be unsocial in outlook. I seek my own advantage, but I cannot inconsiderately take advantage of others. Eventually, the best interests of each square with a reasonable advantage for all, and this suitable balancing, or harmony, of contending claims distinguishes fair trading that leads to real prosperity.

So convinced was Smith of the socially beneficent operation of the normal economic processes, that he advocated free enterprise as a basic principle of government. This is the doctrine of laissez faire; emancipate industry and commerce from official interference and restraints. In pursuing unhampered their best advantage, men learn that trading requires regard for others. Rapacity defeats its own end; reasonable and equitable commerce enriches a nation. Only a stupid employer is callous to the well-being of his men; only a stupid merchant swindles the customers on whom he depends. The same principle applies in international trade; British commerce should not envy, but welcome the prosperity of its customer, France. Like ethics, enlightened economics points to broad philanthropy as the normal and perfect expression of human character. And men will proceed to this philanthropic consummation readily on their own, and, under free enterprise, they will prefer to advance the general welfare rather than to exploit and oppress their fellows. The social-economic doctrines of Adam Smith expressed his complacent optimism even more strikingly than did his moral doctrine. Ironically, *The Wealth of Nations* was published in 1776, and its author died the year after the storming of the Bastille.

Thomas Reid and the Scottish Philosophy of Common Sense

We may consider here the philosophy of Thomas Reid (1710–1796), whose initial significance is found not so much in his specific ethical doctrines as in his radical criticism of the method and principles of empiricism. Hume's development of Locke's philosophy of experience led to conclusions which Reid regarded as wholly untenable and, in morals and religion, intolerable. Convinced, therefore, that Locke's premises must be wrong, he undertook to establish reasonable conviction on sounder foundations.

If, like Locke, we begin with sense impressions, we must perforce be left finally with a collection of ideas. The stirring of ideas can no more yield a cosmos than can a swirl of atoms. The Lockian school had successfully emptied nature of all reality. First, the primary qualities of objects were rejected, and, thus, material substances; then minds and bodies were reduced to a congeries of ideas, and no basis of objective reality remained.

Reid regarded this as a philosophical collapse, showing the need of a radically new design in construction. The elements of experience are not mere items of perception, nor are the patterns of knowledge mere aggregates of sense data. Intelligence never operates as bare receptivity, a blank tablet. Whenever it acts, from the very outset, it proceeds on basic judgments of nature, or first principles. Without these initial convictions of essential order, we should never reach or recognize the laws derived from experience. Philosophy, Reid thought, must start with this immediate responsiveness of the understanding. It is itself the condition of all knowledge in detail; it has the stamp of certainty and sanity that is evident to all clear-thinking men.

This, then, was to be the philosophy of plain common sense. It claimed that our mind possesses certain first principles; thus initially endowed, our understanding expands its detailed knowledge by experimental inquiry and reflection. This doctrine recalls Leibniz's principle that the basic power of intelligence is not derived from the particulars of sense. But Reid also maintained the mind's inherent grasp of certain definite truths. Like Henry More, he tabulated them, and, from them, inferred and elaborated his philosophical doctrines. Thus, for his conclusions, he relied on good logic, but his initial premises were derived by the fiat of intuition.

The systematic exposition of this philosophy of common sense may be seen in Reid's ethics. From fundamental and very general convictions, his argument proceeded toward more and more specific rules of judgment and action. Thus, two rational principles are innate in our moral intelligence: regard for our own good on the whole, and a conviction of duty or conscience. By direct intuition, furthermore, we recognize a whole series of truths essential to morality—that our actions merit approval or disapproval when they are voluntary, but not when they have been performed as a result of unavoidable compulsion; that neglect of the right, as well as the doing of wrong, is blameworthy; that duty itself must be kept enlightened lest it lead us astray. From these general moral foundations, Reid proceeded to more specific precepts, urging farsighted prudence, regard for the normal realization of our powers and constitution, a philanthropic outlook on life, fairmindedness in all social relations, and pious devotion to God's will.

This method of inquiry had the merit of extensively exploring the plain judgments and attitudes of unprofessional everyday minds, and, thus, expanded the range of man's self-understanding. But it was also liable to grave misdirection. Common conventional tenets might be proclaimed as innate and incontestable principles. Philosophy, having renounced its initial test or analysis, might proceed to enjoy, through edifying reflection, what it had not earned by critical appraisal.

SUGGESTED WORKS FOR FURTHER STUDY

HISTORIES AND DISCUSSIONS OF EIGHTEENTH-CENTURY BRITISH ETHICS. Albee, Ernest, *History of English Utilitarianism;* Selby-Bigge, L. A. (ed.), *British Moralists* (selections); Stephen, Sir Leslie, *History of English Thought in the Eighteenth Century;* Tsanoff, Radoslav A., *The Moral Ideals of Our Civilization* (Chaps. XIV–XVIII).

SHAFTESBURY. Shaftesbury, Earl of, *Characteristics of Men, Manners, Opinions, Times, etc.* (J. M. Robertson, ed.); *Life, Unpublished Letters, and Philosophical Regimen* (B. Rand, ed.).

BUTLER. Butler, J., *Works* (W. E. Gladstone, ed.); W. L. Collins, *Butler;* W. E. Gladstone, *Studies Subsidiary to the Works of Bishop Butler;* Mossner, E. C., *Bishop Butler and the Age of Reason.*

ADAM SMITH. Smith, Adam, *Theory of Moral Sentiments, The Wealth of Nations,* and *Adam Smith's Moral and Political Philosophy* (H. W. Schneider, ed.); Haldane, R. B., *Life of Adam Smith;* Hirst, F. W., *Adam Smith;* Macpherson, H. C., *Adam Smith;* Morrow, G. R., *The Ethical and Economic Theories of Adam Smith.*

REID. Reid, Thomas, *Works* (W. Hamilton, ed.); Fraser, A. C., *Thomas Reid.*

23. The Philosophers of the French Enlightenment

The Influence of English Philosophy on French Thought

Descartes has been called the "father of systematic modern philosophy," and, during the seventeenth century, his influence—and with it the influence of French ideas—was a major factor in the development of outstanding thinkers like Hobbes, Spinoza, Leibniz, Locke, and Berkeley. But Cartesianism did not achieve any extensive original expression in France. Aside from the work of Malebranche and Pascal, for over half a century the history of French philosophy was of no consequence. The hundred years of Fontenelle's life (1657–1757) yielded some popular expositions of Cartesian cosmology and a few brave essays in the history and criticism of religious beliefs, but no work of commanding, systematic thought was produced during this time.

The monarchical centralization of power in France by Louis XIV was accompanied and followed by the exaltation of traditional ideas and by political and theological authoritarianism. Freedom of thought and expression were stifled. Cartesian rationalism itself, though at first opposed by surpliced minds, was adapted to orthodox and conservative demands, and it supplemented Scholastic orthodoxy as a medium of acceptable reflection. Voltaire could not obtain a copyright for his book on Newton's philosophy, because in it he opposed Descartes.

In contrast to this reactionary constriction of French intelligence was the situation in eighteenth-century Britain. The British had subdued royal and theological absolutism, and had expanded the range of free discussion. Newton and Locke were leaders into new regions of understanding. Critical deism, and even freethinking infidelity, were evidences of the interplay of ideas in unshackled minds. To increasing numbers of French thinkers, England came to represent the reality of a social ideal that shamed their own actualities. English ideas gained both intellectual and moral prestige in France.

Enlightened Frenchmen turned especially to Locke's philosophy of experience which, in their judgment, expressed the moving spirit in the new unchanneled currents of free English thinking about nature, man, society, and religion. Here was a philosophy without innate ideas or axiomatic first principles—without vested rights or prerogatives—that relied on the plain course of experience in theory, and which respected the plain, practical needs of people. It was a pliable, malleable philosophy, suitable for an age in need of radical reconstruction, such as the *ancien régime* in France. John Locke's empiricism held the promise of a new day to forward-looking French spirits—the "fathers of the Revolution," as they have been called.

Locke's own reasonable moderation, eminent respectability, and piety gained response from critical minds that were still averse to any radical excesses. His characteristically English reserve calmed any initial alarm, and gave the new ideas a chance to make an impression. But the French logical drive was eventually to carry them on their way. The English freethinkers, infidels, and radicals not only were read in France, but eventually, were far exceeded by their followers there.

Thus, the French development proceeded along its own lines to its more extreme final outcome. Locke's disciples in France were not content to entertain his tentative speculation that God might have endowed some kinds of matter with the ability to think. They restated his conjecture as a scientific conclusion, expanding it as a materialistic account of all human nature and all existence, and leaped the whole length of the ancient Lucretian arguments to a denial of God and immortality. When Hume was in Paris, he remarked one evening to Baron Holbach, his host, that he had never met a real atheist, whereupon Holbach replied, "You have been a little unfortunate; you are here at table for the first time *with seventeen of them*."[1]

Montesquieu's Sociological Jurisprudence

It would be as misleading to overemphasize as to overlook Locke's influence on French philosophy during the eighteenth century. Locke himself would not have admitted the conclusions which some French radicals drew from his empiricism, but the new experimental method of inquiry which was being applied to various problems led to basic revision of traditional principles. We may consider in this perspective Montesquieu's *Spirit of the Laws*, a work of widespread significance in the development of modern social ideas.

Montesquieu (1689–1755) was a well-to-do, retired magistrate and country gentleman whose high social standing gained a respectful hearing for his criticism of established institutions. Midway in his career, he had visited England, and he remained deeply impressed by the growing liberalism and capacity for progress which he noted in English society.

[1] Quoted in James Orr, *David Hume and His Influence on Philosophy and Theology*, Edinburgh, Clark, 1903, p. 69.

The Spirit of the Laws was described in part, on its long title page, as dealing with "the relation which the laws should have to the constitution of each government: manners, climate, religion, commerce, etc."[2] Instead of deriving his system of jurisprudence by abstract deductions from certain axiomatic first principles, and thus using Cartesianism to uphold vested rights and institutions, Montesquieu traced the entire legal structure to its historical sources and to its foundations in environmental factors of human experience in various societies. His actual procedure was prevailingly inductive, yet he intended to demonstrate his conclusions as validly deduced from his ascertained principles; he even believed himself to be still a dependable Cartesian. His book suffered somewhat from this duality of motive. He sought inductive merit for an inquiry that demanded and included direct exploration of empirical data. If his treatment impressed his more exacting critics as unsystematic, it also showed that a system of jurisprudence could not be reasoned out abstractly, a conviction that was itself a principal merit of the book. He removed laws from the lofty region of pure demonstration to the homely soil of social experience.

Montesquieu's work utilized the resources of his historical erudition in showing the vital relation, which the laws of any people should maintain, to actual conditions of life. Three sorts of government were distinguished: in a republic, the body of the people has the sovereign power, or a select part of the people exercises it, as in an aristocracy; in a monarchy, a single person governs by fundamental laws and is sustained by the intermediary power of the nobility; and, in a despotic government, the only law is the will of the tyrant. Montesquieu examined these types of government in relation to the systems of laws, or edicts, by which they are maintained, the social conditions that sustain or unsettle and corrupt these laws, their military security and defensive and offensive power, and the status and relative freedom of the citizens or subjects. He then explored the natural and social environments in which these governments and systems of laws tend to arise and thrive, in terms of climate and other physical conditions, the natural temperament and customs of the people, the suitable forms of livelihood and the prosperity of the people, the density of population, the social standards, and the religious beliefs and practices.

The historical objectivity of Montesquieu's treatment made the application of his conclusions to existing conditions in France doubly evident to his readers, without any radical propaganda. Already, in the *Persian Letters*, he had subtly, but unmistakably, criticized the political, social, and religious corruption in his own country. When he exposed the iniquities of despotic rule in Turkey or Russia, their parallels under the French monarchy became transparently clear, and there was no need to point specifically to them. When he explained English constitutional government, with its explicit division and balance of legislative, executive, and judicial powers, he showed

[2] Translated from *Oeuvres complètes de Montesquieu* (E. Laboulaye, ed.), Paris, Garnier, Vol. III, 1876, p. 81.

how the people of France, too, could preserve and enjoy real freedom and the protection of law, if their king reigned with justice and was responsible to the expressed will of the citizens. He saw the pressing need for thorough-going reform, but, like Bodin, he was reluctant to shake the unsteady social structure lest he upset it altogether. He explicitly opposed certain crying evils—slavery and serfdom, torture of prisoners, disgraceful prison condi-tions, and religious persecution. The wide popularity of his book—there were twenty-two editions within two years, and it was translated into many languages—spread his liberal principles of constitutional government and hu-mane laws throughout Europe.

Voltaire's Skeptical Deism and Humanism

François-Marie Arouet (1694–1778), the son of a bourgeois Parisian no-tary, was frail of body but strong-minded and of boundless ambition. He aspired to literary fame and devised for himself the high-sounding name, Voltaire. He boasted that, unlike aristocrats who inherit their names, he was making his own; and he made this name known above any other in his time. The eighteenth century may be described as the "age of Voltaire." And not in France alone; his name came to express a direction of thought in western civilization which is still preserved in the dictionary definitions of Voltairism, signifying infidelity, or skepticism, about revealed religion.

The cultural dominance of Voltaire's thought was out of all proportion to its solid substance. It was not systematic. He contributed to the history of philosophy neither original conceptions nor thoroughgoing elaborations of basic principles. He had, however, a genius for the effective popular clarifi-cation of ideas. The most gifted man of letters of his day, he fought for radical reforms with all the weapons in his abundant arsenal: historical es-says, ironical poetry, and satirical romances and fables. In his *Philosophical Dictionary*, he followed Bayle's example in discussing the disturbing topics and problems which upset staid orthodoxy and traditional conformity. Again like Bayle, but more brilliantly, Voltaire voiced the protests of an unde-ceived age—protests against superstition, intolerance, arrogance, and injustice. His purposes were not always lofty; he was greedy for fame and money, and he was capable of unscrupulous tactics and of shameless writing. But, despite the blots on his character, he strove more effectively than anyone else of his period for the emancipation of the human mind from bigotry. His words were relished by libertines, but they also nourished a new epoch of greater liberty in which men could think and live more freely.

Two terms of imprisonment in the Bastille convinced the young Voltaire that even a brilliant success in literature could not safeguard the son of a bourgeois who was in ill favor with high aristocrats and ecclesiastics. Sub-sequently, he lived on the Swiss border; his houses on both sides of it provided him temporary refuge from the police. When he went to Friedrich the Great, in Berlin, he soon learned that royalty was oppressive even when it had philosophical pretensions. His own insecurity made him sympathize the more with the hopeless condition of the uncounted plain, good people, who were the victims of imposture and oppression. So he struck at the foundations of the evil edifice, at tyrannical dogmatism and its eternal "verities."

Voltaire's skepticism was practical in motivation and in aim. His visit to England had taught him that man's principal hope of reaching a modicum of truth lay in a society that permitted a free interplay of ideas. But he was also convinced that this modicum of knowledge was slight. English ideas, the ideas of Locke and Newton, confirmed his resolution to eschew dogmatic certainty and to adhere to the evidence of experience. He championed this experimental philosophy in France, wrote a popular exposition of the Newtonian method and its results, and applied and developed Locke's philosophy of experience.

Locke's reluctant, or tentative, metaphysics, and the skeptical aspects of the *Essay* which Hume developed effectively, indicated the direction of Voltaire's empiricism. He was skeptical about ultimate principles; how can a body of clay feel and think? How can an immaterial soul have sensations? Between these two mysteries, we should suspend judgment; but the former is the less baffling. "I am a body, and I think; more I do not know."[3] Though he was inclined toward materialism, the Epicurean finality of it seemed absurd to him: "A stone can produce no Iliad, not even in an eternity."[4] The evident order in nature turned his mind toward the recognition of God's existence. If God did not exist, men would have to invent Him. But, while atheism makes no sense, theism does not make sufficient sense for pious assurance. Nature's ways seemed to Voltaire by no means convincingly just and beneficent. He saw no sufficient grounds for trust in a divine providence. The poem which he wrote on the Lisbon disaster after the earthquake in 1755, and the satirical romance, *Candide, or Optimism*, which followed this poem, indicated the definitely pessimistic tone which his skepticism was taking—a tone that darkened increasingly during his later years.

He felt tethered to uncertainty about the ultimate nature or direction of the world and of human lives, and he found no real conviction in theology or metaphysics. Scorning and hating the dogmatists, he never missed a chance to expose the hollowness of some alleged first principle, or to strip the vestments of sanctimony that covered imposture and decay. He respected religion, but he despised the ecclesiastics. "Throughout the world religion has been used to evil ends, but it was instituted everywhere to yield good."[5]

[3] Quoted in F. A. Lange, *History of Materialism* (trans. E. C. Thomas), 2nd ed., London, Kegan, Paul, 1892, Vol. II, p. 18.
[4] Translated from the quotation in Paul Sakmann, "Voltaire als Philosoph," in *Archiv für Geschichte der Philosophie*, 1905, Berlin, Reimer, Vol. XVIII, p. 201.
[5] Translated from Voltaire, *Oeuvres Complètes*, Paris, Garnier, Vol. XIII, 1878, p. 182.

In this world of dubious twilight, what is our only hope and chance? Voltaire's counsel was plain: we should use our limited intelligence productively, within its limits: "Let us cultivate our garden." He was not assured of God's final justice, but he could and did struggle to vindicate the innocence of tortured prisoners like Calas, and to secure justice for other victims of bigotry and oppression. For he believed that we are on more solid ground in morals than in metaphysics. Man's speculation formulates conflicting theologies, but his uncorrupted conscience agrees regarding probity, justice, and beneficence.

In its direction and general tone, Voltaire's thought recalls that of the English deists, but he was more radical than many of them in his own skeptical conclusions. In contrast to whited sepulchers like the orthodox Cardinal Dubois, Voltaire was ironical about the supernatural revelation of the Gospel, yet he held fast to its teachings about brotherhood and humanity.

Condillac's Treatise on the Sensations

The Abbé Étienne Bonnot de Condillac (1715–1780) undertook a recasting of Locke's doctrine of experience that would emphasize sensation as the source and foundation of all that we think and know and are. In an age of propagandists and reformers, his was a theoretical mind, engaged mainly in psychological inquiry. Locke had declared that knowledge is derived from sensation and reflection. In Condillac's judgment, Locke had not explored the initial sources thoroughly. Condillac turned his attention to the first sense reactions; how do we get our first ideas of sight, hearing, taste, smell, and touch, and how are they combined into our so-called "knowledge" of the external world? He would start with Locke's supposition of an initially blank mind, a clean slate, and trace the first writings of experience.

In order to show vividly that sense data are the beginning of all mental activity and the sources of knowledge, Condillac used a fantastic illustration. Locke had written about a man who was born blind but who was enabled to see. Condillac imagined a marble statute, or better, a living human mummy in a marble case, supplied with sense organs which have never been exposed to any impressions. Such a mummy would be void of any ideas; its so-called "mind" would be a blank. If, now, just the marble over its nose were removed, it would have its first sniff of the world. All its impressions and ideas would be olfactory: perceptions, memories, comparisons, recognitions, abstractions—all would involve odors. If we next uncovered the statue's eyes, a new mass of impressions—for example, ideas of colors—would be assembled, and they would be related to the earlier ideas of smell. And so for the other senses. In this way, Condillac brought out the increasing range of the mind in the process of experiencing sense data.

The practical aspects of mental activity were similarly traced to sensation.

Sense impressions yield pleasure or pain, and rouse desires or aversions which grow into the various passions. Thus we are the accumulated results of our sense experiences. Our preferences and our principles are all derived from our stock of sensations.

Condillac's immediate aim was to examine closely the several regions of sensation in a man limited to smell, sight, hearing, taste, or touch, or to these several senses in various combinations. Like Locke, he was reluctant to consider the finalities of metaphysics. Shall we distinguish the statue's mind and its ideas from external objects which are said to impress it? But it begins with its impressions, and its whole range of activity consists of a stock of ideas. Or, shall we move in another direction, and view sensations physiologically as organic reactions of nose, eyes, or ears? This materialistic inference, which many of Condillac's contemporaries drew, was contrary to his purpose. He preferred to explore the spreading range of experience without reference to a materialistic or any other sort of cosmology. But, if he had to make a choice, he would decide against the materialists. Besides, he reflected, he was observing men's minds in their present condition. Before the original sin in the Garden of Eden, the soul in its pristine innocence was presumably a simple substance that did not depend on sense organs for its ideas; this was the Platonic-theological comment the abbé would make to the psychologist.

Helvétius: Selfishness and Social Order

Claude Adrien Helvétius (1715–1771), collector-general of the French taxes, was also a collector, rather than a begetter, of wit and wisdom. Mme. de Graffigny said that his books contained the sweepings of her salon. As a writer, he must have been a typical reader, for the anecdotes and scandalous tidbits which crowded his pages made his books best sellers. Parliament condemned and burned his volume *On Mind*, but not before all of its members and their wives had read it. From Paris to Petersburg, it circulated in fifty editions.

The notoriety of Helvétius' work is not hard to understand. Here was a rich, estimable public official, a generous man famous for his hospitality, who used fourteen hundred pages of sprightly argument and gossip to prove that, far from being just and benevolent, people are generally selfish, and they keep their promises and obey the laws only when it suits their interests to do so. Had he not really told abroad the ugly secret familiar to all but admitted by no one? He found human physiology and psychology more absorbing than any metaphysics, but, though he did not expound explicit materialism, he actually treated men like living machines. The springs that move them to action are desires craving gratification. Like Hobbes, Helvétius saw man as always spurred by insatiate wants. With this estimate of man, he combined Condillac's description of human experience. Our minds are the accumulated stock of sensations and of the pleasures and displeasures aroused by our experiences. The dynamics in our conduct are the passions. Instead of expounding hollow principles of rationality, we should recognize men, others and ourselves, for what we all are. In personal relations, we should rely on these actual human incentives; in legislation and administration, government should never forget to make its laws and measures advantageous to the people, thus making it worth their while to be law-abiding.

In deriving all intelligence and character from the process of sense experience, Helvétius denied anyone's inherent superiority of mind or personal worth. The premises of aristocracy are null. There are no born Homers and Newtons. A great man is a man who has had great sensations, who has had an opportunity to have them. Not only individuals, but whole nations, are like wax, molded by experience, and, in time, are completely transformed. It was of none other than the Parisians that Emperor Julian said he loved them, for their character, like his, was austere and serious. What matters in human life is the actual course of experience; it raises and it debases men. The careers and societies of men are pliable; men may be completely transformed by a redistribution of their opportunities. The revolutionary dynamic of these reflections is unmistakable.

Helvétius believed he had based his ethics on the facts of human experience by explaining moral judgments as selfish considerations of eventual advantage, and by relating virtue and vice to pleasurable or painful consequences. As in ethics, so in politics: the strategy of effective living must reckon with the selfish incentives of men. There is nothing wrong in this; egoism is the natural expression of human nature, and statesmanship consists in devising laws that reconcile men's common interests with their private desires.

Diderot and the Encyclopedists

The new critical-radical ideas of the French Enlightenment were advocated on an extensive scale in the great *Encyclopedia*, which appeared in more than thirty volumes during the third quarter of the eighteenth century. Its importance exceeded that of Bayle's *Dictionary*, for it was not the work of one man, but brought together the leading minds of France, giving their views cumulative weight and influence. Voltaire, Turgot, Holbach, and Rousseau were among the contributors. The outstanding mind and will that organized and directed this project, and that brought it to a conclusion, was Denis Diderot (1713–1784). Diderot had a fertile, versatile mind, and he was always an aggressive protagonist. From traditional piety, he turned to liberal deism, and then to an unbelief which was resigned and derisive in turn. Since no regular profession suited his protean intelligence, he became a literary freelance. Like Carneades in ancient Rome, he argued eloquently both sides of every moral question, reveling in the transitions of emphasis. His mind, thought, and career expressed the characteristically unsettled, but vigorously upsurging, radicalism of his age.

His speculative sweep and mental fertility vied with his social-revolutionary ardor. The intellectual motive was primary. Diderot was not content to unsettle bigotry; he wanted to confute it utterly. Man's knowledge is limited, but he loses even his small chance of understanding if he renounces experimental inquiry to rely on dogmatic assertion. Diderot's violent scorn of the ecclesiastics was due not only to their support of the reactionary monarchist regime, but also to their impeding of man's sole path to knowledge. "Astray at night in an immense forest, I have only a small light to guide me. A stranger comes along and tells me: 'My friend, blow out your candle so as to see your way better.' This stranger is a theologian."[6] Diderot would replace the priestly teleology by a cosmic theory that conforms to the facts of modern science. He revived the spirit of Bruno and Lucretius. The new cosmology, he was sure, required an adequate view of the complexity of nature. The theologian should not be allowed his imagined easy victory over the materialist because of a meager conception of matter. Matter is complex and most abundant in potentialities; it is not merely so much occupied space, inert and brute, it is capable of life, of sensation, and of thought. If we duly acknowledge the versatility of material existence, we shall not have to import illegitimate hypotheses of immaterial principles in order to explain any activity of human life, even that which is highest. Confident of accounting for all the complex activities in nature through his revised and expanded interpretation of matter, Diderot was still convinced that he was confirming a strict materialism.

Diderot's ethics led in two directions, between which he seemed unable to choose, for each of them appealed to strong and contending motives in his personality. His first philosophical publication was a version or paraphrase of Shaftesbury's *Inquiry Concerning Virtue or Merit*. Shaftesbury's aesthetic-moral naturalism had appealed to Diderot's loftier aspirations. Later, however, he was led to dignify or to tolerate his lower impulses as quite natural. Spiritual aspirations and sensuality, philanthropy and philandering, contended in his nature, and he made an ethics of each one. The noble ideals of the French Enlightenment were advocated by the man who wrote some of the lewdest pages in philosophical literature. Critical subtlety may overtax itself in trying to arrive at a reconciliation of Diderot's moral ideas. Were they not, like his own life and personality, expressions of the instability of an age of radical transition?

[6] Translated from D. Diderot, *Oeuvres Complètes* (J. Assézat, ed.), Paris, Garnier, Vol. I, 1875, p. 159.

The Materialism of La Mettrie and Holbach

The French materialistic revision of Locke's philosophy of experience was generally opposed to Cartesian rationalism. This was a peculiar turn in the materialistic argument that had been derived from Descartes' cosmology. For, had not Descartes described all animals as mechanisms, and had he not treated human physiology as would a physicist? Since animals have sensations and feelings, and since sense impressions are physiological processes from which all our knowledge is derivable, the traditional view of the mind becomes superfluous. Men's thought and activity may be explained in terms of matter. So reasoned Julien Offray de La Mettrie (1709–1751) in his *Man a Machine* and other similar books.

During a severe illness, La Mettrie had observed that bodily infirmity was followed by mental and moral disturbance. It became obvious to him that thought must be a physiological process or condition, and he assembled psychological and medical evidence in support of his materialistic thesis. Our so-called "rational" ideas are elaborated from sensations, and sensations are reactions of our bodily organs, with which they originate, grow, and eventually decay. Different states of soul are always correlative to different bodily conditions. Man's intelligence exceeds that of animals even as his brain is relatively larger and more furrowed. All direct and comparative study of mental activity must lead us to its ultimately material source.

The conviction that mind is essentially material led La Mettrie to revise the usual ideas about matter. He followed Diderot in regarding physical nature as versatile. It moves, it lives, it can perceive and think. Whether matter has these capacities inherently, or whether it acquires them only as a result of a certain organization of bodily particles, we cannot say. The fact is simply that all sensations and all so-called "intelligence" are inextricably bound up with a brain and a nervous system. This does not imply that all material particles are capable of consciousness, but it should rule out any reference to immaterial reason. Human nature shares certain qualities with animals and plants, and, like these, it is a part of the mechanism of nature. But neither the human nor the animal machine can be explained simply in terms of the more elementary mechanisms of inorganic bodies. Observe the complexity and variety of material existence; it will teach you its own lessons, and you will not require any transcendent rational essences to explain its natural operation.

If we realize once and for all that all mental activity is a physiological process, our ideas of human knowledge and human conduct will be transformed. We shall see ourselves for what we are, as organisms which react for a while to their environment, and then decay and pass away. This rules out any question of eternal truths; we have only habitual and limited impressions. There can be no meaning in alleged eternal principles of right or wrong, but only in peculiar and transitory pleasures and satisfactions. Like the Epicurean atomists, La Mettrie was led to hedonism in morals, but he preferred the Cyrenaic indulgence to any critical gradation of enjoyments. His hedonism was avowedly quantitative, and, in two treatises, he explored the voluptuous art to make sure he missed no delight within his reach. He did not, it is true, ignore death, but he saw no reason for considering that unpleasant subject until he had to. Having, with Lucretian scorn, rejected all beliefs in immortality, he was resolved to taste to the full the delights of his one life while he had it. The Stoic's serene resignation is a fine doctrine, he thought, if one keeps it only for one's last breath.

Paul Heinrich Dietrich von Holbach (1723–1789) was a German baron who had settled in Paris; his dining table was the meeting place of the radical philosophers twice weekly. He listened well and had efficient secretaries at the gatherings to note every brilliant sally by Diderot or sharp criticism by Rousseau. Only his intimates knew that, while his was not an original mind, he was the most systematic and thoroughgoing of them all. The troubles that Diderot and Helvétius had had with the authorities had taught him a lesson. He preferred safety to literary fame, and he twitted the censors by publishing his *System of Nature* under the name of the deceased Mirabaud, a sedate former secretary of the French Academy. The secret of Holbach's authorship was kept for years. The author of the book needed a disguise on the title page, for inside it he was most outspoken and emphatic in his negation of all the respectable verities. He was unqualified in his materialism, atheism, denial of free will and immortality, contempt for all religious doctrines, and political and social incitement to revolt. His volume soon became the bible of the radicals.

Holbach began with a strictly materialistic account of human nature. He recognized only bodily processes. So-called "rational" thought and "moral" conduct are simply special reactions of the human organism under certain conditions. Our ideas and actions can be traced to elementary sense impressions and responses, all of them strictly physiological processes. These processes are causally determined in each case. The notion of human freedom or spontaneous choice is illusory. Man is never free for a moment. His actions are determined by his nature, temperament, and the counterplay of motives and ideas in his being. And these are all derived from sensations, which are physiological processes. The so-called "soul" is thus reduced to the organic behavior of the body; its whole career begins, grows, and ends with the body. What can justify us in expecting survival and eternal life in a world where everything changes, comes into being and passes away? Such an anticipation is only empty arrogance on our part, and no lofty religious pronouncements can really sustain it. The Christian hope of immortality is a vain dream. Matter is eternal, but its particular combinations which constitute you and me are changing and transitory.

That Holbach's system of nature should uphold atheism was inevitable from the outset. He saw no evidence in human life or in the external world of any immaterial, spiritual principle. The second part of the *System* is devoted to an elaborate refutation of the traditional proofs of God's existence. Holbach's negative conclusions were not only emphatic, but scornful. He professed no regret in exposing the hollowness of men's hopes; he considered religious beliefs to be harmful superstitions, and emancipation from them to be a boon to mankind. "Theology and its notions, far from being useful to mankind, are the real sources of evils which afflict the earth, of errors which blind it, of prejudices which make it stupid, of ignorance which makes it credulous, of vices which plague it, of governments which oppress it."[7] These words epitomize the spirit of Holbach's work.

The practical philosophy to which Holbach was led was philanthropic hedonism. People are stirred to action by the urge for satisfaction; they seek pleasure and avoid pain. In this drive of human passions, some men find gratification at the expense of their fellows; others pursue pleasure in acts which promote the general happiness. We call the first kind of individual, "bad," the second, "good." Morality is simply bodily behavior that expands social security, peace, and satisfaction.

Holbach extended his ethical conclusions to politics. The good man enjoys the good will of his neighbors and seeks to deserve it, both in his lifetime and in their grateful memory of him after he is dead. Good governments also should be concerned with the people's happiness and should appeal to their approval. Despotism runs counter to the people's interests; it thrives on superstitious belief in the divine right of kings. An enlightened nation needs only firm resolution to sweep away hateful oppression and regain its conditions of general happiness.

SUGGESTED WORKS FOR FURTHER STUDY

GENERAL.   Lévy-Bruhl, L., *History of Modern Philosophy in France.*

MONTESQUIEU.   Montesquieu, *The Spirit of Laws* (trans. T. Nugent).

VOLTAIRE.   Voltaire, *Philosophical Dictionary* (selected and trans. H. I. Woolf), and *The Living Thoughts of Voltaire* (André Maurois, ed.); Morley, John, *Voltaire.*

CONDILLAC.   Condillac, É., *Treatise on the Sensations* (trans. G. Carr).

DIDEROT.   Diderot, D., *Early Philosophical Works* (Margaret Jourdain, ed.); Cru, R. L., *Diderot as a Disciple of English Thought;* Morley, John, *Diderot and the Encyclopaedists.*

LA METTRIE.   La Mettrie, J., *Man a Machine* (trans. G. C. Bussey).

[7] Translated from P. H. von Holbach, *Système de la nature*, London, 1781, Vol. II, p. 245.

24. Rousseau: The Upsurge of Romanticism

The Personal Tone of Rousseau's Philosophy

The topic of this section might well comprise the entire chapter, for the philosophy of Jean Jacques Rousseau (1712–1778), and his life and personality reflected each other. His thought was lyrical; his arguments were confessions, and his conclusions were intense feelings.

The Philosophers of the Enlightenment criticized and rejected dogmatic theology, Cartesian rationalism, monarchical principles; they appealed to the new science and the new philosophy of experience. By more thorough experimental inquiry and more rigorous reasoning, they meant to reach more valid conclusions. Even their skeptical inferences were inferences of the understanding. Rousseau put small faith in all this display of discursive thinking. He appealed, beyond all impressive proofs, to his direct emotional conviction. Philosophers might try to prove to him that the belief in divine providence was not logically valid, and scientific investigators of human society might conclude that poverty and prostitution are inevitable. But, against the first conclusion, Rousseau reaffirmed his imperious faith, and the second callous inference he rejected as intolerable and, therefore, false.

Rousseau was a philosopher of the heart, and he might have used Pascal's words as his own: "The heart has its reasons, which reason does not know at all."[1] There was no arguing with him on the basis of evidence, for it did not impress him if it seemed alien to his intimate assurance. He began his essay on the origin of inequality with a frank disclaimer: "Let us begin by setting aside all the facts."[2] The Encyclopedists undertook to spread abroad the new knowledge in the sciences and the arts, and through this enlightenment to lead modern society to a higher level of civilization, progress, and welfare. But Rousseau denounced science and art as corruptions of man's primitive integrity, and civilization as baneful and a fraud. The philosophical

[1] Translated from B. Pascal, *Pensées*, 277, in L. Brunschvicg (ed.), *Œuvres de Blaise Pascal*, Paris, Hachette, Vol. XIII, 1904, p. 201.
[2] Translated from J. J. Rousseau, *Oeuvres Complètes*, Paris, Furne, 1885, Vol. I, p. 535.

radicals repudiated traditional theology by exposing its invalid premises and its unsound reasoning; Rousseau was still more radical: he rejected theology altogether for usurping the place of religion in men's lives—religion, which is not concerned with doctrines and proofs, but is the devout outpouring of the heart.

Rousseau's philosophy was the direct expression of the romantic spirit that had characterized him from his youth, even before he ran away from his native Geneva. Throughout his life he was always gazing at a romantic mirror in which the facts of his own life and other external events were refracted to suit the sentimental perspective to which his mood inclined him. His *Confessions* should be read, not as a biography that is objectively reliable in all details, but as an exceedingly intimate revelation of his feelings and attitudes.

His adventurous life provided emotional incitements to his philosophy. While serving as a lackey, he consoled himself with an inner feeling of superiority over his master. The great achievements of which he dreamed atoned emotionally for his actual vagabondage. He paid court to great Parisian ladies who obtained for him some official recognition, yet he scorned their high society as corrupt. During the latter part of his life, after his early books had made him famous and infamous, the contention of motives in his emotional life continued along new lines. Intoxicated by his sudden and expanding celebrity, he was also obsessed by the hostility he aroused and by his fear of persecution. The heart of mankind had spoken in his words, but the masters of men's lives hated him for it and burned his books. He felt himself homeless and helpless in a wicked world; he unbosomed himself in endless letters to men and women whom he also distrusted as being in the foul cabal against him. He professed the pure, intimate spirit of friendship, but when David Hume took pity on his worries and infirmities, brought him to safety in England, and cared for him generously, Rousseau grew suspicious and accused his benefactor of conspiring with his numerous enemies.

These and other tensions and morbid strains, like faults in the strata of Rousseau's character, wrought havoc in his life. Recognition of them may help us to understand some problems in his philosophy of life. But the living Rousseau that embodied them, also transcended them. Out of this vagabond life and this unstable personality came some of the most dynamic ideas of modern times, piercing to the heart traditional ideas of culture, education, social order, and religion. Rousseau spoke brave and burning words for the long-suffering, submerged masses, the injured and insulted in our gaudy, heartless civilization. He had been one of them, and he always felt with them and for them; he felt their indigence and squalor, their moral ignominy that tainted the image of God in men and women. In the evil gloom and boredom of an artificial society, Rousseau had visions of a bright world of uncorrupted nature for free and happy men and women; and his dreams fired the imagination of millions. His spirit evoked a new romantic literature in Europe. Voltaire called him "the arch-fool," but Rousseau's portrait was the only one in Kant's study, and Tolstoy even wore it on a medallion around his neck. This dynamic influence cannot be dismissed offhand as morbid; it calls for a fair examination.

Rousseau's Attack on Civilization

Rousseau's first philosophical work was a prize essay on a subject proposed in 1749 by the Academy of Dijon: "Has the restoration of the sciences and the arts contributed to purify morals?"[3] Rousseau read the announcement of it in a journal while he was walking to Vincennes to visit Diderot in jail, and suddenly he felt a flash of inspiration, in which the whole meaning of his life's message became clear to him. Whether this, his own account of the experience, is to be believed, or whether Diderot's reported claim that he urged Rousseau to denounce civilization should more properly be credited in this respect, cannot, and perhaps need not, be definitely settled. Diderot's fertile mind was quite capable of suggesting the essay, but Rousseau was the one intended to pour out his heart in writing it.

The first-prize essay answered the Academy's question emphatically in the negative. Rousseau began by exposing the corruption of the proud civilizations of the past; Egypt, Greece, Imperial Rome, and the oriental empires had decayed as they became civilized. The ancient races which were honored for their virtues and their integrity were uncivilized tribes, such as the early Persians and the early Romans. The civilization produced by the spread of science and the arts is artificial; it cultivates the vain curiosity and luxury of a minority which arrogantly exploits and oppresses the common people. Man's primitive, simple freedom and virtue have been lost, and men have become tyrants and slaves.

Rousseau's essay won the Academy prize and immediately aroused wide discussion. In his replies to his critics, its author probed further the corruption of civilization. He exposed the root of the evil as inequality: "From inequality came riches; . . . from riches, luxury and idleness. From luxury came the fine arts, and from idleness, science."[4]

He was thus ready for his second-prize essay, also for the Dijon Academy, on the subject: "What is the origin of inequality among men, and is it authorized by natural law?"[5] Rousseau's answer, which did not receive the prize, was much more extensive, and even more radical than his first essay. He portrayed the primitive life of men as free, untainted, and virtuous in a savage way. These men of the uncut forests and unfenced plains lived close to nature. They had unequal strength and varied powers, but no one was master and none slaves. In untamed freedom and vigor, they supplied their

[3] Translated from *ibid.*, p. 463.
[4] Translated from *ibid.*, p. 491.
[5] Translated from *ibid.*, p. 555.

natural wants and realized their simple felicity. Rousseau's account, in this essay, of life in the state of nature was in rosy contrast to Hobbes' dark picture in the *Leviathan*.

Against this nostalgic dream of primitive life, Rousseau portrayed the nightmare of civilized society. When he asked how men had lost their original free equality, his reply pointed to the institution of private property as the initial, fatal defection. Science and technology served to enslave mankind. Some men learned how to work metals, how to make axes, spades, and plows. These tools multiplied the power of their hands and the produce of the earth they tilled. If they could have the land for their own and force others to work it for them, they could be masters and fulfill all their desires. So with private property came wealth and poverty, landlords and slaves, luxury and squalor, and the whole ugly system of modern civilization.

In this essay, Rousseau went continually from what was meant to be historical exposition to ardent rhetoric:

The first man who, having enclosed a piece of ground, could think of saying, *This is mine,* and found people simple enough to believe him, was the real founder of civil society. How many crimes, wars, murders, miseries, and horrors would not have been spared to the human race by one who, plucking up the stakes, or filling in the trench, should have called out to his fellows: "Beware of listening to this impostor; you are undone if you forget that the earth belongs to no one, and that its fruits are for all."[6]

We can understand why Rousseau was read to Parisian crowds by street-corner agitators during the Revolution. His own intentions may not have been violent, but his ideas were incendiary.

It would be labor misapplied to undertake specific criticisms of the historical accuracy of Rousseau's two discourses, the validity of his social analyses, and the adequacy of his interpretations. Overwhelming evidence from modern studies of primitive men and societies has discredited his romantic vision of the free savage. His portrayal of primitive life is unwarranted, and his account and his judgment of civilization are one-sided. The increasing complexity of civilized society which, in so many ways, has constricted and shackled human lives has also given mankind a new and expanded freedom of self-expression. To be content with such a fair reflection, however, would be to miss Rousseau's importance in the history of liberalism. He portrayed the ugly side of the human scene in grim colors that could not be ignored; he drew vital problems of civilization to the center of attention. His emphasis was one-sided, but the side he emphasized was one to which attention had been long overdue.

[6] Translated from *ibid.,* p. 551.

The Social Contract

Rousseau drew practical inferences from his doctrines. He undertook to practice what he preached: he would return to nature, to primitive simplicity. If this aroused derision among his former friends—the courtiers and Encyclopedists—so much the worse for them. He would support himself by copying music; it seemed to him the smallest concession to social formality by which he could obtain his livelihood. In long controversies with various critics he was formulating his philosophy of life. How are men to realize, even in this corrupt civilization, some freedom of self-expression? This problem had educational, political, cultural, and religious aspects. Rousseau pondered on his manifold plans of reform. Within a decade after his first prize essay, he developed his thought more adequately in three major works: *On the Social Contract*, *Émile, or On Education*, which includes "The Savoyard Vicar's Profession of Faith," and a novel of romantic love, *The New Héloïse*.

The Social Contract is, of all Rousseau's work, the least emotional and the most reasonable in exposition. He stated his problem and his purpose definitely. "Man was born free, and everywhere he is in chains."[7] In what kind of social order can he realize the greatest degree of liberty? Life under law is not a life of nature in which no one is obligated; it must have been established by contract. This contract cannot have been made between the citizens and the king, for before a monarchy or any other government can be instituted, the people must become a nation. By organizing themselves as a nation, each individual authorizes the community to legislate in his name as a citizen, and submits to the legislation as a subject. The first principle of Rousseau's political philosophy, which he shared with, and probably derived from, Locke, is the people's initial and final sovereignty.

Each individual, submitting to the general will, is not subjected by other individuals; since all are law-abiding, each one enjoys freedom within the framework of the social order. The citizen-legislator obliges himself, on principle, to obey the laws of the general will, even when they have been passed over his dissenting vote. On principle, he even orders his own punishment if he transgresses the laws. The individual obeys laws with which his will is politically identified as a citizen, though not always as an individual. The primitive, private freedom in nature is here exchanged for a political liberty under law. If this principle is not to become an empty formula, the people who obey the law must periodically reaffirm their character as legislating citizens. In public assemblies, they must exercise their basic authority to reaffirm established laws, or revise or abrogate them. Since the royal or any other type of executive is charged with enforcing the popular authority, his tenure of office is to be subject to the people's periodic approval. It is

[7] Translated from *ibid.*, p. 639.

obvious that the greater a state, the less directly effective can be the will of each citizen in it. Rousseau therefore advocated small states patterned on his native Geneva.

Rousseau's discussion of the various forms of government is not as significant as his basic doctrine of safeguarding popular rights. He agreed with Montesquieu that, in different countries and environments, different political systems may prove most suitable. Though we cannot state absolutely which government is best, the test of good government remains the same: the preservation and prosperity of the people. Rousseau here concurred with Aristotle.

This doctrine of human emancipation has its own strict discipline. Man's political freedom as a citizen is compatible with certain stringent state controls on his life as a subject of the state. The sovereign will of the people may promulgate not only a code of laws, but also a creed, or articles of faith, conformity to which is exacted with due penalties for transgression. Those who refuse to believe in God or in immortality and future retribution should be exiled, not for their impiety but for their rejection of these socially binding convictions. *The Social Contract* even stipulated capital punishment for anyone who, though professing these religious beliefs, remained an intractable atheist. Rousseau, who claimed unqualified sovereignty for the people in an assembled council, allowed, and even demanded, the harsh constraint of nonconformist citizens when he deemed them unsocial and recalcitrant. This part of his political doctrine had ominous implications, some of which were soon to be illustrated by Marat and Robespierre—and the guillotine. Was the Genevan patriot siding here with Calvin against Servetus, against the modern leaders of man's liberation from intolerance? Or did the contrast between *The Social Contract* and the individualist cult of untrammeled freedom in the prize essays show how readily Rousseau could forget consistency when he was advocating a doctrine to which at the time he was ardently devoted?

Educational Reforms Proposed in Rousseau's Émile

Rousseau's radical views on educational aims and methods carried to extreme conclusions the resistance to the classicism of the Renaissance humanists, which had been started by reformers like Comenius and Locke. The new emphasis—not on mastery of the classics, but on preparation for life—was noted in our discussion of Locke, but even with the introduction of new studies, the emphasis remained on discipline of the mind. Rousseau took the really radical step. He declared that the proper education of children is not schooling—not preparation for the university, for an intellectual career, or for a learned and polite life. The right education should afford the child the fullest experience and self-expression of childhood, in which, alone, the natural development of youth can be realized. The school child should not be a little man in a little uniform with a little powdered wig; the child should not be in school at all. He should be saved from the stiff grip of social conventions and allowed to range freely in the glories of nature.

The details of the new method were as radical as its guiding principle of letting children be children. Through a vigorous outdoor life, the child's bodily constitution was to be strengthened. Rousseau drew an educational inference from Locke's empiricism by insisting on the initial expansion and perfection of sense experience. Open the senses, the child's immediate avenues to sound understanding. But, while the young nature is thus aroused, and its normal capacities are unfolding, the teacher should not undertake premature, formal discipline. Let the intellect lie fallow. Rousseau portrayed this ideal vision in his account of the education of little Émile. Living in direct contact with nature, Émile knows things, not words; he knows actions before abstractions. And he knows them directly, from his own experience; he does not learn them from a teacher reading a book in a stuffy school room. For, while Émile is, of course, provided with a tutor, he is instructed as little as possible. The tutor's main function is to guide the boy toward fields of experience and activity where his curiosity will be aroused and developed, where nature will teach him its own lessons, as it taught Robinson Crusoe. Émile achieves practical dexterity; he becomes not erudite, but handy and resourceful in any natural eventuality.

Thus childhood is lived to the full. However, with the dawning life of adolescence, Émile's natural education takes new turns. Heretofore, he has been a child alone with nature; now he is youth reaching out socially toward others. His social education begins, and it, also, must be natural. Émile is to live a life of normal responses to others, both men and women. His moral and religious sentiments are to be given normal expression. In men, he is to see and to respect humanity, and, in nature, he is to recognize and to love God.

The vital influence of Rousseau's ideas on modern education may be traced: his advocacy of child study, individual and collective, to provide suitable outlets for characteristic self-expression; and his emphasis on nature study, on manual training, on direct contact with external things, and on intimate and genuine inner emotional experience. The procedure which Rousseau proposed was scarcely feasible—a solitary forest for each pupil instead of a classroom for thirty—and no one but Rousseau could have advocated it seriously. It was also unsound in emphasizing first the child's solitude in nature and then the adolescent's budding social sentiment. Had Rousseau realized the active interplay of unique individuality and social participation, which actually characterizes all of human life, his Émile would have been offered a different, more normal, and more humane education.

Likewise, the initial emphasis on roaming alone in the forest, away from any contamination by society, reflected Rousseau's stubborn contrast between nature and culture. His educational theory, like his basic philosophy of life, suffered from his inability to realize that civilization, with all its cramping and corrupting effects on mankind, is also the normal medium for the fulfilment of human capacities, and that man's nature reaches maturity through the life and activities of his society and culture.

Romanticism in Literature, Morality, and Religion

The intense emphasis on emotion, and the cult of primitive innocence in the bosom of nature, affected Rousseau's views of literature and art. To him, human life was a romance; he felt that the truly poetic version of it must also be romantic; it must express and satisfy the longings of the heart. Our imagination must realize the transports we have missed in actual experience. The novel, *The New Héloïse*, was both an emotional release and a literary declaration for Rousseau. Its unmistakably personal impulsion fortified its romantic appeal. The readers of these ardent confessions felt intimately revealed to themselves. This undisguised passion, ardent in its Alpine solitude, was in sharp contrast to the elegant amours of the neoclassical salons. It seemed convincing and it proved infectious. Rousseau's conclusion, in his novel, on a note of quiet family life disarmed the scruples of its readers, who returned avidly to its earlier flaming pages. This upsurge of emotion drew poets, novelists, and dramatists into strong currents. A deluge of sentimental novelizing swept over European literature; but here, also, creative genius could, and did, slough off the trappings of the new fashion in order to produce original expressions of the romantic art.

Rousseau was outstanding among the French moralists of the eighteenth century, but he was characterized by the intense feeling with which he expressed his moral convictions, rather than by any systematic exposition of his ethical principles. Unlike the egoistic interpretation of human motives by men like Helvétius, Rousseau regarded selfish greed as a perverted, not a natural, incentive. To be sure, human nature seeks to preserve itself. This natural regard, *amour de soi*, is not naturally hostile to the welfare of others; it may develop into active social good will. The corrupting influence of civilization turns this normal self-regard into rapacious selfishness, *amour propre*. But the primitive, generous reaction of our hearts may be seen in the admiration we give to noble benevolence, even when it profits us not a whit.

Morality and religion alike, according to Rousseau, find their heart and essence in the sentiment of a devout conscience. Virtue is not found in the external action; it is in our dutiful spirit—in pure dedication to the right— that we identify ourselves with the noble choice without regard to any advantage or satisfaction. This emphasis on conscience is given exalted expression in the *Savoyard Vicar's Profession of Faith*:

Conscience! Conscience! Divine instinct, immortal and celestial voice; assured guide of an ignorant and limited, but intelligent and free being; infallible judge of good and evil, which renderest man like unto God! In thee is the excellence of man's nature and the morality of his actions; without thee I feel nothing in myself which would raise me above the beasts, except the sad privilege of groping from error to error, helped by an understanding without laws and a reason without principles.[8]

Rousseau's religious philosophy is absorbed in intimate communion with God. Love of God expresses and satisfies the inexhaustible heart in an infinite measure. Rousseau gave an emotional version of St. Augustine's great thought—that the restless soul seeks in God the peace that nothing else can supply. This peace not only passes understanding but, according to Rousseau, does not require understanding or systematic doctrine; it need not be bound by ecclesiastical forms and regulations. The Savoyard Vicar expresses this apotheosis of devout sentiment in religion above any orthodox theology: "Keep your soul in the state of always desiring God's existence, and you will never doubt it."[9]

Rousseau's ideas do not lend themselves to systematic exposition, but their characteristic features are unmistakable: intense humanism, resistance to form and structure, emphasis on mood and sentiment. These explain his opposition to both the dogmatic theologian and the infidel materialist. They also reflect the larger outlines of his philosophy. He was convinced that neither his own character nor the world in which he was active could be explained adequately in merely physical terms. Philosophy must recognize the reality of spirit, of our unique wills, of real persons facing nature and seeking to come to terms with it and to realize in it their hopes and ideals. Man's distinctive activity is not so much mechanics, and, thus, it cannot be extinguished by the dissolution of the bodily mechanism. Rousseau cherished a trust in immortality to afford scope for man's inexhaustible moral career and to satisfy his boundless yearning. His philosophy was not based on cited evidence, but was rather an expression of Rousseau's emotional demands.

SUGGESTED WORKS FOR FURTHER STUDY

WORKS BY ROUSSEAU. Rousseau, Jean Jacques, *The Social Contract* (trans. H. J. Tozer; C. Frankel, ed.), *Emile, or On Education* (trans. B. Foxley), and *Political Writings* (C. E. Vaughan, ed.); Rolland, Romain (ed.), *The Living Thoughts of Rousseau;* Hendel, C. W. (ed.), *Citizen of Geneva;* (selections from Rousseau's correspondence).

BIOGRAPHIES AND CRITICAL STUDIES. Gran, Gerhard, *Jean Jacques Rousseau;* Hendel, C. W., *Jean-Jacques Rousseau, Moralist;* Höffding, Harald, *Jean-Jacques Rousseau and His Philosophy;* Josephson, Matthew, *Jean-Jacques Rousseau;* Lemaître, J., *Jean-Jacques Rousseau;* Morley, John, *Rousseau;* Wright, E. H., *The Meaning of Rousseau.*

[8] Translated from J. J. Rousseau, *Oeuvres Complètes*, Paris, Hachette, Vol. II, 1914, p. 262.
[9] Translated from *ibid.*, p. 284.

IV.   THE PHILOSOPHERS OF THE NINETEENTH AND TWENTIETH CENTURIES

25. Immanuel Kant: The Critical Gate to Nineteenth-Century Philosophy

The German Enlightenment

German thought was slow in achieving distinguished philosophical expression. During the two centuries that passed between Boehme and Kant, Leibniz was the only German thinker of commanding importance. In astonishing contrast to this situation, toward the end of the eighteenth century German minds manifested great productive power in every field of philosophical inquiry. The stimulating influence of Kant's genius was the major factor in this epoch-making advance in thought that put Germany in the forefront of modern philosophy. But the ground for Kant's achievement had been prepared, by popular interest and systematic reflection, during the German Enlightenment.

The period of the Enlightenment was marked by an alertness to the significant achievements in French and English philosophy and literature. French learning was the main topic among those engaged in discussions at the Prussian Academy of Friedrich the Great, and Voltaire was court philosopher at Friedrich's palace of Sans Souci; English theories were zealously studied, and the philosophical poetry of Pope initiated a literary fashion. Of more direct importance, however, was the influence of Leibniz's philosophy. His teleology and optimistic theodicy, sustained by the similar tendencies of Shaftesbury, spread a tolerant liberal spirit in popular social and religious thought. His firm reliance on rationalistic methods set the tone of philosophical instruction in the German universities. This intellectualism was evident in various lines of inquiry; it was resisted by theologians and by experimental scientists, and it gained systematic ascendancy in the treatises of Wolff. But the abstract formalism of the latter's exposition demanded a radical revision, which it received through the works of Kant.

The outstanding academic rationalist was Christian Wolff (1679–1754) who combined philosophy with mathematical studies. On Leibniz's recommendation, he was appointed professor at Halle. Although his own rationalism was derived largely from Leibniz, Wolff was not an avowed disciple; in fact, he radically revised the philosophy of his great predecessor; however, this revision was not an advance in philosophy. Wolff achieved abstract, systematic coherence by abandoning or neglecting some of Leibniz's really original ideas. Thus the monadology and the teleology of preestablished harmony were both modified and greatly limited.

In a long series of German and Latin treatises, Wolff undertook to cover the whole territory of knowledge, all of which he classified under his abstract rubrics, and thus, rationalism became an elaborate system of tabulated concepts. The pure sciences, for example, were arranged under three heads: rational theology, rational psychology, rational cosmology, and dealt respectively with God, the soul, and the physical world. Practical philosophy was covered under ethics, politics, and economics. Further distinctions from other points of view yielded still other classifications. Every type of problem in every conceivable perspective was assigned its place in Wolff's vast conceptual scheme.

This intellectualism was rigidly formal. All theoretical knowledge and logical principles were deduced from the law of contradiction. The laws of physical science were derived from the principle of sufficient reason. Morality became an elaborate series of analytic inferences; religion, a system of abstract rational theology. This sort of doctrine seemed to lose the soul and spirit of Christian religious conviction, and it was accordingly resisted by the more devoutly pious theologians. Opposition to Wolff spread and became violent; until finally royal authority was secured to expel him from the university and to banish him from the province. But his reputation in intellectualist circles persisted; a later king, Friedrich the Great, recalled him to Halle, where he lectured with distinction until his death.

The liberal leader in the struggle for tolerance, in the critical revision of traditional ideas and in the expansion of the cultural outlook of the Enlightenment, was Gotthold Lessing (1729–1781). The great master of German literature before Goethe, especially in the drama, Lessing also invites attention as a philosophical thinker. He was influenced, in the development of his ideas, by his study of Spinoza and Leibniz. With Spinoza, he shared a pantheistic view of deity, but he demanded a more adequate recognition of the active ongoing process of reality than Spinoza's philosophy provided. This more dramatic view of nature he found in Leibniz; yet he resisted the latter's concessions to dogmatic theology, advocating instead Spinoza's uncompromising devotion to the truth.

His general method was to proceed from criticism of traditional forms to new fruitful reconstruction. As a dramatist and art critic, he emancipated Germany from her servitude to French neoclassical formalism and laid the foundations for a free and creative self-expression. His active work in Biblical criticism was likewise motivated by his resolution to liberate man's mind from rigid traditional forms, to give the more enlightened spirit of the age genuine religious utterance. It is precisely in religion, the heart of the spiritual life, that men most need unhampered activity in their striving after perfection. No stiff conformity to doctrine avails here, only a genuine yearning for the boundless plenitude of truth.

In their common spiritual endeavor, Lessing saw all men as brothers by right; racial and religious tolerance must mark any reasonable view of social liberalism. This principle of tolerance and enlightened humanitarianism inspired his great drama, *Nathan the Sage*, and it was also developed in a historical-religious setting in his *Education of Mankind*. Lessing was not content, like so many deists, to uphold natural religion in general terms against dogmatic tradition. He undertook to trace man's spiritual growth in the ongoing process of traditions: the advance from naïve and crude to more mature ideas of God, from engrossment in ritual to the pursuit of righteousness, from pious concern for rewards and punishments to a pure and disinterested devotion to the godly life.

Kant's Life and Philosophical Development

The critical philosophy of Immanuel Kant (1724–1804) was epoch-making. It became the principal task of nineteenth-century philosophers to adopt, to reinterpret, to develop, or to oppose it. It was rightly called "critical," for it issued from the contending ideas of the earlier modern systems of thought, and it was a critical settlement of their difficulties. We shall appreciate Kant's achievement better if we keep in clear view the philosophical traditions in which he was trained and with which he struggled in his critical advance.

Kant's real biography is found in his inner life of thought. His outward career was uneventful. His father, believed to have been of Scotch descent, was a poor saddler in the city of Königsberg. There was neither wealth nor learning in the family history, but both his parents were deeply religious members of the sect called Pietists, who emphasized the nonintellectual and more intimate spirit of religion. Though his mother died when he was 14, her devout spirit, shared and continued by his father, affected the boy's entire spiritual life. His intellect, however, resisted the dogmatic strain in the Pietist teaching to which he was subjected in the sectarian school he attended. But he was also stirred by the rich personality of his teacher Schulz, who combined a mastery of rationalistic doctrine with a prevailing intensity of moral convictions and Pietist ardor.

When he went to the university, two motives contended in Kant's mind: a respect for moral-religious ideals, and a demand for critical understanding. He was fortunate in having as professor Martin Knutzen (1713–1751), a philosopher with mathematical-scientific interests and competence. Knutzen modified his Wolffian rationalism, not only by pursuing direct scientific inquiry, but also by trying to appreciate the Pietist objections to Wolff's too rigid intellectualism, especially in religion. Knutzen gave young Kant a chair in his library where he studied Newton's *Principia*, thus being grounded directly in modern scientific methods. His appeal to direct moral and religious experience found sympathetic appreciation, and his distrust of metaphysical and theological abstractions was shared and confirmed. But the underlying framework of his philosophical training was still a modified Wolffian rationalism.

Kant's father had not been able to contribute to his son's support at the university, and he died when the youth was 22. The young scholar then spent several years as private tutor in the homes of several country squires in East Prussia. He continued his own studies, mainly in the sciences; his first writings were on scientific topics. In 1755, he obtained his doctorate at the University of Königsberg. For fifteen years, he served there as an ill-paid lecturer, and later, as assistant librarian. Despite his straitened circumstances, Kant's productive work was uninterrupted, and, eventually, it gained him academic recognition. Erlangen and Jena had both offered him a professorship when, finally, in 1770, Königsberg appointed him to a chair in logic and metaphysics, which he held for thirty-four years until his death.

Kant's mature life and old age were as uneventful as were his earlier years. He lectured, of course, on logic, metaphysics, ethics, and natural law, and on mathematics, physics, physical geography, and anthropology. His daily program was most methodical. Every day he was awakened on the stroke of five by his servant Lampe, and he spent his mornings preparing his university lectures and writings. Some friends would join him for dinner and a discussion, but would leave in time for his afternoon walk, which was timed with such regularity that the merry wives of Königsberg set their clocks by the thump of the philosopher's cane on the cobblestones. He never married; he took no active part in any social or political movement; his whole life was lived within the boundaries of his native province. He had read some great literature, but no masterpieces of painting, sculpture, or music had enriched his life. His world was a world of ideas, of reading, writing, and lecturing on philosophy and science.

Yet, from his study, Kant revolutionized western civilization. Science, morality, art, social life, religion, the world-outlook, and the principles and ideals of human life all gained new meaning and perspective through his reflection. Where can we find a more impressive example of the single strength of thought? Kant's works do not owe their power to clarity or eloquence of style. Goethe remarked that, on reading Kant again and again, he felt as though he were stepping into a brightly lighted room. However, "again and again" does not suffice for most of us, for Kant's writing often impresses us as a dark labyrinth.

Kant's was not the only labyrinth. Unlike the leading French and British thinkers—who, as a rule, wrote clearly and effectively, and among whom many were literary masters—the modern German philosophers were very opaque writers. Schopenhauer was a remarkable exception. After we have read, studied, and then *thought*, Kant, we begin to understand Schopenhauer's praise of the *Critique of Pure Reason* as the highest achievement of human reflection.

The Critique of Pure Reason

The year of publication of Kant's first *Critique*, 1781, has been regarded as memorable in the history of modern culture, for it was marked by the death of Lessing and the appearance of Schiller's drama *The Robbers*, a masterpiece of German romanticism. Actually, Kant's work had been planned and in preparation for more than a decade, although its publication had been delayed several times. During these years, Kant's whole philosophical orientation was shifting and was being revised. His inaugural dissertation upon assuming his professorship in 1770 was a forecast of the new philosophy which he realized in the *Critique of Pure Reason*.

The disturber of Kant's thought was David Hume. Kant said that the reading of Hume roused him from his "dogmatic slumber." The remark may puzzle us at first, for Kant was never a dogmatist in the usual sense. His earlier works showed a characteristically original mind; they were critical of established doctrines and traditions, and alert to new alternatives in scientific theory and in philosophical construction. The impact of Hume's skeptical thought may be regarded not as a sudden and radical crisis, but as a notable stage in the critical development of Kant's philosophy. It served to accentuate the contending alternatives between or within which he was proceeding to a more adequate theory.

These alternatives were rationalism and empiricism, which had broadly distinguished the dual course of systematic modern philosophy, and of which the doctrines of Wolff and Hume, respectively, were the emphatic versions in Kant's time.

The rationalist regarded sense experience as unreliable, and emotion as confusing; he demanded axiomatic first principles, analytic mastery of them, and systematic deduction of their implications. His method yielded coherent structures of universal ideas, but it was abstract and unresponsive to man's direct experience of things, or to the experimental procedure of modern science—Newton's physics had not been achieved by Wolffian reasoning.

The empiricist, on the other hand, relied on the immediate impressions of sense, from which, by association, he proposed to elaborate his whole structure of ideas. But does sense experience warrant any necessary inference of one idea from another? Hume's examination of causality had reduced the idea of necessary connection to our subjective habit of associating ideas that have been constantly conjoined. The empiricist was thus immersed in the process of sense experience, but this experience yielded him no universally valid laws or principles of science.

Between, or rather through, these two philosophies, Kant sought a theory of knowledge and of nature that could explain the actuality of modern science. For science, he knew, was true. Its laws predicted results which experiment or observation of nature verified. A sound philosophy must be capable of understanding and explaining the mind's actual scientific achievement, its universal laws of experience. The data of sense perception and the concepts of the understanding are both required for a system of real knowledge. "Thoughts without contents are empty, perceptions without concepts are blind."[1] Kant's scientific and philosophical thinking demanded a critical solution of the question, How is scientific—that is, universally valid—knowledge of nature possible? This is the initial problem of the *Critique of Pure Reason*, and, in this philosophical vindication of science, Kant perfected his distinctively critical method.

Kant formulated his problem in logical terms. Logic has distinguished two kinds of judgment, analytic and synthetic. The predicate of an analytic judgment is implied in the subject, and the judgment is simply the explicit statement of this conceptual analysis. Thus, the judgment "All bodies are extended" requires only the analysis of the subject. "Body" implies or signifies "extended being." Since, in this judgment, we do not have to go beyond the analysis of the subject, it can be made independently of any particular observation or experience; it is universally valid of any body whatever. All analytic judgments are thus prior to experience, or *a priori*.

It is otherwise with synthetic judgments. Here the predicate is not necessarily implied in the subject, but is connected with it in the judgment. If I judge that swans are white, clearly "whiteness" is not implied in "swan," and such a judgment is not a statement of analysis, but a report of experience; I have looked at swans and have seen that they are white. This is a synthetic judgment which comes after experience, or *a posteriori;* it is not universal or necessarily true.

These two types of judgment, respectively, mark the rationalist and the empiricist. Wolffian rationalism was an elaborate system of conceptual analysis *a priori*, whereas Hume was always aiming at synthetic judgments *a posteriori*. Kant believed that science demands and includes a third type of judgments which he called "synthetic judgments *a priori*." If we say that bodies have weight, or that bodies are expanded by heat, these predicates are not derived by mere analysis of the subject. This sort of judgment is synthetic. But it is not merely the record of a particular experience; it is universally valid in all experience of bodies and can be made prior to any specific perception. It is thus *a priori*. The laws of science are such judgments. In this logical way, Kant raised his problem: How are synthetic

[1] Paraphrased from Kant, *Critique of Pure Reason* (trans. F. Max Müller), 2nd ed., New York, Macmillan, 1911, p. 41.

judgments *a priori* possible? That is to say, how can we have universally valid knowledge of experience? Clearly he was here undertaking to meet the challenge which Hume's radical empiricism presented to the philosophical understanding of scientific knowledge. How can scientific laws of nature be established truly?

Kant's initial problem concerning real knowledge has many implications in mathematics, physical science, and metaphysics. He indicated them more definitely in his *Prolegomena to any Future Metaphysics*, which he published in 1783. He did not regard the mathematical judgments as merely analytic. The conclusion of the Pythagorean theorem really adds meaning to our concept of a triangle, and it is a universal judgment *a priori*. In pure natural science, the universal judgments of causal connection are likewise synthetic *a priori*. The same kind of meaning is claimed for ultimate judgments in metaphysics. So Kant expressed his problem in several questions: How is pure mathematics possible? How is pure natural science possible? How is metaphysics in general possible? The third question leads to a fourth—since we are concerned, not only with the mind's ultimate reflections, but with the validity of its ultimate judgments—How is metaphysics as a science possible?

Kant proceeded to the solution of his problem by examining the process and character of experience. We seem to know objects through sense experience, and our sense perceptions are thought out through our understanding. What *a priori* elements in our knowledge are produced in these two stages of experience?

The first part of the *Critique of Pure Reason* is entitled "Transcendental Aesthetic." This title calls for explanation. In Kant's use, the terms *transcendental* and *transcendent* are related but differentiated. Both of them signify more than mere data of particular sense experience. A *transcendent* idea is one that refers to what transcends or is entirely beyond the limits of any possible experience. A *transcendental* idea likewise goes beyond particular data of experience, but expresses the universal and necessary character of experience. It is an essential form, a principle, law, or uniformity of experience. The term *fundamental* may be suggested as a synonym for it. Kant was not always consistent in distinguishing these two terms, and the reader must be on his guard to avoid confusion. Kant used the word *aesthetic* in the old Greek sense, meaning a doctrine of sense experience. Kant was asking: What is fundamental to sense perception? His answer presented his doctrine of space and time. Through sense perception, we become aware of the data of sensation as being in space and time. Space and time, according to Kant, are not derived empirically by abstraction from sense perception; nor are they general concepts; nor yet are they realities apart from perception. They are the pure forms of sense perception. Sense perceptions are fundamentally spatial and temporal; space and time are the essential forms of outer and inner sense experience. We perceive objects in spatial and temporal reference simultaneously and in succession. Thus, Kant noted, as the first stage in attaining a systematic order of experience, the two fundamental forms of sense perception, space and time.

This spatial-temporal ordering in sense perception makes scientific knowledge possible, but does not itself attain it. Knowledge is achieved through the process of thought. To the examination of this, Kant devoted his "Transcendental Logic." In the first division of it, called "Transcendental Analytic," he examined the elements and principles of knowledge of the understanding in the field of possible experience. That was, in effect, his vindication of science in reply to Hume. The second division, called "Transcendental Dialectic," exposed the confusions of human reason when it ventured to reach universal knowledge beyond the limits of possible experience. This was Kant's criticism of rationalistic metaphysics, and, to it, he devoted the latter half of his *Critique of Pure Reason*.

Kant's real problem in the "Transcendental Analytic" was to establish the synthetic *a priori* character of scientific knowledge. His exposition here was confused by its traditional logical involvements, but it yielded a statement of some basic conclusions. Kant was convinced that the intelligent mind and the intelligible order of nature reveal each other, and make each other possible through the process of experience. The mind's fundamental forms of judgment, and the forms of organization in the world of our experience— logical order and cosmological order—are thus correlative. They reveal and reflect each other. Kant explored and presented in schematic detail this mutual correspondence by constructing the logical table of judgments and the table of the pure concepts, or categories of the understanding. He arranged each table under the four heads of quantity, quality, relation, and modality, as follows: [2]

TABLE OF JUDGMENTS	TABLE OF CATEGORIES
I. *Quantity*	I. *Quantity*
Universal	Unity
Particular	Plurality
Singular	Totality
II. *Quality*	II. *Quality*
Affirmative	Reality
Negative	Negation
Infinite	Limitation
III. *Relation*	III. *Relation*
Categorical	Substance and Accident
Hypothetical	Cause and Effect
Disjunctive	Community or Reciprocity

[2] *Ibid.*, pp. 58, 66 f.

IV. *Modality*	IV. *Modality*
Problematical	Possibility or Impossibility
Assertory	Existence or Nonexistence
Apodictic	Necessity or Contingency

It is readily apparent that this tabulation is incomplete. Should he not have considered similarity and difference, identity and contradiction? Would a more comprehensive list have upset the schematic balance of his fourfold table of threes? In any case, is it possible to draw up a really complete table of categories? Ten for Aristotle and twelve for Kant—their number has varied and will vary with the progressive scientific interpretation of nature. The significance of genetic categories in the biological sciences is an instance of this flexibility of tabulation. Furthermore, the categories or types of organization in nature are not of the same significance. As we shall see, causality was the principal category in Kant's interpretation of scientific knowledge. The important point here is not the detailed execution of the above two tables, but their parallelism, the mutual correspondence of logical and cosmological order.

A very difficult part of Kant's analytic, which he modified in the second edition of the book for reasons that are not very clear, is the so-called "transcendental deduction of the categories." He was undertaking to trace "the conditions *a priori* of the possibility of experience."[3] His account of the forms of space and time in the process of sense perception pointed to the first stage in the organization of experience which attains knowledge, the "synthesis of apprehension." The time form is essential to this synthesis. By distinguishing the temporal succession of our impressions, we perceive and hold them together.

The perceptual unity clearly requires, not only the sense impression of the moment, but also the retention, in memory, of past sensations. This power of reproducing past experiences becomes a reconstructive process in the imagination. Kant called it the "synthesis of reproduction," but he also regarded it as really productive. By evoking past impressions, the process recombines them and weaves the data of perception into various patterns. Through this reconstructive power, "an art hidden in the depth of the human soul,"[4] we become capable of organized experience and knowledge.

The capacity of intelligence is explicitly realized in the third synthesis, "recognition in concepts." In this "unity of apperception," the content of consciousness is integrated into an intelligible system. The mind is now aware of itself grasping the elements of experience in a significant unity. We express the meaning of this unity to ourselves in a concept. Consciousness becomes apperceptive, self-consciousness; a subject knows of its experience of objects.

[3] *Ibid.*, p. 78.
[4] *Ibid.*, p. 116. See also p. 97.

The progressively realized unity of consciousness through these three syntheses is a condition for the possibility of knowledge. In the pure concepts or categories of the understanding, the knowing mind is revealed to itself as is the system of nature which it knows. Physical nature is a world of experience, a world in which the logic of the mind reflects categories of reality, and a world in which the data of sense experience engage the synthesizing activity of the mind.

The synthesis of the imagination not only connects the senses with the understanding, but also colors our conceptual representations. This imaged, or pictured, version of the categories was presented by Kant in his "Schematism of the Understanding." This part of his work has been depreciated by some critics; he conformed too stiffly to his former tabulation—quantity, quality, relation, modality—but, in his exposition, he brought out his characteristic interpretation of nature. The general conclusion toward which his thought was moving in this so-called "analytic of principles" is that physical nature is a causal continuum. Such a view excluded or resisted any rigid atomism as well as the doctrines of empty space, chance, and miracles.

The general conclusion of Kant's theory of knowledge emphasized the dominance of the category of causality. The world of which we have scientific knowledge is a necessarily connected world in space and time, a causal system in which every event is conditioned by some prior event. Every new experience expands the causal nexus and perfects our knowledge of the system.

In his answer to Hume, Kant vindicated scientific knowledge, but he also limited it to the objects of experience. These objects are not "things-in-themselves"; they are phenomena, experienced objects, and, in this sense, they are ideas. But Kant distinguished his view from Berkeley's, which he thought implied the denial of reality to objects. Kant maintained that our experience must be the experience of something; he expressed it as the "transcendental object = x." But this transcendental object, or implied objective reference, is not to be identified offhand with the thing-in-itself. We recognize that there are things-in-themselves, but we do not cognize them; we do not know what they are except as they appear in our experience of them. All we know is the content of our experience; the "transcendental object = x" is a pure concept expressing our conviction that our experience must be the experience of something, of an object. Kant called this pure concept a *noumenon*, but he was not uniform in his use of the term. In its negative sense, a noumenon signified what is not the object of sense perception. But Kant also used *noumenon* in a positive sense to connote the object of nonsensible intuition. This latter use of the word is not very clear. It is in the negative sense that Kant's theory requires the term *noumenon* as a limiting concept. His theory of knowledge was called "phenomenalism." It maintained that all our scientific knowledge is of phenomena—that is, of the objects of possible experience in their systematic organization under the categories of the understanding. We have no knowledge of noumena, of

objects beyond the reach of experience. The strength of the scientific understanding lies in maintaining its firm ground within the scope of experience.
This is Kant's doctrine of the critical limitation of scientific knowledge.

But human reason does not remain content with our reliable scientific
knowledge of the world of experience. It ventures to formulate doctrines
of reality beyond the scope or test of experience, and, thus, it becomes involved in the quandaries of rationalistic metaphysics. These predicaments of
rationalism were examined by Kant in the second half of the *Critique of
Pure Reason* called "Transcendental Dialectic."

Reason insists on raising problems concerning the ultimate reality of
things, of things-in-themselves, beyond the mental representation of them;
and also concerning the nature of the mind in itself, apart from its perceptions and concepts. The self-conscious mind that we know is the unity of
apperception in the process of experience. But is there not a thinking soul
substance that has its ideas and also transcends them, now and in eternity?
The world of our experience is a system of causally connected events. Does
this preclude any ultimate spontaneity and freedom? What can we know
about the universe itself? Is it finite or infinite in space and time? Is it
infinitely divisible or is it composed of ultimately irreducible particles? Is
the natural order of things evidence of an eternal, infinite, creative Being?
These questions proceed from the three "transcendental Ideas" of the soul
and its immortality, the world totality and freedom, and God. Evidently
Kant was here subjecting to criticism the Wolffian doctrines of rational
psychology, rational cosmology, and rational theology. To these three doctrines, he devoted the three parts of his "Dialectic," entitling them, respectively, the "Paralogism," the "Antinomy," and "Ideal of Pure Reason." His
general conclusion was that it is beyond the competence of our mind to deal
with the problems raised by these ideas. Our reason can neither prove nor
disprove God, freedom, immortality.

Taking up, first, rational psychology, Kant maintained that pure reason
is involved here in a paralogism or confusion of ideas. The active unity of
self-consciousness is confusedly regarded as implying a unitary soul substance. This is defined as a metaphysically simple entity, and its uncom-
pounded character is interpreted to preclude decomposition. It is therefore
imperishable, an immortally self-identical person, itself real amid the ideality
of all its perceptions. The notions of the soul's substantiality, simplicity, and
personality, and the ideality of its experiences, are all confused, paralogisms.
The only self of which we have any knowledge is the unity of self-consciousness; it is the self, or mind, of experience. Therefore, no valid scientific
or theoretical proof of personal immortality is available.

The rational cosmology, in contemplating the world totality, involves
reason in conflicts with itself, which Kant called antinomies. He exposed
four such conflicts vividly by presenting on opposite pages the contrary
arguments of reason in dealing with four ultimate problems. Thus in the
first antinomy we have the thesis: "The world has a beginning in time, and

is limited also with regard to space," and the antithesis: "The world has no beginning in time and no limits in space, but is infinite, in respect both to time and space."[5] Kant presented the two conflicting sets of arguments, both plausible, neither one of them conclusive or valid. Rejecting both dogmatic extremes, he held that the spatial and temporal regress in nature is neither infinite nor finite, but indefinite—not assignable. The solution of the problem as stated by reason is beyond our competence.

Kant reached the same kind of conclusion in examining the second antinomy. Here the thesis regards the universe as ultimately composed of simple, indivisible parts, and the antithesis denies any such atomism and admits no limit to divisibility. Again he maintained that there is no assignable limit to the analysis of compounds; the regress here also is indefinite.

The third and fourth antinomies were treated differently. The third concerns the free production of events in nature. The thesis affirms this. The antithesis denies any such spontaneity and upholds the causal necessity of all events in nature. Kant granted the validity of the antithesis in the world of phenomena with which physical science is concerned. But he allowed that we may entertain freedom as a principle in certain ultimate realms beyond the province of science. Freedom, which Kant here admitted only as a possible notion, he was later to maintain firmly as a postulate of morality.

The fourth antinomy is an extension of the third; it also anticipates the cosmological argument for God's existence. The principle at issue concerns the reality of an absolutely necessary Being, either as a part of the world or as a cause of it. This the thesis affirms; the antithesis rejects this idea and maintains that every being is relatively necessary, causally determined by something else, and so on indefinitely in the world of which we have knowledge. Here again, Kant admitted the scientific position of the antithesis, but also conceded the idea of an absolutely necessary Being in an ultimate, spiritual perspective.

Kant's "Ideal of Pure Reason" is a criticism of the principal theoretical arguments advanced by rational theology to prove the existence of God. He reduced these traditional proofs to three kinds: the ontological, the cosmological, and the physico-theological, and he maintained the impossibility of proving God's existence by them.

The ontological argument advanced by St. Anselm was examined by Kant with special reference to its advocacy by Descartes and Leibniz. In his earlier days, Kant had regarded this argument as the only possible ground for a demonstration of God's existence, but he revised this conviction. To maintain, as the ontological proof does, that the most perfect Being must necessarily exist is to regard existence as a predicate of perfection to be elicited from it by conceptual analysis. Kant regarded this as fallacious: "Whatever . . . our concept of an object may contain, we must always step outside it, in order to attribute to it existence."[6] It is not by analyzing

[5] *Ibid.*, pp. 344 ff.
[6] *Ibid.*, pp. 484 f.

my concept of a hundred dollars that I can really learn whether or not I have them in my pocket. Existential judgments are synthetic; they depend on actual experience, not on formal analysis. The rationalist might reply that the example of a hundred dollars is irrelevant, as was the perfect island which the monk Gaunilo used as an example against Anselm. That is to say, the idea of God is not an idea of a particular being presented in sense perception, but an idea of the supreme reality, evident to reason. In his criticism, Kant reaffirmed his critical limitation of knowledge within the framework of experience.

The cosmological argument, like the thesis in the fourth antinomy, infers the existence of an absolutely necessary Being from the relatively necessary or contingent character of all particular things in nature. This is the so-called "first cause" argument. Kant criticized this argument for its misuse of causal reasoning. The inference from effects to causes applies only in dealing with particular events in nature and "has not even a meaning outside it."[7] Cause and effect are correlative terms; each ascertained cause in nature must in its turn be considered as the effect of another cause. Therefore, so long as we reason in causal terms, we cannot proceed validly to an unconditioned first cause. Kant admitted that the ideal of a supreme Being remains as a regulative principle of reason; we should consider the order of events in nature as having an ultimate absolute ground of cause. But this regulative principle, he maintained, should not be changed into a constitutive one by asserting the actual existence of the absolutely necessary Being.

The proof which Kant called "physico-theological" is the teleological, the argument from design in nature. It surveys the purposive order and the clear indications of intelligent operation throughout the world and regards them as evidence that not blind nature, but a sublime and wise Author directs the course of existence. Are we then warranted in inferring from such reasoning that God is the Author and Creator of the world? By such proof we could at most conclude only a world Architect; the argument from design could not prove more than the existence of a Designer. Even if valid, this proof would not be adequate for theology; it must be sustained by the cosmological proof, just as the latter, in turn, must rest ultimately on the ontological argument. In thus emphasizing the ontological argument, Kant was, in a way, reaffirming the conclusion of his earlier treatise with the addition of a radical proviso: It is the only possible proof—that is, if any theoretical proof of God's existence is possible at all.

It must be noted that Kant did not regard his criticisms of the arguments for God's existence as a warrant for an atheistic conclusion. Speculative reason cannot prove God's existence; neither can it disprove it. The general outcome of Kant's entire dialectic is to show that God, freedom, and immortality are ideas beyond the competence of speculative reason. In his destructive critique of rationalism, Kant thus reached the same position he had established constructively in his analytic, as a reply to Hume's challenge

---

[7] *Ibid.*, p. 491.

to scientific knowledge. Science is concerned with the system of nature, a system of causally connected events in space and time. In this self-limitation to phenomena, to the world of possible experience, lies the validity of scientific knowledge.

So much for science. But what of morality, or art, or religion? To say that physical science does not require them and cannot include them need not mean that they are to be dismissed altogether. It may mean that physical science is not the only possible interpretation of reality. Unlike the specialized problem of science, the problem of philosophy is comprehensive. Kant realized that his dialectic had not utterly disposed of God, freedom, and immortality. He was convinced that they would have to be reconsidered in a spiritual perspective of ideals and values. And this additional perspective could not be ignored. The reality of the moral law and duty was no less imperative to Kant than the validity of scientific knowledge. His critical philosophy demanded a theory of ethics, art, and religion, just as it required a vindication of science.

Kant's Moral Philosophy

Kant's thought, from its earliest development, was dominated by two convictions which he was bound to explain and to correlate: the validity of scientific knowledge and the authority of the moral law. Newtonian physics and Pietistic earnestness provided the contending motives in his reflections.

The Pietists combined devout moral and religious feeling with dogmatic formalism in their theology. Early in his schooling, Kant had reacted against this stiff doctrine, but the moral fervor of the Pietists had not ceased to move him, and so he was naturally impressed by the ethics of sentiment. The study of Shaftesbury, Hume, and Rousseau confirmed some of his own early moral convictions. The goodness of an action and the perfection of character cannot be conceived in terms of any external results or advantages. They are the expressions of the inner worth of any man. Kant remembered the high spiritual qualities revealed in the lives of his parents, a poor saddler and his humble wife. Moral insight reaches beyond externals. It demands a feeling of respect for the personal dignity of all men.

But the ethics of sentiment could not satisfy Kant's demands. He resisted the hedonistic strains in Hume and Shaftesbury. And, while Rousseau had stirred Kant by his moral-democratic recognition of plain human dignity, and by his exaltation of the inner loyalty to conscience, he was too perfervid to satisfy Kant's reflective character. The earnest feeling of loyalty which Kant emphasized had to be a loyalty to imperative principles. His view of the moral ideal was moving from an emotional to a rational perspective. He had rejected the abstract formulas of dogmatic rationalism, but he could not remain content with mere emotional ardor, no matter how lofty it might be. He sought a rational conviction of duty beyond Rousseau's transports of conscience. In ethics, as in the theory of knowledge, Kant's thought advanced by a criticism of contending alternatives, toward a more significant reconstruction.

Kant's lectures on ethics at Königsberg, given for almost twoscore years, reflected the gradual development of his moral philosophy. We can study this doctrine as it approached its perfected statement in the volume, *Lectures on Ethics*, compiled and edited from three students' notebooks which, happily, have been preserved. In some of his earlier works, Kant had interested himself in descriptive ethics, the historical survey of actual human behavior. But he became convinced that true ethics is concerned only with duties and moral ideals—what ought to be done. The moral imperative is not a technical requirement of providing the means needed to realize some end, nor is it a prudential obligation to use the means to the general end of happiness. The moral imperative legislates universally, irrespective of any particular expediency or advantages; it is inherently authoritative and worthy of respect.

This moral law is the essential and supreme standard; by appealing to it, we can settle particular moral issues. Specific virtues like fidelity and benevolence may be convincingly derived from it. Kant's classroom lectures indicate his very real interest in applied ethics, both personally and in the various social relations of life. His emphasis on the beauty and dignity of personal worth is exemplified in his exposition of friendship, in his critical discussion of truthfulness, in his advocacy of religious tolerance, freedom of belief, and critical investigation.

The dutiful moral will is not moved by any considerations of selfish regard. It is disinterested, and its moral worth can be tested by an appeal to universality; what it wills for itself it is rationally prepared to will for all men. Dutiful actions performed in this spirit yield high satisfaction, but their end and purpose is not happiness. They express pure devotion to the moral ideal, and their true fulfillment is in the perfection of the dutiful will itself. Kant's fuller expression of these principles was presented in his *Foundations of the Metaphysics of Morals* (1785) and the *Critique of Practical Reason* (1788). To these may be added the later work, *Metaphysics of Morals* (1797).

Kant required of his reader critical understanding of his works; "Don't read my book; think it."[8] He is said to have stopped lecturing when he heard the scratch of his students' pens, preferring to have them ponder on his ideas, not merely to take down his words. We should heed his warning when we study his ethics, especially when we read the *Critique of Practical Reason*. Kant entangled his exposition by forcing it into the schematic framework of the *Critique of Pure Reason*, to which he resolutely adhered. Once more he must have his doctrine of elements and his methodology, an analytic and a dialectic, with its antinomy, of course! We shall follow Kant's own advice

[8] On Kant's method in teaching, *cf.* E. Caird, *The Critical Philosophy of Kant*, 2nd ed., Glasgow, Maclehose, 1909, Vol. I, p. 60.

and consider his basic ethical ideas, not retrace his conceptual diagrams.

There are two fundamental relations between the second and the first *Critique* which should be kept in mind: the analogy between their respective problems, and the raising of the second problem by Kant's solution of the first. In the *Critique of Pure Reason*, Kant had asked, How is science possible? How should we interpret the nature of the mind and of the world in the process of experience, so as to explain the possibility of universally valid knowledge? An analogous problem confronted Kant's ethics: How is morality possible? First of all, in what does moral action consist, and second, what larger interpretation does morality imply, of man as a moral agent and of the world of moral values?

The question of the character and possibility of moral action had been emphasized by Kant's conclusions in his theory of knowledge. The world, as science knows it, is a world of causal connections, and, in it, men and their behavior must be considered as in each case determined by necessary antecedent conditions. This account of human nature and conduct would constitute simply another descriptive and explanatory science, anthropology. Kant did not by any means ignore or depreciate it. His lectures on anthropology attracted wide attention, and he also pursued the related subject of man's historical-cultural development. Factual knowledge of people and peoples, he was sure, would safeguard the moral philosopher from entanglement in abstract notions. But such factual knowledge would not yield a genuine ethics. After learning how people behave and have behaved in the past, we still face the real questions: How *ought* we to act? What makes an action morally good, the right thing to do?

Moral goodness, according to Kant, could not depend upon any external empirical condition, or upon the eventual consequences of an act. A person is not good because he is charitably inclined, or bad because he is emotionally callous. These are empirical qualities. Some metals corrode more easily than others; some men are more easily affected than others. Nor is an act morally good because it yields pleasure, bad because it is unpleasant. These are consequences often beyond our control; they cannot provide a standard for comparative appraisal. Goodness must be in the quality of will, in the principle on which we act.

Kant expressed his basic idea of morality in the first sentence of his *Foundations:* "Nothing can possibly . . . be called good, without qualification, except a Good Will."[9] By a "Good Will," Kant did not mean any emotional inclination, nor what are loosely called "good intentions." A good will signified to him an upright will, a will acting solely on the right principle. This disinterested loyalty to essential rightness he regarded as fundamental to morality, the spirit of duty imperative in action. Not the aim to achieve a certain result, but single-minded rectitude is decisive in moral conduct.

[9] Immanuel Kant, *Critique of Practical Reason and Other Works on the Theory of Ethics* (trans. T. K. Abbott), 6th ed., London, Longmans, 1909, p. 9.

"Duty," Kant declared, "is the *necessity of acting from respect for the law*."[10] And mere conformity to the moral law does not suffice; one must act not only *as* duty requires, but also *because* duty requires. Respect for the moral law does not mean achnowledgment of any specific requirement or duty, but is pure unqualified uprightness. It cannot, therefore, be affected by any particular or individual considerations; it has its essential worth, it is entitled to universal adoption. This is Kant's maxim or test of a moral action: "I am never to act otherwise than so *that I could also will that my maxim should become a universal law*."[11] In proclaiming the pure dutiful respect for the moral law as the essence of morality, Kant recognized in moral obligation a new kind of necessity, different from the causal necessity analyzed in his vindication of scientific knowledge. Laws of nature express relative necessity, the dependence of a certain event on certain determining conditions. So with practical affairs of expediency: if we want a certain result we must provide the requisite means. Kant called all such laws and determinants *hypothetical imperatives*. Lock your doors at night, put on your gloves, avoid rich food, pay your bills. To all these precepts, an *if* is attached. But, when we consider a moral behest to tell the truth, the obligation is unconditional. Here there is no qualifying *if;* should we ask the question *why*, we would only be exposing our moral deficiency. Therefore, Kant called the moral law a *categorical imperative*, the unqualified obligation of pure duty.

The moral man exemplifies in his choice the unconditional, imperative worthiness of the right, and thus he himself expresses inviolable moral dignity. This principle, which is of vital importance in all social ethics, is formulated by Kant as a second version of the moral law: "*So act as to treat humanity, whether in thine own person or in that of any other, in every case as an end withal, never as means only*."[12] Human beings are not to be treated as bare instruments of profit or pleasure, as merely means to private advantage of any sort; for man is not mere goods to be utilized; he is capable of goodness, he is to be respected in his own right and dignity as a person. The worth of persons is not relative and replaceable, as the utility value of things in nature; it is like the obligation of the moral law, unconditional and absolute. This principle must be the moral basis of all social order and all social reform. But it is also a principle of moral self-respect, an ethical piety essential to virtue. In acting from pure respect for duty, a man is himself the spokesman of the law which he fulfills. He is both subject and legislator. Kant formulated this conviction as the third main principle of his ethics: The moral will is universally self-legislative.

After considering Kant's ethical exposition without critical interruption, we may inquire into the adequacy of Kant's formal maxim, his appeal to

10 *Ibid.*, p. 16.
11 *Ibid.*, p. 18.
12 *Ibid.*, p. 47.

universality. And we should consider what his recognition of the categorical imperative implies regarding his view of human nature and of the world in which man is active morally.

By his maxim of universality, Kant rightly intended to distinguish a genuinely moral choice from a pursuit of mere expediency. But his statement was too formal; in its strict form, it emptied morality of all content in experience. Actually, Kant was not so strict; in several specific demonstrations of his principle, despite his basic disavowal of appeal to consequences, he perforce considered the self-confuting operation of wrong maxims in long-range experience. In actual experience, the selfish dismissal of charity, though we all disapprove of it, can scarcely be refuted as self-contradictory. On the other hand, a formal appeal to universality will not enable us to disown morally the anarchist, the assassin, and the promiscuous free-lover, who may themselves be acting on principle and who may wish to make their practices universal. How is the pure ethics of duty to be cleared of any possible imputation of fanaticism? This is, of course, an old problem of the ethics of conscience. Kant would meet the difficulty by maintaining that the fanatic's maxim cannot rationally be universalized; but if, by this, we are not to beg the question, we must appeal to moral experience that reaches beyond Kant's formalism. Kant pointed a way out of these difficulties, in both personal and social morality, by his principle of moral respect for men's inviolable personal worth and dignity. But this idea, capital in ethics, was not developed sufficiently by him.

The second question we raised concerns a problem in the metaphysics of morals. If we take morality seriously, to mean moral action as Kant understood it, what view of a person is implied in our moral judgment of his acts? This problem becomes the more emphatic the loftier is our conception of Kantian morality. Kant himself faced this challenge in his famous apotheosis of duty, which we may regard as the climax of his moral aspiration and the acknowledgment of his philosophical demand:

Duty! Thou sublime and mighty name that dost embrace nothing charming or insinuating, but requirest submission, and yet seekest not to move the will by threatening aught that would arouse natural aversion or terror, but merely holdest forth a law which of itself finds entrance into the mind, and yet gains reluctant reverence (though not always obedience), a law before which all inclinations are dumb, even though they secretly counter-work it; what origin is there worthy of thee, and where is to be found the root of thy noble descent which proudly rejects all kindred with the inclinations; a root to be derived from which is the indispensable condition of the only worth which men can give themselves? [13]

In answering his questions, Kant was led to the doctrine that freedom, immortality, and God are "postulates of pure practical reason," fundamentally implied in any serious recognition of moral agents and moral activity. The first postulate of morality is freedom. The unconditional and universal obligation of duty can be respected only by a person acting on principle,

13 Ibid., p. 180.

that is, freely and responsibly. The idea of freedom which, as we have seen, speculative reason could only entertain is espoused by practical reason to express the essential character of a moral agent. The moral activity of persons reveals an aspect and a prospect of reality beyond the causal framework of scientific knowledge. As members of the world of nature, men are subject to physical necessity. But, as moral beings acting on principle, men are free members of a "realm of ends," a world of values and ideals. The two other moral postulates, personal immortality and the reality of God, connect Kant's ethics with his philosophy of religion; we shall consider them in the next section.

This recognition of man as a free moral agent corresponds to the vindication of the scientific view of nature in the *Critique of Pure Reason*. In both cases, Kant achieved a philosophical conception of a cosmic order. The causal mechanism of nature and of human nature, considered from the standpoint of physical science, does not warrant any unqualified materialism. On the contrary, by his doctrine of the critical limitation of scientific knowledge, Kant ruled out materialistic metaphysics even as he ruled out speculative dogmatic theology. The moral activity of people reveals the character and range of the spiritual world of values. On this note of a twofold contemplation of universal order, Kant concluded his *Critique of Practical Reason*:

Two things fill the mind with ever new and increasing admiration and awe, the oftener and the more steadily we reflect on them: *the starry heavens above and the moral law within*. . . . The former view of a countless multitude of worlds annihilates, as it were, my importance as an *animal creature*. . . . The second, on the contrary, infinitely elevates my worth as an *intelligence* by my personality.[14]

Kant's Philosophy of Religion

Kant's ethics and his philosophy of religion are closely related. When thoroughly interpreted, morality is shown to have religious implications, while religion must have its true basis and motivation in moral activity. Two fundamental religious convictions, the belief in God and in immortality, were regarded by Kant as postulates of morality. He proposed to restore through ethical argument the convictions he had unsettled by his criticisms in the "Transcendental Dialectic."

Kant gave two moral proofs of immortality and of God which derive from his interpretation of the highest good. We may regard the *summum bonum* as the supreme good, meaning virtue, perfection in dutiful activity; or as the complete and consummated good, meaning virtue prevailing and triumphant. The virtuous will does not aim at happiness, but it is worthy

[14] *Ibid.*, p. 260.

of happiness, and, in a rational universe, it should attain it. This consummation is not realized in this life, and, hence, we are warranted in expecting it in the hereafter. This belief in immortality implies a belief in God as the infinite judge and director of men's moral destinies in eternity. Kant's revised versions of the old arguments for divine retribution are stated in more rigorously moral terms, but they do not overcome the radical difficulties of the traditional proofs. The reader who has been convinced by Kant's ethics of the purely disinterested pursuit of virtue is disturbed by this discussion of the forthcoming emoluments of righteousness. He may recall Hume's doubts whether any men are good or bad enough to deserve or to need eternal retribution, and he may question whether, by this sort of argument, we can get either a religiously adequate conception of God or a really eternal view of the divine activity.

Kant's further reasoning on this subject was far more significant. His argument now proceeded from his deeper interpretation of the implications of the ethics of duty. What every true moral act really aims to achieve is moral perfection, the complete dominance of moral reason over all the inclinations and impediments of sense. Morally speaking, the will endeavors to become perfect and holy; but this perfection cannot be consummated in any finite career. Immortality, therefore, is postulated as the eternal, ideal progress essential to moral activity. Furthermore, the dutiful commitment of the moral will points to the eternal ideal reality of infinite perfection. This is our moral conviction of God. It may be remarked that the recognition of the implicit demand for perfect moral attainment raises difficulties in an ethics which conceives of moral good as essentially involved in the struggle of duty with inclination. In seeking to overcome these and other difficulties, later thought has been led toward an active or dynamic view of perfection, human or divine, as infinite perfectibility, which has far-reaching implications for the philosophy of religion.

The argument Kant stated in moral terms may be expressed in terms of other spiritual values which are likewise eternal-infinite in prospect. Kant's merit and great influence in modern critical theology have been in the central emphasis he gave to values in his religious thought.

Religion within the Limits of Mere Reason (1793), the late work of Kant's full maturity, is a radical reinterpretation of religion and, more specifically, of the central Christian beliefs, in terms of his characteristic emphasis on moral values. According to him, the basis and heart of religion is the conviction of the moral direction and perspective of the world. Kant depreciated the reliance on revelation and on supernatural, miraculous intervention in the processes of nature as evidences of God. The Kingdom of God is within us; the divine is truly manifest in our moral career, in our dutiful self-dedication to infinite perfection. Rigid conformity to orthodox doctrine should not be exacted of an active mind as an essential of religious communion; nor should any external observances and ceremonial forms usurp the important role of virtuous conduct.

Yet religion is not to be identified offhand with morality. In his religious outlook, man views his moral activity in a divine perspective. "Religion, subjectively considered, is the recognition of all our duties as divine commands."[15] But this religious-divine orientation of our moral thinking involves us in the problem of evil. Though religious conviction may not depend on a rational theology, it demands a theodicy. How are we to account for man's evil corruption in the spiritual world of values? Evil must affect more than our sensuous nature, yet it cannot be a real expression of our rationality. Sin as a defection of reason is conditioned by the activity of the rational will in the phenomenal world of impulses and inclinations. The story of the original fall is a pictorial statement of man's empirical character.

The ideal of perfection as rational emancipation from the chains of sensuality finds Christian expression in the doctrine of redemption. Kant's interpretation of salvation proceeds from his ethical conviction that, while we should promote the happiness of others, each of us must pursue and achieve perfection himself. The traditional doctrine of divine grace, in his judgment, requires revision, according to the closing sentence of his book: "The right way is not from the divine grace to virtue, but from virtue to the divine grace."[16] The Christian Church under divine providence is the communion of saints dedicated to perfection. In its historical development, it has been an organized society of persons striving to do the right, and urging each other's good endeavor by profession and example. The ritualistic-ecclesiastical framework of this common spiritual life has, of course, its historical motives and explanation, but Kant regarded it as inessential. Imperative is our resolution to "do the will of [our] Father which is in heaven."[17] We are to live our lives, not as if limited and bound to the world of physical necessity, but as free members of the ideal world of values—to live our lives as if God and immortality were real.

Kant's Aesthetic Theory

Kant regarded a critical theory of art as part of his philosophical program. By a "critique of taste," he hoped to relate the natural system of causal necessity to the realm of moral freedom, to the world of facts, and to the world of ideals. Aesthetic taste expresses a judgment of something "as it should be," corresponding to the "must" of causality and the "ought" of the moral law. Kant undertook to trace the *a priori* principles of this aesthetic appreciation. This is, in part, the theme of his *Critique of Judgment* (1790). As in his second *Critique*, so in this third one, Kant forced his ideas into the

[15] Translated from Immanuel Kant, *Religion Within the Bounds of Mere Reason*, in *Kant's Werke*, Prussian Academy ed., Berlin, Reimer, Vol. VI, 1914, p. 153.
[16] *Ibid.*, closing sentence.
[17] Matthew 7:21 (Revised Standard Version).

abstract framework of his theory of knowledge, including a fourfold "Analytic of the Beautiful" under the respective heads of "Quality," "Quantity," "Relation," and "Modality," and a dialectic with its antinomy of the beautiful. The merit of his aesthetic ideas is more evident, however, if they are examined less schematically.

The object called "beautiful" is judged to give rise to disinterested delight. This aesthetic delight differs from empirical pleasure and from moral approval. The aesthetic judgment is not concerned with any use or advantage, nor is it a deduction from any concept. Since it is not due to any peculiar desires, the object judged beautiful is regarded as universally delightful. Hence, we are apt to speak of beauty as objective, apart from the subjective judgment of taste. I need not expect you to share my preference in foods, but in judging that anything is beautiful I intend to express a delight which I expect to be shared universally. This appeal to universality implies a certain necessity; though not everyone will do so, surely all *should* judge this to be beautiful.

The three "moments" of quality, quantity, and modality are already evident in this brief account. The aspect of relation is of special interest as it indicates Kant's aesthetic outlook on reality. According to Kant, "Beauty is the form of *finality* in an object, so far as perceived in it *apart from the representation of an end.*"[18] The aesthetic view of things is somehow teleological, but it has no reference to any specific goal; it manifests a sort of purposiveness without purpose. Beauty engages our evaluative activity, but the pursuit of it, disinterested, seeks no specific accomplishment; it is free, a holiday self-expression, content in its delight.

In his examination of aesthetic values, Kant analyzed the idea of sublimity. He distinguished the mathematical from the dynamic sublime; the former is the sublime of vast magnitude in space and time, the latter is the sublime of overmastering power. The aesthetic contemplation of the sublime humbles our short-fingered sensibility; but it also evokes the reaffirmation of reason, particularly its moral pursuit of the ideal, infinite, eternal, and irresistible.

The greatness of Kant's philosophy is to be measured, not by the technical and specific adequacy of his doctrines, but by the depth and fertile significance of the problems which he raised. Some of the doctrines he subjected to criticism were in their way more consistent than his own; but they were onesided and insufficient. Kant attacked the philosophical problems thoroughly, full front and flank; his criticism brought out principles and difficulties which no thorough thinker after him could ignore. In this way, his work signalized a new philosophic epoch. Through the *Critique of Pure Reason*, modern philosophy transcended the abstract limitations of both rationalism and empiricism. Though we may not find in Kant's conclusions regarding ethics the one definitive system of morals, any modern ethics that

18 Immanuel Kant, *Critique of Aesthetic Judgment* (trans. J. C. Meredith), Oxford, Clarendon Press, 1911, p. 80.

ignores his principles must appear shallow. True further progress in ethics has been possible, not outside the course he pursued, but through it and beyond it.

A thinker of such critical thoroughness and such stimulating power as Kant was bound to raise more problems than he solved or even faced. After him, the formulation of a philosophical system was a more deeply significant, but also a more difficult, undertaking. In Germany first of all, but also throughout western thought, his influence is seen in the resistance he aroused as well as in the development of his ideas by his followers and in their further original reconstructions.

SUGGESTED WORKS FOR FURTHER STUDY

LESSING. Sime, James, *Lessing*.

WORKS BY KANT. Kant, I., *Critique of Pure Reason* (trans. F. Max Müller, N. K. Smith); *Prolegomena to Any Future Metaphysics* (trans. L. W. Beck); *Lectures on Ethics* (trans. L. Infield); *Critique of Practical Reason and Other Works on the Theory of Ethics* (trans. T. K. Abbott); *Critique of Practical Reason and Other Writings in Moral Philosophy* (trans. L. W. Beck); *The Moral Law* (trans. H. J. Paton); *Critique of Judgment* (trans. J. H. Bernard); *Critique of Aesthetic Judgment* and *Critique of Teleological Judgment* (trans. J. C. Meredith); *Religion Within the Boundary of Mere Reason* (trans. J. Semple); *Immanuel Kant's Religion within the Limits of Reason Alone* (trans. T. M. Greene); and *Selections* (T. M. Greene, ed.).

BIOGRAPHIES AND CRITICAL STUDIES. Adamson, Robert, *On the Philosophy of Kant;* Caird, Edward, *The Critical Philosophy of Immanuel Kant;* Lindsay, A. D., *Kant;* Paton, H. J., *The Categorical Imperative;* Paulsen, Friedrich, *Immanuel Kant;* Prichard, H. A., *Kant's Theory of Knowledge;* Schilpp, P. A., *Kant's Pre-Critical Ethics;* Smith, Norman Kemp, *A Commentary to Kant's Critique of Pure Reason;* Wallace, William, *Kant;* Webb, C. C. J., *Kant's Philosophy of Religion;* Wenley, R. M., *Kant and His Philosophical Revolution*.

26. The German Idealists After Kant

The Critical Reactions to Kant

Kant's philosophy rapidly became the crossroads of German thought. It found both opponents and constructive critics; the influence of Kant's critical spirit expressed itself through the manifold efforts to supplement and to revise his own solutions of the problems on which he had centered philosophical thought. These problems were both theoretical and practical. The basic concern of Kant's successors was the relation of experience to reality. In limiting knowledge to the world of phenomena, the causal network of nature, was Kant, after all, conceding Hume's main point? Can we ask, but in no way answer, questions concerning ultimate reality, the thing-in-itself? Kant had unsettled the theoretical metaphysics of rationalism, but had reestablished its ultimate ideas of God, freedom, and immortality as postulates of morality, and he had proclaimed the primacy of moral reason in the settlement of ultimate philosophical issues. Does this position signify a definitely idealistic metaphysics, so that, in living our lives as if God, freedom, and immortality were real, we may be said to reach the heart of reality? Between a phenomenalism that resisted a skeptical outlook and an idealism that inspired metaphysical ventures in various new directions, Kant's successors explored the many resources of the human spirit in reaching a finality of philosophical conviction. Yet Kant aroused opposition among many who felt that his philosophy spurned the demand of the heart for the intimate certainties of faith.

Johann Georg Hamann (1730–1788) was a man of turbid passions and mystical yearnings. He was repelled by cold reason and he disdained its analysis and principles; he also scorned the scientific understanding which chewed its causal cud. According to Hamann, the whole tenor of the eighteenth-century Enlightenment—empiricism and rationalism alike—could yield only distortions of the truth and misleading dualisms of sense and intellect, nature and spirit, human and divine, reason and revelation. Against factual evidence and logical proofs, he cherished the mystical assurance of the heart.

Like Kant, a native of Königsberg, Hamann called himself "the Magus of the North." His philosophy was meant to be, not piecemeal knowledge, but the wisdom which God grants to those who believe with utter devotion, with a divine passion.

A far more reasonable advocate of the philosophy of feeling was Johann Gottfried von Herder (1744–1803). At Königsberg, he had been deeply influenced by Kant's lectures, but also by Hamann's spirit. Later, in Weimar, his aesthetic taste was cultivated by his association with Goethe. Because his logical intelligence and his poetic and religious emotions all demanded satisfaction, his philosophy of life was an attempted reconciliation of these contending motives; it was mainly sentimental in emphasis, but it intended to pay due tribute to natural facts and historical evidence.

Herder's strength lay, not in systematic philosophy, but in historical-cultural interpretation. His principal work, *Ideas for the Philosophy of History of Mankind*, aimed to trace humanity's march toward civilization and spiritual fulfillment. In man's progressive mastery of his physical environment, as the higher spiritual powers find expression in social institutions, in science and philosophy, in art, poetry, and religion, nature itself reveals its deeper meaning and directs the soul to God. Rejecting any doctrine of the final duality of the physical and spiritual, Herder sought a cosmic synthesis that would satisfy the demands of faith. He approached Spinoza's monism, but with a mystical emphasis. Certain of the spiritual purport of existence, he endeavored to express it in convincing naturalistic terms, as physical and mental facts, ideal significance. In nature, as in culture, he felt that the divine purpose is progressively being realized. This realization has no assignable limits, for, beyond any present achievement, history can contemplate the infinite prospect of still higher unattained perfection.

Kant's influence contended in many minds with that of romanticism. Friedrich Heinrich Jacobi (1743–1819) was a sentimental thinker of confessional-intimate tone, resistant to any logic which did not yield his cherished convictions. How could he trust his spiritual treasures to reason, reason that had led even an ideal character like Spinoza to his blighting conclusions of stark determinism? Reason can arrange and organize, but it lacks creative power. Reason is ever inconclusive and ambiguous; it looks in two directions simultaneously and is unable to arrive anywhere. Kant might expose this quandary in his antinomies, but his own constructive philosophy is also affected by it. Did he not somehow imply the causal action of the thing-in-itself, while conceiving of causality as strictly a category of the understanding? The way out of these perplexities is through intuitive insight and affirmation. Behind all reasoning is an initial challenge which calls for a decisive and unreasoned response of faith, spirit answering to spirit.

In practical as in theoretical philosophy, Jacobi championed the primacy of faith and feeling above rational principles. The good life requires, not a purely rational respect for the moral law, but love and devout expression in feeling; not postulates of practical reason, but intuitive certainties of moral faith. Rooted in man's most intimate nature, Jacobi's morality was to be as genuine and uncalculating as the Kantian, but not rationally austere. In place of the stern earnestness of the call to duty, his ethics preferred the warm, rhapsodic effusions of "beautiful souls."

Goethe and Schiller's Aesthetic Idealism

The idealizing of nature which characterized the romanticists—poets and philosophers alike—served as a sort of religious faith that took the place of the traditional orthodoxy. This pantheistic appeal spread the influence of Spinoza, and may be noted in Goethe and Schleiermacher. The dualism of nature and spirit, a basic problem of the Kantian philosophy, required a solution pointing to an ultimate synthesis. Even before his study of Kant, Goethe (1749–1832) had striven with this fundamental issue and had sought a way through it in Spinoza's principle of "God or Nature." But Goethe would revise Spinoza's monism so as to recognize the ongoing life of nature, to see the world as a drama of ceaseless activity in which each person has his unique role. Goethe's cultural dominance during the Kantian and post-Kantian period in philosophy was not due only to the creative mastery of his genius. His presence in Weimar made that city the German Athens, and his official influence helped to make the nearby University of Jena a great productive center of philosophy. Schiller, Fichte, Schelling, and Hegel were all Jena professors. Week ends and vacations brought philosophers, historians, and poets together in Weimar. Never before had German creative intelligence reached such a summit of social expression. Even after the newly founded University of Berlin drew some of the main thinkers away from Jena, the interplay of philosophy and poetry continued in Weimar.

This account cannot give due recognition to the poetic genius of Goethe and Schiller. Schiller (1759–1805), however, is noteworthy for combining poetic creation with philosophical criticism, in which Kantian ideas were significantly revised in a philosophy of artistic culture. Schiller's rich personality had voiced in his youth the loftiest aspirations of the Enlightenment and the noble strains in the romantic protest, without its excesses. From romantic poetry and drama, he turned to an increasingly classical outlook on life, both as a literary artist and as a thinker.

Two influences in Schiller's life were decisive in his spiritual development: the philosophy of Kant and the poetry and personality of Goethe. Schiller had struggled with untoward circumstances in his private life and had learned to distinguish the real inner worth of character from external mastery or advantages. The contending principles of nature and spirit in Kant's philosophy impressed Schiller not so much for their metaphysical import as for their dramatic significance. Kant's conception of sublimity—in which man, overwhelmed by the vast magnitude and irresistible forces of nature, responds with the still higher sublimity of intelligence and moral resolution —influenced Schiller's poetry and philosophy of life. Schiller's upright character was inspired by Kant's ideal of duty and disinterested pursuit of perfection. The categorical imperative was interpreted by Schiller as a clarion call to noble resolution. Schiller reaffirmed Kant's moral maxim with literary mastery:

If you confess the truth because it is the truth, and if you practice justice because it is justice, you have made of a particular law the law of all possible cases, and treated one moment of your life as eternity. . . . The judgment of all spirits is expressed by our own, and the choice of all hearts is represented by our own act.[1]

But the ethics of the moral law could not express the final word in Schiller's philosophy of life. His view of perfection emphasized the classical principle of harmony, not the austere Kantian "ought." Surely the good life is not essentially and always a life of stern obligation; at its best, virtue chosen for its own sake may well be chosen spontaneously, without moral tension. Will not the true saint find his "delight in the law of the Lord?"[2]

Schiller expanded the meaning of Kant's principle of freedom. Man's spiritual activity manifests his ability to act, not merely in conformity to causal necessity, but also "on principle," from pure respect for the moral law. But this freedom of the human spirit is not always involved in the issue between duty and inclination. Spiritual freedom may reach toward the empirical level and idealize the inclinations themselves, harmonize duty and pleasure. This, according to Schiller, is the function of aesthetic experience, and, in his aesthetic idealism, he gave the finest expression of one alternative solution of the Kantian problem. Schiller was led to this solution by the progress in his own thought and in his poetic activity, and also by his study of Kant's theory of beauty, of the aesthetic judgment as mediating between the causal judgments of science and the moral law of duty. He was likewise influenced by the living embodiment of his ideal that he found in Goethe. He did not idolize Goethe uncritically, but he recognized that the categorical imperative by itself could not explain the Olympian serenity, the free integrity of sense and passion and critical intelligence which were expressed harmoniously in that creative genius.

In his work, *Grace and Dignity*, Schiller had already contemplated an ideal of aesthetic spiritual achievement, in which duty and love, arduous and spontaneous perfection, may exist in unison. He developed his ideas further in his *Letters on the Aesthetic Education of Man* (1795), which he addressed to Goethe. Art is the daughter of freedom; through art and poetry the ideal personality that is latent in everyone may be aroused and be given living expression. The creative process by which we give form to our artistic

[1] F. Schiller, *Essays Aesthetical and Philosophical*, London, Bohn's Libraries, 1916, p. 62.
[2] Psalm 1:2 (American Standard Version).

moods and ideas is itself a molding and creative achievement of personality. Man's motive in this artistic activity is a free dynamic of playful utterance. This play of art engages the plenitude of our powers, which is also fullest integrity and harmony; no low impulses and appetites drive the soul, no dictates of stern duty direct its conduct; reason and sense, contemplation and feeling, are here in perfect accord. Yet Schiller acknowledged the imperative character of the ideal, which infinitely transcends any man's achievement, and which ever challenges his pursuit in aspiration. By bringing "form" into their enjoyments, men may prepare themselves for this higher spiritual loyalty. This is the aesthetic education of mankind.

Fichte's Ethical Idealism

Johann Gottlieb Fichte (1762–1814) reconstructed Kant's critical system of thought by emphasizing and developing the principle of the primacy of moral values. In an interview with Fichte, Mme. de Stael asked for a brief exposition of his philosophy. Satisfied after ten minutes that she had the kernel of it, she turned her questions to his ethics. "Grasp my metaphysics, Madame," Fichte replied; "you will then understand my ethics."[3] This ironical comment is a key to his philosophy. Fichte intended his ethics to issue logically from his metaphysics. The fullest understanding of nature and of man, according to him, was to be gained through insight into moral activity. The highest theory points toward moral practice. He settled the issue between nature and spirit by subordinating nature to spirit, and interpreting spirit as ideal productive activity, manifested preeminently in the moral life. In his philosophy, ethics became the heart of metaphysics.

This ethical idealism was Fichte's conclusion and the deepest utterance of his character. Young or old, he himself might well have been called "the categorical imperative," for he was the principle of duty incarnate, sovereign moral will prevailing over all external circumstances. His early upbringing was even humbler than Kant's. The son of a poor Saxon peasant weaver, he earned his bread as a child by herding geese. He had a sharp memory, and this gave him his chance in life. A land baron who had missed the Sunday sermon was referred to the little gooseherd, who repeated it verbatim. The nobleman, deeply impressed, thereupon undertook the boy's education. Fichte's mother urged him to prepare for the pulpit, but he had a growing conviction that his destiny was philosophy.

An ideal demand to express some truth of lasting worth possessed his soul even before he had any clear idea of the content or direction of his intended philosophy. His wide reading confronted his mind with critical issues. The

[3] Translated from the quotation in Maurice Paléologue, *Vauvenargues*, Paris, Hachette, 1909, p. 87.

untrammeled freedom cherished by the romanticists was challenged but not silenced for him in the logic of Spinoza's determinism. While he was convinced by the criticisms to which the Enlightenment had subjected dogmatic theology, he found his own enlightened generation spiritually barren. He sought a philosophy of life which would both meet the test of critical intelligence and recognize man's ideal aspirations.

While tutoring a student in the works of Kant, Fichte experienced a philosophical conversion. The moral philosophy of duty became for him the way of truth, or better, the way to the truth and the light. Kant's ethics needed only a fuller recognition of its ultimate implications in order to become the foundation of the true philosophy. To this purpose, Fichte now consecrated his life. He went to Königsberg, where he attracted Kant's interest and confidence by his book, *Essay on the Critique of All Revelation*. When it was published, Fichte's name by some slip was omitted from the title page, and the German public mistook the anonymous work for Kant's expected fourth Critique. By the time the error was explained, a second edition was being demanded. Fichte's sudden fame brought him a professorial call to Jena in 1794. His career there was brilliant and productive, but very stormy. His moral rigorism made him unpopular with dissolute students and easy-going professors, and his radical critique of traditional theology outraged the clerics, who charged him with atheism. Fichte refused, on principle, to make the slightest concession, and he left the university.

The next decade, the first in the nineteenth century, was fateful in the history of Europe. It marked the summit of Napoleon's power and foreshadowed his eventual ruin. Fichte's ethical idealism during this period gained in systematic formulation, but it also found more popular and practical expression. In a series of eloquent works, radically different in style from his earlier treatises, Fichte undertook to arouse his people to resolute spiritual self-affirmation as the only true way of preserving the nation during a period of continually impending disaster. The decade which he spent as a public lecturer and author included only short terms of university teaching at Erlangen and Königsberg; but, in 1810, he accepted a professorship at the newly founded University of Berlin. Four years later, he died from a fever which he had caught from his wife, who had contracted it while nursing wounded soldiers.

Even this brief biographical sketch should suggest how deeply rooted Fichte's philosophy was in his own upright, stern, aspiring moral will. But his resolute reconstruction of Kant's principles should not be taken as merely temperamental. The implications of morality prevailed in his thought and were imperious in his character. Because to him philosophy implied profound insight into reality, a philosophy could not be formulated by any external inspection of things. It required the deepest and most intimate self-penetration. Both the merits and the defects of Fichte's character issued from its imperative tenor. Was not his severity with people due to their falling so far short of his standard for man? His impatience with actualities expressed his self-dedication to the ideal.

In his philosophy, theory of knowledge and cosmology were steps on the way to the fuller establishment and final reaffirmation of the initial moral conviction. Moral and theoretical integrity were thus to sustain each other. Beyond multiplicity, no matter how interconnected and systematic, and beyond external determination, Fichte sought unity and creative activity in the inner life. Likewise, in his use of the critical philosophy, which had taught him more than had any other, he was concerned less with his conformity to its specific doctrines than with his development of its fundamental principle. He aimed not so much to repeat Kant's words as to interpret "the utterance of the Holy Spirit" in Kant.

Philosophies, according to Fichte, are of two kinds: dogmatism and idealism. Dogmatism begins with things, substances, manifold contents, and, from them, seeks to derive some unity, meaning, knowledge. But this method is bound to fail, whether the substances are material or mental. The only way in which man can attain real spiritual meaning and activity is to recognize it from the outset, for it is indeed the primary, certain reality. This is the merit of idealism, the only true philosophy, that it starts at the center instead of straying along the periphery. Central in all reality is the immediate self-evident ideal activity.

St. Augustine and Descartes had started with the indubitable act of thinking and the implied reality of the thinking self. Fichte began with the undifferentiated primary-ultimate activity. It is not *a* process, *an* activity distinguishable from others. It is not a *thing*-in-itself. It is the principle of active self-affirmation, basic to all reality. Fichte expressed this conviction in his formula, "The Ego posits itself." This is the fundamental and infinite *I am* of all true idealism. The infinite activity evokes, sets for itself a field of operation, something to act upon. This negative principle was stated in Fichte's second formula: "The Ego posits a non-ego." But this second principle affects the infinite character of the first. The Ego has in effect hemmed itself in by its relation to the non-ego, even as the knower implies, and is bound by, what he knows. Hence, Fichte proposed his third principle: "The Ego posits a limited ego in opposition to a limited non-ego."[4] This is the familiar conscious self of empirical knowledge.

In these three formulas Fichte abstractly conceived the idealistic threefold view of reality. He tried to put his conviction in an analytic statement. These first principles of his system were elaborated, qualified, and reaffirmed extensively in his *Science of Knowledge*, or as Coleridge called it, *The Lore of Science (Wissenschaftslehre)*. The detailed deduction yielded various logical laws and categories of nature. Important for our understanding of Fichte's philosophy is our recognition of his primary emphasis on activity.

4 J. G. Fichte, *The Science of Knowledge* (trans. A. E. Kroeger), London, Trübner, 1889, pp. 68 ff.

As Goethe's *Faust* put it, "In the beginning was the Act."[5] Reality is fundamentally infinite doing.

Furthermore, from this primal, active self-affirmation of the "Ego," the opposite "non-ego" cannot be deduced logically. Yet the Ego does not posit itself without, by its activity, positing its field or medium of activity, a non-ego. More precisely, Fichte held that in his theory "only the *act of opposition* was not provable."[6] But the "only" here raises more than a minor point. Fichte recognized the question that imposed itself: Why does this self-opposition arise in the infinite activity, how does the infinite activity get itself a world? This metaphysical issue cannot be solved theoretically, by thought; but it can be resolved practically. Our entire moral activity involves striving and struggle; it involves ends to be pursued and barriers to be overcome. The reality of nature may thus be recognized analogically in the basic activity. Likewise in religion, theological reasoning cannot prove God's existence, but in religious practice "we are only to speak of his acts, and to vivify, strengthen, and keep in consciousness always the faith in them."[7]

In their opposition, we may regard the ego and the non-ego as each limiting the other. In theoretical-cognitive activity, the knowing subject is affected by the object of its knowledge. But there is a cleavage between the knower and the known, a subject-object dualism which no theoretical reflection can surmount. True idealism can never be realized in terms of cognitive intelligence; there must eventually be an ethical idealism. Only the practical ego can overcome this dualism. In moral activity, the object is the end that expresses the character or meaning of the activity. A moral act is an event realizing the will, the self. Morally speaking, every object or condition is to be recognized as being whatever our will wishes to make of it. It is a possible means to a goal or a barrier to be overcome, a stage in the active career of the will. The moral agent, like the creative artist, always makes, and must make, a cosmos of whatever confronts him.

Fichte's philosophy gave Kant's doctrine of the primacy of practical reason a metaphysical emphasis. Beyond the reach of the cognitive mind, the heart of reality is approached directly by the activity of the moral will. Morality is purely dutiful, ideal, creative endeavor and fulfillment. Unremitting activity is its essence; stagnation or placidity is the root of evil. Virtue is dynamic, forward-reaching, it challenges us to achieve freedom, to rise above the limitations that face each step in our advance, to realize our ever-expanding vocation. Our true personality is our unique role in the ideal drama; it is our duty and our free self-expression. Our moral career is our progressive self-discovery and self-recognition. This is the life of conscience in which we unmistakably confront, acknowledge, and achieve our true selves. It is also the course of true religion, and life in God; as Fichte said

[5] Goethe, *Faust*, Part I, I:iii (trans. B. Taylor), Boston, Houghton Mifflin, n.d., Vol. I, p. 51.
[6] J. G. Fichte, *The Science of Knowledge, op. cit.*, p. 79.
[7] *Ibid.*, pp. 376 f.

in his work, *The Way to the Blessed Life:* "Divinity itself enters again into thee, in its first and original form, as life, as thine own life that thou shouldst live and wilt live."[8]

Fichte's ethics emphasized the free, unique, moral personality, but it also recognized the social system of relations and its manifold opportunities and problems for moral activity. A man is fully a man only among men. In respecting each other's rights, we recognize the system of social cooperation in which our humanity progressively matures. Social activity may be religious fellowship. This is the Church, in which people deepen their common dedication to the blessed life. It uses traditional forms and symbols by which men give utterance to their devotion. But these symbols cannot usurp the place of righteousness. They must heighten and fructify spiritual-moral activity.

The state is the social system of rights and laws. In all the various relations and dealings among men, the state is a system for the mutual adjustment of claims and obligations. Each person's freedom must continually be limited by his respect for the freedom of others. And this freedom, his own and that of others, is not abstract; its concrete actuality involves all the particular external conditions and instrumentalities of effective personal life. In discussing the economic problem of property rights and the system of production and distribution of goods most likely to satisfy human needs, Fichte was not reluctant to advocate radical measures. He outlined a plan for state control of foreign trade; but he was also concerned lest the individual be swamped and mechanized in a rigid industrial system.

In the more personal relations of social life, Fichte was resolved to preserve, at all costs, the dutiful integrity of conscience. He felt that to surrender his moral will to another's keeping was to abdicate his true vocation. He who would follow the traditional or popular "better course" against his conscience would be guilty of sin. What matters morally is not whether this or that action may turn out well, but whether free self-determination in genuine conviction and loyalty to it remain dominant for the moral will. It is only when we keep in mind Fichte's conviction of his moral ideal that we can understand his uncompromising spirit, which seemed to be intractable fanaticism to many of his contemporaries.

One merit of this philosophy was his undeviating single-mindedness in advocating his chosen principle. He refused to make any concessions, and the alternatives he resisted were brought out sharply. In its imperative emphasis on the moral will, on spirit over nature, his philosophy was a radical solution of the Kantian problem. But it was not a solution that the modern scientific mind could accept. In Kant's philosophy, scientific naturalism was confronted with the demands of the human spirit for the recognition of the world of values. This issue could not be settled by emphatically exalting one

[8] Translated from J. G. Fichte, *Sämmtliche Werke*, Berlin, Veit, Vol. V, 1845, p. 471.

side. The Kantian problem still called for a more thorough and balanced solution.

Schelling: Idealistic Metaphysics

The philosophies of Friedrich Wilhelm Joseph Schelling (1775–1854) may well be described as an odyssey. It should properly be mentioned in the plural, for, in his speculative voyages, he sailed through four or five systems of thought. An adventurous mind and an aggressive protagonist, he was ever ready to turn from his good to his better theories. Hegel spoke of him ironically as carrying on his studies in public, which described Schelling correctly, for his mind did not excel so much in originality as in the enthusiasm with which he absorbed and uttered anew the great ideas of the past. He let these ideas have their way, and they often led him to weird conclusions, but they also opened expansive philosophical vistas. His speculative excesses in cosmology discredited metaphysics in the judgment of scientific minds, but his stimulating power influenced several systems of nineteenth-century philosophy. In his imaginative drive, fertility, and spontaneous abandon, he was the most characteristically Romantic philosopher of his day.

Schelling was very precocious, and, before his twentieth year, his philosophical studies were yielding fruit. He came to be known for his brilliant expositions of Fichte's philosophy; in 1798, he joined Fichte at Jena and remained there for several years after Fichte's departure. This first, or Fichtean, stage of his philosophy need only be mentioned. Schelling was on his way to a more satisfying view of the world. The moral-dutiful emphasis did not appeal to his own temperament, which was poetic, sensuous, alert to the living reality of nature.

The artistic Weimar circle of which he was an active and enthusiastic member inclined toward the idealizing of nature. Could not the Kantian problem be solved, as Leibniz had solved the problem of mind and body, by regarding nature as the lower stage of a developing activity which reaches its higher summits in spirit? Schelling came forth as the champion of a philosophy of nature. Nature, he held, tends toward spiritual realization, but it is not to be regarded negatively, as a mere non-ego. Nature is positively real as latent spirit. Schelling undertook to trace the progressive budding, blossoming, and fruiting of spiritual powers in the processes of nature. Natural and human history are two periods in the continuous biography of spirit. Schelling's general principle here was a basic idealistic conviction which he could have discussed with the Platonists or with Goethe. But, in his enthusiastic advocacy of his idea, Schelling ranged through all the sciences at will, took what suited him, and supplied himself with whatever he needed

—attraction, repulsion, electricity, magnetism, gravity or body or female, light or soul or male, all impressively scheduled on Nature's calendar. This fusion of scientific ingredients, romantic notions, and bold symbolism was distasteful to the rigorous naturalists, and it brought philosophy into disrepute. But Schelling's philosophy of nature also had ideas of fertile significance—the unity and continuity of nature and its evolving processes reaching ever more complex and higher stages of realization.

Schelling proceeded to supplement his philosophy of nature by a system of transcendental idealism that interpreted the progressive self-expression of intelligence, morality, and aesthetic activity. This part of his theory was meant to be the history or biography of self-consciousness. In theoretical philosophy, truth expresses the agreement of thought with its object. The stages in the process of acquiring knowledge were indicated by Schelling: from sense experience to reflection, through judgment—which relates as well as distinguishes perception and conception—to the will—in which the self is productively active. In practical philosophy, he interpreted the moral career of the will as a process of achieving personal self-recognition and realization: "Cease to be yourself a phenomenon, strive to become a reality!"[9] From conditioned behavior, in which our life is only a series of states, we must rise to genuine acts revealing our own moral dignity and our respect for it in other persons, our active membership in the ideal order. From this moral social outlook, history can be seen as the drama of the progressive realization of spirit in which every person has his unique part, and can choose and achieve his role. The creative mind manifests itself further in aesthetic activity, in which the antithesis of subject and object is transcended. The work of art is the sensuous expression of the ideal; spirit here becomes flesh, and nature utters its innermost meaning through the creative power of genius.

Throughout this idealistic philosophy of nature, the metaphysical problem of ultimate interpretation confronted Schelling. Is ultimate reality more adequately described in terms of spirit, or in terms of nature, or are these two absorbed and transcended in the absolute ground of reality? Schelling's thought tended toward the third of these views. He was influenced in this by Bruno and by Spinoza's monism of the infinite Substance. He advanced a so-called "system of identity." The absolute, ultimate reality absorbs and transcends all finite distinctions. It is beyond definition; no predicates qualify it—neither body nor mind, object nor subject, nature nor spirit, the material nor the ideal, fact nor value. But, for all his insistence on the ultimate identity, the idealistic motive still prevailed in Schelling's thought, for he regarded the spiritual attribute as a more adequate manifestation of the absolute than the physical.

In formulating his system of identity, Schelling retained and expanded many of his notions in his philosophy of nature, and the romantic tenor of

---

[9] Translated from F. W. Schelling, *Sämmtliche Werke*, Stuttgart, Cotta, 1856, Vol. I, p. 247.

his speculation was now inclining toward mythological symbolism, mysticism, and theosophy. These later forms of his philosophy showed the influence of Neoplatonism, Boehme, and other mystics. In this philosophy of revelation, the religious note was dominant, but Schelling's philosophical use of mythology and symbolism had an aesthetic as well as a religious motivation. His active leadership in the artistic culture of his day expressed his conviction that art and poetry reached deep into spiritual realities, and also reached high in man's aspiration toward the ideal.

Schleiermacher: Religious Faith and Philosophical Insight

The contending demands of nature and spirit, fundamental in the Kantian philosophy and in the development of post-Kantian idealism, were living issues in the character of Friedrich Schleiermacher (1768–1834). His early school teachers were deeply pious, but also dogmatic, Moravian brethren. Schleiermacher reacted toward them as Kant did toward the Pietists; their devotion won his heart, but their doctrines did not convince his critical reason. From their godly school, he went on to study theology at the University of Halle, a center of the Enlightenment and of abstract rationalism. When Schleiermacher left the university, he was struggling with the conflict between reason and faith. As a clergyman he found himself in a society where scientific and other worldly minds dismissed religion as groundless, and pious minds disdained science and philosophy as godless. Resisting both of these judgments as one-sided and spiritually sterile, he sought a way of reconciliation in fruitful harmony.

He invited the unwelcome lot of reconcilers. His theological colleagues suspected him of heretical leanings; to the scientists and philosophers, he appeared as a compromiser. But he would not yield to either extreme, and he sought, by a truer reinterpretation of religion, to meet the spiritual crisis of his times. This reinterpretation was outlined in his work *On Religion: Speeches to Its Cultured Despisers*, in which Schleiermacher declared that the finality of religion lies neither in a system of doctrines nor in a system of churchly or moral observances. Theology and religious practices are both important, but they are not the heart of religion; it does not depend on them. Beliefs in God, creation, miracles, revelation, immortality—all of these are ways in which men's intellects formulate or explain their religious experience. They are variable doctrines which reflect men's intelligence and are subject to critical revision. Ecclesiastical forms and other observances are the practical vestures of religion. But religion itself is deeper and more intimate than mere doctrines or conduct. It is man's intimate and indubitable experience of God, a feeling of absolute dependence: a "sense and taste for the Infinite."[10]

[10] F. Schleiermacher, *On Religion* (trans. J. Oman), London, Kegan, Paul, 1893, p. 39.

This view of religion, championed in Schleiermacher's first important work, and, with some revisions, maintained in his major treatise, *The Christian Faith*, also determined his position in relation to Kant and the idealists after Kant. Kant's moral grounding of religion, of which Fichte's ethical idealism was an accentuated version, impressed Schleiermacher as showing insufficient appreciation of the mystical intimacy of religious experience. He honored Fichte's spirit of consecration, but he could not share his solemn ascetic attitude toward nature. Like Schelling, he was convinced that nature was somehow latent spirit, but his reason distrusted Schelling's alleged proofs of this principle, which yielded pseudo-scientific schemes but no vital spiritual meaning.

Our emphasis on the mainly Kantian orientation should not overlook the major influence of Spinoza on the romantic circle in which Schleiermacher moved. His philosophy of religion was inspired by Spinoza's "intellectual love of God" and may be said to include meditations on the fifth part of the *Ethics*. But these meditations were Christian. Schleiermacher was convinced that a true pantheism must grasp the tragic actuality of sin. Otherwise, though it may declare the infinite perfection of nature, it is bound to end with a neutral evaluation and a religiously unavailable view of reality. Schleiermacher also resisted the cosmic gloom of some of the romanticists. His Christianity taught man's utter need of redemption, and also his blessed hope for it.

Philosophical intelligence may formulate a theological doctrine of God's nature in relation to the world, or a secular-scientific account of the order and unity of nature. The moral view of human conduct is neither a view of man as a purely spiritual character nor a description of him as a certain natural structure and system of reactions. Morality is concerned with the interplay and mutuality of reason and nature. The defect in Kant's and Fichte's ethics, according to Schleiermacher, was that they represent man's moral career as supersensible, and moral principles as solemnly imperative but not assuredly operative in the actual lives of men. Schleiermacher voiced the need for a more realistic emphasis in post-Kantian moral philosophy.

Nature and reason are not two separate worlds in each of which we have ambiguous citizenship. They are two aspects of one ongoing reality. As in Goethe's dramatic revision of Spinozism, Schleiermacher, in his ethics, revealed man as pursuing and realizing a spiritual destiny in his natural medium. Moral good and human perfection lie in the achievement of this rational-natural harmony. This direction of thought pointed toward a Christian-Platonic perfectionism, and it is shown also in Schleiermacher's interpretation of the cardinal virtues. Virtue essentially involves conviction and readiness that are manifested in insight or discernment and expression. The four cardinal virtues thus yielded are wisdom, love, composure, and steadfastness —four manifestations of rational living. The insight of right conviction is wisdom; its expression is love. The insight of a ready and vigorous spirit is composure; its expression is steadfastness. This system of virtues reveals a blend of a Platonic and a Pauline-Christian perspective, with the latter prevailing. Wisdom inclines toward faith; composure (temperance) and steadfastness (courage) blend into hope; justice yields its dominant role to love.

SUGGESTED WORKS FOR FURTHER STUDY

ANTHOLOGIES OF POST-KANTIAN IDEALISTS. Howard, W. G., *Laokoön: Lessing, Herder, Goethe* (selections).

JACOBI. Crawford, A. W., *The Philosophy of F. H. Jacobi;* Wilde, Norman, *Friedrich Heinrich Jacobi.*

GOETHE. Croce, Benedetto, *Goethe;* Lewes, G. H., *The Life of Goethe.*

SCHILLER. Schiller, F., *Essays, Aesthetical and Philosophical;* Carlyle, Thomas, *The Life of Friedrich Schiller;* Thomas, Calvin, *The Life and Works of Friedrich Schiller.*

FICHTE. Fichte, J. G., *The Science of Knowledge, The Science of Ethics,* and *The Science of Rights* (all trans. A. E. Kroeger); *The Vocation of Man* (trans. W. Smith); Everett, C. C., *Fichte's Science of Knowledge;* Talbot, E. B., *The Fundamental Principle of Fichte's Philosophy.*

SCHELLING. Schelling, F. W., *Of Human Freedom* (trans. J. Gutmann); Watson, John, *Schelling's Transcendental Idealism.*

SCHLEIERMACHER. Schleiermacher, F., *On Religion* (trans. J. Oman); *Soliloquies* (trans. H. L. Friess); Brandt, R. B., *The Philosophy of Schleiermacher;* Chapman, J. A., *An Introduction to Schleiermacher;* Selbie, W. B., *Schleiermacher.*

27. Hegel: Dialectical Idealism

Hegel's Character and Philosophical Development

Georg Wilhelm Friedrich Hegel (1770–1831) was a colleague of Schleiermacher at the University of Berlin for thirteen years. The systematic philosopher and the philosophical theologian each faced the Kantian problem of the tension between nature and spirit; they each felt the romantic demand for a final spiritual unity in nature. But they differed radically in their proposed satisfaction of that demand, and in their philosophical solution of the critical problem. Schleiermacher's ultimate appeal was to the self-attested certainty of mystical faith. In Hegel's mind and method, reason was dominant; his metaphysics had to be logical. For all his mastery of doctrine, Schleiermacher's basic conviction was religious, with "sense and taste for the Infinite."[1] Hegel reached a different conclusion: "What is Rational is Real, and what is Real is Rational."[2] This contrast should be kept in mind. It will enable us to understand and evaluate Hegel's relation to Fichte and Schelling, and to recognize his central role in the history of post-Kantian idealism.

Hegel's mind seems to have been temperamentally prepared for the Kantian and the romantic issues. He was ever alert to conflicts in ideas, motives, or directions of action. At school, and also at the theological seminary of Tübingen, he was confronted by the issue which Matthew Arnold later called "Hebraism and Hellenism." His early classical education had fired his enthusiasm for the free human perfection of Plato, Aristotle, and Sophocles, and he composed a German version of *Antigone*. But, in planning his life work, he was committed to the Christian ideal. His theological professors, however, repelled his intelligence by their stiff Biblical dogmatism. Even at the seminary, Hegel pursued his classical studies enthusiastically with his intimate friends, Schelling and the gifted young poet, Hölderlin. How was he to reconcile these two strains in western civilization? The outlook of Greek humanism—from the heights of rational perfection to the abysses of tragedy, man against nature and Nemesis—and the Christian view of man as tainted from birth with original sin but a blessed, though an undeserving

[1] F. Schleiermacher, *On Religion* (trans. J. Oman), London, Kegan, Paul, 1893, p. 39.
[2] G. W. Hegel, *Philosophy of Right*, in S. W. Dyde, *Hegel's Philosophy of Right*, London, Bell, 1896, pp. xxvii.

recipient of God's saving grace—these two views contended in Hegel's mind, and demanded a philosophical synthesis.

The romantic plea for unconstrained individual self-expression moved young Hegel deeply. The social-political outburst of this protest against institutional repression in the French Revolution aroused young German dreamers of the new freedom. Already Schiller had sounded the call of "storm and stress" in his romantic drama, *The Robbers*. At the Tübingen seminary, the students were singing the *Marseillaise* in a German version that was attributed to Schelling. Hegel was not in the thick of this commotion— he was never a firebrand—but, in his radical youth, and even in his later, more conservative years, the ideal of free self-realization remained dominant in his social philosophy.

His mind excelled in systematic solidity rather than in brilliant intuitions. He did not impress his teachers at Tübingen, who reported his good character and his conscientious study of languages and theology, but also that he had an insufficient grasp of philosophy! This reminds us of the classroom of Albert the Great, where the students called young Thomas Aquinas "the dumb ox." Hegel laid the foundations of his structure slowly, but he did not have to alter its design continually. When he joined Schelling at Jena, the initial philosophical agreement of the two was bound to be temporary. Schelling was always reaching toward some new theory; Hegel was developing the fuller implications of his basic principles. Two fundamental ideas were gaining clear recognition in Hegel's mind. In his social and religious philosophy, there was a positive evaluation of the human spirit; in his philosophical method and metaphysical outlook, an unmistakably rational emphasis. The first of these ideas was manifest in his solution of the Hellenic-Christian issue and in his ethics of the social realization of personality. His philosophy was a program of spiritual development, not a gospel of salvation. The second idea distinguished Hegel from the other leading idealists after Kant, and from the romanticists generally. He would not accept any substitutes for reason. He did not share Fichte's renunciation of a logical solution of Kant's problem, or his exaltation of the moral will as the core of reality; he was suspicious of the romantic appeals to faith, intuition, and mystical feeling, whether they found utterance in enthusiastic poetry or were brilliantly molded into philosophical systems, as by Schelling and Schleiermacher. He was firmly convinced that the issue between nature and spirit must be reasoned out, that the right solution must be rational, for spirit expresses the rational essence of reality. Hegel's idealism was resolutely logical.

Logic and Metaphysics: The Dialectical Process

The treatment of the Kantian problem of nature and spirit in the course of German idealism pointed to a principle of solution which Hegel grasped and formulated in his philosophical method. In this principle, he combined two significant, but insufficiently developed, ideas of Fichte and Schelling, respectively. Fichte had emphasized a certain antithetical process in reality: the ego posits a non-ego, spirit evokes nature. Schelling had contemplated the cosmic tendency toward ultimate unity—nature is latent spirit. But, whereas Fichte pursued a synthesis of opposites, he actually exalted one of these opposites, the moral will, or spirit, rather than nature. And Schelling went on to exhibit the basic synthesis, not as a real unity of differences but as an identity, a transcendence or effacement of differences.

In distinction from his two idealistic predecessors, Hegel sought a true synthesis, a unity-in-differences. The right principle of solution was implied in the Kantian problem itself, when fully understood. The whole structure of nature, as known by the mind, is a system of different, but related, events. The philosophical issue of nature and spirit expresses a contrast—a contrast to be resolved. The mind is involved in a double operation, two aspects of its basic activity. Its every idea points to its contending opposite; in its every opposition, a further, more integral idea is emerging. Kant regarded the intelligent self as the organic unity of experience. Hegel described the activity of thought as the progressive organization of differences into higher and higher unities, a dialectical activity. The dialectic is the scientific application of the orderly procedure inherent in the very nature of thought; it is fundamental in all thinking. Philosophy must start with it.

Hegel's dialectical process was, in the first place, a logical method. But the mutual opposition of ideas and their progressive organization into higher unities, the dialectic as he understood it, was more than a conceptual manipulation. It was the logical, operational expression of a deep-lying ultimate principle, the ongoing movement and rhythm of all reality. His logic was thus, in his basic intention, a metaphysics. When Fichte described ultimate reality as an ideal activity, he was stating a principle whose meaning he himself did not fully grasp. Hegel did not regard thought as merely a logical system of abstract concepts, unlike the rest of existence. If we once understand the dialectical principle where it is most perfectly revealed to the mind, in thought, we can recognize its less obvious manifestations in the world of factual existence. Hence, we can see the reason for Hegel's logical approach to philosophy, and we should not make the common blunder of regarding his system as simply an elaborate operation of concepts.

We may first consider Hegel's logic as a logic. Its dialectical principle at once impresses us as questioning Aristotle's laws of thought. For Aristotle, A is A, and we cannot predicate of it B and non-B at the same time. These laws of identity and noncontradiction are essential in a formal logic of concepts. But they need revision in Hegel's logic of the thinking process itself. For B and non-B, in any significant judgment, are not only distinguished in opposition; they are also related in distinction. Underlying their contradiction is a more ultimate interrelation which renders their opposition significant and points to its synthetic revision. So the mutual antithesis of the two judgments, *A is B, A is not B,* may lead us to the judgment, *A is becoming B.*

This reconciliation of Being and non-Being, in Becoming, was Hegel's first example of his dialectical procedure. Most historians of modern philosophy have formulated this logical process as a triad of thesis-antithesis-synthesis. Some more recent critics have pointed out that Hegel himself did not use this precise formula, and that it is too abstract to do justice to his more concrete view of the nature of thought. This protest is debatable. Even though the triadic formula was not used literally by Hegel, it may well express his dialectical process, provided we heed the warning of undue formalism.

The resolution of abstract opposition of concepts into more concrete unities is an ongoing characteristic of thought. The logical advance toward a synthesis is followed by a concentration on the realized solution, and then, in its turn, it also exposes its limitations and leads the mind to its respective antithesis, demanding another more adequate interpretation. Thus Hegel proceeded to explore and to trace the logical organization of ideas, from the most abstract concepts—that is, the barest and least comprehensive—to the most concrete, significant, and integral ideas. At the lowest level of this scale are concepts like quality, quantity, and measure; at the highest are the notions of life, knowledge, and the absolute Idea.

The dialectical advance in thought is an advance in insight and comprehension. We contemplate our ideas in their ever fuller perspectives of relations, and thus we grasp their essential meaning. Hegel was ready to illustrate his guiding principle by examples from every field of experience. Perhaps we ourselves may supply the most concrete instances when we try, for example, to do full justice to a great personality. Every biography is an attempted synthesis, but, actually, it propounds some kind of thesis. The biographer is likely to fit within some formula of interpretation a character that, in reality, repeatedly negates, absorbs, and transcends the elaborate thesis. Rousseau strikingly exemplifies this dialectical process. On the one hand is the romantic radical zealot indulging his passing moods and carried away by his emotions; on the other hand is the champion of plain human freedom and dignity, the devotee of the gospel of duty and disinterested conscience. These are both Rousseau; each of these sets of characteristics involves both its negation in the other and also its synthesis with it in the deeper understanding of his character.

Hegel also recognized in the dialectical triad a threefold, progressive mental activity which characterizes, respectively, common sense, science, and philosophy. At the common-sense level of thought the mind perceives, adopts, and affirms. It entertains a multiplicity of things in an unsystematic array; it may describe, measure, and sometimes compare, but it does not really distinguish or organize its ideas. The scientific mind seeks order by overcoming the vague confusion of ideas that are present together in the common-sense mind. It undertakes precise definition, an indication of limits; this necessitates clear distinctions. It specializes in abstractions; it traces specific relations, in terms of which it classifies its ideas systematically. But, because of its very methods of specialization, it does not attain to a fully integral insight, an organic total interpretation of reality. This integral interpretation is the purpose of philosophy, the ultimate synthesis of ideas.

Hegel traced this evolution of categories in the three main divisions of his logic. We shall review them broadly. In the first division, the categories of Being are those used by the unreflective mind. As noted already, Being poses and opposes non-Being, and so a higher category, Becoming, is established. Determinateness of Being, or Quality, is thus reached, but as determination is limitation, Quality manifests itself as both reality and negation. Limit involves the distinction and relation of the finite and the infinite. The true infinite, or Being-for-self, involves the opposition of the one and the many with which Hegel related repulsion and attraction; the union of these two is Quantity. Under this category, pure Quantity points to the distinction of continuous and discrete magnitude, and thus to limitation of Quantity, or Quantum (How much). Quantum, in turn, may be viewed as both a sum and a unity, and thus indicates number, or extensive magnitude. But Quantum is also intensive magnitude, or Degree. Degree involves an infinite series and a quantitative ratio; but, in this ratio, Quantity and Quality are combined in the category of Measure.

Such a bare summary accentuates unduly the abstractness of the logical deduction, but it may suggest Hegel's actual detailed exposition. The other two divisions of the logic will be described more briefly. The second, the doctrine of Essence, emphasizes both the unity and the difference of Quality and Quantity. The categories of Reflection, Identity, and Difference lead to the category of Ground. From this are derived the ideas of Existence, of this thing in relation to others, and the distinction of Matter and Form. In and through the opposition of these, Essence as the Ground of Existence involves the categories of Appearance and Actuality. Under the latter, Hegel included Kant's categories of Relation: substance and accident, causality and reciprocity, or action and reaction.

The third division, the doctrine of the Notion, relates Being and Essence. Notion is a mediated being that organically relates the differences to which it gives rise, which, on becoming differentiated, expresses its deeper and more concrete unity. Here Hegel expounded first the subjective Notion in judgments and syllogisms, and then the objective Notion, which he explored through the categories of Mechanism, Chemism, and Teleology. The highest categories of the Notion are stages in the manifestation of the Idea: Life, Cognition (Knowledge and Will) and the Absolute Idea.

In a vaster metaphysical perspective, the dialectical logic may point beyond itself to a cosmic-philosophical triad, the dialectical process of reality itself. Here Hegel indicated his solution of the Kantian problem of Spirit and nature, through a revision of it. The logical dialectic of Ideas is itself a sort of thesis, a basic way of contemplating reality. This thesis of Idea is confronted with its antithesis, Nature. Idea and Nature find their synthesis in Spirit. For Hegel, the philosophy of Spirit is the full insight into reality. But Spirit in turn is revealed for interpretation subjectively and objectively, and beyond these two in their opposition is the highest synthesis of all, Absolute Spirit, which Hegel found manifested in art, religion, and philosophy.

Philosophy of Nature

From his logical analysis of the rational Idea of reality, Hegel proceeded to explore its actualization. The logical system represents only the possibility of the actual world. Hegel undertook to deduce, first, the unfolding material existence of Nature, and then the progressive self-manifestation of Mind, or Spirit, in which the rational character of reality finds more nearly perfect expression.

Nature, the system of sense-perceived things and processes, is the opposite of the rational Idea, the antithesis, "the other" of the logical principle in reality. Reason explores nature like a stranger seeking his way home. This exploration, however, reveals a progressive resolution of the antithesis; from the lowest types of externality, estranged reason proceeds toward less and less alien types of material existence; these point toward mind, in which the rational idea recognizes itself as actualized. Thus, we may contemplate again the dialectical triad: from the Idea to material nature and then to Mind, or Spirit.

In the system of nature, objects and events are connected externally. The lowest determination is mechanical in the framework of space and time. In mechanical changes and processes, matter is viewed abstractly. Any moving body, of whatever dimensions or specific characteristics, will exemplify the laws of mechanics. Physics is a more concrete view of matter as having various distinguishable qualities and modes of operation. Thus,. we pass from processes like abstract motion, inertia, and gravitation to sound, heat, and light, and to the various chemical processes.

From mechanics and physics, Hegel's analysis proceeded to the third level, organic nature. Organism, in its turn, is distinguished as threefold: geological, plant, and animal. The geological-mineral kingdom may be regarded as a transitional stage between physical-chemical existence and the vegetable and animal worlds, a realm of nonliving organisms. Plants are living bodies, assimilating external material for their appropriate forms and processes, and reproducing according to their kind. On the higher, or animal, level, nature continues the formative, assimilative, and reproductive characteristics of plants, but, within the framework of externality, it turns to subjectivity, consciousness. At the highest stage, this consciousness becomes self-awareness; material nature achieves mental character.

This broad survey of Hegel's philosophy of nature suggests its kinship to Schelling's doctrine of nature as a dormant or latent spirit. Like Schelling, Hegel was guided in his exposition by his own scheme of progressive inferences rather than by his direct knowledge and grasp of the scientific facts. This procedure betrayed both thinkers into serious blunders and misconceptions which discredited their philosophies in the judgment of scientists.

Philosophy of Spirit

Our words "mind" and "spirit" may be used alternately or together to express the meaning of Hegel's term *Geist*. To him, *Geist* signified both the ultimate divine spirit—the summit of reality—and mind, human intelligence. This ambiguity was not due to any actual indefiniteness of the German word. For Hegel, the human mind was a finite token of the infinite Reality. His twofold use of *Geist* followed the same principle as his use of "Thought" and "Idea"; in all these, the interpretation of finite processes is intended to reveal the inmost nature and the highest reaches of Reality. Logic, psychology, and ethics have metaphysical implications in Hegel's philosophy.

In 1806, the night before the battle of Jena, Hegel completed his *Phenomenology of Mind*. This treatise, in some respects the most remarkable of Hegel's works, was intended to be an exploration and interpretation of the entire span of spiritual activity, from its most elementary states of consciousness to the more developed processes of self-conscious intelligence and reason; the objective realization of spirit in the ethical order and in culture and civilization, and its highest expressions in art, religion, and philosophy.

As the title, *Phenomenology*, suggests, Hegel's purpose in this treatise was to trace the continuity of the entire process of experience through all its stages and at the same time to reveal the characteristic place and role of each type of experience in the common process. Each experience, and all of them together, point toward the essential culminating expression of absolute Spirit, their supreme destiny. In all experience, there is a consciousness of subject and object in a relation of mutual interplay within a comprehensive, integrating, and universal reality of Spirit. In its own way, Hegel's idealism brought out the philosophical meaning of St. Paul's words: "In Him we live and move and have our being."[3] He called this book his "voyage of discovery." His pathway of reality in consciousness and experience is a pathway to God.

Hegel's final contemplation recalls the theological climax of Aristotle's *Metaphysics*. Aristotle had written of deity that "it thinks itself, and its thinking is a thinking of thinking."[4] Hegel concluded that "self-conscious-

---

[3] Acts 17:28 (American Standard Version).
[4] Aristotle, *Metaphysics*, in Richard McKeon (ed.), *The Basic Works of Aristotle*, New York, Random House, 1941, 1074b.

ness, which knows this pure knowledge of pure inwardness to be spirit, is not merely intuition of the divine, but the self-intuition of God Himself."[5] But the road to reality that leads to this sublime vision is also a course of the mind's tragic contention with itself. Man that seeks after God, if haply he might find Him, is also resistant to God. He is dedicated to the eternal, and he feels himself shackled to his own changing moment. This is the un-happy, or Contrite Consciousness, "divided and at variance within itself . . . a personality confined within its narrow self and its petty activity, a personality brooding over itself, as unfortunate as it is pitiably destitute."[6] In the unfolding of civilization, this state of consciousness was especially characteristic of the medieval mind. In contrast to the undivided estate of man's soul which marked classical antiquity, the medieval spirit was a devout, yet prodigal, son. Mind must rise above and beyond this tension to a natural self-recognition of Reason. This is the prospect revealed in the history of the modern spirit.

PHILOSOPHY OF SUBJECTIVE MIND

In 1817, ten years after his *Phenomenology of Mind*, Hegel presented, in the *Encyclopedia of the Philosophical Sciences*, a systematic exposition of his idealism, including his logic and philosophy of nature—both of which we have already considered—and his philosophy of mind. In this, Hegel first examined its subjective manifestation. This included psychology in our broadest sense; but Hegel designated as "psychology" only the third sec-tion of this topic, preceding it by his discussions of anthropology and what he now entitled "phenomenology of mind" in a more restricted sense. These three parts deal respectively with the soul, consciousness, and mind; although his use of terms is somewhat at variance with ours, it should not confuse us if it is indicated plainly.

Anthropology, as Hegel regarded it, deals with the soul, that is, with the bare elementary conditions for conscious activity. Intelligence is not really active here; it is present only in remote prospect. There is a dim feeling of vitality in a body which is not clearly aware of itself. This borderland be-tween nature and spirit is a state of latent sensibility in which physical qualities are still the prevailing ones. Sleeping or awake, man's sentience is first of all a bodily condition. But the stages of emerging mental activity are here—elementary feelings and reactions which eventually come to definite awareness as the "soul rises to become *consciousness*."[7]

Physiological conditions which dominate the anthropological view are not completely ignored, but they are subordinate in considering conscious-ness. The definitely conscious soul is aware of its feelings and sense percep-

---

[5] G. W. Hegel, *The Phenomenology of Mind* (trans. J. B. Baillie), London, Sonnen-schein, 1910, Vol. II, p. 807.

[6] *Ibid.*, Vol. I, pp. 200, 215.

[7] G. W. Hegel, *Philosophy of Mind* (trans. W. Wallace), Oxford, Clarendon Press, 1894, p. 195.

tions. Consciousness distinguishes itself from its object; it has a feeling of itself and its desires as related to, yet unlike, the experiences of other selves. Potentially, a more clearly intelligent organization of itself and its conscious states will be realized, but the soul has not yet attained this.

The third and mature stage of subjective mind is Mind in the proper sense of the term. Intelligent mind organizes its ideas and volitions in a universal order; it devises language as a medium for preserving and communicating its ideas; it not only cognizes, but recognizes, understands, and interprets its reflections in a rational pattern. It actively and consciously enjoys its activity, and it realizes a certain freedom of self-conscious contemplation.

But this free self-expression of Spirit cannot be fully realized on the subjective side alone; it naturally seeks objective manifestations. This is the field of the objective mind, and Hegel's interpretation of it contained his ethics and social philosophy.

THE OBJECTIVE MIND: SOCIAL SELF-REALIZATION

The outline of moral and social theory in the *Encyclopedia* was developed by Hegel in his *Philosophy of Right* (1821). For Hegel, as for Aristotle, ethics and social-political philosophy are two stages in the rational perfection of personality. Hegel's moral philosophy brings to fulfilment the principles of the right social order as implied in the Kantian ethics. The moral law imperative in individual and social conduct is stated explicitly by Hegel: "Be a person and respect others as persons."[8] Hegel recognized the Christian influence in his acknowledgment of this principle. *The Philosophy of Right* aims to reveal the self-recognition and social realization of personality.

Hegel distinguished three stages in this activity of the objective mind that proceed in a dialectical movement. On the stage of abstract right, or mere legality, the character and dignity of personality are not yet recognized; men submit to laws and contractual obligations with which they are not yet fully identified. The stage of morality marks the subjective emergence of the moral will, self-expressive and self-directive in conscience, but not yet socially integrated. Beyond abstract right and morality, beyond contract and conscience, is the stage of the ethical system of society, in which legal sanctions become moral imperatives, and moral ideals find objective realization in ethical institutions. Here men become truly persons and respect others as persons, in the ethical interpenetration of minds which characterizes the true family, civic community, and the ideal state.

The principle of expansion through participation, basic in the Hegelian ethics, finds its primary expression in elementary terms on the low level of abstract right. Man allies certain things in his external environment with himself; he is their owner, they are his possessions. Private property is the first step in the objective realization of personal character. Here Hegel

---

[8] G. W. Hegel, *Philosophy of Right*, in *op. cit.*, p. 45.

noted three principal points. The fundamental moral dignity of persons precludes their being the property of another and hence rules out all slavery as immoral. The importance of private property as a primary condition of self-realization establishes the essential right of all persons to own something. But, while Hegel thus rejected both expropriated serfdom and communism, he regarded the demand for economic equality as unwarranted. People vary in their ability to own and to use property, just as they vary in their other capacities.

My ownership of anything is my right to use and to dispose of it, and so to relinquish it to another. This transfer involves contract between persons, but such a contract can concern only things. Thus, I can relinquish my house, but not my life; suicide is not admissible under any condition. Furthermore, marriage is not to be regarded as a mere contract; nor is the traditional idea of the "social contract" reasonable. In the truly ethical system, both family and social relations require the attainment of a higher level of personality than that of abstract right.

Contract, the mutual transfer of property, involves a cooperation of two wills, but also contention between them. A person may willfully violate the rights of property. This is wrong, a transgression of abstract right, and the criminal must be repudiated by the legal system. In his penology, Hegel rejected all doctrines of protection or deterrence, and advocated a reinterpreted principle of retribution. Crime is a negation of the system of law, and the system must reaffirm and vindicate itself through the punishment of the criminal.

Abstract right, or the legal system, regards persons as related to one another externally through a system of property rights. But, although personality finds this outward objective expression, it involves, also, a subjective inwardness. A man that owns things, also seeks his own intimate self-possession in unique freedom. This is the scrupulous life of conscience that respects the claims of duty. Purpose and responsibility, and, likewise, intention and well-being, on this level of morality, concern the inner integrity of the will's motive, rather than any outward benefit from the action performed. Hegel, however, did not follow the extreme Kantian formalism here. He recognized that the rational moral will, when it chooses to act, must view the proposed action in all its eventual consequences and bearings.

Conscience, regarded by Hegel as "the deepest internal solitude,"[9] is most scrupulously subjective in deliberation and decision. Without its sovereignty, true morality cannot be attained; a person may act effectively or beneficially, yet not virtuously. But the purely conscientious spirit, in its self-consecration, runs the ethical peril of disregarding the actual well-being of the social-ethical system. The enlightened conscience must ever seek the right path so as not to stray into either mere accommodating expediency

[9] *Ibid.*, p. 130.

or fanaticism. "In a self-certitude, which exists for itself, knows and decides for itself, both morality and evil have their common root."[10]

The full objective realization of Spirit becomes possible in the ethical system of social-institutional life. Here people can participate in one another's self-expression, each eliciting and responding to the spiritual growth of others. Individuality now attains social fruition; man finds his own enhanced significance in the life of the family, the civic community, and the state.

The close intimacy of the family affords an especially suitable medium for the active self-identification of its members with each other's purposes. Marriage is essentially an ethical union. The love which inspires it fuses sexual, emotional, and practical bonds into a deeply spiritual communion of man and wife. In this spirit of ethical interpenetration, the growing lives of the children are integrated. This view provides the justification of monogamy, that it makes this intimate social-personal expression an abiding lifelong experience. As the children grow up and establish their own families, this social expression of personality is realized—in a less intimate degree, but on a larger scale—in the civic community and the state.

The civic community provides a range of activities in which its members can share in the objective realization of their aims. The economic, legal, and administrative interplay of claims and obligations which engaged men on the level of abstract right, now affords opportunities for free and genuine cooperation. An ethical community must face the problems of economic and social inequities, the cramping of personal lives by the external conditions under which individuals have to live, the unsocial and inhuman relations into which industry and trade force multitudes of people. The administration of justice and the maintenance of order by the police should be guided by a basic regard for the rights and dignity of individuals as well as for their duties to the social order. Not abstract conformity to law and orderly behavior for their own sakes, but the safeguarding of men in communal cooperation and growth must be the directive principle, "to oversee and foster the ways and means calculated to promote the public welfare."[11]

In the realization of these social-personal values the civic community grows naturally into the state. According to Hegel, the state provides the society fully developed for ethical self-realization. Something of the shy, uncommunicative innocence of the child may remain in the adult man; yet the full-grown person is the standard by which a youth's range of capacities is to be judged. Even so, although no state may quite eclipse the individual, an individual attains ethical maturity in his life as a citizen. The ethical citizen does not regard the state as an instrument of advantage or protection, nor chafe under it as hindering his private ventures. He is fully identified with the larger life of his people. This is true patriotism—not merely readiness to die for one's country in the hour of destiny, but whole-hearted willingness to live generously in a truly national spirit.

[10] *Ibid.*, p. 133.
[11] *Ibid.*, pp. 226 f.

In his political theory and his philosophy of history, Hegel did not always maintain the high level of his idealistic principles. Like Coleridge and Wordsworth, in his youth during the French Revolution, Hegel dreamed of a brave new world of free men; but later in life all three men settled or stiffened conservatively. More than once, the great objective idealist wrote like a Prussian official. He preferred constitutional monarchy to a democratic commonwealth. Though he had exalted the state as the great medium of the people's fullest ethical self-realization, he could also despise the people's will and glorify the great man who could tell his age what to think and want. We should expect him to condemn war as unreservedly as he condemned suicide; instead he maintained that wars preserve the ethical health of nations, and that, in any case, modern wars are prosecuted humanely!

Hegel's social ethics reached its climax in his doctrine of the state, but, to be consistent, it should have found its consummation in an international perspective, the universal life of civilization. He did consider this implication of his ethics in the brief concluding sections on international law and world history; but he did not recognize it adequately nor develop it thoroughly. He repeated Schiller's great words, "The history of the world is the world's court of judgment."[12] We should expect him to conclude that above all nations is Humanity, or, like Marcus Aurelius, to declare himself a rational citizen of the universe,[13] a fellow participant with mankind in the vast historical life of civilization. Actually, the closing pages of *The Philosophy of Right* review, in rapid survey, the historical evolution of mankind, and discover "the unity of the divine and the human"[14] in the German Empire, or the Germanic realm, *Germanische Reich.*

In his lectures on the philosophy of history, Hegel undertook a systematic review of the historical evolution of humanity. The course of civilization, in Hegel's discussion, revealed the world Spirit in its chief progressive manifestations, notably in the oriental realms, in the culture of Greek antiquity, in the Roman Empire, and in the Germanic world. Careful historians can readily point out his errors regarding details, and some social-philosophical critic may dispute his adherence to the Germanic, or may we say even more broadly, western slant, which affects his appraisal of the ideals and institutions of other cultures. Nevertheless, in his *Philosophy of History*, Hegel continued in the path which Herder before him had opened. Beyond historical studies of specific events and periods of human development, Hegel sought to unveil a philosophical pattern of the inner meaning and increasing purpose that could he read in the history of humanity: "The history of the world is nothing but the development of the Idea of Freedom."[15]

[12] *Ibid.,* p. 341. See also Schiller's poem, "Resignation."

[13] Cf. *The Thoughts of the Emperor M. Aurelius Antoninus* (trans. George Long), London, Bell, 1891, p. 98.

[14] Hegel, *Philosophy of Right, op. cit.,* p. 348.

[15] G. W. Hegel, *Lectures on the Philosophy of History* (trans. J. Sibree), London, Bell, 1914, p. 476.

ABSOLUTE SPIRIT IN ART, RELIGION, AND PHILOSOPHY

Aristotle had ranked the contemplative virtues above the virtues of moral conduct; the most nearly godlike is the purely rational activity of the mind. Hegel, likewise, regarded as the highest expression of reality absolute Spirit, in which the opposition of subjectivity and objectivity has been absorbed in the integrally spiritual life. Hegel interpreted three forms, or stages, in the manifestation of absolute Spirit: art, religion, and philosophy. He regarded the first two as finding their culmination in the third; the philosophy of fine arts and the philosophy of religion are fulfilled in philosophy.

Hegel viewed beauty as essentially spiritual. The so-called "beauty" of nature is misapprehended. Aesthetics is therefore a philosophy of fine art. The domain of art is the expression of Spirit in sensuous form. This definition of aesthetic value indicates the range and limitations of art. The development of the fine arts proceeds from abstract inadequacy to a more harmonious relation of Spirit and the sensuous form in which it is expressed, and then to the transcendence of the form by the growing depth or scope of the meaning that seeks expression. Hegel designated these three stages or types of art as the symbolic, the classical, and the romantic.

Symbolic art is vague in its idea and inarticulate, or inappropriate, in its form of expression. It achieves only indefinite embodiment of inchoate abstractions. Here natural structures are violated to express the meaning which is imposed on them—as in oriental statues of gods with twenty arms. Symbolic art embodies the yearning and fermentation of Spirit, not its concrete expression in sensuous form. The perfect equivalence or harmony of the idea and its sensuous form in artistic expression is achieved in classical art. What the Greek thinks, he utters in marble. Here is complete concord of meaning and embodiment. But the Idea, spiritual significance, is not to be confined within sensuous form. There is a felt overplus of meaning, and it taxes the resources of artistic embodiment. This is the characteristic of romantic art; here are works of art that do not quite "speak for themselves," but need interpretation and raise problems. Though, at this stage, art seems to point toward philosophy, it cannot be regarded as philosophy. Art here is transcending itself, but it is still within its own range; hence, the felt insufficiency of its sensuous molds.

A broad historical survey would recognize oriental art as typically symbolic, Greek art as preeminently classical, Christian art as romantic in tendency. Hegel similarly distinguished the symbolic strain in architecture, and sculpture as the basic type of classical art form, and painting, music, and poetry as arts in which the romantic surcharge of meaning is manifested more characteristically.

The exposition of Hegel's aesthetics cannot be reviewed here in further detail. No philosopher before him had undertaken a systematic interpretation of the fine arts on such an encyclopedic scale. Through more than 1500 pages, Hegel reviewed modern aesthetic theories, analyzed the fundamental ideas of beauty and artistic activity, undertook a thorough interpretation of the three stages of art mentioned above, and then proceeded to examine the particular arts—architecture, sculpture, painting, music—in their historical development and in their role as spiritual expressions. He placed his greatest emphasis on poetry, which he estimated as the most profound and greatest of the arts, reaching its summit in the drama.

"The Greek god is the object of naive intuition and sensuous imagination. His shape is therefore the bodily form of man."[16] But the more mature Christian intelligence recognizes that God is Spirit, to be worshiped in spirit and in truth. The deep insight expressed by the conviction of aesthetic insufficiency in romantic art is manifested especially in tragedy. Poetry in its highest achievements marks the rise from sensuous to inner spiritual expression, from art to religion.

"Religion is the Divine Spirit's knowledge of itself through the mediation of finite spirit."[17] Hegel's fundamental view of religion identified it with philosophy, but with an important distinction. Both religion and philosophy are "knowledge of that which is eternal, of what God is, and what flows out of his nature."[18] In philosophy, this knowledge of the highest and ultimate reality is thought; in religion it is imaged, expressed in figurative representation. Philosophy contemplates the universal, basic reality as manifested in particular, existent things. Religion presents God, in the first week of the universe, creating heaven and earth. In the development of the popular consciousness, Spirit seeks religious utterance; but, at the most mature stages of consciousness, Spirit turns to philosophy for its expression.

Hegel traced this progressively more philosophical insight in the evolution of religion. At the lowest level of definite religion, which Hegel called "the religion of nature," man uses worship as a means of controlling and exploiting nature through magic. Advancing somewhat on the same level, men seek by various paths to reach out for and to use a deity represented by boundless power, but not yet conceived as Spirit. The Chinese deity, T'ien, is the sovereign but indeterminate universal Being; the Hindu Brahma is formless, abstract Essence; Buddhism exalts empty Nothingness. Hegel traced the transition from these forms of natural religion to the religions of spiritual individuality. Approaches to the higher stage are represented by the Zoroastrian religion of Light, or Good, striving with Darkness, or Evil, by the Syrian religion which Hegel called the "religion of pain," and by the Egyptian religion of world mystery. In all three, an insistent hope illumines the baffled dismay of men. The Zoroastrian Ahura-Mazda will eventually prevail over Ahriman and nullify his evil realm; the Syrian Phoenix rises to new life from his ashes; like Adonis, Osiris dies to live again.

The second main stage of development in the religions of spiritual indi-

16 G. W. Hegel, *The Philosophy of Fine Art* (trans. F. P. B. Osmaston), London, Bell, 1920, Vol. I, p. 107.

17 G. W. Hegel, *Lectures on the Philosophy of Religion* (trans. E. B. Speirs and J. B. Sanderson), London, Kegan, Paul, 1895, Vol. I, p. 206.

18 *Ibid.*, p. 19.

viduality was seen by Hegel as represented by the three religions which provide the cultural background of Christianity. The Jewish religion is the religion of sublimity; the Greek religion is the religion of beauty; the Roman religion is the religion of utility.

The summit of absolute religion is Christianity, and Hegel interpreted its truths as religious-figurative representations of the true philosophy, Hegelianism. Christianity is the religion of the freely self-conscious, absolute Spirit. Its fundamental doctrines are the basic convictions of idealism, and can be so interpreted by philosophical intelligence. The Trinity signifies the threefold self-manifestation of deity, God as the eternal all-embracing universal; God as the infinite, particular self-manifestation; God as the Holy Spirit of individual, eternal love. Man's sinfulness and his redemption and atonement by Christ's death express, in the language of religion, the alienation between the finite and the infinite and their ultimate reconciliation. Hegel contemplated three religious prospects: the Kingdom of the Father, or God in His eternal Being; the Kingdom of the Son, or God creatively active and manifest in a finite world that is also temporarily estranged from Him; and the Kingdom of the Spirit, or God as the living, infinite presence in the Church, the spiritual community of godly men.

Hegel's philosophy of religion included his examination of the proofs of the existence of God, in which he developed critically the main arguments of theology. His reinterpretation of the ontological argument of St. Anselm is especially noteworthy. The ontological argument is analytic; "It starts from the notion or conception, and passes by means of the conception to existence."[19] How is this transition accomplished? The idea of God is the idea of an absolutely perfect Being; and, surely, ultimate and supreme Being cannot be conceived as nonexistent, a sublime nonentity. Being is the poorest of categories which the least grain of sand can afford; the supreme notion "is not so poor as not to contain this determination in it."[20] The ontological argument, rightly understood, does not make an unwarranted leap from meaning to existence. When Gaunilo urged his idea of the most perfect island, and Kant his concept of a hundred dollars in his pocket, their inferred disproof of the ontological argument was not relevant. It is a mark of finite things that a logical idea of them does not necessarily involve their objective existence. But the scale of reality points toward the synthesis of idea and existence. The highest reality of absolute Spirit, God, must necessarily comprehend the utmost of idea and existence.

The truth of absolute Spirit, of which Christianity gives the highest religious or figurative utterance, can be expressed fully only through the rational thought of philosophy. Philosophy is thus the final synthesis of spiritual experience. But this absolute synthesis does not emerge full and complete as Pallas Athene did from the head of Zeus; it has a progressive historical development and realization. The history of philosophy is the dialectical

19 *Ibid.*, Vol. III, p. 244.
20 *Ibid.*, p. 365.

unfolding and self-revelation of philosophical truth, and, in Hegel's interpretation of reality, the history of philosophy is preeminently important. It is the epic of absolute Spirit; in philosophy, ideas are no mere concepts, but are living realities that express the dialectical rhythm of the spiritual world.

Beyond his patient historical record of the various specific doctrines, Hegel sought to trace the significant currents and crosscurrents found in the principal movements of thought, the synthesis of extreme, contending doctrines in a more integral and adequate principle, which, in turn, exposes its limitations, is opposed by a counter theory, and points to a further and deeper ground of reinterpretation. As in his logic, so in his history of philosophy, Hegel exhibited the dialectic of thought, not only in the counterplay of specific categories, but also in the main distinguishable stages of the ongoing process. We may note, for instance, how the solution of the issue between Heraclitus and the Eleatics involved a transition from monism to pluralism, which in turn required reconciliation. The problem of universals in medieval Scholastic philosophy, the modern opposition of empiricism and rationalism and its critical synthesis by Kant provide other instances of the same process. On a vaster scale, the history of philosophy manifests in its three major periods, ancient-classical, medieval-Christian, and modern, its fundamental dialectical movement.

Hegel's *History of Philosophy* was left in rough and incomplete form as lecture notes, and this may account for his uneven treatment of the various periods and systems of thought. We should expect a much more adequate examination of modern philosophy. Hegel's critical discussion of post-Kantian problems and issues proceeded to a "Final Result" in which his own philosophy was presented as the culmination of the historical self-expression of absolute Spirit. But, surely, he himself should have been a better Hegelian; he should have recognized that there could be no such definite assignable limit to the unfolding perfection of philosophical thought and no such specific "Final Result." In fact, Hegelian idealism was soon to be confronted not with one but with several alternative antitheses. These issues complicate the later history of philosophy; they expand and deepen the philosophical problem, but they also confirm us in regarding a definitive solution of it as unlikely.

SUGGESTED WORKS FOR FURTHER STUDY

WORKS BY HEGEL. Hegel, *Early Theological Writings* (trans. T. M. Knox); *Phenomenology of Mind* (trans. J. B. Baillie); *Works on Logic* (trans. W. H. Johnston and L. G. Struthers, or H. S. Macran, or W. Wallace); *Philosophy of Mind* (trans. W. Wallace); *Philosophy of Right* (trans. S. W. Dyde or T. M. Knox); *Philosophy of Fine Art* (trans. F. P. B. Osmaston); *Philosophy of History* (trans. J. Sibree); *Philosophy of Religion* (trans. E. B. Speirs and

J. B. Sanderson); *History of Philosophy* (trans. E. S. Haldane and F. H. Simson); *Encyclopedia of Philosophy* (trans. G. E. Mueller); *Selections* (J. Loewenberg, ed.).

BIOGRAPHIES AND CRITICAL STUDIES.   Caird, Edward, *Hegel;* Cunningham, G. W., *Thought and Reality in Hegel's System;* Hibben, J. G., *Hegel's Logic;* McTaggart, J. E., *Studies in the Hegelian Dialectic, Studies in Hegelian Cosmology;* Marcuse, Herbert, *Reason and Revolution: Hegel and the Rise of Social Theory;* Mure, G. R. G., *A Study of Hegel's Logic;* Seth Pringle-Pattison, Andrew, *Hegelianism and Personality;* Reyburn, H. A., *The Ethical Theory of Hegel;* Stace, W. T., *The Philosophy of Hegel;* Stirling, J. H., *The Secret of Hegel.*

28. Arthur Schopenhauer: Irrationalism and Pessimism

Personal Strains in Schopenhauer's Philosophy

The philosophy of Schopenhauer, in its substance and tone, reflects the character of the man behind it. A biographical introduction is essential to an understanding of Schopenhauer's view of the world and of human nature. Though he prided himself that, unlike the idealists after Kant, he had built his system on solid ground, the reader of his works is impressed, not by their scientific objectivity, but by their intensely lyrical utterance. His works are philosophical poems of unreason and gloom. They owe much of their power to his literary style; for, unlike most German philosophers, Schopenhauer was a master of living expression. His ideas are not stiff concepts; as recorded, they carry the direct message of experience. His appraisal of life is intensified by his dramatic account of it. Even warped evidence and misfit logic might produce conviction in a reader swept by Schopenhauer's flood of eloquence.

Arthur Schopenhauer (1788–1860) was born into a family in which violent emotional tensions were characteristic. There was an emotionally tainted strain in his paternal heritage; the only sound one of this stock, his father, also was consumed by pride, ill temper, and dejection. He had been a solid banker of Danzig who remembered that his grandfather had once been host to Peter the Great. When that oligarchic city-state was taken over by Prussia, the unsubmissive magnate wound up his affairs and moved to Hamburg. But the change proved financially and personally depressing, and one day, during a fit of melancholy, the banker drowned in the Hamburg canal.

His widow—twenty years younger, and possessed of a gay temper and social and literary ambitions—soon consoled herself. Leaving Arthur to work in a commercial office, she took her young daughter with her to Weimar, where she established a salon that attracted poets and artists, including Goethe. But Arthur hated his ledgers, and, mentally grappling with the problem of evil, he wrote black letters to his mother in which he begged her to let him prepare for the university. When she finally consented, he required only two years of concentrated study to be ready for Göttingen. There—and later, at Berlin—he studied classical literature, science, and philosophy. The conviction possessed him that he was destined to solve the miserable problem of life. But, to his complacent mother, his despondency was just bad temper; she had neither the ability nor the taste for his developing philosophy. When he showed her his doctor's dissertation, *On the Four-fold Root of the Principle of Sufficient Reason*, she held her nose, because the root in the title, she said, smelled like a pharmacy.

Goethe understood the young man better, and befriended him; the two cooperated for a while on a study of the theory of colors. But Schopenhauer was no one's disciple. Within five years after entering the university he was at work on his philosophical masterpiece, *The World as Will and Idea*. It was completed when he was 30, but its publication failed to shake the philosophical world as the young author had confidently expected. His attempt to lecture at the University of Berlin in direct rivalry with Hegel proved a failure. No one took notice of the new philosophy, and Schopenhauer became convinced that he was the victim of a conspiracy of neglect.

His patrimony, despite some financial upsets, sufficed for his support, and he settled in Frankfort-on-the-Main as a philosophical freelance. He kept on writing philosophical works—although scarcely anyone read them—*The Will in Nature;* a successful prize essay, *On the Freedom of the Will;* and an unsuccessful prize-essay, *The Basis of Morality*. With unyielding courage, twenty-five years after the failure of his main treatise, he persuaded his publisher to bring out a second greatly enlarged edition, which also missed recognition. Finally, however, the tide turned during the mid-century period of depression that followed the frustrated revolutions of 1848. The great popularity of a collection of Schopenhauer's essays published in 1851 created interest in his other works, and the last decade of his life was one of expanding fame.

When he was 17 years old, like the young Buddha, he had been gripped by the universal misery of life. At 70, after lifelong rebuffs and frustration, he wrote, "So roses are strewn in my path also, but of course, only white roses."[1] His embitterment at the apathy of the philosophical world for thirty years was his greatest grief in a life of continual annoyances. He spoke with contempt of professors, publishers, reviewers, and editors; he wrangled with landladies and neighbors. He whom no one read was ever suspicious of plagiarists. He was sensual, irascible, arrogant, and morose. The only living thing that commanded his steady devotion was his dog. The virtues a zealous biographer might finally discover in his character would prove to be reflections of his vices. Was ever a major system of philosophy propounded by so negative a personality? Yet, between our enchantment with Schopenhauer's style and our aversion to many traits of his character, we should strive for a fair examination and appraisal of his philosophical ideas.

[1] Quoted in Hermann Frommann, *Arthur Schopenhauer*, Jena, Frommann, 1872, p. 6.

Reason as the Tool of the Will-to-Live

Schopenhauer never mentioned the names of the post-Kantian idealists without a diatribe. To him, Fichte was a windbag, and Hegel was a charlatan, an intellectual Caliban, and a Beelzebub. Denouncing in just such terms these two and Schelling as false pretenders to Kant's crown, Schopenhauer declared that he alone was the true heir. Actually, he owed many of his ideas to his contemporaries, but these did not include the fundamental, dynamic principle of his philosophy and its pessimistic tone.

In an appendix to *The World as Will and Idea*, Schopenhauer presented his "Criticism of the Kantian Philosophy." He esteemed highly Kant's theory of space and time as the fundamental forms of sense perception, but he believed that, on this basis, he could establish a new geometry proceeding, not by rational proof, but by direct perceptual evidence. He apparently did not grasp the full meaning of Kant's integration of perceptions and concepts in the process of experience. His criticism of Kant's system of categories was very searching, and he exposed many of its defects. Likewise, in his critical examination of the transcendental dialectic, especially the antinomies, Schopenhauer disclosed Kant's artificial procedure in unduly balancing theses and antitheses in the various conflicts. But in his correction of specific defects in Kant's method and theory, and in his admiration of the Kantian principles that suited him, he failed to grasp and to develop the constructive value of Kant's critical account of experience. He did not go through and beyond Kant as Kant had gone through and beyond Hume.

Schopenhauer's theory of knowledge is a phenomenalism of skeptical tenor. Kant's doctrine of critical limitation affirmed the universal validity of scientific knowledge within the scope of possible experience. The metaphysical pretensions of dogmatic rationalism, according to Kant, transgress the limits of the mind's competence. Schopenhauer gave a negative version of this mainly constructive doctrine. Scientific knowledge and all intellectual cognition, he said, concern only phenomena and can never grasp ultimate reality. The mind does not know things-in-themselves; its so-called "knowledge" is an intellectual construction of the causal nexus of events in our experience. "The world is my idea."[2] Physical science is simply an explanation of our version of nature, but physics can never yield metaphysics, can never yield insight into the nature of reality as it is in itself.

In his doctoral dissertation, Schopenhauer had already analyzed the fundamental scientific category of causality, the ground of becoming, in its relation to the other three forms of the principle of sufficient reason—the reason, or ground, of being, of knowing, and of doing. The first, the ground of

[2] A. Schopenhauer, *The World as Will and Idea* (trans. R. B. Haldane and J. Kemp), 7th ed., London, Kegan, Paul, n.d., Vol. I, p. 3.

being, or *ratio essendi*, is manifested as the perceptual order of ideas, in spatial coexistence and temporal succession. The ground of knowing, *ratio cognoscendi*, is the required dependence of each judgment on its adequate reason. The third, the ground of doing, *ratio agendi*, concerns the determining motivation needed to explain any action. These three forms of the principle of sufficient reason express the basic character of necessary order in our experience, of which the outstanding expression is the ground of becoming, *ratio fiendi*, the causal nexus of events with which physical science deals.

Schopenhauer's version of Kant's phenomenalism was an unacknowledged reaffirmation of Fichte's rejection of a theoretical metaphysics. Fichte maintained that the intellect can never span the cleavage or the dualism of subject and object. So Schopenhauer held that all the objects of the understanding are objects for a subject, conditioned and colored by the subjective forms of space, time, and causality. Fichte sought ultimate reality in the infinite striving of the ideal Will. But Schopenhauer's view of the striving Will was radically different, and it is here that he struck his original note in philosophy.

Schopenhauer included both materialism and idealism in his repudiation of theoretical metaphysics. The materialist mistakes his own physical-scientific constructions for ultimate realities. "The materialist is like Baron Münchausen who, when swimming in water on horseback, drew the horse into the air with his legs, and himself also by his queue."[3] Physical, material objects are all objects of experience, objects for a subject. The thinking mind cannot reason itself out of existence, as it undertakes to do in materialistic metaphysics. But no more can it exorcise material existence and contemplate its own pure subjectivity, as is attempted in the cloud-cuckoo-towns of the idealists. The intellect is lashed to its subject-object dualism, and can never pierce beyond it to grasp the nature of ultimate reality. "We are like a man who goes round a castle seeking in vain for an entrance, and sometimes sketching the façades."[4]

The solution of the metaphysical problem which has baffled all theoretical philosophy is unmistakable, according to Schopenhauer. He prided himself on having first pointed it out. The thing-in-itself, the ultimate reality at every stage of existence, is the will to live. Recognize it in human nature; our mental and bodily processes, distinguished and also related, are both of them modes of appearance and means of the craving, insatiate activity, the desires and purposes of our will to live. That vital dynamic constitutes each one of us fundamentally and finally; all the rest is but the medium of operation.

When we have thus faced the living kernel of our own being, we can recognize its kin throughout nature at various stages of its manifestation and activity. This ceaseless, self-assertive drive, which, at our level of conscious

[3] *Ibid.*, pp. 34 f.
[4] *Ibid.*, p. 128.

experience, manifests itself as desire and volition, finds its various expressions throughout nature. The phenomenal means and processes differ; the permeating dynamic is the same:

The force which germinates and vegetates in the plant, . . . through which the crystal is formed, that by which the magnet turns to the north pole, . . . the force which appears in the elective affinities of matter as repulsion and attraction, . . . even gravitation, which acts so powerfully throughout matter, draws the stone to the earth and the earth to the sun.[5]

These are only different manifestations of the identical ultimate reality, which is most intimately known to us in our daily life as "will."

Schopenhauer's book, *The Will in Nature,* had a similarity of pattern to Schelling's and Hegel's philosophies of nature. Schelling interpreted nature as latent spirit and sought to trace the progressive realization of spiritual character in the process of existence. Hegel, similarly, endeavored to unveil in nature the dialectical process of the progressive organization of differences. Schopenhauer's treatise was intended to exhibit the operation of the will to live throughout the range of existence. Against "Hegel's philosophy of absolute nonsense,"[6] a clacking mill that ground no flour, his report of solid evidence was meant to carry its own proof and convincing power.

Schopenhauer traversed the field of physiology, pathology, and comparative anatomy, citing scientific writers—ancient and modern—who had unwittingly testified in support of his doctrine of the will to live. And he found it significant that his fundamental principle, which was sustained by science, could be shown also to clear up borderline subjects like animal magnetism and magic.

Theologians and philosophers have sought to prove God's existence from the evidences of an intelligent design in nature. Schopenhauer rejected the theistic inference and interpreted the seeming unconscious adaptation in terms of his voluntaristic irrationalism. *The World as Will and Idea* continually cites instances of this world-wide operation of the will to live:

The eye is adapted to the light and its refrangibility, the lungs and the blood to the air, the air-bladder of fish to water, the eye of the seal to the change of the medium in which it must see, the water-pouch in the stomach of the camel to the drought of the African deserts, the sail of the nautilus to the wind that is to drive its little bark. . . .[7]

When we turn from all these lower manifestations of the will to live to its activity on the human level of consciousness, we should recognize in all of them the essential identity of the ultimate active power. We should not, however, make the egregious blunder of regarding the will to live as con-

---

[5] *Ibid.,* p. 142.
[6] A. Schopenhauer, *The Will in Nature,* Introduction, in Mme. Karl Hillebrand, *Schopenhauer on the Fourfold Root of the Principle of Sufficient Reason and on the Will in Nature,* revised ed., London, Bell, 1910, p. 222.
[7] A. Schopenhauer, *The World as Will and Idea, op. cit.,* Vol. I, p. 208.

scious throughout its entire range simply because it is conscious in human experience. Schopenhauer employed the term "the will to live" analogically. Just as Hegel, in his conviction of the essentially rational character of reality, gave the word "thought" a metaphysical connotation, so Schopenhauer described ultimate reality with the expression "will to live," which characterized the higher stages of its manifestation. His will to live was not intended always to signify volition.

In emphasizing will rather than thought, Schopenhauer meant to affirm the basically irrational character of reality. Reason is not the primal creative power in the universe. It is an episode in the saga of existence. It is an instrument of the will to live, like the dog's keen scent or the snake's venomous fangs, a means of survival in the struggle of life. "The magnet that has attracted a piece of iron carries on a perpetual conflict with gravitation. . . . Many insects . . . lay their eggs on the skin, and even in the body of the larvae of other insects, whose slow destruction is the first work of the newly hatched brood. . . ."[8] Similarly, man, in his rational ways, devises his schemes of attack and defense. The characters and the stage setting differ, but the reenacted drama of existence is the same.

The cosmic drama is a tragedy, and its woeful character becomes evident to consciousness on the human level. The will to live is manifested in us as the pang of desire. Want, the distress of insatiate craving, is our primary experience. Desire is the consciousness of some actual lack or deficiency. So long as it is unsatisfied, the experience of it is painful. But pleasure is only a temporary relief from this common misery, for the satisfaction of one desire leads to a new want and its gnawing distress. In rarer cases of more readily gratified cravings, consciousness may sink into the empty longing for nothing in particular, deadly tedium. This, in bare outline, is the sorry biography of each of us. Our religious visions find us enmeshed in the same dilemma; "After man had transferred all pain and torments to hell, there was nothing left for him in heaven but boredom."[9]

The recognition of this miserable round of human existence becomes clearer with the perfection of intelligence. The mind of genius is possessed by the tragic spectacle of human life and all nature. As Gautama Buddha expressed it, the universality of misery is the cardinal truth of existence. Were human life only miserable, however, it would be pitiable but it would still have dignity. Its corruption, though, is more widespread. The life of insatiate desire is a life of selfish, wicked, and futile greed. Hobbes had pointed out that men's rapacity makes them rivals and enemies, so that, in a state of nature, human existence is a universal war of each against all. Even in society, Schopenhauer said, men are only muzzled wolves and tigers. We devise polite conventions to screen the ugly actualities, but the least stir of conflicting interests exposes the greedy beast behind the courteous pretense.

[8] *Ibid.*, pp. 190, 192.
[9] Paraphrased from *ibid.*, p. 402.

Human wickedness is only the conscious expression of the natural ruthlessness which the striving and self-rending struggle of the will to live exhibits at every stage of existence. The ant bear's extensible, glutinous, and long tongue is a manifestation of its will to live by preying on the fat brood in the termite nests. This example can be multiplied a hundredfold. The whole world is a "scene of tormented and agonized beings, who only continue to exist by devouring each other, in which, therefore, every ravenous beast is the living grave of thousands of others, and its self-maintenance is a chain of painful deaths."[10] Hegel's idealism portrayed history as the gradual realization of freedom, but Schopenhauer called it "a wretched series of cat fights." At the end of its long chapters devoted to this or that war, there may be some blank half-pages; they are for the dubious intervals of peace.

Our life is as futile as it is miserable, selfish, and wicked. We crave a finality of satisfaction which we never experience. We struggle to avoid this peril or that, but even if we succeed, we are always coming nearer the inevitable shipwreck, death. And because, despite our lofty pretensions, we have throughout been activated by low greed, our eventual frustration lacks the tragic relief of heroic dignity; our downfall is inglorious, and, in its details, it is comical, a wretched jest. Men, themselves without worth, realize nothing worth having: "If we could lay all the misery of the world in one scale of the balance, and all the guilt of the world in the other, the needle would certainly point to the center.[11]

Pure Intelligence in Aesthetic Contemplation

From all this grim portrayal of the wretched and wicked lives of men, and the reasonless sweep of existence, the reader turns in search of some redeeming light. Actually, Schopenhauer had his gospel of salvation, but even as we hear it, we ask ourselves, how he could have any gospel, any glad tidings for the world which he saw? If we accept his metaphysics of the will to live, the irrational, ceaseless drive and insatiate craving, what else can our lives be but selfish, wicked, wretched, and altogether futile? The black secret has then been told, and all is known. Yet, in his pessimistic account, Schopenhauer prided himself on his straightforwardness; he had spoken right out, reported the plain facts of human life. If now he turns to other pages of the book of life and cites other facts from which he infers his gospel, this new evidence will have to be included in our critical estimate of his complete theory. It will surely affect his metaphysics of the irrational will to live. We need this reserve of judgment as we turn to his aesthetics and ethics. His portrayal of these heights of human experience is brilliant. However, its connection with his earlier dismal exposure is not clear.

10 *Ibid.*, Vol. III, p. 392.
11 *Ibid.*, Vol. I, p. 454.

The usual retort to the eloquent pessimist has been to urge suicide. If the air in the room is foul beyond endurance, why not open a door and walk out? Even if we could somehow circumvent the will to live in ourselves, with its strong attachment to life, Schopenhauer warns us that suicide will not relieve the basic evil. Not life is to be denied, but the will to live and the evils it breeds. But our intelligence is itself the tool of the will to live; how can it ever perceive and pursue the road that leads to the denial of the will?

Schopenhauer pointed out two paths to salvation, and, in both of them, he revealed capacities of man's intelligence for which he had made no provision in his metaphysics. The first path is through aesthetic experience. The intellect usually acts as an instrument of the will to live. We consider everything as a source of possible advantage or satisfaction. We ask what there is in it for us. But, in rare instances, a man may relinquish this common exploiting view of things. His intelligence may become the clear mirror of its object. This purely disinterested contemplation is the mark of artistic genius, and, in various degrees, it characterizes all aesthetic experience.

Schopenhauer compared this will-less perception of reality in art to the rational contemplation of the Platonic Ideas. The various arts represent the various stages of existence as viewed disinterestedly by pure intelligence. Accordingly, Schopenhauer drew up a table of the principal arts of this hierarchy of nature, in the following order: architecture, sculpture, painting, poetry, music.

Architecture presents to our contemplation the counteraction of the elemental forces of material existence, especially the conflict of gravity and rigidity, burden and support. To see the roof press the earth through its columns, the arch support itself, to see these opposed forces in a counteraction in which each is held by the other—this is the essence of architectural perfection on its own level. Sculpture affords the pure contemplation of animal and human forms in their beauty, without lust or desire of any kind. Here artistic genius may even improve on nature, present to nature in hard marble a living form surpassing actuality, as if to say, "This is what you wanted to express!" Intelligence may stamp its vision on matter so that the stone attains character. In painting, the will-driven tumult of life is both portrayed and stilled in the portrayal, in the perfect harmony of design and color, in the peace of still life and landscape, in the blessed serenity of saintly resignation.

A much higher art is poetry. Its medium is man's own experience, feelings, and thoughts. They may find direct lyrical expression, or the poet may portray the far-flung careers of men and nations on an epic scale. The greatest poetry is dramatic. It finds its summit in tragedy, which portrays human life as revealed to our deepest insight, life in its essential distress, frustration, and final ruin.

In these ways, the artist disinterestedly contemplates the various stages of objectification of the will to live. But music, the highest art of all, is unique in that it contemplates the will itself, "disclosing the most profound ultimate and secret significance of the feeling expressed. . . ."[12] The longings and the anxieties of our hearts, our occasional relief in moments of happiness, our far rarer peace of stilled desire—all find their expression in the chords and harmonies of music. This deep insight into reality is not presented to us in the explicit terms of intellectual understanding; it is communicated directly, and no abstract verbiage can convey its meaning. "We might, therefore, just as well call the world embodied music as embodied will."[13] Thus, he who could penetrate the full significance of music would grasp the secret of reality in true metaphysics.

Disinterested aesthetic contemplation gives relief from the drive of the will to live, but it is not permanent salvation. We turn our glance from the beautiful statue or painting, the curtain falls on the great tragedy, or the last note of the symphony fades away, and once again we are gripped by our insatiate desires. Art gives us only passing visions of the blessed peace of emancipation, but this abiding peace points beyond art, to morality and saintly renunciation.

The Morality of Compassion and the Denial of the Will

The idealists after Kant were committed to the principle of a spiritual unity in the universe. Their philosophy of life did not ignore the actuality of evil—this problem engrossed Schelling's attention—but the prevailing tone of idealistic metaphysics was optimistic, and so the idealistic ethics emphasized perfectionism, the normal fulfillment of personality. This sort of moral philosophy was unthinkable in Schopenhauer's irrationalism and pessimism. He considered any positive, optimistic view of the good life—self-realization or general happiness—not only unwarranted, but a gratuitous insult to wretched humanity. Morality, if one could speak of morality at all, could be conceived only as some alleviation of our evil and miserable lot, some escape from it.

Schopenhauer was thus in radical opposition to the varieties of traditional moral philosophy, and here his theoretical admiration for Kant was replaced by a contemptuous repudiation. He rejected Kant's categorical imperative as void of sense. An unconditional obligation is self-contradictory; all imperatives are hypothetical; that is, they appeal to consequences, and in usual human motivation they reveal a selfish incentive, and hence, are morally worthless. I ought to keep my promises; why? because otherwise men will break their promises to me. Instead of excogitating an abstract ethics for purely rational beings, and proclaiming solemnly and loftily a moral law of duty—merely formal content and without real substance—Kant should

---

[12] *Ibid.*, Vol. III, p. 233.
[13] *Ibid.*, Vol. I, p. 340.

have based his ethics on direct examination of human nature, of men's motives and actions.

Schopenhauer thus came forward as a pronounced ethical realist. He rejected as an empty abstraction the Kantian supersensuous realm of ends or a world of values, and, along with it, the alleged spiritual principles of the idealists. He recognized only men and women of flesh and blood, and, therefore, he refused to listen to any word about moral freedom. Already in his criticism of Kant's third antinomy he had taken a firm stand on determinism. In his prize essay, *On the Freedom of the Will*, he systematically examined the historical development of that problem, and reaffirmed his adherence to the strict necessity of human actions. Motivation is only a more involved causal operation. An animal responds to the stimulus or irritant of the moment. Man may look beyond it to more remote considerations harbored in his memory, or to further aims and anticipations. But across these spans of experience the causal chain is unbroken. The careers of men are as determined as are the courses of the stars in their orbits.

Schopenhauer declared that Kant's doctrine of the empirical and the intelligible character had a deeper meaning which was unperceived by its author. The empirical character, as Kant held, is a man's bodily and mental make-up. But, what Kant called the "intelligible character" should properly be recognized as the inmost kernel of our being, namely, the will to live. Each action has its motives and determinants, but the whole character and purport of a man's life is ultimately the expression of what he is. If we now insist on asking why I am thus myself and not another, we shall be pushing beyond the limits of specific explanation. This does not mean that man's basic character is free, but that causality concerns only specific events.

All ethics is a proposed judgment on human lives, but Schopenhauer insisted that it be based upon a direct examination of human lives. This examination had already led him to a pessimistic conclusion in his philosophy. Men are wretched, selfish, wicked, and the usual run of human actions is empty futility, and without worth. If any morality is possible, it can be only by denial of the characteristic human motives. Schopenhauer recalled the cardinal truths of Buddhism: Human life is altogether miserable; the misery is due to selfishness; and it can be overcome only by the extinction of self; to this goal leads the blessed eightfold path of salvation.

Schopenhauer distinguished three possible incentives to action: egoism, malice, and compassion. The first two mark the wretched affairs of men. Any conceivable virtue can lie only in their negation, in compassionate acts. Egoism and malice should not be confused. Schopenhauer proposed to formulate their respective "maxims." The egoist acts on the principle, "Help no one, but so far as it is to your advantage, hurt others."[14] That is, the egoist disregards the well-being of others, but he is not bent on hurting them unless they are in his way. He is intent on his own advantage, and

[14] A. Schopenhauer, *The Basis of Morality* (trans. A. B. Bullock), London, Sonnenschein, 1903, Part III, chap. 3.

may accordingly trample others or entirely ignore them. The malicious man finds his own satisfaction in hurting others. This is spiteful conduct, "sheer cussedness." From egoism and malice stem all the vices of human conduct. Greed, gluttony, lust, avarice, covetousness, injustice, hardness of heart, pride, and arrogance are due to egoism. Envy, ill will, prying curiosity, pleasure in seeing others suffer, slander, insolence, petulance, hatred, anger, treachery, fraud, vindictiveness, and cruelty are due to spiteful malice.

Compassion, or sympathy, is radically opposed to the evil incentives in human life, and it alone characterizes virtue. The compassionate man acts on the principle, "Hurt no one, but so far as you can, help others."[15] Sympathetic motivation indicates a curbing of the will to live. In contrast to the selfish desires which make each man opposed, or at least callous, to the well-being of others, sympathy involves active concern for the sufferings and needs of those we feel to be our fellow men. The compassionate man no longer says of his neighbor's burden of sorrow: "What is that to me? Let him see to it." Even as pure intelligence in aesthetic experience disinterestedly contemplates all nature, so in compassionate conduct morality expresses a man's disinterested self-identification with others. Both experiences, artistic and moral, are most exceptional. Thus, we read in *Hamlet*: "To be honest, as this world goes, is to be one man picked out of two thousand."[16]

The two clauses in the maxim of compassion indicate its negative and positive aspects. These are the two cardinal virtues, justice and loving-kindness (*caritas*). Justice in a miserable world consists in not adding to the heavy burdens of others, but carrying our own load. The just man at least restrains his selfishness; he does not oppress or exploit others; he takes no unfair advantage. Loving-kindness is positive sympathy; it seeks to relieve the distress of others; it is active self-forgetting concern for the common well-being.

The fundamentally pessimistic tone of Schopenhauer's philosophy persists in his idea of compassion as the only possible good in life. The very meaning of the word, the same in different languages (compassion, sympathy, *Mitleid*), is negative. Compassion is suffering with others, a fellow feeling of common distress. Morality is thus a tragic experience arising from a tragic outlook on life. But, in this gloomy perspective, the promotion of the common welfare no longer has the complacent meaning found in traditional ethical theories. In place of the hedonist's bland pursuit of the greatest happiness of the greatest number, Schopenhauer's ethics expressed a grim, deepening conviction that happiness and well-being are unattainable. The good man seeks to promote his fellow men's well-being but finds in the lives of them all only miseries crying for some relief. And, in his endeavor to alleviate this distress or that, he is led to the tragic realization of the essential wretchedness of us all in our miserable and futile will-driven existence.

The morality of compassion, therefore, points beyond itself to the ascetic

---

[15] Paraphrased from *ibid.*, p. 175.
[16] Shakespeare, *Hamlet*, II:ii.

curbing and, finally, to the utter denial of the will to live. The moral saint renounces the life of will-driven desire in all its expressions, and he must start with the basic and strongest impulse, the sexual. "Voluntary and complete chastity is the first step in asceticism."[17] From chastity, the hermit proceeds to his renunciation of all the lusts and ambitions of men. His fasting is a daily curb on bodily appetite; he adopts holy poverty; he dismisses worldly ambition; he patiently bears ailments and the blows of fortune, endures ignominy meekly, returns good for evil, is slow to anger and alert to mercy and charity.

Schopenhauer was as eloquent in his eulogy of the compassionate, ascetic life of the denial of will as he had been in his pessimistic portrayal of a will-driven existence. "He . . . who has attained to the denial of the will-to-live, however poor, joyless, and full of privation his condition may appear when looked at externally, is yet filled with inward joy and the true peace of heaven."[18] This peace, Schopenhauer said, infinitely surpasses everything else in life. But he also recognized that this denial of the will is a negation of the ongoing course of human life. Since the will to live is the ultimate reality that manifests itself in the world, how can it be extinguished without blotting out all existence?

Schopenhauer met this challenge boldly in the concluding sentence of *The World as Will and Idea:* "What remains after the entire abolition of the will is for all those who are still full of will certainly nothing; but, conversely, to those in whom the will has turned and has denied itself, this our world, which is so real, with all its suns and milky-ways—is nothing."[19] This is a brilliant passage, but does it meet the problem? If by "suns and milky-ways" Schopenhauer referred to the course of phenomenal existence, then he might mean that asceticism probes the kernel of reality which the scientific knowledge of phenomena cannot reach, and which worldly selfish activity misses altogether. This would only accentuate, not solve, the problem; if the will to live is the ultimate reality, how can it ever "turn and deny itself"?

Aesthetic disinterested contemplation; moral, compassionate conduct; and ascetic renunciation and self-denial may be as rare as they are excellent; but, however exceptional, they express the nature of reality even as physical existence and the egoistic desires of men express it. And the ultimate reality for Schopenhauer is the will to live. When he extolled the ascetic saint for probing the inmost heart of reality, could he mean that the higher saintly life is a truer expression of the will to live than the grim manifestation of it which he had exposed in his metaphysics? We can scarcely believe that this was his intention, for, if it were, he should have recognized that the conclusion drawn in his philosophy required a radical revision of his metaphysics. But, whatever his intended position may have

[17] A. Schopenhauer, *The World as Will and Idea, op. cit.,* Vol. I, p. 491.
[18] *Ibid.,* p. 503.
[19] *Ibid.,* p. 532.

been, Schopenhauer's gospel of salvation and his irrational, pessimistic account of reality are in radical conflict. The opposition cannot be overcome by logical synthesis without rejecting his irrationalism. We might interpret the conflict as not irreconcilable, and trace a dramatic deepening of insight in his philosophy of life. But then the question of right emphasis would confront us. These radical issues in Schopenhauer's philosophy had to be faced by his followers, who sought a way out by a critical redistribution of emphasis on the various discordant parts of the master's system. The most noteworthy development was Eduard von Hartmann's proposed synthesis of Schopenhauer's and Hegel's philosophies, which will be considered in a later chapter.

SUGGESTED WORKS FOR FURTHER STUDY

WORKS BY SCHOPENHAUER. Schopenhauer, A., *The World as Will and Idea* (trans. R. B. Haldane and J. Kemp); *The World as Will and Representation* (trans. E. F. J. Payne); *The Basis of Morality* (trans. A. B. Bullock); "Essays" (under various titles, trans. T. B. Saunders); *On the Fourfold Root of the Principle of Sufficient Reason* and *On the Will in Nature* (trans. Mme. K. Hillebrand); *Selections* (DeWitt H. Parker, ed.); *Essay on the Freedom of the Will* (trans. K. Kolenda); *The Living Thoughts of Schopenhauer* (T. Mann, ed.); *The Philosophy of Schopenhauer* (Irwin Edman, ed.).

BIOGRAPHIES AND CRITICAL STUDIES. Caldwell, William, *Schopenhauer's System in Its Philosophical Significance*; McGill, V. J., *Schopenhauer: Pessimist and Pagan*; Tsanoff, R. A., *Schopenhauer's Criticism of Kant's Theory of Experience*; Wallace, William, *Life of Arthur Schopenhauer*; Whittaker, Thomas, *Schopenhauer*; Zimmern, Helen, *Schopenhauer*.

29.   Opponents of Idealism

Herbart: Pluralistic Realism

Schopenhauer's irrationalism and pessimism represented a violent reaction against the idealistic systems of Kant's successors. But idealistic metaphysics was also opposed on several other fronts. The principle of a spiritual unity in nature was challenged in a realistic philosophy which revived the doctrines of atoms and monads. Kant's phenomenalism, the critical limitation of scientific knowledge to the actual course and causal connection of events in experience, led some thinkers to resist the metaphysical *élan* of the idealists, and to advocate empirical psychology as the reasonable philosophy. The discrediting of Schelling's and Hegel's philosophies of nature, in the judgment of scientists, emphasized the naturalistically opposite view that idealism is incompatible with physical science, and this judgment evoked a systematic revival of materialism. These movements were further strengthened by those who deserted the Hegelian camp.

The leader of the realistic reaction was Johann Friedrich Herbart (1776–1841). A younger contemporary of Kant's idealistic successors, Herbart turned against them early in his university studies, even while he was in Fichte's classroom at Jena. Thorough study of Leibniz, Wolff, and Kant confirmed him in his temperamental distrust of any philosophy deduced from initial unitary principles. He resisted the philosophical development from Fichte to Hegel, and he called himself a Kantian of the year 1828, after the idealistic misdirection. He continued his university education in intensive private studies while he was engaged in tutorial work in Switzerland. His acquaintance there with Pestalozzi turned his attention actively to pedagogical problems, which shared his interest with philosophy throughout his life. After four years of lecturing at the University of Göttingen, he went to Königsberg, where, for more than twenty years, he occupied Kant's chair. The closing years of his life found him back at Göttingen, the leader of an expanding group of philosophical and educational disciples.

According to Herbart, philosophy is the elaboration and explanation of the concepts of common reflection and science. Logic clarifies these concepts. Metaphysics develops them critically so as to expose, and then overcome, their inherent confusions and contradictions. Philosophy of value, which Herbart called aesthetics, completes this critical examination with judgments of approval or disapproval. Philosophy is a comprehensive and evaluating criticism of general ideas.

Descartes had recognized doubt as the beginning of philosophical thought. Herbart started with the recognition of radical inconsistencies in our basic concepts. He probed the shaky structure of human knowledge, but his guiding intention was not skeptical. He criticized for the sake of construction. Several of Kant's pure forms of sense perception and his categories of the understanding were subjected to reinterpretation. The agelong problem of the one and the many engrossed Herbart; how is the unity of a thing compatible with its multiplicity of qualities? In particular, the unity of the subject, the ego, was cleft by seemingly irreconcilable dualisms. How are we to understand the unity of self-consciousness when the self as subject must be both distinguished from and identical with the self as object? Turning to the objective world of consciousness, Herbart considered the confusions in man's ideas of space and time and their finite or infinite divisibility.

The problems of change and causal determination presented a basic confusion of ideas. Herbart exposed this confusion in the form of a trilemma, three unacceptable alternatives. The popular view, that every event, A, has an external cause, B, involves an infinite mechanical regress. But this can never provide an adequate explanation of, nor can it account for, the process itself as a chain of determinants. If we entertain the second alternative view, the existence and action of A must be ascribed to an internal cause; A determines itself and its processes. But, in addition to the above difficulties, this theory somehow splits A, regards it both as a determinant and as determined, as both cause and effect. If we entertain the third alternative, if we proceed, beyond the doctrines of causal determination, to the idea of an absolute becoming and production, we regard change as itself a quality of permanent self-identical being. If a being is viewed as preserving its identity *by* changing, the quandary in our conception of it becomes glaring.

Metaphysics is thus embroiled in the manifold inconsistencies of its basic ideas. But the confusion is not hopeless. Herbart, like Descartes, regarded doubt as philosophically productive. Though we may doubt the existence of things, surely they appear to exist, Herbart reasoned, or else we should not entertain any doubts about them. Nothing would appear to exist unless *something* existed. Hence, some form of being must be real. This real being cannot be regarded as single and uniform, for all our sensations are experiences of manifold unities and differences. Therefore Herbart was led to postulate a world of many "reals" which we perceive in various combinations. We can thus reconcile and explain both the persistent identity of ultimate beings, and the confusing variety of ways in which they are manifest to us. This view of existence may recall the ancient doctrine of Democritus, but Herbart, like Anaxagoras, regarded his "reals" as differing not only in size and shape, but also in kind. He described his cosmology as a "qualitative atomism." It may be regarded as a realistic version of Leibniz's monadology.

Some of these reals act consciously; we call them "souls," or "minds." A soul preserves its identity while reacting toward or against other conscious or unconscious reals. Some of these unconscious beings and processes stand in an especially direct relation to the soul; they constitute the body in which the soul is active. The soul operates immediately in and through the brain and nervous system. In self-conscious reflection, the soul is aware of both its own conscious states and the objects of its conscious experience, and it distinguishes between them. The mind organizes its ideas into groups that yield universal ideas. Its complex, organized experience provides a background of materials and meanings within which new perceptions find a suitable place and significance. This growing range of apperception expresses the character of a certain soul, its mental temper. But, while we can follow the growing complexity of mental life in this way, it is important always to keep in mind the elementary reactions out of which the system of personality is built up. Without postulating any spiritual faculties or principles, Herbart believed that the simple processes of association of ideas—by means of similarity and of contiguity—could explain the entire complex procedure of mental operations. He hoped that his view of the mental mechanism would relate psychology more closely to the other natural sciences, and that the application of mathematical measurements to conscious processes would lead to greater precision in psychological statements and laws.

The theory of values in such a realistic philosophy is important. The idealists claimed that materialism cannot account for real values in our experience, and idealism was essentially a proposal to integrate the world of causal necessity and the realm of values in a dominantly spiritual universe. Herbart rejected this idealistic program. Value, he maintained, must be distinguished from existence. In judging anything to be good, just, or beautiful, I am expressing my estimate of it irrespective of its existence. I may judge that it ought or ought not to be, but that is my way of appraising its worth.

The basic theory of value concerns judgments of taste. Herbart called it aesthetics. He did not center his attention on aesthetics in the usual and stricter sense, but on the theory of worthy and unworthy wills and actions, ethics. In this section of his system, moral philosophy, Herbart's thought was marked by a prevailing formalism that was unlike Kant's, and far more elaborate. He listed five basic will relations, or ethical ideas, in terms of which he proposed to organize the entire practical activity of human life. Two of these express individual personal worth. The other three find social expression.

The "idea of inner freedom" signifies the harmony of the will and its own evaluation. I will as I judge that I ought; this is the life of free moral concord. This freedom requires clear insight and vigorous espousal. Both qualities of mind may be developed. As they reach their fulfillment, we recognize a pattern of personality which we express in the "idea of perfection."

In its free self-expression and attainment of perfection, each will is involved in relation with other wills. When several wills are actively concordant, each willing the freedom, perfection, and satisfaction of the others, we have an expression of the "idea of benevolence." But individual wills also contend with each other, in convictions, in conflicting interests and claims. The reconciliation of this conflict is the essence of the "idea of right, or justice." And justice in turn demands effective approval or condemnation of beneficent or unsocial conduct. This yields the "idea of retribution."

Herbart's social philosophy translated these five fundamental will relations into basic institutions. The idea of justice is socially exemplified in the legal organization of society; the idea of retribution operates effectively in the economic wage system; the idea of benevolence is expressed in the administrative system of government that aims to promote the general welfare; and the idea of perfection is manifest in the social process of expanding culture. Thus, organized society may be seen to aim at the ideal of a moral community of persons which realizes the idea of freedom.

The cultivation of the available values of human character is the task of education. Herbart's contribution to educational principles and methods was very important. We can note here only his moral conception of the teacher's mission, to guide the mind and the heart of youth in the unfolding of character values, or as he put it, in the aesthetic revelation of the world. When moral perfection is thus set as the whole purpose of humanity, a deepening of insight is achieved, and men's entire career is seen to hang on their choice of values. Educational wisdom in the training of youth is concerned with several main points: the way in which young wills may be directed, intelligent and misguided judgments of taste, the use of precepts and principles, and the organization of these precepts and principles into a life pattern and system of ideals. In his religious thinking, Herbart was marked by his refusal to base ethics on theology, and also by his insistence that our idea of the divine should express our highest spiritual vision and thus be conditioned by the integrity, vigor, and maturity of our moral life. Morality does not depend on theology, but it sustains and elevates religion.

Feuerbach: Positivism and Anthropology

The unsettling of idealism—and especially of its principal system, Hegelianism—was due both to incursions from without and to inner disruption. The spiritual emphasis in Hegel's metaphysics, and his constructive philosophy of religion, inspired Protestant theologians with the hope that Hegelianism might provide a new philosophical basis for Christian orthodoxy. The conservative note in Hegel's social-political philosophy was accentuated by reactionary advocates of the established order during the period of seething discontent and strife which led to the revolutions of 1848. It was natural that the leaders of religious and social radicalism should turn against the conservative "Hegelians of the Right," and then against the entire system of dialectical idealism. The scientific disdain for Schelling's and Hegel's philosophies of nature led some German opponents of idealism to materialistic philosophy. This materialism professed an aversion to systematic metaphysics; it claimed for its doctrines the status of positive, scientific conclusions. Positivism, the restriction of philosophical thought to specific, ascertained, factual results of the sciences, gained converts within the Hegelian camp. These young "Hegelians of the Left" had lost confidence in the ultimately rational nature of reality. They were insurgents who were ready for radical reconstruction in religion and society. To them, positivism seemed to offer a likely transition to the principles of a scientific philosophy and a new social order.

The leading spirit in this rebellion against idealistic absolutism was Ludwig Feuerbach (1804–1872). In his adolescence, Feuerbach planned to be a theologian; during his 20s he turned to Hegelianism, but he found its conclusions more and more questionable, and, finally, he rejected its basic principles. "God was my first thought," Feuerbach wrote, "Reason my second, Man my third and last thought."[1] By this he meant that the truth about man and nature could be attained only by examining the whole man in nature—not man with or against God, nor yet man as some kind of finite logos or embodied reason. Philosophy should turn from theology and speculative rationalism to sound, factual anthropology.

Feuerbach's chosen principle, in his mature thinking, was humanistic positivism. His various systematic works were intended as chapters in a philosophical anthropology. His chief treatise, *The Essence of Christianity*, viewed God as the infinite expression of man's religious experience. What concerned him was not God's existence or attributes, but how man came to form his ideas about God's existence and character. The secret of theology is anthropology. Feuerbach would humanize and secularize religion. He rejected the theological basis of religious devotion, but he did not avow himself a materialist. His anthropology and positivism, however, acquired an increasingly materialistic cast and tone, and those who followed him proceeded to emphatic materialism.

Feuerbach, a vigorous writer, was always outspoken about whatever he believed. His works are a remarkable record of the sharp reversals of his thought as it progressed through the years. During his Hegelian period, he had written, "The Copernican system is the most glorious victory which idealism has achieved over empiricism, and reason over the senses."[2] For, in a merely material universe, how could there be a theory of materialism? At the age of 25, he had asked, "Man also eats and drinks, . . . but can we fairly define him as a being that eats and drinks?"[3] Yet, fifteen or twenty

---

[1] Quoted in F. A. Lange, *History of Materialism* (trans. E. C. Thomas), 2nd ed., London, Kegan, Paul, 1892, Vol. II, p. 247.

[2] L. Feuerbach, *Sämmtliche Werke* (W. Bolin and Fr. Jodl, eds.), Stuttgart, Frommann, Vol. II, 1904, p. 136.

[3] *Ibid.*, Vol. I, 1903, p. 55.

years later, he came back to this very idea and startled Germany with his notorious pun, "Man is what he eats (*Der Mensch ist was er isst*)."[4] He liked the idea so well that he proposed to develop a dietetic theory of religious sacrifice and of social-cultural processes. In dealing with thought, and with mental activities generally, he found them all reducible to bodily conditions. Infancy, adolescence, sex, senility—these cannot be understood as states of an immaterial soul. The "philosophy of spirit" must learn its real facts from physiology.

Materialism had been criticized as incompatible with a genuine recognition of ethics. Feuerbach, on the contrary, held that physiology provides the only solid basis of morals. Idealism may lift men to the clouds of speculation, but their aching bodies force them to see themselves as they are. Religion, as well as philosophy, needs the corrective of physiology. Thus the German Reformation brought the Christian religion down to earth, and Luther's son became not a theologian but a physician. Man's need of his doctor humiliates his lofty speculations and is a strong argument for materialism.

Philosophical anthropology reveals men and women as they are; in origin, nature, and destiny, they are part and parcel of the material world. Materialism also enables us to understand man's pathetic refusal to reconcile himself to the facts. This refusal stirs him religiously and philosophically to idealistic visions. The traditional beliefs in God and personal immortality are his tragic protests against the inevitable. We should study the development of these illusions in order to deepen our understanding of human nature. Thus Feuerbach examined the Christian doctrine of Christ's resurrection, the God-man's victory over death. By this belief, men have sought to convince themselves of their abiding communion with the eternal and divine that goes beyond death and destruction. Faith in God and in life everlasting are fundamentally the same; both of them are sublime expressions of the demand for survival.

In exposing these illusory beliefs—in showing that they are illusory and that men have been lured by them—Feuerbach also undertook to show how they can be outgrown and replaced by true insight into the mature reflection of men. Modern humanity requires an outlook, human and cosmic, that will fulfill man's intelligent expectations even as his traditional visions have satisfied his deluded mind. Mature men can find this intelligent perspective of their role and destiny right within their social sphere of activities. Their traditional faith in God may yield to their sound faith in man, a secular, humane religion. Yet, Feuerbach did not aspire to be the prophet of a humanistic cult; his aim was to divert a traditional religious devotion into the channels of social reform and cultural upbuilding.

The practical philosophy of this materialistic positivism emphasized social organization and reconstruction for human welfare. The essential characteristic of moral activity is social-mindedness. Conscience is socialized con-

---

[4] *Ibid.*, Vol. X, 1911, p. 22.

sciousness—*con-science*—thinking, feeling, and acting with others. Both legal and moral obligations rest on the fact that the striving and satisfaction of each of us involve the wants and satisfactions of others, as obstacles, conditions, or consequences. The legal system expresses the organized will of society to secure the conformity of recalcitrant individual wills. But intelligent individual wills may, of their own accord, espouse the common interests and well-being. This is the moral system of conduct, and the best wisdom of mankind has championed it—from Confucius to the golden rule of the Christian Gospel. Even with this moral program for life, men may go astray, glorifying self-abnegation and then seeking consolation in the hope of heavenly rewards. But truly moral social-mindedness is the affirmation of an enlightened will which cherishes life and the satisfactions and possibilities of human social activity, and which finds its fullest fruition in the promotion of the common happiness in a progressive social order.

Karl Marx: Dialectical Materialism

La Mettrie had explained the vigorous ferocity of the English as due to their diet of beef—pointing out, in contrast, the dullness of the Irish with their diet of potatoes. Feuerbach made dietary reform a first principle in his program of a new culture. If the masses had at least peas in place of potatoes, the prospects for a successful revolution would be improved. An important strain in the complex and confused social philosophies of our time has been the alliance of the socialistic and communistic programs for social-economic reconstruction with the materialistic doctrines of human nature and of the whole historical process.

The leading mind in the so-called "scientific socialism" was Karl Marx (1818–1883). He was scarcely mentioned in the standard histories of philosophy—even Höffding accorded him only half a sentence—nevertheless, 100 years after his *Communist Manifesto*, the world is still torn by the struggle he inaugurated. Soviet Russia and other communist governments have reorganized the entire life of their nations on Marxist lines, and they tolerate no philosophy but Marxism within their borders. Even a brief discussion of the basic philosophical principles of "scientific socialism" should indicate its relation to the conflicts within the Hegelian idealistic camp which, philosophically speaking, gave rise to it.

Marx combined jurisprudence and history with idealistic philosophy during his university studies. His own early materialistic bent was shown when he wrote his doctoral dissertation on Epicurus. On leaving the university, he soon identified himself with revolutionary movements throughout Europe as a radical journalist and agitator. Banished successively from Prussia, Belgium, and France, he found asylum in London. He hailed the revolutionary uprisings of 1848 with the *Manifesto of the Communist Party*, written with Friedrich Engels (1820–1895). The lifelong collaboration of these two men is a notable chapter in socialistic history. The main work to which Marx devoted his life as a writer is *Das Kapital,* the second and third volumes of which appeared posthumously, and this was edited by Engels.

Marx's revolutionary career in the socialist movement, his leadership in organizing the First International, and the details of his communist economics are beyond the scope of our survey; but his fundamental ideas are an effective alternative in modern philosophical thought. His theory has been designated as "dialectical materialism," and an explanation of this term should clarify his relation to Hegel's idealistic dialectic.

We saw that Hegel's *Logic* traced the progressive self-organization of thought from its barest and most abstract forms to its most complex, and most highly integrated and significant expressions. This process, according to the Hegelians, is dialectical. Each idea exposes its limitations as a thesis which leads to its negation in an antithesis, and, out of this contraposition of alternatives, emerges a synthesis—an idea more significant and adequate than the alternatives it replaces. This synthesis, in turn, becomes a thesis, evoking an antithesis, and proceeding to another synthesis, and so forth. This ongoing movement of dialectical triads in the various fields of experience was regarded as the basic characteristic of reality.

Marx agreed with Hegel in recognizing a dialectical process in reality, in nature, and in history. But he rejected Hegel's idealistic conception of the dialectic as the progressive self-manifestation of reason. He followed Feuerbach's lead in maintaining that the Hegelian pyramid was set upside down, on its peak, and should be turned over on its natural material base. Thus, Marx wrote in *Das Kapital:*

My dialectical method is not only different from the Hegelian but is fundamentally its direct opposite. For Hegel the thought process . . . is the demiurge (or creator) of the actual, and actual existence is only the outward manifestation of the Idea. But I, on the contrary, regard the ideal as nothing else than the material reality, transposed and translated in the human head.[5]

According to Marx and Engels, the materialistic dialectic operates in the historical process, determining the necessary succession of social-institutional structures. This process was traced especially in the economic sphere. In this ideology, not only the actual forms and operation of the various social processes, but the dominant ideas and the so-called "spirit" of an age or a culture are directly dependent upon the material-economic conditions and framework of society. The dialectic of this materialistic interpretation of history is a dialectic of factual structures and systems—slavery, serfdom, feudalism, trade guilds, modern bourgeois economy, the rise of capitalism, the industrial revolution, the pyramiding of capital structures, the labor struggle, the eventual collapse of the capitalistic system, and the establishment of the socialistic state.

[5] Translated from Karl Marx, *Das Kapital* (K. Kautsky, ed.), Berlin, Dietz, Vol. I, 1928, p. 47.

In every historical stage of society, a certain dominant system, itself the result and social expression of certain natural material conditions, has been supported by those to whom it is advantageous, but resisted by the multitudes whom it irks and oppresses. The historical process is one of continual strife between opposite forces, and its eventual resolution only transposes the scene or direction of the conflict. This materialistic dialectic operates with the necessity of the laws of nature; it is itself the course of nature on the historical level.

Marx traced with especial care the processes that produced modern capitalism, and that direct the movement to its eventual dissolution. The modern amassing of capitalistic fortunes has been the result of the appropriation of "surplus value" by the masters of industry. The owners of the machinery and other means of production control the livelihood of the workers, who have only their labor to sell. The laborer receives as wages only a certain part of the value of what he produces. The rest of this value, the surplus value, is kept by the employer. This accumulation of profits swells the capital controlled by the owner, expands his mastery of the means of production, and confirms the individual workman's dependence on the system which exploits and expropriates him.

This entrenchment of the capitalistic system points inevitably to strife, crisis, and revolution. The stupendous capitalistic system of enterprise—against which the individual laborer is helpless—depends, for its very existence, on the collective labor which it exploits. Collectively, the laboring masses have the power to resist their exploiters, to alter and, finally, to overthrow capitalism, to replace its economy for private profit by an economy for social cooperation and welfare.

Marx regarded the modern, historical-economic process as necessarily moving to its socialistic climax, but he was also a vigorous leader in the social revolution that would speed the great day. The conclusion of the *Communist Manifesto*—"Working men of all countries, unite!"—was a stirring appeal to the inevitable flood of revolt to sweep over the dam. Despite his materialistic commitment to mechanical necessity, Marx did not overlook the productive power of people's wills, convictions, and purposes.

Scientific socialism has been distinguished from the earlier utopian visions of the perfect society. The Marxist dialectic, like the Hegelian, cannot consistently be regarded as leading to a final consummation. Yet, in both cases, a grand finale was contemplated. Marx's communistic ideal of a classless society was like Hegel's Absolute Idea; his "dictatorship of the proletariat" was, in prospect, like Hegel's notion of the perfect Germanic realm, "the union of the human and the divine."[6] As Hegelians have given us revised versions of their master's ideals, so Marxists, of course, explain that the attainment of the communistic state will provide its own scope for human development, reveal new values, and place human aims on new planes of achievement.

[6] G. W. Hegel, *Philosophy of Right* (trans. S. W. Dyde), London, Bell, 1896, p. 348.

A radical problem, with its implied criticism of the materialistic dialectic, can only be mentioned here. Materialism in its many varieties has been confronted with the difficulty of accounting for the reality or the gradation of human values. Marx's scientific socialism would combine a strictly materialistic account of human nature and the social-historical process with an active espousal of social reform, and of the values to which the program of reform is dedicated. On a strictly materialistic basis, how is the social injustice of capitalistic exploitation to be understood, and how is the higher worth of the communistic state to be vindicated? Was not Marx confronted by a demand for a revision of his initial definition of human nature that would include and account for its eventual manifestation in his own social program? More recent history has shown, tragically, that, unless men's lives are seen as the lives of persons with spiritual character and worth, professed plans for social reform and reconstruction may readily allow brutal policies to prevail, in which the human individual is lost and men are treated as mere machines.

Kierkegaard and Existentialism

Philosophical ideas in their development have a past, present, and future which do not quite agree with their chronological order. In the history of philosophical discussion, some remarks are made too late, when they no longer matter; other comments have no effect because the proper state of mind to receive them is lacking, although these may return later to realize all their power. Schopenhauer, unshaken by thirty years of public apathy to his philosophy, declared: "I must die before I can be born. My burial will be my baptism." A striking instance of this resurrection of philosophical ideas is provided by the Danish thinker Søren Kierkegaard (1813–1855). Although he lived a century ago, his thought, in its real influence, belongs to today; his ideas have stimulated some strong tendencies in contemporary life. They have been taken up by various writers, and, in some of their versions, have recently gained wide popularity under the name of *existentialism*. We shall consider some of them in our last chapter. Our unsettled age is embroiled in a variety of conflicting ideologies, and many issues do not admit of solution. Yet, the choice is imperative; we must decide. Kierkegaard's books are dramatic expressions of this thinking in crisis.

His philosophic theory has been called an "existential dialectic," and it can best be described by contrasting it with the Hegelian dialectic. Kierkegaard plowed through Hegel's logic, but he saw no hope of any harvest there. He was attracted by Hegel's keen sense of antitheses in human life and thought, but he could not share Hegel's sublime confidence that all will be resolved in the progressive syntheses of the dialectical triads. To Kierkegaard, abstract reflection that so complacently ironed out the contending issues seemed artificial; it evaded the living problems.

Kierkegaard turned from the formulas of reason and centered his thought on the unique, existing individual, on the actual existing crisis. Objective truth—truth in general—could not meet his demands. His own truth had to be existentially vital, truth in his own struggle, truth for which he could live and die so that he would not only know it, but it would own him and be himself. If he could thus probe himself to the heart, he could reach bedrock in reality, he could face God.

By his existential dialectic, Kierkegaard sought self-penetration. But, in the drama of his life, he played different roles. Kierkegaard traced the existential search for, or achievement of, the self through three characteristic self-expressions or value levels of individual activity: the "aesthetic," the ethical, and the religious. The issue between the first two is the theme of his work *Either-Or*. In his so-called "aesthetic" career, the individual is an ironic sensualist who indulges his whims or who is swept along by his passions. But, withal, he feels emptiness and dismay. Contending with this avid enjoyer is the ethical self which is moved by scruples and duties, and which faces decisions of grave import, heroic and tragic in their resolution. Beyond these two that contended in his own life—even for his soul—Kierkegaard could see a third, which to him, was his truest and highest fulfillment: the religious life of utter devotion. But this religion could not be one of stiff doctrines and dead forms. It must be a religion that could consume and refine him entirely, that could pierce through the slime of indulgence and the fog of doctrine, a flaming sword of consecration.

SUGGESTED WORKS FOR FURTHER STUDY

HERBART.   Herbart, F., *The Science of Education* (trans. H. M. and E. Felkin); De Garmo, Charles, *Herbart and the Herbartians;* Harris, W. T., *Herbart's Doctrine of Interest.*

KARL MARX.   Marx, K., *Capital, the Communist Manifesto, and Other Writings* (M. Eastman, ed.); Croce, Benedetto, *Historical Materialism and the Economics of Karl Marx;* Hook, Sidney, *Towards the Understanding of Karl Marx;* Spargo, John, *Karl Marx.*

KIERKEGAARD.   Kierkegaard, S., *Either-Or* (trans. D. F. Swenson, *et al.*); *Philosophical Fragments; or, A Fragment of Philosophy* (trans. D. F. Swenson); *Stages on Life's Way* (trans. W. Lowrie); *The Journals of Søren Kierkegaard* (trans. A. Dru); *A Kierkegaard Anthology* (Robert Brettall, ed.); Lowrie, Walter, *Kierkegaard.*

30.   French Philosophers of
the Romantic Period

The Ideologists

The Encyclopedists and the other philosophical radicals of the eighteenth century have been called the "fathers of the French Revolution." Voltaire, Rousseau, Condillac, Diderot, and Holbach all died before the revolutionary storm, and it is doubtful whether they would have gone much beyond Mirabeau, or have come near Marat and Robespierre, but the revolution was translating into action the ideas of these radical philosophers. The course of action which ran in the bloody streams of the Terror went far beyond the logical inferences. It horrified both liberals and conservatives throughout Europe, many of whom blamed the godless philosophy for the guillotine. Some keener minds, however, distinguished the atrocities of the Terror from the ideas which had inspired the revolution, and they remained loyal to these ideas. When Napoleon was rising to power, he inspired great hopes in liberal circles that he was the expected French George Washington, and, for some time, he wooed these philosophers. His imperial ascendancy disillusioned them, however; he spurned the radicals, preferring to be anointed by the monarchical Church which had decided to interpret his victories as seals of divine approval.

The philosophers who adopted the materialistic version of Lockian empiricism followed the lead of Condillac's sensationalism, in particular. These came to be known as *idéologues*, or ideologists. They emphasized the direct observation of sensations and the reduction of general ideas to the simple impressions from which they are derived, and the physiological conditions which produce them. Madame Helvétius—whose devotees included Benjamin Franklin—provided a meeting-place for them in her salon. The most substantial contributors to this doctrine were Pierre Jean Georges Cabanis (1757–1808) and Destutt de Tracy (1754–1836).

Cabanis' procedure—a clinical method and a liberal political-social outlook—was characteristic of the school. His main treatise investigated the relation of physiological conditions to mental processes. Although he considered the effect of conscious-cerebral activity on the rest of the organism, his chief interest lay in examining the determination of the so-called "mind" by the body and by nature. Sense perceptions, feelings, thoughts, volitions, and the whole character and personality of men are the results of natural, physiological conditions. Age and sex, health and disease, climate and diet, all affect a person's mental life. Instead of repeating the old confused notions about an immaterial soul, we should plainly realize that thought is a secretion of the brain, analogous to bile. This explicitly physiological view of mind has practical implications for the education of individuals and the reform of societies. Just as there are no innate ideas, there are no inevitable human states. The teacher and the social reformer, like the capable physician and the animal or plant breeder, can correct human ills and transform minds and societies by providing proper physical conditions of existence. This work of active philanthropy was regarded by Cabanis as the intelligent application of the golden rule and a good working religion.

Destutt de Tracy opposed all metaphysical speculation, and emphasized both the direct exploration of the sensations as physiological processes, and a cautious inspection of the order and connection of impressions into general ideas. Like Hume, he insisted on never accepting any alleged general principle until it has been traced to the simple data of consciousness from which it is derived. All the primary elementary states confronting us are physiological changes.

A basic experience, or bodily reaction, is the self-affirmation of the will, and will should be recognized as the expression of desire, as an organic urge toward something. We value what we want, and our moral judgments are motivated by the desire for pleasure and the avoidance of pains. Our life is one of self-preservation, but also one of living with others; hence arise our feelings of self-regard and social-mindedness, or sympathy. Morality involves the reconciliation of these feelings in justice and reason. What justice and reason would signify in basically physiological terms was not explained by the ideologists.

Revival of Religion: Traditionalists and Radicals

The French Revolution undertook to sweep away all the forces of oppression; not only the king and his extortionate officials, but also the Church that, in the name of Christ, shackled men's minds and feasted on the produce from one-fifth of the French lands. But the bloody struggle for freedom bred its fanatics and demagogues, and, finally, in Napoleon, met its master, and regarded its submission to him as glorious. Yet, even before his rise to power and his imperial restoration of ecclesiastical authority, the opponents of the revolution had stigmatized it as the evil work of godless men and had urged France to return to the Christian fold. Some of these men identified Christian truth with the monarchical policies of the Church, but others preached a new gospel of social redemption as the heart of Christianity. The broad variety of social programs—reactionary, liberal, romantic-mystical, radical-socialistic—each had its devout Christian advocates.

The most rigid conservative among the traditionalists was Louis Gabriel Ambroise de Bonald (1754–1840), who regarded the revolution as the ruinous finale of the entire modern misdirection of thought and life. The Renaissance and the Protestant revolt had spurned the eternal authority of God for the passing desires and opinions of men. Lacking any sovereign, divine principles, modern science and philosophy put their faith in human reason. Rebellious against the righteous rule of God, people could recognize only prevailing force. The spread of empiricism and democracy was even more flagrant evidence of the dissolution of universal principles in modern society. The apotheosis of the popular will, like the trust in the fleeting round of sensations, portended imminent chaos in ideas and institutions; the Revolution and the Terror were its disastrous consequences.

Bonald saw no path to redemption except the path of the prodigal son, the humble return of France and Europe to God, and to Mother Church. He championed Catholic monarchic absolutism without any reservations. "The revolution began by a declaration of the rights of man. It must finish by the declaration of the rights of God."[1]

On the vaster scale of history, beyond Bourbon and Bonaparte, Bonald envisioned the whole structure of the social-institutional order as a divine texture woven by the centuries. Christ is the eternal Word, and the holy life of Christian tradition is the age-long building of the City of God. Willful men may mar the holy edifice, or try to wreck it, but their evil designs will be confuted, and divine authority will prevail in the end.

Joseph de Maistre (1753–1821) shared with Bonald the leadership of the traditionalists, but his reflections on the collapse of the godly civilization in France led him to the deeper issues of theodicy and the problem of evil. Why had God allowed France to betray her historical role as Europe's teacher in Catholic divinity? Why had Christ seemingly forsaken his most devoted worshippers in France and yielded the leadership of his people to unprincipled and unspeakable men? What mysterious divine destiny was being realized through all the havoc and ruin that had devastated Europe? Maistre grappled with the problem presented in the book of Job. His theodicy, like that of Bossuet and Butler, sought hope and reassurance in the infinite scope of God's design, beyond any immediate human reckoning. Besides, he reasoned, God is "no respecter of persons";[2] his justice is meted out eternally to the entire, sinful human race.

Maistre resisted individualism in his tragic theodicy, even as he opposed

---

[1] Translated from the quotation in G. Gogordan, *Joseph de Maistre*, Paris, Hachette, 1894, p. 41.
[2] Acts 10:34 (American Standard Version).

it in his social philosophy. The godly life is a life of disinterested devotion to God, and to pure philanthropy. The saintly man illumines the dark caverns of human existence; his godliness brings all mankind nearer God, and his innocent suffering is an expiation for the guilty. Both his life and his death are Christlike.

A radical swing from traditionalism to Christian socialism marked the thought and life of Félicité de Lamennais (1782–1854). His first work, *Essay on Religious Indifference*, traced the spiritual and social chaos of his day to the rejection of Catholic authority. Infidels and Protestant heretics must return in humble submission to the holy, universal Church, which Christ had established and through which, alone, he redeems mankind. But Lamennais demanded that the Church devote itself whole-heartedly to this social redemption, abandon its worldliness, and, in the spirit of Christ, minister to the weary and the heavyladen. This social gospel outraged the ecclesiastical hierarchy and was condemned by the Pope. Lamennais thereupon followed Christ's gospel according to his own conscience. His program of reform, which had advocated liberal democracy even in his *Words of a Believer*, became increasingly Christian-socialistic.

Maine de Biran: from Physiology to Mysticism

The demand for a thorough understanding of the active powers of human intelligence, and for genuine recognition of spiritual values, led some critical ideologists to abandon their preoccupation with the passive reception of sense impressions. The most noteworthy expansion of outlook in this direction marked the philosophical development of F. P. G. Maine de Biran (1766–1824). Philosophy was his interest, although his career was that of a public official. His lively responsiveness to social amusements contended with his zeal for high achievement, and he found his projects always ahead of his performance. By temperament, also, he was ever inconclusive and forward-looking. His keenness of self-observation and his psychological analysis were astonishing.

Maine de Biran began as a follower of Condillac and Cabanis, but he found himself dissatisfied with the theory of mental process as initially and fundamentally passive. For him, the evidence of an active soul was too clear to be ignored; its positive effort was the primary dynamic in experience. In his endeavor to explain the soul, he went beyond the doctrine of the ideologists to a voluntaristic account of mental activity.

Condillac and his followers, the ideologists, could not explain self-consciousness. The self is not a sense impression, nor a sum of sensations; nor, on the other hand, is it eventually derived from the organization of the data of consciousness. The self is manifested in the active tendency, or effort, that is apparent in every experience. In each mental process, we can distinguish an active and a passive aspect. Habitual repetition of certain mental reactions, because it diminishes our active attention to them, may tend to make them routine and scarcely conscious; in other cases habituation may perfect our ready grasp and mastery of perceptions. But the active element in consciousness is unmistakable. We see and hear in passive sensibility, but we also look and listen in active will. This initial and basic reality of will action is essential to an understanding of mind. It cannot be explained in physiological terms as the effect of sense impressions. It exposes the inadequacy of materialism and points to the recognition of spiritual principles in reality.

The growing emphasis on activism in the philosophy of Maine de Biran shows the influence of Leibniz. The voluntaristic account of the self has a kinship with Schopenhauer's doctrine of the will to live, but is not dependent on it. Maine de Biran's view of the self is much closer to Fichte's doctrine of the ego as active will-striving, especially in view of the spiritual emphasis that characterized them both.

The development of Maine de Biran's practical philosophy was as farreaching as that of his psychology. He began as an Epicurean, and defended Epicurus from the charge of gross sensuality, but avowed himself a hedonist in his emphasis on immediate enjoyment. He noted, however, the instability of pleasure and passion; they are as unreliable as intellectual zest, itself one of his chief delights, but precariously subject to bodily conditions. The round of sensations which could not, by itself, reveal a self-consciousness was likewise incapable of yielding a sovereign principle of conduct. How can man find real satisfaction in life without some central and dominant principle to give meaning and character to all his actions?

Mastery comes only through self-discipline. It is mastery of ourselves, but is it not also a subjugation? Resolute endeavor is itself the practical consciousness of the active self, but an imperative emphasis on duty was opposed by Maine de Biran as the wrong note in morals. The true aim in life must be not submission, not even to reason, but the active emergence and self-affirmation of intelligence; not stern loyalty to law, but free devotion, the soul actively one with its ideal, conviction and blessedness in love. Thus Maine de Biran moved from Epicurus to Marcus Aurelius, and, perhaps, to Kant, and then to St. John.

Pascal distinguished three orders of reality, a material order, a mental order, and an order of values. So Maine de Biran traced three stages in the self-realization of personality; from mere animal reaction of the sense organs to external impressions—pleasant or unpleasant—to definitely human experiences of voluntary endeavor and self-mastery, and, finally, to the perfect fulfillment of the human spirit in loving communion with God.

The soul's approach to God is twofold: by way of reasoning, and by immediate vision. Our will prefers the better, the higher value, and our reason is bent on recognizing it. This is the urge for the divine which leaves us restless this side of perfection. And, in our holy striving, we are not alone, for it is our life in God, and God is closer to us than we are to ourselves. Neither rational insight nor moral resolution expresses the full spiritual fruition, only loving communion and union with the divine which the mystics call the "vision of God."

Cousin and the Eclectic Idealists

The demand for a guiding principle in an active spiritual life, which drew Maine de Biran to the Stoics and to the New Testament, led many French minds to search for other philosophies as alternatives to the materialism and hedonism of the ideologists, and to the revival of traditional authoritarianism. A new eclecticism arose which was influenced first by the Scottish philosophy of common sense, and later, by German idealism. The correlation of these two by the leading eclectic thinkers involved a skillful exploration of the treasures of philosophy, and produced many broad, and some masterly, studies in the history of ideas.

Victor Cousin (1792–1867), the leader of the eclectics, began with the common-sense verities, but he ranged more widely, and showed astonishing versatility in his critical use of the ideas of others. He agreed with Maine de Biran that the true philosophy must conserve spiritual values, and he gleaned the rationalistic and idealistic philosophies of antiquity and of his own day, from Plato and the Neoplatonists to Kant and Hegel.

Eclecticism was Cousin's method and his creed. "The time of exclusive theories has gone by,"[3] he wrote. Philosophy needed to assay and to integrate its great heritage of ideas, and, in the words of St. Paul, to "prove all things; hold fast that which is good."[4] The true eclectic thinker should avoid the errors in the old doctrines, assimilate their truths, and organize them so as to realize their contribution to each other. Cousin's eclecticism pretended neither to originality nor to finality of doctrine; both were regarded as vain illusions. Just as it was nourished on the great ideas of the past, so Cousin expected philosophy to respond to the living thoughts of the present and the future.

The misdirection of French philosophy by the materialists and ideologists could not be righted by a return to exploded authoritarianism. Cousin championed the spiritual outlook of German idealism as a corrective of both sterile sensualism and rigid orthodoxy. But he made clear his resistance to the German *a priori* procedure, and he preferred the French method of observation and specific analysis. Observation and analysis, however, should be thorough; they should go beyond the reactions of our sense organs; they should probe the primary consciousness of self, the basic conviction of

[3] Victor Cousin, *Lectures on the True, the Beautiful, and the Good* (trans. O. W. Wight), Edinburgh, Clark, 1864, p. 346.
[4] I Thessalonians 5:21 (American Standard Version).

principles and standards, truth, beauty, and the affirmation of the will in moral choice. The eclectic method should lead to the recognition of the fundamental characteristics of human experience and it should reveal spiritual nature.

Cousin's ethics sought to blend Platonic perfectionism with the Kantian emphasis on the imperative character of the moral law. He assailed the ethics of self-interest as effacing the basic difference between good and evil, and as failing to recognize genuine moral nobility of motive. The common hedonism cannot understand clearly either vice or virtue. It cannot explain remorse as distinguished from mere pain. It runs counter to the plain judgment of men who resent injustice and insult, not mere injury. Does not language itself sustain the distinction between interest and virtue? Without this distinction, esteem and contempt lose their meaning. But, while Cousin thus emphasized a dutiful respect for right principle as essential to morality, he also advocated the rational direction of life by ideal principles as being truly in the best interests of human nature. The moral life is the life of our most abundant realization, and it should not be pursued in a spirit of resignation and sacrifice. Hedonistic ethics, in truth, has value; its positive emphasis on happiness is a corrective reaction to misguided asceticism.

The social ethics derived from these principles acknowledged the inviolable dignity of persons which Kant and the idealists had emphasized. The democratic declaration of the rights of man finds its true warrant in this moral recognition, and it is the bulwark of a really just society. But, beyond justice is the recognition of the rights of our fellow men, and, beyond dutiful respect for the moral law, and the inviolable dignity of persons, is our spiritual perfection expressed in love. Our self-identification with the ideal values—the true, the beautiful, and the good—leads us toward "the common centre, the last foundation of all truth, all beauty, all goodness, [which is] above all, God, always God."[5] Religion represented to Cousin the integration and culmination of the supreme values; here, also, critical eclecticism should lead us aright. Although he avowed his feeling for the deep insight and lofty aspirations expressed in the various great religions, he paid highest tribute to "the Christian religion, incomparably the most perfect and the most holy."[6]

This eclecticism has been criticized as a well-meaning, but shallow, compilation of ideas, that evaded problems and compromised with issues instead of meeting them squarely. Cousin, personally, was distrusted as being more diplomatic than forthright. The progress of philosophic thought has sustained some of these criticisms; the real solution of problems is not likely to be attained if it is undertaken with the prevailing intention of reaching an agreement. The great merit of Cousin and his school was in expanding the philosophical background and outlook of a whole generation of French thinkers. Especially in the field of the history of philosophy, the various

[5] Cousin, *op. cit.*, p. 419.
[6] Paraphrased from Victor Cousin, *op. cit.*, p. 419.

eclectic studies produced fruits of lasting significance. Beyond the immediate circle of the school's disciples, Cousin's eclectic idealism—and Maine de Biran's activism and spiritualism which preceded it—exercised an influence which can be traced in the thought of two or three generations of French thinkers.

SUGGESTED WORKS FOR FURTHER STUDY

FRENCH PHILOSOPHY OF THE ROMANTIC PERIOD.   Boas, George, *French Philosophies of the Romantic Period*; Cousin, V., *Lectures on the True, the Beautiful, and the Good* (trans. O. W. Wight).

31.   Auguste Comte: Positivism and Social Philosophy

Comte's Predecessors: Vico and Condorcet, Philosophers of History

In Italy, the fertility of philosophy during the Renaissance was followed by a barren period. Giambattista Vico (1668–1744) was the only noteworthy thinker for more than a century after Bruno and Campanella, and he had no immediate followers or critics of any particular merit. His Italy had not responded constructively to the great systematic philosophers of the age. Naples was in the grip of the Inquisition; among Vico's contemporaries, diluted, abstract Cartesianism passed for modern philosophy. Only the driving power of his own genius led Vico out of this stagnation. He came to philosophy by way of jurisprudence. His brilliant originality was hemmed in and confused by traditional notions which he could not outgrow. The fertility of his thought is especially apparent in his philosophy of history. In this area, he was a modern pioneer, a precursor of Condorcet and Herder, and an earlier reader of the social-historical epic of humanity of which Comte was to become later the great rhapsodist.

Vico's main work, *The New Science*, included an analysis of mind, a philosophical interpretation of the origins and development of universal history, and a specific examination of political and social institutions. He combined a critical-naturalistic account of human affairs, which would have shocked a Scholastic doctor, with unquestioning conformity to Biblical tradition. Thus he traced the natural history of mankind; that is, of the nations that descended from Noah's sons and daughters after the Flood. This confusion of critical-original ideas and their uncritical version disturbs the reader who must distinguish the two in his estimate of Vico's thought.

Against Descartes' seeming victory over skepticism, Vico maintained that simplicity is not the essential mark of truth, nor is self-evidence the property of ideas themselves which compels our acceptance of them. Our minds achieve ideas by creative acts of intelligence, even as God knows eternally the infinite truth of all things that He has created and formed into a cosmos.

The geometer, who forms in his mind the figures which he contemplates and knows in his theorems, ponders the pattern which intelligence approximates in other fields of truth. These truths may be clear and simple, as in the most abstract sciences; but they may also become turbid in the deeper and more complex reflections, some of them of boundless significance. Mechanics is less certain than geometry, and the history of civilization is much less certain than physics. But the most complex and profound inquiries—history, morals, jurisprudence, poetry, and religion—engrossed Vico's mind, and he sought to probe their essential principles.

The laws of nature and of the human-social order express God's creative activity, in which will and intelligence are eternally one and integral. In examining and understanding the historical rhythm, the laws and patterns of humanity's universal career, we are sharing in God's truth and in his ways with men. Vico distinguished three main stages of historical development: the divine, the heroic, and the human. These stages express three kinds of natures, and are paralleled in a triad of customs, systems of laws and governments, and reason and judgment, in the whole span of human life. The first stage is one of robust imagination, religious devotion, theocratic rule, mystical wisdom, and revelation. During this stage, the family was instituted, and language and myth had their origin. The second, or heroic, stage is marked by the rule of valor and force, "the law of Achilles, who referred every right to the tip of his spear."[1] Its government was aristocratic, its discipline military, and its language one of epic nobility, which reached perfection in Homer. The third stage, which Vico called the "human stage," is an age in which reasonable and responsible persons recognize duty and conscience. Its governments acknowledge the people's equality before the law, and are either popular self-governments or responsible monarchies. Its language achieves alphabetical simplicity, order, and precision, and is suitable for rational discourse and the communication of knowledge.

The eventual decay of the third, or human-cultured stage, brings the historical cycle to a close; civilization stagnates and finally collapses. Out of this social dissolution arises another historical movement which repeats the previous triad of stages. This doctrine was Vico's version of the idea of eternal recurrence, which had had several advocates in oriental and classical antiquity and which was to find its most famous modern protagonist in Nietzsche.

The *Historical Outlines of the Progress of the Human Spirit* by Marquis de Condorcet (1743–1794) gave a hopeful account of advancing civilization that was resolutely entertained during the French Revolution. This treatise was written amidst the atrocities of the Terror. Condorcet was a vigorous and confident advocate of reform—vigorous because he was confident. He did not recognize any basic depravity in human nature; the evils and miseries of men are due to the poor social conditions under which they live, to their

[1] G. Vico, *The New Science* (trans. T. G. Bergin and M. H. Fisch), Ithaca, Cornell Univ. Press, 1948, p. 304.

ignorance and superstition, to their oppression by Church and State. Education and social reconstruction can abate and abolish these evils. And these reforms will disclose man's unlimited capacity for intelligent conduct and for philanthropy. The study of history cures us of complacency and despair, for it shows us man's long upward march from savagery to civilization, and, as it reassures us of the reality of human progress, it also exposes our still persisting ineptitudes and inequities, and our grievous, unsolved problems.

In disowning the theology of his youth, Condorcet also disavowed any other metaphysical ventures. Indeed, he would cling to the biographical and historical actualities of human lives. But he discerned a general correspondence between the course of individual development and the historical process; a basic principle of human nature seemed to operate in the lives of people and peoples. In tracing the vaster outlines of history, he was also exhibiting the characteristic features and laws of human nature.

Condorcet's treatise should not be understood as a mere digest of universal history. His purpose was to interpret human progress, man's capacities and achievements as they have been manifested during the successive historical periods. He distinguished nine stages in the course of civilization. The first three are marked by the beginning of a social order—progressively expanding and reliable—in fishing, hunting, herding, and farming life. The next two are stages of recorded history that reached their summit of intelligence, culture, and political organization in Greek and Roman antiquity. The sixth period, that of medieval theological domination, was, in Condorcet's view, a period of cultural stagnation; but his confidence in progress was vindicated by the seventh, the period of the Renaissance with its advance in science and human achievement. The last two stages, periods of modern progress, have manifested unprecedented human powers and capacities for boundless perfection in the discovery of the laws of nature, in man's self-understanding, and in the curing of physical and social ills.

Condorcet was always ready to draw precepts for the future from his historical review. In struggling to abolish religious and political-economic oppression, men must recognize their aim to achieve a more and more humane society, in which people can realize perfection through activities that assure all a fair chance. Like Montesquieu, Condorcet was not satisfied with generally advocating justice and the common good; he advanced to specific programs of needed reforms, in which he expresses some of the highest purposes of the revolution at the very time when they were being sullied by fanatics and demagogues.

Claude Henri de Saint-Simon

Many of the prophets of the perfect new society were seers of romantic visions; but some combined with their dreams a practical grasp of social needs and reforms. No one manifested this interplay of insight and fantasy more strikingly than did Claude Henri de Saint-Simon (1760–1825). His biography is a stirring tale of bold, noble, and disreputable adventures; of far-seeing projects and extravagant notions, of generous philanthropy and unprincipled servility. He grasped and expressed many of the fundamental ideas which the far more thorough mind of Comte developed in his philosophy of positivism. And he had brilliant technological projects which were realized later in the construction of the Suez and the Panama Canals.

Saint-Simon advocated social reconstruction along scientific-industrial principles. He was also the evangelist of a *New Christianity*, as he phrased it in the title of his last important book. The union of these two ideas was his message to his age. Free Christianity of outworn dogmas; translate the Christian ideal of godly living into a vital modern gospel of social redemption here and now; establish the kingdom of God in men's daily lives and in a social order of justice and brotherhood and love. Traditional theology is scientifically untenable and religiously irrelevant. The priests had their day and their role in the Dark Ages, but the civilization of science and industry has outlived them, and they should now step out. The leaders of the new Christianity must be abreast of the modern sciences, expert in technology and industry, immersed in the daily productive enterprises of civilization, and thoroughly permeated with the divine purpose of human betterment. Thus directed and inspired, our civilization will control and master disease, wipe out poverty and insecurity of livelihood, and abolish oppression and injustice, the exploitation of labor, and the enslavement of less developed races. It will dispel ignorance and superstition, and make freedom and human fellowship living realities on earth. Saint-Simon expressed his golden rule of loving collaboration in two precepts: "Man should work,"[2] and "Love and succor each other."[3] He proclaimed himself the apostle of this social-industrial gospel: "Earth, rejoice, Saint-Simon has appeared! . . . The Man-God of the Christians has become in Saint-Simon the Man-People."[4]

Comte's Method of Positive Philosophy

Auguste Comte (1798–1857) was, for several years, Saint-Simon's secretary and collaborator. Some critics have depreciated his philosophy as a mere elaboration of his chief's, but this judgment overemphasizes the ideas and purposes which Comte shared with Saint-Simon and other social thinkers

[2] Translated from C. H. Saint-Simon, *Oeuvres Choisies*, Brussels, Van Meenen, 1859, Vol. I, p. 220.
[3] *Ibid.*, Vol. III, p. 5.
[4] C. H. Saint-Simon, *Religion Saint-Simonienne. Recueil des Prédications*, Paris, Globe, 1832, Vol. I, pp. 303, 597.

of the period, and fails to recognize Comte's original approach to philosophy. We should note the similarities, but we should see them in their proper perspective. Comte parted with Saint-Simon because he did not think that the social or religious utopians could solve the basic problem which confronted that age. Later in his life, he, in his turn, became a prophet and the head of a cult, and some of his adherents and sympathizers, like John Stuart Mill, disagreed with him as he had disagreed with Saint-Simon. As Comte expressed it himself, he was Aristotle first, and then St. Paul. To understand Comte, we should keep in balanced view both aspects of his mind, and also consider his own lofty self-appraisal. Comte's professed apostolate is important in the history of modern religious thought, but his role in the history of philosophy was played mainly during his "Aristotelian" period. The substance of his philosophy lies in his positive-scientific method and its application to the interpretation of man and society. But even during this rigorous intellectual construction, a prophetic motive was impelling his thought and sentiment toward their ultimate devotional utterance.

Comtism is the philosophy and the religion of sociality, though perhaps the outstanding characteristic of its author's life is his solitariness. Comte was the son of intensely devout Catholic parents, but, early in his youth, he struggled and broke with orthodox beliefs and practices. He then dedicated himself to the pursuit of science, and found welcome among the radical groups of the polytechnic school which he attended in Paris. When the school was closed by a bigoted ministry, Comte decided to direct his studies himself. Before long, his mastery of the sciences was unquestioned, but it did not have the official academic stamp; hence he could not get a professorial appointment. He was assigned to subsidiary educational tasks, and had to resort to tutoring. His married life was unhappy from the first. His Catholic parents refused to recognize the civil-ceremony marriage, and his wife's independent spirit extended beyond her own consent to such a ceremony. She had a mind of her own, and she was not duly submissive to his intellectual dominance. Later in life, Comte's idealized love for Madame Clotilde de Vaux, and, after her death, his devotion to her as his Beatrice, "irradiated" his solitude. But the mystical effusions to which he was then inspired in his propagation of the religion of humanity alienated many of his closest followers and associates. The "Occidental Republic" which he proclaimed to the world was not without citizens, but its founder died, as he had lived, a lonely spirit.

In his later apostolic years, Comte interpreted his whole philosophy as pursuit of the sound foundations of true religion. During his earlier period of philosophical activity, he had no religious aims or sympathies. Even as late as 1846, he used the term "religious" depreciatingly. This may only mean that Comte resisted the usual theological implications of religiosity; yet, in the final volume of his last major treatise, *Positive Polity* (*Politique Positive*), he included some of his earliest pamphlets as evidence of his search for a final religion of humanity. He seemed, in fact, to have been seeking a true ideal which would replace the untenable, traditional religious devotion.

There was a practical dynamic in Comte's scientific-philosophical thought from the very outset. It was the problem of social regeneration. He was convinced that the social-political unsettlement and chaos of western civilization were due to the confusion of ideas by which men directed their lives. The dissolution of social order was the outward expression of the root evil, the mental anarchy of the age. Saint-Simon had recognized this truth, but Comte undertook to probe it and to elicit its full significance. No mere change of government, and no radical or utopian schemes of social reconstruction, could solve the fundamental problem. The real revolution must take place in men's minds and thoughts, for the order and civilization of a society are the practical expressions of its outlook on the world and of its self-understanding.

THE LAW OF THE THREE STAGES OF THOUGHT

The study of the evolution of ideas and of men's progress toward the right method of attaining truth was, in Comte's judgment, the primary task of philosophy. Condorcet and Saint-Simon had sought to trace the historical course of intellectual development. Comte, continuing their work, proposed, as a general principle, the law of the three stages of thought: theological, metaphysical, positive-scientific. He regarded this law, not only as manifested in the general history of ideas, but also as exemplified in the advancement of each particular science and in the development of each active mind.

In its first, or theological, stage, the mind entertains fictions. This is the age of myth-making. Men explain each event in nature as due to the action of some god or goddess. At first, they may feel the presence of these weird beings all around them, in every stick and stone. Later, their imaginations may people the world with a pantheon, a hierarchy of divinities, and theologians may conceive of all existence as ruled by one universal deity that they seek to comprehend and to worship.

As the growing mind thus proceeds from imagining to speculation, it passes beyond theology to the second, or metaphysical, stage. In this stage, men still speculate instead of investigating; but now they emphasize conceptual instead of mythological construction. Rational abstractions replace the myths of folklore and popular faith. The various processes in nature are ascribed to ultimate entities and directive principles—nature of things, the logos, design in nature.

When the mind reaches maturity, it outgrows both theology and metaphysics. It renounces futile speculations about the supreme Being, cosmic reason, and ultimate reality, and concentrates its inquiries on specific processes and causal connections in various fields. It disavows alleged absolute principles to ascertain particular data and causal uniformities. This is the stage of positive science, the attainment of real knowledge in detail. Saint-

Simon had advocated the pursuit of "positive philosophy," but the thorough elaboration of the method was Comte's achievement.

Thought has not progressed steadily all along the line. It has reached the positive-scientific stage earlier in some fields of inquiry than in others. The same society, even the same person, may think scientifically in some fields, speculate metaphysically in others, and still retain some persistent theological fictions.

The advance of thought to the positive-scientific stage can be understood more clearly if we consider Comte's classification of the sciences. When arranged in the order of their generality—mathematics, astronomy, physics, chemistry, and biology—they are arranged also in the order in which they have attained the positive-scientific stage. This hierarchy of the sciences exhibits their progressive growth in complexity. Each science in the list serves as a foundation for the next, less general and more complex, science. It should not be difficult to see why positive scientific methods were attained in physics earlier than in biology, or why mankind has been so slow in formulating an adequate science of human nature.

As we thus trace the progress of thought—from fictions to abstractions to positive knowledge—and perceive the reasons for the advance and for the limitations of past knowledge, we are in a position to take the next step forward. Comte regarded this as the most important step of all, the formulation of a positive science of man. He called it "social physics," the science of social nature, or sociology. This sociological emphasis expressed his interpretation of human nature and his program for man's true career. Comte exalted social science as the summit and crown of all knowledge. He early made it his aim in life to lead mankind to this summit, and, in his last years, he wrote of it with religious fervor. But this supreme importance of sociology demands a thorough study of its relation to the other sciences. Thus, we can understand the indefatigable zeal with which Comte explored the entire scale of the positive sciences in the first three thick volumes of his *Course of Positive Philosophy*, before he took up sociology and social philosophy to which he devoted the rest of his vast treatise.

SOCIAL SCIENCE AND PHILOSOPHY

Comte's classification of the sciences omitted psychology. This was not an oversight, but was due to his interpretation of mind and human nature. He rejected the traditional notion of an immaterial soul, and he also criticized the psychologists of his day who examined mental processes by methods of introspective analysis, without due regard for their physiological basis. The scientific study of human nature is properly a chapter in biology, and must be in the closest possible relation to the investigation of animal behavior. The recognition of the organic basis of intelligence was the merit of the Encyclopedists and the ideologists; but they distorted this truth into a serious error by their one-sided materialistic conclusion. The full understanding of human nature requires, not only its physiological explanation, but also the recognition of its social character. Man is an animal, but he is preeminently a social animal. The full meaning of the word "human" is "social." Thus, the advance of the study of man to the positive-scientific stage, according to Comte, required sociology, which followed biology in his classification of the sciences, and which represented the summit of intellectual attainment.

Comte distinguished two scientific inquiries in his sociology, or social physics: social statics and social dynamics. Social statics, he understood to be the general theory of the natural order and organization of human societies. His social dynamics was the science of humanity's natural progress through its historical periods. His two main ideas were order and progress, and he gave these prominence later on the title pages of his books.

Social statics leads us to the principle of the harmonious interrelation, or solidarity, of the various social activities and forms of institutional order. Man's fundamental sociability expresses itself in the various characteristically human attainments—domesticity, economics, politics, morality, religion, art, and science. These may be distinguished, but they should be seen in their bearing on each other. During the Renaissance, Bodin had described the state as a system, or the tissue, of social relations, the basic relation being the institution of the family. Comte regarded the family as the veritable and primary social unit or nucleus of order. Society is a system of families; it is, in fact, the great human family. It is in family life that individuals first realize their self-identification in interests and purposes with the lives of others, their essentially social character. The family cultivates the social-altruistic tendencies in human nature, and an abiding social order depends on the dominance of these altruistic tendencies. An abiding social order, in turn, will perfect human character. Social life is a system of cooperation of individuals and families. It involves a division of labor that is particularly necessary in large undertakings. But this specialized distribution of activities should not be allowed to isolate men from each other, or to make them lose their feeling of active collaboration in the common social enterprise. By instruction and direction, both public education and public administration should aim to keep alive and deepen men's conviction of their essential social bond, the principle of social cohesion.

Comte's study of social dynamics, the science of human progress, involved a vast investigation of the history of civilization in every field. In its general pattern, this progressive movement, according to him, follows the law of the three stages of thought. The theological stage corresponds to the military spirit in the social order; the metaphysical stage is paralleled by a social regime of legalism; and the positive-scientific stage gives prominence to an industrial social order.

Comte claimed for his positive philosophy the merit of having a truly historical sense, a tolerant, but critical, interpretation of past epochs. Unlike the eighteenth-century atheists, he could recognize the significance of medieval-Scholastic culture and philosophy for its age, but he did not take its truth for his own. Progress in social order, as in ideas, must proceed through and beyond traditional forms. The reactionary traditionalist misunderstands both human nature and civilization.

Social science reveals man's progressive realization of his essentially social character. Social philosophy is thus warranted in inferring a social principle and standard of morality. If the truth of our being is that we live *in* humanity, our sovereign ideal and highest good must be that we should live *for* humanity. The good and virtuous life was conceived by Comte as a life of thorough social-mindedness. Our thought and outlook on life, our sentiments, purposes, and actions, must become consciously socialized. *"Vivre pour autrui,"* Comte declared: we should not merely "live for others," as it were, by self-sacrifice; we should live the fullest and most significant life as active members of our own society and of the vaster society of civilization. Actively be one with the great life of humanity; feel its joys and sorrows, think its great thoughts, share its noble purposes, and pursue the realization of its ideals! This was also the vision George Eliot expressed in her poem "The Choir Invisible."

COMTE'S RELIGION OF HUMANITY

The altruistic morality of active sociality which Comte inferred from his sociology led him, beyond science and intellectual construction, to advocate a new religion. The fruition of wisdom, according to his later views, required that "the Intellect should always serve the Heart, and should never be its slave."[5] The life of moral perfection takes us beyond rights to duties, and beyond duties to a spirit of loving devotion to mankind, humane piety. In this thoroughly and universally human consecration, we can experience intimate communion with the immemorial, heroic nobility and leadership of mankind, and with the greater life of civilization.

In this religious prospect, Comte sought to translate certain spiritual values which religious tradition had misapprehended. Instead of worship of God, he advocated intense devotion to Humanity among whom we live and move and have our being. Instead of the communion of saints commemorated in the calendar of the Church, he composed a positivistic calendar, in which each day was dedicated to meditation on a great genius of attainment in some field of civilization. This devout daily consecration of thought and sentiment served as prayer in his religion of humanity. Thus, feeling, thinking, and acting in generous social-mindedness, and identified in his every present moment with the great all-human life of the past, a person would contemplate his future fulfillment in social terms. In place of the traditional belief in personal immortality, Comte advocated the ideal hope of survival in the larger life of mankind. The idea of living in the memory of others, survival in posterity, was exalted by him to an all-human perspective. He advocated his religion of humanity with great fervor and confidence, convinced that it would gain increasing recognition as the true faith for enlightened minds.

[5] A. Comte, *A General View of Positivism*, Paris, 1848, title-page.

If he could live to be 90, might he not see the Pantheon in Paris consecrated as the world temple of his new religion?

This apostolic direction of Comte's later activity, of great interest in the study of the varieties of religious experience, cannot be pursued further in our history of philosophy. The positivistic cult had followers who established meeting houses in many parts of the world. In our day, a revival of this religious strain has led to humanism, a movement which has attracted some notable adherents in America. The more definitely philosophical influence of Comte has also been widespread. As may be expected, it affected the philosophical interpretation of various fields of human experience—psychology, literature and art, religion, and the critical method in the social sciences.

SUGGESTED WORKS FOR FURTHER STUDY

WORKS BY AUGUSTE COMTE.   Comte, A., *Positive Philosophy* (trans. and condensed Harriet Martineau); *A General View of Positivism* (trans. J. H. Bridges).

BIOGRAPHIES AND CRITICAL STUDIES.   Caird, Edward, *The Social Philosophy and Religion of Comte*; Lévy-Bruhl, L., *The Philosophy of Auguste Comte*; Lewes, G. H., *Comte's Philosophy of the Sciences*; Mill, J. S., *Auguste Comte and Positivism*; Watson, John, *Comte, Mill, and Spencer*; Whittaker, Thomas, *Comte and Mill*.

32.   John Stuart Mill: Revival of Empiricism and Utilitarianism

The Utilitarianism of Bentham

The principal fruitful philosophical movement in Britain during the first part of the nineteenth century took the form of a revival and continuation of empiricism, with emphasis on its hedonistic inferences in ethics and with definite application to problems of social reform. Jeremy Bentham (1748–1832) was the leader of this school of so-called "philosophical radicals"; its members were known as Benthamites, and in morals, as utilitarians.

Bentham's mind, precociously brilliant and radical, was given every educational opportunity to realize its promise. His father, an attorney, hoped to see his son become a great judge. Young Bentham turned to the criticism of English law and aspired to establish a truly enlightened jurisprudence. His extended residence in Europe, ranging from France to Russia, not only gave him a cosmopolitan outlook, but also familiarized him with the writings of the French empiricists and hedonists. Their influence on him explains the difference between Bentham's thoroughly secular utilitarianism and that of the earlier theological hedonists. But Bentham did not dismiss certain respectable English provisions from his radicalism. His projected reforms stopped short of revolution, be it American or French.

Bentham's empiricism was not a theory of knowledge, but a practical procedure. He relied on no universal principles and accepted neither the doctrine of natural rights nor the social contract as the basis of legal sanctions. In his first work, *Fragment on Government* (1776), he argued that political obligation and obedience to law are dependent on the people's welfare which they safeguard. The basis of political society is utility. This term was used by the Benthamites to signify the general good interpreted as happiness or prevailing pleasure. Instead of the lofty but abstract "declaration of the rights of man," they proposed "the greatest happiness of the greatest number" as a more definite aim, a standard issuing from men's direct experience.

In Bentham's judgment, both ethics and jurisprudence are concerned with producing the greatest possible quantity of happiness. Ethics considers the direction of one's own conduct to that end, whereas jurisprudence and the art of legislation provide for the direction, and even the compulsion, of people's actions to the attainment of the general happiness. The warrant of the hedonistic appraisal of conduct lies in men's basic motivation; the incentive for every action is the expected pleasure. Other proposed ethical principles are dogmatic, and, if pressed to justify themselves, must lead finally to utility; this alone is the self-sustaining standard that expresses man's natural desire for the greatest possible quantity of pleasure.

Bentham proposed a method for the comparative calculation of pleasurable consequences of acts to be used as a guide to choice. In this "hedonistic calculus," the pleasure and displeasure of two or more courses of action were to be compared as to their intensity, duration, certainty, nearness or remoteness, fecundity, purity (that is, the likelihood that the pleasure will be followed by other pleasure or by pain), and, finally, their extent, the number of persons they may affect. Bentham proposed this "calculus," not only as a general statement of the various aspects of hedonistic appraisal, but as a method of scientific, hedonistic measurement. In this latter sense, it has repeatedly been criticized as defective.

Bentham defended his altruistic hedonism by declaring that his own motive was as selfish as other men's; he desired pleasure for himself. But he found this pleasure in promoting the happiness of others. This, we recall, was Holbach's definition of a virtuous man. Bentham stated explicitly that the moral value of an action is determined not by its motive, but by its intention, that is, by its intended and willed consequences. Society provides inducements to moral-altruistic behavior; these are the utilitarian sanctions, which are variously enumerated in Bentham's writings. The principal sanctions recall Locke's list: the political, the moral or social, and the religious.

John Stuart Mill

Bentham's astonishing precocity would attract more attention were it not so overshadowed by that of his critical disciple, John Stuart Mill (1806–1873) who is regarded as the premier infant prodigy on record. His record is incredible. The child began the study of Greek at 3, and of Latin—along with algebra and geometry—at 8. Before adolescence, he had read the ancient classics (he started with Plato while he was still in the nursery), he had begun calculus and economics, and he soon learned French. He never went to school, but was tutored by his father, James Mill. A strict teacher, he heard the boy's lessons during their walks in the late afternoon, explained nothing to him that he ought to think out for himself, asked him to write a criticism of every author he read, and appointed him teacher of his younger brothers and sisters.

This strenuous regime achieved for young John intellectual mastery, but caused an emotional crisis, in which the youth felt like a logical machine in whose expert operations cold reason could see no meaning or worth. Fortunately, this gloomy season was brief. Aesthetic and moral influences aided his return to a life of animation and earnest purpose; one of these influences was his study of Wordsworth's poetry. With fresh enthusiasm, he resumed his active participation in the utilitarian movement in morals and social reform. The gospel of the greatest happiness of the greatest number became the spiritual dynamic in his life. It deepened and clarified the liberalism to which his father's influence had early inclined him, and it accentuated his critical demand for reconstruction in philosophical method as well as in the political order.

Mill's mature years realized in abundant degree the promise of his brilliant youth. In logic, ethics, and political economy, his philosophical contributions were of prime importance. His role in the social reconstruction of England was equally noteworthy. For him, as for his father and Bentham, utilitarianism was not merely a theory of morals; it provided a basis and a platform for achieving a fairer and happier nation. Mill identified himself actively with educational and economic reforms, advocated women's rights, and in other ways was in the forefront of the modern struggle for the emancipation of mankind. Gladstone said that, during his brief term in the House of Commons, Mill raised the moral tone of parliamentary debate.

MILL'S EXPERIMENTAL LOGIC

From 1823 to 1858, Mill was employed by the East India Company, first as clerk in his father's department, and later, rising to the positions of chief examiner and general superintendent. During these years, his books were written after office hours, which makes his intellectual production the more remarkable. His first and most substantial philosophical treatise was *A System of Logic* (1843). Its chief merit is its examination of the experimental methods of inductive proof. Mill perfected Francis Bacon's analysis of inductive procedure, but he did not, as did Bacon, neglect the importance of deduction in systematic science. While he recognized the interplay of inductive and deductive methods, however, Mill did emphasize the importance of induction in the scientific ascertainment of facts and causal connections in nature. A syllogism subsumes a particular case under a class of subjects which have been noted to have certain predicates. The basic reasoning in the major premise is inductive.

Science does not merely classify the objects of experience; its main interest is the investigation of causal relations. Mill revised Bacon's three Tables of Essence and Presence, of Deviation or Absence in Proximity, and of Comparison. He named these, respectively, the Method of Agreement, of Difference, and of Concomitant Variations. He examined their operation in great detail, and he formulated their canons. He also distinguished from them his so-called "Method of Residues," as needed for more complete causal determination; after a part of any phenomenon has been causally explained as due to certain antecedents, the residue of it must be regarded as due to other remaining antecedents. A fifth method, required in certain complex fields of investigation, where the Method of Agreement and the Method of Difference cannot be used effectively, was called by Mill the "Joint Method of Agreement and Difference." Mill's canon of this method not only states its logical procedure, but also gives us a sample of his formulations of the five methods. "If two or more instances in which the phenomenon occurs have only one circumstance in common, while two or more instances in which it does not occur have nothing in common save the absence of that circumstance, the circumstance in which alone the two sets of instances differ is the effect, or the cause, or an indispensable part of the cause, of the phenomenon."[1] The general basis on which causal reasoning proceeds is that the sole invariable antecedent of an event is its cause, and the sole invariable consequent of an event is its effect. The five methods attain various degrees of certainty in discovering these uniform connections in otherwise variable conditions. The basic method would seem to be the method of difference, in which the inclusion or exclusion of some factor or circumstance is accompanied by the presence or absence of a certain other condition or behavior. When this method cannot be used completely, the method of concomitant variations may provide inductive proof and yield formulas of precise correlation.

Mill's experimental logic investigated the specific causes and effects in nature, but it proceeded on an initial declaration of the fact of causal connection in nature. Can we say that this most preeminent of all major premises, "Events in nature are causally connected," is to be regarded as an inductive summary of observed data? The circular reasoning in this sort of procedure should disturb the cautious empiricist. It disturbed Mill. He tried to meet this difficulty by examining the evidence of the law of universal causation. His candor in inspecting his possibly precarious foundations is as impressive in logic as it is in his utilitarian ethics.

Mill did not regard himself as a disciple of Comte, but he agreed with the positivist disavowal of any metaphysics. All our knowledge is of the data and connections of experience, not of any ultimate realities. Mill regarded mind, not as an immaterial substance, but as a texture of perceptions, ideas, and emotional and volitional states. Bodies, likewise, are known to us as so much experienced material. Mill described matter as the "permanent possibility of sensation."[2]

MILL'S UTILITARIANISM AND SOCIAL PHILOSOPHY

In his ethical views, Mill began as a Benthamite and then proceeded to radical revisions which really led him beyond strict utilitarianism. His loyalty

[1] J. S. Mill, *A System of Logic*, new impr. ed., London, Longmans, 1911, p. 259.
[2] J. S. Mill, *An Examination of Sir William Hamilton's Philosophy*, 2nd ed., London, Longmans, 1865, p. 198.

to his father and to Bentham kept him from admitting his disagreements with the utilitarian position, but his correspondence indicated that he was not unaware of them. From the outset, he took a firmly teleological position in ethics. The moral value of actions depends on their consequences; that is, as he specifies further, on their tendency to promote happiness. But, whereas Bentham depreciated the moral bearing of the motive, Mill admitted that the motive makes a difference in morality when it makes a difference in the act. But is it not evident that the motive always affects the acts in its entirety? He agreed with Bentham in espousing altruistic hedonism—the promotion of the greatest happiness of the greatest number—but he went beyond Bentham's professedly selfish pleasure in promoting the happiness of others. Mill believed that people have a genuinely benevolent, sympathetic regard for others, and that utilitarian altruism has a direct empirical basis.

In the last chapter of *Utilitarianism*, Mill traced the evolution of justice in human social relations. His exposition recalls Hume's treatment of a similar theme. Men may begin by selfishly seeking retributive punishment, but this desire is gradually extended to a demand for punishment to check all evildoers, and tends to take a firm stand against actions that endanger the common welfare, a negative form of the promotion of the general happiness.

Mill's most important departure from Bentham, and from strict hedonism, was his insistence on qualitative differences in pleasures. Pleasures are not simply amounts to be reckoned; they are also of different kinds, to be graded and subjected to preferential choice. This eighth factor of "quality" was Mill's addition to Bentham's hedonistic calculus. To Mill, the greatest happiness of the greatest number meant the best, the highest, happiness. By this radical revision, he sought to meet the severe criticism that hedonism was the ethics of the trough. "It is better to be a human being dissatisfied than a pig satisfied; better to be a Socrates dissatisfied than a fool satisfied."[3] For this choice of the higher pleasure, Mill relied on man's higher intelligence, which can discern between two values, and which can choose the better.

In this grading of the relative worth of various pleasures, Mill had already gone beyond the strict hedonistic position, and was appealing to other standards, both of the value pursued and of its appraisal. He realized—and, in his candor, he stated explicitly—that a fool's pleasures have the greater chance of being fully satisfied. A society of men like Socrates, with their high purposes, would miss the happiness of full satisfaction. Yet Mill, while still believing himself to be an advocate of the general-happiness theory, applauded Socrates' choice. This may have been an inconsistency in Mill's utilitarianism, but it was also a real gain in ethical insight. His analysis exposed some basic deficiencies in hedonistic ethics, and called for a radical revision of that theory. Mill preferred to reconstruct Benthamism rather than to abandon it, but he was not unaware that he had given up the traditional utilitarian position. Carlyle had good ground for telling Emerson that

[3] J. S. Mill, *Utilitarianism*, New York, Dutton, Everyman's Library, 1951, p. 12.

Mill had "worked himself clear of Benthamism."[4] Mill's letters to Carlyle record his gradual, but eventually radical, shift of thought. Though he continued to call himself a utilitarian, it was, he said, "in quite another sense from what perhaps anyone except myself understands by the word."[5] How far he had moved toward perfectionism—and even toward Kantian ethics—is indicated by his eulogy of "the cultivation of a disinterested preference of duty for its own sake."[6]

Mill's application of his ethical principles to social problems is marked by a spirit of vigorous, but sober, liberalism. In 1848, the year of social revolutions, and when Marx and Engels issued their *Communist Manifesto*, Mill published his *Principles of Political Economy*. The pattern of his social-economic criticism recalls his treatment of utilitarianism. Basically, he adhered to the system of private enterprise. The communistic alternative to competition is state ownership and direction of the means of production, but this will not evoke the full exertion and development of men's powers which are essential to progress. Nevertheless, Mill recognized the evils in the existing system, especially in the distribution of the fruits of industry, and he advocated radical reforms. He would combine mainly private initiative in production with social control of the owners, and with protection of the landless and laboring classes, to the degree required to correct or mitigate existing flagrant evils, and to assure a steady rise in the general standard of living.

In political theory, Mill sought a reasonable middle ground between the conflicting tyrannies of the few and the many which threaten modern societies. All good government is *for* the people, but not *by* the masses. The wisdom needed for the direction of the state is best provided by its few, superior minds, but the people cannot entrust their destiny even to enlightened despots. The ideally best state is one that has representative government. It requires educating all toward an organized respect for the general welfare; this is the political expression of utilitarian morality. Sovereignty must be vested, ultimately, in the people, for whose sake laws are enacted and public measures administered. But the common people must not be flattered by this; instead they must be taught to recognize their need of expert guidance. The chief purpose of this guidance, in turn, must be the social betterment and political education of the people; on these alone any true commonwealth must depend.

Mill continued his active promotion of the specific reforms in which his father and Bentham had been engaged, and which achieved marked success in the parliamentary Reform Bill of 1832. Mill was also a leader in the struggle for the political and social rights of English women. An enlightened

[4] R. W. Emerson, *Journals* (E. W. Emerson and W. E. Forbes, eds.), Boston, Houghton Mifflin, 1910, Vol. III, p. 182.

[5] Quoted in J. Seth, *English Philosophers and Schools of Philosophy*, London, Dent, 1912, p. 249.

[6] J. S. Mill, *Dissertations and Discussions*, New York, Holt, Vol. IV, 1874, p. 292.

society should recognize and respect women as persons; it should not defend their subjugation. For women, as for men, Mill advocated the fullest individual self-expression as would be compatible with the regard for the rights of others. In his essay, *On Liberty*, he examined the interrelation of personal initiative and social control. The concern of good government is to safeguard and to promote the common welfare, and it has a right to interfere with individuals only in exercising its socially protective role. In his own life, where he does not injure others or interfere with their rights, the individual should enjoy liberty of thought and expression, of choice and action. Mill advocated the emancipation of mankind, not only from political and economic oppression, but from the social control of the individual mind, which perpetuates traditional opinion and which holds in check the original creative thought that is the dynamic of progress. The fullest realization of the common welfare depends on the free interplay of ideas in a society of free minds.

Mill's reflections on religion were marked by an empiricist distrust of the metaphysical speculations of theologians and a distaste for churchly forms. Although he saw no tenable ground for believing in a divine providence, his life and thought were devoted to the moral and other kinds of human values for which traditional religion claimed to have supernatural warrant. He therefore welcomed Comte's positivism as a sound philosophy that preserved the kernel of human values without the theological shell. But, when Comte declared himself high pontiff of his new religion, it meant a parting of the ways for Mill.

Mill's posthumously published *Three Essays on Religion* reveal his deep concern for man's religious quest, but without the resolute venture of faith. His study of nature and human nature revealed no certain prospect of life beyond the present scene. A belief in immortality in its various forms was, in Mill's judgment, sublime, but not really warranted—although he did not reject the hope as a bare possibility. The eminent arguments for God's existence, he criticized as unconvincing, and he found little evidence for the moral attributes of omnipotent deity that are most essential to traditional religious assurance. The nearest approximation to theistic belief which he suggested on the grounds of natural religion was belief in a finite God, "a Being of great but limited power, how and by what limited we cannot even conjecture."[7]

SUGGESTED WORKS FOR FURTHER STUDY

BENTHAM. Bentham, J., *Introduction to the Principles of Morals and Legislation* (several editions are available); Baumgardt, David, *Bentham and the Ethics of Today*.

[7] J. S. Mill, *Three Essays on Religion*, London, Longmans, 1874, p. 194.

JOHN STUART MILL.   Mill, J. S., *Autobiography* (J. J. Coss, ed.); *The Ethics of John Stuart Mill* (Charles Douglas, ed.); *A System of Logic; Principles of Political Economy; Utilitarianism, Liberty, and Representative Government* (A. D. Lindsay, ed.); Courtney, W. L., *Life of John Stuart Mill;* MacCunn, John, *Six Radical Thinkers;* Watson, John, *Comte, Mill, and Spencer.*

33. German Philosophers, 1850–1900

Lotze: the Issue of Naturalism and Idealism

The idealistic philosophy—especially in its Hegelian version—which had dominated German thought during the first part of the nineteenth century, was opposed by the resurgence of naturalism and materialism, and by Schopenhauer's doctrine of the will to live. These two basic issues, in various forms, engaged many German thinkers during the latter half of the century. The first pair of alternatives, materialistic naturalism and idealism, was approached from both sides; or rather, thinkers in search of a synthesis shifted their emphasis to one side of the issue or the other.

Rudolf Hermann Lotze (1817–1881) was, like Aristotle, the son of a physician. At Leipzig he studied physics and physiology; he graduated simultaneously in medicine and in philosophy, and, for a while, was a practicing physician. He then entered into a distinguished university career, during which he combined his philosophical and scientific ideas into a system he described as "teleological idealism." He aroused the hopes of the materialists with his *Medical Psychology*, but he promptly corrected their misunderstanding. In exploring the physiological aspects of mental processes, he nowise upheld the materialistic reduction of mind to a series of mere organic reactions.

We may both compare and contrast Lotze with the idealists of the romantic period. He shared many of their ideals and truths, but not their philosophical methods. He reached his conviction of the spiritual character of reality neither by romantic affirmation nor by a derogation of physical science. Strict application of the scientific method, which he held valid in its own province, led him to consider more ultimate spiritual problems which science raises but cannot solve. The mechanism of physical science is cosmic in its extent, but it cannot express the significance of nature or the values of man's experience.

Lotze's procedure in metaphysics was not quite the same as Kant's. He would not "abolish *knowledge* to make room for *faith*,"[1] but he denied to

[1] Immanuel Kant, *Critique of Pure Reason*, in N. K. Smith, *Immanuel Kant's Critique of Pure Reason*, New York, Macmillan, 1929, p. 29.

natural science the full possession of our spiritual range. He meant to pursue steadily a rigorous scientific procedure in tracing the mechanistic pattern of physical and mental processes. Beyond this naturalistic frame of description and explanation, Lotze brought up the question of meaning and values. To understand the construction and operation of a machine, we must consider the purpose it serves. Human experience and the whole structure of nature raise the same problem of basic interpretation, which no mere description of the operating mechanism can solve. Lotze, therefore, insisted on viewing nature and human nature in the various perspectives in which they present themselves to a contemplative mind. Those perspectives do not reveal equally the range and meaning of reality.

Deeper than the technical knowledge of the modern naturalist is the wisdom of Plato who pointed to the Idea of Good, or the principle of value, as the supreme expression of reality. Lotze concluded his *Metaphysic* with a Platonic conviction: "I feel certain of being on the right track, when I seek in that which *should be* the ground of that which *is*."[2] This conviction of teleological idealism was derived from his scientific account of nature, but it was intended to complete and to transcend it. Any being, he held, involves interrelated activities with other beings. This interrelation as investigated by science is causal. If we consider only the cosmic mechanism, our view of nature will be a pluralism. But Lotze did, not accept the Herbartian cosmology of "reals" any more than he accepted the atoms and atomic clusters of the materialists. Even Leibniz's monadism, though it influenced the development of Lotze's thought, did not satisfy him. Both analysis and direct experience raise objections to the finality of pluralism and to a monadism which does not place its emphasis on a divine monad of monads. Herbart had already pointed out the confusion inherent in the principle of causation. Lotze held that we must somehow explain the interconnection of distinct beings as indicating their ultimate fellow membership in a basic reality. Our own direct experience expresses, not only the connectedness of different mental states, but also the concrete unity of self-consciousness. Lotze's cosmology resisted abstract pantheistic monism as well as bare pluralism. He recognized the unique individuality of persons as well as their spiritual community. Like all-comprehensive nature is the infinite divine spirit in which all souls find their common summit.

This final conviction cannot be fully attained by discursive intelligence. It is expressed by feeling, for which Lotze claimed recognition as an essential approach and response to reality. He mediated between stiff intellectualism which dismisses feeling and effusive romanticism which mistakes emotional fervor for logical demonstration. He did not equivocate in his scientific reasoning, but in his final account of reality he included emotional tone, which is essential to the appreciation of values.

Moral and aesthetic experience each reveal the feeling element in the

---

[2] Hermann Lotze, *Metaphysic* (trans. B. Bosanquet), 2nd ed., Oxford, Clarendon Press, 1887, Vol. II, p. 319.

acknowledgment of values. In conduct, feeling is manifested as pleasure or displeasure. But Lotze did not proceed from this explicit recognition of happiness, or satisfaction, as central in moral judgment to expound the usual hedonistic doctrine. Pleasure is a response to value, but our satisfactions and dissatisfactions reveal our range of values and our spiritual reach and maturity. The implied teleological idea of moral perfection was expressed in Lotze's *Microcosmus:* "That would be of supreme worth which caused satisfaction to an ideal mind in its normal condition, a mind which had been purified from all tendency to diverge from its proper path of development."[3] Aesthetic experience manifests an analogous span of spiritual growth. We appreciate the beauty of whatever corresponds to our actualized spiritual organization. In our enjoyment of beauty, we respond, as much as we are capable, to the integral spiritual appeal in nature and in art.

Lotze's deeper view of the nature and destiny of persons was expressed in his philosophy of religion. Personality had been interpreted as essentially involving social relations and therefore as being finite; Lotze emphasized unity and self-completeness as the basic attributes of personality. Personality, in the full sense of the term, can be ascribed only to God. Finite individuals, at best, strive toward the attainment of personality. Their aim is to become godlike. Their destiny depends on their spiritual attainment. Regarding personal immortality, Lotze was sure of his principle but not of its application. "Every created thing will continue, if and so long as its continuance belongs to the meaning of the world; . . . [but] we certainly do not know the merits which may give to one existence a claim to eternity, nor the defects which deny it to others."[4]

Hartmann's Philosophy of the Unconscious: A Synthesis of Schopenhauer and Hegel

Schopenhauer's pessimistic doctrine of the will to live as an opposition to Hegelian idealism gained strength during the period of depression that followed the frustrated social revolutions of 1848. The disciples of Schopenhauer preached his gospel with a redistribution of emphasis on its various discordant strains. Thus, among some factions, the irrationalism and pessimism of Schopenhauer's doctrine were resisted, and his metaphysical recognition of intelligence was emphasized; among others, Schopenhauer's irrationalism was accentuated, with rejection of all gospels of salvation as weak concessions to optimism.

Among these consoling or bleak sages, Eduard Von Hartmann (1842–1906) advocated systematic reconstruction. His own experience had shown him

---

[3] Hermann Lotze, *Microcosmus* (trans. E. Hamilton and E. E. Jones), 4th ed., Edinburgh, Clark, n.d., Vol. I, p. 690.
[4] Lotze, *Metaphysic, op. cit.*, Vol. II, p. 182.

the senseless frustration of high purposes, and his final valuation was tragic, but he resolutely sought some meaning in life despite its miseries. The son of a general, he had originally planned for a military career, but an accident which crippled his knee also twisted his entire life. He tried to unlock the doors of art and music, but he did not possess the keys of genius; as he said, he found himself bankrupt save for his powers of thought, and he was forced to find his real destiny in philosophy. He was a very fertile writer who gained great popularity. His books ran to some 16,000 pages, and he saw twelve editions of his first treatise, *The Philosophy of the Unconscious.* Especially noteworthy among his other works is the *Phenomenology of the Moral Consciousness*, an analytic survey of the development of moral ideas, given from a pessimistic point of view.

He believed that, like Kant, he had found philosophy at the crossroads and that it required a new orientation. He depreciated the resurgent materialism of his day and agreed with Schopenhauer that crass atomism had definitely been refuted by Kant. The crucial philosophical issue was between Schopenhauer and Hegel, and, in dealing with it, Hartmann neither took sides nor compromised. He would integrate these two alternatives into a more adequate cosmology. His proposed synthesis was analogous to Spinoza's resolution of the Cartesian dualism of mind and body. Body and mind, Spinoza had said, are not two irreducible substances but two parallel attributes of the one infinite Substance. In a similar way, Hartmann recognized an implied mistaken dualism in the conflict between Schopenhauer and Hegel. Neither the will to live nor the Hegelian Idea could qualify as the ultimate reality. A philosophy which ignored either of the two would be one-sided, but a synthesis of the two could be achieved only through the recognition of them both as two phases or attributes of the ultimate reality. Hartmann undertook this metaphysical reconstruction.

He maintained that even on good Hegelian premises the philosophical dialectic demanded a synthesis of the issue between Hegel and Schopenhauer. Guidance toward this synthesis could be found in the advance of Leibniz's dynamic rationalism beyond Spinoza's geometric method. But Hartmann derived his more immediate direction from Schelling, whose versatile and brilliant notions had stimulated both Hegel and Schopenhauer. Schelling regarded nature as latent spirit, but he also perceived a certain dynamism in nature, a cosmic urge which he called "will." Ultimate reality was somehow both spirit and will, and yet transcended them both. Hartmann pursued this speculative lead of Schelling. The will to live expresses the ultimate drive in reality that makes the existence of things possible. But it is because of the idea, Logos, or spirit in ultimate reality that the existent world is a cosmos, has a certain character. Hartmann distinguished these two, will and idea, drive and significance, as the *That* and the *What* of existence, two basic aspects of the absolute substance. The absolute had been signified by Schelling as $\pm$ A. Hartmann called it neither "will" nor "idea," but "the Unconscious"; hence, the title of his first main treatise. The term proved to be a striking catchword for his doctrine, but Hartmann admitted that he might just as well have called his principle, "the Superconscious." He emphasized that the kernel of all being is dynamic, an activity analogous to will, which, even prior to any definite consciousness, operates as if it were intelligent.

This metaphysics was meant to reach beyond materialism and idealism. No merely mechanistic cosmology can explain the natural attainment of eyesight or of rational intelligence. But the actual teleology in nature neither warrants nor requires the doctrine of a creative, divine reason or an analogous, idealistic logos. The teleology in nature appears prior to consciousness. Consciousness itself arises at a certain level of existence as the reaction of "will activities," or processes in nature which counteract the resistant medium they encounter.

Thus far, Hartmann had adhered to strictly metaphysical reconstruction. But his definition of consciousness revealed the pessimistic slant in his view of all existence. The most elementary sensation is a baffled state of checked activity. We become aware of whatever is in our way, whatever counteracts and hems us in and would thwart us. In this cosmic struggle of existence, our conscious experiences issue from the stir and shock of intrusion, and rise to pursue the lure of desired satisfaction and mastery, but in which pursuit they suffer repeated frustration, and they end in a sense of futility and disillusionment.

Now it may be asked, despite Hartman's cosmological reconstruction, does not Hegel seem to yield here to Schopenhauer? What avails the metaphysical recognition of intelligence, if it finally proves incapable of assuring meaning and value of life? Hartmann's position with regard to this crucial problem reflects progressive revision through the years, and his pessimistic tone is more prevailing in his earlier works than it is in his later ones. He was, and he remained, a "eudaemonological pessimist," as he called himself, but his philosophy of life inclined increasingly toward "evolutionistic optimism." In plainer terms, Hartmann believed that, in the quest for happiness, life is a losing venture; but that it is worth living, nonetheless, because it affords development and the attainment of other values.

The Philosophy of the Unconscious traced the three historical stages of man's great illusion, the pursuit of happiness. The first stage was characterized by the belief that individual happiness was attainable in this life. Men's disappointment in this belief marks the lowering gloom and the decline of classical antiquity. Disillusioned in this life, the ancient world was converted to the Christian Gospel with its glad tidings of heavenly happiness in the life to come. This is the second stage of the great illusion. This faith marked medieval civilization, but it lost its power with the spread of modern scientific ideas. The quest for happiness next assumed the form of a belief in social progress that will speed the greatest happiness of the greatest number. But modern civilization is teaching us its grim lessons. Men realize that they may make their life more active, productive, and intelligent, but no happier; as far as happiness goes, life is a wretched business which will finally be renounced by all of us. When mankind has become sufficiently enlightened, a universal pessimistic resolution could lead people to vote this wretched world out of existence! In his later writings, Hartmann did not explicitly disclaim this project of world extinction, but he showed a tendency toward a more positive valuation, which, be it noted, was still tragic in its finality.

Hartmann looked beyond Schopenhauer to Kant as the founder of the true pessimistic view of life. Kant's ethics rejected the idea of the virtuous life as the most pleasurable and satisfying, and advocated a life of disinterested, upright will. He saw life, not as easygoing enjoyment, but as dutiful endeavor. Only in such a life did he see moral dignity and worth. Hartmann held that the surest basis of morality is pessimistic, a perspective of life as a duty that ought to be fulfilled, but which is tragic in the end. He rejected Kant's arguments for belief in God and personal immortality, as required to crown virtue with happiness or to afford eternal scope to the moral pursuit of perfection. His appraisal of man's present life led him to recognize real worth in the quest for intellectual, aesthetic, moral, and other values. But his judgment always inclined toward a tragic note. His prospect was grim; he called his outlook "peiorism"—things are getting worse. Man's best choice is heroic devotion to recognized values and duties, against the inevitable ultimate ruin. This was the spirit of his "cosmotragic religion." Ultimate salvation for God, as well as for man, must be salvation from the nullity of existence.

Nietzsche's Philosophy of the Will to Power

Friedrich Nietzsche (1844–1900) was an aristocratic individualist in rebellion against the dominant values of civilization. His contempt for modern life was ruthless. He scorned the sterile, abstract science of the learned, the dull ignorance of the masses, the philistine democracy with its sordid wealth and abject poverty, the Christian gospel of charity as sentimental, and Christian ascetic ideals as sickly. He would wipe the cultural slate clean, or, rather, on new tablets he would engrave a new decalogue for untrammeled men with free minds and prevailing will to power. His style was that of poet and prophet. He ignored logical coherence and relied for his convincing power on brilliant terse utterances that were like hammer blows of driving truths, or like lightning flashes of insight—with unlit intervals.

Nietzsche's father and grandfather were Saxon-Lutheran pastors who were supposed to have been descended from Polish nobles named Niétzky. Early in childhood he lost his father, and he was brought up and spoiled by his mother and two spinster aunts. He disappointed their hopes by refusing to enter the Church. His brilliant scholarship earned him a professorship of classical philology at Basel when he was barely 25. His health, which had never been good, deteriorated. Migraines, ailing eyes, sleeplessness, organic disorders, and an eventual nervous breakdown finally forced him to give up his professorship in 1879. For the next ten years, Nietzsche was a wandering, invalid scholar, seeking a public for his ideas and some relief from his ills. In 1889 he suffered a mental collapse from which he never recovered. His mother, and later, his sister—the devoted editor of his papers—cared for him until his death in 1900.

Careful readers of Nietzsche's writings have distinguished three periods in his philosophical career. He began as a brilliant classical philologist, thoroughly versed in the philosophy, art, and literature of Greco-Roman antiquity. A zealous protagonist of the aristocratic spirit in Hellenism, he was dominated by the idea of a creative dynamic in human life and culture, the prevailing will of genius. Schopenhauer's *World as Will and Idea* captivated him by its masterly style and its doctrine of the will to live, but he could not follow its ascetic gospel of salvation. He advocated not the denial, but the heroic affirmation of the will. Affirmation had to be heroic to meet the tragic demands of life.

In his first important work, *The Birth of Tragedy*, Nietzsche traced in Greek culture and dramatic art the interplay of the two contending vital impulses. The "Dionysian" assertion of the will to live—insatiate, passionate, and unrestrained—was at war with "Apollonian" reasonableness, harmony, and justice. Genius must bring lawless instincts under the direction of intelligence, in order to transform the wild orgy of life into a work of art. But the living music and rhythm of life should not be wholly subjected to the abstract rules of reason, else creative utterance will be stifled by historical learning and traditional abstractions. Human life is fully realized and justified in creative artistic achievement. Nietzsche lauded this summit of living in his interpretations of Greek culture, but he hailed its manifestation in his own day also, in the heroic music dramas of Richard Wagner. Wagner, however, disappointed his admirer shockingly when he published his *Parsifal,* in which he exalted the ascetic ideals of medieval Christianity. Nietzsche broke with Wagner forthwith and violently, but he also realized that his own ideas were taking a new course.

He was turning from classical studies to modern scientific and social-philosophical ideas. His book, *Human, All Too Human*, was dedicated to Voltaire, and the flavor of his ideas was reminiscent of the French, skeptical *moralistes*. His emotional tone varied from bitter gloom to occasional high spirits—as in *The Joyful Science*—but the prevailing note was intellectual emphasis. Heroic mastery of life was now revealed by Nietzsche as manifested not so much in artistic creation as in the integrity of free scientific inquiry that unlocks the truths and resources of nature. He championed this free spirit of investigation against the dead hands of theological dogma, and his opposition to Christianity was expressed with increasingly violent hatred.

The last stage of Nietzsche's philosophy was signalized by the publication of his most famous book, *Thus Spake Zarathustra*, in 1883. To this period belong also his *Genealogy of Morals, Beyond Good and Evil,* and *The Will to Power.* He now seemed to combine his ideals of creative art and anti-Christian naturalism into a proud and ruthless philosophy of life for men of prevailing will to power.

Nietzsche rejected idealistic metaphysics along with Christian theology. His cosmology was a revised version of Schopenhauer's doctrine of the will to live, revised so as to describe the world-wide struggle for mastery, the will to power. Nature, in every place and at every moment, is a contest. Each organism is in armor, girt for battle in its own way. On different levels of existence the will to power is dominant, and most strikingly so in all living beings and in human individuals and their societies. Our intelligence does not manifest any essential rationality in nature. Reason, as Schopenhauer said, is only an instrumentality of the will to live, a means to survival. Thinking is directed toward action and is tested in action. This may be called the pragmatic strain in Nietzsche's philosophy.

Corresponding to this biological-evolutionary account is Nietzsche's physical view of the world as a vast mechanism in which every event is a combination of energy factors. From the law of the conservation of energy, Nietzsche inferred that the total energy in the universe, however vast, must still be a finite, calculable amount. In the eternity already elapsed, therefore, everything that could possibly have taken place must have taken place already, and more than once; it can only be repeated in the future. Nietzsche should have known that this doctrine of eternal recurrence had its Stoic and other philosophical advocates in classical antiquity, but he believed that it had come to him by a flash of cosmological insight: "Everything has returned: Sirius and the spider, and thy thoughts at this moment, and this last thought of thine that all these things will return. . . ."[5] He tried to reason this out, and, for a while, he planned to resume systematic studies so as to come forth with a scientifically proved cosmic philosophy of eternal recurrence. But his eyes and his head were not fit for sustained work, and, therefore, he had to be content with his flashes of wisdom.

Nietzsche wrote that he found the idea of eternal recurrence both great and terrible. All our acts, from the greatest to the pettiest and most contemptible, will recur eternally in the cyclic round of existence. How are we to endure this dismal prospect? There is only one way to meet this most tragic problem of life, and its right solution is the essence of morality. There can be only one maxim of virtue: Perform only the actions which you will be willing to repeat countless times! Such actions, in which we reach our summit, should reconcile us to the endlessly rehearsed pettiness of existence.

The life that is worth accepting and living must, therefore, be a life of heroic affirmation. Nietzsche declared that it required a transvaluation of all traditional values. Conflicting moral notions and standards express men's different characters and ways of coming to terms with life. He distinguished between a master morality and a slave morality. The man of mastery is self-

[5] Nietzsche, *Complete Works* (O. Levy, ed.), Edinburgh, Foulis, Vol. XVI, 1911, p. **248.**

reliant, brave, candid, and honorable in word and action; he is the creative mind, the maker of laws. The slave, the beggar, and the weakling cherish the virtues in others on which they have to depend if their mean lives are to be succored—the sickly virtues of pity, charity, and forgiveness—because their vices are as despicable and cringing as themselves.

The great epochs of human history, like the great days in a man's life, are those of heroic affirmation of mastery. But the moral tragedy of civilization is its infection with the sickly slave morality of the Christian Gospel. Nietzsche opposed Christianity with hatred and contempt; one of his last books was called *The Antichrist*. Unless men reject the spirit of Christian charity, they will perpetuate mediocrity, incapacity, and invalidism, which have already tainted our godly, philistine democracy. Civilization can be reclaimed only by reawakening heroic nobility in the human soul, the will to be ruthless with the weakness and meanness in oneself as one is with these in others is boundless in its reach, firm in its grasp, overabundant with the plenitude of life and power.

Nietzsche advocated a social order, rooted in eugenics and education, to achieve his goal. A society dedicated to greatness will discover and develop the men of genius, the masters of nature and men. Such a society will let the defective strains die out, and will perfect the human stock, and eventually beget supermen.

There is something pathetic in the ailing Nietzsche—on the verge of the breakdown and madness that were to leave him helpless in the merciful care of others—blaring his trumpet call to ruthless disdain for all weakness, and his eugenic gospel to generate supermen. Recent history has proved as ironical as Nietzsche's doctrine. Hitler and his master race of self-styled supermen worshiped the will to power; it seemed to justify their ruthless plans of aggression. Nietzsche himself would probably have scorned the Nazi philistine misconception of nobility. But how was the cult of power to be kept scrupulous in its purposes? And what did this cult have to sustain it in defeat, when it had sacrificed fundamental spiritual values on its one stake of victorious might?

SUGGESTED WORKS FOR FURTHER STUDY

LOTZE. Lotze, R. H., *Metaphysic* (trans. B. Bosanquet); *Microcosmus* (trans. E. Hamilton and E. E. C. Jones); *Outlines of Aesthetics, Metaphysics, Philosophy of Religion, and Practical Philosophy* (all trans. G. T. Ladd); Jones, Sir Henry, *A Critical Account of the Philosophy of Lotze;* Thomas, E. E., *Lotze's Theory of Reality.*

HARTMANN. Hartmann, Eduard von, *The Philosophy of the Unconscious* (trans. W. C. Coupland).

NIETZSCHE. Nietzsche, F., *Works* (Oscar Levy, ed.); *Thus Spake Zarathustra* (several editions); *The Living Thoughts of Nietzsche* (Heinrich Mann, ed.);

Brandes, Georg, *Friedrich Nietzsche;* Brinton, Crane, *Nietzsche;* Halevy, D., *The Life of Friedrich Nietzsche;* Kaufmann, W., *Nietzsche: Philosopher, Psychologist, Antichrist;* Morgan, G. A., Jr., *What Nietzsche Means;* Salter, W. M., *Nietzsche the Thinker.*

34.   The Philosophers of Evolution

Charles Darwin

The fundamental idea of evolution as a cosmological pattern—that is, the interpretation of nature as a process of developing forms—found modern expression in various fields of scientific and philosophical inquiry. Montesquieu, Herder, Hegel, and others had applied the principle of development to the history of civilization. In 1809, the year of Darwin's birth (he died in 1882), Lamarck (1744–1829) published his *Zoological Philosophy*, which proposed to explain the variety and complexity of animal species on the basis of the use and disuse and variations of organs. The vital urge leads animals to develop needed organic changes for self-preservation; these changes are propagated and serve to form new species. This theory rejected the traditional theological doctrine that all plant and animal species are God's specific and distinct creations, but it supplied no adequate natural explanation in causal terms. It asserted that animals could somehow develop what they required and could transmit it to their offspring.

Darwin sought a natural, causal explanation of the origin of species. That species do originate in nature was, in his judgment, an indubitable fact, abundantly attested by the record of fossil remains. In successive geological epochs, life on earth has proceeded from elementary forms to species of increasing organic complexity. Skillful gardeners and breeders are continually producing new races of plants and animals by means of selection. How can this selective process operate in nature? Darwin's *Autobiography* records how he reached his decisive idea by a flash of theoretical insight while he was reading Malthus' essay *On the Principle of Population*. Malthus pointed out that the increase in population is always limited by the insufficient food supply. Darwin proceeded by analogy to infer his broader principle:

Being well prepared to appreciate the struggle for existence which everywhere goes on from long-cultivated observation of the habits of animals and plants, it at once struck me that under these circumstances favorable variations would tend to be preserved, and unfavorable ones to be destroyed. The result of this would be the formation of a new species.[1]

[1] Quoted in Francis Darwin (ed.), *The Life and Letters of Charles Darwin*, 2nd ed., London, Murray, 1887, Vol. I, p. 83.

This theory of the survival of the fittest in the struggle for existence—as it was developed by Darwin in detailed exposition and supported by abundant citation of evidence in his book, *On the Origin of Species by Means of Natural Selection* (1859)—signalized a new epoch in the biological sciences. The causal explanation of the formation of new species ruled out the need for any appeal to a design in nature, and placed biology alongside of the other physical sciences. The survival of the fittest in the struggle for existence was not planned or designed; it occurred. The occurrence in each case was determined causally. The fittest species in each environment were those having the variations that enabled them to survive. The ancestral ptarmigan did not change its plumage white in winter in order to protect itself from attack. The bird that had white feathers in winter was invisible in the snow; it was protected from attack, and thus survived to multiply its species. Not purpose, but causation, provides the explanation.

The evolutionary principle was not limited to biology. It was a fundamental category that soon proved significant in many fields of scientific investigation. Before long, genetic-historical methods were fruitfully being applied in various humanistic studies—in tracing the evolution of language, of social-economic institutions, morals, and religions. Even before he formulated his theory, twenty-two years prior to the publication of the *Origin of Species*, Darwin had written in his notebook: "My theory will lead to a complete philosophy."[2] Our modern view of nature and human nature has been radically modified by Darwin's evolutionary trend of thought.

The thorough application of the evolutionary method was bound to include man in its zoological survey. Should all the humanistic sciences, then, ultimately be considered as chapters in the biological science of anthropology? Darwin recognized the problem of interpreting mind and morals in evolutionary terms. With his characteristic candor, he did not evade the difficulties in giving an adequate account of human character, but he indicated some lines of likely explanation. In investigating the genesis of mind, we may trace our mental powers to their primitive human origins, to the earliest and most rudimentary beginnings of conscious responses. If, then, we consider animal reactions, though we may not find instances of deliberate reflection and rationality, we may ascertain in them more or less distant approaches to intelligence. The evidence is sufficiently varied and extensive to warrant our including the mind with the rest of the human organism in the evolutionary scale.

In his evolutionary ethics, Darwin started by viewing moral conduct as social-minded and philanthropic, and then undertook to show its evolutionary genesis. Animal gregariousness and the mutual attachment of parents and offspring could be traced in their advance from instinctive reactions to elementary sympathetic affections, to habitual responses and sentiments sustained by social pressure, and, on higher mental levels, to customary

---

[2] Quoted in H. Höffding, *A History of Modern Philosophy* (trans. B. E. Meyer), London, Macmillan, 1900, Vol. II, p. 438.

forms of behavior and to convictions and recognized principles of conduct. Darwin's inquiries in these fields, especially those presented in his *Descent of Man* (1871), stimulated extensive work in descriptive ethics on the origin and growth of the moral instinct, and of moral ideas and practices in the evolution of justice, of hospitality, of respect for life and property, and so forth.

On this issue, Darwin's followers have not been able to reach agreement. Some maintained that the gregarious solidarity of animals had survival value no less effective than aggressive or defensive equipment in the struggle for existence, and that, similarly, on the human level, social-mindedness has been the safeguard of life and the condition of man's maximum welfare. But others regarded the morally commendable versions of evolution as unwarranted. The biological evidence does not indicate that philanthropy and conscience have greater survival value than ruthless selfish behavior. Virtue has another and a higher justification. The golden rule would lead man out of the evolutionary jungle to a higher plane of existence. The basic difficulty of expressing moral values and standards in terms of survival was a crucial problem in evolutionary ethics. It was given a radical turn in Nietzsche's new morality of self-assertive will to power.

The philosophical interpretation of evolutionism has been complicated by the fact that Darwinism explained the survival results of fit variations, but he did not provide an explanation of the causes of variations, nor did he proceed to ultimate cosmological inferences. Regarding the heritability of variations, opinions differ. The Lamarckians have definitely lost ground, though they have never been without allies. The theory of mutations, as developed and interpreted by careful geneticists, has reached specific conclusions regarding the evolutionary results of changes in the germ plasm. But the larger pattern of evolutionary cosmology can scarcely be regarded as ascertained. Is it a pattern of strictly mechanical determination? Or, does biological evolution produce results that cannot be reduced to merely antecedent causal determinants, and that indicate a certain natural creative activity? Or, does the stream of existence, unlike water, somehow rise higher than its source; do lower processes produce their self-transcendence, in higher types of being? Philosophy since Darwin has explored these and various other theories. We shall indicate, in brief outline, several main alternative lines of evolutionary cosmology. In the theories selected for consideration, it will be noted that the evolutionary interpretation is a part of a larger philosophical outlook.

Herbert Spencer

In his day Herbert Spencer (1820–1903) was the acknowledged and most influential advocate of evolution as a fundamental philosophical principle.

Darwin accepted Spencer's broad alliance; he called Spencer "our philosopher." But Spencer was not merely Darwin's philosophical disciple. He had used the basic principle of development before the publication of Darwin's *Origin of Species;* it was a part of his more general philosophical theory.

A contemporary of John Stuart Mill, and, like Mill, a brilliant youth who was privately tutored by his father, Spencer showed early determination to follow his own bent. He would not be a schoolmaster as was his father; he followed for a while a career of engineering, after which he tried journalism. But once he made philosophy his final decision, and outlined his program of synthetic philosophy, he never wavered in its elaborate execution. No English philosopher since Bacon and Hobbes had undertaken such a comprehensive system of thought. Spencer's indefatigable persistence in his work for forty years, despite his ill health, recalls Comte's devoted prosecution of his *Course of Positive Philosophy*, which had appeared a generation earlier. These two grand syntheses are comparable philosophical reviews of scientific knowledge, although they appeared separately during the first and the second halves of the nineteenth century. A significant shift in emphasis is indicated by Spencer's disposing of the physical sciences with a general reference, which he did in order that he might concentrate on biology and psychology. Like Comte, Spencer emphasized sociology and ethics. He shared Comte's philosophical concentration on scientific methods, but he could not, like Mill, be classified among Comte's adherents. Although he stressed the principle of development in nature, he did not exemplify it in his relation to other thinkers. His doctrines were meant to be his own, spider-spun. He confessed openly that he could not bring himself to study Plato or to peruse even a page of Locke's *Essay*, or to read Kant beyond his account of sense perception.

Spencer's philosophical position may be approached through his theory of knowledge. This is indicated by his way of relating philosophy to science and to religion. Whereas "Science is *partially-unified* knowledge, philosophy is *completely-unified* knowledge";[3] but unlike both of these, religion deals with the unknowable. Spencer began with a disavowal of metaphysics. We can know things only as we relate them to other things in our experience or thought; we know only what is finite or limited. At this point, Spencer's reflection recalls Kant's in regard to the thing-in-itself. Our knowledge proceeds by relations and limitations, but we must admit that there is an ultimate reality that is manifested in the world we know. Our mind must acknowledge the Unknowable, though it can never conceive or formulate it; it is unknowable but undeniable. Although Spencer disavowed metaphysical knowledge, he did not, as did Comte, dismiss metaphysical problems or the metaphysical principle in philosophy. His agnosticism is an admission of man's ignorance, not an insistence on his unconcern.

We can know only the manifestations of the unknowable, and these are basically of two kinds, minds and bodies. We have vivid impressions of the

[3] Herbert Spencer, *First Principles*, New York, Appleton, 1896, p. 136.

objective things we perceive, and we have less vivid ideas of our subjective experiences. But, both the subjective and the objective, both self and not-self, express operations of some force. For Spencer, this force was the ultimate principle, but he protested against its crassly materialistic interpretation. He would use it, as it were, metaphorically, to express his dynamic view of reality, be it physical or psychical. Spencer's cosmology would have been virtual dualism if he had not insisted on regarding mind and matter as phases, or manifestations, of the ultimate force. Although this absolute was declared to be unknowable, it actually reveals its nature in a variety of perspectives. By far the greater part of Spencer's philosophy surveys the extensive fields of available knowledge. We know things in relations, and our basic concepts express types of relation. Thus, for instance, we experience things in sequence and coexistence. "The abstract of all sequences is Time. The abstract of all co-existences is Space."[4]

Spencer insisted on the principle of conservation of energy, or, as he preferred to call it, the "persistence of force." All events are changes; all physical and mental states are transformations. The special sciences involve investigations of these changes in various particular fields. The discovery and formulation of the universal law, or pattern, of the transformations in nature would give us unified philosophical knowledge of the structure and course of nature. This universal law, according to Spencer, is the law of Evolution, and he formulated this law as "an integration of matter and concomitant dissipation of motion; during which the matter passes from an indefinite, incoherent homogeneity to a definite, coherent heterogeneity; and during which the retained motion undergoes a parallel transformation."[5]

Spencer traced this process of evolution through the entire course of nature, and he distinguished its main characteristics. Evolution involves a concentration and combination of parts. This integration may be only an assemblage, and its product a mere aggregate; or it may be an extremely complex organization of tissues and processes. The formation of the solar system from the primal nebulous diffusion is a case of astronomical evolution. The integration of a planet goes through the several stages of nebulous ring, gaseous, liquid, and then externally solidified spheroid. On the biological and mental levels, similar, but more complex, processes of integration take place. The organism grows by the assimilation of various materials in the environment. Mental activity connects its multifarious data into a system of ideas and principles.

Two other characteristic processes—heterogeneity, or differentiation, and definite determination—should be noted in compound evolution. The concentration of incoherent parts involves their distribution to form different bodies or organs with their appropriate structures and ways of functioning. Biological evolution manifests an increasing heterogeneity that distinguishes elementary simple organisms from highly complex birds and mammals.

[4] *Ibid.*, p. 167.
[5] *Ibid.*, p. 407.

Social-historical evolution, likewise, proceeds from elementary hunting or fishing groups and the more or less homogeneous tribal cultures to civilized industrial societies with increasingly differentiated systems of activities.

The concentration and the differentiation are both marked by an increasingly definite determination. Evolution is a progressive advance from confused incoherence to coherence and determined order. Both structure and function exhibit this growing coordination of parts and the systematic organization of material. The highly evolved organism does not react indifferently like a conglomerate mass; the reaction of each organ is specific and has a definite relation to all the other organs as well as to the organism as a whole. A highly developed mind manifests similar definition and order in its systematic thought. Also similar is the complex coordination of functions and activities in a civilized society.

The survival of the fittest in the struggle for existence is always relative to the specific environment. A glacial flood would wipe out the highly evolved fauna and flora of a continent; the fittest species that would survive in that environment would perhaps be lichens and elementary microorganisms. Spencer's evolutionary cosmology included a bold speculative venture. He viewed the cosmic process as oscillating between eons of evolution and dissolution. In this vast pendular sweep, the evolutionary process would eventually arrive at a state of equilibrium in which the maximum possible integration, differentiation, and definite order have been attained. The cosmic cycle would then reverse its direction, and move toward dissolution, disintegration of structure, disorder and confusion, and ultimate undifferentiated chaos. Again, the constructive, cosmic process of evolution would be resumed. This was Spencer's variety of the old doctrine of eternal recurrence, which was, at the same time, being revived by Nietzsche.

As Giordano Bruno, during the Renaissance, had undertaken to reason out the ultimate corollaries of the Copernican astronomy, so Spencer sought to elicit the widely ramified implications of the evolutionary theory. Just as Spencer himself had arrived at evolutionism with his agnostic metaphysics of the unknowable, persistent force, so he undertook an evolutionary demonstration of an ethical theory already adopted. He advocated a utilitarian ethics, which called for the promotion of the greatest happiness for the greatest number, and he undertook to show the evolutionary evidence for his philanthropic hedonism. In this field, he regarded himself as a pioneer, having published an earlier version of his moral theory, *Social Statics*, eight years before Darwin's *Origin of Species*. His later work, *The Principles of Ethics*, represented a substantial revision of his views, but he claimed that it included no basic change in his principal theory.

The pursuit of the general happiness was traced and appraised by Spencer, in a fourfold examination of conduct, in its physical, biological, psychological, and sociological aspects. Moral conduct, physically speaking, is efficient conduct, well adjusted to the conditions under which man operates; biologically, the moral good involves perfect functioning, maximum health, and well-being; psychologically, the moral life involves the subordination of direct pleasures to more remote, but fuller, satisfactions; and sociologically, the good life is one in which reasonable social-philanthropic ends increasingly prevail over stubborn and lawless selfishness. In every aspect, according to Spencer, the promotion of the general happiness is sustained and fructified by the individual's adaptation to the evolutionary course and conditions of life. Human evolution proceeds from prevailing strife to greater and greater cooperation, from a ruthless and precarious existence of conflict to a state of security under law, justice, and beneficence. Man's natural pursuit of happiness leads him increasingly to seek his satisfaction in social-philanthropic activities. Thus human conduct and social order progressively gain moral significance. "Ethics has for its subject-matter, that form which universal conduct assumes during the last stages of its evolution."[6]

Henri Bergson: Spiritualism and Creative Evolution

Evolutionary ideas in French philosophy were used to sustain both positivism and spiritualism. In both directions of thought, evolutionism served to emphasize the dynamic principle in nature as essentially a system of activities.

An original and radical reinterpretation—not only of evolution, but of many other scientific and philosophical problems—marked the brilliant works of Henri Bergson (1859–1941). No philosopher of our day has surpassed Bergson in his combination of mastery in literary exposition, classroom eloquence, and radically stimulating power of ideas. Like his contemporary, William James, he opened a significant prospect on reality, which critical thought might not adopt without serious revision, but which it could scarcely dismiss or neglect.

Bergson undertook a scientific approach to philosophy, but his approach ran counter to established scientific ideas and procedures. In *Time and Free Will*, his first book on the immediate data of consciousness, he criticized the usual scientific accounts of our experience as artificial constructions. Thus, we describe the pure qualities of conscious states in inappropriate quantitative terms, as when we try to calculate intensities. We miss the real character of time when we think of it in terms of extent, as longer or shorter, as divided into stretches, hours and minutes. Against this misconstrued "spatial" time, Bergson urged recognition of the pure time of direct experience, real duration (*durée réelle*). This real time is not a succession or causal chain of discrete occurrences. The moments of duration permeate one another, and time is a stream, not a series. When we overcome the confusion of quality with quantity, and of time as pure duration with time as extension, we can realize the misdirection of the usual controversies over determinism and free

[6] Herbert Spencer, *The Principles of Ethics*, New York, Appleton, 1897, Vol. I, p. 20.

will. The fundamental self is free because it is never a definite result, but is ever active, ever achieving itself. And our acts are free in so far as they express and realize our whole fundamental self. Freedom is thus real, but not definable in abstract analysis, "For we can analyze a thing, but not a process; we can break up extensity, but not duration."[7]

Bergson has been described as a decided antiintellectualist, but he did not question the value of scientific analysis and its categories when applied to the mechanical, static, and spatial world. He questioned—or, rather, he denied —the value of this analysis in dealing with the living whole of direct experience. Philosophical insight into life and mind requires the concrete immediacy of intuition. Thus, we can never grasp the real nature of mind if we consider it as an immaterial substance somehow related to its body and other material things. The essential difference and relation between mental activity and matter can be understood better by an examination of memory.

In *Matter and Memory*, Bergson considered pure memory as the whole sweep of past experience, whether related or unrelated to present mental activity. The pure perception of the present moment stirs this pool of conscious or unconscious experience, and evokes specific memories for selective adjustments of the body, which is the mind's medium of action. Neither psychophysics nor associationism can explain the sounding of these depths of available, yet not directly conscious, memories which at any instance may yield a free new creation of thought. The psychic range widely exceeds the cerebral. One's body and—by extension—other bodies, are to be regarded as the mind's instruments, or channels, of specific action and response. "Spirit borrows from matter the perceptions on which it feeds, and restores them to matter in the form of movements which it has stamped with its own freedom."[8]

Bergson's insistence that the mechanistic interpretation of mind distorts the living character of our experience was strikingly expressed in his *Laughter: An Essay on the Meaning of the Comic*. The laughable, or comic, has its source in the confusion of a person with a mechanical thing. As persons, we expect to be our own unique and supple selves, not run-of-the-mill products from stamped molds. We object to any routine mechanizing of personality, to any stiff formalism, snobbery, stupidity, or inertia. When a man seems to be a puppet or a mechanism, swallowed up in his uniform, rigid modes or mannerisms, we laugh at him. How can he forget *himself* to such an extent?

The free creative activity so clearly manifested in mind is not an exceptional peculiarity, but a deep characteristic of nature. In his most famous work, *Creative Evolution*, Bergson interpreted the ongoing stream of life

[7] Henri Bergson, *Time and Free Will* (trans. F. L. Pogson), 3rd ed., London, Allen, 1913, p. 219.
[8] Henri Bergson, *Matter and Memory* (trans. N. M. Paul and W. S. Palmer), London, Sonnenschein, 1911, p. 332.

as evidencing the creative operation of the universal vital impulse or urge, the *élan vital*. The appearance of certain variations, and their preservation, in certain species in certain environments cannot be regarded as inexplicably fortuitous, nor can it be explained in terms of mechanical determination. But the traditional teleology of a divine program, or design, in nature is also open to radical objections. Both the mechanist and the traditional teleologist view the stream of life as a result, causally determined or initially planned. According to Bergson, life is not something which has already been completed, but something which is actively and creatively going on. In life, as in mind, nature manifests itself inexhaustibly. We can never say retrospectively, "All is given."[9]

Life achieves and explains itself progressively. From the lowest to the highest stages of evolution, the *élan vital* is the creative flood which is ever checked by the channels it has formed, and which is ever overflowing its banks to stream out in new directions. On the animal level, two main directions of creative evolution may be distinguished: instinct, which attains full development in insect life, and intelligence, which is developed in the vertebrates, and which culminates in man. Instinct should not be mistaken for imperfect intelligence; nor should intelligence be regarded as derived from instinct, or as a developed instinct. Intelligence is acquired knowledge, comprehension which uses constructions, forms, and concepts in dealing with its material. But instinct is innate knowledge, a direct unanalyzed awareness, a sort of sympathy and an unfailing adaptation. "When a paralyzing wasp stings its victim [caterpillar] on just those points where the nervous centres lie, so as to render it motionless without killing it, it acts like a learned entomologist and a skillful surgeon rolled into one."[10]

Analogous to instinct in human mental activity is intuition, that is, a developed and self-conscious instinct, an expansive and penetrating insight. It is the immediate response of the living mind, not to the structure and form, but to the living reality and spirit of whatever it considers. The perfection of spiritual life requires an interplay of these two powers. Whereas intelligence alone can analyze and formulate its problems, intuition resolves them unformulated. "There are things that intelligence alone is able to seek, but which, by itself, it will never find. These things instinct alone could find; but it will never seek them."[11]

Bergson traced these two movements of the vital urge, intelligence and instinct, in the spiritual life of men. *The Two Sources of Morality and Religion*, his last major work, raised the question: What would human morality have been if our minds had been merely instinctive instead of intelligent? Bergson distinguished our implicit conformity to traditional ways —the social cohesion which invokes individual responses, like instinctive

[9] Henri Bergson, *Creative Evolution* (trans. A. Mitchell), New York, Holt, 1913, p. 39.
[10] *Ibid.*, p. 146.
[11] *Ibid.*, p. 151.

reactions—from the continual rebound of analytic, critical, and insurgent intelligence. The interplay of these two motives in our daily lives raises the question of morality and outlines the direction of moral activity.

Beyond the direct and obligatory urge of instinct is its analogous activity on the highest levels of religious intelligence, mystical intuition. Religious practice and doctrinal belief engage rational, systematic, and reliable intelligence, but living religion needs also the dynamic faith and love of mystical piety. God, in Bergson's contemplation, is the cosmic heart of the *élan vital*, the creative urge throughout the sweep of evolution. The divine reality in all things is the productive life in nature, pregnant with abundant fulfillment, boundlessly and inexhaustibly achieving. No formula or concept of our own can grasp God in definition; only the creative intuition of mystical genius can respond to Him in loving devotion. "The ultimate end of mysticism is the establishment of a contact, consequently of a partial coincidence, with the creative effort of which life is the manifestation. This effort is of God, if not God himself."[12]

Samuel Alexander: Emergent Evolution

The various philosophies of evolution are usually evolutionary versions of their respective authors' outlooks on life. The cosmic pattern of development was used by Spencer to frame his cosmology of persistent force and his utilitarian ethics; by Nietzsche to sustain his haughty proclamation of the will to power; by Bergson to substantiate his dynamic-creative spiritualism. The evolutionism of Samuel Alexander (1859–1938) proceeded from an ethical to a cosmological perspective in the development of his basically realistic philosophy.

Alexander's education, begun in his native Australia, was continued at Oxford. Here he came under the strong influence of the new idealists, whose ideas he resisted, but whose Hegelian bent toward systematic speculation he retained. The evolutionary theory proved to be the more powerful influence in the development of his view of the world. Definitely inclined toward a naturalistic philosophy, he responded constructively to the modern developments in physical science, and he allied himself with the new realism in his theory of knowledge.

The continuity, as well as the radical advance, in the development of Alexander's philosophy may be seen by comparing his early book, *Moral Order and Progress* (1889), with his major treatise, *Space, Time, and Deity* (1920). The first expounded a prevailingly evolutionary ethics, in which the young author interwove utilitarian and positivistic ideas, and gave some emphasis to the self-realization he had learned at the idealistic Oxford Uni-

---

[12] Henri Bergson, *The Two Sources of Morality and Religion* (trans. R. A. Audra and C. Brereton), London, Macmillan, 1935, p. 188.

versity. Alexander inquired into the nature and standard of moral values, and into the origin and growth of goodness. He reached a social-philanthropic conception of morality as a system of satisfactions effected by our willing aright, and culminating in active, generous cooperation between persons. He shared Spencer's evolutionary optimism that the historical process points toward increasing social-mindedness, and, thus, he expresses a moral dynamic deeply rooted in nature. He interpreted virtue, not as austere and obligatory, but as evoking man's normal social fruition in a positive way.

Alexander's characteristic principles found their systematic fulfillment in *Space, Time, and Deity*. With these two volumes of Gifford Lectures, in which he organized the ripe reflections of a lifetime, he stepped to the forefront of contemporary British philosophy. Although we shall consider his evolutionism in particular, a brief introductory statement regarding his generally realistic position may facilitate our understanding of his cosmology.

To Alexander, philosophy mainly signified metaphysics, which he regarded as differing from physics and the other sciences, not in method, but in scope. True philosophy is comprehensive, the scientific study of the problems of nature in their widest range. His theory of knowledge was meant to accentuate the characteristics and requirements of a scientific philosophy, but it was only a preface to his major inquiry, which is metaphysical. Alexander regarded knowledge as one type of the simplest and most universal relation in nature, namely, "compresence," two things existing together. When one of these things is a mind, the relation is cognitive: the mind knows the thing. The object which we may thus know is an external object and has an external relation to us; it is not altered by our knowledge of it. Although Alexander had a realistic view of the objects of knowledge, he regarded all the images and other contents of perception as objective, as parts of the perspectives or selected portions of the thing presented to us, to which we stand in the cognitive relation of compresence. His revision of Locke was contrary to Berkeley's; to him, the secondary qualities of objects were quite as objective as the primary.

While the mind may thus know its objects, it can also be conscious of its knowing. Alexander distinguished these two mental processes as "contemplating" and "enjoying." "The mind enjoys itself and contemplates its objects."[13] Whatever the mind contemplates or knows has an external relation to it, whether the object is a sunset or one's own hand. The mind may enjoy itself, but it has no contemplative knowledge of itself. What is sometimes called "introspection" is not the mind's contemplation of itself, but merely an experience of our mental state, or the process of remembering or imagining—for example, Stonehenge at sunset, or how it might have looked on a ceremonial day of old.

Alexander's philosophy is a speculative cosmology in which he undertook to weave together the ultimate implications of evolutionism and modern physical science. The basic reality, the matrix of all existence, he called

[13] S. Alexander, *Space, Time, and Deity*, London, Macmillan, 1920, Vol. I, p. 12.

"space-time." Unlike some contemporary scientists, Alexander did not regard time as, in some way, a dimension of space. He paid tribute to Bergson for taking time seriously, but he did not follow Bergson in divorcing time from space, or in describing reality in terms of pure duration. For Alexander, the primal reality is space-time: "They are interdependent, so that there neither is Space without Time nor Time without Space."[14] Every instant of time is an event at some point of space, and conversely. The primordial nature of things is a sequence of such point-instants. Space-time is all-comprehensive; it is also infinitely differentiated and concretely individual. The fundamental space-time character of all nature persists throughout its ongoing stages, both the physical and the mental.

Like a modern Heraclitus, Alexander contemplated the world as a process of ceaseless activity; but, throughout its changes, he traced certain characteristic phases of existence. Some of them mark the various and variable, particular things or stages of being; these he called "qualities." Others, called "categories," he regarded as pervasive. He considered these categories to be real and constant aspects of nature, not merely universal principles of our understanding. His list of them was intended to comprise the various perspectives in which the world can be studied by science: existence, universality, relation, order, causality, substance, quantity and intensity, whole and parts, one and the many, and motion.

In this general framework of the categories, Alexander contemplated the world as a process of inexhaustible self-enhancement. Although the basic qualities of space-time are retained in this process, new stages of being are reached, new qualities that somehow arise from the lower, but that are not merely reducible to them. These higher stages are "emergents." In the cosmic perspective of Emergent Evolution, the causal determination, or the explanation of effects by their causes, do not account fully for the periodic, seemingly original and unpredictable attainments of nature, such as life and mind. From primordial space-time arises elementary, material-mechanical nature, and, in its progressive emergence, the so-called "primary" qualities (such as figure, size, motion) precede the "secondary" (color, smell, sound, etc.). Out of these lower stages of being, life—and subsequently, mind—emerge. Alexander resisted the materialistic reduction of mind to matter, but he likewise opposed any dualism of life and matter, or of mind and matter. He also rejected any spiritualism, such as Bergson's, which regarded the world process as the creative expression of a cosmic Mind. Alexander's naturalism emphasized both the continuity of nature and its periodic emergence to new levels. Life and mind are respectively fuller manifestations of the range of nature; they are continuous with the lower material forms of existence, but they are not merely reducible to them. Thus, we could distinguish the emergents as matter, life, and mind; or we could recognize their continuity as material, inorganic, organic, living, conscious, and thinking space-time.

[14] *Ibid.*, p. 44.

The interpretation of values is a difficult problem in realistic philosophy, which Alexander did not evade. He distinguished values from the primary and secondary qualities of objects by calling them "tertiary," maintaining that tertiary qualities express certain relations between minds and objects. The rose is round and red whether or not it is perceived by me or by anyone else, but it can be beautiful only for a contemplative mind. Truth, likewise, is realized by minds in their experience and correlation of facts. Moral goodness implies the mind's similar organization of its interests and satisfactions in social correlation with those of other minds.

Alexander's philosophy, as a comprehensive, scientific system of nature, was a survey of the hitherto attained stages of cosmic evolution. But his adoption of the principle of emergence led him to a speculative venture of the prospect of further, still unrealized summits of reality. The range of evolution, in Alexander's own cosmological vision, extends beyond minds like ours, and is divine in its ultimate reaches. This ever-higher, emergent quality is deity. The sublime achievements of genius, creative intelligence, or saintly aspiration may be adumbrations or foregleams of it. But we cannot, from our level, indicate or delineate the character of deity, for deity does not yet exist; we can only envision God as ever potential and progressively emerging. Were the next level above mind to be objectively realized in evolution, the deity thus attained would be, we might say, a race of beings higher than human minds; we might call them angels or archangels. Their contemplative aspiration, in turn, would aspire to a still higher summit, deity for them. Alexander used the term deity for this still higher level of reality, reserving the word God to signify "the whole universe, with a nisus to deity."[15]

SUGGESTED WORKS FOR FURTHER STUDY

DARWIN. Darwin, Charles, *The Origin of Species; The Descent of Man;* Darwin, Francis (ed.), *The Life and Letters of Charles Darwin.*

SPENCER. Spencer, H., *First Principles; The Principles of Ethics; The Principles of Sociology,* and *Autobiography.*

BERGSON. Bergson, Henri, *Time and Free Will; Matter and Memory; Creative Evolution; Laughter: an Essay on the Meaning of the Comic; Mind-Energy;* and *The Two Sources of Morality and Religion.*

ALEXANDER. Alexander, S., *Moral Order and Progress; Space, Time, and Deity,* and *Beauty and Other Forms of Value.*

---

[15] *Ibid.,* Vol. II, p. 362. See also p. 365.

35. Idealistic Reconstruction

British Reactions to Kant and Idealism

The intellectual leadership of British minds during the eighteenth century was followed by a period of relatively undistinguished work in philosophy. This was the more disappointing in view of the great achievements of British genius in other fields during the same period. The subsequent revival of systematic philosophical activity in Great Britain, after the middle of the nineteenth century, showed the vital influence of Charles Darwin, but also of Kant and the German idealists—preeminently, Hegel. Kant—who had been "roused from his dogmatic slumbers" by Hume—in turn, aroused Hume's successors. Hegel's influence on modern British idealism was as strong as Locke's influence had been on the French empiricists before the revolution.

Two men, Samuel Taylor Coleridge (1772–1834) and Thomas Carlyle (1795–1881) were especially important in introducing British minds to German philosophy and literature. Coleridge explored Kant and the post-Kantian idealists, revived Berkeley, stirred English interest in Spinoza, and returned to the ancient fountains of spiritual philosophy, Plato and Plotinus. Against empiricism, "sensualism," and common-sense precepts, he championed the creative reality of spirit. He revised Kant's distinction between understanding and reason in a way that recalls Jacobi. The understanding organizes the data of experience according to its categories. But reason is the primary creative intelligence, the divine logos, which is immanent in our minds and in the world. Despite his theosophical meditations, Coleridge resisted pantheism, both the Spinozistic and the post-Kantian varieties. While criticizing traditional Christian orthodoxy, he avowed his devotion to the deeper esoteric truths contained in Christianity, and expressed them in his spiritual metaphysics. His heart was with St. Paul and St. John, but he taught the theologian to understand these mystics better by learning to think with Plato, Plotinus, Schelling, and Hegel.

Carlyle was no metaphysician, but he had an intensely thought-out philosophy of life. A man of profound sympathies and convictions, he uttered his feelings with a prophetic fervor that moved Goethe to recognize in him a new moral force in Europe. Carlyle advocated German romantic poetry and idealistic philosophy for their spiritual values and for their emphasis on the creative powers of personality. He did not expound German epistemology or cosmology, however. Fichte's vision of reality as infinite ideal activity influenced Carlyle, but Goethe's *Faust,* with its final wisdom of unceasing productive endeavor, inspired him even more.

Against these spiritual realities, he regarded the causal network of nature as merely an external vesture of appearance. This is part of his "philosophy of clothes," in *Sartor Resartus.* He was not satisfied with the garments and trappings of existence which science investigates. He demanded the kernel within the shell—the person, and not the attire, the inner spirit and meaning of life. Hence, he would strip orthodox theology of its outworn vestments of dogmas and superstitions, but only in order to reveal and to preserve its inner heart, its faith in the saving truths of life. He also exposed the empty negations of the soulless philosophy of materialism and the philosophy of profit and pleasure, which he scorned as the hedonistic gospel of the pigsty.

Carlyle championed a vigorous, idealistic faith in spiritual realities, to be expressed in productive activity. This was his moral philosophy of salvation through work. The intellect is sterile unless it is fructified by the will. The meaning of life is not revealed to us in speculation, nor is it confirmed by analysis, but is both attested and achieved only through action. Man's duty and true happiness are realized when he finds and does his work. His dignity lies in his own work. Great genius is characterized by this unique self-expression. The main chapters of human progress may be read in the biographies of the heroes of civilization, in whose lives the deep hopes of men have found utterance; the will of nations has realized itself in personal achievement and social institutions. This heroic conception of history recalls Comte's positivist calendar of great men, but Carlyle entertained it in a spirit of romantic exaltation. The right social principle is not that of the mechanical, leveling process which produces nondescript uniformities; it is manifest in man's forthright self-respect, in the absence of vanity and envy, and in men who honestly plow their own furrow. "Produce! Produce! Were it but the pitifullest infinitesimal fraction of a product, produce it, in God's name!"[1]

This emphasis on spiritual values characterized the poetry of Shelley and Wordsworth and a number of their Victorian successors. It was sustained by many thinkers who sought in philosophy a revindication of religious convictions that had lost their dogmatic, theological warrant. The traditional emphasis on classical studies, especially the Platonic, inclined some of these men toward modern idealism.

[1] Thomas Carlyle, *Sartor Resartus,* in *The Works of Thomas Carlyle,* London, Chapman and Hall, n.d., Vol. I, p. 157.

Thomas Hill Green

Green (1836–1882) was the first outstanding leader in the new idealism. A descendant of Cromwell and a student of Plato, he combined social reform with his metaphysics. His study of Kant's ethics emphasized the principle of man's inviolable moral dignity. There is little direct reference to Hegel's text in Green's works, and he seems to have found Hegel's expository style uncongenial: "It must all be done over again."[2] But Green was deeply moved by the main ideas in Hegelian idealism, and he expressed and developed them in his own way.

He felt that the thinking of his time was being misdirected into barren channels. He repeatedly urged his students to close their Mill and Spencer, and to read Kant and Hegel. His critical *Introduction to Hume's Treatise* was intended to expose the inadequacy of the empiricist account of human knowledge and man's real character, and to show the need for the Kantian reinterpretation. But Green proceeded from Hume to Kant with a principle that took him beyond both. Hume's empiricism was a sort of atomism in theory of knowledge. Just as the atomist regards the world as an immense swirling assemblage of particles, so Hume viewed the mind as a bundle of sensations. Kant pointed out the organizing activity of the mind, the synthesis of self-consciousness. The unity of self-consciousness is not an external bond; it is not derived from lower mechanical conditions. It expresses a spiritual principle that is essential in nature. In this sense, we know a real world; our mind's relating or organizing experience itself reflects and constitutes the real nature of things. Thus Green reinterpreted Kant's doctrine that the understanding makes nature possible. Green did not, however, follow Kant in his sharp distinction between phenomena and things-in-themselves. Our experience yields adequate knowledge of reality as it progressively expresses all its interrelations. The mind grasps and possesses real nature in this concrete universality. Reality is fully experienced Being.

To Green, this idealistic principle in knowledge implied a spiritual universe both rooted and culminating in God. The life of intelligence reveals infinite but unrealized capacities. The moral, social, and religious implications of this conviction were apparent to Green, and he pursued them especially in his main work, *Prolegomena to Ethics*. He raised the problem of man's real character and vocation. The right course of conduct, and the right kind of society—ethics and social philosophy—were both contemplated by him, not only in the framework of the current scene, but in the ultimate perspective of men's fellow membership in the Kingdom of God. Plato and Aristotle, as well as Kant and Hegel, influence Green's philosophy of self-realiza-

2 Quoted in James Seth, *English Philosophers and Schools of Philosophy*, London, Dent, 1912, p. 345.

tion. How am I to act, considering what I am? How are men to realize together their spiritual character with its infinite implications?

Unlike the evolutionists, who traced man's descent from ape and worm, Green viewed human life as a foregleam of man's full meaning; he saw, or sought, the oak in the acorn. Ethics must begin with an unwavering certainty of man's ideal spiritual character. Morality, rightly conceived, is man's true career; its goal is his full self-realization. How are we to recognize our true purpose among our many hankerings and impulses? Moral insight and the moral achieving of value come from a self-legislative will which recognizes a common and absolute good as its own good, even though it may not suit the individual liking at the moment. This resolute self-identification with one's higher and more universal self distinguishes conscience and dutiful loyalty. But we should not think of this identification as any occult or separate moral sense. It is the same spiritual principle of personality—the same true insight—whether it is expressed in knowledge or in conduct.

Green regarded all values as personal—values "for, of, or in a person."[3] He agreed with Hegel in considering the practical realization of these values as a social process. From the lower greed for goods that, because they cannot be shared, embroil people in conflict, moral advance points toward the higher values that are shareable, and that must be shared to be truly realized. The social-mindedness of moral intelligence manifests this acknowledged principle, "The true good must be good for all men, so that no one should seek to gain by another's loss."[4]

Green's social-political philosophy applied his moral principle of the spiritual character of man with Christian-democratic emphasis. He resisted Hegel's occasional arrogance toward the common people, as well as the Platonic and Aristotelian aristocratic grading of men, and reaffirmed Kant's Christian recognition of every person's inherent dignity and right, man's eternal worth in the sight of God.

Bradley's Absolute Idealism

The most original speculative thinker in the new idealistic movement was Francis Herbert Bradley (1846–1924). His followers and critics agree in hailing his books as epoch-making, and many have ranked him with Hume. The comparison is pertinent in two respects: in the bold thoroughness with which these two men applied their respective methods, and in the various uncertainties to which their inferences led them. But Bradley differed from Hume in somewhat the same way as Pascal differed from Montaigne. He admitted—but would not accept—the mind's inconclusiveness in its quest of

---

[3] T. H. Green, *Prolegomena to Ethics*, 4th ed., Oxford, Clarendon Press, 1899, p. 218.
[4] *Ibid.*, p. 289.

finalities, and he sensed infinite reality in the very conviction of finitude to which his thinking brought him.

Bradley's three main works are *Ethical Studies* (1876), *The Principles of Logic* (1883), and *Appearance and Reality* (1893). All three are inspired by the same basic motive, and they all follow a similar pattern—a searching analysis of experience to expose the unsoundness of many traditional methods and doctrines, and to establish some reasonable principles; but, in going beyond these principles, which are relatively stable in their respective contexts, he recognizes that, somehow, they all come short of finality. A line from Goethe's *Faust* comes to mind: "How grand a show! but, ah! a show alone."[5]

In *Principles of Logic*, Bradley undertook a refutation of empirical logic by exposing the psychological invalidity of traditional associationism. He, of course, admitted the plain fact of the association of ideas, but he rejected the "psychological atomism" of Hume and Mill, according to whom particular perceptions are linked in the mind by fortuitous concurrence. "No particular ideas are ever associated or ever could be. What is associated is and must be always universal."[6] Bradley maintained that mental activity, from the very outset, reveals a principle of integrity—an organizing process —in which each datum is perceived in a certain context or perspective. The development of the mind is a development and systematic perfection of this organization; but the mind is always, in some degree, intelligence. We do not begin with bare particulars, and, from them, somehow derive general ideas. However vague and imperfect in its intention, the mind is always understanding, and its ideas are universals.

The view of the mind as essentially an interpretative activity is shown in Bradley's treatment of logical judgment. Judgment does not presuppose certain prior, discrete concepts which it links together; it is itself the elementary and fundamental act of thought. The process of inference, again, is not a colligation of discrete propositions, but a more complex and expanded judgment. We may say that, in all our ideas, the mind is, on the one hand, apprehending a certain datum in a certain context, and, on the other hand, pursuing the further reaches of that context, or its connections with others. Judgment and inference may be said to express these two aspects of the mind's organizing activity.

Throughout his discussion, Bradley intended to distinguish his logical analysis of thought, not only from physiological, but also from psychological accounts of mental activity. Yet these various approaches to reality demand eventual correlation. The problem of the validity of inference may be considered in strictly logical terms—that is, whether or not the conclusion and the premises are coherent. Or, we may ask further whether our reasoning is true in reality. This latter problem gets us deep into metaphysics,

---

[5] Goethe, *Faust*, Part I, I:i, "Night" (trans. B. Taylor), Boston, Houghton Mifflin, n.d., Vol. I, p. 20.

[6] F. H. Bradley, *The Principles of Logic*, 2nd ed., Oxford Univ. Press, 1922, Vol. I, p. 304.

and here the last chapter of the *Principles* is not very reassuring. If we are to judge and to infer at all, we must proceed discursively; we must work with ideas. But every idea is, after all, a version. Its very fidelity to the mind's intention and experience precludes its unqualified factual reality. Our ideas are "nothing in the world but adjectives, and adjectives whose substantives we fail to state. . . . Our principles may be true, but they are not reality."[7] Bradley seemed concerned to retain two convictions. First, the logical activity is not a mere linkage of prior discrete factual data; it is itself an expression of a basic principle of intelligence in reality, a process of judgment and inference. Second, this logical version is, after all, a version; the mind's discursive account does not exhaust the nature of reality; it does not even fully conform to it.

This final upshot of Bradley's philosophy may also be noted in his *Ethical Studies*, his first book, which enchanted its readers with its brilliance, but which left its author dissatisfied, and, for many years, he refused to republish it. Bradley built his ethics on the principle that man, a moral self, is integral in principle, and he ought, therefore, to realize this integrity in his individual conduct and social relations. Morality as self-realization has both its immediate province and its further ultimate prospect. " 'Realize yourself' does not mean merely 'Be a whole' but 'Be an *infinite* whole.' "[8] A person's very consciousness of his finite and imperfect character is, in principle, a recognition of his infinite, ideal nature. This essential recognition does not imply adequate cognition of his ideal character and destiny. Bradley first turned his attention to man's nearer moral prospect. He considered what he called "my station and its duties"; the wide range of individual careers and social institutions in which each person, in cooperation and fellow membership with others, can realize an increasing degree of spiritual meaning and personal worth.

In his ethics, also, Bradley was finally confronted with the mind's inconclusiveness. Morality implies recognition of an ideal reality of infinite perfection; the practice of morality is an unceasing, finite effort to achieve a perfect consummation which no finite activity can realize, and which, were it ever realized, would negate the activity. This, then, is Bradley's paradox of morality, that if anyone ever were perfectly moral, he would be no longer moral. Morality does not give final insight into reality, for reality is a system, not of pursuit, but of perfection.

The ultimate issues with which Bradley's thought was concerned were metaphysical, and he probed them in *Appearance and Reality*, aptly subtitled "A Metaphysical Essay." This 600-page essay promptly achieved recognized rank with the subtlest achievements of British philosophical genius, but it accentuated the skeptical and unyielding tenor of Bradley's reflections.

Bradley devoted the second part—more than three-fourths of his treatise—to "reality," though most of the proposed attributes of reality which he

---

[7] *Ibid.*, Vol. II, pp. 585, 591.
[8] F. H. Bradley, *Ethical Studies*, London, King, 1876, p. 68.

examined were shown to be varieties of appearances. Reality can be nothing partial, conglomerate, or abstract; it must be a concrete whole; but all our thoughts about it, even our truest truths, are more or less abstract. Our knowledge of anything is a contemplation of that thing in a certain context of relations. This knowledge points toward a systematic view of a reality that is expansive and harmonious throughout. In its ideal, final knowledge would be all-comprehensive, concrete, and, therefore, real. As finite knowledge, it can never have this character; it must always be *a* knowledge of a specific system, and, thus, relational; it falls short of full reality. All our intellectual and practical versions or perspectives are, in this way, shown to be mere appearances—qualities and ways of predication, the various categories of the understanding, spatial and temporal forms, motion, change and permanence, and causal necessity. Both truth and goodness, if we examine them thoroughly, finally point beyond their reach, and are transcended in a reality which they cannot definitively qualify. Even the supposed finality of religion does not escape the judgment of this dialectic. Religion, also, is appearance, not ultimate reality. There is no way in which we can qualify reality that, on careful scrutiny, would not be exposed as inadequate.

Though no appearances are ultimately real *as* they appear, we cannot question that, somehow, they are all appearances of reality. Reality, which transcends them, also comprehends them; it comprehends all specific systems of relations, all multiplicity, variation and contradiction, all change and striving. The intellect can never fully grasp or entertain reality. Bradley could not accept Hegel's magisterial declaration that "What is Rational is Real, and what is Real is Rational."[9] But he concluded his metaphysics with the assurance that reality is essentially spiritual. Our mind approximates to ultimate insight only in intuitive feeling. Thus, Bradley wrote in a later essay: "The real, to be real, must be felt."[10] We cannot know or define it. Yet we can achieve this feeling of reality more fully in some views of it than in others. Though they all are views of mere appearances, they are not all equal in their degrees of reality or truth, and it is the wisdom of philosophy to perfect the recognition of this hierarchy.

The closing paragraph of Bradley's *Essays on Truth and Reality* expresses the contending motives in his philosophy:

On the one hand it is the entire Reality alone which matters. On the other hand every single thing, so far as it matters, is so far real, real in its own place and degree, and according as more or less it contains and carries out the indwelling character of the concrete Whole. But there is nothing anywhere in the world which, taken barely in its own right and unconditionally, has importance and is real. And one main work of philosophy is to show that, where there is isolation and abstraction, there is everywhere, so far as this abstraction forgets itself, unreality and error.[11]

---

[9] G. W. Hegel, *Philosophy of Right* (trans. S. W. Dyde), London, Bell, 1896, p. xxvii.
[10] F. H. Bradley, *Essays on Truth and Reality*, Oxford, Clarendon Press, 1914, p. 190.
[11] *Ibid.*, p. 473.

Bernard Bosanquet

Bradley's influence was a prime factor in the philosophy of Bernard Bosanquet (1848–1923), and though Bosanquet acknowledged this influence, he also subtly resisted it. He redirected the course of Bradley's thought, especially in his *Logic or the Morphology of Knowledge,* to which Bradley acknowledged a real obligation in revising his own *Principles of Logic.* Bosanquet was in no sense a disciple of Bradley, nor of Green or Hegel, although his philosophy represented a shift from Bradley toward these latter two. In a real sense, his philosophy was his own reconstruction which he applied in all fields of philosophical inquiry. His work was an original, expanded version of the idealistic system.

In view of Bosanquet's close relation to Bradley, we shall first indicate the central point of their divergence. Although Bosanquet reaffirmed Bradley's idealistic conviction of the ultimately spiritual character of reality, he departed from Bradley in favor of Hegel's declaration of the rationality of this spiritual character. Bosanquet regarded rationality as an essential expression of the basic, all-comprehensive, integral nature of the Absolute. The difference between this and Bradley's view is primarily one of emphasis, but the difference extends far. Bosanquet admitted what Bradley accentuated: the inconclusiveness of intellectual metaphysics. So Bosanquet pursued constructively the main pathways to reality—logical, aesthetic, moral-social, and religious. In the course of increasingly concrete experience, he found incomplete, but not unreliable, adumbrations of reality. Our experience does not fully comprehend the spiritual nature of reality, but it reaches toward it, spirit revealing spirit. Thus logic, for instance, does not yield an explicit formula of the real but it does express the rational structure of being. In his general statements, Bosanquet inclined toward synthesis. One of his last books had a significant title, *The Meeting of Extremes in Contemporary Philosophy.*

Bosanquet's central philosophical problem, individuality and destiny, was given its best systematic treatment in his two volumes of Gifford Lectures, *The Principle of Individuality and Value* (1912), and *The Value and Destiny of the Individual* (1913). Working primarily in the field of values, Bosanquet examined the careers of individual persons in order to deepen his insight into the principle of individuality. Individuality, as he understood its metaphysical sense, is ultimately spiritual unity, integrity, and a reconciliation of opposites—necessity and freedom, part and whole, one and many, activity and peace, and striving and perfection. This reconciliation, or harmony, is the ideal aim and destiny of the individual person. But, while the realizing of this ideal marks our higher life, its perfect realization must absorb and transcend individual personality. Bosanquet was a thorough student and translator of Lotze, and the latter's idea that human beings are only approximations of personality, and that God is the only real and perfect Person, may be compared to Bosanquet's interpretation of the principle of individuality. Bosanquet felt bound to revise the traditional ideas of personal immortality. Man's destiny cannot be his eternal personal continuance; it is, rather, the transfiguration of his finite being into the infinite, eternal absolute. Bosanquet held that the religious motive—spiritual absorption in God—expresses a deeper strain of reality than does moral self-realization.

The finite individual person, according to Bosanquet, is a product of nature and a foregleam of reality. The world—Bosanquet quotes John Keats—is "the vale of soul-making."[12] Rooted in nature, people are destined to spiritual fruition, but their transitional character is reflected in their adventurous career. Bosanquet traced the molding of souls, the hazards and hardships of finite selfhood, and its stability and security. Personality is characteristically self-surpassing in nature; its fullness is also its transcendence. Yet although he centered his reflections on the principle of individuality, Bosanquet resisted any form of individualism or personal idealism. Ultimate reality, in his view, is the only Absolute. He was a deeply poetic spirit; his *History of Aesthetic* is a fine expression of his extensive and mature artistic understanding. He not only regarded beauty as a fundamental manifestation of spiritual reality, but, in his more allegorical moments, he envisioned the Absolute as the perfect artist who contemplates his cosmic masterpiece.

Unlike Bradley, who was a metaphysical hermit, but like Green, Bosanquet was actively engaged in social reform. As he declared, "[the self] will not admit that it *really* is what it is *in fact*,"[13] and, recognizing the converse of this, also, he devoted himself to the realization of greater spiritual values in human lives. For Bosanquet, as for Green, the social strain in ethics was paramount, and should not be mistaken for a merely Hegelian trait; it should be considered as the expression of deep and vigorous, humanitarian convictions, the concrete response to all the uttered and unuttered demands of spirit in modern society. Out of the idealistic classrooms and discussion groups in Balliol and Scotland came some of the leaders in the moral and social emancipation of Britain.

American Idealism: Emerson and Royce

The British idealistic reconstruction was paralleled by similar philosophical activity in America. It would be erroneous to regard American idealism as an importation from Oxford and Glasgow to Harvard, Yale, and Cornell.

[12] Quoted in Bernard Bosanquet, *The Value and Destiny of the Individual*, London, Macmillan, 1913, p. 64.
[13] *Ibid.*, p. 247.

American philosophy—like American life and institutions—has reflected the influence of European thought, but the influence is always modified to suit the native temper and conditions. While American idealism had close kinships with the British, it had other sources as well. The New England transcendentalists drew their inspiration from Plato, Plotinus, and the Upanishads, and they read Goethe even before they read Hegel.

In considering American idealism, we should recall that Jonathan Edwards —the first American thinker of real philosophical rank, and a contemporary of Berkeley—related his Calvinist theology to a Platonic or Neoplatonic philosophy. Between Edwards and Royce lies a century and a half of American growth in cultural maturity. The most outstanding American thinker during those 150 years was Ralph Waldo Emerson (1803–1882). Emerson's greatness was not achieved by a systematic philosophy; his writings belong to the so-called "wisdom literature" of mankind. No one in this country has expressed more finely the deep conviction of the reality of spiritual values.

Emerson's theories of knowledge and metaphysics, if such terms are at all applicable to his philosophy, are each dominated by his ideal conviction. From Kant, via Coleridge—or, perhaps, from Edwards or Plotinus, or even from his own meditation—he learned the distinction between understanding and reason. To him, the distinction was to be made between particular knowledge about the detailed qualities and connections of objects in our experience, and direct intuition or penetrative insight into the heart of things. He did not scorn the detailed knowledge in the special sciences and in daily routine experience, but, where all the finalities of thought and life were concerned, he trusted only spiritual insight.

This concentration on inwardness brought Emerson into deep sympathy with the great mystics, although he remained indifferent to the various occult mysteries and utopias with which his native New England was swarming. Spiritual insight was not to be gained by escaping from Boston to the utopian colony of Brook Farm. Like the Kingdom of God, wisdom is not here or there; it is within us. Emerson felt he could reach the infinite only through himself. Like Carlyle, he stripped the random externals of his being to see and to feel himself to the heart, and, in nature, he saw beyond bark and husk. As he reached the root and the kernel, he achieved unwavering certainty of one universal life and spirit throughout, the over-soul. Emerson's wisdom lay in keeping unified what might easily have become a dualism. By the most thorough penetration of himself, he sought union of self with the infinite world spirit. Therefore, his religion could not be other-worldly, and his self-concentration could not be egocentric.

Emerson's ethics and social philosophy expressed a similar reappraisal of daily experience. He did not gauge the moral worth of life in terms of external gains or satisfactions, nor did he hope for the redemption of society by any outward schemes of reform. True reformation can be found in the inner life alone, in absorbing into one's self the ideal aims and principles with which men and societies become identified. But just on this account are human acts and institutions important, as our living commitments to certain ideals of ourselves. We must personally overcome our lesser selves to conceive of and to achieve our true, universal destiny through thought and action. To Emerson, this road to perfection was also the path to reality. "My creed is very simple, that Goodness is the only Reality. . . . Itself is gate and road and leader and march. Only trust it, be of it, be it, and it shall be well with us forever."[14]

Josiah Royce (1855–1916) studied in California and Germany, and at Johns Hopkins University, and he spent a lifelong career of teaching and philosophical writing at Harvard. During his lifetime, he attained a most profound, systematic reconstruction of American idealism. It is significant that both his first book and his last major work had religious themes. His main problem concerned God and the soul. How are we to understand thoroughly the reality of the individual person and his full reality in God? Royce's interpretations of nature and of the community contributed to his central inquiry; *The World and the Individual,* the title of his principal treatise, comprised two volumes of Gifford Lectures.

Royce, like Emerson, sought God through the individual man, through the deepest reality and fullest implications of man's experience as a person. Our experience—in both its truth and its error—points to its transcendence, yet it is also essentially involved in the self which transcends it. Royce grasped the problem of knowledge first by turning it inside out. He asked, What is an error? Taken by itself, my judgment about an object cannot be regarded as true or erroneous; it cannot be said to agree or to disagree with the object. For, "as a separate fact, a judgment has no intelligible object beyond itself."[15] Like truth, error is possible only in the interrelation of ideas; idea *A* can be judged as an error only when it is viewed as a part —an inadequate part—of idea *B,* which is the higher truth because it better reveals how each relates to the larger idea *C.* So Royce concluded that "*either there is no such thing as error, which statement is a flat contradiction, or else there is an infinite unity of conscious thought to which is present all possible truth.*"[16] Infinite knowledge of infinite mind would be true knowledge of all relations in absolute rational unity. This is implied ultimately in every logical act of thought.

As in theory, so in practice—the finite individual has infinite involvements and prospects. Royce conceived of individuality positively, not as a discrete object, but as a unique purposive will. An individual is a distinctive pursuer of values, "a being that adequately expresses a purpose."[17] To realize fully this character of individuality should be the aim of every person. Yet this aim is never fully realized by anyone. Our finite acts, like our finite truths,

---

[14] Quoted in Bliss Perry, *Emerson Today,* Princeton, Princeton Univ. Press, 1931, p. 59.
[15] Josiah Royce, *The Religious Aspect of Philosophy,* Boston, Houghton Mifflin, 1885, p. 393.
[16] *Ibid.,* p. 424.
[17] Josiah Royce, *The Conception of Immortality,* Boston, Houghton Mifflin, 1900, p. 48.

are as partial in their actual worth as they are whole in their ultimate significance. Here is the tragic insight of philosophical wisdom. Pascal called it man's grandeur and misery, but Royce's idealism made no skeptical or pessimistic concessions. Error and evil are both explicitly finite; they involve the challenge which must ideally overcome them. My consciousness of my finite limitations is essential to my personality, but it signifies that my fuller meaning, even now, ideally transcends my meager actuality. "God who here, in me, aims at what I now temporarily miss, not only possesses, in the eternal world, the goal after which I strive, but comes to possess it even through and because of my sorrow."[18] The tone of this passage, which is not exceptional, may suggest Royce's moral-religious intensity, a deep strain in his logically rigorous mind.

Royce was convinced that man's moral career is, in principle, the eternal pursuit of perfection, but he resisted the pantheistic idea of utter absorption in the infinite as the destiny of personality. He used mathematical analogies to express the eternal reality of individual persons as unique and infinite in themselves and also in and of the absolute. The series of powers of prime numbers, say 2-4-8-16, 3-9-27-81, 5-25-125, and so forth, are each infinite, each of them is unique and distinct from any other, yet all of them are related and comprehended within the entire collection of whole numbers. Even so, may we think of persons in their eternal individuality and their abiding reality in God.

Christian devotion has entertained the ideal of the communion of saints, and Royce's ethics and social philosophy explored the ultimate spiritual meaning of the ideal community. He sought to include the Kantian ethics of duty in a perfectionist theory in which man's moral career centered on the principle of loyalty. Loyal devotion is the practical and genuine self-identification of my will with a purpose and cause which expand my bare self and realize its fellow membership with other selves and other lives. Loyalty is the heart and essence of any moral society. Its various expressions find objective form in institutions; loyalty is the living spirit in them that gives character to a community. Royce pursued the religious implications of the ideal, beloved community which he interpreted as a central principle of Christianity, the Kingdom of God within us. It is significant that the harmonious note of social-spiritual community, on which Royce's moral, social, and religious philosophy concluded, had been sounded in one of his early works which dealt with social conditions and problems in California's unruly countryside during the gold rush of the mid-century.

American idealism followed several lines of development with corresponding shifts of emphasis. While Royce's thought led toward a conception of the absolute that would preserve the reality of moral agents, his philosophy was fundamentally an absolute idealism. Borden Parker Bowne (1847–1910) fused Kantian and Lotzean ideas into a philosophy of unambiguous theism

[18] Josiah Royce, *The World and the Individual*, New York, Macmillan, 1901, Vol. II, p. 409.

that emphasized the principle of personality as the core of reality. He could see how things in external nature might be explained as created by the infinite mind, and ordered according to the categories of intelligence; but he could not admit that minds of persons could ever be derived from an ultimately irrational material reality. Personal intelligence, if it is to be real at all, must be basically so. In this personalism—discounting the traditional notion of soul substances, and viewing the self as actively manifested in the process of experience—he conceived of God and men as living, personal realities, all spiritually related. Bowne was a gifted teacher and a vigorous writer. His disciples have continued and developed his teaching in many classrooms, and his influence may also be noted in certain liberal tendencies in contemporary theology.

Critical Idealism in Germany and France

The development of idealism in Germany and France will be noted here very briefly in some of its representative thinkers in several fields of interpretation. The philosophical interpretation of the history of ideas in their entire, social-cultural setting distinguished the brilliant writings of Wilhelm Dilthey (1833–1911). Dilthey's guiding purpose was to recognize and to reveal the integrity of meaning in a complex historical situation, so that not only the ideas and personalities of the thinkers, but the spirit of their whole epoch would come alive. This was his conception of real biography and history; it was not merely an external or abstract, special exposition. A truly integral historical interpretation of man in his world. Dilthey regarded as the right introduction to philosophy. We can thus distinguish and appraise the basic types of philosophy in the history of ideas—materialistic naturalism, the idealism of freedom or creative spirit, and the objective idealism of a significant cosmic order.

The history of ideas and their problems, of which Wilhelm Windelband (1848–1915) became the acknowledged master in his day, led to his systematic work on the philosophy of values. His philosophy was essentially an organization of logical, moral, and aesthetic values. These three values, regarded in a transcendent perspective, express the religious attitude.

Rudolf Eucken (1846–1926), winner of the Nobel prize for idealistic literature, was an eloquent champion of spiritual ideals and strivings as the heart of man's life and the core of history. His books, which had wide popular appeal, interpreted the unfolding of man's spirit as the higher self-manifestation of ultimate reality. Religion is man's burning conviction of this truth. God and man reflect and reveal each other in the spiritual life. Social order, in its historical traditions and development, provides the medium of man's moral, religious, intellectual, and aesthetic activity. But

Eucken also reaffirmed the Christian and Kantian idealistic emphasis on the unique worth and self-expression of each person.

The positivistic impact on metaphysics in general, and on idealism in particular, produced critical reactions in French thought. Two French philosophers express significantly the idealistic resistance to empiricist naturalism and positivism. Charles Renouvier (1815–1903), a pupil of Comte, had been associated with the Saint-Simonians, but he later turned against them. He advocated, on what he regarded as critical-Kantian foundations, an idealistic theory of monadism that emphasized the unique personal character of the centers of activity which constitute reality. His universe is a society of finite, active beings. The theory of knowledge in this "neocriticism" rejects all things-in-themselves. We can know only the system of phenomena, representations in experience. Each representation has a subjective and an objective aspect. The critical analysis of experience reveals the significant aspects and operations of nature as a system of calculable relations in space and time; its changes are causally connected; we perceive its qualities; it manifests teleological and personal characteristics. With these categories of the structure of phenomena, Renouvier proceeded toward a pluralistic spiritualism. He was one of the leaders in modern personalism.

Jules Lachelier (1834–1918) was an idealist from beginning to end. Against the skeptical inferences of empiricism, he expanded the Kantian analysis of knowledge to emphasize the productive character of thought; the understanding makes nature possible. Existence demonstrates itself in the organizing activity of the mind. The levels of being correspond to the degrees of thought activity. Like Maine de Biran, Lachelier maintained a gradation of spiritual ascent in the field of conduct, from animal-sensual reactions to rational responses and choices, and up to the divine life of higher spiritual contemplation.

Croce and Italian Idealism

For almost 100 years after Vico, Italy produced few systematic philosophers of distinction. This was a period during which Italian thinkers imported mainly British empiricism and French materialism. There were, however, a few men who became aware of Kant's works and of the idealistic philosophy, which was to have its Italian harvest at a later season. The philosophical response to all manifestations of culture, which characterized the development of idealism in Italy, was in its way a new humanism, and no one has expressed this spirit more eminently than did Benedetto Croce (1866–1952).

Croce has called his system a "philosophy of spirit." By stretching the use of the term *evolution* to suit our intended meaning, we could call Croce an idealistic evolutionist. Reality, according to him, is essentially history;

that is, reality is ongoing, significant activity. We do not have a history of a nonexistent past; rather, mind, or spirit, is itself the historical process. Mind is both intelligence and will, a simultaneous knowing and doing, both theoretical and practical activity. Each of these is manifested in two ways, and so there are four basic phases of reality; to these Croce devoted the four main parts of his philosophy of spirit. Theoretical activity, knowing or beholding, is either intuition or conceptual judgment. Intuition is the mind's immediate concrete experience, and its direct expression is the essence of art. The aspect of reality which is thus revealed we usually call "beauty." In conception and judgment, the mind contemplates its ideas in their relation to each other; it is bent on verification, on the establishment of a universal and valid order. The practical activity, mind as a doing, is volitional. The will seeks ends and is identified with them. The ends may offer particular advantage, or they may be of universal and ideal worth. Thus, we may recognize and distinguish four basic phases of reality: beauty, truth, utility, and goodness. Corresponding to these are Croce's four fundamental philosophical sciences: aesthetics, logic, economics, and ethics.

Croce's aesthetic theory has proved very influential, not only in the contemporary philosophy of art, but also in literary-artistic creation and criticism. According to Croce, art is not a physical fact, not a utilitarian or moral act, nor yet any kind of intellectual knowledge or conceptual form. Against hedonistic, moralistic, or intellectualistic aesthetics, Croce declares that true art is pure intuition. It is the mind's direct beholding activity; it is a vision of reality, not a judgment about it. The poet is a seer, and his poem is his expression. The painting or the statue directly objectifies the artist's impressions. In beholding them, we are sharing in immediately expressed intuitions.

Logic is the philosophical science of the pure concept. By "pure concepts," Croce does not mean general terms that refer representatively to groups or classes of particulars, such as house, cat, triangle. These he calls "pseudo concepts." The pure concept has a universal character that is not exhausted in specific representative content—such are the pure concepts of quality, development, finality, and these are concretely and universally expressive. They are essential to the philosophical understanding of reality. The pseudo concepts enable us to classify our knowledge, but it is the pure concepts that enable us to understand. Philosophy, strictly speaking, is logic, the science of the pure concepts, or rather, the science of the system of pure concepts. The historical development of philosophy reflects the mind's progressive recognition of the great fundamental concepts and their synthesis or systematic organization.

In his *Philosophy of Practice: Economics and Ethics*, Croce considers the volitional-active phase of reality. He opposes voluntarism, and regards will as dependent on knowledge, which, in some form, is always prior to will activity. But he does not advocate intellectualism, for he recognizes the active character of knowing. His fuller truth seems to be that theoretical and practical activity are correlative, basic phases of reality. Croce also recognizes both determinism and freedom in the volitional act. The will does not operate in a historical vacuum of spontaneity. It acts in a certain personal and social setting. It achieves creative self-expression, and is thus genuinely an action, not a bare effect. In this sense, the will is responsible; its action has really molded the historical pattern.

Economic and ethical activity represent, not two divisions of practice, but two aspects of it. The same action may, of course, manifest both of these phases. Economic processes deal with the will's pursuit of specific ends or advantages. Ethics is concerned with ends of universal worth. Some theories of ethics have confused moral and economic volition and have adopted as a standard the satisfaction of certain, particular desires. This, for instance, is the error made by utilitarianism. The opposite confusion is found in ethical rigorism, which denies any role to satisfaction or utility in the moral life. Morality includes, but also transcends, utility. The moral man finds his own interest and satisfaction in the universal end; this is the really moral ideal. Croce insists on the universality and sovereignty of moral values above any standard of utility or expediency, but he also maintains that, in pursuing and attaining them, man finds his fullest welfare and satisfaction.

Giovanni Gentile (1875–1944) advocated a so-called "actual idealism." His most important work is entitled *Theory of Mind as Pure Act*. According to Gentile, the mind is not a thing in space and time; its nature is not factual, a particular effect of particular conditions. It is pure act, perennial and inexhaustible activity. Although it is not in space and time, time and space are in it; they are its forms or its framework of empirical representation. The mind's activity is its self-realization. This is the essence of morality, that I achieve myself, I become actual in conduct. Myself and my worth are both realized and vindicated in my act. But the mind's activity reveals an *other*. This *other* may be an *other than* mind; we call it "nature." It may be an *other in* mind; we then call it history. The world is both nature and history, and the mind's relation to the two is revealed in the whole range of experience. This range is infinite in the absolute mind, in which all human minds actively share. "Nature and history *are*, in so far as they are the creation of the 'I' which finds them within itself, and produces them in its eternal process of self-creation."[19]

Gentile collaborated with Croce for some years, but they eventually parted. Their philosophical divergence was followed by their opposite stands towards fascism. Croce held fast to truth and right, never yielding to Mussolini, but Gentile became the Duce's minister of education. Did Gentile have an ideal vision of fascism as the political embodiment of the principle of creative and self-justifying action? Or was he, a Sicilian born across the island from ancient Syracuse, venturing to emulate Plato's endeavor to reform a tyrant?

[19] Giovanni Gentile, *The Theory of Mind as Pure Act* (trans. H. W. Carr), London, Macmillan, 1922, p. 264.

SUGGESTED WORKS FOR FURTHER STUDY

GENERAL DISCUSSIONS AND ANTHOLOGIES. Adams, G. P., and Montague, W. P. (eds.), *Contemporary American Philosophy*; Barrett, Clifford (ed.), *Contemporary Idealism in America*; Cunningham, G. W., *The Idealistic Argument in Recent British and American Philosophy*; Metz, Rudolf, *A Hundred Years of British Philosophy*; Muirhead, J. H. (ed.), *Contemporary British Philosophy*; and *The Platonic Tradition in Anglo-Saxon Philosophy*.

GREEN. Green, T. H., *Prolegomena to Ethics*.

BRADLEY. Bradley, F. H., *Ethical Studies; The Principles of Logic; Appearance and Reality*; and *Essays on Truth and Reality*.

BOSANQUET. Bosanquet, Bernard, *Logic; The Principles of Individuality and Value; The Value and Destiny of the Individual*; and *The Philosophical Theory of the State*.

RALPH WALDO EMERSON. Emerson, R. W., *Essays; The Heart of Emerson's Journals* (Bliss Perry, ed.); *The Portable Emerson* (Mark Van Doren, ed.).

JOSIAH ROYCE. Royce, J., *The Spirit of Modern Philosophy; The World and the Individual; The Philosophy of Loyalty; The Conception of Immortality*; and *The Problem of Christianity*.

BOWNE. Bowne, B. P., *Metaphysics* and *Personalism*.

EUCKEN. Eucken, Rudolf, *The Meaning and Value of Life* (trans. L. J. Gibson and W. R. B. Gibson) and *Life's Basis and Life's Ideal* (trans. A. G. Widgery).

CROCE. Croce, Benedetto, *Aesthetic; The Breviary of Aesthetic; Logic; Philosophy of the Practical: Economic and Ethic*; and *History, Its Theory and Practice* (all trans. D. Ainslie).

GENTILE. Gentile, Giovanni, *The Theory of Mind as Pure Act* (trans. H. W. Carr).

36.   Pragmatism, Realism, and Other Recent Philosophical Tendencies

The Contemporary Scene in Philosophy

The preceding chapter surveyed the main lines of development which idealistic thought has followed, and it examined some of the more important versions of this idealism. These are the later currents of a long historical tradition that streams from German idealism, but which has its springs in antiquity, in the Academy of Plato. With classical dignity, its more confident advocates have called this traditional *philosophia perennis*, the perennial basic truth to which reflective minds have returned, and will continue to return through the ages to come. But contemporary critics readily state that modern idealism belongs to history, the history of systems that have had their day, even though, for some obsolescent minds, they have not yet ceased to be.

It is quite otherwise with other tendencies in contemporary thought. These seemingly new departures may prove to be real philosophical alternatives, and they may vitally engage the future historians of philosophy. But some of them may turn out to be merely winds of doctrine that make a stir only in and for their day. Even within the span of one generation of philosophers, unkind critics observe that the storm of pragmatism seems to be subsiding.

The case of contemporary realism is different. Here is a great variety of modern doctrines that not only have revitalized certain old tendencies of thought, but that are really original philosophical developments, like the new ideas and principles in physical science to which they productively respond. The future historian of ideas may appraise contemporary realism as the fruitful philosophy of the modern scientific reconstruction. But this scientific reconstruction is still in process; even more fluid is the realistic movement in its various philosophical channels. Groups of realists may publish their common platforms, but their members reinterpret and revise the announced doctrines. This current of realistic thought may prove to be the life blood of a strong, growing philosophy. Although it seems too early to survey and to appraise it in true, historical perspective, the historian of philosophy who refrains from any comment fails to convey to his readers a living sense of the contemporary scene.

We might consider all the contemporary thinkers who appear to be significant in any way. But this procedure runs the risk of creating an impression of a multitudinous confusion of voices. The very multiplicity of productive thinkers—which is one of the real elements of power and promise in philosophy at the present time—may seem quite unwieldy in a serial summary. As an alternative, we might attempt an analytic examination of these principal philosophical theories and tendencies in their relation to each other. This procedure, however, would give the termination of our survey a different character from its main substance, which is that of a history of ideas and not a systematic reorganization.

In preference to both of these methods, we shall follow a third course in this closing chapter. We shall survey, in very broad outline, some of the main directions of contemporary philosophical thought, and we shall consider the methods and ideas of the most outstanding representatives. The selection, in some cases, will appear to be incontestable, and it is hoped that in the others, also, the selection will be regarded as well advised. Any thought of finality in appraisal is liable to be dogmatic, or, at least, premature. We are in the midst of a discussion—a common search—but we are also in the midst of a contention of ideas, in which none of us, not even the unphilosophical, are entirely neutral auditors.

American Pragmatism: William James

William James (1842–1910) brought to philosophy one of the most alert, variously responsive, and hospitable minds in the history of modern thought. He acquired early the spirit of radical conformity from his father, who cherished traditional values, but who could not pursue them in orthodox ways. Having disavowed Calvin, the elder James explored Swedenborg and entertained Emerson, both in person and by reading his books of transcendental wisdom. William and his brothers were educated in various schools overseas; they learned foreign tongues and customs, and they sampled the varieties of human experience. While his brother Henry was showing a definite inclination toward literature at an early age, William was slow to find his true career. He tried painting, he explored chemistry and biology at Harvard, he went on a scientific expedition to Brazil with Agassiz, and he graduated from medical school. His health, never very robust, failed him, and the problem of life and its meaning confronted him sharply.

Crass materialism led to no final sense or purpose for him, but benign transcendentalism could not provide the spiritual assurance which his scientifically trained mind required. James' reading of Wordsworth's poetry sustained Emerson's influence on his thought. At that stage, his study of Renouvier's philosophy led him through and beyond physical science to the recognition of a reasonable basis for belief in spiritual realities, in free moral choice, and in genuine individual careers. While he was teaching anatomy and physiology at Harvard, his interest was turning to psychology and philosophy, which he felt to be his true vocation.

The Principles of Psychology, on which he labored for a decade, sealed his fame as a master in this field. For the rest of his life, he planned to do an equally solid work in philosophy. But, unlike many philosophers, he never completed such a systematic tome, nor would it have been James' true contribution to philosophy. He said that he liked his summer house at Chocorua because it had fourteen doors, all opening outward; his own books were so many doors—from each of them a path led outward. Did these paths join somehow, somewhere, or were they like so many spokes, with their only hub his many-sided personality? His *Varieties of Religious Experience*, for example, became one of the best known books in its field. He had planned to write, in its stead, a systematic volume on religion; but would it have been half as dynamic and significant in its influence on modern thought as the book he did write?

The reader of James is likely to feel that his excellence lay in the stimulating power of his ideas, not in their systematic order. Nevertheless, there is a dramatic, if not a logical, unity in his thought. In the many new fields which he plowed, he always raised the crops he preferred. James was himself the best illustration of his pragmatic method. He went to philosophy for what it could give him. Pure logic—or neutral, uncommitted, unexpectant reflection—had no appeal for him. Even when he was digging at fundamentals, he was always thinking of his eventual harvest: "By their fruits ye shall know them, not by their roots."[1]

We have referred to James' pragmatic method as though it were generally familiar. James got its first statement from his friend Charles Sanders Peirce (1839–1914). Peirce had proposed a "pragmatic" maxim for testing the real meaning of an idea. In an article, "How to Make Our Ideas Clear," Peirce said that believing or thinking is essentially a rule for action. We can understand what we mean by an idea by considering "what effects . . . we conceive the object of our conception to have. . . . Our idea of anything *is* our idea of its sensible effects."[2]

James adopted this experimental view of the meaning of ideas and the test of their truth, and then proceeded to formulate from it a theory of the nature of truth. When we test the truth of an idea, what are we testing? What is the definition of truth? Is truth found in the degree of consistency with a coherent system of ideas? Is it embodied in the direct presenta-

[1] William James, *The Varieties of Religious Experience*, New York, Longmans, 1902, p. 20.
[2] C. S. Pierce, *Collected Papers* (C. Hartshorne and P. Weiss, eds.), Cambridge, Mass., Harvard Univ. Press, Vol. V, 1934, p. 258.

tion of the object known by the mind, or in its correspondence to the object? James regarded the process of verification or validation as itself the verity or validity of the idea. "The truth of an idea is not a stagnant property inherent in it. Truth *happens* to an idea. It *becomes* true, is *made* true by events."[3] Truth is not a solemn, logical value to be acknowledged by us. It characterizes certain practical ways in which we use ideas to serve our purposes. "The true is only the expedient in the way of our thinking." Truth is workable. The truth of our scientific ideas is their experimental verification, our handling of them and our coming to terms with nature. By his way of writing the word "veri-fication" James meant it to connote more than ascertainment or discovery of truth. Ideas are veri*fied, made* true in the process of experience.

Our true judgment in moral experience is expressed in its practical fruition, wherein it produces the greatest available good and satisfaction toward which we normally aim. Truth may be realized or achieved by people that value it, adopt it, and fulfill their lives by acting on it. James followed this principle in moral and religious matters. This was one prospect of his *The Will to Believe.* "My first act of free will," he said as early as 1870, "shall be to believe in free will."[4] Belief in God does not rest on objective knowledge. Religious conviction yields rich experience. Even more than moral action, it leads to our inmost dealings with life. "We and God have business with each other,"[5] and the truths of religion signify this vital spiritual involvement.

It is clear that here James was combining two conceptions of truth: in terms of its verification, and in terms of its various personally satisfactory qualities. Both of these are, to be sure, pragmatic in engaging our experience practically. But the second interpretation of the nature of truth has been widely criticized as not recognizing the distinctive character of logical values. To some of James' readers, his will to believe has seemed too much like unphilosophical wishful thinking. Croce spoke sharp words against it: "Whoever in thinking says, 'Thus I will it,' is lost for truth."[6] Preferring to understand rather than merely to decry James' procedure, we may note that he was emphasizing his concern with the course of direct experience, but he was also expressing concern for the safeguarding of his cherished values and principles.

He described his pragmatic philosophy as a theory of "radical empiricism." According to this theory, philosophers should discuss only such matters as can be defined in terms drawn from experience. Furthermore, as a statement of fact, experience includes not only the things with which we deal but all the relations between them. Hence, the parts of experience—things and re-

---

[3] William James, *Pragmatism*, New York, Longmans, 1912, p. 201.
[4] Williams James, *The Varieties of Religious Experience, op. cit.*, pp. 516 f.
[5] *Ibid.*
[6] Benedetto Croce, *Philosophy of the Practical* (trans. D. Ainslie), London, Macmillan, 1913, p. 37.

lations—form their own structure that is to be studied directly, without any extraneous or transcendent substratum or absolute of whatever sort.

In this radical and direct exploration of experience, James was satisfied to see the validation of certain ideas that were of prime importance to his philosophy of life. As he sought reality in the direct course of experience, so he recognized that our views of reality reflect our peculiar experiences, our characteristic turns of mind. In his *Pragmatism*, he traced a far-ranging distinction between two kinds of minds:[7]

The Tender-Minded	The Tough-Minded
Rationalistic (going by "principles")	Empiricist (going by "facts")
Intellectualistic	Sensationalistic
Idealistic	Materialistic
Optimistic	Pessimistic
Religious	Irreligious
Free-willist	Fatalistic
Monistic	Pluralistic
Dogmatical	Skeptical

This distinction could not be regarded as an unbridgeable gulf. James himself preferred tough-mindedness in theory of knowledge, but, in his further reflections on life and nature, he could be very "tender," as will presently be seen.

His radical empiricism plunged into the living stream of experience, and he was impressed by the primal fact of concrete individuality throughout nature and, especially, in human life. We should never accept mere concepts and abstraction, substitutes for the direct unique truth of experience. He called the desire to formulate truths a virulent disease. Similarly, we should not lose the real individual in the types of routine classification. Each one of us identifies himself as "me-myself-nobody-else." And, though, for example, we may call this crab a crustacean, we misapprehend it. "I am no such thing," it might say, "I am MYSELF, MYSELF alone."[8]

This firm insistence on the inexpugnable reality of the individual led James to pluralism in his cosmology. He resisted Emerson's pantheistic outlook and the idealists' Absolute in all their forms. He opposed absolutism for two reasons: first, because it swallowed up unique individuality, the outstanding characteristic of the only experience that he knew directly; and second, because it similarly absorbed all genuine activity, individual purpose and achievement, in the eternal absolute. "There is no such superstition as the idolatry of the *Whole*."[9] This second point was very important to James. He had rejected the eternal, mechanical necessity of the materialists because

---

[7] William James, *Pragmatism, op. cit.,* p. 12.
[8] William James, *The Varieties of Religious Experience, op. cit.,* pp. 516 f.
[9] Quoted in Henry James (ed.), *The Letters of William James,* Boston, Atlantic, 1920, Vol. I, p. 247.

it left no ground for recognition of genuine living ideals. He opposed absolute idealism for a similar reason.

He advanced, instead, the idea of a pluralistic universe, or "multiverse." In place of the venerable contemplation of the world as an all-comprehending, infinite sphere, James preferred to view it as a living stream, or, we might say, an ongoing multitude. In the multitudinous stir of existence, he saw real events with real beginnings. In this existence, things are neither eternally set nor foredoomed. The real world always has another chance. This was an idea which James owed to Peirce, who, using the Greek word for chance, *tyché*, propounded a theory of *tychism*, or fortuitism, to include the element of indeterminacy in nature. James combined this idea with that of unique untrammeled individuality, advocating free will and personal moral creativeness. The world of our experience is, to be sure, a world of our necessary involvement in nature, but it is also, to an undetermined degree, a world in our own hands, of our own making—a truly dramatic universe.

This view of life is reflected in James' moral philosophy in his treatment of the problem of evil. The moral struggle is real, for evil is a fact, but it is not a futile struggle, for evils can be overcome. He taught "meliorism," which offered a prospect of progressive improvement. It is never complete, for new shortcomings and hardships beset us, but it is a real progress in which the resolute wills of people count for something. James had a keen sense of the essential role and unquenchable vitality of each person. His reflections did not reject the hope of immortality; they insistently returned to it. To be sure, minds, as we know them, operate through bodies, but this may not be the one exclusive framework of experience. We are told that thought is a function of the brain. But, James asked, is thought a productive function of the brain? May it not be only a transmissive function? The mind that, in life, acts through the body may conceivably function in disembodied ways. Even now, if we only knew how, we might be able to communicate with the souls of the dead. In his exploration of possible new roads to the undiscovered country of the hereafter, James was ready even to take part in séances with mediums.

The kinship of his view of the world with other forms of activism may be pointed out, but more important is his divergence from some of them. James did not leave his ongoing multiverse to make a final monistic concession. He valued piety if he could have it on the terms of pluralism. Like John Stuart Mill, he advanced the idea of a finite God, a God to whom the evils in the world are real problems even as they are to us, a heroic, achieving God. The religious life is the mutual experience of God and man of one another in a productive spiritual activity that verifies our own higher personal reality and also that of the divine. "The universe is no longer a mere *It* to us, but a *Thou*, if we are religious."[10]

---

[10] William James, *The Will to Believe*, New York, Longmans, 1912, p. 27.

Further Developments in Pragmatism: John Dewey

It should now be clear that James' pragmatic method could be adopted without accepting all his other conclusions in philosophy. One could start with his "tough-minded" radical empiricism and never swerve to the "tender-minded" column. Like Peirce, one could use the pragmatic test of verification by experiment, without confusing logical validity with personal satisfaction. The emphases on activity and growth may ally the pragmatic method with an evolutionary outlook to yield a new theory of naturalism.

The philosophy of John Dewey (1859–1952) is the fullest statement of pragmatism. Like other fulfillments, it grew beyond its originating idea. Dewey preferred to call his theory "instrumentalism," and his theory has also been described as a type of evolutionary naturalism. By an interesting coincidence, Dewey, Bergson, and Alexander—all of whom formulated original philosophical versions of evolutionism—were born in the year in which Darwin's *Origin of Species* was published.

Evolution was not the only formative idea in Dewey's philosophical development. His earlier work reflected the influence of common-sense intuitionism and of Hegelianism. Even at the age of 70, Dewey still avowed his preference for Hegel over any other systematic philosopher except Plato. But early he rejected the whole Hegelian schematism as artificial, although Plato he continued to prize as "the dramatic, restless, cooperatively inquiring Plato of the Dialogues, trying one mode of attack after another to see what it might yield."[11] The evolutionary struggle of ideas and the struggle for survival in James' psychology impressed him, also; Dewey felt that James showed a genuinely biological approach to the mind in his theory of mind and life in action.

As Dewey was turning from the Hegelian dialectical progression of categories to the direct testing of ideas in the active process of experience, educational problems naturally engaged his attention. His influence on contemporary educational theory and practice has spread from the University of Chicago—and later, from Columbia University—to every American schoolhouse and to schools in several countries overseas. Emphasis on the social vocation of the pupil was central in his doctrine. He recommended his *Democracy and Education* as a good introduction to his philosophy. Just as he would develop the minds of school children by having them spin and weave, mold clay figures, and share their experiences in oral and written discussions, so he interpreted the entire educational process, the active life of intelligence, in terms of progressive social adjustment in a variety of ever-expanding zones of cooperation.

[11] G. P. Adams and W. P. Montague (eds.), *Contemporary American Philosophy*, London, Allen, 1930, Vol. II, p. 21.

In this program for the cultivation of intelligence, Dewey also expressed his "instrumental" view of mental activity. Thinking should not be regarded as the contemplation of realities beyond direct experience, but as a way of coming to terms with actual problematic conditions. An idea in a specific case is an experimental project, a proposed way of meeting the supposed demands of the total situation. Its validity, or truth, is tested by the outcome. To the extent that it fails to yield adequate adjustment, the idea falls short of being real knowledge. We should observe Dewey's revised pragmatic statement of how ideas work; they are valid or invalid, not only in the way they fulfill our expectations, but also in the way they exhibit more fully the problem of our situation and show which of our expectations are most appropriate to meeting this problem. Thus, Dewey wrote in his volume of Gifford Lectures, *The Quest for Certainty*, "Knowing consists of operations that give experienced objects a form in which the relations, upon which the onward course of events depends, are securely experienced. . . . It comes between a relatively casual and accidental experience of existence and one relatively settled and defined."[12]

Both the standard, or test, and the role of knowing can be understood only in relation to the total experience of vital adaptation to an ongoing process of events and situations. Intelligence is immersed in the activities of impending adjustment, and this is not the only part or role we play in the drama of existence; we also eat, fight, fear, and reproduce. "Hopes and fears, desires and aversions, are as truly responses to things as are knowing and thinking."[13] Dewey's instrumental method was meant to avoid both metaphysical pretensions and arid intellectualism. His philosophy pursued the various important ways of practical adaptation, but it was especially concerned with knowing and with moral activity. The aesthetic response also interested him.

We now turn to consider briefly the directions his pragmatism took. Dewey insisted that a theory of knowledge should not divorce thinking from action. Knowing is instrumental; it is a means to practical adaptation. This view of intelligence is biological-evolutionary; but, in its development, Comte's influence seems to blend with Darwin's. Thinking is a vital adjustment to a biological situation, but the environment in which ideas operate and seek adaptation is a social environment. Dewey's emphasis on the mind's operation in a social medium was evident at an early stage in his educational theory, and he developed it farther in his general theory of knowledge. Thinking does not take place in a historical vacuum; our ideas are likely to be heirlooms; habit and custom mold them. Even when we face the world anew, the critical ideas which we validate in our personal experience seek a social outlet in appeal or advocacy. The formal aspects of our ideas are usually public, and thus they tend to become traditional. Their content also is determined by situations which are largely social-cultural. Thinking

[12] John Dewey, *The Quest for Certainty*, New York, Minton, Balch, 1929, p. 295.
[13] *Ibid.*, p. 297.

and knowing are adaptations of minds to minds, as well as of individual minds to their own experiences of the objective world. The social-cultural environment, and each person's private experience are ongoing activities. Socially and individually, ideas are in a process of continual readjustment.

In this stressing of the social character of experience and thought, Dewey was closer to Royce than he was to James. The latter regarded the philosopher as "a lone beast dwelling in his individual burrow."[14] Dewey's social emphasis is evident in his *Human Nature and Conduct*, which bears the subtitle, "An Introduction to Social Psychology." His thought proceeds from evolutionary naturalism which recognizes the social environment of human conduct, and which, in particular, advocates the values of tolerance and a fair-minded democratic regard for the common good.

A moral problem is in effect an issue between the contending demands of a self that is operating in a natural social situation. The eventual decision made from among these contending demands calls for a certain kind of will that is committed to certain interests and satisfactions, and to the promotion of a certain kind of society in which these demands can be more securely realized. Thus, the social medium and the individual will continually reflect and mold each other. "Democracy has many meanings, but if it has a moral meaning, it is found in resolving that the supreme test of all political institutions and industrial arrangements shall be the contribution they make to the all-around growth of every member of society."[15] The social, economic, and political issues in which our moral life is involved were always of vital concern to Dewey. In this age of continual unsettlement and crises, his record as an unwavering leader of constructive liberalism was preeminent.

In his philosophy of art, Dewey endeavored to avoid the abstract deduction of aesthetic values from fundamentally intellectual and moral theories of experience. The values of art must be distinctively aesthetic values of integration, or enjoyment of immediate experience. But aesthetic values share with logical and moral values a vital relation to their real need and demand for satisfaction. Art, in its own way, is "also a remaking of the experience of the community in the direction of greater order and unity."[16] The aesthetic integration of experience involves a reinforcement of the present moment by an intensity that makes it significant and somehow representative, so that it stands out as *an* experience. Choice feelings and perceptions may thus stir the imagination with a fine suddenness. When we are deeply moved about something, all our past ideas and feelings may be aroused and may yield a refined expression:

Art . . . quickens us from the slackness of routine and enables us to forget ourselves by finding ourselves in the delight of experiencing the world about us

[14] Quoted in E. P. Aldrich (ed.), *As William James Said*, New York, Vanguard, 1942, p. 196.

[15] John Dewey, *Reconstruction in Philosophy*, London, Univ. London Press, 1921, p. 186.

[16] John Dewey, *Art as Experience*, New York, Minton, Balch, 1934, p. 81.

in its varied qualities and forms. It intercepts every shade of expressiveness found in objects and orders them in a new expression of life.[17]

This aesthetic expression is, in its characteristic way, the mind's perfect adaptation to a situation; for, while it is thoroughly subjective, it is also saturated in the object. In the aesthetic experience, the subject and the object mutually reflect and express each other.

Dewey's radical empiricism, unlike James', is inhospitable to metaphysical excursions. The varieties of religious experience reveal men's immemorial ventures into the supernatural. In Dewey's judgment, however, these flights do not attain knowledge or reach conclusions that are material for philosophy. But Dewey, like Comte, believed that human social experience achieves a consummation of values analogous to those of traditional religion. Without the liturgical vestments of the Comtist cult of humanity, Dewey's homespun "common faith" would arouse a vital sense of human solidarity and would inspire men's devotion to the social ideal of the most abundant life for all. A religion of humanism should be totally immersed in human life and values. "Nature, including humanity, with all its defects and imperfections, may evoke heartfelt piety as the source of ideals, of possibilities, of aspiration in their behalf, and as the eventual abode of all attained goods and excellencies."[18]

The Contemporary Realistic Movement

Realism in philosophy has expressed the conviction that the mind's experience points to real objects existing independently of mind. In opposition to the views of the world as ultimately a spiritual reality or process, as eternal reason or a system of minds, or as an exclusive concentration on the process of experience itself—realists have argued that experience is an experience of objects, and that the real existence and character of these objects is neither conditioned nor affected by our knowing them. Knowledge is an "external relation" between the knower and the known. The main types of contemporary realism may be distinguished by their account of the objects of our experience in relation to our consciousness of them.

In our day, German neorealism has found its most exploratory statement in the "phenomenology" of Edmund Husserl (1859–1938). For Husserl, our every idea is, by intention, an idea of some object. In examining our experience, we are involved in considering the objects to which it refers. The descriptive study of our consciousness of objects—or "phenomenology"—requires a philosophically reflective attitude in which the mind does not directly feel the objects of its ideas, but examines its own ideas as they refer to their objects, and so distinguishes the subjective and objective aspects of

---

[17] *Ibid.*, p. 104; *cf.* p. 35.
[18] John Dewey, *The Quest for Certainty, op. cit.*, p. 306.

experience; for example, a statesman may view himself as affixing or as not affixing his signature to a certain treaty. When we examine consciousness in its subject-object relation, we note that, while the physical object is perceived or intended by the idea, the object is not entirely comprehended by the idea, as, for instance, universals or essences are comprehended. The mind reaches toward its object in apprehension, but also feels the externality of what it apprehends. It implies its object, but its idea does not constitute the object, nor exhaustively encompass it. In his exploration of experience, with its real objects which are also objects of consciousness, Husserl combined some idealistic views of the implications of his theory with its realism.

British and American realism may be regarded as a vigorous and fertile growth of contemporary philosophy. It has already proliferated in numerous directions, yet it is still in the process of actual development. The historian may feel reluctant to undertake an exposition of doctrines that, to a considerable extent, are still in mid-career. But the main varieties of realistic theory can be distinguished.

The British and American realists include a number of former idealists who have sought a more convincing theory of knowledge and metaphysical inferences which will be, at the same time, more harmonious with modern science. A scientific background has given the doctrines of other realists a definitely naturalistic tone, which, with expert use of mathematical analysis, has served to perfect the logical aspects of realistic theory. A principal center of British realism has been Cambridge University, long noted for its mathematical-scientific researches. We can only mention two of the leading Cambridge realists, George Edward Moore (1873–1958) and Bertrand Russell (1873–   ), but either could be selected for an extended, representative discussion of realism. Moore advanced a realistic doctrine by way of his acute critique of idealism. Russell, whose famous *Principia Mathematica* was written in collaboration with Whitehead, has brought to his realistic philosophy, not only his mathematical-logical mastery and his wide knowledge of modern science, but also a lively interest in current problems of human conduct and social order, which he has attacked with radical boldness.

American realists reflect the influence of their British colleagues, but they have also proceeded to independent construction, and, in their turn, they have exerted an influence overseas. This realistic movement gained impetus by the publication of a collaborated work, *The New Realism* (1912), which contained "The Program and First Platform of Six Realists."

The authors of *The New Realism*, despite their published common platform, showed considerable divergences. Some features which they did hold in common may be pointed out; they maintained that the existence and the nature of the objects we know are not determined by our knowing them. While we should thus say that the known is related to the knower externally, nevertheless, the object is immediately present to the knowing mind. When I see this tree, it is precisely this tree that I see. "This was the *presentative* realism of Reid as contrasted with the representative realism or epistemological dualism of Descartes and Locke."[19] Furthermore, seeing or knowing this tree is only one transaction, between me and it. Both of us have many other relations, and they need not be all involved in the specific experience. While I am seeing the tree, it may be rotting at the roots, and I may be missing my bus. A particular experience of knowing does not necessitate or depend upon an ultimate or all-comprehensive, metaphysical absolutism. The world may be as diversified in its being as our experiences of things are varied. The new realists have tended to regard the knowing mind as similar in character to the physical objects it knows. But they have also been careful to distinguish this behavioristic psychology from crass materialism by recognizing in physical nature itself the evidence of some logical entities. Here the new realism raises some important problems of more basic formulation which can scarcely be regarded as resolved.

An alternative version of American realistic philosophy was outlined in *Essays in Critical Realism* (1920). Critical realism differs from the new realism in important details, the most important of which concerns the objects of knowledge. According to the new realism, the external object itself is directly present to the mind. But how can the star which you and I both see be simultaneously and directly present to both of us, and how can it be present to either of us now, if, as astronomers tell us, it may actually have been extinguished 100 centuries ago? The critical realists held that the objects known directly in our consciousness are our ideas. Or, we may say that we know "essences," which are somehow intermediate between, and corresponding to, the ideas in the mind and the external objects themselves. At any rate, we infer the existence of external physical objects to account for our ideas of them. The objects themselves are represented by our ideas. Critical realism has been described by the new realists as returning to some variety of epistemological dualism. It has been criticized as deficient in its explanation of truth. For example, when one person sees a brick as red and another sees it as gray, we may call the latter color-blind, but what can a critical realist mean by declaring that the first observer's idea of the brick as red is true? The critical realist would rejoin by asking the new realist whether the brick directly present to the two minds is both red and gray, and furthermore, what is meant by saying that the idea of it as gray is erroneous?

Realistic philosophy has manifested much controversial skill, acute analysis, and logical talent in the elaboration of specific doctrines and in systematic philosophical construction. Realism has reflected in contemporary philosophy, also, the influence of the modern reconstruction in physical science. Some of the realists have inclined toward a materialistic emphasis, but others have included the higher values and principles of intelligence in their views of nature.

[19] W. P. Montague, "The Story of American Realism," in *Philosophy*, April, 1937, p. 143.

Alfred North Whitehead

Alfred North Whitehead (1861–1947) began one of his best-known books, *Science and the Modern World,* by describing philosophy as the critic of cosmologies. "It is its function to harmonize, refashion, and justify divergent intuitions as to the nature of things."[20] We may say that it seeks a conspectus of reality without confusion. The gifts of philosophers are many, and all of them have their use and value. Each doctrine must have undeviating proponents who reason out the utmost that the doctrine can yield by itself. But the creatively systematic minds can also penetrate beneath the periphery of technical abstractions and distinctions. They criticize the defects of alternative doctrines, but they also perceive limitations in their own. As they reach toward the center and summit of their inquiry, they come to other paths whose origins were remote from their own. This tendency in fruitful philosophical thinking Bosanquet called "the meeting of extremes." It is no shallow compromise, but a productive reconciliation of contending abstractions by means of a deeper insight into the problems. The main progress in philosophy has been achieved, not through sectarian precision, but through the creative reconciliation of significant, alternative views.

No philosopher of our time has personified this spirit of original systematic reconstitution more eminently than Whitehead, and he expressed this spirit in his achievement and in the urbanity of his expansive contemplation. Whitehead named four great thinkers who have contributed to the "philosophic process of assemblage"[21] (a significant phrase here): Plato, Aristotle, Leibniz, and William James. Despite his "sharp disagreement with Bradley," Whitehead acknowledged that, in his own ultimate conception of the cosmological problem, "the approximation to Bradley is evident," and he himself raised the question as to whether his own philosophy may not be "a transformation of some main doctrines of Absolute Idealism onto a realistic basis."[22]

Whitehead was preeminently equipped to supply another vital need of contemporary philosophy—its correlation with the fundamental reconstruction of modern science. He did not approach the mathemathical foundations of the new physics from the outside. He was past 60 before he turned from his great achievements in mathematics and mathematical logic at Cambridge University to his second career at Harvard, where he devoted himself to organizing his philosophical ideas. His system of thought may well come to signify, in future years, the philosophical implications and basic problems

[20] A. N. Whitehead, *Science and the Modern World,* Cambridge, Cambridge Univ. Press, 1927, p. ix.
[21] A. N. Whitehead, *Modes of Thought,* New York, Macmillan, 1938, p. 3.
[22] A. N. Whitehead, *Process and Reality,* New York, Macmillan, 1929, pp. vii–viii.

of our present scientific outlook. In this sense, it may prove to be the greatest work of contemporary realism.

The materials which Whitehead undertook to organize were conglomerate, and his synthesis demanded a radical reinterpretation of many traditional philosophical ideas. He used familiar philosophical words in unfamiliar ways, and he changed their meaning and his use of them as his thought developed, without always giving the reader due warning. He also devised many new terms to express his revised concepts. In this brief discussion, it has seemed advisable to attempt a paraphrase of some of Whitehead's leading ideas, although we thus run the risk of frequently missing his distinctive tone and enunciation. Where his own terms have seemed essential for a statement of his thought, an effort has been made to explain their meaning. The steady reader of his works is rewarded by passages of brilliant and clear exposition, as some of the citations here will illustrate.

Whitehead may be called a "twentieth-century Leibniz." The two are similar in their mastery of mathematical analysis, in their demand for a philosophical synthesis, and in their reconciliation of alternatives. Another basic kinship is their cosmological activism. Whitehead developed the view of nature as a system of activities. Unlike Bradley's *Appearance and Reality*, Whitehead's *Process and Reality* was not meant to express any antithesis. "Nature is a structure of evolving processes. The reality is the process."[23] The early Greek explorers of nature used the term *physis* to signify the form or constitution of things that resulted from their growth; that is, how things come to be what they are, their essential generation. Whitehead translated *physis* as "process."[24]

How are we to think of the world, and of the things in it, in terms of process? Whitehead recognized three ultimate facts of direct experience: actual entities, or "occasions"; "prehensions"; and "nexuses." Actual "occasions" or entities are the final real things. They may be meager or vast —God, or "the most trivial puff of existence." In each case, they express a certain concurrence of the basic eternal essences that are implied by our experience—this or that specific process. "Prehension" is distinctively characteristic of experience, a relational process in which we distinguish the prehending subject from the prehended datum, and the subjective form or manner of the prehending process. Occasions and the relational processes involve extended togetherness, which Whitehead called "nexus." Nexuses become more or less complex events in active situations. They cross, affect, and reflect each other. In various perspectives, their correlation of processes constitutes the ongoing drama of existence. "The reasons for things are always to be found in the composite nature of definite temporal actual entities."[25] This is Whitehead's "ontological principle."

Let us note some traditional views and doctrines which were considered

[23] A. N. Whitehead, *Science and the Modern World, op. cit.*, p. 90.
[24] A. N. Whitehead, *Adventures in Ideas*, New York, Macmillan, 1933, p. 192.
[25] A. N. Whitehead, *Process and Reality, op. cit.*, p. 28.

by Whitehead. He acknowledged both the isolation of an individual thing, in which it is simply itself, and also its togetherness with other things: no thing is only private or only public. The philosophical application of the idea of relativity is evident here; "There is no possibility of a detached, self-contained, local existence. The environment enters into the nature of each thing."[26] Whitehead extended this dual recognition to essences or eternal objects. These also have their public or universal nature, and likewise, their private aspect or characteristic in which they may be uniquely enjoyed. As a general principle, "the crux of philosophy is to retain the balance between the individuality of existence and the relativity of existence."[27]

This view enables us to escape the two opposite pitfalls of atomism and absolutism. The unique and the universal both require recognition. Whitehead criticized the misleading abstractness of crude atomism and the concept of simple location, according to which a thing is simply itself at a certain place and time. No longer can we think of our experience as merely a collection of similarly simple and discrete sense impressions. Everything is what it is in the variety of settings and perspectives in which it is active. But, on the other hand, nothing is ultimately absorbed as a mere phase or a mere appearance. In the variety of processes, each being is itself constituted and expressed; it is both "the least puff" and the alleged Absolute.

We are reminded of Bradley and Bosanquet's warning not to forget the use of abstractions. Whitehead exposed "the fallacy of misplaced concreteness," consisting in the neglect of the degree of abstraction involved in considering an event or process only in a particular, selected perspective. A thing is misunderstood if some of its qualifying predicates are wrongly regarded as providing its definition. "The success of a philosophy is to be measured by its comparative avoidance of this fallacy."[28] Just as misleading is the theory of a bifurcated nature—for example, my view of a hurricane as an objective process in nature that follows its own course, and that is external to me, though it causes my experience of it, as opposed to my other, subjective view of it that is contained in my perception and still stirring memory. In place of a world thus split in two, Whitehead demanded the clear recognition of the interplay or correlation of these two perspectives.

His cosmology resists both materialism and mentalism as unwarranted abstractions in philosophy. He was as firm in recognizing mental activity as he was in rejecting the existence of any mental substances apart from the events of mental experience. Subjective experience and objective nature are interrelated; each involves the other. The conscious character of experience does not admit of ready definition, however; Whitehead regarded it as "that quality which emerges into the objective content as the result of a conjunction of a fact and a supposition about that fact."[29] Consciousness is itself an

[26] A. N. Whitehead, *Modes of Thought, op. cit.,* p. 188.
[27] Quoted in Paul A. Schilpp (ed.), *The Philosophy of Alfred North Whitehead,* Evanston, Northwestern Univ. Press, 1941, p. 680.
[28] A. N. Whitehead, *Process and Reality, op. cit.,* p. 11.
[29] A. N. Whitehead, *Adventures in Ideas, op. cit.,* p. 347.

event, the event of the summation of several events. It is an experience, not only of these events, but also of itself as an event concerning these events. Consciousness includes selection and negation of events, as well as their composition. Consciousness "originates in the higher phases of integration and illuminates those phases with the great clarity and distinctness."[30] But its selective activity involves abstractions from which it, alone, can deliver itself. "Philosophy is the self-correction by consciousness of its own initial excess of subjectivity."[31] Realistic philosophy was preferred by Whitehead for its insistence on this self-correction. "The things experienced and the cognisant subject enter into the common world on equal terms."[32]

Whitehead called his theory a "philosophy of organism." He interpreted reality as a system that is organic throughout; each part of it is, itself, an active system, a correlated process. Each part manifests a natural conformity or determinate adaptation, but, in some unique way, it also reveals creativity. Each actual entity has a genuine career. It is not merely an effect, but also a *causa sui*. "All actual entities share with God this characteristic of self-causation."[33] For it is as correct to say that this particular crossway or occasion of activity conditioned and constituted this unique expression, as to state that essences correlated here determined the event. The concrete truth comprehends the two abstractions. So we may say, in Goethe's words:

> The unattainable
> Here becomes an event—[34]

It becomes an event, not in the mystic, heavenly choir only, but also in each unique experience.

As Whitehead recognized no bare determinateness, but a unique creativity in each event, so he maintained that reality is not inevitably, and only, as it actually is. There is a boundless range of possibility which is perhaps the matrix of unique unrealized events. We could contemplate, not only specific, but also cosmic, contingence. Yet each actual entity serves to limit this boundless abstract possibility to a real and particular potentiality. Thus the world is actually a cosmos that manifests the correlation of certain essences in certain systems of events.

This cosmic-rational character of the world process would seem to indicate the presence of a dominant rationality that is dynamic throughout existence. Whitehead called it "God," intending no concessions to traditional theology, but was not unresponsive to the deep implications of the religious insight. "Today there is but one religious dogma in debate: What do you mean by 'God'?"[35] Philosophically, God is Whitehead's ultimate "principle of concretion." Wary of any eventual surrender to substantialism,

30 A. N. Whitehead, *Process and Reality, op. cit.*, p. 362.
31 *Ibid.*, p. 22.
32 A. N. Whitehead, *Science and the Modern World, op. cit.*, p. 110.
33 A. N. Whitehead, *Process and Reality, op. cit.*, p. 339.
34 Translated from Goethe, *Faust*, Part II, last page.
35 A. N. Whitehead, *Religion in the Making*, New York, Macmillan, 1926, p. 67.

Whitehead maintained that God is "not the world, but valuation of the world,"[36] and that God's purpose is "the attainment of value in the temporal world,"[37] value inherent in actuality. Whitehead saw life as a process of contending values, higher and lower. He conceived of evil as "a destructive agent among things greater than itself,"[38] and noted the state of degradation to which it leads. Somehow he included God in his dramatic contemplation of reality as process. He did not set God up as a perfect reality against our imperfect world of fact or appearance. The profoundly enigmatic conclusion of *Process and Reality* expresses the contending aspects of naturalism and spirituality in his final insight into reality: "Neither God, nor the World, reaches static completion. Both are in the grip of the ultimate metaphysical ground, the creative advance into novelty. Either of them, God and the World, is the instrument of novelty for the other."[39]

Dialectical Materialism

In the struggle for world power which has marked our century—especially since the communist revolution in Russia at the close of the first world war —the conflict of ideologies has spread beyond the scope of philosophically contending ideas and methods into the field of propaganda. The rigid restriction of thought and instruction to dialectical materialism in the communist countries is a significant fact for the social historians of our time, but it has afforded little or no range for the critical development or revision of Marxist ideas. It has not contributed material of intellectual substance to the student of contemporary philosophy. From the Baltic to the China Sea, any suspected deviation from the Marx-Engels-Lenin doctrine is accounted not only wrong, but culpable. Even now we are witnessing a cleavage in the erstwhile monolithic structure of communist power, with Moscow and Peking accusing each other of heresy. Our closing review can only note this aspect of contemporary thought as gravely significant—and indeed, ominous in its social-political implications—but philosophically unproductive.

Existentialism

A century ago, Kierkegaard sought existential truth beyond any doctrinal forms, be they scientific, philosophical, or theological. This radical, or root-probing, spirit has aroused a strong response in contemporary religious

[36] *Ibid.*, p. 159.
[37] *Ibid.*, p. 100.
[38] *Ibid.*, p. 95.
[39] A. N. Whitehead, *Process and Reality, op. cit.*, p. 529.

thought, but it has also seemed to inspire an upsurge of irrationalism, and in two directions. Kierkegaard's subjection of conceptual thought to vital re-solution has been treated as an unreasoning but august will-to-believe. By its fiat, the religious convictions, regarded as all-important, could be re-affirmed despite any rational objection to them. In the opposite camp, how-ever, existentialism has also been espoused by moral skeptics and atheists. If you begin with an initial and unqualified denial of God or of any hierarchy of values, then what? With what standards do you then meet the crises which confront you?

We may consider these two opposite varieties of the existential resolution-in-uncertainty. The list of thinkers in this cleft encampment are many; only three can be noted here. Outstanding in his existential religious fiat has been the Protestant theologian, Karl Barth (1886–   ). Barth has not been neutral in his social or political views and commitments, but his basic outlook, be it in social reform or in personal concern and choice, has been religious and providential. He would not secularize Christ, or reinterpret the Christian gospel as any kind of a political or economic program of reform. Beyond morality, and deep within any human planning or execution, is the one centrally important act: the act of utter devotion to God's will. That devo-tion itself is not our work but the working of God's grace in us. Barth would thus press beyond goodness to godliness, and rely, not on reason or philoso-phy, but on faith and utter consecration.

In less devotional or confessional terms, Karl Jaspers (1883–   ) has em-phasized his view of personality, not in any analytic account of definable qualities and faculties, but in a characteristic active commitment to chosen values. You and I are what we espouse, and by this, our present character, our eventual course is determined. Our life is a quest and our loyalty to our commitment affects our relation to others. No rational formulation of our-selves, no schematic mapping of our career, can do us full justice. In a similar vein, while Jaspers has traced the important stages in the historical process, he regards them as indications of deeper tendencies which do not yield to abstract definiteness.

An insistent, initial negation marks the existentialism of Jean-Paul Sartre (1905–   ). In his philosophical and literary works, he has stated in unmis-takable terms that he starts with an utter denial of any belief in God, or in a fundamental standard of values. His philosophy is the existential elabor-ation of atheism. I am myself alone, and I am what I choose and must choose to make of myself. In this necessary freedom, I must go my way in a world of irrational abyss—a ground of nothingness. What meaning can my life have for others, or theirs for me? I am continually in changing situations in which I have to choose; I do choose, and this choice of my course—and indeed of myself—is my *engagement*. As I have no other standard of evaluation, either for myself or for others, what ground for approval or condemnation can I have? My only relief would seem to be the freedom from any remorse or compunction. The words of Mephistopheles in Faust come to mind: "After all, you are what you are!"

Neo-Scholasticism

The progress of modern science and of modern Biblical criticism impressed many Catholic thinkers with the need for some fundamental revision of the orthodox position. Abandoning their rigid adherence to questionable beliefs of tradition, these so-called "modernists" advocated a new intellectual policy for the Church. Let it come abreast of the present established knowledge, let it realize the living and developing character of truth. Instead of unyielding conformity to the forms of Scholastic theology, the modernists pleaded for a truly inquiring spirit that could achieve a Christian philosophy which would be responsive simultaneously to the spiritual outlook and to the needs of modern intelligence. Catholic modernism, and related liberal movements in Protestant circles, indicated a natural, and perhaps inevitable, religious reaction to modern ideas. This theological radicalism affected a far greater number of minds than those who were outspoken in their criticism. The Church replied officially to modernism with a solemn reaffirmation of Scholastic orthodoxy. It condemned the philosophical radicals and confirmed the *Summa Theologica* of St. Thomas Aquinas as the true Christian-Catholic philosophy.

Neo-Scholasticism has maintained the perennial truth of the Thomist—or, more broadly, the Scholastic—doctrine, but within this conformity, it has sought the most effective ways of bringing conviction. Whitehead wrote of medieval philosophy: "What scholasticism gave to the European world, was penetration in the handling of ideas."[40] To this age of fertile variety and instability of ideas, the neo-Thomists have expounded their systematic doctrine of Christian Aristotelianism. Does not this philosophy recognize and trust reason in the establishment of scientific truth? Does it not also realize that, while reason leads us in the right direction, it does not take us the whole way, and so must find its consummation in faith? Neo-Scholasticism is a faith, but it is a faith seeking to understand; it is a philosophy, but it is a philosophy which seeks God. It aims to clear up modern confusion and error through Christian intelligence.

Neo-Scholasticism stands in several significant relations to the contending movements in modern philosophy. It is suspicious of the idealistic substitutes for theism. It resists skepticism in all its varieties; it opposes Kantian phenomenalism and the positivist renunciation of metaphysics; it criticizes the strong naturalistic bias of many realists, but, in its way, it may be regarded

[40] A. N. Whitehead, *The Function of Reason*, Princeton, Princeton Univ. Press, 1929, p. 36.

as a variety of realistic philosophy. Our minds, neo-Scholasticism holds, can gain rational knowledge of externally existing things, of material and immaterial substances, of universal essences and principles, of God's existence.

The neo-Scholastic revival of Thomistic Aristotelianism should be appraised in more than one way. As a dogmatic self-reaffirmation of Catholic orthodoxy, it is a significant expression of present cultural tendencies, though not a new chapter in the history of philosophy. The neo-Scholastic doctors of our time have served philosophy well by greatly increasing our direct knowledge and understanding of the masters of medieval thought, whose doctrines they have sought to make convincing in modern terms. The vigorous advocacy of Thomistic Aristotelianism has likewise served to revive general philosophical interest in Aristotelian realism. And it is interesting to note that, in the neo-Scholastic field, orthodox sowing has sometimes proceeded to a more or less critical harvest.

Concentration on Philosophical Analysis: Logical Positivism

The history of philosophy and the history of mathematics meet in the work of numerous modern thinkers. Pascal called the geometrical method the most perfect afforded by our limited minds; the rationalism of both Descartes and Leibniz reflected their mathematical mastery. Contemporary thought, likewise, shows the influence of the new mathematical ideas on philosophy and the logical reinterpretation of mathematical principles. Russell and Whitehead's *Principia Mathematica* is the most eminent expression of this interplay of mathematical and logical analysis in the philosophy of our day.

The new analysis has subjected the Aristotelian formal logic to radical criticism. The expert operation of mathematical symbolism has achieved a reformulation of logical procedure. The new symbolic logic not only has perfected the statement of the older syllogistic logic, but also has explored and exposed its limitations, and, through keener analysis, has advanced and perfected the self-examination of thought. This more competent formal procedure, itself an advance in method, has, in the judgment of its exponents, also made possible a deeper understanding of logical processes. But the new symbolism has been criticized as even more abstract than the Aristotelian. For all its formalism, the traditional logic did concern itself with actual reasoning in daily experience. The new symbolic logic has seemed to be very far removed from the "logic for use" that pragmatists advocate.

Another field in which preoccupation with formal analysis is evident is the new British intuitionism in ethics. Instead of the traditional ethical theories of the moral standard and the organization of human values, some of these analysts have devoted themselves to ethical grammar and the semantics of moral ideas. The ethical problem has been reduced to a question of basic definitions, of the meaning of "good" and "right." By subtle arguments, the priority of one or the other of these two terms has been urged as fundamental in ethics. The definability of both these ideas, especially of the one regarded as primary, has been questioned, and they have been treated as underivative intuitions.

A more general emphasis on analytic method as the chief and proper concern of philosophy characterizes a contemporary movement known as "logical positivism." Its exponents believe that philosophical error and confusion can be overcome by the more reliable initial analysis of terms and propositions. Instead of expounding the nature of reality, philosophers should first clarify their ideas. The primary, important questions are, "What do I mean by this term or proposition?" and "How do I derive it and know it?"

These new expert analysts are confident that their more thorough analysis will show many venerable philosophical ideas and tenets to be meaningless, logically futile. Traditional metaphysics, in their judgment, suffers from this fatal inconsequence. But they are not professed skeptics. They rely on modern mathematical methods and on the physical sciences for their accounts of nature.

As the historian of philosophy reaches the end of his last chapter, he should not assume the mantle of a prophet; he is well advised to make his closing remarks very brief. Ours is a transitional age, unsettled in its thinking and in its social structure, facing exceedingly grave perils, yet having the possibility of unprecedentedly rich fruition. Of one thing in philosophy we may be sure: the solution of our problems can only deepen our insight to reveal still more fundamental issues. Philosophy disposes only of its routine tasks. Its major inquiries may become more enlightened, but they cannot be terminated. This is not a skeptical reflection. It signifies, not that philosophical thought is futile, but that it is inexhaustible.

SUGGESTED WORKS FOR FURTHER STUDY

ANTHOLOGIES OF CONTEMPORARY PHILOSOPHY. Adams, G. P. and Montague, W. P. (eds.), *Contemporary American Philosophy;* Feigl, H. and Sellars, W. (eds.), *Readings in Philosophical Analysis;* Muirhead, J. H. (ed.), *Contemporary British Philosophy;* Schilpp, P. A. (ed.), *Library of Living Philosophers; The New Realism* (multiple authorship); *Essays in Critical Realism* (multiple authorship).

PEIRCE. Peirce, C. S., *Collected Papers* (Charles Hartshorne and Paul Weiss, eds.).

WILLIAM JAMES. James, William, *The Principles of Psychology; The Will to Believe; Pragmatism; The Meaning of Truth; The Varieties of Religious Experience,* and *A Pluralistic Universe.*

DEWEY. Dewey, John, *Democracy and Education; Ethics* (with J. H. Tufts);

Experience and Nature; Human Nature and Conduct; The Quest for Certainty; Logic, the Theory of Inquiry; Reconstruction in Philosophy, and *Art as Experience*.

WHITEHEAD.   Whitehead, A. N., *Science and the Modern World, Process and Reality, Adventures of Ideas, Modes of Thought*, and *Religion in the Making*.

Index